Europe Since 1715

A Modern History

Work, by Ford Madox Brown. Reproduced by courtesy of the City Art Galleries, Manchester, England.

Europe Since 1715

A Modern History

EUGEN WEBER

UNIVERSITY OF CALIFORNIA, LOS ANGELES

W · W · NORTON & COMPANY · INC · New York

Cartography by Harold K. Faye

Library of Congress Cataloging in Publication Data

Weber, Eugen Joseph, 1925–
   Europe since 1715.

   "Comprises parts III and IV of [the author's] A
Modern history of Europe" published in 1971.
   Bibliography: p.
   1. Europe—History—1492–   I. Weber, Eugen
Joseph, 1925–   A modern history of Europe.   1972.
II. Title.
D208.W42   914'.03'2   70-39865
ISBN 0-393-09404-9

CONTENTS

Contents

Contents

Contents

Contents

ILLUSTRATIONS

Illustrations

MAPS

PREFACE

This book attempts to tell the story of Europe in the past two hundred and fifty years and to reconcile the reality of the times themselves with what they mean to us. It is a compromise between historical narrative, synthesis, and analysis. It is divided into two major parts, each of which has its own internal unity and logic: first, the revolutionary period 1715–1848, during which the ideological and industrial base of the contemporary world evolved; then, the most recent period, an age of masses in material as in human terms, ending in our own day.

Each of these sections begins with some chapters that give an overview of international and political affairs in general: the continent and the world in which the events that it describes took place; the economic background, the atmosphere, the mentality of its times. Then follow sections devoted to internal affairs and to the development in particular states and regions—Britain, France, Northern or Eastern Europe—which had relevance to contemporary events.* Last, but not least, come the chapters about how people lived and the things that affected and reflected their way of life and thought. These chapters of social and cultural history take up at least half the book and will, I hope, prove its most useful contribution.

This organization is not strict. The pattern varies as it has seemed appropriate, and does so notably in the last part of the book, where 1945 marks a major limit. With the visible ending of Europe's hegemony (on the decline for a generation before), the continent reverts to its real dimensions and its history becomes a part of the history of the surrounding world with which it shares common problems, perplexities, and pressures. Hence the more general treatment of the years since 1945

---

* Countries are mentioned in terms of the role they play. Eli Hecksher remarks somewhere that a small country has no right to demand that its history be studied just because it happened. Space and prejudice both have persuaded me that he is right.

when Europe ceases to hold the center of the stage.

An enterprise on this scale cannot be brought to a conclusion without the help of others. I am beholden to the resourcefulness of my research assistants: Mr. Ronald Behling, Dr. Vlad Georgescu, and Miss Vivienne Thomas, the last of whom especially afforded immense help. I have derived much profit from the comments of colleagues and friends who read and criticized portions of the manuscript: my friend and editor, Donald Lamm; Isser Woloch of Columbia University and David D. Bien of the University of Michigan for the earlier portion; Hans Rogger of the University of California, Los Angeles, and Charles Delzell of Vanderbilt University for that beginning in 1848. The fiercest arguments about the text, however, were with my wife, who stubbornly insists that what I write should be both readable and clear. The text will show that she got her way sometimes.

E. W.

Los Angeles, 1972

INTRODUCTION

You should not expect to find here . . . the immense details of wars,
of the storm of cities taken and retaken by arms, given and ceded by
treaties. . . . All that was done, and does not deserve to be written.
We shall only attend, in this history, to that which deserves the attention of all times, to that which can illustrate the genius and the customs of men. . . .

(Voltaire, *The Century of Louis XIV*)

A Modern History: the subtitle of this volume is intended, first, to warn
that here is *one* interpretation among several, not ultimate but tentative.
It is *modern*—less as a part of the traditional triptych of ancient, medieval, and modern, whose arbitrariness becomes increasingly awkward,
than in the relative sense of "recent": a contribution and response to
ways of life and thought and action which are ours today. It is of
Europe, not because the greater world is irrelevant, but because for the
past three centuries Europe was the most significant part of it. Not so
naïve as to believe that the variety of mankind is exhausted by one of
its physical incarnations, I am convinced that the mode and models
evolved in Europe have provided the dynamo and the coloring of the
modern world. Moreover, this period of European supremacy came to
an end a quarter of a century ago and may be treated as a dramatic
whole: the age when Europe found, organized, and affirmed itself, scattering its children, notions, and techniques over the world's surface. And it
is history: *a* history.

What kind of history? A glance through the coming pages will show
very soon. Above all it tries to touch on matters that fifteen years of
teaching courses in so-called Western Civilization have made me feel
students want to know. Not just the peaks but the valleys too. Not just
the epic of collective deeds, but the tissue of the times. Not just what
happened, but to whom and how. Not just wars and politics, the doings
of a relatively restricted group, but the way people lived—humbler and

middling people, and the rich as well—their food, their housing, the warp and woof of their existence. Not just great artists and philosophers and their works (and, it is to be hoped, not long, forgettable lists of dates and names), but the times and public to which they addressed themselves and to which they—somehow—responded. Above all, men and women.

Movements, ideologies, regimes, and trends are abstract. Great events are the poetry of fate. We remember them more for their lyrical impact than for the results that we attribute to them later. Only people are real, and what really matters is not Liberalism but Mill, not Cubism but Picasso, not electricity but its uses for factories and homemakers. History is the story of them, not as contributors to a present which soon becomes the past, but living their own lives. One can apply to history what General de Gaulle said about war: "No universal system, but only circumstances and personalities."

The difficult thing to understand is that past lives and events were not a preparation for what succeeded them, let alone for our own day, but autonomous: heavy with their own past but not with subsequent events, which only *we* now know would follow. Inevitably, knowing what happened, we look on Frederick the Great or Robespierre or Marx as predecessors, on events and situations as antecedents. In fact, they existed in their own right and deserve to be so considered: because otherwise they would not be free—not of history but of the future. Times make men, but men make ideas and make them in their image. After all, a time of distress could spark pessimistic reaction or optimistic escape; a time of change could suggest withdrawal or enthusiastic commitment. Man thinks alone and his thoughts, while affected by history and memory, by prejudice past and present, by circumstances social, economic, and physical, are still his own—not a social product, though they may become a social force.

History is not a sum but a synthesis, and one that goes on changing and accruing even while observed. The past, writes Marc Bloch, is by definition a fact that nothing can modify, but the knowledge of the past is a thing in process, which changes and progresses without end.

No account divided into chapters can really represent the continuing interaction between part and whole. An account on the present scale dwells too much on the general and only hints at ways in which the particular affects it. Those who lived through events cannot see them in perspective. Those who explain them cannot share their experience, reproduce the specific character of a given moment and its uncertainty. All we can do is *try* to distinguish the symptomatic and functional from the rest; attempt to approach situations concretely, by way of men and things; grapple with some of the living essence of history, of time, of the things men did and felt and wanted—the homely as well as the stately, not only those that were said in speeches, written in treaties and books, which have their place but not the exclusive significance so long attributed to them.

None of this is easy. When Rousseau proposed to write Prince Eugene's biography, Eugene warned him that history is a much more dangerous enterprise than poetry. Rousseau wisely forbore. Others are not so wise. In any case, it seemed to me worth doing, for the embarrassment of failure was outweighed by the possibility of some provisional truth. "Silence (Stravinsky *dixit*) will save me from being wrong but it will deprive me of the possibility of being right." Or, at least, suggestive.

Inevitably, things have been telescoped, compressed, omitted. The result is one man's view, one possible interpretation of events. No book can be all-inclusive. This one is far from it. Those who miss one thing or another may be moved to supply it for themselves. I hope they will concede that this was the particular story that I chose to tell. In telling it I have avoided singling out any particular theme: there are many themes, or trends, or views, but no dominant thesis. To impose one particular pattern on centuries so diverse would be to squeeze them into a corset built for one moment in time.

Despite such relativism, any account of such scale and nature is bound to be selective, and all selection is a form of prejudice. I have preferred to show my prejudices, without pretending to offer an ultimate or balanced chronicle. My presuppositions and my sympathies color choice and text. It will be for the reader to aim off for wind: take what he wants, leave or adjust the rest. He must not accept, but question: the facts perhaps (though those, I hope, are right); the interpretations certainly. He must invent his own questions too: is there a direction in history, or is the world spiraling in incoherence? Is there progress or eternal return? Is there coherence, can one make sense, and what is it?

The historian, said Lucien Febvre, is not the man who knows but the man who searches. His reader must search too.

PART I

An Age of Revolutions

1715-1848

EUROPE IN 1789

Prussia

Habsburg possessions

Boundary of the German Empire

RUSSIA

St. Petersburg

BLACK SEA

Dniester

Danube

OTTOMAN EMPIRE

Constantinople

CYPRUS

CRETE

Athens

POLAND

Warsaw

Vistula

Danzig

Oder

P R U S S I A

AUSTRIA-HUNGARY

Budapest

Vienna

BOHEMIA

Prague

Elbe

Berlin

Hamburg

Danube

VENETIA

PAPAL STATES

TUSCANY

NAPLES

Naples

Rome

Po

SICILY

SARDINIA

CORSICA

M E D I T E R R A N E A N   S E A

SEA

BALTIC SEA

SWEDEN

NORWAY

DENMARK

NORTH SEA

NETHERLANDS

Amsterdam

AUS. NETH.

Brussels

Rhine

SWITZ.

Rhône

FRANCE

Seine

Paris

Loire

Marseilles

Barcelona

GREAT BRITAIN

London

IRELAND

Dublin

Bordeaux

Garonne

SPAIN

Madrid

Duero

Tagus

Guadalquivir

Cádiz

PORTUGAL

Lisbon

A T L A N T I C   O C E A N

500 miles

0

The Great Lines of Change

The turn of the eighteenth into the nineteenth century is generally regarded as the focus of a revolution which has its roots in the preceding hundred years and whose effects are still felt today. For Robert R. Palmer the period 1760 to 1800 is *The Age of the Democratic Revolution;* for E. J. Hobsbawm, *The Age of Revolutions* runs from 1789 to 1848. Without quibbling too much over dates, one cannot deny the number or importance of the changes and convulsions of this time. They led from absolute monarchies to constitutions and republics, from feudal institutions to representative ones, from political passivity alleviated by sporadic risings to participation and reform, from the speed and productivity of men and beasts to that of machines, from cottage industries to great manufacturing hives in factories and cities, from parochialism to world vision. Change has today become a part of life. It was not so in the eighteenth century, when stability was the norm, even in a life and world beset by the murderous spasms of war and insurrection, famine and plague. At the beginning of the period we are about to examine, environment, way of life, institutions, altered so little, so slowly, that to most men they could have seemed unchanging. By the time the period ended, for most Europeans this would never be so again.

Perhaps this shift from stability to mobility was the greatest revolution of the age and we still live within its shadow. Its groundwork was laid within the eighteenth century, its decisions were made by the middle of the nineteenth. One generation laid the foundations for the advances of the next, one generation worked on foundations laid down by the last. Not without trouble, convulsions, and pain. Here is a time of ideas in turmoil, techniques in transition, society in evolution, economies in flux, the whole world view modified. Religion collapses into privacy or secularism. Institutions, hierarchies, long taken for granted, are questioned, criticized, exposed, overturned, replaced by others. Against the background of international conflicts, social conflicts acquire new importance, forging new worlds in the embers of their fires. Wars themselves change, in mood and scale, from professional and dynastic enterprises to ideological crusades or national undertakings; and politics, no longer the preserve of a restricted circle, take the same coloring as war. The wars of princes become the wars of nations; the politics of courts come down into the street and marketplace, assemblies, and exchanges. Their mood, scale, tempo, also change; and so do the terms in which they are conducted as more and more people are involved.

The seeds of novelties to come had been sown in Holland and in England and in France, where new attitudes to state and trade, to administration and finance and public opinion (a term first forged at this time), had been formulated and, sometimes, even felt. In England especially, the political institutions, the social structures, bent to new winds; and England it would be which, after Utrecht, dominates not only the seas but the affairs of the century. It was to England that the French philosophers looked, who formulated the criticisms and yearnings of the time, who lent their pens to the campaign for change which, in due course, would bring much change about. It was in England that the rebels inspired by French examples to gain their liberty often took refuge and, from these wards and offspring of the English realm, others would draw the hope that they could do as much. England, her colonies, then France, provided example, inspiration, and then proof that radical change could be brought about, new institutions set in place of old. Many would want, many would have, to follow.

Meanwhile, another revolution was taking place. What we now call the Industrial Revolution brought radical change in business and in industry—again a change in scale but also in conditions, frames of mind, and life—no less important than what happened in politics. Based on new wealth acquired and new stability achieved during the prosperous decades of the eighteenth century (roughly 1730–1770), this development took off in England, surged to the continent, holding out prodigious expectations for a new well-being belied at first by its ferocity. Carried on the new tide of wealth and opportunity, some grew affluent, the middle classes settled more firmly in power. But the poor workers who provided the human capital of the new industries felt little gain. Their clamor, their incipient struggles, introduced a new note in the cacophony of politics. Their very presence was a new factor which after 1848 would not be discounted again.

Their growing number was another. The population explosion is one of the great events of the late eighteenth and nineteenth centuries. Demographic pressures worked on political structures, burst out in revolutions and political unrest, spread outward from Europe in a vast exodus whose scale would make it the greatest migration that history has known.

In 1848 all these conflicts came to a head: the sheer weight of increasing numbers of people and their growing demands, notions of popular sovereignty and national consciousness, the political ambitions of the middle classes, the social claims of the workers, the feudal leftovers in many parts of Europe, traditional authorities and new interests, clashed, crashed, and were in great part settled. Not always resolved but, for a while, decided. The trends which the eighteenth century announced were fulfilled at last, the feudal age was buried, the middle classes or their values eclipsed the older hierarchies for good, the new contenders for a hearing and a say on class and national grounds had put in their claim, and their defeat set the pattern of struggles yet to come. The hopeful affirmations of the eighteenth century had been fulfilled with all the disillusions only fulfillment brings. Europe believed in progress because it had been proved. The questions progress begged were still unsettled in 1848; their innings would come later.

Chapter 1

THE WORLD
AND ITS HORIZONS

Industrial Revolution

"In every country a traveller can pass through," writes an English voyager of the 1780's, "he will find some mechanical contrivances, some modes of expediting work, which are of late invention, or at least new to him . . ." The Industrial Revolution has given rise to almost as many arguments as the Renaissance: was there an industrial revolution or was there an industrial evolution? Should events strung out over a century and sometimes more be described as a sudden, radical change? The debate, suggestive though it is, need not detain us here. G. M. Trevelyan seems to have solved the problem by calling the vast changes in the means and results of production which had their start in the second half of the eighteenth century a *process*, not an *event*. If we think of the Industrial Revolution in that way, we shall have no need to waste time on quibbles.

What actually happened seems to be fairly clear. It all started in Britain where, beginning in mid-eighteenth century, better medical schools, better midwifery, more orphanages and lying-in hospitals, kept more children alive, provided more migrants to the growing towns, a bigger reservoir of labor and consumers, above all a lower-middle class with the education and the technical background gathered in schools, and ready to take advantage of the opportunities held out by expanding markets.

Early in the eighteenth century Abraham Darby had discovered how to replace charcoal by coke in smelting iron, thus opening the way to expansion now that timber no longer commanded fuel needs. In 1759

5

The Duke of Bridgewater Canal. Opposite: the Staffordshire collieries. The "whimsey" or engine at the right is used to draw coal from the mines at the left.

the Duke of Bridgewater began the famous canal leading from his colliery to Manchester, and its success persuaded others to invest in the fundamental base without which a spurt in production would have been impossible. Then, in 1784, the puddling process to convert pig iron into malleable iron doubled and redoubled production, providing lasting iron rails to replace frailer wood.

Puddling and rolling made cast iron cheap. England rose to first rank among European iron producers—a handy accomplishment when sixty years of war lay ahead. John Wilkinson, the greatest of ironmasters, built the first iron bridge (1779), the first iron boat (1787), a Methodist chapel in iron, and was buried in an iron coffin (1805). At his works at Coalbrookdale, where coke first replaced charcoal in a blast furnace, even tombstones were made of iron. Wilkinson seems to have been an epic figure: he had a ballad written about him in his lifetime, and after his death the legend spread that he would rise again in seven years. But iron itself caught the imagination of the age; and a utopian novel of 1849 presents an ideal city erected entirely of iron. Perhaps more important, by 1825, cast iron cost two and a half times less in England than it did in France, and lower costs meant extraordinary possibilities for its use.

Iron called for coal, coal called for power and hence for steam, and steam spurred the mills. By 1757, the new industrial areas of the English Midlands set the imagination of the poet soaring:

> Thus all is here in motion, all is life:
> . . . th'echoing hills repeat
> The stroke of axe and hammer; scaffolds rise
> And growing edifices . . . and new streets . . .
>   So appear
> Th'increasing walls of busy Manchester,
> Sheffield, and Birmingham, whose redd'ning fields
> Rise and enlarge their suburbs.

As shallow ore veins became exhausted, mines had to go deeper, engines were needed to pump out the water or provide ventilation. Power engines were devised to work the pumps—driven by human beings, horses, goats, and dogs. Something more sturdy was needed. The first successful piston steam engine appeared around 1712, the brainchild of two English engineers, Thomas Savery (1650?–1715) and Thomas Newcomen (1663–1729). But a really commercially successful design would be the work of James Watt (1736–1819), and did not come until 1776.

A poor man's son who had obtained a post of laboratory assistant and instrument maker at Glasgow University, Watt had to repair a Newcomen steam engine and was shocked by the heat it wasted as it worked. To remedy this, Watt devised a separate condenser (patented in 1769), which would subsequently be patented into the rotative steam engines that became standardized in the 1780's. By 1800, some 500 of these had been built by Watt and by his partner, Matthew Boulton (1728–1809) at their great Birmingham plant, in Soho.

Boulton and Watt sold, as the former put it "what all the world wants —Power." But the source of this power came from coal, and coal consumption jumped as the demand increased by leaps and bounds. So, coal, the need for which had spurred development of steam engines, would be needed even more as steam engines spread. And rising coal consumption, for quantities no longer small enough to be shipped by cart or packmule, in turn sparked the construction first of canals, then railroads, to link main rivers and industrial towns with ports, and also with the mining areas. Coal became the first raw material to be measured and carried by millions of tons; and, after coal, bricks and iron followed, and all the other heavy goods that stood as the foundation of heavy industry.

There was one industry where demand was even greater. Overseas trade and a growing home market called first of all for textiles to clothe the swelling masses of the globe. Increasing demand, in this field as

James Watt's first "sun and planet" steam engine, named for the manner in which the driving gear rotates around the flywheel gear. Right: the spinning jenny, invented by James Hargreaves in 1767.

in others, incited men to search for more efficient methods: division of labor, which replaced the craftsman's slow and careful work by a series of simple processes enabling unskilled labor to turn things out much faster; simplification of the product, by eliminating decoration and refinement; last but not least, technological improvements—the development and introduction of machines.

The first weaving machines may be dated back to the 1730's, when John Kay devised his flying shuttle, although they took some two decades to come into wider use. When they did, the faster rate of weaving increased the demand for yarn, which part-time spinners still spun on spinning wheels, and which tended to run especially short at harvest time when home producers left their cottages for the fields. In the 1760's, when British victories in India opened the Indian market to Lancashire cotton goods, this shortage became particularly acute. Result: the jenny of James Hargreaves (1767) enabling one man to work first eight then eighty spindles; then Robert Arkwright's water frame driven by water power (1769); then Samuel Crompton's mule (1774–1779) combining previous ideas to produce a much finer yarn. Greater yarn production pushed weavers to catch up, lest excess yarn be exported to continental competitors. Cartwright's power loom followed in the 1780's, using the possibilities provided by Newcomen and Watt.

The English textile industry progressed and expanded because the markets it supplied grew rapidly. Economic historians have expressed doubts whether before the nineteenth century the world market could have accommodated more than one industrialized economy able to provide (or needing) mass-produced goods on a modern scale. Holland, France, and Britain struggled for a market that the seventeenth and eighteenth centuries still regarded as fixed and unvarying. They assumed that one man's gains cut down the possibilities of other com-

8

petitors; and perhaps this view, proved wrong in the nineteenth century, fitted the conditions of earlier times. The Dutch lacked the territorial base and the industrial tradition. French possibilities were limited by the weakness of the money market which hamstrung industrial expansion, but also by the fact that in the crucial eighteenth century France lost potential colonial outlets to Britain. By the late eighteenth century the British had captured or controlled most of the world's colonial areas; and this victory gave their industrialization a flying start, both from windfall profits and from demand.

Again, English settlements were more likely to provide such demand than the purely trading and mining posts of earlier days. Even more, the slave trade. Importation of slaves into the Americas grew five- or tenfold from about 10,000 a year in the 1640's to 50,000 and 100,000 a century later. The increase created a great demand for European goods in Africa, and plantation products increased demand for these and other goods on the plantations themselves and throughout the hinterland. In 1700, about 20 per cent of English exports were going to colonial areas; by 1759 over one-third of all British exports went to British colonies alone; by 1784 about half, if we include the new United States. And if we take the staple of the new Industrial Revolution—cotton goods—then the colonies, including Ireland, took almost 90 per cent of Britain's products until 1770.

Capitalism

But if all this brought in money, it also cost money. Machines need capital much greater than the tools of individual artisans. Raw capital was flowing in from overseas. Nationalist historians and some others have asserted that the capital of England's Industrial Revolution was supplied by Indian plunder, funneled back by returning nabobs. In actual practice, another source was far more important. Through Portugal, which in the eighteenth century became almost a British economic preserve,* Brazilian gold flowed into London banks to the tune, sometimes, of 50,000 pounds a week. The consequent accumulation of gold reserves enabled London to wrest the financial supremacy of Europe from Amsterdam, and provided the treasure which permitted England to carry on her wars without facing ruin. Meanwhile, English manufacturers were clothing and equipping Brazil as well as Africa.

But, while the bullion imports afforded much needed liquidity, the basic capital came out of the societies which it served, much as the spider's web is spun from the very substance of the beast. Serious indus-

---

* The British had supported Portugal's long seventeenth-century struggle to assert its independence from Spain, and in 1662 Charles II of England married a Portuguese princess whose dowry included Bombay. The two countries' alliance was enshrined in the Methuen treaty of 1703, promoting the exchange of port wine for English woolens and giving English merchants a commanding position in Portuguese trade.

9

trialization on a large scale required more money than even Brazil could provide. If the capital to set up one large enterprise might not seem overwhelming, the economic substructure of roads and docks and buildings and various means of transport was still largely lacking. It continued to be so everywhere until the eighteenth century, and in most places much later than that. Government after government tried to industrialize, but few really succeeded until—as in eighteenth-century Britain—the initial equipment had been accumulated for the Industrial Revolution to get off the ground. So England had a basic foundation which other countries had to build up while she thrived on hers.

There was, however, one obvious way to accumulate capital which others too could use. Throughout this time, and even more on the continent than in England, prices seem to have risen way ahead of wages, thus providing profits—that is, capital—with which the country's industrial and manufacturing strength could be built up. This stern lesson is clearly drawn in Earl Hamilton's *War and Prices in Spain 1651–1800**: "By involuntarily sacrificing real incomes through the price-wage squeeze, the laboring class bore the burden that implemented material progress, just as laborers and peasants in Soviet Russia, sacrificing through governmental directives, have largely financed the mechanization of industry . . . Along with other social groups, later generations of workers have reaped the rewards."

Capital now appeared, massive, mobile, created by labor rather than by land, available for reinvestment, circulating rapidly, contrasting with the rather stiff and stolid land economy in a society where money and men are on the move. And so appeared modern capitalists, whom one of Rousseau's correspondents mentioned in 1759 ("I am neither great lord nor capitalist"), whom Turgot defined in 1777 as "possessors of money," whom a speaker in the Convention of 1792 denounced: "Of whom is our republic composed? Of a small number of capitalists and a large number of poor. Who carries on the grain trade? That small number of capitalists. Why? To get rich. How can they get rich? By raising the price of grain. . . ."

There was one other source of capital and, in the late eighteenth century perhaps the most important, and this was trade. In the sixteenth and seventeenth centuries, shares in business ventures had come to be sold on the open market and impersonal capital, in shares of enterprises, began to take over the functions previously exercised by individual investors. Companies organized for periods longer than single voyages or ventures, warranted and acquired a separate impersonal "personality" of their own. Directors, investors, "managers," became replaceable, interchangeable, no longer absolutely crucial as the Fuggers or the Medicis had been.

In 1602, the foundation of the Dutch East India Company had brought into being the first giant stock-holding corporation. Others fol-

* (Cambridge, Mass.: 1947), p. 225.

The Royal Exchange in London.

lowed. The London Stock Exchange was incorporated under William III, the English Board of Trade set up in 1696, the French Council of Commerce in 1700, "The wealth of the nation, that used to be reckoned by the value of land, is now computed by the rise and fall of stocks," wrote Jonathan Swift in his *Examiner*. Large corporations and private trading ventures provided the original accumulation of modern capital, especially in France and England where overseas trade flourished. This was particularly true of England, where profits of trade tripling between 1715 and 1790 helped subsidize much of industry: Welsh iron works were backed by the money of London and Bristol colonial shippers, the Clydeside industry grew out of Glasgow's tobacco trade.

Where merchants would not lend a hand and private capital was lacking, there were banks. The seventeenth century saw state and private banks set up throughout the west, whose paper—guaranteed by their deposits—provided credit at more or less moderate interest. Holland had led the way, but Holland concentrated more on trading and finance operations than industrial production. In France, the crash of speculative banking schemes in 1720 discouraged the development of banking activities, and thus restricted investment credit there until Napoleon founded the Bank of France in 1800. So England had an advantage here as well. To carry the story forward, since industrial development fed on capital, banks became its mainstay and the indispensable turntables of modern economy. The nineteenth century would be the age of bankers—or else of usurers like Balzac's Grandet or Gobseck, Dickens' Murdstone or Ralph Nickleby, men who made a fortune out of a credit-hungry world. "The bank heads the state," noted the French novelist Stendhal in the 1830's. "The bourgeoisie has taken over from the nobles and the bankers are the nobles of the bourgeois class."

The Rothschilds must have been the greatest of these bourgeois nobles

11

and the origin of their fortune throws a useful light on the services that bankers could provide. In the 1790's, the landgrave George William of Hesse-Cassel—a colossal brute who had shut his wife in a fort in order to be free to enjoy his mistress in his Cassel palace—worried that the invading French revolutionaries would take his fortune accumulated largely by Hesse's trade in soldiers, entrusted it to Meyer Amstel Rothschild of Frankfurt, who paid regular interest on the wealth and returned it to the landgrave when the danger had passed, much increased. The landgrave then turned over the management of all his financial affairs to Rothschild, and publicized his trustworthiness all over Europe.

In the meantime, Meyer's sons, established in Frankfurt, Vienna, London, Paris, and Naples, had rendered signal services to the princes allied against France by conveying British subsidies to Britain's allies, and had increased their capital as well. Their reward came after the war was over, as Metternich helped secure baronies for all of them, and also moved to improve the condition of the Frankfurt Jews. Karl Rothschild, head of the Naples branch, was decorated by the Pope himself. Baron James, in Paris, supported composers like Meyerbeer and Berlioz, novelists like Balzac, poets like Heine, while his balls and dinners were no less famous than his artistic interests. Lionel in England, elected to the House of Commons in 1847 by the City of London, could not take his seat because of his religion; he was re-elected in 1858, and the form of the Parliamentary oath was changed partly to accommodate him.

These men provided the capital for French railroads and United States bonds, for steamship companies on the Danube and railroad enterprises in Bohemia, for paying Austrian troops in Lombardy and equipping the rebel student corps in Vienna in 1848. They seemed indispensable, omnipotent, and omnipresent. In 1844, G. Toussenel, a follower of Fourier, the socialist reformer, published a significant attack, *The Jews, Kings of Our Time,* in which he argued that it was not the people but the Jews who reigned and governed, above all the Rothschild Bank. Toussenel's allegations would echo down the ages. Of course, it was not the Jews who reigned; but, to some extent, the bankers—of whom some of the more visible were Jews. They were, true enough, the harbingers and symbols of great changes which, without capital, without a banking structure that could collect and distribute it, could not have taken place. And they were hated as representatives of change —of that change which, for better or for worse, was affecting all people in its turmoil.

The Price of Change

With the nineteenth century, the price of change, the pressure of progress, seemed to increase. In France the textile worker's wages in the second quarter of the nineteenth century were half what they had been in 1800; the wage index for miners, 100 in 1792, was 49 in 1850. In England, the domestic weaver who made thirty shillings a week around 1820, was making seven or nine shillings twenty years later. Industry, once dependent largely on home production, was organized in factories: "This temple, where is offered up/To gain, the master-idol of the realm,/Perpetual sacrifice"; and factories reminded observers, and not least their inmates, of barracks, or convents, or prisons.

In 1817, Mary Shelley invented *Frankenstein* as a symbolic tale of science creating slaves out of men and also creating monsters that could master and destroy them. It seemed as if Leviathan had been reborn. The ideal factory was, in the words of one of their leading advocates, "a vast automaton," its various organs—mechanical or human—"subordinate to a self-regulated moving force." Machines fitted well enough in this, but workers were less reliable; and the main difficulty lay in "training human beings to renounce their desultory habits of work and to identify themselves with the unvarying regularity of the complex automaton."

The author of these remarks, Dr. Andrew Ure, even advised mill owners "to organize their moral machinery on equally sound principles with their mechanical," meaning presumably that moral discipline and religious enthusiasm could help chain or channel passions and emotions which could otherwise endanger the regularity and discipline of work, productivity, or social order.

This could go a long way. Wordsworth, in his *Excursion* (1814), described the boy deprived of "the short holiday of childhood":

> Creeping his gait and cowering, his lip pale,
> His respiration quick and audible;
> And scarcely could you fancy that a gleam
> Could break out from those languid eyes . . .
> —Can hope look forward to a manhood raised
> On such foundations?
>   Hope is none for him!
> And tens of thousands suffer wrong as deep.

Yet

> Economists will tell you that the state
> Thrives by the forfeiture—unfeeling thought
> And false as monstrous!

When the great French wallpaper manufacturer, Oberkampf, was ennobled in 1787, the decree congratulated him for employing in his factory many children "from the age of five and six." In fact, even babies of three and four could be put to work plaiting straw or making lace. By 1804, the poet William Blake was singing bitterly about "those dark

Children at work in
a textile factory.

Satanic mills" to which little boys and girls trudged at three in the
morning, from which they tottered home after ten at night, after a
day in which the hour off for meals was partly spent cleaning the
machines.

Apprentice children from workhouses or bankrupt enterprises were
sold in batches like slaves to factories where the day shift often collapsed into the night shift's bunks without giving them time to cool.
Small boys worked from dawn till dusk in squalid, filthy shops. Many
toppled from weariness into the machinery to be maimed or killed. Many
were flogged or tortured, had weights hung down their backs, heavy
hand-vices screwed to their ears, or were tied, three or four at a time,
"on a cross-beam above the machinery, hanging by our hands, without
shirts or stockings," as a witness told a British Commission of Inquiry
in 1833.

Not only boys squatted solitary daylong in the dark beside the shaft
trap of a mine, beaten to keep awake, facing walks of a mile or more to
and from work. Girls and women, man's earliest beasts of burden, did
so too. More and more of them worked in factories and mines where
some, bare to the waist and crawling on all fours through the long, dark
shafts, pushed or pulled the wagonets of coal, then carried huge loads
of it on their backs up long ladders from pit to surface. They cried as
they climbed, one witness tells us, all the way. Draught animals. Or
drudges like the little sweeps sent up to clear chimney flues in which
they often stuck and died, even as late as 1863 when Charles Kingsley
wrote his *Water Babies,* based on a Royal Commission report of that
year. This should remind us that the worst conditions were not necessarily in industry, but among small masters and independent journey-

14

men struggling to survive in the new industrial world.

However much mechanization increased, at this stage it was still only a portent. The greatest raw material of the Industrial Revolution was human, and human brawn and sinew long continued to be its chief source of power: the backs of men to carry coal, the arms of men to push wheelbarrows full of sand for nine miles sometimes and nine miles back empty for one shilling a day, the ditches dug, rails laid, coal chipped, wool and cotton woven and pottery turned by the fists and the picks and the skills of human beings, hundreds of thousands of them, more and more of them, competing with one another for jobs when the economy faltered, for demeaning, exhausting, abasing, occasional and seasonal and casual labor, immolated on the altars of supply and demand. As the men who sowed and plowed and harvested went hungry, so the men who wove the cloth went in rags, the men who baked the bricks lived in cellars, the men who mined the coal went without fire, the hundreds of thousands of domestics who catered to the increasing comfort of their masters were banished to basements and garrets.

"It is as if the English nation entered a crucible in the 1790's and emerged after the wars in a different form," writes E. P. Thompson. Contemporary observers, too, reflect this sense of catastrophic change, in class relations, in economic activities, in political and social attitudes, in scale and speed of movement, of change and of transition. The catastrophic view of industrial revolution has been much challenged of late by an almost semantic re-evaluation of phenomena: enclosures are not harsh dislocating measures, but contributions to agricultural efficiency; starvation wages and squalid slums are seen as part of a necessary process of capital accumulation and relocation of labor, shaking a whole new world into place; popular unrest becomes social tension, and the grim horrors of unemployment and hunger disappear behind tables of statistics, cycles, food prices and wage scales which document a steady improvement.

It has been argued by W. W. Rostow that all this was the price that society had to pay before it could "take off into self-sustained economic growth," that present consumption and existing welfare had to be sacrificed to accumulate the capital base, the long-term investments and substructure, buildings and equipment and roads and railways, without which expansion and future prosperity would have been impossible.

But maybe we should forget the determinism that we read into events after they have happened, think less about standards and more about ways of life: loss of independence, loss of status, monotony, discipline, conditions of work, the conscious sense of becoming a machine like others, or a bookkeeping item rather than a person. In the end, people suffered. Lives were dislocated, social relations disrupted. The industrial development multiplied and practically created before it ground them down, domestic workers, miners, factory workers, transport workers, and plantation slaves, all of whom increased in numbers to answer the demand for cotton and calico, iron and coal, stuffs and steam. It crowded them together in horrid lives no less awful for being necessary and, if their conditions of life in earlier days may not have been more sanitary, they were almost certainly less unpleasant, less ugly, and less open to disease and crime.

The Agricultural Revolution

In the age of the Industrial Revolution, the greatest industry remained agriculture; and agriculture also was revolutionized, so that fewer men on the land were eventually able to supply and feed far greater populations. The seventeenth century had counted seven important agricultural inventions; the eighteenth brought forth thirty-eight, the greatest part during its second half; and sixteen more would see the light between 1815 and 1848. A new, much heavier plow, allowing deeper plowing, was being widely used by 1800, so were manure to improve the soil, and forage corps to see more cattle through the hungry winters. Cattle breeding and animal husbandry made great strides, so that in Germany and the Netherlands where cows had given 150 gallons of milk a year in 1750, by 1800 cows gave up to 400 gallons a year. Butter churns, cheese presses, also were improved and wool production rose to meet demands—permitting, for example, British imports to rise from an average of 2.5 million pounds a year before 1799 to over 35,000,000 pounds in the 1830's.

The crux of agricultural changes lay in the fact that, sometime in the eighteenth century, an industry geared to provide subsistence turned to production for markets and for profit. The seventeenth-century Dutch had already set this trend; and soon the English followed. In 1733, Jethro Tull's book on horse-hoeing outlined the new principles: rows cleaned of weeds, economy of seed, a sowing machine sowing in regular rows. A great reforming landowner fascinated by the possibilities of root crops, especially turnips, Charles, Viscount Townshend (1674–1738) inspired by Tull and by Dutch methods, showed that practical improvements could bring a profit. Then, in the 1760's Robert Bakewell (1725–1795) turned attention to stock-breeding.

The new root crops provided better fodder. Sheep, once bred for wool, would now be bred for meat, to answer the needs of a growing population. The average weight of oxen sold at the London slaughterhouse between 1710 and 1795 more than doubled, that of calves trebled, that of sheep went up two and a half times. Breeding and fodder made the roast beef of old England. Last, came the most impressive of the land reformers: William Coke, Earl of Leicester (1752–1842) who made 48,000 acres of poor Norfolk land at Holkham fertile by turning the subsoil to the top, surrounded his estate with a high wall and turned it into an experimental farm for trying out all sorts of crops, which do not seem to have done too badly, since we learn that his revenue increased from £2,200 a year to £20,000. What was, perhaps, equally remarkable, this gentleman married at sixty-nine a girl of eighteen and produced five sons and a daughter.

While English reformers showed an empirical bent, the French seem to have been more theoretical. Tull's ideas spread to France in mid-eighteenth century, but few took them up. More popular were the new physiocratic doctrines put forward by François Quesnay (1694–1774), personal physician to the royal mistress, Madame de Pompadour. Quesnay, who had set out to find a way to improve the tax yield, concluded (rightly for his time) that the best source of revenue was land. *Physiocracy* (from two Greek words meaning the force of nature) was a reaction against the mercantilist insistence on industry which the French associated with Colbert. Not industry but land, argued Quesnay's followers, is the real basic source of riches. The existing fiscal system discouraged intelligent enterprise by undertaxing land and overtaxing trade and industry. Landowners were stupid, selfish, and protected. Their lack of enterprise slowed down the growth of industry and commerce, and left these to bear the charges of the state. The only remedy was for all existing taxes to be abolished and replaced by a single tax on land property, estimated not on the revenue the land might bring but on the value of the land itself—that is, on its capacity of production. Landowners would then be forced to draw out of their ill-exploited lands profits proportionate to their real potential, or else to sell them to those who could and would.

Going beyond this, and carried by the logic of their arguments, the physiocrats became the advocates of free trade and *laisser faire,* calling first of all for abolition of restrictions on the internal movement of goods, especially of grain, and on its export too. They reasoned that a free grain trade would raise prices, encourage grain production—especially large-scale cultivation, which would be most economical and productive—and hence bring larger crops and also better revenue from taxes. The physiocrats stood against all anachronistic trammels: mercantilistic regulation, feudal privileges and exemptions; and on this they agreed with their Scotch contemporary, Adam Smith, who also objected to the artificial distribution of social resources under the existing system but, being British, thought more about encouraging trade and industry.

Under the impact of argument in France and proof in England, under the more direct pressure of population growth and economic need, the surface of land under cultivation increased throughout western Europe. Drainage and irrigation brought into use fens in Yorkshire and Lincolnshire, polders in Holland, marshes in Italy, Germany, and France. The English, Dutch, and Belgians led the field. But men like Frederick II in Prussia, Turgot in France, Grand Duke Leopold in Tuscany, did their best to stimulate agricultural progress. Veterinary schools were founded, some before 1789; between 1770 and 1850 new tools and techniques appeared, especially on large estates, where—sometimes in a lifetime—factory-made cast iron plows replaced the local product, seed no longer broadcast would be sown by drills, harvesting and threshing came to be done by machines which drove out flails and sickles. McCormick's reaper, patented in 1834, began to be mass-produced in 1846.

Clover, turnips, and other fodder crops increased supplies of animal feed for winter. More and fitter livestock provided larger quantities of manure to fertilize the soil, but increasingly artificial manure came into use as fertilizer: waste, shreds, peat, turf, crushed bones especially (to such extent that old battlefields were scoured for more), had to serve until the 1820's saw the first shiploads of Peruvian guano and Chilean nitrates. England was using 220,000 tons in 1847. That same decade, the artificial fertilizer industry was taking shape, with the manufacture of calcium superphosphate in England by Sir John Bennett Lawes (1814–1900) and in Germany by Justus Liebig (1803–1873). Agriculture was becoming scientific. *The Journal of the Royal Agricultural Society* was founded in 1838. Justus Liebig published his *Organic Chemistry in its Relations to Agricultural and Plant Physiology* in 1840.

The Napoleonic wars and the British blockade of continental Europe led to a search for substitutes for articles that the blockade cut off. Sugar was so rare that in those rich homes which could still secure it, a piece was sometimes hung from the ceiling so that everyone could plunge it for a few seconds into his cup. The first factory to make sugar from beet roots was built in 1801; by 1836, Europe produced three-quarters of a million tons. By then the agricultural market had broadened and altered quite a lot: freight trains and steamships were carrying prod-

An excerpt from a survey book of Strellington, Sussex, showing individual land-holdings in 1781.

uce and cattle, Odessa was shipping almost as much wheat as Danzig.

All this took money. That was partly why initiative for innovations came from the authorities (as we have seen already), from agricultural societies, rare landowners with progressive views, and, only very rarely, from peasants themselves, little inclined to any innovation. Gentlemen or vicars fired by reading the works of agronomists, some country ironmaster, frequently postmasters eager for sources of fodder to feed their horses, might venture on applying the newfangled methods. In any case, modern agriculture called for capital which the smaller farmer could not hope to find. Rural credit appeared first for the rich, and smaller men were driven to the wall or left to linger in their backwardness.

This was true in all countries, but especially true as one moved eastward or southward across Europe, and the different levels of development can be discerned from the way in which population shifted from the country to the cities. By 1830, only 25 per cent of English population lived in rural parts, France and Italy had 40 percent of their population in cities, Belgium and Holland more than that. But over 70 per cent of Prussian population, over 90 per cent in Spain, over 95 per cent in Russia and eastern Europe still lived on the land—and off it. And there, as on the small, chopped-up, impoverished holdings of central and southern France, sowing and harvesting were still done by hand, with gestures that an ancient Egyptian would have recognized; livestock remained costive; goats, the poor man's cows, nibbled away at everything they could; average productivity remained low. The revolution in agriculture progressed like that in industry and, if it went at a slower pace, it left behind as many casualties.

This had significant results and for a while Europe, which had always been an agricultural economy, lived on two levels: with part of its economy industrial and part still agricultural. Agricultural and industrial economies have a different incidence on general well-being. The former is less flexible. Politically, every bad harvest could become a civil danger. Any grain shipments, carts on the roads, barges on rivers and canals, government convoys, or merchants heading for the highest market, gave an impression of abundance in the midst of scarcity which persuaded the common people that the high prices were not due to shortage but to speculation, conspiracy, and ill will.

Popular notions are always anthropomorphic, their economic conjectures always come down to personalities: the government, the brokers, or the owners are to blame. What bad harvests really mean is high prices, when the farmer has little to sell after deducting his own needs for food, seed (one-fifth or a quarter of the average old-fashioned harvest), and dues; and the high price of bread affects both the landless laborers and industrial workers at the very time when lower revenues would shrink demand and cause unemployment. Only very large farmers with reserves, or landlords cashing in on fixed rents, could prosper while

19

all others suffer. Industrial prices on the other hand rise with greater demand which reflects greater possibilities—that is, greater prosperity. In agricultural societies high prices mean low production. In industrial societies (except when raw materials run short, as cotton would do in the 1860's high prices mean prosperity and invite greater production.

Higher agricultural prices cannot be answered with greater production by small farmers, whose flexibility is limited by capital, means, land, and shortage of seed. Only large landowners can put more land to the plow and they are reluctant to do so, thinking that they are doing well enough as it is. From this there follows unemployment, which only aggravates the economic crisis. This was the situation in 1789 and it appeared again in 1847 and 1848. But by then it was an exception; and railroads, steamships, international trade, would soon be turning it into an anachronism. Agriculture like industry was becoming modern and, in the age of industry, it would become a secondary factor, no longer dominant, no longer threatening the livelihood of men or the stability of industrialized society.

Society and Societies

More Food, More People

A historian of Britain in the 1750's begins his description with a revealing phrase: "To understand how human life looked and felt," he writes, "we have to begin by removing six out of seven persons in its present population." The world of 1700 or of 1750 was a much less crowded world, for objects and for people. But it would become more crowded, it was growing so, and this is when demography changes gears. In 1750 the process was only starting; by 1850 it was rolling fast.

Estimates of population figures in the eighteenth century are still somewhat approximative, especially beyond western Europe; but it would seem that the world population, about 600 million in 1700, stood around 900 million in 1800. Within this population, that of Europe increased faster than Asia's, much faster than Africa's, spilling over into the Western Hemisphere, where American rates of population growth were a magnified reflection of those in the European homeland. European population, which probably hovered around 100 million in 1650, about 140 million a hundred years later, has been estimated at 187 million in 1800 and 274 million in 1850. Within Europe itself demographic relations were changing: the British Isles went up from 9 million in 1700 to 16 million in 1800 and over 27 million in 1850; Italy rose from 18 million to 25 million between 1800 and 1850; Germany without Austria almost matched France's 35 million in 1850, second only to the 57 million of Russia. But some nations had higher birth rates than others: the French birth rate fell; the British stabilized around 32 per 1,000 in 1850, while the Germans boasted 40 per 1,000 and the United States 43.3.

Life expectation figures can also be revealing, though only in a very general way: life expectancy seems to have risen from 33 to 40 years in Sweden between 1755 and 1840, from 35 to 41 years in the United States between 1789 and 1850. In France the average life span increased from 21 in the years around 1660 to 32 in the years around 1780, and averaged 38 in 1832. Such figures can easily be misleading, for they ignore the vast variations between the rich and poor, the fact that at a time when the average age was 38, that of an Alsatian cotton spinner would be 22; and that in 1830 in an industrial center like Lille in northern France, half of the children died before they reached the age of five. They tell us one thing, however: people lived longer, though nowhere near as long as they do today. When at 46 Diderot visited the town where he had been born, he found that most of his childhood friends were dead. Life was still brief in 1759.

What caused the population explosion, we do not know. Did the death rate decline because of better medical practice, better drugs, and better midwives, improved housing, water, food supplies and general hygiene? Did the birth rate rise because social taboos were breaking down and the illegitimacy rate was soaring, or because of a conscious attempt to produce more potential wage earners for a family?

There was more food: not greater food consumption *per capita,* but there were more regular supplies and fewer periodical shortages. Some people may have eaten worse, but most ate more regularly. Endemic illnesses disappeared, especially smallpox, which had killed almost a third of children before the age of four. Yet scholars tell us that mortality remained terribly high. Undernourished, unresistant, recurrent epidemics knocked down the poor like ninepins. Smallpox drew back as vaccination advanced, but typhus, cholera, syphilis, and consumption raged, while malaria ruled over Mediterranean countries. The terrible thing about death, Proust has said, is that it nearly always simplifies life for the survivors. This was a young society (in France in 1815 44 per cent of the population were below twenty, only 7 per cent over sixty), and one where the weak went to the wall.

As for the survivors. they went to the city. In England where the population was growing 30 per cent in every generation, the cities grew still faster. Manchester had some 12,000 inhabitants in 1760, 50,000 in 1780, double that by 1801, 400,000 in 1850, doubled again in time for the First World War. Liverpool had 26,000 in 1670, 77,000 in 1800, 375,000 in 1850. Glasgow, 30,000 in 1750, was ten times as populous a hundred years later. Such figures may not seem overwhelming in twentieth-century America; they were so then. The crux of the demographic

21

revolution lies in the migration of country people to the towns and in the growth of big cities at the expense of small ones. In 1850 England, of the 3,336,000 inhabitants of London and the sixty biggest cities, only 1,337,000 had been born in the cities where they lived. In London, as in Paris, far less than half the people had been born there. *This* was a revolution.

As we have seen, the basis of the eighteenth-century economy was still agricultural. By increasing the mass of workers in an economy which had little flexibility because of its agricultural basis, the demographic revolution of the eighteenth century may be said to have worsened the workers' lot. In industrial societies high prices mean high demand and encourage the employer to grant higher wages; in agricultural societies dependent on the harvest, high prices generally mean low production and low demand, so that the employer is readier to fire workers than to give them more pay just when they need the money to buy the dearer bread, while periods of prosperity mean cheaper bread, hence less pressure to improve a pay which seems relatively more adequate.

In Padua in the eighteenth century, masons earned 384 lire a year, foremen 512—the same as the cost of a theater box for three months. In the countryside, the day-laborers, the *braccianti*, when fully employed, earned 161 lire, of which a minimum of 128 were needed for food and 20-30 to pay for lodgings. That left little or nothing for taxes, heat, or emergencies. In France, on the eve of the revolution, an agricultural laborer made 10-12 sous a day, an artisan 15–18 sous, skilled workers 26–30. With bread at 3 sous a pound, beef 7 sous a pound, coffee (a luxury) 27 sous a pound, wine 4 sous a bottle and milk 2 sous a pint, the cost of a day's food came to a minimum of 18–19 sous at least. Some workers worked for eighteen hours a day—when they found work. The printers and bookbinders who worked only fourteen hours were regarded as the aristocracy of labor. In 1808, the English House of Commons was told that a skilled workman made eight shillings a week for ninety hours' labor (fifteen hours a day for six days a week). No wonder that within a few years textile workers like the Luddites were rioting through the Midlands, breaking up the machinery which put them out of work or chained them to it.

Unlike today, the price of food was even more important than a worker's wages. Wage rates stayed fairly steady: prices varied. When a poor harvest made food prices rise, popular effervescence would begin. That was what happened in 1787–1789, in 1838–1840, and in the hungry 40's. In 1847 and 1848 the price of bread doubled, and sometimes worse than that: a catastrophe for those whose diet consisted largely of bread. As a greater proportion of working-class income had to turn back to food (assuming it had ever been spent on something else), the industrial sector was affected, sales receded, unemployment rose, and a revolutionary situation was created.

POPULATION GROWTH
DURING THE
INDUSTRIAL REVOLUTION
1820–1840

▲ City populations over 200,000 in 1820
▲ City populations over 200,000 by 1840

POPULATION INCREASES
BY PERCENTAGE, 1820–1840

10–25

25–50

50–75

Industrial areas

◣ Coal mining

500 miles

0

BLACK SEA

OTTOMAN EMPIRE

GREECE

Moscow

St. Petersburg

RUSSIA

SWEDEN

NORWAY

BALTIC SEA

DENMARK

Copenhagen

Hamburg

Berlin

GERMANY

Warsaw

Breslau

Prague

Vienna

AUSTRIA–HUNGARY

Budapest

Munich

ADRIATIC SEA

Venice

Florence

ITALY

CORSICA

SARDINIA

SWITZ.

Milan

Turin

Genoa

Marseilles

NETHERLANDS

Amsterdam

Brussels

Lux.

Paris

FRANCE

Bordeaux

NORTH SEA

GREAT BRITAIN

Edinburgh

Glasgow

Leeds

Liverpool

Manchester

Sheffield

Nottingham

Birmingham

Bristol

London

Dublin

SPAIN

Madrid

PORTUGAL

Lisbon

MEDITERRANEAN SEA

ATLANTIC OCEAN

"No one ignores," wrote a Lyons manufacturer in 1786, "that price of food sets the price of labor," and that low cost of labor makes the low price of goods and hence better sales. But "it is necessary that the worker should never grow rich, that he should have precisely what he needs to clothe and feed himself." For "in certain classes too much ease dulls industry, breeds laziness and all the vices that depend on it." Most of this time there was little chance for ease to dull industry. The buying power of the working classes depended on the harvest—we might say on the weather. Meat in the eighteenth century was still considered a luxury by most. It would be only in 1789 that the French National Assembly mentioned it as "an aliment of secondary necessity." A family would eat 2–3 pounds of bread a day in good years, less than one pound in bad, and little else. To make clear what this means, one must know that two and a half pounds of bread are the equivalent of 3,000 calories, which would be the absolute minimum required by a family of five. They could expect to get this one year out of four. Potatoes in northern and western Europe, corn in the southeast, enabled more people to survive on smaller wages and possibly put off revolt until production increased or society organized enough to give some satisfaction or crush dissatisfaction. Yet the poor must have lived all the time on the verge of hunger. The specter of famine returned every bad harvest year. Fear of the panics and riots which might arise from this accounted for the cumbersome and complicated system of regulations and surveillance, which were intended to keep markets and bakers supplied with flour, but which hindered and clogged agricultural development, movement and initiative, and burdened the state with heavy charges and with the worst suspicions too.

The Dark Side of the City

By the nineteenth century, living space in the cities had become horribly restricted. A German visitor to England compared working-class quarters to the worst ghettos of the continent. In Bristol, half the families visited by official investigators lived all in one room. In London, the proportion was much greater. In Paris, a mason who came to town in 1830 lived in a room where twelve lodgers shared six beds. Martin Nadaud who remembered this, worked hard, got rich, and became a deputy. Others did not, like the old woman quoted by Blanqui: "I am not rich, but I have my heap of straw. God thanks." By the 1820's, research conducted in Paris had established a direct relation between the height of men and their position on the tax rolls—that is, between wealth and physical development. Death rates in the poorer quarters were two and three times those of the wealthier ones. An official French report of 1840 found that where four out of ten conscripts from agricultural regions would be rejected as unfit for service, the proportion among recruits from industrial departments was nine in ten.

Wentworth Street, by Gustave Doré, a print depicting "the dangerous classes" in the slums of nineteenth-century London.

Thousands lived underground, in cellars and in basements with no light or heat, only the eternal bone-searing dampness. In Manchester, in 1832, the Board of Health found 20,000 such lodgings; in Liverpool, Engels counted 45,000 troglodytes and, thirty years later, Taine found that things had not changed. In France, at Lille, thousands were crowded in basements with earthen floors full of filthy puddles, lying on beds of straw that crawled with vermin or on potato parings or, even, sand and ashes. Privies were scarce: one for 120 people in Manchester's Little Ireland, so that most used the courtyard, the stairs, or hallways. Piles of excrement stood in yard or close, rising sometimes as high as fifteen or twenty feet, awaiting the contractors who carted if off once a week, or even once a month, to sell to farmers.

Fed on adulterated provisions, their sugar mixed with soap boiler's refuse, their flour mixed with gypsum and with chalk, their pepper with pounded nutshells, their cocoa with brown earth; clad in rags they seldom took off and even more seldom washed, freezing in the cold, stifling in the heat, dying like flies in recurrent epidemics or just of anything that can attack worn and weakened constitutions, to be buried in loosely covered ditches from which the putrefaction spread to the neighborhood; misshapen, brutalized, unwashed (of course, since few houses had water and some streets had no pumps), untaught, and hopeless—these were the cholera-incubators of the early 1830's and the late 1840's, the men and women with reference to whom the moralists justified the moral depravity of the lower classes.

"The workers" wrote a French observer, "are as free of duties towards their masters as their masters are towards them; they consider them as

The Stonemason's Yard, by Canaletto. National Gallery, London.

men of a different class, opposed to them, even hostile. Cut off from the nation, cast out of the social and political community, alone with their needs and their misery, they agitate to escape this frightening solitude and, like the barbarians to whom they have been compared, perhaps they meditate an invasion." Savages and outcasts, these people were both a threat to society and a necessity, a little like the black laborers of South Africa today: potential criminals whom circumstances continually turned into actual ones. One observer estimated some 115,000 criminals living in London around 1800, when the population was somewhat less than a million: Not only thieves and harlots, coiners and receivers, but wonderful types whom he enumerates, like scroungers, mudlarks, scuffle-hunters, bludgeon men, morocco men, flash coachmen, grubbers, bear baiters and strolling minstrels.* There was little security, and less sense of it, since the general assumption held people without a steady job or source of income to be actual or potential criminals; and the general assumption was not far wrong. This is the age that gave birth to the revealing description "poor *but* honest."

"The laws are spiders' webs through which the great flies pass and in which the small are caught." This phrase, written by Montesquieu in the eighteenth century, would be Balzac's conclusion to his epic of nineteenth-century finance: *La Maison Nucingen* (1837–1838). Police were extremely scarce; smugglers, bandits, highwaymen pullulated. As

* Patrick Colquhoun, *Treatise on the Police of the Metropolis* (1797), quoted in Edward P. Thompson, *Making of the English Working Class* (New York: 1964), p. 55.

26

late as the 1830's, great pitched battles were fought on the English coast between smugglers and newly organized coast guards. Cutpurses and criminals existed in every street. The arm of the law was short but its penalties were terrible, making up in savagery what they lacked in efficiency. In Paris in the 1830's, criminals were still exposed at the stake before the town hall, to be publicly branded with a red-hot iron. It was in the 1830's, also, that public executions were shifted from that central spot toward the city gates, and began to take place at dawn, which only partly discouraged attendance in this early rising age. In the 1820's Hans Christian Andersen and his schoolfellows near Copenhagen were taken to witness a triple execution as an edifying sight. Similarly, in *The Fairchild Family,* a juvenile best-seller of those days, the father takes his children to see a man hung in chains, in order to warn them by example.

When police were almost nonexistent, spies and informers provided an essential cog in the machinery of government. Since they were paid by results, such men tended to become *agents provocateurs,* stirring up the very crimes they were hired to detect—whether by planting forged bank notes to collect blood money or by sparking conspiracies to do better still. Paradoxically, the more police, the more humanity. The London metropolitan police was founded in 1829, and policemen called bobbies after Sir Robert Peel who organized them. A rural police appeared only after 1839. Capital offenses became restricted in the 1820's and 30's, the pillory went out in 1837, about the same time as cockfighting, bull- or bearbaiting; but public executions continued until 1865.

If sewers play such an important part in the writings and the terminology of the time (as in the novels of Victor Hugo), it is because never have sewers resumed and subsumed so utterly the hidden realities of city life. Crime was no longer a sort of marginal waste—the offal, so to speak, of urban life; no longer an exceptional but a normal part and consequence of it. The memoirs of Vidocq, criminal and policeman, published in 1828, inspired Balzac, Hugo, and Sue; became a legend that struck sparks off the everyday reality of crime to inflame the popular imagination. "If we write terrible things," a correspondent wrote to Sue in 1843, "it is because everything around us is terrible. If we are anxious, ill at ease in our society, it is because the future is here, more terrible and perhaps more bloody than the past."

The suicide rate rose. Illegitimacy and infanticide went up by leaps and bounds, until one enthusiastic English Malthusian suggested that all working-class children after the third should be asphyxiated, which caused some debate. On the other hand, of babies in the Paris foundling hospital —which received twenty a day in 1835—a quarter died in their first year. Slower than infanticide, perhaps, but more legal.

Death, banished from the imagery of the lighter-hearted eighteenth century, reappears in the nineteenth as symbol and as fact, hovering over the minds, the works, the lives of the Romantics, but more concretely over the masses, whose mortality rate rose to fearful peaks, running wild in the great cholera epidemics of 1832 and 1848, cutting its widest swath where misery, overwork, and underfeeding had prepared the ground. There was no equality there, and no fraternity either: the cold and death which Victor Hugo evokes in *Les Misérables* as leading to the barricades, turned disease into revolt and social malady into political malady. When people speak of revolution as a fever, the fact shines through the image to reveal the biological basis of social unrest.

Social unrest there was aplenty, often what Eric Hobsbawm calls "collective bargaining by riot." Where the machines appeared, low wages, unemployment—first of all in England, but also in France and Belgium, Switzerland, the Rhineland, and Saxony—the workers struck or rioted. In French textile towns the revolution of 1830 flared up to cries of "Break the machines!" The workers claimed to fight for bread and work. But the bourgeoisie was not about to grant them bread without work, and it would give them work only when it needed them. No interference was tolerated with the free operation of the market (except occasionally in order to impose tariffs), labor must be free, unorganized, unconstrained, divided before employers. Calls for regulation, maximum hours, minimum wages, or anything that interfered with the laboring man's freedom were similarly opposed. Interference to defend the poor was denounced as tyranny; and if the poor preserved from tyranny rebelled, they must be crushed. "No quarter," ordered the French prime minister, Thiers, in 1834; "All must be killed," decreed General Bugeaud who carried out his orders. "No quarter, be pitiless . . . we have got to slaughter 3,000 rebels." The figure would be upped in 1848, and a year later we find Bugeaud muttering to Thiers: "What brute ferocious beasts! . . . there are the true enemies, not the Russians or the Austrians!"

So, poverty was a crime. But it was also an economic phenomenon, an outgrowth of market oscillations, of demand and supply, or growth of population. This point of view was new and its effects insidious. Having become a factor of production, the poor man would soon move ahead to a larger role. In the medieval or Catholic view, the poor man is the image of Christ, the one who is sure of a place in heaven. Beggars are hallowed by the begging friars, by St. Francis, and by the opportunity which they afford all men to exercise charity. In the modern view, poverty is not virtue but a vice or the result of vices; charity only an encouragement to idleness, not just a social ill but the Devil's playground. The best kind of charity is work, or giving work. Where there were many mansions in Christ's father's house, now there was just a workshop.

This kind of attitude could be, and generally was, very harsh indeed, providing a good conscience to those in comfortable circumstances who could look down on misery and disapprove it without feeling involved by it. But those who did feel involved, affected, now found that charity was not enough. Resignation to individual and mass misery, which beggar and philanthropist both accepted, was not possible to minds for which poverty was evil and must be cured not by benefactions but by labor, discipline, social organization, and education. If poverty is a failure of character, reform would be the training of character: schooling and, if need be, forced labor. But if labor is a duty, it is also a right which society cannot refuse to those who ask for it. Asking for charity had been dishonorable, asking for work was honorable and manly. Here lay the justification of new social claims.

The Brighter Side

The obverse of this suffering was profit, progress, and prosperity. Between 1800 and 1851 the English population grew 111 per cent, coal output increased 470 per cent, the production of pig iron 946 per cent, cotton imports 1400 per cent. Power looms had become really serviceable only in 1803; by 1820 there were 14,000 of them in England, by 1829, 55,000, by 1833, 100,000. Domestic industry gradually disappeared; small workshops gave way to larger ones. Workers no longer owned their instruments, much too costly to be bought by one man, too demanding to be used only by one. The new dominant class would be that of machine owners. And not only were machines beginning to be shipped all over the world, as far as India, as far as Peru; so was the know-how. The French and Germans sent their young men (like Friedrich Engels) to learn industrial techniques in England, the English sent operatives and entrepreneurs to teach skills or found new firms, like those of Thomas Cockerill whose Belgian works would be the largest on the continent by 1830.

Standardization progressed and so did mass production. From Josiah Wedgwood's potteries, at Etruria in Staffordshire, popular chinawares flowed out, serviceable, cheap, to replace the trencher, the pewter plate, the tin cup. Many backward villages remained outside the distribution network, depending on a subsistence economy and on traveling hawkers. But Balzac in 1833 describes the portent of things to come, the commercial traveler Gaudissart, as "one of the most curious figures created by the ways of the present," announcing "the rule of uniform but levelling power, equalizing products, throwing them out in masses . . ." And Cobden, the English radical, had ridden twenty-five to thirty miles a day in his youth, trying to sell muslin. Bazaars, chain stores, department stores appeared, with shopwindows, clearly marked prices, periodic sales; retailing cheap, ready-made clothing more or less mass-produced, and even, at the end of this period, foods (Felix Potin's stores in Paris, 1850); or cutting prices by eliminating middlemen and selling direct from manufacturer to consumer. Advertising appeared—publicity posters, eye-catching in color and design, forerunners of a whole new art form—and advertising agencies (the first set up in Paris in 1845, by followers of the philosopher Saint-Simon), as well as newspaper publicity, which set the press free from political backers before enserfing it to business ones.

A way of life was dying. By mid-nineteenty-century it had died. And with it died a certain speed of life, of life and of experience and perception. Perhaps the Industrial Revolution lay not in *change,* but in the *rhythm* of change it introduced. Change had existed before, and change would be more vertiginous later. But here in this harsh period, the *rate* of change altered in spectacular fashion. So did the energy available to man. The Industrial Revolution set on foot the use and the production of new energy sources beyond the plants, the elements, and animals which men had harnessed some time during the Stone age. Coal and steam were only a beginning. The more energy produced, the more was sought, the more consumed. Nor have we seen the end of the revolution.

The Urban Environment

"In this great town," Descartes had written from seventeenth-century Amsterdam, "where apart from myself there dwells no one who is not engaged in trade, everyone is so much out for his own advantage that I should be able to live my whole life here without ever meeting a mortal being." Evidently, the sense of alienation amidst the impersonal vastness of great cities did not first appear in the twentieth century. Yet it would be in the eighteenth that such cities really grew in size and problems to proportions which we today would recognize as urban.

Urban agglomerations had grown higgledy-piggledy until the central power began to rationalize them in the late seventeenth and eighteenth centuries, to light, straighten, and pave streets which until then had catered rather to their dwellers than to traffic, and to eliminate or regulate refuse disposal, gutters, signs, stalls, outbuildings, and projections. Special oil lanterns for public places had begun to appear in the last third of the seventeenth century, but were primitive and rare.* Oil lamps steadily improved throughout the eighteenth century, were fitted with better wicks, glass mantles, and reflectors, and were eventually overtaken by gas lamps, burning first wood- then coal-gas. By the first decade of the nineteenth century, English industrialists were lighting their works and houses with new gas lamps. We have to make an effort to imagine the utter revolution which artificial light produced in public and private life, the hours which it added to the day, the possibilities it opened. In Louis XIV's time, the friends of Madame de Sévigné used

---

* Naples, whose king had tried to introduce street lights, only succeeded when holy shrines were set up at every convenient street corner, and the inhabitants persuaded to keep lamps burning below them—the only regular illumination which the city had from the 1750's to 1806, when street lamps actually appeared.

two candles a day, which suggests that, at least in winter, such noble households must have dined before five and gone to bed about six. The safety of the streets, the comforts of the home, the possibilities of study, play, or movement were all immeasurably increased.

Even in daytime, light could be a problem if it found no way of shining in. The eighteenth century would see the spread of window-glass in the urban west. Indeed, the economic advance of a city or region can be related to delays in its appearance. By the time of the Revolution the lodgings of the poorest Paris workers could boast windowpanes, but in the provinces oiled paper still held sway. In Serbia, glass windows became the norm only in the nineteenth century. The bright hues in which furniture, walls, and ceilings were often painted, or peasant rugs woven, reflected the hunger for light, for some liveliness and color in dark places—the homes, or hovels, palaces, churches, or stores where men had to live and work.

Much more than lighting, straightening of streets was one of the passions of an eighteenth century which wanted to replace "Gothic" disorder with rational uniformity. Demolished city ramparts were replaced by malls, boulevards, gardens, promenades. Urban improvement flourished—at least in theory—and English urban architects in particular built towns or sections of them in squares and terraces, planned as coherent wholes whose charm and harmony still survive today. The regulation of shop signs (many of which impeded traffic on narrow thoroughfares) and straightening out of streets also removed the peculiar personality of houses, which had to be given a new identity in numbers. In Paris this began under Louis XVI, but only spottily and inconspicuously. In 1780, the painter Greuze lived in the "Rue Pavée, first door on the left after the Rue St. André des Arts" and Fragonard in the "Rue de la Bucherie, the gate after the corner of the Street of Rats." The official and compulsory numbering of houses would come only in Napoleon's time. In Rome, the first street signs with names on them appeared only in 1803, and houses would not be numbered until mid-nineteenth century. Until then, addresses seem to have been indicated as "the house with green painted shutters in the street which goes from X to Y."

Streets were not only nameless, they were also dirty. Stendhal, in Napoleon's Paris, once had to spend the night at a friend's house, having his trousers dried for having tried to cross the street gutter and got them completely muddy. Yet, slowly, mud was being paved over (first in London), new sewers built which drained the filth from streets into some river, cemeteries in the churchyards of residential quarters transferred into the suburbs, to the indignation of priests and relatives and to the benefit of sanitation. In mid-eighteenth century steam pumps and iron pipes improved water supplies. Wells and fountains in insufficient number (Lyons under Louis XIII had only six public fountains) were

31

supplemented by new aqueducts, fountains, and water towers. Public washhouses for the laundry, public baths for people, were built at municipal expense. Water also served to put out fires and, while the water flowed only at certain hours, a messenger could be sent to the offices of the water company to have the mains opened in an emergency. At least the eighteenth century would see the equipment of trained fire companies with real pumps, as well as the spread of fire insurance companies.

Since most people still got around on foot, cities could not grow too much without solving the transportation problem. Sedan chairs served only the wealthy few. Tradition attributes the invention of omnibuses to Pascal, and public transportation vehicles appeared in the 1660's. By the end of the eighteenth century they had been replaced by cabs and—later—"hansoms,"* catering to those who had the means for transport but not for keeping a carriage of their own. Poor people had to walk until cheap public transportation developed in the following century.

The cleaner, more orderly cities that the eighteenth century sought to build were soon overrun by the pressure of growing population. The cities of the Industrial Revolution were a jumble of houses put up without order or reason, obeying only profits. Space shrank again and dirt advanced, ugliness triumphed, house piled on house, street on street, with no plan, no open space except the waste allowed by hazard, factories in the midst of residential quarters, workshops taking over great houses with no reference to history, art, let alone aesthetics. Fine old buildings were demeaned or completely destroyed. In 1817, William I of Holland handed the Castle of Seraing over to John Cockerill the ironmaster; even Louis XIV's elegant pavilions at Marly were turned over to a cotton weaver and, in the new urban maze, no one knew his neighbor or his name. Speculators built fast and speed pared quality just as it would do in the early days of Soviet Russia, when passage from underdeveloped economy to intense industrialization would cause somewhat similar conditions.

Cleanliness, too, had its ups and downs. Country squires, like Richardson's Sir Charles Grandison or Fielding's Squire Western, were coarse, brutal, stinking and hard-drinking, gluttonous and dirty, seldom changing their linen or their shirt. Yet there was more soap about. And, now that cottons and calicoes replaced wool and silk, cotton cloth could be boiled without damage, thus killing lice and vermin. As snuff became the passion of all who could afford it, handkerchiefs became a necessity, soiled shirts began to be changed more often. Not by the poor, of course, and many even of the better off still wore them fifteen days at a time. But beaux and dandies changed as often as three times a day, and impeccable linen became the mark of the fastidious man, good personal hygiene a sign of social status. The eighteenth century rediscovered the possibilities of cleanliness. Thomas Sheraton de-

* J. A. Hansom registered his "patron safety cab" in 1834.

signed washstands. Lavabos and bidets appeared—one Paris dealer of the 1740's advertising the latter as "a porcelain violin case on four legs" and Boucher painting a portrait of a lady using one. As soap became cheaper, patents were taken out for mechanical washing machines. Lavatory stools, sometimes quite sumptuous, which played such a conspicuous part in the appointments of well-furnished rooms that we find important personages granting audience while seated on them (it was on his *chaise percée* that Louis XIV announced his forthcoming marriage to Madame de Maintenon), began to be replaced by water closets. An English cabinet maker had made 6,000 such by 1797, and W.C. became one English term to enter universal speech.

Baths caught on more slowly. Fifteenth-century Nürnberg had had thirteen vapor baths, and it was one of these that Dürer sketched in 1496. The Reformation and the Counter-Reformation, with their prejudice against nakedness and sin, stifled medieval respect for the body's welfare and equated sin and "stews." Concern for physical well-being returned only slowly, as eighteenth-century doctors and nature-lovers worked on the public mind. Rousseauist and therapeutic views spread the vogue of cold baths, even of sea-bathing. On the educational front, reformers like J. B. Basedow (1724?–1790) and J. H. Pestalozzi (1746–1827) were coupling swimming with gymnastics. Ludwig Jahn's gymnastic societies sought to harden German youth after 1807. "Military exercises," declared Jahn in 1816, "even without guns, build a manly character, awaken and stimulate the sense of order, and inculcate obedience to leadership." These too went with cold baths, and the English public schools—that is, those private schools in which the upper classes were brought up to muscular Christianity—soon applied a variant of Jahn's point of view.

Water had other uses too. It could be drunk at spas and, in 1765, a private lunatic asylum in Norwich used baths both hot and cold to calm unruly inmates. The sane followed more slowly, but it seems that Napoleon liked very hot baths indeed and, since Wellington liked them cold, it has been suggested that Waterloo may have been won in the bathroom. Yet, in most places, baths had to be limited to pails and sponges, while tubs and showers long remained rare luxuries for the rich. A French writer, we are told, "died of a cold caught by washing," and Joseph II would pay his brother-in-law, the king of Naples, a dubious compliment: "He is clean, except for his hands; and at least he does not stink." When Voltaire built a bathroom at Ferney, with hot and cold water, he placed it in the park, rather like a privy, which made it awkward to use and suggests that use was not his first consideration in its building. In 1837, Victoria found no bathroom in Buckingham Palace and Parliament had to vote an allocation to meet the cost of conveying water to the portable bath in the young queen's bedroom. Public baths appeared in mid-nineteenth century, in conjunction with public laundries, but did not really catch on until the century's end. Running water only began to be common in the second half of the nineteenth century, and then it took its time reaching the upper stories.

Running hot water only really came with the turn of the nineteenth into the twentieth century—wash basins equipped with taps as well—and permanent bathrooms with tubs and running hot and cold water are really twentieth-century installations beyond a very few rich houses.

Meanwhile, drainage and sewers posed pressing problems. Sewage from cesspools and privies seeped into wells, or ran into rivers, thence to be drunk by those living on their banks, while noxious gases from the cesspits gave residents in the houses above them vapors, sore throats, and worse ills. At Buckingham Palace in 1845, " a room in the basement painted freshly with white lead paint was blackened by the next morning owing to putrefactive gases. The kitchens were fitted with charcoal fires with no flues, the fumes going straight up to the royal nurseries." In mid-nineteenth century, the smell from the Thames "was sometimes so bad," noted Lord Malmesbury, "as to make it questionable whether Parliament could continue to sit." And Prince Albert alone had the drive to replace the overflowing cesspits under Windsor Castle with more modern conveniences.

We shall soon see that these descriptions apply largely to the better off. Yet, before leaving this class, it should be noted that many of the changes taking place were indeed for the better. More jobs, more salaries, more quarters, encouraged young couples to move out of the parents' house into independent lodgings where husband, wife, and children formed a separate unit, one in which the children in their turn stood out more clearly, as also did the cost of their upkeep and education, an argument in favor of family limitation and planning. Apartments and houses grew smaller, and their design reflected the new interest in privacy. Rooms no longer opened one into the other, so that everyone was always passing through, but onto a corridor or hall. Beds, once present throughout the house, were concentrated in specialized rooms and such specialization was marked by the English prefix indicating the function a room might serve—bedroom, dining room, etc.

Servants were given their own quarters, increasingly distant from their masters' lives, and hand-bells which could only be heard from nearby were replaced by bells that could be rung to summon help from a distance. Privacy was increasingly preserved. Not only against servants but against all intruders who formerly could come and go much as they pleased. Now "family quarters" appeared, and also "days" or hours when people were "at home" to visitors. Light, comfort, privacy, are very modern concepts—and modern conquests too—for which we might give thanks. Yet for most of this period, their enjoyment was limited only to narrow sections of society. Now we must turn to the rest.

The Populace

The immense majority of Europeans lived on the land. East of the Rhine, more often of the Elbe, these people were serfs and remained so until mid-nineteenth century or, in Russia and Romania, later. In 1842 the *Farmer's Magazine,* defending British Corn Laws, referred to the low wages "paid to German boors, Polish serfs and Russian slaves." Further west things were different. By the late seventeenth century countries like England and France knew hardly any serfs, only villeins. Was it much better? It is hard to say. Peasants were the invisible men of their time. "One sees certain wild beasts," La Bruyère had written in the golden years of Louis XIV, "males and females, scattered about the countryside, dark, leaden, and all tanned by the sun, bound to the soil which they dig and stir with invincible stubbornness; they have something like an articulate voice, and when they rear up on their legs they show a human face, and in truth they are men. At night they take refuge in lairs where they live on black bread, water and roots; they spare other men the trouble of sowing, toiling and reaping to live, and thus deserve not to lack the bread which they themselves have sown."

Wheelless plows made labor harder; rye bread full of bran was black and heavy as lead, so that little girls of four had stomachs round as pregnant women. There is little difference to be found in the living conditions appearing in the seventeenth- and eighteenth-century paintings of peasants like those by Le Nain and Fragonard, and those illustrated in fourteenth-century works like the *Riches Heures du Duc de Berry*: the furnishings sparse, the clothes worn, ill-fitting and rough, the bread gray. In Auvergne peasants baked 20- to 30-pound cartwheels of bread that could be kept for a month. In Dauphiné, the bread was baked twice a year and kept as long as eighteen months. Little country lads sent to city schools took bread for six months, broke it with a hammer, and soaked it in order to eat.

That was under Louis XV. Under his heir, the English traveler Young was struck by the poverty of peasant houses, the lack of windows and of chimneys—the smoke getting out by a hole in the roof; at Souillac, the women were "walking dunghills"; near Amiens, in Normandy, men, women, children had neither footwear nor stockings. A year later in Brittany, Young found "a hideous heap of wretchedness" round the home of a future romantic hero: "To Combourg the country has a savage aspect; husbandry not much further advanced, at least in skill, than among the Hurons, which appears incredible amidst enclosures; the people almost as wild as their country, and their town of Combourg one of the most brutal filthy places that can be seen; mud houses, no windows, and a pavement so broken, as to impede all passengers, but ease none. Yet here is a chateau, and inhabited; who is this Mons. de Chateaubriand, the owner, that has nerves attuned for a residence amidst such filth and poverty?"

On his way to Metz, on July 12, 1789, while walking up a long hill to ease his mare, Young would fall in with a poor woman who complained of the hard times: "God send us better, for the *taille* and the services crush us."

"This woman, at no great distance, might have been taken for sixty or seventy, her figure was so bent, and her face so furrowed and hardened by labor,—but she said she was only twenty-eight. An Englishman who has not travelled cannot imagine the figure made by infinitely the greater part of the country women in France; it speaks, at the first sight, hard and severe labor. I am inclined to think, that they work harder than the men and this, united with the more miserable labor of bringing a new race of slaves into the world, destroys absolutely all symmetry of person and every feminine appearance. To what are we to attribute this difference in the manners of the lower people in the two kingdoms? To *government.*"

Such people have no recognizable personality and their contemporaries seem to have allowed them none, not even surnames which, in the common people, began to be handed on only in the early nineteenth century. The same was to some extent true of servants—an immense proportion of the working force,* who seem to have been regarded more as objects than as beings, so that Voltaire's mistress, the enlightened Marquise du Châtelet, bathed before her *valet* just as the Madisons, in this country, did not bother to conceal their marital affairs from the slave sleeping on a pallet at the foot of their bed.

The urban poor (and this included most workmen) lived, as we have seen, close to the margin of starvation, often over it. And things in the countryside were not much better. Thomas Smart testified before the Select Committee of 1824 on the Rate of Agricultural Wages that he had "by good luck and hard work" always enjoyed steady employment and received relief only to bury six of his thirteen children. "He lived almost entirely on bread and cheese, had often touched no meat for a month, got now and then a little bacon and sometimes a half-penny worth of milk, but the farmers did not like selling it." Those who were not as lucky or hard-working "mostly lived on bread" or bruised bean porridge.** It was in the 1790's that the agronomist Antoine Parmentier (1737–1813) published his famous *Treatise on the Uses of the Potato*, which would provide a base for economical soups and keep people alive when wheat was scarce. And in the early 1800's, when popular pretensions had begun to rise, horse meat would be the answer: a popular source of cheap meat for the people, its use encouraged by philanthropists and by the armies for whose old horses the horse butcher provided a perfect end. Yet fresh horse meat was sometimes inaccessible and, in the hungry 40's, we hear stories of weavers unburying the carcasses of dead animals and fighting over dogs and cats. Scrofulous, rachitic, consumptive, syphilitic, these people—working people unable to find work and sometimes to find relief—looked on prosti-

---

* In 1795, Vienna, with a population of 260,000, counted 40,000 domestic servants—15 per cent of the population—a proportion often repeated in many central and east European towns.

** Quoted by John Burnett, *Plenty and Want* (Edinburgh: 1965).

tution as a welcome addition to the family income and on drink as one
of the few escapes from grim reality.

Gin was the opium of the eighteenth-century masses, a passion that
swept over England, ruined their health, their morals, their sanity, and
what little respect they might have had for the law. From the classic
sign "Drunk for a penny, dead drunk for twopence," to Hogarth's illustration of *Gin Lane,* gin was the poison and the sop of the poor, "the
principal sustenance (wrote Fielding) of a hundred thousand people in
this metropolis."

From 1714 to 1733, English consumption rose from two to five million gallons of gin a year, and only receded in the 1750's when stringent
laws began to restrict sales. The rich, of course, drank too: "All the
decent people in Lichfield," recalled Dr. Johnson, "got drunk every night
and were not the worse thought of." But where the poor drank gin, the
rich drank port and brandy in incredible quantities. Five or six bottles a man were par for an evening; and Dr. Johnson once drank thirty-
six glasses of port without moving from his seat—a feat in more ways
than one. Addison and Steele, Goldsmith and Boswell, Sheridan and
Fox and Pitt—and Walpole before them—were bottomless wells of liquor,
frequently drunk, often dead drunk, and little the worse for it, except in
health and that only eventually. It was, evidently, an age of titans.

Where the wealthy drank for pleasure, the poor drank for solace;
and not only in England. Around 1700, Vauban estimated 40,000 taverns
and cabarets in the 36,000 parishes of the French kingdom. In 1789 one
country parish of 400 souls counted eight taverns, beside lesser cabarets.
In 1875 France would have more than one dram shop for every hundred inhabitants.

Warder Collection

Gin Lane, by William
Hogarth. Courtesy of
the Metropolitan Mu-
seum of Art, New
York.

No wonder life, like men, was coarse and callous. Beneath the exquisite veneer of eighteenth-century manners, behind the screen of polite punctiliousness, the mass of men appear as savages, much closer to their savagery (and to its results) than we. Barbarians, savages, nomads, are terms which recur endlessly in the press and the social novels of the early nineteenth century when they describe those who dwell, in Eugène Sue's words, in "the sinister regions of misery and ignorance," those sinister depths which Victor Hugo plumbed in his *Les Misérables,* which he began to write in 1842. Such wretchedness could not but stir some response. The poor who begged and stole and robbed among their betters, as Fielding, magistrate and novelist observed, also starved and rotted and froze among themselves; and if a man were to hang for stealing, why should he hold back from murder, which would not kill him twice? Like Smollett's Humphry Clinker, they stood convicted of sickness, hunger, wretchedness, and want.

Going by Somerset Maugham's notion that "the degree of a nation's civilization is marked by its disregard for the necessities of existence," all nations of this time appear excruciatingly civilized. Yet, of the three great elements of modern civilization—gunpowder, printing, and an effective system of police and law—the last was still missing.

"To civilize" is an old legal term describing the transfer to civil law of a case which had been classed as criminal. Given the barbarous penalties of eighteenth-century criminal law, we may well say that law, and then society, would be civilized by legal reforms undertaken at the behest of the enlightenment but also under the pressure of utilitarian arguments. "We live in an age of commerce and computation;" wrote the *Annual Register* of 1759: "Let us, therefore, coolly inquire what is the sum of evil which the imprisonment of debtors brings upon our country . . . What shall we say of the humanity or the wisdom of a nation that voluntarily sacrifices one in every three hundred to lingering destruction?"

"We live in an age when humanity is in fashion," a London magistrate observed in 1787. Humanity maybe; utilitarian concerns certainly. The shocking thing was the waste of imprisoned men who might have been productively employed. Whatever the motivation, reform advanced: in prisons, in penalties, even in madhouses. Then it was stifled by fear and counter-revolutionary hostility. Then it began again, again on utilitarian lines, less to save lives—of which there were too many—but effort and resources, save souls, induce sobriety and order, make better citizens. The poor were still expected (as Edmund Burke had put it in 1795, which was a famine year) to rely on "patience, labor, sobriety, frugality and religion . . ." But, increasingly, their claim to better things was voiced and heard. However bad their conditions, never had there been so much talk *about* them: "One of the most marked characteristics of the present time," wrote the *Edinburgh Review* in 1846, "is the

large amount of public attention which is given to the working classes."
Here, too, change had broken the web of habit; and poverty, which
had been taken for granted until then, became a subject for comment
and concern. The poor were after all the people, as Carlyle and Michelet argued with a new pride and love. And the very fact of this new
attention seemed to foretell a firmer future hope.

Transport and Communications

It would be in the eighteenth century and most especially in the nineteenth that the scale of time cut down the scale of space, broadening
the horizons of the latter by lowering the time it took to get from one
place to another, making journeys not only shorter but safer and more
comfortable, improving means of conveyance and the ways by which
these moved, contributing yet one more factor of mobility to a rapidly
fluctuating world.

Transport in the seventeenth century had still been risky, primitive,
and costly. In 1612 Barbary pirates inflicted 40,000 pounds' worth of
damage on Newfoundland fishermen. Coastal shipping in the Atlantic
was continually threatened by them, the coal flow from Newcastle to
London was interrupted for a year or two together, and at one time
measures against the Mediterranean pirates planned by the admiralty
in London were suspended because the Lord Admiral had been bribed
by English pirates. The Barbary pirates were no fiction. Robinson
Crusoe, in Defoe's novel published in 1719, was a slave at Salee, near
Rabat. Robinson was fictional but Salee-men were not: in 1625, off
the Newfoundland banks, they seized forty ships from Le Havre and many
others besides. In 1631, Algerian pirates captured the whole able-
bodied population of Baltimore in County Cork; in 1634 they got 800
slaves in Iceland; and mid-seventeenth century Cornwall lived in fear of
them. In 1679 still, Algerian pirates based on the Scilly Isles took thirteen
Virginia ships; and Barbados sugar shipments to London had to sail
around Scotland instead of taking the southern route.

Slave raids on the coasts of Spain, France, and Italy—not to mention
the Mediterranean islands—remained a commonplace of seafaring life
until the French conquest of Algeria in 1830. But, by the eighteenth
century, trade in coastal Atlantic waters had become fairly safe and long-
range voyages increasingly so. Besides, canals were being built which did
a lot to cut the freight rates, as in the case of the late eighteenth-century
ship canal built between Manchester and Liverpool which cut the cost
of shipping goods to and from Manchester 700 per cent. The late

eighteenth and early nineteenth century was the great age of canals, when all of western Europe was crisscrossed with them; but perhaps the most successful of them all was dug not in Europe but in America, where in 1825 Lake Erie was linked to the Hudson River, opening the west to trade, and cutting the cost of shipping a bushel of wheat from Buffalo to Albany from $108 to $7. The Erie Canal brought cheap western flour to the northeast, thus integrating the midwest with the east and driving immigrants into the Great Lakes basin, before it created a whole new grain shipping situation in the western world.

The eighteenth century was still an age, as one chronicler has described it, that was short on lamp posts and long on highwaymen. The latter only disappeared with railroads, but the safety and structure of the roads improved. Slowly: parts of Sweden would only see their first wheeled vehicles in 1790; and Odensee, where Hans Christian Andersen was born, less than a hundred miles from Copenhagen as the crow flies, was, at his birth in 1805, two and a half days by coach and ship from the capital. But on the major routes the speed and comfort got much better. In France, in the 1780's, coaches took five days from Paris to Bordeaux, about 400 miles, two and a half to Lille, about 150. Half a century later they took thirty-six and fifteen hours respectively. In 1750 England, the journey from London to Edinburgh (comparable to that from Paris to Bordeaux) lasted ten or twelve days; by 1786 reforms improving postal and passenger services had reduced this to seventy-two hours. Eighteenth-century roads introduced one of the great revolutions of the time: the taming of space, the liberation of land transport, the opening of possibilities which dominated eighteenth-century warfare before defeating Napoleon's armies, lost in the roadless spaces beyond the Elbe and the Vistula when their triumphs had been based on facilities unknown outside the West.

Still, travelers took accidents, spills, or getting stuck for granted. Traveling was an adventurous enterprise. Then, in the early nineteenth century, McAdam's method of surfacing roads with a layer of granite lumps and chips improved surfaces, hence safety and speed. The French had led the way in establishing the first body of public works experts in the Road and Bridge Corps of civil engineers, who were given their own training school in 1747. Stone highways took the place of ruts and trails in France, Germany, Austria; traffic increased. In 1830 coaches logged 500,000,000 passenger-kilometers (1 kilometer = .62 mile); and by then protests were being heard against the speed at which they traveled. Trains pulled by steam engines were beginning to run. In 1840 the railroads carried 113,000,000 passenger-kilometers, 800,000,000 in 1851, 4,270,000,000, in 1870.

At the same time, roads with really strong foundations were spreading over Europe, built by men like Telford and McAdam. In the cities the presence of more wheeled vehicles demanded better pavements: bricks,

George Stephenson's "Rocket." The winning entry in a competition among railroad engines in 1829.

cobblestones, wood coated with tar and pitch, were pressed to use, although concrete, tar, or asphalt roadbeds caught on more slowly and hardly counted until the advent of the motorcar. Roads were a symbol of liberalism and progress: Sicily had no real ones before mid-nineteenth century; in Russia the first modern highway, between Moscow and Petersburg, was finished only in 1834; the Spanish corps of highway engineers, set up on the French model by the reforming Charles III, was abolished by Ferdinand VII on his restoration in 1814, re-established by liberal revolutionaries in 1820, dissolved again by the reactionary king in 1823, and only came to stay when re-established again by liberals in 1834. Italian disunity was reflected in the disjointedness of the Peninsula's transportation network. In 1849, Giuseppe Verdi, leaving Naples where he had overseen the first production of his opera *Louisa Miller*, would take five days to reach his home near Parma, by steamboat, then by coach. Today, by train or car, the journey takes less than one day.

Yet Verdi took a steamship from Naples to Genoa, and that probably helped shorten his journey. Steam had appeared first on rivers and canals, ruining haulers and barges, but developing river traffic on the Rhine, the Elbe, the Vistula, the Danube, and the Mississippi—which latter river boasted 200 steamboats in 1830, over 1,000 in 1860. One could not cross oceans as yet by steam alone, with no port of call for refueling, but it was possible to combine steam and sail. The first such lines began in 1816, and Samuel Cunard's steamers took only seventeen days from Liverpool to Boston. But in 1848 sailing ships still dominated navigation: 10,-000,000 tons of sail towered over 750,000 tons of steam-driven ships.

Steam transportation on land and sea appears as a significant fact only after 1850. Before that time one could regard it as hopeful or as ominous as one might choose. Still, it was a fact. In 1814, George Stephenson's engine *Blucher* had pulled eight carriages weighing 30 tons at five miles an hour; in 1825 the Stockton-Darlington Railway had opened in England, with trains that could do up to 26 m.p.h. going downhill; in 1830 Manchester and Liverpool were linked by rail. By 1850 trains could do 35-40 miles an hour, and passenger fares were about half those of the former coaches. The United States took the invention up: in 1830 there were 316 kilometers of rail in Europe (279 in England) and 65 in the United States; by 1840 Europe had 3,534 kilometers and the United States 4,509. In the political crisis of 1834, Sir Robert Peel, returning "at the utmost speed" from Rome to London, took twelve days to do it. Thirty years later the same journey would take two and a half days. That was the sense of the revolution in transportation. The leisurely pace of coaches and of barges was left behind for good. Perhaps for ill, as some critic said who saw in the new speed the ruin of carters, a danger for cattle, and madness for men. But more thought differently: "The iron rail has proved a magician's road," wrote Samuel Smiles, the popular moralist. "The locomotive gave a new celerity to time. It virtually reduced England to a sixth of its size. It brought the country nearer to the town, and the town to the country . . . it energized punctuality, discipline, and attention; and proved a moral teacher by the influence of example."

Better means of transportation encouraged specialization in agriculture, modified techniques, replacing the habits and trade of past centuries with new ones they evoked. In the next decade, American wheat, Argentine meat and leather, Australian wool, Egyptian and American cotton, Japanese silk, Asian rice, the oils and oleaginous grains of Africa, would begin to compete with European products and eventually push them out. Equally important, as road and then railroad networks spread, their tracery had profound effects on the economic and social geography of the lands they covered. Old cities withered from want of transportation, villages grew into towns, great cities were allowed to expand unreasonably because food could be shipped in from very far away, the provinces—once so distant—were much more closely tied to metropolitan centers, and the metropolis itself, its shops, its cultural life, even its politics were affected in turn by the far greater facility with which provincials could now visit them—even for the day. Men traveled more: for every Englishman who had gone abroad under the first two Georges, ten faced the glories and the weariness of foreign travel under the third George, a hundred under Queen Victoria. Men traveled more, and more men traveled, and far more kinds of men.

Power and Profit Overseas

Now we must turn to the colonial struggles which played a growing part in the history of this time. Some of the major conflicts of the eighteenth century, many of the major enterprises of the next, took place on the seas or across them. The old colonial powers—Dutch, Spanish, Portuguese—gradually lost their grip on colonies and trade, while France and Britain struggled for colonial power and the latter won.

European countries had had colonies in Europe before they ever struck out across the oceans: in the Baltic, in the Mediterranean, even in the Aegean. The crushing of the population, the withering of the cities in these areas during the sixteenth and seventeenth centuries, narrowed the outlets for western manufactures and redirected the attention of some merchants toward more distant colonies in the Americas and Indies. The chief purpose of colonies, a Bristol merchant declared in 1717, was "to take off our product and manufactures, supply us with commodities which may either be wrought up here or exported again, or prevent fetching things of the same nature from other places for our own home consumption, employ our poor and encourage our navigation." *

At first the need for naval stores, raw materials, and "colonial" goods, could be fulfilled by a few planters controlling a large subject labor force. But colonies, it was thought, could also provide a safety valve for population problems caused by a laggard agriculture, a point of view voiced by many writers of the early seventeenth century. When that century ended, the idea of drawing off the surplus population or funneling the discontented overseas had worked only too well. Greater economic stability brought new appreciation of human material and the fear that too much of this was being lost by emigration. Already an English pamphlet of 1674 had complained about "the ruinous numbers of our men daily flocking to the American plantations, whence so few returned . . ."

In due course, those who did not return would win independence. By that time, at the end of the eighteenth century, the North American colonies which became the United States had built a sizable trading activity of their own (see pp. 486–492). Less economically enterprising, but no less relevant, Spanish colonies in Latin America would be moved by Yankee example and by the opportunities offered by the French revolutionary wars to assert their own independence in the first quarter of the nineteenth century (see pp. 572–575).

Sugar and Slavery

For a long time, however, influential men in the city of London, in Paris, Nantes, or Cadiz thought less of the American plantations or, indeed, of territorial possessions *as such* than of the profitable trade to be conducted in the southern seas. There, two things dominated: bullion and

* Quoted by J. F. Reese, *The Cambridge History of the British Empire* (Cambridge: 1929), Vol. I, p. 566.

sugar. Brazil had both: sugar in the north, gold mines inland and also diamonds, which sent a seemingly inexhaustible flow to Portugal and thence to her ally, England. Spain had silver in Mexico and Peru, whose flow revived remarkably in the eighteenth century under the impact of new technologies, and sugar in her Caribbean islands.

This last commodity stood at the center of a complex trade. Sugar had come to America from the cane-producing islands in the East Atlantic—Madeira, the Azores—first to Brazil in the sixteenth century, then to the Caribbean isles where the introduction of cane in the early seventeenth century promised prosperity to planters and to their backers in the metropolis. Sugar was scarce and very highly prized. British Barbados began to export it in 1646, the French from Martinique and Guadeloupe, the Spaniards from Cuba and San Domingo in the next decade, Jamaica in the 1660's. But cane plantations needed a large labor force, able to stand the heat and hardships of back-breaking work in equatorial sun. So did the refining process. European settlers lent themselves ill to these needs; the native Indians were either soon exterminated, as in the Caribbean, or ill-adapted to the labor, as in Brazil. Sixteenth-century Spaniards and Brazilians sought a solution in the importation of black slaves, stolen in Africa, as the historian David Williams put it, to work the lands stolen from the Indians in America. Between 1570 and 1670 an average of 4,000 slaves entered Brazil yearly, who seem to have enjoyed an average life span of about seven years. There and in other colonial territories, slave labor permitted the development of a large-scale mining industry, sugar refining, and agricultural plantations. Exploited by the whites, the blacks in turn affected local culture—the language, literature, art, and culinary taste of Brazil and the Caribbean—which turned into an Euro-African society, mixed in blood and mentality.

Slaves being ordered into the hold of a ship. A pathetic but edulcorated view fit to move the magazine-reading public.

A print from revolutionary France which asks the question, "Am I not your brother?"

By the seventeenth century, the slave trade had passed largely into the hands of French, Dutch, and English shippers, and these nations, too, were using slaves for their own account. By 1701, the slave population of the French Caribbean islands was double that of whites, by the end of the eighteenth century the proportion would be ten to one: half a million to 50,000.

The slave trade was a link in a great trade triangle which shipped shoddy goods and textiles from European ports to Africa, thence slaves to America, and sugar, precious metals, or other colonial goods from there to Europe. The African captives not only facilitated production by their labor, but exchange by their very being. Bought from African chiefs who captured or who pressed them, men, women, children were crowded below the decks of slave ships for the two- or three-month-long voyage to the isles. Mortality of a slave cargo would vary between 5 and 34 per cent, and probably averaged 12 or 15 per cent.* Trade grew with demand. In 1725, Bristol ships alone carried 17,000 slaves, London ships more. By 1750, ships from Liverpool—close to the Lancashire textiles which provided the main source of payment and exchange—carried 35,000. In the thirty years before 1793 some 80,000 slaves a year were shipped out of west Africa, a quarter of them in French ships and over half in British.

Soon, slaving became the preserve of a few large shippers in ports like Liverpool or Nantes. Profits were very high, sometimes as much as 300 per cent, but turnover was slow, losses were large, and enterprises risky. Opposition was appearing, invoking Christian principles or the Rights of Man, but also arguing that labor which did not appeal to personal profit would be less productive. Here was an ominous note. The enlightenment had not criticized slavery. Montesquieu's *Spirit of the Laws*, which rejoiced that slavery had been banished from Europe, considered it natural in certain countries and pointed out that sugar pro-

* A figure somewhat higher than that in other long-range voyages on the high seas at that time.

duction, for example, would become too expensive if not done by slaves. The *Encyclopedia*—most influential compendium of the age—treated slavery as a colonial necessity. In 1774, one French slave ship owner even named the three slavers of his fleet: the *Artless,* the *Huron* (after the noble savage), and the *Social Contract.* The French National Assembly refused to abolish slavery at the expense of the property rights of owners. It even refused to enfranchise mulattoes and free negroes. However, neither enlightened relativism nor property could hold out very long against the Rights of Man, and especially against evangelical reformism. For a brief moment, the Convention of 1794 abolished slavery

OVERSEAS TRADE IN THE SEVENTEENTH AND EIGHTEENTH CENTURIES

and declared all men, whatever their color, French citizens with all a citizen's rights. This did not last and slavery was restored, at least partly, by Napoleon, while in Haiti the first black independent modern state arose in 1804, out of revolt and torment.

In England meanwhile, the antislavery campaign inspired by evangelical enthusiasm and under the determined management of William Wilberforce (1759–1833) progressed. Since 1787, annual motions to abolish the slave trade drew ever stronger support in the House of Commons, until their passage was only prevented by the merchants' opposition and the sugar interest in the House of Lords. Almost half

47

the working population of Manchester and Birmingham produced goods for the African trade. Were they to lose their livelihood, it was argued, or ship captains their cargoes? By the early 1800's, however, most merchants and shippers had become convinced that they could make as much or better money in other ways, now that they had won almost complete dominion of the seas and of overseas markets. The opposition to reform became less bitter and a bill prohibiting the slave trade was passed in 1807. Having prohibited the trade in their own vessels and possessions, the British now had every interest to prevent others from carrying it on. Hence, we shall see that they applied great pressure at the conclusion of the peace treaties of 1815, though only with delayed results. The Danes had banned the trade in 1804, the Americans one year after Britain, in 1808, the Netherlands in 1814, and other powers followed. But many still found the opportunity for profit irresistible; and more or less open smuggling flourished, especially in French, Spanish, and North American ships, to feed new demands arising in Brazil, Cuba, and the American south where cotton now revealed a great new source of riches in need of slave labor. Instead of diminishing, the slave trade increased, so that by 1840 about 135,000 slaves were being imported into the Americas yearly.

Between 1831 and 1838 slavery was finally abolished in British territories and the Second French Republic followed suit in 1848. But, while the institution persisted in Brazil and the United States, little improvement was to be expected; nor were the English themselves without second thoughts. "We know that for all mercantile purposes we are one with the States," said an editorial leader of the London *Times* in 1857, "and that, in effect, we are partners with the southern planter; we hold a bill of sale over his goods and chattels, his live and dead stock, and take a lion's share in the profits of slavery . . ." The same people who cried over Uncle Tom backed Simon Legree.

Britain negotiated treaties to abolish trading and allow inspection of merchant ships with one country after another. But the real problem was to stifle slavery at the source. Naval patrols could not put an end to smuggling. So, antislavery interests began to seek some legitimate rival to compete with the deadly trade, to develop a new climate among Africans themselves and suggest new sources of wealth both to the Africans and to those who preyed upon them. One way or another, this led to the exploration of an African interior that Europeans had hardly plumbed before, and to progressive involvement in the new continent which, in its turn, created new situations and new problems. From this point of view, African colonialism was born of good intentions.* We shall return to this situation at a later stage.

* And so, quite specifically, in the 1820's were the settlements of freed slaves at Freetown (Sierra Leone) and Monrovia (Liberia), the former a British, the latter an American abolitionist enterprise.

A street in Canton at the time of the Opium War, from a painting by Thomas Allom.

The Farther East

While empires in America were collapsing, others were being won in Asia. There, the quest for spices had sent the Dutch after the Portuguese, and the English and French after the Hollanders. During the seventeenth century, the Dutch succeeded in defeating all their rivals and set up a great spice-carrying and producing empire that stretched from Batavia (1619) to Colombo (1636) and the Cape (1652), with trading posts radiating outward as far as Nagasaki and Isfahan. But, as the century ended, the Hollanders were getting out of breath. Their great joint-stock East India Company, set up in 1602, still made impressive profits, but greater resources and a broader base enabled the English East India Company to forge ahead. Dominion of the east would be disputed not between the Dutch and English, but between English and French; and it would turn not on possession of the Spice Islands but of India, control of which could provide control of the eastern seas.

Part of the issue was that the trading companies needed both goods and bullion to secure the silks and porcelain, the tea and spices and the lacquer wares that they would sell at home. Far Eastern trade, though most impressive, was not yet carried out on a scale which could supply sufficient capital for significant expansion, and until the middle of the eighteenth century Europe's bullion shortage starved eastern traders of the major means of exchange Asiatics would accept. To put the matter blunt, things would be better if they could find a source of loot with which to finance their operations, and this India provided.

There, the great Mogul Empire which Shah Akbar had founded in the seventeenth century was slowly disintegrating. Akbar had done his best to reconcile the Hindu peoples of the peninsula to Muslim rule. Those who followed Akbar were increasingly intolerant and rapacious, until the disastrously bellicose Aurangzeb (1659–1707) ruined the peasants and the administration, while his religious fanaticism raised the Hindus and the Sikhs against him. The army, on which Mogul power rested, deteriorated as its Hindu and Sikh contingents broke away. Revolts broke out throughout the Mogul empire, while Aurangzeb's successors struggled for throne and treasury. Chaos reigned. In the south-center, the marauding Maratha federation grew; in the north, the Persian Nadir Shah took Delhi and almost put an end to Mogul rule (1739). Afghan raids seared the northern plains. The empire fell to pieces into a series of principalities.

Amid this chaos, the English and French companies, trading mostly in the south of the continent at first, were caught both in the rivalries of local rulers and in the wars precipitated by governments at home. Competing for the support of native princes, they found themselves in turn supporting them, then putting up their own candidates against others, then ruling through their puppets, or alone, in territories secured in exchange for aid. Both the French and the British used these methods, drawn ahead most of the time insensibly, without deliberate purpose, to turn a trading interest into a political one. Eventually, superior leadership, as well as the fortunes of naval warfare, enabled the English East India Company to establish its power firmly in Bengal (Plassey, 1757) and then in the Carnatic in the south (Wandewash, 1760). Political commitment became military occupation. By 1800 the British had a serious problem on their hands, a problem not only political but moral: they had come to India to trade. Should they stay to govern?

By what reason were they entitled to inflict themselves on the Indians? And what would they get from it? The latter question was most readily answered: gain. And this in turn would suggest a justification for the first. It was God who willed that the enlightened British should rule benighted Indians for their good, and such imperial destiny could not be lightly evaded. The evasion might have had to take place, had Divine Providence not provided opium, which, prohibited in India, could be exported to China in large quantities, so that the profits of the China trade might pay for governing India, a subcontinent full of heathens unable to rule themselves—a self-enforcing argument if ever there was one.*

* In 1839–1840, the first Opium War opened five Chinese treaty ports to British trade and consuls, gave Britain a firm base on Hong Kong Island, and assured the East India Company of a sound means of exchange for its Chinese trade. Through the breach that the English blasted in Chinese isolation, other nations soon followed, led by France and the United States.

The seventeenth century had admired Chinese and Hindu cultures, learned from them that virtue and society could be founded even without Christianity, adopted practical ideas like that of the Chinese national census. Now all this changed. Once the Asians had been conquered they did not seem so admirable anymore. The philosophical count of Saint-Simon discouraged research in the history of Hindus or Chinese, peoples —he said—which had remained in a childish state. Another philosopher, Auguste Comte, seeking the "laws of social development" would pay attention only to "the major part of the white race," since other societies "have not followed the march of progress." Everyone apparently felt confronted by childish races, to be paternally governed, missionized, and taught. The old colonial system that collapsed in America would be replaced by a new one, more moral, or at least more moralistic, more committed, and, on the whole, more profitable. This is the time when English colonists turn from being nabobs into sahibs, from buccaneers to moralists with a sense of mission, from tolerated merchants to a ruling caste. The crude old greed and swagger is overlaid by a sense of duty; the appetites, though no less great, are now indulged in for the sake of authority rather than of wealth; the eighteenth-century expediency and openness to local institutions, natives, and native cultures is overcome by sentiments of class, caste, and racial superiority.

By mid-nineteenth century, Sir Fitzjames Stephen would see the British task as "introduction of the essential part of European civilization into a country densely peopled, grossly ignorant, steeped in idolatrous superstition, unenergetic, fatalistic, indifferent to most of what we regard as the evils of life, and preferring the repose of submitting to them to the trouble of encountering and trying to remove them." All this must mean a vast social revolution imposed upon the Indians and unpopular with them, bound to go against the feelings, opinions, prejudices of most of the population. Yet such a revolution must be tried. "The English in India," wrote Stephen in 1883, "have been by circumstances committed to an enterprise which is in reality difficult and dangerous to the last degree, although its difficulties and dangers have thus far been concealed by the conspicuous success which has attended their efforts. That enterprise is nothing less than the management and guidance of the most extensive and far reaching revolution recorded in history. It involves the radical change of the ideas and institutions of a vast population which has already got ideas and institutions to which it is deeply attached . . ." Thus it was that imperialism, which had begun as a series of expedients, became by the nineteenth century an emotional commitment, its secular objectives translated to a religious plane and pursued with evangelical zeal.

Chapter 2

STRUCTURES IN TRANSITION

The State in Flux

Mid-eighteenth century saw European economies refloated on a tide of gold from Brazil and silver from the Spanish Indies, where new extractive methods improved lagging yields. The stock of precious metal doubled, then tripled, quadrupled even, sending new energy coursing through the arteries of exchange and trade. Even more important, the eighteenth century saw the stabilization of currency first in England (1719), then in France (1726), where the gold value of the pound and of the *livre* (which would become the *franc* in 1801) remained unchanged for two centuries, until the aftermath of the First World War. This monetary stability, already achieved by Holland, would eventually be attained by most countries of western Europe and would provide a base of stable values and certainties on which liberal economy and liberal society could be founded. The state no longer manipulated currency, no longer expropriated cash by nibbling at its value, no longer imposed its will on economic exchanges based on currency. The autonomy of the economy vis-à-vis the state would parallel and render possible the autonomy of the individual, and the growth of capital.

There was stability and confidence in another way as well: the social massacres of the past few centuries spaced out, became rarer, milder, then disappeared. 1848 saw the last great famine, more horrible because people had grown unaccustomed to it. Meanwhile, an economy based wholly on agricultural revenues, flourished as agricultural production increased and, with it, population. Even the poorest, who in the past had been decimated by recurrent famines, now survived in greater numbers, their fate commuted from death to hard labor. The massive birth rate began to overtake the death rate, creating more hands and more mouths, but also more revenues, however low, at every level. As long as the land paid off, these changes vitalized all sectors of the economy. The rural population began to buy the clothes and tools which it had always needed but never could afford. Industrial production grew even more for, while few could eat twice as much bread, many wanted to dress better or improve their lodgings. Colonial trade brought in luxuries—sugar, coffee, spices—which all coveted and more could now afford. Manufacture and trade prospered most of all, and the bourgeoisie increased in numbers and in power, spreading its hold further over the land in which it also invested. Gold and silver, decreed Dr. Johnson in 1778, destroy feudal subordination. The men of substance who felt they had a stake in their country's fate wanted a voice in its government but were excluded from it. The owners of government bonds and of annuities, the various creditors of the crown, were deeply concerned in public finance, wanted a say in it, had such a voice in England and Holland, claimed it elsewhere, and finally grappled to get it.

Prosperity made people feel that the economy would take care of itself, that it did not need state interference which only hamstrung enterprise. Machinery created for periods of scarcity and need began to look anachronistic in times of affluence: corporations, monopolies, subventions, regulations, appeared a nuisance when expansion ruled. Free the artisans, free the trades, free industry, allow enclosures and agricultural enterprise, and let profit reign. Nature will take care of its own if you open the doors to market economy, sweep out the bureaucrats and the fetters that hinder free movement and free enterprise. Reflection of an expanding economy, this was the mentality of liberalism from the eighteenth to the nineteenth century, from Turgot, in the 1770's, through Camille Desmoulins at the turn of the century, to François Guizot in the 1840's.

Such views clashed with existing institutions and traditions elaborated by secular experience, with the anarchic structure of rules and regulations accumulated over the centuries, with the absolutist tendencies and the interventionism of almost every European state and of the monarchies which the state machinery served.

With few exceptions—like the United Provinces, Genoa, Venice, or the Swiss cantons, all on their decline—monarchy and state were still pretty much identical. The monarchy was, was expected, or tried to be all-powerful. Though waning, the old idea of kings as agents of God and fathers of their people had left behind the image which Lord Bolingbroke described in 1738 as "that of a patriarchal family." And this was supplemented by the utilitarian view that a strong monarchy alone could develop an effective bureaucracy and a powerful army, guarantee civil peace and security, overcome provincial particularism, introduce necessary reforms. Strong or not, all governments sought to do these things in part as continuations of earlier policies. For monarchs had long tried to secure control over their territories, unify their administrative and legal institutions, subject all classes, corporations, and provinces to their writ, ensure a larger and a steadier flow of revenue for their treasuries and recruits for their armies from a more prosperous, more productive, and more pliable body of subjects.

Most of the rulers tried very hard to introduce reforms, but found that the very conditions of their power restricted their ability to move with the times. Monarchy had become absolute by depriving the intermediary authorities of the feudal world of their independent power, but guaranteeing their nonpolitical privileges. Public power, once divided among a host of lords (religious and secular) and of corporations, had become concentrated in the state, that is—England excepted—in the *entourage* of the ruler. What survived was *property,* a hierarchy of revenues and benefits, in which the right of property was guaranteed and whose existence became the chief obstacle in the way of the exercise of royal power. Privilege itself became a property of which the possessors could not be deprived without risk for the whole system; and this paralyzed royal power by forbidding change in the existing society and economic order.

Having suppressed the organized representatives of orders and groups which could have facilitated reform, monarchy found nothing but opponents to innovation. Having failed to suppress these orders and groups, it found them ranged against any reform. Only in a country like England, where politically significant and effective bodies existed and where economic and social differences were not underscored by law, could social relations be recognized to operate on a basis of ability and wealth, and reforms keep up (however sluggishly) with contemporary needs. In England, the nobility was actually a politically effective class, as in some countries of eastern Europe, but one whose members were prepared to work for their position and even to tax themselves. This was the fundamental distinction that saved them when others crumbled before the revolution in France and this is why many of the following generalizations do not apply to England, or do so only with a difference.

Enlightened Despotism

Absolute monarchy of the traditional kind—the sort which culminated in Louis XIV—had to respect rights, privileges, and property. "The first rule of justice," argued the parlement of Paris against the King's reforming minister, Turgot, "is to conserve to everyone that which belongs to him"; and that included the prerogatives of rank and birth. Despotism, on the other hand, need recognize no difference between its subjects and could assert the interest of the state, superior to any prior right an individual subject might refer to. Some despots may indeed have been benevolent or enlightened, as described in the term which still survives today; the fact is that all were autocratic and that their main characteristic was less the adjective than the noun. The Belgian historian Henri Pirenne has defined enlightened despotism as the rationalization of the state; and that is why it was called benevolent or enlightened. Frederick II in Prussia, Charles III in Spain (and before that in Naples), Joseph II in Austria and then his brother Leopold, Gustavus III in Sweden, all sought to achieve prosperity, efficiency, and reform.*

A good example of enlightened despotism may be found in Gustavus III of Sweden (1771–1792), who began his reign with a *coup d'état* that put an end to the long struggle between the aristocratic and popular factions which had enfeebled Sweden for two generations. The King imposed a new constitution, abolished torture, granted foreign immigrants freedom of worship, freed the grain trade, developed elementary education, founded the Swedish Academy, reformed army and navy, finally increased the taxes to the point where he lost popular support and allowed the nobles to rise again. Force allowed him to defeat his enemies, but in the end force killed him: a dagger at a masked ball. Here in a capsule we have most of the measures such men were concerned with, most of their methods too.

Almost all these rulers felt that the best source of wealth lay in a numerous population, and the best way to ensure this was to make the population prosperous. The mass of the people being on the land, the crux of things lay in improving the lot of peasants; and royal administrators everywhere sought to advance and protect the peasants against those who exploited them and the land without working and, above all, without paying the same taxes. "Populationist" doctrine stressed this new concern for the welfare of the masses: a concern which tended toward an alliance of people and prince against the nobles who both exploited the people and opposed those measures that reason of state suggested to the prince. It drew support from natural law ideas which saw the prince's absolute power as an economic necessity: the crown being the natural supporter of the people against an arbitrary and spendthrift feudalism. It also leaned on the progressive ideas of the period and, most particularly, upon the arguments of contemporary Physiocrats who advocated a single tax on land, sweeping away old exemptions for those best able to pay (nobles and clergy), old exactions from those most likely to produce (peasants), old restrictions upon the free movement of grains and goods and persons.

* Catherine II in Russia talked better than she did in practice; while King Stanislas of Poland meant well but could achieve very little indeed.

Of all existing institutions none was more hated by all "enlightened men" than serfdom. Wherever they could, therefore, progressive rulers sought to change labor service into cash payments. This did not always work: sometimes because of the fierce opposition of landowners dependent on the labor services of peasants, sometimes because the peasants lacked the cash which would release them from their obligations. One of Maria Theresa's advisers went so far as to suggest the use of black slaves to ease the lot of serfs in Habsburg territories; but even he could not devise a way to solve their credit problem. Generally, results were highly uneven. It might be said that where (as in Austria, Bohemia, and Hungary) rulers really insisted on their emancipation programs, they failed; and that where they did not fail (Prussia or Russia) it was because they did not insist.

Nevertheless, almost everywhere, reforms went some way in improving the peasants' lot. Not much east of the Elbe, where, despite all the efforts of Frederick the Great, a Frenchman commented that while in France the peasant held the land, in Prussia the land held the peasant. And the situation was the same in Russia and Poland. But in the Habsburg lands, in Denmark, in many German and Italian states, some dues were limited, some services commuted, the peasant gained freedom of movement and from manorial justice, and certain rights of tenure in the land he worked. On behalf of the crown—and against the landlord if need be—local government would protect the peasant: at least in theory, for in practice local government itself was often administered by local noblemen. In theory, too, the government got more eager cultivators, more prosperous taxpayers, fitter recruits. That was in principle and, sometimes, in practice.

Trade was a second source of wealth for the ruler and very much in evidence at the time when world commerce and shipping were undergoing a tremendous change of scale, with British exports doubling between 1720 and 1763 and French exports quadrupling in the seventy years before 1789. The fortune and prestige of maritime companies were so great that even inland states would seek to set them up. After the kings of Denmark and of Prussia, the rulers of Russia and Austria, Saxony and Bavaria, founded their own companies, none very successful, but an indication of the hopes that trade held out.* But trade not only promised; it demanded. More and more, merchants and producers criticized the old controls of prices, quality, movement, and production. They wanted to turn out all they could as cheaply as they could, sell all they could on the best terms they could, when and where they could. Political economists agreed. Jurists and legislators should do in politics "what the philosophers of our times do in the physical and natural sciences": free themselves from prejudice and tradition, revise existing laws according to "the natural rules of right and reason," give way

---

* They did lead, however, to the creation of new ports at Trieste and Ostend.

Instruction in an Austrian classroom in the time of Maria Theresa. State Historical Museum, Vienna.

to a market economy. Trade was, indeed, freed from old restrictions, in Tuscany and France and even in the dominions of the king of Spain; though only partly and in piecemeal fashion, which did not satisfy either those who resented change or those who called for more.

It was a complicated situation. Economic freedom is seldom the true ideology of private interests, which are generally inclined to deny to others the freedom demanded for themselves. Complaints against the rigidity of protectionism do not mean that the plaintiff is liberal, only that he wants his particular interest freed from some anachronistic burden, while protected from somebody else. Business interests tend to be liberal in general, protectionist in particular, each with its own interest to defend. Liberalizing moves at this time seem to have come more often from the royal administration than from any interest groups. The royal administration was ahead of business, ahead of landed interests, ahead even sometimes of intellectuals; and it came up against the jungle thickets of rights and customs where everyone had something to defend—even the poorest peasants, concerned to preserve the common lands, their wood-gathering, gleaning, and grazing rights. This is why enlightened opinion could think only of a despotism equally enlightened (that is, of the same mind) to cut through the mass of particular privileges and carry through a revolution for the public good, not against the monarchy, but by and for it.

Monarchs and governments agreed, and were determined that nothing should stand in their way. It was a question, as a French philosopher put it, of "joining absolute authority to the force of reason." Men, equal before God, should be equal before the law as well: same taxes, same courts, same opportunities to show their talent. But, equal before God, men are not equal before nature. Their unequal capacities must be reflected in their unequal fortunes. Property, born of the free exploita-

tion of opportunities, was natural and sacred. Liberty was not necessarily so. Political freedom was not for the great mass of the people. For
them, thought Voltaire, "a yoke, a goad and plenty of hay" should
suffice. Joseph II of Austria drew the conclusions of enlightened philosophy: "all for the people, nothing by the people."

Rulers and Churches

There were other conclusions that rational men would draw from the
enlightened pursuit of their self-interest. Private morality did not apply
in politics, reason of state ruled supreme and, in its service, the virtues
and the worst passions of mankind might properly be enlisted. To
strengthen and to modernize the state, religious tolerance and religious
persecution were both valid methods, to be used if necessary for secular
ends. "Any religion is as good as any other," declared Frederick II, "provided that it teaches obedience to men." Napoleon, in due course,
agreed. Inevitably, in this process, some of the despots clashed with the
established church. They were determined on social and economic
development, and insisted that the church should make its financial
and physical contribution. The typical example is afforded by Joseph II
(in so many ways a prototype of his kind), who abolished the contemplative orders in his dominions, because, he claimed, the realm could not
afford their cost. What Austria and Bohemia needed were "virtuous,
educated priests who teach love of one's neighbor; not beggars, barefoot and ragged." Orders which nursed the sick, maintained schools or
some scientific activity were welcome. Others were turned away. While
founding new parishes and churches, Joseph was determined to force
the church to use its vast wealth for the social purpose for which—many
argued—it had originally been intended.*

The negative side of this appears in the fate of the Jesuits, resented
by a great many governments as an obstacle to their policy and a rival
focus of influence and opposition in the state. In the Iberian peninsula
especially, they had also incurred the popular ire by being among the very
few to stand out against the brutish anti-Semitism that other religious
orders encouraged and the Inquisition exploited, pleasing the masses and
stripping Spain and Portugal of some of their most enterprising elements. For this and other sins the Jesuits would pay in the eighteenth
century. In 1758, a Jesuit missionary had the bad inspiration to describe
the terrible earthquake which in 1755 laid low most of Lisbon and killed
thousands of people as a divine punishment of the Portuguese govern-

* After 1945, communist regimes have referred to the Josephist tradition in their
policy of restraining the material power and spiritual influence of the Catholic Church.

ment. The Portuguese government at that time was headed by the Marquis of Pombal (1699–1782), who had played a great part in destroying the flourishing Jesuit colonies in Paraguay. Pombal, a ruthless authoritarian, was a typical "enlightened" minister in a backward, poor, priest-ridden state.* Pombal established the absolute power of the crown by humbling the great noble houses, strengthening state control of the church, harnessing the Inquisition in his service. Robert Southey, the English writer, who found no conscience or humanity in the great minister, thought him devoted to restoring Portugal if not to greatness at least to plenty. But Pombal did not get far with this, failing to develop the home manufactures that he hoped for, and his most concrete achievement was the rebuilding of Lisbon after the earthquake. At any rate this was the man the Jesuit was attacking.

Pombal retaliated in a pamphlet denouncing the Jesuits as exploiters of the natives of Paraguay, and arguing that the state which the Jesuits had set up in South America, at the natives' cost, was but a pattern of the way in which they planned to enslave the world. The pamphlet achieved great effect in enlightened circles. In 1759, the Jesuits were expelled from Portugal, followed in 1760 by the Papal Nuncio, while the Portuguese Inquisition was used to scourge supporters of the Jesuits and of the Pope who vainly tried to stand by the Order. Reconciliation between the Pope and Portugal could only be achieved at the cost of accepting their expulsion. Once the Pope agreed, other governments followed. Expelled from France in 1764, suppressed in Spain in 1767, in other Italian states in 1768, the order was finally dissolved by the Pope in 1773, under the steady pressure of its royal enemies.** The latter much preferred the "Jansenists" (see p. 260 ff.) or Febronians (after the name of an Erastian German Bishop), who combined a simpler, sterner, more scriptural moralism with opposition to papal supremacy, support of local bishops and of the secular power. In the long struggle between church and state it seemed at last as if the state was winning clear decisions.

Enlightened despots regarded the state as the ultimate touchstone of all policy, declared themselves the servants of the state, seeking to be its masters only in order to serve it better. Frederick the Great defined the sovereign as the first magistrate, the first general, the first financier, the first minister of the community: "He is only the first servant of the state, obliged to act with integrity, wisdom and complete disinterestedness as if, at any moment, he were bound to render an account of his

* In early eighteenth-century Portugal, the church owned two-thirds of the land and boasted nine hundred religious houses in a population of three million. Prelates were as thick on the ground as Kentucky colonels, the King having invested much of the gold of Brazil to turning his court chaplaincy into a cardinal patriarchate and securing special privileges for the canons of his new foundation in Lisbon.

** The Jesuits survived in Russia until expelled from there in 1820, because Tsar Alexander found them converting too many of his Orthodox subjects. The order was revived in 1814.

59

administration to his fellow citizens." This was confirmed from an even better source, a letter that Leopold II of Habsburg wrote to his sister in 1790, on the eve of his accession to the Imperial crown:

> . . . I am firmly convinced that each country needs a constitution, that is a contract between the people and its sovereign . . . I am convinced that the sovereign who does not respect that contract, renounces thereby his throne . . . I am convinced that the executive power belongs to the sovereign, while the legislative power belongs to the people and its representatives . . . I am convinced that the sovereign is accountable before his people . . . I am convinced that the supreme reason for the existence of societies and governments is the happiness of individuals . . .

There is little evidence that Leopold really believed all this, but every reason to think he was convinced it was the right thing to believe at this time. Constitutional monarchy in the English fashion was obviously in the air, and the French Revolution would go to war against an emperor who seemed to hold much the same views as many of its leaders.

Yet revolution came. It came because reforms were too slow and sporadic, because the enlightened despots, however much they tried, could only scratch the surface of their problems, because in many places—and especially in France—no reforming despot could appear. It came to some extent because, especially in countries like France, changes had been taking place, things had been getting better, and revolutions, at least according to Tocqueville, "spring not from despair but from rising expectations." It came, above all, perhaps, because too many rulers, heedless of real priorities, indulged in ruinous wars which aggravated the debts and financial difficulties of their treasuries, the social and economic tensions between classes resulting from their incapacity to reform, or else frustrated those reforms they had managed to introduce. The beginning of the end was precipitated by costly conflicts which showed no real awareness of how precarious was their position and that of the existing order in most countries.

International Conflicts: Wars and Revolutions

Most international conflicts of the early eighteenth century turned on inessentials. The ideological wars of an earlier day, to be revived as the century ended, the great power struggles like those in which Bourbon and Habsburg had locked horns, do not appear until midcentury or later. Only one power, England, followed a line of conduct which, despite twists and turns, consistently reflected its national interests. In peace and war, with the one sometimes not very distinct from the other, England struggled to assert her naval and colonial supremacy, not as a matter of royal policy but as reflection of trading and manufacturing interests which showed a familiar mixture of selfishness and rectitude, and of popular policies in which self-interest was salved by good conscience. The moralization of self-interest was a practice in which the eighteenth and nineteenth centuries excelled. Here, as in other areas, England was supreme.

On the continent, the powers kept their eyes fixed on dynastic rather than economic objectives. There is a reality about dynastic conflicts which our day may be tempted to underrate, yet there is no underrating the great dynastic clashes of the fourteenth or the sixteenth century when lives, thrones and the control of kingdoms were at stake. The dynastic interests of the eighteenth century appear less consistent and less basic, their contests less tuned to the realities of an age of markets and finance; and the succession problems of Poland, Austria, or Parma were of little direct concern to the subjects of the princes who pursued them. If that itself was no novelty, the rise of a public opinion which formulated and expressed such an impression was. As a result, subjects felt little involvement in, and less commitment to, their masters' wars: in 1733, Goldoni, the Venetian playwright, joined the citizens of Parma watching the battle fought beneath the city's walls—a battle which ended with 25,000 dead, including the Austrian commander; in 1744, the Romans on their walls watched Austrians and Neapolitans slaughtering one another below; a year later, at the battle of Fontenoy, the trees were full of curious onlookers. In more favorable circumstances, ladies actually got seats on fortification bastions to watch hostilities from a comfortable place.

War was for the soldiers; a rabble of rankers, the sweepings of city streets and country taverns, officered by professionals who recognized one another across the fortuitous barriers of war as members of the same fraternity and caste. "No man in his right senses," William Pitt told the House of Commons in 1759, "would ever enlist in the army." * So, armies were made up largely of jailbirds released on condition they joined up, of paupers, of "any sturdy beggar, any fortune teller, any idle, unknown, suspected fellow in a parish that cannot give an account of himself"; and, in central Europe, of recruits called up, kidnapped, or captured among the prince's subjects or his foes.

In the nation, such troops were a foreign body. In the seventeenth century, the greatest punishment one could inflict on a city had been to quarter troops in it. There are cases of the inhabitants fleeing their cities at the soldiers' coming, deserting their houses and shops to save

---

* In Dr. Johnson's opinion no man would be a sailor who could get into jail, for the ship was equivalent to a jail plus the risk of drowning. And not only drowning: in the Seven Years' War, 1,512 seamen were killed in battle, 133,708 were missing or dead of disease.

what they could. Then came barracks, first for the garrisons in border towns, then, in the eighteenth century, inland too. Barracks were a relief for the citizens; but they only emphasized the isolation of the soldier, with his dissolute and brutal manners and his point of view oriented to, and by, what was in those days a lifetime occupation from which only age or desertion offered an escape.

To guard against desertion, discipline was tightened, marching and battle order organized to keep the soldier in the ranks, affording the least possible chance for a man to slip off unnoticed. There would be no marauding or foraging expeditions, during which troops could desert in droves. Magazines, stores, ovens, heavy supply trains, regular arrangements with contractors en route, limited mobility, excluded winter campaigning, precluded swift movement or pursuit, made sieges rather than battles the preferred form of war, imposed parade ground order even on the battle ground, and thus enhanced the importance of drill.

The ragamuffin soldiers learned to move with the precision of automatons. Their officers, versed in drill, convinced of the superiority of position over movement, unaccustomed to initiatives which their cumbersome machine discouraged, became used to fighting by the book, deciding some encounters by rule and precedent rather than waste their shot and men. An enemy in a strong position meant that you should march away. A city meant a siege to the attackers, or else a breadbasket to protect with stout fortifications. Supply lines became all-important, and soldiering an enterprise from which the civil population should ideally be left out. Gone were the days when the soldiers of Louis XIV, sent to put down a French peasant rising, roasted the children on spits. War was still full of atrocities; but mostly in the somber east where the Russians, for instance, hung the inhabitants of conquered Memel after cutting off their noses and ears, "tore off legs, opened innards and heart." Further west, hostages, requisitions, reprisals, were part of the logistical arsenal, brought in to secure order or supplies; no longer the commonplace of every land where troops appeared.

So, there were wars and the horrors of war, but there was no fighting for sheer survival or for a dominant ideal. War was part of the business of the state—perhaps the greatest part. Like every business, it often turned around land and trade but—like a business too—its directors generally knew when they should cut their losses. One did what one could, and gave up when one had to without too much fuss. And, since the actual fighting and the duration of the wars were relatively limited, the suffering they caused was less than that to which the seventeenth century had grown accustomed.

Men have called this relatively mild period the time of lace-cuff wars— *la guerre en dentelles*—even though thousands of corpses still strewed the battlegrounds whose hideousness only gave way to the rich meadows grown out of their bones, so that old battlefields offered a lush contrast with the sparse-cropped fields nearby. Perhaps this only stresses how alien the servants of war and their pursuits were to the society of that time. Rather than war in lace cuffs, European alliances and entanglements in the eighteenth century evoke a minuet, that superficial dance in which partners pair and separate, evolving gracefully and somewhat gratuitously amid the scenery of a stately world.

As in the days of Louis XIV, the great perennial contest for dominion in this time was waged between England and France, the richest and most powerful nations of the West. No great wars broke out while they were at peace; but no tenuous *entente* could conceal for long the power struggle between them. From 1715 to 1740 and from 1815 to 1848 peace between the two powers, if it put no end to European wars, at least kept them from spreading. The rest of the time, France and England were the core of more widespread power struggles, which rose to a great climax in the Napoleonic wars. When these ended, the issue had been settled. France lay defeated, decimated by two decades of murderous campaigns, humbled by foreign occupation. And Britain ruled the seas. In a sense the long years of unrest and war that began in the 1790's provide a natural transition from the "old regime" which had evolved out of the feudal order, to the new conditions of the "modern" nineteenth century. The transition would only be accomplished in 1848, when the agitation and convulsions of fourscore years culminated in revolution continent-wide.

The next few pages carry the chronicle of major international events to the eve of the French Revolution. Subsequent chapters will sketch their background in more detail, and bring the story to the watershed of 1848.

From Utrecht to the Peace of Versailles

The Peace of Utrecht, the accession of a Hanoverian prince to the English throne, the death of Louis XIV, all drew England and France, so long at daggers drawn, closer together. Louis XV (1715–1774) was a child, and the Regent sat uneasily in his place. George I (1714–1727), was the occupant of a contested throne. French recovery depended on British co-operation. The peace of both countries hung on maintaining the terms agreed at Utrecht, keeping the Stuarts from the English crown and the Spanish Bourbons from the French. Spain and Austria, on the other hand, were both dissatisfied with the Utrecht settlement. Charles VI had been frustrated in his Spanish aspirations; Philip V, encouraged by his Italian wives, sought further gains in Italy. When in 1717 Spain opened the attack in Italy at last, England and France intervened on Austria's side, forcing Philip V to moderate his ambitions and to accept a settlement which promised the succession of the duchies of Parma and Piacenza to one of his younger sons (1720).

Italy was not yet over her troubles. The young king of France had been affianced to an even younger Spanish Infanta. His kingdom could not wait for her to grow up before the succession problem was resolved. In 1725, the Spanish engagement was broken off, the incensed Infanta returned to her parents in Madrid, and Louis XV was married to Marie Leczinska, the plump and pious daughter of the pretender to the Polish crown. When, in 1733, Augustus II, the reigning king of Poland died, the French naturally supported the claims of their king's father-in-law, the Austrians a rival candidate—Augustus's son. War broke out with France and Spain on the one side, Russia and Austria on the other. Stanislas Leczinsky was soon driven out of Poland, the French armies occupying Lorraine—Empire territory—while the brunt of fighting took place in Italy, where Spaniards vied with Austrians for territorial gains. In 1738, the Peace of Vienna gave Stanislas the Duchy of Lorraine for life, after which it would revert to France to complete her eastern border. Francis, Duke of Lorraine and husband of the Emperor's daughter, Maria Theresa, was compensated with Tuscany and Parma, while Prince Charles of Spain gave up Parma for the Kingdom of the Two Sicilies.

Like the wonderful game that Alice witnessed in Wonderland, everybody had won, everyone must get prizes—though no one consulted the inhabitants of places which rulers were treating as musical thrones. Everybody had won—except England. England had kept out of war and saved her resources for business. Now she began to feel that her interests were threatened. France was increasing her power once again, not only in Europe but in the Mediterranean too, where French merchants were elbowing Englishmen out of the Levant trade. Spain, too, was regaining strength, and her refurbished fleet interfered with the multitude of English smugglers who had long poached so profitably on her South American preserves. In 1739, the government of England was forced to give in to popular outcry and mercantile pressure and to declare war on Spain, whose fleets in the South Seas would shortly receive support from French warships.

Then, in 1740, Emperor Charles VI died, to be succeeded by his daughter, Maria Theresa (1717–1780). Charles had spent much energy and money to secure recognition of the Pragmatic Sanction by which the Salic Law, banning succession in the female line, was laid aside and his daughter's right to the family heritage assured. But the agreements Charles secured were written on the wind. The young king of Prussia, Frederick II, considered the opportunity too good to miss and marched into Austrian territory, occupying Silesia. In Frederick's wake, the Elector of Bavaria asserted his rights to the Austrian succession, Spain attacked Austrian lands in Italy, finally France—not to be outdone—attacked the

Austrian Netherlands (i.e., Belgium). This brought England into the general war.

The English, already at war with Spain, might have kept out of the wider conflict but for the French threat to their interests overseas and—through Belgium—to their own coasts as well. Having been drawn into war, they fought it mostly overseas, where French and Spanish forces divided by the continental war did not show up in a good light. Fighting in Europe as well as overseas, the French and Spanish had to scatter their forces over several fronts, apportion their resources between the fleet and the army. The British, of course, did too, but nowhere near as much. This disproportion, and her freedom to concentrate on colonial questions, stood Britain in good stead in this as in future conflicts. And we shall see that the only war she lost was lost when France was free to concentrate on fighting her enemy of long standing, free of commitments on the continent.

Despite British support, the weight of the enemies leagued against her told against Maria Theresa; and the Peace of Aix-la-Chapelle was concluded in 1748 at Austria's expense. Spain received Parma and Frederick received Silesia. France gave up Belgium, which her forces had occupied, and left the war no better off than when she started, partly because her merchants were clamoring for peace and the reopening of sea lanes which the English had cut. Britain made no gains either, although she had asserted her power in the Western hemisphere.

But the peace was only a truce. None of its signatories felt quite satisfied or quite secure. Maria Theresa wanted Silesia back. Frederick was waiting for the first opportunity to defend himself by attacking her. England, her attention focused overseas, wanted an effective guardian for her king's Hanoverian possessions and thought she could find one in Frederick, who hoped that, already assured of the French alliance, he could detach England from Austria and thus achieve the isolation of his chief enemy. But the rapprochement of England and Prussia threw France into the arms of Austria, herself in search of an ally who could help check the dangerous might of Prussia. The secular hostility of Bourbons and Habsburgs was abandoned and a diplomatic revolution brought Paris and Vienna together, turning the tables on Frederick, who found himself isolated, with no great expectation of effective armed support from his new British allies.

Yet both France and Britain were less interested in Europe than in their struggle overseas, where population pressure and the search for markets spurred their imperial ambitions, leading to frequent clashes. In 1754, the long-standing friction between French troops and trappers moving south and west from Canada and British settlers and traders moving north and west from the seashore colonies exploded into fighting. The interest of France was to concentrate her forces against Britain, in America and in India, where trouble also brewed. Yet, once again, she would be caught between her continental commitments and her colonial interests. In 1756 the colonial war became a general one, as England and Prussia faced Austria, Russia, and France in what became known as the Seven Years' War. While Frederick fought a series of brilliant but desperate holding actions against Russian and Austrian armies, the French were losing their empire to the British. Quebec fell in 1759; Canada was forfeited soon after; most of the Caribbean sugar islands too; in India, Pondicherry surrendered to the British in 1761. When Frederick had been saved on the brink of defeat by the death of the Tsarina Elizabeth (1762), whose successor preferred to leave the war, France's hope of redeeming her losses overseas by European victory had to be given up. So had Maria Theresa's hope of recovering Silesia. Frederick was left in possession of his loot and the Treaty of Paris (1763) gave England Canada and effective, if temporary, dominion of the North Atlantic. France recovered the sugar islands, which her merchants and economists regarded as far more important than "a few acres of snow," as Voltaire called Canada.

Two things came out of the Seven Years' War quite clearly. The first was its impact on the finances of all participants, an impact which had a great deal to do with subsequent events. The budgetary troubles resulting from the conflict inspired the legal and administrative reforms of the Habsburg empire; the British policies which eventually set off rebellion in their American colonies; the fiscal reforms of Louis XV and his clashes with the privileged orders and institutions; not least and most successful, the various reforms of Frederick II in Prussia. The second effect of the Seven Years' War was on the international scene: it left Prussia ruined but one of the great powers. Her population had been quite literally decimated, her land devastated, both friends and funds seemed to have melted away, the state of her provinces—wrote Frederick—resembled that of Brandenburg at the end of the Thirty Years' War. But she was a power now, and none could count without her. Her isolation imposed one course: alliance with Russia, whose change of front in 1762 had saved Frederick and with whom Prussia shared a common greed for Poland. This alliance would dominate Prussian diplomacy for a hundred and fifty years.

The Anglo-French struggle had remained unresolved; and the French prepared for the next round in it by buying Corsica from the Genoese (1768), hoping to use the island as an advanced Mediterranean base, and by feverishly rebuilding their navy. Meanwhile, with British and French attention focused on a future naval conflict, Prussia, Russia, and Austria were free to prey on their weaker neighbors. Poland and Turkey would have to pay the price of the preoccupation of the western powers, their fate strangely interconnected as Catherine of Russia and Frederick of Prussia, reluctantly joined by Maria Theresa, stepped in—they claimed—to rescue Christians from benighted Ottoman opression, or from Catholic intolerance and governmental anarchy on

ATLANTIC OCEAN

NORTH SEA

SWEDEN

NORWAY

DENMARK

BALTIC SEA

RUSSIA

GREAT BRITAIN

PRUSSIA

POLAND

PRUSSIA

AUS. NETH.

SAXONY

SILESIA

UKRAINE

FRANCE

BAVARIA

AUSTRIA - HUNGARY

SWITZ.

SAVOY

PIEDMONT

PAPAL STATES

BLACK SEA

PORTUGAL

SPAIN

CORSICA

SARDINIA

KINGDOM OF THE TWO SICILIES

SICILY

OTTOMAN EMPIRE

MEDITERRANEAN SEA

ALLIANCES TO 1756

France, Prussia

Great Britain, Austria, Russia

THE DIPLOMATIC REALIGNMENT OF EUROPE · 1756

ATLANTIC OCEAN

NORTH SEA

SWEDEN

NORWAY

DENMARK

BALTIC SEA

RUSSIA

GREAT BRITAIN

PRUSSIA

POLAND

AUS. NETH.

SAXONY

SILESIA

UKRAINE

FRANCE

BAVARIA

AUSTRIA - HUNGARY

SWITZ.

SAVOY

PIEDMONT

PAPAL STATES

BLACK SEA

PORTUGAL

SPAIN

CORSICA

SARDINIA

KINGDOM OF THE TWO SICILIES

SICILY

OTTOMAN EMPIRE

MEDITERRANEAN SEA

ALLIANCES AFTER 1756

France, Austria, Russia

Great Britain, Prussia

the banks of the Vistula.

The War of the Polish Succession had not closed the tale of that kingdom's woes. Further succession struggles in the 1760's had turned Poland into something close to a Russian protectorate. A Polish rising at the end of that decade brought Turkey into war with Russia, when Russian troops pursuing Polish foes violated Ottoman territory. The war went badly for Turkey, and in 1774 the Treaty of Kuchuk-Kainardji deprived her of vast territories between the river Bug and the Sea of Azov. Before that, however, as Russian troops advanced in the southern Ukraine, Prussia and Austria came to feel that the balance of power could only be maintained if they secured compensation for the Russians' gains. Where could this be found better than in Poland? The first partition of Poland, therefore, was carried out in 1772 and gave all three of Poland's neighbors important chunks of new territory.

A new Russo-Turkish war (1787–1792), which ended with more annexations of Turkish territory by Russia, suggested further compensations at Poland's expense in 1792, when France, deep in the throes of revolution, was once again incapable of intervening. It has been suggested that, in turn, preoccupation with the affairs of Poland saved the young French Revolution from being crushed to death by an effective Austro-Prussian intervention. At any rate, in 1794, the Poles who understandably enough refused to accept the role of victim with equanimity, were finally dispatched and their kingdom, which once had stretched from the Black Sea to the Baltic and even reached out to Moscow, fell victim to Romanov, Hohenzollern, and Habsburg greed.

While all this happened in the eastern borderlands of Europe, France and England had gone to war again when England's American colonies had rebelled against her. Between 1778 and 1783, French military and economic aid on land, the skillful use of the rebuilt French fleet at sea, ensured the defeat of the British. In 1783, the Peace of Versailles lost England an empire: thirteen colonies, the island of Minorca to Spain, several islands and African lands to France. Leopold of Tuscany noted sadly that the great power which had balanced the might of France had fallen completely and forever. But if the American war brought England defeat, it brought economic and political collapse to France. Unable to face the financial problems which the cost of war had exasperated, France broke into revolution, thus apparently removing yet another counter from the international checkerboard.

Several revolutions had preceded the French: in Geneva, in 1766 and 1781 French intervention had curbed serious risings; between 1774 and 1783 Britain's North American colonies had gained their freedom; between 1783 and 1787 there had been civil war in Holland, and in 1789 a revolt in Austria's Belgian provinces. But the troubles which began in France in 1787 would set fire to Europe, then to the Caribbean, and, finally, to Latin America, adding their own fuel to existing conflicts and fundamentally affecting the international situation itself.

Chapter 3

CONSTITUTIONAL EVOLUTION IN BRITAIN

Like Italy in the fifteenth century and France in the seventeenth, England seems to have been the pilot country of the eighteenth century, its economic and industrial advances, its political institutions, the ideas it generated, inspiring envy or emulation elsewhere.

To trace the internal policies of European countries during the century and a half in which an older order fumbled for new forms, it seems best to begin with a look at Great Britain (so called since the official union with Scotland in 1707, when the crosses of St. Andrew and St. George were joined in the Union Jack), and at her American offspring whose self-assertion played an important role in subsequent events in Europe.

Both England and France underwent "revolutions" which were to leave their mark on their neighbors and on the whole world. But England's "revolution" was both similar to and different from that of France: less immediately evident, yet in some ways more far-reaching. Above all, it began sooner.

The eighteenth and nineteenth centuries saw England preserving extraordinary stability in the midst of changes no less extraordinary. Popular agitation, political and industrial riots, rebellions and invasions, as well as bitter and wide-flung wars, did not manage to shake either the Protestant settlement or the parliamentary system, each of which underwent profound reforms that strengthened rather than endangered the established order. Government by cabinet, party politics, a wider franchise, radical social and economic changes, a demographic explosion which increased the population from six million in 1750 to eighteen million a hundred years later, and the total national income in far greater proportion, succeeded only in affirming the dynasty and increasing attachment to a system which, with all its faults, had proved able to adjust to fast-changing conditions and to accept the new world rather than battle it.

When Queen Anne, last of the Stuarts, died in 1714, she was succeeded by her nearest Protestant relative, the Elector of Hanover, first of a string of Georges destined to rule for 116 years.* One consequence of their accession was a revival of Jacobite** hopes for a restoration of the Stuart dynasty. In 1715 James II's son—James III—landed in Scotland, only to flee after defeat a few months later. Further attempts to raise the Highland clans in the 1720's met with no success. But in 1745, while France and Britain were at war, Louis XV supported a fresh attempt to upset the Hanoverians: James's heir, Charles Edward (1720–1788)—Bonnie Prince Charlie—landed in Scotland, rallied the clans still faithful to the Stuart cause and even invaded England. By spring of 1746, however, he too had been defeated and hopes of Stuart restoration dashed for good, while the Scots, crushed and persecuted, were forced out of their secular isolation to win a paradoxical revenge in their increasing share of the trade and administration of their English victors and of England's empire.

Another result of the Hanoverian settlement, and one which affected the kingdom's European policy, was that fifty-two years after giving up her last continental possessions England had once more to bear in mind the interests and security of her king's electorate. The interlude was brief. The fate of Hanover only mattered to the first two Georges, still close to their German roots. George III showed little interest in what he called "that horrid electorate;" and this progressive detachment culminated in 1837 in the accession of another branch of the family to what had by then become a kingdom, to whose throne Victoria, as a woman, was not entitled to succeed. But for a while, the Hanover connection affected the policies of England.

Much has been made of the idea that George I could speak no English, which left his ministers very much to themselves and allowed cabinet government to develop unpresided by the King and increasingly independent of his direct authority. Despite tales of George I communicating with his ministers in dog-Latin, it would appear that he did know a bit of English, and quite a lot of French, which he generally used like many other monarchs of his time. State documents destined for the King's examination were translated into French, and George's

---

* George I, 1714–1727; George II, 1727–1760; George III, 1760–1820; George IV, 1820–1830; followed by William IV, 1830–1837, and Victoria, 1837–1901.

** From Jacobus, Latin for James: partisans of James II, exiled in 1688, and of his direct heirs.

George I of England.

conversations with English ministers were in that language.

The situation changed under his son, less boorish than his father. It was said that the sight of a book made George I angry; his grumpy "I hate all boets and bainters!" has often been quoted. George II liked books and patronized their authors—and musicians too. What is more important, the new king was familiar with English ways. Thereafter, and to the end of the century—even though George II long left his affairs in the hands of his father's great minister, Robert Walpole—the crown once more dominated British policy. Yet, with a difference: for it never ruled with the arbitrary power wielded by the kings of France, let alone of Prussia; or long ignored the wishes of the lords, the money interests of the city of London, and even of public opinion taken in the broadest sense. So that, henceforth and quite significantly, the tale of English politics would be told in terms of ministries, not reigns.

King and Parliament

England was ruled by the King-in-Parliament, and for most of the eighteenth century this meant that to rule England the king—or rather his ministers—had to manage Parliament, and the great families or interests which controlled elections to it, so as to secure a majority in the House of Commons. This turned politics into a vast spoils system, in which support was bought with offices and the perquisites of office supported the cost of politics. In 1726, one quarter of the English peerage held either court or government office, and most of the offices left over went to peers' friends, their clients, or their relatives, in a great round of venality, nepotism, and corruption. Archaic survivals, like the post of Taster of the King's Wine in Dublin, became sinecures in the gift of ministers eager to ensure the loyalty of some man or clan. Failing

71

office, bribery would do. The visiting Voltaire recorded the remark of an English member of Parliament, threatening that if he did not receive a bribe he would be forced to vote according to his conscience. On the other hand, Walpole once explained he was obliged to bribe members, not to vote against their conscience, but for it. One way or another, it may be argued that the system seems to have worked; and that, bad as it was, corruption was better than force.

Walpole and Pitt

The man who made it work was Robert Walpole (1676–1745), a country gentleman of great managing ability, who held office from 1715 to 1717 and again from 1721 to 1742. In Louis Kronenberger's words "he ascertained that men are vain, self-interested and stupid, and proceeded to act on the information." Most people are content to bewail the fact. Not that many did so in those days, when most generally admitted that they went into public affairs for what they could get out of it. As one of Walpole's chief opponents put it, speaking of his own Tory party, "our principal views were the preservation of this power, great employment to ourselves, and great opportunity of rewarding those who had helped to raise us, and of hurting those who stood in opposition to us." Hence, the matter-of-factness with which Walpole could remark about the House of Commons "All these men have their price." Much the same could be said of any other ruling group of the time, but it is significant that it was said in England.

Controlling the Commons and strong in the King's support, Walpole kept England at peace as long as he could, avoiding commercial wars and higher taxes. After he resigned in 1742, influence, patronage, and low taxes were followed by influence, patronage, and high taxes raised to pay for aggressive enterprises which were designed to exploit every possibility of commercial expansion. The change in policies can be seen in the comparison between the two great prime ministers of the time: solid, all-too-human Walpole, the politicking country squire, himself the scion of an old established country family; and the man who succeeded him, dynamic William Pitt (1708–1778), grandson of an East India merchant who promoted himself from interloping buccaneer to governor of Madras. Cold, aggressive, egoistic, and unstable, Pitt believed in his destiny and in that of England—which meant that of her sailors and her merchants. William Pitt had learned from his fierce grandfather that trade and wealth came by risk and war. In 1735, at twenty-seven, he entered the Commons from the family borough of Old Sarum, where proprietorship of a mound of earth on which a village had once stood gave the right to a seat in Parliament. In 1739 he spoke for war with Spain: "When trade is at stake, you must defend it or perish." It was a language which the merchants of London and Bristol, and the city people whose livelihood depended on them, liked. For the next fourteen years, England would be almost constantly at war, in India, in America, and over all the seas, conquering the empire that would serve her trade; and Pitt—later the Earl of Chatham—would be the symbol of her imperial gains.

Yet Pitt would be removed from power in 1761 and reduced to protest bitterly against the mealy policies of lesser men,* and against the Peace of 1763, in which, he complained "We retain nothing although we have conquered everything" and which, above all, failed to curb France's power at sea. His warnings went unheeded and Britain paid the penalty in the American war, during which the old statesman died, the empire he had helped build foundering, his son William reading to him from the *Iliad* the death of Hector. Burke wrote the inscription of his tomb in Westminster Abbey, praising the first statesman by whom commerce was united with and made to flourish by war.

G. M. Trevelyan, the English historian, has called the days of Pitt "an age of aristocracy and liberty," when law and money ruled but reform was kept at bay. Such stability could rest only on prosperity and expansion, and figures bear this out. Between 1720 and 1802 the value of British imports increased fivefold, that of British exports sixfold. "Our ships," Addison boasted in his *Spectator* in 1711, "are laden with the harvest of every climate: our tables are stored with spices, and oils, and wines: our rooms are filled with pyramids of china, and adorned with the workmanship of Japan: our morning's draught comes to us from the remotest corners of the earth: we repair our bodies by the drugs from America and repose ourselves under Indian canopies . . . nature indeed furnishes us with the bare necessities of life; but traffic gives us a great variety of what is useful, and at the same time supplies us with everything that is convenient and ornamental." That year, the penny post introduced in London and nearby facilitated letter writing and business communications, providing frequent and regular deliveries of mail. That year too had seen the foundation of the South Sea Company, set up less to trade in the southern seas than to finance the taking over of the national debt and strengthen public credit.

The wave of speculation that the maneuvers of the South Sea Company set off, and the eventual crash in which they finally resulted when this and other bubbles burst in 1720, threatened for a while to have just the opposite effect. Yet Walpole's astute policies righted the situation and, as the 1720's ended, trade was booming once more and public credit had been restored. The very venality of the administration approached that of the business interests and, while ministers made no bones about their greed, rapacity did not prevent scrupulous discharge

---

* Like George III's tutor, the Earl of Bute; or, briefly, the Duke of Newcastle, of whose bumbling ways Louis Kronenberger quotes some characteristic examples: "Oh—yes—yes—to be sure—Annapolis must be defended—troops must be sent to Annapolis—pray where *is* Annapolis?" "Cape Breton is an island! Wonderful! —show it to me in the map. So it is, sure enough. My dear Sir, you always bring us good news. I must go and tell the King that Cape Breton is an island."

of governmental debts. This policy paid off. Public confidence in the government enabled it to draw on private resources to an amazing extent. The national debt, one million in 1688, was nearly eighty million in mid-eighteenth century, and yet government securities which paid 5 per cent in 1717 paid only 3 per cent in 1749. Government was constitutional; propertied men knew that their peers controlled expenditures and made accounting public. Public obligations would no more be canceled. That was why the government could borrow cheaply and use what it got for policies which only advanced the interests of its merchant creditors.

Perhaps England was ruled less exactly by an aristocracy than by an oligarchy—or a plutocracy. Rank meant wealth and wealth brought rank. The English, as Burke put it, were "entitled to equal rights, but to equal rights to unequal things." Magnates grew rich on the rents of their lands; lesser gentry yearned for a better past and turned against them, but prosperity tempered social animosity. Among the rural lower classes many went hungry but some prospered. Workhouses fed, housed, and hired out the poor to manufacturers or landlords, who got cheap labor for the cost of their keep. Some workhouse children wore manacles, or rings round their necks, to keep them from running away. Riots were commonplace in leaner years, but the countryside was well in hand.

The pivot was the volunteer Justice of the Peace, who acted as neighborhood administrator and supervisor, licensing inns, fixing wages, supervising the jail and the workhouse, meting out rough justice, setting the rates, and keeping highways in indifferent repair. The J.P. could become a petty local tyrant; he was certainly a very influential man.

"You are the slaves of laws," Voltaire remarked wistfully to Boswell. "The French are the slaves of men." Any reader of *Tom Jones* will know that some English magistrates were also arbitrary and unjust. But they were the stern defenders of the order they incarnated. As late as 1763 a seventy-three-year-old schoolmaster would be put in stocks and thrown in jail for translating Voltaire and publishing freethinking tracts. But that itself reflected a new public, for which the literature of this kind was meant. As early as 1727, a Swiss traveler had been impressed by the way English workmen started their day by going to a coffeehouse to read the newspapers, discussing politics and even the King. By that year the English provinces boasted twenty-five newspapers. By 1753, seven and a half million newspapers were being sold in England: forty years later this number had more than doubled. Literacy grew, thanks largely to charity schools for children of artisans, small shopkeepers, the lower middle class. Clubs sprang up devoted to discussion and debate. Political awareness increased in London and the provinces. And all this would be reflected in the Wilkes affair.

John Wilkes (1727–1797) was the son of a parvenu distiller: a great talker, winebibber, and womanizer, a brash and exhibitionistic man.

Robert Walpole Before the British Cabinet, a painting by Joseph Coopy. British Museum, London.

But he was also the owner of a newspaper and member of Parliament, in which he supported the politics of Pitt. In 1763, angered by the peace which made too many concessions to France and none to the city merchants, Wilkes denounced the treaty, the ministry, and even George III, in his *North Briton,* in ferocious terms that brought charges of seditious libel and a general warrant to arrest both him and his printer. George III had used general warrants much as the king of France used *lettres de cachet,* but with explosive results. The English public were not about to see a printer, let alone a Member of Parliament, arrested and pursued against what seemed to them the law of the land. From the Tower, Wilkes claimed wrongful arrest and instituted a countersuit. Popular imagination sizzled, "Wilkes and liberty" became the slogan of the day and, when a friendly judge declared general warrants illegal, Wilkes triumphed and won his damages. But the King had other strings to his bow, and Wilkes was expelled from the Commons on obscenity charges and had to flee the country. In 1768, he returned to stand as candidate for Middlesex. Elected, rejected by the Commons unwilling to displease the King, he became a hero once more, was repeatedly re-elected by Middlesex votes and repeatedly rejected by the Commons which finally declared his defeated opponent elected in his stead.

Wilkes lived on to become Lord Mayor of London, proof that blundering governments could not blunder too far and that popular temper could not be denied too long; but also that—in the end—England was not fated to revolution but to adjustment. Meanwhile, the long battles waged around him established the right to report Parliamentary debates; political agitation, complete with public meetings and propaganda

John Wilkes, as depicted by William Hogarth. British Museum, London.

organization, indicated that politics could not remain the preserve of a narrow coterie; and Parliament itself was discredited for the prejudice, corruption, and unrepresentativeness which had been taken for granted until then. A new mentality was appearing, fertile ground for the reform agitation to come, and one soon to be raked over by the great controversy that would arise over the rights of Britain's American colonies,

From Colonies to Nation in America

By a curious paradox, the land which today symbolizes the western hemisphere and arrogates to itself the name of America was one of the last parts of the New World to be discovered, settled, and organized. English colonists reached Virginia almost a century after Columbus had sighted Cuba; French travelers preceded English ones in the Canadian wastes. While English settlers were scrabbling between the Bay of Fundy and the Savannah River, empires had been built to the south and an empire was growing in the north. Yet, unexpectedly, it would be the latecomers who triumphed, to build new Jerusalems throughout the continent.

More than any other country, the history of North America is that of men tackling nature, wrestling with the physical environment and with the elements, taming and shaping them to their will and being shaped in turn by the experiences they encountered and the challenges they overcame. Men, not states; men, not heroes; men who turned a continent of forest and waste into the immense demonstration of what men can do.

Two great cohesive forces seem to have dominated the formation of these new societies: the one was the pressure of the environment, the hostility of Indians and Frenchmen; the other idealism, diversely manifested, but chiefly—to begin with—in religious terms. Many colonists, especially in New England and the middle colonies, had left their homelands or been forced from them to be free to follow their conscience, to worship in their own way. Seeking freedom of conscience and worship for themselves, they denied it to others, as it had been denied to them. Their new societies would be founded on a common faith, which, once responsible for their own exclusion, now suggested the exclusion of others. Religion provided unity and counseled intolerance, as well as the moral right of society to intervene in its members' private lives, private morality becoming a matter of public concern. And though this applies largely to the New England colonies, religious beliefs would inspire other settlements, including that of the Quakers in Pennsylvania, who would be tolerant on principle as others were intolerant, and who would also leave their mark on American minds in centuries to come.

Since so many immigrants were nonconformists, they left their mark in yet another way: in their interest in popular education, in reading, in libraries and printing presses, above all in representative institutions from the town meeting to the colonial assembly, whose members consented to the taxes levied by the royal government. Conditions varied immensely among settlements stretching for nearly 1,500 miles across fifteen degrees of latitude; but one thing is evident: the colonies were growing fast. The twelve colonies of 1713 numbered about 360,000 people; in the thirteen colonies of 1763 the population had increased fivefold and the area of settlement had tripled. Much of the increase can be attributed to favorable conditions in a country where land was plentiful, and large families useful and easy to feed. Most of it, however, came from immigration: Huguenots, Highlanders, Swiss, about a quarter of a million Ulstermen, Germans driven by war or poverty or religious persecution, black slaves who numbered some 300,000 by the close of the Seven Years' War. The population seems to have doubled every generation. By 1775 it was approaching two and a half million; the first census in 1790 counted nearly four million, including 750,000 Negroes.

"You may depend upon it," said an American patriot, "that this is one of the best Poor Man's Country's in the World." Driven by land hunger, by dissatisfaction with the rule of churchmen in New England or great planters in the south, the poor men moved inland, pushed forward an irregular but ever-advancing frontier which served both as a safety valve and as a source for further development. Where the tidewater was prosperous and sophisticated, the hinterland was rebellious and self-reliant. Indifferent or hostile to the English culture of the seaboard, to the mercantile preoccupations of wealthy merchants and planters, to religious or political conformism, frontiersmen were nomadic, homespun, tough; they looked west across the continent, not east across the sea. Only the threat of Indians and the competition of Frenchmen held them back.

There were only 60,000 Frenchmen, but enterprise and military organization allowed them to hold their own. Sixty thousand against seventeen times as many. But not all British colonists were confronting the French, and most of their militiamen preferred to remain close to home rather than fight in the Canadian wastes. The so-called French and Indian wars of the 1750's which led into the Seven Years' War, would not have gone against the French but for the troops shipped over to do the fighting, and for the British fleet commanding the sea lanes over the Atlantic.

No wonder the British general, James Wolfe, did not mince his words: "The Americans are in general the dirtiest, the most contemptible cowardly dogs you can conceive. There is no depending on 'em in action. They fall down dead in their own dirt and desert by battalions, officers and all." As long as the French Empire lasted, the fate of the colonies, especially their chances of expansion, remained in doubt. Once the French threat had been removed in 1763, they would have little use for government from the outside, still less for taxes that might keep it up.

Issues of Conflict

Hardly more than a decade passed between the Peace of Paris and serious trouble in the colonies. The most evident sources of trouble were two: trade and taxes. The first was connected with the basic principle of the old colonial system, according to which colonies were supposed to supply the home country with raw materials and provide a market for its exports, never competing with them. American colonists could buy only English goods or foreign goods imported by way of England, could sell their goods only to the English, who might not want them if they competed with their own, or who would make a profit reselling them to others. So, the Americans fell back on smuggling, which became so successful that it enriched the colonists and angered the English.

Incapable of stopping contraband, the British government sought at least to cash in on the prosperity it fostered, by taxing the colonists. Walpole tried it and caused such a stir that he retreated. Then, after 1763, the cost of war and of its aftermath counseled other attempts, especially a stamp tax whose revenue should pay for the upkeep of British troops in America. But the victorious war had just removed the chief need for such troops, and the colonists felt that for defense against Indians they could do as well more cheaply, the more so since the presence of the British troops also hampered their own attempts to encroach on Indian territories. Moreover, they would not be taxed without their consent and there were many men in England who agreed.

Here we come to the second issue, that of taxes. After 1763, the British government felt that economies were in order and that these could best be achieved by stopping westward expansion which would avoid Indian wars, and by devising means whereby Americans assumed the burden of their own defense. The government's effort to raise revenue by customs and taxation caused opposition and protest which remained only local until the Stamp Act of 1765, requiring revenue stamps to be fixed on legal documents, bills, and newspapers, roused the most vocal classes among the colonists and produced a violent reaction. Repealed in 1766, chiefly because revenue did not live up to expectations, the Stamp Act was followed by new import duties, which raised a fresh uproar and a boycott that frightened conservative interests in the colonies as much as it did the government in London. For the moment most of the duties were repealed and protests simmered down again until, in response to the East India Company's financial needs, the Tea Act of 1773 permitted the company to ship its tea direct to American ports and retail it there more cheaply, thus injuring both established colonial merchants and the smugglers who had supplied them.

These two influential groups now joined with the constitutional radicals who opposed the measure on principle. The Boston Tea Party of December, 1773, which destroyed the cargo of tea ships in Boston harbor, shook the British government out of appeasement into coercion, attempts at which in turn united the remaining colonies in support of Massachusetts, groaning under the British Coercive Acts of 1774.

Growing resentment and distrust of London in the colonies was matched by growing exasperation in London over the obstreperousness of the colonists. By 1774, as Burke reported to the New York Assembly, not only government but opinion felt the need to assert themselves by *"some* act of power." Such acts, when they came, unleashed first a storm of popular fury against the supporters of imperial authority in the colonies and, then, armed conflict.

Meanwhile, as the American debate grew ever more heated on both sides of the Atlantic, Parliament, discredited by recent events, bore the brunt of criticism. Old William Pitt, now Earl of Chatham, supported the colonists, arguing that there could be no taxation without representation.* A high judge, Lord Camden, formulated their greatest argument: "Taxation and representation are inseparable; this position is founded on the laws of nature"; and quoted Locke: "The supreme power cannot take from any man any part of his property without his own consent." In British eyes government was a trust, a *delegation,* not an absolute, unchallengeable force as on the continent. Yet, in defiance of nature and of Locke, this was something to which no government of the

---

* The friends of liberty took their watchword from a pamphlet by James Otis, *Rights of the Colonies* (1764): "No parts of His Majesty's dominions can be taxed without their consent."

day could resign itself.

The issue had ceased to turn on taxes. It was now one of Parliamentary and governmental supremacy facing the traditional and theoretical rights of free men. If the Americans "would submit and leave to us the constitutional right of supremacy," Lord North told Parliament in 1775, the quarrel would be at an end. The colonists, on their part, would not give way to what George Washington—in a letter of 1774—called "a systematic assertion of an arbitrary power, deeply planned to overturn the laws and constitution of their country, and to violate the most essential and valuable rights of mankind . . ." To do so would mean that they were no longer free. "None of them will ever submit to the loss of those valuable rights and privileges which are essential to the life of every free State, and without which life, liberty and property are rendered totally insecure."

In May of 1774 the first Continental Congress, meeting at Philadelphia, petitioned the King for redress and organized to withstand the mother country, while provincial congresses collected stores, organized militia, and prepared for trouble. In April, 1775, at Lexington, British troops sent to seize the arms and stores which colonists had gathered at nearby Concord, were fired upon. These were the shots heard round the world. By the end of the day, the British were besieged in Boston. By the end of May, a second Continental Congress had authorized a Continental Army "of the United Colonies," which George Washington was soon appointed to command. In July, 1776, after a year's fighting, Congress approved the Declaration of Independence.

If the language of this great document is familiar today, it is worth noting that it was familiar in its own day as well, and that much of its success came from the fact that it voiced in magnificent terms the basic tenets which Locke and his successors had inculcated in educated westerners since the beginning of the century:

> We hold these truths to be self-evident, that all men are created equal, that they are endowed by their Creator with certain unalienable Rights, that among these are life, liberty and the pursuit of Happiness.—That to secure these rights, Governments are instituted among Men, deriving their just powers from the consent of the governed.—That whenever any Form of Government becomes destructive of these ends, it is the Right of the People to abolish it, and to institute new Government . . .

These things were worth repeating. If they were not original, that only meant that they could be the more effective on minds prepared to receive them and on which their effect was electrifying.

For the moment the issues were to be decided not by words, but arms. Chiefly, it might be added, French arms; for the news of the first real rebel victory in forcing General Burgoyne's surrender at Saratoga (1777) persuaded the French government that the time had come to take revenge against the British. Four years later, another surrender—that of Cornwallis cornered in Yorktown by the French fleet and the Franco-American army—would persuade the British to open negotiations for peace, which was finally signed in 1783.

"New Government"

Independence had been won. Patriots had actually shown that the ideas of Locke and Montesquieu could be put into practice and that governments could be founded by social compact. They had developed the arsenal of revolution, from correspondence societies and clubs to constitutional conventions. The Declaration of Rights (1776) stated the basic rights of men or, at least, of American citizens, for slaves were still excluded; the Articles of Confederation (1781) organized the new republic as a federal state; finally, the Constitution (1787) laid down the working structure of the state to be: the separation of powers (executive, legislative, judiciary), the separation of church and state and the disestablishment of the church; the faith (as every dollar bill reminds us) that they were ushering in a new order of ages.

The new order did not apply to slaves or to indentured servants; and, oddly enough, it was a reactionary swing back to an older order, a reaction against modernist reforms which had inspired those who fought for it. Yet the state whose first President was inaugurated just four months before the fall of the Bastille, was a new thing: it was republican, it was federal, it was a symbol of hope. This new hope, this promise, this American myth, would be as strong in Europe as in the new federal republic. Here was the proof that philosophical ideas could really be put into practice: in Budapest a Masonic lodge called itself *American*, the new American Constitution was translated, commented upon, and set a pattern for the future. "We talked of nothing but America," Talleyrand would remember later; and Benjamin Franklin in Paris provided a dubious but impressive example of republican virtues for everyone to see.

What was less obvious at the time, the long debate during which the Constitution was hammered out gave a prophetic foretaste of future conflicts which the Republic—and other democracies too—would have to face. To oversimplify, it was conducted between "Republicans"—defenders of state rights against the central power, of small free men, preferably landowners, against the ambitions of some selfish faction of the powerful and greedy—and the Federalists, who stood for stronger federal power, for an executive which could maintain order and run a modern state. The former, with Rousseau and Jefferson, believed in the individual; the latter in order, hierarchy, and sound laws. Elitist, the Federalists wanted the minority's rights protected from the possible oppression of majority rule. Democratic, the Republicans wanted the majority freed from the oppression of the powerful and rich. The Federalists looked to England and to a National Bank to maintain sound money; the Republicans looked to France, to schools, and newspapers, and easier credit. The former would rule with Washington and John Adams; the latter with Jefferson, Madison and Monroe between 1801 and 1825. But while Republicans stood for a small man's democracy, and sympathized with the French Revolution, neither party really envisaged social revolution on these shores.

"A little rebellion now and then," thought Thomas Jefferson, "is a good thing." The author of the Declaration of Independence was the new republic's minister in Paris in 1789, and General Lafayette, who had won his spurs on Washington's staff, gave him a key of the Bastille to convey to his old commander. But conservative Federalists like Washington did not like the way in which the French Revolution evolved, or the Jacobin propaganda of Citizen Genêt, the French Republic's representative in the United States. Washington stood for neutrality, American opinion shifted from sympathy for France to co-operation with England, and the Alien and Sedition Acts were voted to defend this neutrality.

America, "kindly separated by nature and a wide ocean from the exterminating havoc [in Europe]," as Jefferson would put it, meant to keep further revolution from its shores. That was not easily done. Napoleon's Berlin Decree of 1806 was to be answered by the British Orders in Council of 1807: blockade by counterblockade. These led to Jefferson's Embargo Act (1807) forbidding U.S. ships to sail outside their territorial waters. And, while this hurt the French and English, many of whose imports came in U.S. vessels, it hurt American shipping more. After Madison took office in 1809, the Embargo Act was repealed and replaced with the Non-Intercourse Act, permitting trade with all but Britain and France, which was itself revoked in 1810. The Americans needed to trade, as the Europeans needed their goods.

Then, Napoleon managed to trick the Americans into thinking that their continued difficulties were to be attributed solely to the British refusal to withdraw the Orders in Council, pretending that he was willing to withdraw his own blockade decrees. This suited the anti-British partisans of western expansion, the war hawks, who seized on these differences as a pretext for war with Britain, hoping to annex Canada and, anyway, to put a stop to aid which the Indians received from there. Despite British anxiety to avoid conflict, war was declared in 1812, just two days after the Orders in Council had been withdrawn. This, in a way, illustrates the most remarkable aspect of a war begun after its ostensible reason had evaporated and ended two weeks before its most important battle, since the news that peace had been signed did not reach New Orleans in time to prevent the bloody fighting there.

Distances were so great and news so sluggish, that things like these were bound to happen. The one great result of the war was that the young United States became conscious of themselves as one nation that stretched from Erie to New Orleans, complete with a war hero (Andrew Jackson) who would become one of her great Presidents.

"These United States"

When the thirteen ex-colonies had given themselves a new federal Constitution in 1789, their total population was below four million, less than that of Switzerland today, less than that of contemporary Spain (ten million) or Mexico (six million), and including several hundred thousand Negro slaves. This tiny nation held immense territories, which were increased by the acquisition of Louisiana from Napoleon for $15,000,000 in 1802, and of Florida from Spain in 1819. With Texas acquired in 1845 and the Pacific Northwest wrenched from England in 1846, the Southwest from Mexico in 1848 and 1853, finally with Alaska, bought from Russia in 1867, the continental empire would be complete. The continent soon filled with people, for not only immigrants came but more people were born and fewer died in the spacious new republic than elsewhere. It was the economist Adam Smith who had noted in 1776 that the population of the North American colonies tended to double every twenty or twenty-five years, whereas in Britain the same process took twenty times as long. This continued to be true in the nineteenth century; and the disproportion, although less striking, remains marked: the American rate of population increase in recent years being still twice that of France, nearly three times the German, three and a half times the British.

The American colonies had early produced most of their necessities. The development of the sugar islands in the Caribbean provided Northerners with a hungry market for wheat, rum, fish, and lumber, and stimulated their shipping. The war of independence, interrupting imports of manufactures from England, further stimulated home production. Then came the Revolutionary and Napoleonic Wars, which left the new United States the only neutral with a large merchant fleet, a fleet that grew sevenfold between 1789 and 1810. Its earnings alone could pay for more imported goods than the colonies had used before the Revolution. Eli Whitney's invention of the cotton gin in 1793 turned the South into a cotton kingdom and established a new symbiosis beween the Southern states and Lancashire, which was soon taking about three-quarters of all the raw cotton they exported. Expansion of textile industries in continental Europe also created a vast and growing market for American cotton. The British mills alone increased their consumption from 2,000 to 250,000 tons a year, between 1780 and 1850. In the United States the number of spindles rose from

8,000 in 1808 to 500,000 in 1815. The parallel rise in American production went with large-scale productivity, which, cutting the price of raw materials, allowed the price of British manufactures to be cut by two-thirds in the same years. Cotton exports and those of similarly bulky goods like timber and wheat meant that ships sailing westward, back to the United States, had lots of space which they could sell at low rates to passengers from Europe. Lower passage fares encouraged immigrants who might otherwise find the journey's cost impossible to bear, while the expanding market for American goods meant that the immigrants could sell their labor and its products when they arrived on these shores. The demand fed not only an increasing supply of goods but of people too.

The decade following 1815 is known in U.S. history as the era of good feelings. It was perhaps more, as the historian George Dangerfield suggests, an era of mixed feelings, when geographical divisions would take the place of political ones, when slavery began to threaten the delicate balance of the union, when the Missouri Compromise of 1820 prohibiting slavery north of 36°30′ provided a temporary solution to the conundrum whether a nation can exist half slave half free, and an introduction to the sectional controversies which colored the rest of the century. In 1823, with the Monroe Doctrine, the new nation had established the basis of a diplomacy which unilaterally—though taking the Royal Navy for granted—kept both Russians and reactionary Europeans from enterprises in its hemisphere.

The greatest land power in the West—modest though its real power still was at that time—was the first to have farmers who thought in terms of movement not stability, of cash when they talked of crops, of markets and enterprise. The first, too, effectively to offer equal chances to all (although not to slaves) in the great economic race that now opened up. The Jacksonian confrontation of the 1820's would revive the two-party system which had faded away during the era of good feelings. The Democrats now stood for Jacksonian equalitarianism, freedom of enterprise and trade, states' rights. The Whigs, heirs of the Federalists of yore, had no real program but shared a common distrust of the masses. With Andrew Jackson (1829), the transition from East to West, from mansion to log cabin was established, and democratic politics rose on a firm foundation of spoils and wider suffrage.

American democracy was rude, its structure was clumsy, its politics were wasteful, but it worked. Or so it seemed to foreign observers like Alexis de Tocqueville who saw in it, with little enough satisfaction for some of them, the shape of things to come. Not only did American democracy work; it moved: Louisiana in 1803, Florida in 1819, Texas in 1845, Oregon in 1846, California and New Mexico in 1848. After 1853, only Alaska and Hawaii would be missing from the present constellation.

The year 1850 would actually see the United States reach its continental limits. From 9 million in 1820, the population by 1850 had grown to 23 million. The sprawling union was still a colony of its eastern seaboard. The railroad only reached Chicago and St. Louis in 1853. In this expanding land, where every tenth man was an immigrant, a new nationalism was taking shape. "We have listened too long to the refined muses of Europe," wrote Ralph Waldo Emerson. "We shall walk on our own feet, we shall work with our own hands, we shall speak according to our own convictions."

Britain Resurgent

"A great empire and little minds go ill together," Burke had said. Events had borne him out. As the American conflict unfolded the spectacle of division at home and incompetence abroad, the King's bid toward a "despotism" only dimly lightened ran on the rocks. So did his supporters. In 1780, the Commons narrowly passed the famous motion "that the influence of the crown has increased, is increasing, and ought to be diminished." By 1783, this was done.

Domestic reforms introduced salaries for public servants whose services had formerly been paid by fees, bit into political patronage and sinecure-appointments, diminished the influence of the Court—partly by the Civil List Act which fixed a yearly sum for the king's expenditures, simplified the tax structure and the funding of government debts. Parliament resisted its own reform, but the country's administration was gradually rationalized. The executive became less corrupt, more stable, more sensible too. Economies were effected, revenue was increased, a financial reconstruction was achieved which would stand the country in good stead in the years ahead.

The Americans had saved Britain from monarchic despotism, if such a threat existed. They had also shaken her badly. But that did not last long. The 1780's would be a time of economic and industrial boom, and the loss of empire soon proved to be no loss to trade and, hence, to prosperity. But the war had portentous effects in many ways. One concrete issue raised by the loss of the American colonies was that convicts could no longer be transported westward and had to be shipped southeast instead, to Botany Bay from which Australia grew. Another was that British responsibilities in India would be taken more seriously than those in America had been. Soul-searching following defeat attributed the insurrection to a failure to realize and face imperial responsibilities, which were to bring up the colonists in paternal fashion from childhood to maturity. This implied a mission highly suitable to an increasingly Christian and moralistic society that preferred its economic and strategic interests presented in moralistic terms.

Reform: For and Against

Not unconnected with this mood was the growing agitation for reform—reform of a discredited Parliament, but also of an institutional structure increasingly criticized by vocal friends of liberty and of efficiency, foremost among them the members of the country's dissenting sects.

The Glorious Revolution of 1688 had brought toleration to dissenters (and to Catholics too) but not full citizenship. The Catholics, held to be potential enemies and almost resident aliens, lived very much at the margin of society, their low status emphasized by the poverty of Irish immigrants, most of them Catholic. Decent people loathed and feared members of a church connected with the Inquisition and other dark mysteries.* Dissenters had a much easier time. They were generally accepted but the Test and Corporation Acts hamstrung and hampered them, preventing them from taking municipal office (except in some unincorporated provincial towns) and keeping them second-class citizens. Anyone wanting to get on in public life had to be an Anglican: many became so, more or less sincerely, translating religious into social divisions. Others—among them some of the best and best-educated—lived apart from political activity, depriving the country of their services and concentrating on economic activities in which they were not hampered at all.

Naturally, able men excluded from political life and most aspects of government would be the more critical of them, and the keener to secure the rights of individuals, the civil and religious liberties they needed for themselves. Excluded from the universities, they founded dissenting academies, livelier and more progressive than the old foundations. Excluded from city corporations, they were active in the new unincorporated cities like Manchester and Birmingham. They were moral and rationalistic, and developed a social conscience in localities which had sprung up so quickly, mobilizing the rising middle classes, with no regard for creed, to work for efficient administration and orderly local government. Such men had sympathized with the colonists because they were "virtuous" and with Wilkes because he represented the cause of Parliamentary reform. They were for democracy because they thought it meant their own emancipation: the rights of sober, rational, enterprising men like themselves. English radicalism began as the venture of an assertive middle-class minority group.

The first measure calling for comprehensive Parliamentary reform was introduced in the Commons while war raged in America. It was in 1776, the same year in which Adam Smith's *Inquiry into the Wealth of Nations,* Jeremy Bentham's *Theory of Legislation,* and the first volume

---

* As late as the 1830's a lady alone in a railway compartment with the architect Pugin, who saw him cross himself, cried, "You are a Catholic, Sir! Guard, let me out—I must get into another carriage."

Canvassing for Votes, by William Hogarth. Astor, Lennox, and Tilden Foundation.

of Edward Gibbon's *Decline and Fall of the Roman Empire* also appeared. Members of the Commons were elected in boroughs which had been and were no more, or not elected in boroughs which were but had not been when seats in Parliament were first allotted. Rotten boroughs, pocket boroughs, made nonsense of representativeness. Deserted or near-deserted villages retained two seats in the gift of whoever owned their land; while Manchester and Leeds returned no one at all. Twenty or fifty electors in one borough were as well represented as thousands in some shire. Seats could be bought, and so could their incumbents—paid in sinecures, in pensions, or favors of some kind. No wonder enlightened men thought there was room for improvement.

Yet the agitation for reform, like that for repeal of the Test Acts, which began well, soon ran into the backlash of the French Revolution. The example of France inspired the rise of Jacobin clubs, such as the one in Sheffield where 2,500 "of the lowest mechanics" were enrolled in a constitutional society where "they read the most violent publications and comment on them," keeping up correspondence with other societies in neighboring towns and villages and all over England. Laboring men of every kind were reading Thomas Paine and talking of equality. This was not calculated to reassure men of property.

Burke's *Reflections on the Revolution in France* (1790) denounced the dangers of radicalism which left organic growth behind for destructive and unnatural changes. It was answered by Tom Paine's *Rights of Man* (1791), which found the institutions Burke respected (aristocracy and monarchy) anachronistic, and called for popular sovereignty and universal suffrage. Both books were popular: the one with propertied men and most respectable people shocked by revolutionary excesses; the other with the reform societies and lower-class radicals. The government moved against the latter, suspended the Habeas Corpus Act late in 1790, arrested radical leaders on charges of treason, passed Treason

87

and Sedition Acts in 1795 and again in 1799, suppressed the reform groups, and, by the Combination Act of 1799, closed those clubs which workers had founded to improve working conditions and their wages. Henceforth manufacturers could keep down wages and claim conspiracy if workers organized to protest against them. Any tendency toward unionism was savagely suppressed.

War against France, which came in 1793, meant war against English liberals at home. To face Jacobin subversion, freedom of meeting and expression were suppressed. England was no more threatened by native Jacobins in the 1790's than the United States by home-grown Communists in the 1950's, but the label was convenient and there are always awkward dogs about, to whom it might be well to affix a bad name. There was no revolution in England and there would be none, in the first place because the ruling class was confident and seldom so disunited as to lose its grip on power.

Lenin has pointed out that worse conditions for the masses and wider, more intense political activities can only result in revolution if the rulers are going to pieces and are challenged by men who can make and lead a revolution. In England nothing went to pieces except the party of reform, which split in its reaction to events in France. The failure of the more moderate revolutionaries in France, drove their English counterparts, the manufacturers and commercial classes, into an alliance with landowners and with the Establishment against the prospect of any reform at all. "I wish," wrote Coleridge to Wordsworth in 1799, "you would write a poem in blank verse addressed to those who, in consequence of the complete failure of the French Revolution, have thrown up all hopes for the amelioration of mankind, and are sinking into an almost Epicurean selfishness, disguising the same under the soft titles of domestic attachment and contempt for visionary *philosphes*."

The Pursuit of Grace

Another reason why the revolutionary ideas that spread from France to England never caught fire there was the influence of Methodism, implanted since the late 1730's by pious and passionate creatures, above all John Wesley (1703–1791), whose 40,000 sermons—to deliver which he rode 224,000 miles in fifty-five years—preached salvation by faith and spread evangelical fervor among the masses which, hungry for hope, were ready to renounce a bitter world for a sweeter Providence. The incandescent eloquence of the Methodists* provided the enthusiasm, emotion, and release, which the established church withheld. The wealthy and educated found little need for such febrile escapes from a world quite comfortable enough. The poor found it irresistible. Seventy

* Who soon adopted the contemptuous nickname inspired by the regularity of their lives and their strict observance.

thousand English men and women had joined Wesley by the time he died, and far more in the New World, where the new religion spread like wildfire with the nineteenth century.

The Wesleyan revival improved manners and released emotions; as such it was a harbinger or part of the romantic turn against decorum and against the cold emptiness of reason. Yet its core and focus was God, and in this too it forecast a century when God became anthropomorphic once again, and religious concerns were more closely personal than in the rather detached or indifferent eighteenth century. Frenzied revival meetings, the anguish and burden of sin, the exaltation that a sense of salvation brought, would furnish the days and the feelings of millions in the century to come.

Wesley set up classes—today we might call them cells—bands, societies, a highly co-ordinated pyramid of soul-searching fervent Christians, autocratically ruled by him. By 1784, when he broke with the Church of England which would not ordain his ministers, and began to ordain his own, his followers had built nearly four hundred chapels. Thrifty, industrious, anti-intellectual and narrow-minded, obscurantist in education, abstinent, the Methodists were a dynamic novelty in society but a reactionary force in politics. As Wesley himself noted a few years before his death, diligence and frugality increased their goods but diminished their spirit. That is often the case, but here it was more to be expected, since the movement was the image of its leader.

Wesley would make his followers more respectable but also more grim, suspicious of worldly pleasure, mistrusting worldly rank, hostile to beauty or diversion in any form which could turn the eyes from the supreme concern of personal salvation. This implied the dreary shape of austerities to come, but also an equalitarian and responsible spirit; and the very idea which so revolted the Duchess of Buckingham, that she might have a heart as sinful as that of a wretched commoner, could turn attention to the commoners' wretchedness. If most Methodists, persuaded that equality before God rendered equality before the law irrelevant, were as stoutly conservative as their masters, their interests operated in progressive ways: a more fervent religion, a cleaner, more pious, more decent way of life, built a cleaner, more prosperous, more decent following, although a narrow and a strait-laced one.

In the Church of England itself meanwhile, an evangelical awakening was taking place, which would do for middle-class conversion what the Methodists did among the lower classes: suggest a religion of the heart rather than the mind, but also eventually a formidable social conscience. Conviction of sin and expectation of Grace combined to forge a dynamo of reform: moral, social, and political. The evangelicals criticized the public and private laxness of eighteenth-century morals, the savagery of the criminal law, the selfish mess of anachronistic local government and opportunist industrial conditions, the inhumanity and injustice of slavery which the world had taken for granted time out of mind. They sought to enforce new moral standards, pass new laws, make England a cleaner, safer, more just, more decent country; but also one more prurient, more hypocritical, more dreary.

In pursuit of Grace, the so-called Clapham Sect gathered in the 1790's at Clapham in South London, around the parish rector John Venn: William Wilberforce, Henry Thornton, James Stephen, Zachary Macaulay, Hannah More (a Bishop in petticoats as Cobbett described her).* The party of the saints, as the evangelicals were called after their puritan predecessors of the 1640's, was small but influential. In 1809, the prime minister of the day gave up calling Parliament on Mondays so that members should not have to travel on the Sabbath. The Church Missionary Society (1799) and the British and Foreign Bible Society (1804) cast their net wide throughout the country, where 2.5 million Bibles were distributed between 1804 and 1819, and far beyond its shores, where a free Negro colony was set up at Sierra Leone in 1784.** The African Association (1806) promoted the antislavery cause, while missions and bishops were also sent to India. Beyond the new spirit which they helped to promote, one interesting legacy which the evangelicals left was the organization and propaganda pattern they evolved—tracts and pamphlets, public meetings and voluntary societies, which provided the armory of the organized political activity of the nineteenth century.

Immediately, however, religious revivalism—Episcopal or Nonconformist—provided an alternative to radical politics: sometimes a training for them, sometimes a refuge from them, sometimes a consolation for their failure—a socially sanctioned issue for despair which might otherwise have rocked society gravely.

The Restive Populace

Despair was running strongest in England's nearest and worst-governed colony, across the Irish Channel. There had been troubles in Ireland in the early eighties, echoes of the American Revolution. Reforms sought to restore calm by improving the condition of the Irish. The Test Act was abolished in the island, Catholics allowed to purchase land, the Irish Parliament declared autonomous, the two kingdoms equal. Further reforms came up against the King's conviction that his coronation oath precluded Catholic emancipation and, after 1787, when George III had got down from his carriage in Windsor park and addressed an oak tree as the king of Prussia, his minister, Pitt, Chatham's son, hesitated to press him on any issue that might bring on new attacks of madness. Hence George III ruled on, and Ireland boiled. The Catholics wanted the vote, which Pitt wanted to give them but could not. The nationalist

---

* Her two cats were called "Non-resistance" and "Passive obedience." There is no mention of whether they came when called.

** And a draft from British prisons made good the shortage of women among early settlers.

United Irishmen, led by Wolfe Tone, sought the help of the French, but the projected French invasion went awry and Tone's rising of 1798 was put down with the utmost brutality, while Tone himself committed suicide. The Irish Parliament was abolished, and Ireland "indissolubly" bound to Britain by the Act of Union of 1800, to bedevil British politics for another century and more.

Meanwhile, social unrest was reviving in Britain, born of vast economic changes enhanced by the difficulties of war. The country weathered the storm, the wars with France were won, but never had the situation seemed so uneasy. Shelley portrayed:

> An old, mad, blind, despised and dying king,
> Princes, the dregs of their dull race, who flow
> Through public scorn—mud from a muddy spring—
> Rulers who neither see, nor feel, nor know,
> But leech-like to their fainting country cling. . .

Popular agitation, food riots, machine-breaking, rick-burning, calls for reform, continued in the postwar years, culminating in the Massacre of Peterloo (1819), when armed horsemen cut down a great reform meeting in Manchester's Saint Peter's Fields.

Yet, whatever the misery and sporadic recessions, economic activity poured oil on troubled waters. In spite of Napoleon's Continental System, the value of British exports quadrupled between 1805 and 1811. The volume of international trade had doubled between 1780 and 1800; it would double again by 1840. Between 1700 and 1750 real income per head had grown at an average rate of 0.30 per cent a year. This average rate would increase to 0.45 per cent between 1750 and 1800, 1.1 per cent between 1801 and 1831, 1.5 per cent between 1831 and 1851. In 1830, real wages stood 50 per cent higher than in 1780. Agricultural improvements allowed a smaller number of rural laborers to feed a population which had doubled in number, increased trade revenue took care of the rest. During the first half of the nineteenth century about a quarter of the whole world's trade was in British hands. The exports of

The Massacre of Peterloo, 1819, a contemporary drawing.

the next largest trading power, France, were less than half the value of the British. Britain was the dynamo of the Industrial Revolution, the center of the world's banking structure, the school and inspiration of things to come.

The face of the country was altering at a rate that had not been seen before, population was growing, factories springing up, farming methods changing, masses of people shifting from country to town, crowding around the new manufactory-barracks of production, creating slums, brewing discontent, calling ever more harshly for a remedy to their misery. The young Benjamin Disraeli compared the problems caused by teeming population with those which toppled down the Roman Empire and found the troubles of his day incomparably greater: "What are your invasions of the barbarous nations . . . to our Population Returns!" Already in 1798 a pessimistic country clergyman, Thomas Malthus, had warned that population was increasing faster than the means of subsistence. Laborers who dined on bread and apples, or tried "to make potato flour by grating the half-rotten potatoes into a large tub full of water," plowmen who made tea with burnt crusts of bread and shared a herring among five for Sunday dinner, families subsisting on nauseous messes "that made your inside feel as if it was on fire and sort of choked'ee," bore him out.

Yet reform, sparked by evangelical propaganda and by the arguments of utilitarian thinkers, spurred by popular pressure, was on the march again. In the very year of Peterloo, revision of the criminal law ended the death penalty for over a hundred offenses, such as fraud.* Beginning in 1825, Factory Acts, rudimentary at first but growing increasingly effective, regulated the employment of women and children, the hours and conditions of labor, and provided inspectors to enforce the new regulations. In 1828, the Test and Corporation Acts were at last repealed and Dissenters fully integrated in society.** In 1829, Roman Catholics followed. But the greatest issue remained unsolved: that of Parliamentary reform.

Whigs and Tories

The authority of the Crown had been declining, along with its popularity. George IV and his brothers were, said Wellington, the "damn'dest millstone about the neck of any government that can be imagined." Crown influence shrank as administrative and fiscal efficiency increased. But, while patronage declined, parties were only just taking shape and, without a disciplined party machine, Parliament was bound

---

* The law continued harsh, though not as harsh as some traditionalists would have liked. In the 1840's, a twelve-year-old girl could be sentenced to fourteen days' hard labor for stealing a small prayer book from school, with the magistrate expressing his regret that he could not order her to be whipped as well.

** Although it was not until the 1850's that they could take university degrees.

to flounder amidst a welter of groups and factions.

"Foreigners think parliamentarism a form of government," Oswald Spengler has written: "It is nothing of the kind. It is an English game, like cricket, which only English people can play." The game was played by Whigs and Tories. The latter, on the whole, were the party of landed interests, of the smaller gentry, of opposition to change, to Dissent, to Catholics, to industrial and agricultural developments for which they lacked both sympathy and means. As we might expect, they also opposed parliamentary reform. Their inarticulate loyalties would soon be enlisted in a new Conservative Party, first by Robert Peel (1788–1850) and then by Benjamin Disraeli (1804–1881). The Whigs were not a party that you joined but a connection into which you were born—preferably in a great country house. It was their liberal and radical allies —the City money interests, the manufacturers, the Dissenters—who mobilized them to support the cause of "civil and religious liberty." Although highly exclusive and aristocratic, the Whigs' roots in the Glorious Revolution of 1688 identified them with the cause of constitutional government. They had no particular sympathy for democratic government, let alone for the masses, but would accept innovations in order to avert more catastrophic change. Whig leaders therefore listened to liberal industrialists who wanted representation for their interests and for their growing cities, and to the radicals who expected a reformed Parliament to prove more responsive to the demands of the urban masses; but they were undecided as to what to do.

Reform of Parliament threatened entrenched interests in both parties. It had been fended off for a long time with the argument that even an unreformed House of Commons responded to public opinion and demands; but such a plea sounded less convincing every year. News of the French revolution of 1830, in which the reactionary Bourbons had been swept out with ease, furnished fresh arguments to enemies of aristocratic privilege that seemed embodied in the existing composition of the House of Commons. Shortly thereafter, King George IV died; and the general election following his death turned on the issue of parliamentary reform.

Although the new Whig cabinet, headed by Lord Grey, turned out to be the most aristocratic of the century, its members were persuaded that they must make some concession to popular demands by bringing in a measure which would put an end to further innovations. The bills introduced to this end ran into heavy opposition. While Parliament debated, public tempers rose. There were mass meetings, riots, strikes, and mobs clashed bloodily with army units. Through most of 1831 cholera raged in England, further fraying nerves that brought the country to the verge of rebellion. Business was upset. Some people refused to pay taxes. The radicals talked of setting up a national guard. The Tories saw the struggle as—no longer one for office on traditional lines—a battle between "the conservative and subversive principles."* At last, in 1832, the Reform Bill became law.

Today, the measure which had given rise to so much contention and which was greeted with widespread rejoicing seems a very moderate one. It suppressed the most unrepresentative among the closed or rotten boroughs and gave representation to new ones. It lowered the property qualification for the franchise, thus broadening the Commons' electoral base, and increased the electorate by about 50 per cent—from 435,000 to 652,000: a figure which the country's rising wealth and population would by the 1860's carry beyond the million mark. There was some shift of electoral power from countryside to towns, but this was only slight. The urban electorate was only really strengthened by the second Reform Act, of 1867, which more than doubled the number of electors. For the moment, the composition of the House of Commons changed but little: the landed interest almost held its own, and so did members of the aristocracy, into the 1860's.

New measures needed time to change old mentalities. In 1835, Florence Nightingale's father—a reforming Whig—lost the parliamentary seat he was standing for because he refused to bribe the voters of Andover. They, for their part, felt that, since a vote had always been bought for cash, extension of the franchise simply meant cash for more people who now had the vote: a kind of social subsidy. "How I hate Tories, all Beer and Money," wrote William Nightingale. But, in effect, beer and money flowed on both sides, when the means allowed. Just because candidates talked so much alike and because electors had to choose more between personalities than between policies, money talked and would go on talking until, in 1883, election expenses were limited by the Corrupt Practices Act.

New Politics

Yet 1832 *was* a turning point. The larger franchise drew into politics a mass of new participants, and persuaded others that their turn must come. The new official lists of voters spurred the development of party organizations which would keep registration up and increase the party's voting strength, build local associations, keep in touch with the small voter, and nurse constituencies along from one election to another. Politics were no longer the preserve of a small, charmed circle and of their clientele. Politicians had to adapt to new conditions or face defeat. As

* The prevailing mood may be guessed from the fact that many property-owners expected a bloody revolution followed by confiscation. At Durham, where the Cathedral chapter was fabulously wealthy, the agitation persuaded the chapter to sacrifice some of their revenues in endowing a University, hoping that this at least might survive the coming cataclysm and the confiscation they expected. The cataclysm never came, but the University of Durham was chartered in 1837.

closed boroughs disappeared, patronage crumbled. It would collapse altogether after the introduction of the secret ballot in 1872. The majority
of Englishmen were still voteless, and radical reformers still dissatisfied.
But the rising middle class had been acknowledged, the growing power
of industry and commerce recognized. Many utilitarian liberals, like
Walter Bagehot the economist, or the novelist Anthony Trollope, who
wanted the vote for the educated few but not for the uneducated many,
could rest content.

The uneducated many were going to be taken care of by the Poor
Law of 1834, which forced relief recipients into workhouses: the paupers'
bastilles.

In order to discourage malingering and ease the burden on the tax-
rolls, the condition of paupers sheltered in workhouses was intended to
be worse than the worst they could expect outside. "Our intention is
to make the workhouses as like prisons as possible," declared an assistant commissioner charged with enforcing the law. "Our object . . .
is to establish therein a discipline so severe and repulsive as to make them
a terror to the poor and prevent them from entering," explained another.
Meals had to be eaten in silence, a strict timetable strictly observed, sexes
and families were kept apart, mothers and children separated, work was
endless. This is how the poet George Crabbe described "the pauper
palace":

> That giant building, that high-bounding wall,
> Those bare-worn walks, that lofty thund'ring hall!
> That large loud clock, which tolls each dreaded hour,
> Those gates and locks, and all those kinds of power:
> It is a prison with a milder name,
> Which few inhabit without dread or shame.

By 1843 workhouses had nearly 200,000 inmates. "The most eloquent
testimony to the depths of poverty," comments E. P. Thompson, "is in
the fact that they were tenanted at all."

It is easy to see why sensitive men should find the regime disgusting—
hypocritical, corrupt, costly, and squalid. It is just as easy to see why men
who did well by it wished to retain it, and men who were not actually
maimed by it accepted it as they always had and always would, by force
of inertia and habit. The trouble is that many whom it oppressed and
injured were so stupefied that they could conceive no resistance. Only
a few idealists—radicals, born of Jacobinism, or, like William Cobbett, of
Toryism *—set out to redress the wrongs of the great, obscure, and

* Like Wilkes, William Cobbett (1763–1835) provides another illustration of the
English talent for assimilating critics. He began as a Tory and ended as a radical
opponent of the Establishment and of the bad new times, as well as of "bloody old
Times." But, before his death, the Establishment had got him: he had become a Member of Parliament and a Public Figure; his son, a Chartist at first, became a supporter
of Disraeli; and their descendants, good solid Manchester conservatives, would be the
very image of the values the old man had fought.

much-wronged masses.

Meanwhile, the Whig administration, feeling that reform had gone far enough, knew only how

> To promise, pause, prepare, postpone,
> And end by letting things alone:
> In short to earn the people's pay
> By doing nothing every day.

Exports might be growing, but so was misery; and so was immigration by which some sought to escape it. By the 1840's the trickle had become a flood, directed toward New Zealand and Australia, Canada and the Cape, or the United States. The 60,000 yearly immigrants of the early forties, had grown to 250,000 a year in 1847, and in 1848 some thousand people were leaving the country every day. These figures reflected the depression which began in the late 1830's and rose to a climax in the famine year of 1848.*

Against this sorry background, two parallel agitations developed: the first was directed against the Corn Laws which protected the high price of English grain and kept out foreign foodstuffs by high tariffs. Corn Laws, originally designed to maintain fair prices by regulating the grain trade, had been known in England since the Middle Ages. They had begun by restricting exports to keep bread cheap; then, in the seventeenth century, a sliding scale of import duties had been imposed in order to protect the English farmer. By the end of the Napoleonic wars this had come to operate against the consumer, encouraging speculation and keeping prices high by excluding almost all foreign grain. This was hard on the poor at any time; but in the late thirties a series of poor harvests intensified their hardships and sharpened the agitation for repeal and cheap bread.

The Anti-Corn Law Association, founded in Manchester in 1838, was supported by the manufacturing interests led by Richard Cobden and John Bright, and by the more productive landlords. Its propaganda insisted on free trade and free competition, not only in industry but in the products of the soil; arguing that cheap bread would improve the worker's lot and, also, the competitive position of his employers. What the *Times* called the "incendiary claptrap" of Cobden and Bright stirred up riots and strikes in working-class areas, and consciences at Westminster, including that of Robert Peel. Tea parties and bazaars flanked great free trade meetings; and propaganda, which put out as much as a hundred tons of printed paper a year and made full use of the penny post of 1840 to mobilize middle-class opinion, triumphed with repeal in 1846.

---

* Ireland, dependent on potatoes, suffered more than England. Its population in 1845 was eight and a quarter million; in 1851 six and a half million. About a million had died and another million had emigrated.

Defeat of the Chartists at Newport, 1839.

Repeal of the Corn Laws was seen as the triumph of free trade, and of industry over agricultural interests. It was also a triumph of social consciences stirred by bad times. Robert Peel—"an iceberg with a slight thaw on the surface," said a contemporary, but a deeply conscientious man— had reorganized the old Tories into a Conservative Party which Disraeli would eventually steer toward unwilling reforms. His first Conservative administration in 1841 included a promising young man, William Ewart Gladstone (1809–1898), who would become the heir of his policy though under a different label. It was a great reforming ministry. The Coal Mines Act of 1842 forbade the underground employment of women and of boys under ten; the Factory Act of 1844 set a maximum working day for children under thirteen (six and a half hours) and women (twelve hours); finally, the Ten Hours Bill of 1847 gave workers an endurable working day. Repeal was part of this long list, not unconnected with the second great agitation of those years, that of the Chartists.

Workmen, especially craftsmen, had long tried to organize themselves in associations and unions designed to advance their interests, secure shorter hours, higher wages, effective education, above all universal suffrage which alone would make these things possible. "You have heard, I doubt not, of the trades' unions," wrote Dr. Thomas Arnold of Rugby to a friend in 1834: "A fearful engine of mischief, ready to riot or to assassinate." Some of these people argued that the English middle class, having made its revolution in 1832, was now making a counterrevolution against its erstwhile allies of the working class. It was up to the workers to save themselves and the revolution, by carrying the latter to a logical conclusion in the destruction of the new oppressor class.

In 1838, the London Workingmen's Association drew up the People's

97

Charter, whose six points demanded universal male suffrage, equal electoral districts, no property qualification for Members of Parliament, payment of wages for Members of Parliament, a secret ballot, and annual general elections, that is, direct democracy. Similar reforms had been advocated in 1780 by a reform committee of the House of Commons, and talked about before the great disillusion of 1832, when radical craftsmen found that the Whigs would not give them the vote. So there was a tradition of reform to which the Charter appealed, and current difficulties and disillusions brought it solid support.

The First Petition its supporters presented to Parliament in 1838 bore nearly 1,300,000 signatures. The second in 1842 bore over 3,300,000 signatures. The third, in 1848, with economic depression at home and revolution across the Channel, claimed 6 million and probably got half or two-thirds that many. Parliament rejected them all. Political leaders denounced the Chartist movement as a threat to property. The long series of strikes, riots, demonstrations, and insurrections that marked the hungry forties sharpened class fears so that, as Charles Kingsley—Queen Victoria's future chaplain—tells us "young men believed (and not so wrongly) that the masses were their natural enemies, and that they might have to fight any year or any day, for the safety of their property and the honor of their sisters." Above all, perhaps, repeal of the Corn Laws had satisfied the middle classes and turned them into supporters of order once again. As a result, 170,000 special constables and a considerable military force under the Duke of Wellington faced the Third Petition on "a glorious day, the Waterloo of peace and order" and the great Chartist petition fizzled out in rain and apathy, while Lady Palmerston congratulated herself on "the good spirit of our middle classes."

No wonder the English were complacent. To a ninteenth-century Englishman's mind the best thing between England and Europe was the sea. A widely used elementary text of mid-century reflected English delight that they were not as other people were, certainly not like the French who sometimes "have a king, and sometimes they send him away and will have none." English children could happily

> . . . thank the goodness and the grace
> Which on my birth have smiled.
> And made me in these Christian days
> A happy English child.

Enterprise had made England great. Compromise kept her at peace. But it was the kind of compromise that Tom Brown favored, as Thomas Hughes described him in *Tom Brown's School Days* (1857): "He never wants anything but what's right and fair; only when you come to settle what's right and fair, it's everything that he wants and nothing that you want. And that's his idea of a compromise. Give me the Brown compromise when I'm on his side."

Chapter 4

REVOLUTIONARY CHANGE IN FRANCE

French history did not run so smoothly, or—rather—the French seem to have lacked the English talent for channeling the streams of change to constructive rather than destructive purposes. This would appear as clearly in the vicissitudes of the "Old Regime" as in the ventures of the new.

The last fourscore years of the French monarchy could be divided roughly into three parts. The first of these was the Regency, when from 1715 to his death in 1723, the Duke of Orléans ruled on behalf of his small and sickly nephew, Louis XV. Three important developments originated in these years, each of which was to affect the country's fortunes. First in time was the increased importance of the Paris Parlement whose support Orléans invoked in order to secure full authority as Regent, despite the contrary instructions of Louis XIV's will. In effect, Orléans gained his power by a minor coup, legalized by Parlementary sanction. Louis XIV had confined the Parlement to an insignificant role. Henceforth, it would constantly intervene in politics, providing the opposition with leadership and a focus. When it did not represent the King, this high court of law represented nothing more than itself. Yet these magistrates who owned their offices would become the defenders of all the privileged classes and, against their determination, few reforms which threatened their interests would get by. Nevertheless, the majority of Frenchmen took them at their word when they claimed to stand against monarchic despotism, and rallied to their cause again and again. Only too often, Voltaire would jeer, the people are like flies who take the side of spiders.

The second development was the nobiliary reaction. Released from the stern rule of the old king, the nobility sprang up like a jack-in-the-box and with about as much consequence, to reassert their rights and claim back the influence and revenues of which they had been deprived. Orléans' own prejudices were on their side and, at first, he tried to govern

A contemporary print depicting unrest following the crash of the South Sea Bubble

through councils of nobles rather than through baseborn ministers. This did not last. The necessities of government, the frivolity and inexperience of the nobles, threw Orléans back on the old administrative structure. But the nobles were never jammed back into the box where Louis XIV had squeezed them, or disciplined by his listless successors. Their pretensions and their rebelliousness, allied with the pretensions of the Parlementary nobility, would in due course bring everything crashing down.

The third development stemmed from Orléans' disillusion with his fellow nobles and his search for a more effective policy. The Regent's major problem arose from the heavy debts Louis XIV had left behind. Across the sea, in England, the South Sea Company was booming, apparently taking over the national debt. A Scotsman, John Law (1671–1729), persuaded the Regent that he could do as much, absorbing the national debt and spurring general prosperity. Exchanges, Law argued, depend on currency. Let him create a bank which would accept deposits and issue paper currency redeemable against its deposits. Since depositors seldom claim their deposits back *in toto,* or all of them at once, this meant that the bank could issue more paper than the deposits held, thus creating an inflation that would stimulate economic activity. The principle was sound and Law's bank, founded in 1716, prospered. So did the companies he bought or founded to trade in the East and West, especially the Mississippi Company for the exploitation of Louisiana, where fabulous fortunes were held out to settlers and investors. At last, in 1719, Law proposed a scheme to take over the national debt, converting its obligations to those of his company. The shares soared, speculation ran riot, consumption and prices rose as predicted, Law became head of the state's finances, hailed as the savior of France. Then, in 1720, speculative complications and political intrigue brought a crash, and Law fled to die in poverty at Venice.

The state's debt had, indeed, been very much lightened and, after a brief recession, economic activity returned. Fortunes had changed hands:

many had been ruined, but others (including Law's own coachman) had become wealthy in their stead. But the speculative fever had dealt a hard blow at the idea of economic improvement by hard work and savings; * while its collapse had dealt a harder one at the concepts of paper money or a state bank, thus depriving France of essential instruments of economic activity for a long time to come. Public interest in America also collapsed. The lands which Law had described as choking with gold, emeralds, and diamonds no longer tempted anyone. Only transported convicts made up cargoes for these Godforsaken colonies; and it was soon said that the best thing Louisiana ever produced was the story of the little prostitute, Manon Lescaut, who was deported there. No wonder the empire was lightly abandoned, and Louisiana itself eventually sold to the highest bidder.

This crucial period, during which most subsequent problems were sketched out, ended with the Regent's death in 1723. It was followed by the long, peace-minded ministry of Cardinal Fleury, during which conflict with England was avoided, while French influence and trade slowly increased. The half-century following Fleury's death in 1743 would, on the contrary, be marked by ministerial instability, constant friction between the privileged orders and governments seeking reform, the ever more evident inability of the Crown to put its house in order.

The two latter periods—the final years of the French monarchy—were deeply affected by the personalities of the two kings whose reigns bridged the time between the death of Louis XIV and that of the Old Regime: Louis XV (1715–1774) and Louis XVI (1774–1793). The fact that both had been orphaned at an early age may help account for many of their quirks and inadequacies. It remains that their failings helped demonstrate the awkwardness of entrusting a nation's fate to the arbitrary decisions of birth.

The two men were quite different. Handsome, spoiled, and self-indulgent, Louis XV was five when his great-grandfather died, fifteen when he was married to Marie Leczinska (1703–1768), an unassuming woman seven years older than himself, who gave him ten children in ten years, and whom he soon replaced with a long string of mistresses. The best-known and longest lasting of these was Madame de Pompadour (1721–1764), the most charming of the King's indulgences, intelligent, ambitious, friend and protector of artists and philosophers, but no more effective than her royal lover.

Louis XV lives on in the notorious remark *"Après moi, le déluge."* The words, whether he ever uttered them or not, correctly reflect his

* One of the Persians in Montesquieu's *Persian Letters* of 1721 tells of a visit to a coffeehouse where he meets a landed gentleman who could never collect his rents, a townsman whose house is full of devalued money and who wishes he owned a little country estate which alone produces security, a bitter man complaining that his best friend has had the unkindness to pay him back the money he had lent him, and a genealogist who alone delights in the new society where he expects to grow rich by providing parvenus with fictitiously honorable family trees.

Madame de Pompadour, by her friend and protégé François Boucher. Wallace Collection, London.

rather hopeless detachment and the image of cynical indifference which he left his subjects. Yet there was more to him than that. Louis was intelligent, cultivated, and even his boundless sensuality seems to have been directed toward charming objects. But, as the effective head of a great kingdom, he functioned only reluctantly and spasmodically. This meant that after the death of his tutor and first minister, Cardinal Fleury (1653–1743), the affairs of his kingdom moved in fits and starts, pulled every which way by the passing influence of short-lived advisers. Policy rested in the hands of a small clique at Versailles, whose world turned on the King and on his favorites.

There would be no royal mistresses in the following reign, but a more fatal queen and a king even less fitted for his task. Deprived of parental care, isolated in a hostile and corrupt court, despised by brothers who were his intellectual and physical superiors, Louis XVI was a weaker vessel altogether, decent, dull, awkward, and slow on the uptake. His favorite pastimes (bar one) struck his contemporaries as menial or childish: that he enjoyed forging keys, hammering nails, sweeping out his workshop, or reading police reports was not unusual in his time, or even in our own. But he also liked shooting cats from the terrace of Versailles, or throwing pellets of dirt from between his toes at the courtiers attending his *lever*.* Perhaps the fairest comment on the

---

* The ceremony of the king's rising, washing, and dressing. The *lever* was a fashionable and well-attended spectacle, and so was his going to bed.

man came from his brother-in-law: "His intellectual faculties are weak," reported Joseph II in 1777, "yet he is not altogether an imbecile."

This weak, well-meaning man, admirer of Fénelon and of Rousseau, seriously concerned about his people, lacked the decisiveness or energy to make up his own mind, let alone impose his authority. His marriage in 1770 to Marie Antoinette of Austria accentuated his deficiencies and the crown's incapacity to respond to the country's needs. Marie Antoinette (1755–1793) struck her contemporaries as lightheaded, frivolous, unreliable, interested in politics only as the cat's-paw of Austrian interest, or to find money and places for her friends. She was probably less bad than she has been painted. Gay, warm, loyal, the fifteen-year-old bride found herself isolated in the midst of a court where many opposed the sterile Austrian alliance she represented, married to a man she could neither respect nor love. These two mediocre beings might have performed quite adequately in less demanding times. They would, in due course, pay with their lives for the crime of having been cast in roles that were too great for them.

Only one thing both kings had in common, and that was their devotion to hunting. Both men seem to have invested in this passion time and energies which, some contemporaries felt, might have been more profitably employed elsewhere. "The King is really doing a dog's work for his dogs," complained one of Louis XV's ministers. "From the beginning of the year he arranges all that these animals will do until the end. They say that his majesty would run the finances and the war with far less trouble than all this. But the meetings of the Council weary him, because he has got to remain inactive and because affairs of state bore him." What had been an engrossing hobby for Louis XV was in his grandson a devouring passion. Louis XVI noted in his diary every hunt and every head he got: 1,274 stags and 189,251 lesser trophies between 1774 and 1787. As for his wife, herself a great equestrienne, hunting seems to have offered one more opportunity for diversion and display. In November, 1781, alone, tailors delivered thirty-one riding costumes for the Queen's use.

The Economic Impasse

Since the crux of France's troubles was financial, something must be said about the country's economy. The period that runs roughly from 1730 to 1770 was one of prosperity and expansion. Industry grew. Between 1738 and 1789, production of coal increased 700 to 800 per cent, that of cast iron 72 per cent. Industrial heavyweights began to appear, like the textile manufactures of Mulhouse, the forges of Creusot, Oberkampf's textile printshops, Réveillon's wallpaper factory, and, greatest of all, the coal mines of Anzin, which turned out over 300,000 tons in 1790. With its 4,000 laborers, miners, and carters, Anzin was the biggest enterprise in France. New machines and processes were being developed —Jacquard's silkloom, Berthollet's chlorine bleaching method, Leblanc's artificial soda, Oberkampf's textile printing cylinder—which should remind us that the Industrial Revolution was quite at home in eighteenth-century France. Even criticism of industry and capital began to be heard and, in 1783, we find a Catholic moralist wondering: "Industry multiplies capital; but to whose profit? Of the artisans who contribute their industry? Their share, for the most part, is only labor, misery and degradation. The capital accumulated goes into the coffers of a small number of traders, fattened by the sweat of a multitude of workers who waste away in a somber workshop . . ."

But workshops were fewer than warehouses, and manufacturers fewer than merchants. The great fortunes of the eighteenth century were built on trade, not on industry—especially on colonial trade which enriched the Atlantic ports. Between the 1720's and the 1770's, French foreign trade figures quadrupled, and the noble mansions and public buildings of Nantes and of Bordeaux still bear witness to the profits it could bring. But this prosperity was at the mercy of a fragile credit structure. Reliance on gold meant dearth of credit. England had credit institutions, banks, and notes; France had not. Law's crash had turned the French away from such snares and delusions. Credit was available from the Crown, from great nobles like Orléans, from financiers whose resources came from taxes. Otherwise all enterprises had to be self-financed. This meant that French industry knew little flexibility: no gold, no business. When metal turned scarce, production dried up; so did goods, so did employment, in the cascade of disasters which would fall on the country when hard times returned in the 1770's.

Meanwhile, things went well. There was work for builders and artisans, there was more money for wages and, hence, for food and wine; crops sold well, rents from land increased, and living standards improved at least for some. Not for all since with prosperity there also went inflation. Even as the national wealth increased, individual buying power shrank in many cases; the poor could get poorer while the nation grew rich. And the poor bore the brunt of taxes, so that it was possible for the state to be poor as well, as long as its revenues were drawn from the poorest sections of a wealthy nation.

State revenues were high, higher than the British, but not high enough. All economists agreed that taxes must be rationalized, simplified, privileges and exemptions eliminated, indirect taxes which bore especially hard on the poorest pared down. But every move to introduce reforms met bitter opposition. How could courtiers put an end to waste from which they were the first to benefit, or magistrates correct injustices that fed their revenues? On whom could reformers lean? Royal authority rested on bureaucracy, and this had grown so utterly unwieldy as to clog all development and enterprise. Already in the seventeenth century Colbert complained that justice took 70,000 men to administer it and busied a million others with its pettifogging. By the eighteenth centry, one-third of the active population of a provincial center like Dijon was working in some office, and the King's finance minister could only guess at approximately how many people his services employed.

This civil feudality knew how to guard its rights and would not lose them without protest. The very bourgeoisie that called for changes was strong enough to hamper and prevent them, yet not strong enough to bring them about without convulsions that would unhinge the system as a whole. Aging regimes always face this problem: the impasse between reform and revolution. Original structures decay, support wanes, is lost, or is lacking altogether. The regime finds agony easier to bear than action, and any positive move seems to stir up the possibility of collapse. When the boat is rotten, it should not be rocked. The alternative is to do nothing and await an almost fatal end, or do something and precipitate it. Hence, would-be reformers are often rightly charged with an important part in the eventual catastrophe which they alone might possibly have averted.

Yet reformers did appear, because the need was even more evident than the danger. Rationalization and efficiency were the watchwords of the time. Why should not France put her house in order, abolish privileges, bring the privileged castes in line?

The nobles were changing, largely under the influence of English values and, some of them, in pursuit of opportunities for profit. But none of this meant the abandonment of their privileges. On the contrary. At the very time when new philosophies shed a lurid light on old privileges and abuses, these were taking on a new dynamic life. The nobiliar counteroffensive of the eighteenth century, on which we have touched already, would make the task of reform ever more difficult. Serfdom, often mentioned, was the least of nobiliar impositions. True, while Louis XVI abolished serfdom on crown lands in 1779, elsewhere it was only ended by the National Assembly decrees of 1789. But by that time only vestiges of serfdom had been left, no less irritating for that, but overshadowed by feudal and manorial dues, rents in money (*droits*), labor (*corvée*), and kind (tithes); by the obligation to grind corn in the lord's mill, bake it in the lord's oven, press grapes in the lord's winepress; by subjection to the lord's exclusive hunting rights and sometimes to his right to judge in his own manorial court.

It was such rights and rents and tithes which pressed so hard, the harder when we remember that the nobility, less than two and a half per cent of the nation, owned one-quarter of its land and one-third of its harvests, on which they paid no tax or hardly any. Nor did the clergy pay taxes on their lands and tithes. Fiscal injustice was the nub of the

Anne Robert Turgot, engraving by Francois Drouais.

French problem, and one on which reforming ministers would butt and fall again and again. They could let Parlements expel the Jesuits (1763) and throw the educational system into confusion; they could even free the internal grain trade as Turgot managed to do for a few years; but when they turned to the fiscal system, Parlements stood staunchly against them, raising a cry of liberty which the people echoed with simple-minded enthusiasm.

As a result of this, the French entered the American war in a sorry state, and came out of it looking sorrier still. What with inflation, the war cost France as much as the three other great eighteenth-century wars put together. The annual deficit, 37 million in 1774, had grown to 80 million in 1783 and 112 million in 1787. Merely the cost of handling the public debt accounted for half the annual state expenditure.

Anne Robert Turgot (1727–1781), greatest of the reforming ministers, had been defeated over the question of tax reform. His successors sought to temporize. If taxation could not be reformed, obviously money must be raised by loans. Jacques Necker (1732–1804), who followed Turgot, found loans at high interest until they dried up, turned to tax reform, and fell in his turn. The next finance minister, Charles de Calonne (1734–1802), having tried to govern on credit and exhausted it, came to the same conclusion as Turgot and Necker. But Calonne had a new idea. To outflank the opposition of the Parlement, he decided to convene an assembly of notables, picked by the King, in which he hoped his project would fare better. There is no policy without risks, remarks a contemporary French politician; but there are policies without luck. The notables (including Lafayette) met in 1787 and rejected Calonne's proposals. Only the Estates of the nation, the notables claimed, could declare new taxes; and, when the King turned to the Parlements, he got the same reply. Leaning on enlightened catchwords to defend antiquated structures, notables and magistrates, nobles and philosophers, appealed to "national rights" and "national representation." In 1788 the government gave in. The Estates-General would meet on May

1, 1789, and Frenchmen were free to present their ideas on the reforms to come. Freedom of the press had been permitted.

The political debate had been taking place against a steadily deteriorating economic background. The economic expansion of mid-century had increased population pressure, along with levels of social and economic expectation. In the depression of the 1770's and 1780's, taxes got slightly higher while taxpayers were least able to pay them. In the absence of an urban industrial alternative, the small owner or tenant in time of bad harvest and with more mouths to feed quickly consumed all the crop, had to borrow at high rates and to buy grain in the market. The same man as occasional laborer suffered from the decline in real wages during the price inflation.

Larger peasant owners and tenants were not necessarily hurt by bad harvests. If they still had a surplus to sell in the market, they profited from the very high prices. But the seigneurial dues which added to the small farmer's misery were a critical question to the larger ones, cutting into their profits and joining them to their neighbors in common hostility to aristocrats and cities and government. All cultivators came to resent dues, tithes, taxes, and to blame their troubles on them more than they would have done in better times.

The wine trade, too, had entered a depression which, between 1778 and 1791, would have serious effects. Eighteenth-century French viticulture fed over 2 million people—almost a tenth of the country's population—the very backbone of the small holders, more independent on the whole, more thoughtful, more articulate and argumentative than the mass of small peasants, a kind of bridge between agriculture and industry. Its troubles affected not only vintners and merchants, but the artisans who lived on their trade and worked for them—stave and barrel makers, carters, shippers, and many others—immediately or at one remove.

The financial crisis was aggravated by a seemingly endless series of economic disasters. The terrible winter of 1783–1784 brought things to a standstill for weeks, only to be followed by the worst floods of the century in 1784 and poor crops in 1784 and 1785. The agricultural depression affected industry. Cloth production alone fell by half between 1787 and 1789. This produced unemployment, which coincided with a rise in the price of bread, due to the poor harvest. A free trade treaty concluded with England in 1786, largely for the benefit of the vintners who hoped to sell their wares in that hard-drinking island, flooded the country with English goods and did not really make much difference to the wine trade. There were 30,000 unemployed in Lyons alone, many thousands out of work everywhere. Then came 1788 and a rotten harvest, the most wretched in eighty years, while the following winter was the worst since 1709, the sparrows themselves freezing in the trees. In Provence most vines and olive trees froze. Industrial inspectors were reporting 46,000 unemployed at Amiens, 25,000 in Lyons, 30,000 around Carcassonne, 10,000 in Rouen, many of them flocking to Paris to swell the figure of 80,000 unemployed which the capital claimed in December, 1788. Bread doubled in price in Paris, tripled in some provinces. Riots broke out, peasants and workers pillaged grain stores and bakers' shops, stopped grain transport, threatened their lords. Soon some forms of ration cards would be introduced by local municipalities to ensure that the poor got a minimum of bread.

Principles Take Arms

Meanwhile, elections to the Estates were setting the country by the ears. French intervention in America had been more than a fiscal catastrophe. It had gone against all the principles on which the monarchy rested, supporting rebels against their legitimate king and democratic and republican ideas against traditional authority. Of course, the Very Christian King had never scrupled about aiding his enemies' heretics while persecuting his own. But what could be done with impunity in the sixteenth and seventeenth centuries could not be done in the eighteenth without opening the gates to criticism at home. Intervention on the side of the colonists allowed expression of revolutionary and republican ideas which would soon turn from the majesty of the British crown to that of the French. First of all, in 1782, as a rehearsal of things to come, the republicans of Geneva had to be crushed by French intervention, and Genevan exiles, befriended by the "American party" in France, played a leading role in the agitation which destroyed the government that had first cast them out of their own city and then permitted them to live in France.

Then came the announcement that criticisms and suggestions could be published freely; and a flood of pamphlets and periodicals followed. The first great issue to be settled was whether in the Assembly, which had not met since 1614, clergy, nobles, and the Third Estate would have equal representation or whether the Third, representing more than nine-tenths of the nation, should be granted more deputies. It might be mentioned at this point that, at best, the eventual deputies of the Third Estate represented the masses of the nation only at several removes. Of their 610 representatives at Versailles, one-quarter were lawyers, 5 per cent belonged to other professions, 13 per cent were bankers, merchants, or financiers, 7 to 9 per cent were countrymen, most of them landlords, not peasants. Still, they probably were and they certainly considered themselves representatives of "the people." They were closer to the masses in their daily lives and had the best opportunities of influencing and stirring them. Yet their wishes and—more important—their nuisance value were ignored. A decision that the Third Estate should have double the number of representatives allotted to the other orders was promptly nullified by the announcement that each estate would sit and vote separately. The numerical superiority of the Third, therefore, became a purely formal concession, precluding any effective expression of majority opinion. The possibility of real representative debate and decision had been held out, only to be withdrawn.

Again we see that hope is a dangerous factor in politics. It makes for dynamism, but also increases impatience and embitters disappointments. Now, the public debate on this issue took on ominous tones; and in a tract published in January, 1789, *What Is the Third Estate?* the Abbé Siéyès argued quite simply that the Third was the nation and the other estates nothing, since they played no useful role in society. This announcement of how the Third looked upon them, only confirmed the privileged in their determination not to yield an inch lest they lose a mile. Yet, the fact that Siéyès was a member of the clergy indicates that the first two orders were themselves far from monolithic.

The clergy in particular were split in many cases between the higher clergy—prelates, canons, abbots—nearly all of them of noble birth, and the secular priests, many of them poor and discontented. The French clergy were a small army. The country's 135 dioceses held 70,000 priests, 60,000 monks and nuns, some 3,000 higher clerics. The Church owned about 10 per cent of cultivable land, but incomes varied immensely between the 400,000 livres a year (about $800,000) of the prince bishops of Strasbourg, and the 7,000 livres a year of the Bishop of Vence —itself ten times the pay of an ordinary vicar. The sympathy of what we might call the clerical proletariat often lay with the Third Estate and, while in separate sessions they might succumb to the pressure of their

The first page of Abbé Siéyès' *What Is the Third Estate?*

QU'EST-CE QUE

LE TIERS-ETAT?

Le plan de cet Ecrit est assez simple. Nous avons trois questions à nous faire.

1°. Qu'est ce que le Tiers-Etat? Tout.

2°. Qu'a-t-il été jusqu'à présent dans l'ordre politique? Rien.

3°. Que demande-t-il? A y devenir quelque chose.

On verra si les réponses sont justes. Nous examinerons ensuite les moyens que l'on a essayés, & ceux que l'on doit prendre, afin que le Tiers-Etat devienne, en effet, *quelque chose.* Ainsi nous dirons:

4°. Ce que les Ministres ont *tenté,* & ce que les Privilégiés eux-mêmes *proposent* en sa faveur.

5°. Ce qu'on auroit *dû* faire.

6°. Enfin ce qui *reste* à faire au Tiers pour prendre la place qui lui est due.

A

superiors, if the Estates met jointly many of their votes could be expected to support the Third.

The nobles held together better. Yet, even among them, many who had learned the lessons of Montesquieu looked forward to the same opportunities for political action and distinction as their English counterparts, while a few—like Lafayette—drew their inspiration from America. Of the fifty-four men who presided over the Constituent Assembly between 1789 and 1791, thirty-three would be nobles; and several noblemen also presided over the Jacobin Club. Indeed, the more liberal among them were returned, like Mirabeau, as representatives of the Third Estate in their province.

Meanwhile, the Court havered. The King could not make up his mind. Most of his ministers, led by Necker, who had been restored to office as an earnest of good intentions, leaned toward the Third. The Queen, the King's brothers, and their friends worked against it. When the Estates opened in May, 1789, they were instructed to sit and vote separately. The Third refused to accept this, insisted on common sittings, and balloting by head and not by order. On June 10, the Third invited the other Estates to join it. On the 17th, joined by a few priests, it proclaimed itself the National Assembly. Three days later, locked out of their hall, the members betook themselves en masse to a nearby tennis court, there to take an oath never to separate before having established a constitution. The King could not intimidate the new "Commons," which were being joined by more recruits from clergy and nobility. Popular agitation was growing. On June 27 Louis approved the Assembly and invited the other orders to join it. The Third had won the first round.

But Louis was only trying to gain time while concentrating troops around Versailles and Paris, troops with whose backing he could impose his will. The troop movements in the country helped aggravate the political tension, persuaded the countryside and especially the cities that counterrevolution was afoot, that an aristocratic conspiracy was about to crush the Assembly. A strange crop of rumors spread everywhere, swift to alert villages and cities against nonexistent threats, feeding on the nervous tension caused by food shortages. It was the beginning of the "Great Fear" which would perturb the countryside throughout the summer. And it was in this tense atmosphere that the news of Necker's dismissal (intended to facilitate the reassertion of royal authority) on July 11 sparked an explosion. The word that the minister who symbolized reform had been dismissed set off rioting in Paris. The Paris electors, meeting at the Town Hall, set up a provisional municipal government (the Commune), and organized a citizen militia to be identified by its cockade in which the colors of Paris, red and blue, were joined to the royal white. But the militia had to have arms. Shopkeepers, craftsmen, artisans, soldiers from the regiments around Paris, set off in

The attack on the Bastille. It lasted two and a half hours. Versailles Museum.

search of arms, raided all arms depots, and, finally, on July 14, attacked the Bastille to obtain the powder stored there. The superannuated structure had long outlived its usefulness either as jail or fortress, but continued to loom over the populous quarters of Paris as a constant reminder of arbitrary imprisonments and royal might. The awful symbol of despotic power fell after a brief resistance and, after butchering the governor, three officers, and three soldiers, the jubilant crowd set free the prisoners of oppression: one nobleman imprisoned at the request of his family, two madmen, and four counterfeiters.

Liberté, Egalité, Fraternité

The Court was frightened, Necker was recalled, and the Assembly saved. On July 15 the governess of the Orléans children took her three charges, including the future King Louis-Philippe, to see the ruins of the "dreadful monument of despotism" and bless those tearing it down "whose vengeful hands seem to be those of Providence." On July 17 the King came to Paris to greet the new municipal council and to put on the new red-white-and-blue cockade. Friends of liberty throughout the world rejoiced. In far-off Königsberg, Professor Immanuel Kant missed his regular daily walk to stay at home and read the news about the fall of the Bastille. In the English Midlands, the chemist Joseph Priestley's sixteen-year-old brother burst in upon his friends waving his hat and shouting "Hurrah! Liberty, reason, brotherly love for ever! Down with kingcraft and priestcraft. The majesty of the People for ever! France is free, the Bastille is taken." The nineteen-year-old future poet laureate Wordsworth went to France, where he fell in love and therefore perhaps appreciated better

> . . . a time when Europe was rejoiced,
> France standing on the top of golden hours
> And human nature seeming born again . . .

No less enthusiastic, reverberations nearer home would be more concrete. Unrest spread through the provinces. The Revolution had triumphed. The Revolution must be defended. Aristocrats, bandits, Prussians, Englishmen, were out to crush it, to massacre the friends of liberty, rebuild worse and more terrible bastilles. It was harvest time, and awful rumors strained the far-strung nerves. In the east, they said, the Germans were advancing; in the southeast the armies of Savoy; in Brittany and Normandy it was the English who had landed; in the central region the King's brother was supposed to be marching with a large army from Bordeaux. Dust clouds could start a panic, as at Angoulême in July, where 20,000 gathered in order to oppose bandits who proved invisible. When the church bells summoned the peasants or the burghers and no enemy could be found in sight, the crowd frequently decided that "having found no enemies, they would go visit the nobles, and the priests who supported the nobles," set fire to castles, salt depots, and excise posts, tear up the feudal charters of their servitudes. Thus, the fear of aristocratic reprisal turned against aristocratic privileges. And meanwhile, out of panic and unrest, one city after another decided to set up a militia after the Paris pattern. Before July had passed the National Guard was born and, since this was a burgher guard, its representatives were loud in demanding an end to aristocratic privilege. The reforms of August would follow the fears of July. As Chateaubriand said later: "The patricians began the Revolution; the plebeians completed it."

Faced with a vast peasant revolt, the Assembly reacted with seemingly extreme reforms. On the night of August 4, burghers, priests, and nobles sacrificed the privileges that had set the countryside on fire, abolished the feudal regime, clerical tithes, and decreed fiscal equality.* Finally, on August 27, the Assembly, now known as the Constituent Assembly, voted the Declaration of the Rights of Man, which established freedom of opinion, of the press, of property "sacred and inviolable,"

---

* The measures of August were not as thorough as they seemed. Many rights were to have been redeemed by payments to their owners. But the peasants would have none of it, and they eventually got their way.

and equality of opportunity. Men "are born and remain free and equal in their rights"; one of these rights is the exercise of sovereignty which rests in the nation, no longer in the king and the Parlements, who can only represent it. The law is the expression of the general will, and law courts, no longer arbitrary, must administer the same law for all.

As in the case of American innovations, these moves reflected current philosophical ideas, the enthusiasm of some protagonists, and the pressures under which all labored. Though most of the innovations were more rhetorical than real, the illusions they created stemmed not only from the hopes nourished by the masses but from the self-delusions of their initiators too. In other words, many believed what they were doing.

So did the King, who refused to sanction this "creed of a new age," or the reforms decreed on August 4. Determined to resist, he called new troops to Versailles. But the army was disaffected. For the past few years it had been torn by internal dissensions over reform and promotion procedures. Commoner officers and noble officers distrusted one another. Meanwhile, in Paris food was running short and tempers shorter. On October 5 the market women of the capital, calling for bread, marched on Versailles. The National Guard followed. The King, the royal family, were compelled to accompany their captors back to the royal palace of the Tuileries, where they would be the prisoners of the patriots. The Constituent Assembly brought up the rear. Henceforth it would sit in the capital, its galleries open to the Parisian public.

It was success beyond anyone's wildest dreams. Between the meeting of the Estates-General in May and the King's return to the Tuileries in October, over a century after Louis XIV had moved the court from Paris to Versailles, the profoundest changes had taken place at extraordinary speed. The Revolution seemed accomplished. Yet it was only just beginning.

The End of the Monarchy

The Constituent Assembly was running the country now, with the people of Paris, the orators of the political clubs, the pamphleteers of the popular press, the demagogues and idealists, looking over its shoulder. The first thing to do was establish the nation's finances on a firm foundation. And the attempts to solve the financial problems out of which revolution had come would, in their turn, precipitate further revolution. The general opinion was that the best way of settling the country's deficit would be by selling the property of the church. Church property in 1790 was estimated to amount to some three billion livres, an immense

Giraudon

The March to Versailles,
October 5, 1789.

treasure which could be taken over without offending the principle of property, since the Church theoretically did not *possess* its wealth, but only held it in trust for the faithful—that is, the nation which now stood in need of it. At a time when tax revenue had almost vanished and expenses grew apace, the mass of church property would provide security for a new paper money, the *assignats,* with which the state could pay its debts and which, in turn, could then be used by citizens to purchase portions of the new national property. Accordingly, in November, 1789, church property was nationalized. It seemed that the country's economy had been set on the road to recovery at last. But this was not to be, and from this perfectly rational measure, which a majority of the clergy seems to have accepted, dread consequences would flow: some were economic, others religious, all would affect political events.

The political changes had not improved economic conditions; on the contrary, crops were rotting in the fields, industry was in the doldrums, nobles and the rich were closing their houses and beginning to seek security in emigration, tradesmen were losing their customers, domestic servants by the thousands found themselves out of work.* As for the peasants, most of them felt that liberty must mean an end of all taxation; and, in fact, the administrative structure, severely shaken, was hardly equal to tax collection. The church lands themselves brought less than had been hoped. Their very mass may have spoiled the market and, while buyers with the necessary cash to buy them did very well, many were left unsold. Then, as need pressed, the government took to printing more *assignats.* The paper was supposed to have been de-

* One result of this was the appearance of public restaurants of quality, as opposed to cheap cookshops and taverns, now opened by chefs whose masters had fled the Revolution.

114

stroyed once it had been paid in for a piece of national property. Now it was reissued, along with more. Inflation, which had begun by spurring the economy, was ballooning and the *assignats* deflating in value. The deteriorating monetary crisis would have serious consequences before very long.

Having abolished tithes and nationalized church property, the Assembly became responsible for the upkeep of the clergy. If the state was to pay the salaries of clergy, it had to keep track of them. The Constituent Assembly was restructuring the country into new administrative divisions. The old provincial diversity against which the monarchy had struggled so long was now replaced by eighty-three departments (eventually eighty-five), each subdivided into districts, cantons, and communes. It would be logical for parishes to coincide with the new administrative arrangements. The Civil Constitution of the Clergy followed. Contemplative orders were suppressed as useless, as we saw happen under the "enlightened despotism" of Joseph II. Priests were to serve a social function. They would be paid, but would have to be elected by the local electoral assemblies. Like legislators, priests were representatives and servants of the people, and they were expected to take an oath of loyalty to the nation and to its constitution. This was going too far. In 1791 the Pope condemned the Constitution of the Clergy.

Not the Constitution itself but its extremities proved to be a blunder of the first magnitude, shattering national unity and setting patriotism and religion at loggerheads. The Assembly had wanted the National Church to be as much a bulwark of the new state as it had been of the monarchy. But the Papacy could not condone the democratic Erastianism of a national church whose officers were chosen by the people. Here was an extreme conclusion of Gallicanism when legislators pretended to subordinate the interests of religion to those of the state. Clergy and faithful were caught in the middle, between ecclesiastical authorities which rejected the right of secular ones to legislate in spiritual matters and a secular state demanding the right to adjust the church organization according to the nation's views and needs. Fewer than half the priests took the Constitutional oath, and few of those who did could carry out their office effectively. Religious schism menaced the stability of the new political order.

Louis XVI, in particular, felt that he could no longer reconcile his conscience to compliance with the demands of the new regime. At Easter in 1791 he tried to confess before a priest who had not taken the oath and he was prevented. This precipitated his decision to escape his warders. After an unsuccessful attempt to get away in June, 1791, the royal family was recaptured at Varennes, close to the eastern border. In this sense, the war, the Terror, and the end of the monarchy, may all be traced back to the religious problems which the Civil Constitution cre-

The distribution of *assignats*

ated. In August Louis's failure either to co-operate or to escape brought about the Declaration of Pillnitz, in which his brother-in-law and the king of Prussia invited all powers to help restore order in France.

The French Wars, 1792–1815

A successful revolution in the greatest of Europe's powers was bound to affect the continent and the world more than anything that happened in Holland, Geneva, or distant colonies overseas. Dynastic connections and self-interest led most crowned heads of Europe to support Louis XVI, a fellow monarch imperiled by his subjects. This embroiled them with the revolutionary enthusiasts whose creed threatened their thrones in principle, whose doings would shake them hard in practice.

Far more than the Americans with their *novus ordo seclorum,* French revolutionaries stood for a new order in society as well as state; and the hostility with which they felt themselves surrounded stimulated them into aggressiveness. War might have been avoided even so, for France's British competitors were in a pacific mood and rather pleased than not at her internal troubles. In February, 1792, Pitt, in the House of Commons, advised a reduction of naval estimates because "unquestionably there was never a time in the history of this country when, from the situation in Europe, we might more reasonably expect fifteen years of peace than we may at the present time." As a matter of fact, hostile armies had already begun to concentrate near the French border, not least an army of aristocratic *émigrés* led by the King's brothers, who threatened dire revenge against the rebels. This increased the revolutionary fever at home, and the patriotic appeals against the enemies of revolutionary liberty at home and abroad with whom the King and Queen became increasingly identified For his part, Emperor Leopold II wanted no trouble. There may well have been none had he not died in March, 1792. His successor, Francis II, would speak more sharply, trust in his big stick, and his method achieved at least one end: in April, 1792, France declared war on "the king of Bohemia and Hungary," a formula designed to show that the war was not against any nation, but one of peoples against kings.* The untried armies of the revolution, however, met with seeming catastrophe almost at once. Within weeks the French had been routed and Austro-Prussian forces were advancing on Paris. The soldiers streaming back raised the cry that they had been betrayed. The officers and the King, who sympathized with the reactionary invaders, were letting them down. The assembly voted emergency measures, and the King once more refused to approve them, thus confirming everyone's suspicions. At Louis's secret request, the Duke of Brunswick, commanding the advancing allies, launched a manifesto threatening that if any harm befell the royal family Paris would direly pay for it. The manifesto reached Paris on August 1 and produced exactly the opposite of the effect intended. A popular insurrection, fomented by the popular clubs and led by men like Danton and Robespierre, took the Tuileries by storm. The royal family was suspended from its functions, imprisoned, and new elections announced for a Convention (note the American inspiration) which would endow the nation with a new regime.

The military situation was growing worse. The border fortresses were falling. The fatherland was declared in danger, conscripts and volunteers hurried to the front. Fear of treason filled the air. What if the internal enemies in the Paris prisons should rise behind the army's back? The crowd invaded the prisons (September 2) and 1,368 helpless men and women were massacred—about half the inmates. The murderous new determination gained the army, which, in the rain and mud of the Argonne, at Valmy, on September 20, outfaced the Prussians and forced them to retreat. The nation in arms had triumphed, and now it would go over to the offensive. Before the year was over, Belgium had been overrun and French armies were advancing in the Rhineland, Savoy, and Nice. In Paris the new Convention, elected by universal suffrage while many moderates abstained, contained a strong contingent of republican "patriots." It had met on the day of Valmy. Two days later it proclaimed the Republic.

* The Assembly made very certain this would not lead to misunderstandings. It "adopted in advance all foreigners who, abjuring the cause of its enemies, will come to take their stand under its banners."

While tyrants trembled, the friends of liberty abroad exulted. It was up to France to extend to them a fraternal hand. "The French nation," Paris proclaimed, "will grant fraternity and aid to all peoples who want to recover their liberty." That was in November. In December, it announced that the French nation would treat as enemies countries which supported princes or privileged castes, while guaranteeing the independence of those establishing "free and popular government." Between November, 1792, and March, 1793, France annexed Savoy, Nice, Belgium, the Rhineland. In these territories the political regime was overthrown, the social order changed. Having declared war on both Britain and Holland in February, by March, 1793, France found herself at war with most of Europe. First Holland in 1795, then Italy in 1796, became satellite republics.

> And now, become oppressors in their turn
> Frenchmen had changed a war of self-defence
> For one of conquest, losing sight of all
> Which they had struggled for . . .

Their reception was necessarily mixed. Some people felt that "liberation" did indeed sweep away feudal rubbish of which they were better rid; and many benefited from the political and economic emancipation, the reorganization of laws and courts and administration, which followed in the wake of revolutionary conquests. Yet even liberals who welcomed the removal of old rulers, the demolition of outdated privileges and restrictions, were ambivalent in their reaction to invaders who proved both liberating and exacting. In the service of liberty, French armies plundered all they could lay their hands on. In the Rhenish Palatinate the locks were taken off doors and sent to France. Belgium was sucked almost dry. The treasure of Berne would serve to finance the Egyptian expedition. But propaganda continued to present the conflict as a social war: in Italy, in Ireland, in the Balkans, in Germany, where Baden and Württemberg secularized Church property and abolished feudal rights. The French army included Polish and Irish, Italian and German units. War, like politics, appeared in a new light: an emancipating conflict, appealing to the unprivileged against the privileged and, sometimes, to the poor against the rich as well. A revolutionary conflict too, not only by intent but by its duration. For, while the parties altered, the fighting itself would continue—with only one brief interruption—to 1815.

A New Face for France

War was long and hard, and it would exercise its pressures close to home, more than it did abroad. The men who had declared it were known as

FRANCE IN REVOLUTION
1789–1793

Areas under government control

Areas dominated by Royalists and Girondists

Areas of counter-revolutionary uprisings

Territories annexed to France, 1791–1793

Coalition offensives

Girondins, a group of lawyers, merchants, financiers, and intellectuals whose leading figures came from the area of Bordeaux: moderate in their republicanism, extreme in their nationalism, hoping that internal difficulties would disappear in the exaltation and community of war. They would be overtaken and borne down by more ardent republicans of the Mountain—so named from their location high up on the left of the Assembly. The Mountain drew its main support from the popular clubs which had sprung up in Paris, chiefly on the premises of

119

Marie Antoinette imprisoned at the Temple. Opposite: the beheading of Louis XVI.

abandoned convents, like that of the Dominicans—or Jacobins—or of the Franciscan gray friars—or Cordeliers. This is where its leading figures were recruited: powerful orators like Danton, in the Cordeliers, passionate doctrinaires like Louis de Saint-Just and Maximilien de Robespierre among the Jacobins.

Difficult questions faced the Convention. The Republic had been declared; what should become of the King? Many favored imprisonment. The Mountain called for death. Documents were discovered in the Tuileries proving the King's intelligence with the enemy and, in January, 1793, Louis XVI and his queen went to their execution. The King had betrayed the nation. The Queen was a foreign agent. They clattered toward the guillotine in open carts, and died with dignity beneath the roll of drums. The religious trouble was growing. After war had been declared, a proscription law outlawed priests who would not take the oath. Louis' refusal to sanction this had hastened his end. Thousands of priests fled the country. Many hid. Others preached sedition, resistance to a heathen regime. In the Vendée, over much of the west middle region, peasant rebellion broke out against the middle-class revolution.

Conditions of life were getting steadily worse. During the winter of 1792–1793 the laborer's daily wage hardly covered the price of one pound of bread, bakeries and butchers' shops were looted, queues began at four in the morning and service only at eleven. The *assignat* having lost more than half its value, peasants would not trade food for useless paper. The Convention, on the other hand, would not interfere with the free operation of the market. Popular discontent turned against the Girondists responsible for the war. In June, 1793, a new insurrection brought their arrest and execution. The Mountain took over. Its leaders had opposed the war, defended the interests of the poorer section of the

population: shopkeepers, artisans, small property owners, above all consumers of all sorts, prototypes of the *sans-culottes* who had abandoned
the knee-breeches associated with the old regime for democratic trousers.
The *sans-culottes* might be described as populists. They stood for a
small-owners' society, where proletarians would be kept in their place
but capitalists and privileged would be excluded. The leaders of the
Mountain tried to carry out this somewhat confused ideal.

Economically reactionary, dreaming of a sort of Jeffersonian golden
age, these people were politically revolutionary, calling for direct government and direct democracy. They always remained a minority in the
country—a minority whom the necessities of war and economic crisis
forced to impose conscription and taxation on the people they sought
to rule. But conscription was a horrid novelty, and taxation was associated with the abuses of the old regime. Just as in the days of the Constituent Assembly, the people still felt that revolution was supposed to bring
more freedom, not more encroachments and impositions. It is not surprising that the revolutionary rulers of France had to govern by terror, by coercion, enlisting on their side the nervous strain of the crisis situation
that had brought them into power.

The Road to Terror

Power was exercised by special committees of the Convention, especially
the Committee of Public Safety, dominated by the legendary figures of
Robespierre and Saint-Just: an austere provincial lawyer and a reformed playboy with literary pretensions, hardly twenty-five years old.
Under their rule, freedom of speech became the freedom to say the
right thing; freedom of the press did not include the right to poison

121

public opinion. The public had to be educated by the right side, protected from corrupting views and voices. To such an end, most means were considered good.

Rousseau had attacked the theater as an immoral amusement which turned the minds of men from worthwhile preoccupations to lewd and antisocial diversions. The men of the Mountain admired Rousseau and felt that the theater could and should be used to instill civic virtue, glorify the community, honor the aged and deserving, spread the right social values. They were among the first to recognize the propagandistic possibilities of the stage. In a play like *The Republican Husband,* a man denounces his wife to the Revolutionary Committee and has her guillotined to great applause. In another play—*Last Judgment of Kings*—all the sovereigns of Europe (except for Louis XVI, who has just been executed) arrive in chains on a savage island. All are hungry, and they are thrown a piece of bread for which they scramble and fight. Pius VI throws his tiara at Catherine II, who hits him with her scepter and breaks his cross; the king of Spain loses his nose in the scramble. In the midst of this, a volcano erupts and destroys them all, thus settling the hash of monarchy for ever.

There were more sophisticated means of instilling the new ideas. In October, 1793, as fighting raged on the borders and civil war inside, a new calendar came into effect. It would last for twelve years, until January, 1806, and was meant to mark the opening of a new era: years of twelve months, months of three decades (ten days each), new names replacing the saints of the Gregorian calendar—plants, animals, agricultural implements, names culled from Greek and Roman history—the cycle of history and nature taking over from the traditional nomenclature.*

Even the pulpit was turned into the tribune of a new cult which worshiped Nature and the Supreme Being (unspecified), honored Humanity, its benefactors, and the French people. The pageantry of Reason replaced that of the Church in Notre Dame. Revealed religion gave way to natural religion, masses to Festivals of Reason. Statues represented Reason, actresses embodied her, garlands of flowers wreathed her, poems, hymns, speeches, and morality plays glorified her, massed choirs sang, and cannons boomed her praises.

Those who persisted in the old faith were hunted down, imprisoned, guillotined, shot, or, as at Nantes, "de-Christianized by immersion," that is, drowned in batches. The Jacobins were not deliberately against reli-

---

* Names like Gracchus and Publicola became common, and some enthusiastic Jacobins actually named their sons Conchgrass, Duck, or Dandelion, their daughters Cow, Carrot, or Rhubarb. In the words of Richard Cobb, "The roster of the Jacobin club read like a seed-catalogue." But the real significance of the calendar went beyond this. After struggling against all those wasteful feast days, it was a triumph to have only three holidays a month instead of four Sundays and umpteen saints' days. And what relief for industry! The Goddess Reason triumphed not only over the costly, useless clergy, but over idle workers too.

"The infamous Robes-
pierre," as drawn by An-
toine-Jean Gros, the artist
who would become one of
Napoleon's favorite mili-
tary painters before being
ennobled by Charles X.

gion. "Since my school days I have been a pretty poor Catholic," Robespierre told the Jacobin Club in 1794. "I am all the more attached to the
moral and political ideas I have put before you. If God did not exist, we
should have to invent him." And Hébert, a radical Jacobin speaking in
the same tribune a few days later: "I advise priests to read the Scriptures.
This moral tract seems to me excellent, and one must follow its maxims
to be a perfect Jacobin. Christ seems to me the founder of popular
clubs." But it was Christ and religion with a difference. The object of
worship would no longer be God but society, not His will but Its values.
Civic oaths, patriotic symbols, prophets and priests, martyrs, festivals,
processions, altars of the fatherland and, of course, a creed—the rights
of man and of citizen: these were the marks of a new religion, secular
perhaps, but dedicated to the worship of a new reality with lasting effects:
society, man, ultimately the collective self, directed by historical Providence and fulfilling—that is, directing—it in turn. "Only atheism is
aristocratic," said Robespierre.

Revolutionary fervor has often been compared to religious enthusiasm.
Burke, who saw "a revolution of doctrine and theoretic dogma" taking
place in France, denounced its leaders as theologians and proselytizers.
Tocqueville described it as a "religious revolution." And indeed the
republicans themselves furnished grist for this mill, borrowing metaphors
from ecclesiastical language, intoning civic invocations, reciting a republican creed, drawing up the republican civic Ten Commandments, crossing
themselves in the name of Marat, and sanctifying the "holy Revolution"
or the "holy guillotine." Apocalyptic, messianic, like all revolutions,
the first great modern revolution necessarily borrowed the language that
would suit it.

But that was only one aspect of it. "The eighteenth century had formed man for society," the Goncourt brothers would write. "The Revolution forms him for the state." A textbook, *The Elements of Republican Instruction,* contained the following dialogue between a student and a teacher:

—Who are you?
—I am a child of the fatherland.
—What are your riches?
—Liberty and equality.
—What do you contribute to society?
—A heart to love my country and arms to defend it!

And Saint-Just notes: "The child, the citizen, belong to the fatherland. Common instruction is necessary. Children belong to their mother till the age of five is she has fed them, and to the Republic thereafter, until death." This was total society, born of total crisis and trying desperately to solve its problems by any means at hand. "There are no citizens in the Republic but republicans," declared Saint-Just. "We must oppress the oppressors." Robespierre recommended "the despotism of liberty against the despotism of tyranny." Rigor was only used for the people's good. This was its justification. "Without virtue," said Robespierre, "terror is useless; without terror, virtue is powerless." Here, then, was the Terror, which one survivor later described as "a violent political crisis complicated by no less violent stomach crises."

Yet, as prices continued to rise, blood alone seemed able to assuage popular frustrations. The Revolution again was fighting for its life. The Committee of Public Safety, which called on the people to work, to go hungry, to furnish troops for campaigns on every front, including the Vendée and Toulon where royalist sympathizers had opened the port to the English, had to prove its determination, had to furnish an earnest example of what would befall the treacherous or the halfhearted. The guillotine gave proof. Between October, 1793, and July, 1794, 300,000 to 500,000 suspects were imprisoned, some 17,000 sent to their death. Heads, in the colorful phrase of one Jacobin, fell like tiles: thirty a day in Paris, in the last paroxysm of the Terror. Napoleon, who watched it all in the capital, summed up at Saint Helena: "No social revolution without terror. Every revolution is . . . a revolt which success and time legitimize, but in which terror is one inevitable phase."

Grim ruthlessness achieved its ends. The enemy was repelled, the rebels checked in the Vendée, Toulon recovered, prices regulated more stringently than under the old regime. Yet, if prices were regulated, it stood to reason that wages should be too. When Robespierre set a ceiling for wages, he deprived himself of the popular support which had backed him up. After the middle classes, cowering in terror, the artisan and worker supporters of the Mountain turned away from him.* Yet the

---

* Of the Terror's victims, 31 per cent proved to be workers, 28 per cent peasants.

guillotine worked on, though the emergency of invasion and civil war had passed. It was time for the surviving enemies of Robespierre to act— or shortly lose their own heads. In July, 1794, a coup sent Robespierre and his friends to the guillotine, silenced the popular clubs, brought back the survivors of the Girondins, replaced universal suffrage by a franchise founded on property qualifications, substituted bicameral legislation for the single assembly, and entrusted executive power to a Directory of five.

The Directory

The rule of the Directory was a period of victories abroad and hard times at home. At least the land question which had bedeviled the old regime and the early years of the revolution had been settled by the reforms of previous years, the mass of small landowning peasants was temporarily satisfied, and this ensured that they would pose no major problem. French peasantry, until the twentieth century, would play the role of a largely passive stabilizing force. The first proceeds of this came in the crushing of provincial insurrections.

But if the countryside was relatively quiet, Paris was not. The Directory sought but failed to settle itself firmly. Plots and counterplots, within and outside it, prevented this. Jacobins, monarchists, and sheer opportunists, grasped avidly for levers of power seemingly up for grabs. The image of these few years in the later 1890's remains colored by the brutal cynicism of the ruling clique. Too many of those who had survived the Terror felt what Napoleon described in a letter of 1793: "Among so many conflicting ideas, so many different perspectives, the honest man is confused and distressed . . . Since one has to take sides, it is just as well to choose the winning side, the side that loots, burns and devastates. Given the alternative, it is better to eat than to be eaten."

The victors of 1794 preferred to eat. They would do well and gradually entrench themselves in state and power. Cynical and practical, here was the new aristocracy; it had shed the optimism of the enlightenment and acquired the opportunism of experience. "Yesterday I went to the Chamber of Peers," remarked one of them in 1835. "We were only six when I arrived; we had all been in the National Assembly and we were all over eighty." They had survived the Terror. Henceforth, they would prevail and rule, if necessary by force of arms, calling in the army to suppress further insurrections; or, if not rule, at least they would profit.

The Revolution's Legacy

There were achievements also, and those of the Revolution of which the Directors were a part must be marked. France had been reorganized into "equal surfaces"—departments, which would "facilitate the exercise of [central]' power" and whose capital city would never be more than a day's journey from any of its parts. The departments were given neutral names to help old provincial loyalties fade away. In 1790 the Civil Constitution of the Clergy gave each of them a bishop, and in 1800 Bonaparte would give them all a prefect—the secular agent of the central power. In all aspects of life a new uniformity was being introduced. Trade and industry had lacked any standard of measure.* A decree of 1793 would introduce meters, grams, liters, francs: a set of uniform abstractions divorced from man [foot], experience [rod or pole], tradition [bushel]. Here were products of intellectual concepts and of calculation, which took a long time to gain acceptance but which were destined to simplify and clarify business transactions, just like the new insistence on family surnames and individual (or Christian) names, or the new birth certificates and birth dates that replaced the old certificates of baptism.

Law replaced caprice, a mobile society replaced a static social order. If many of the new municipalities had officers who could not read or write, this was a proof of the new avenues of social promotion and effectiveness that opened under the new regime. Among Napoleon's marshals, Ney was the son of a cooper, Lefebvre the son of a miller, Murat the son of an innkeeper, Augereau the son of a mason, Lannes the son of a stable boy. And in the municipalities, after 1789, a National Guard appeared to drill and strut but, above all, to confirm the revolutionary right of citizens to bear arms—a concept first affirmed in the American Bill of Rights and one which would continue as a liberal ideal throughout the nineteenth century.**

War and revolution offered an extraordinary opportunity to youth. Some of the greatest figures of the Revolution and the Empire that followed were in their teens when the Bastille fell, many in their twenties like Saint-Just (1767–1794), Rouget de Lisle (1760–1836), who composed the "Marseillaise," Camille Desmoulins (1760–1794), or Chateaubriand (1768–1848), who fought in the emigré army. Danton was thirty when he was executed, Robespierre thirty-six; both left their mark in history. Hoche, a corporal in 1789, was an army commander in 1794 at the age of twenty-five. Most of Bonaparte's generals would find fame in their twenties, and Bonaparte himself seized supreme power when he was just thirty years old.

It may well be that, as the eighteenth was a century of growing population and hence of youth, the Revolution was an explosion of these forces. In 1789, only 24 per cent of France's population was over forty

---

* In England, by the 1760's, standard pounds, miles, and quarts had been more or less established for the kingdom as a whole.

** In 1848, in Rome and Milan, in Berlin and Vienna, one of the first popular demands was the right to organize such a body.

years old; 40 per cent were between twenty and forty, 36 per cent were under twenty. These mouths needed land, these hands needed work, these minds sought employment. In eastern and central Europe there was land at least; in England and Ireland emigration offered some escape. France had lost Canada, shed faith in Louisiana, her industrial revolution was not advanced enough to absorb surplus energies and population. Perhaps a political revolution, a great war of expansion, with the opportunities they brought, were needed to give all these men a chance . . . or eliminate them. And that was what happened. The *levée en masse* itself helped stabilize the new regime, transferring men from workshops to the ranks, from the streets to battlefields, from availability for civilian conflicts to more productive foreign ones.

The New Warfare

All this was closely connected with profound changes in the art of warfare. For the revolution ushered in, and its generals perfected, a style of warfare unknown to the eighteenth century, a scale of warfare that the world ignored until that time.

Eighteenth-century armies had been slowed down by cumbrous supply trains. As the century ended, improved economic conditions made more food and forage available, an advantage that revolutionary armies would enthusiastically seize. Formal and limited hostilities had first been abandoned overseas, where the American colonists ignored the milder European manners and treated war as total (as indeed it was), so that Sergeant Lamb in Dublin, remembering his campaigns in the War of American Independence, described the fighting there as "a sort of implacable ardor and revenge, which happily are a good deal unknown in the persecution of war in general."

The American War of Independence persuaded observers that willing soldiers were best. For Lafayette, only citizens could be expected to accept the hardships of military discipline and win. But citizen armies could not exist without political and social changes. Armies, as we have seen, included the most unproductive members of society: nobles as officers, tramps and unemployed in the ranks. Such troops did not prove reliable when facing revolutionary armies made of free men encouraged to heroics and initiative. But it was not really the heroics which won the wars of the Revolution so much as the new strategy and tactics, a military unorthodoxy that grew out of lack of orthodox training and means. The blitzkrieg which the French devised reflected the needs and the shortcomings of their ill-equipped and ill-supplied troops, which had to move fast to seize what they needed and which moved the faster for lack of the stores they sought. But this speed and unorthodoxy of maneuver became effective novelties, which allowed them to achieve decisive superiority at a given place at a critical moment.

The revolutionary armies did have one advantage from the first; and that was numbers. "Only numbers can annihilate," said Lord Nelson, and this was a novelty too: a double novelty, of aim and means. Most eighteenth-century battles were fought with armies of 40 and 50,000. Napoleon himself began his brilliant Italian campaigns with less than that. Ten years later, at Jena, he had nearly 200,000, and almost three times as many for his Russian campaign. His foes had to do as well, so that the allied troops in the Waterloo campaign of 1815 counted about a quarter million. These vast new masses of sometimes poorly trained recruits abandoned the old line-formation which needed well-drilled veterans to keep it up, for a mass column whose battering weight was much greater, but again, whose original source lay in the problems of lack of discipline and of time for drill.

The logic of the new mass armies would be formulated in the works of K. von Clausewitz (1780–1831), a Prussian officer who campaigned with the Russian Army against Napoleon in 1812 and who was present with the Prussians at the Battle of Waterloo. Writing in the 1820's, Clausewitz drew the lesson of experience when he emphasized the psychological factors which would henceforth have to be taken into account. He noted the triumph of spirit over mere form and matériel; he recognized the trend toward absolute and total war, which he described as "an act of violence pushed to its utmost bounds"; and he defined war as only a continuation of state policy by other means. No more limited conflicts were possible, said Clausewitz; war could no longer be the sport of kings now that national existence was at stake. "Since the time of Buonaparte, war, through being first on the one side, then again on the other, an affair of the whole nation, has assumed quite a new nature."

But if Bonaparte exploited its possibilities, the Revolution had created them. Being a movement of youth, the Revolution had all the violence, the color, the passion, and incoherence of youth, all its idealism and all its selfishness. Pompous, solemn, murderously destructive, the Revolution was also exuberant, generous, enthusiastic, naïvely confident in the principles it brandished—sometimes at the end of a pike. It brought not only carnage, but virtue, not only savagery but reconciliation, not only terror but fraternity.

Napoleon

In the 1750's the Corsicans had risen to assert their independence against their Genoese masters. Under the leadership of a remarkable man, Pasquale Paoli (1725–1807), who built schools, founded a university, asked Rousseau for a Constitution, and unsuccessfully tried to forge his supporters into a nation, Corsica held the Genoese at bay for over a dozen years. In 1768, the Genoese, tired of their useless efforts, sold the island to France and French troops defeated Paoli in May, 1769, driving him into exile. In August, 1769, the wife of one of Paoli's chief supporters in Ajaccio gave birth to a son who was christened Napoleone. The boy grew up there, speaking the Italian dialect, offspring of a poor noble family in a poor, primitive land where the Middle Ages still endured, in clans, vendettas, and endless violence. In 1779, before he was ten years old, Napoleon was entered at the Royal Military Academy of Brienne, in Champagne, whence the short, skinny, serious lad was commissioned a second lieutenant in the artillery at the age of fifteen in 1784.

The opportunity to distinguish himself came in 1793 when, as a mere captain, he was charged first with the siege artillery and then with the siege plans of Toulon. He was successful, he was promoted, he hung around Paris—one more political general looking for pickings, escaped the purges of 1794, married Josephine de Beauharnais, discarded mistress of one of the Directors, lent a hand to suppress popular opposition to the Directors, was rewarded with the command of the army of Italy, and thereafter there was no stopping him. By 1798, having just won the victory of the Pyramids and having heard of the infidelity of his wife Josephine, he would write to his brother: "Greatness bores me; all my feelings are dried up. Glory is stale when one is twenty-nine; I have exhausted everything. . . . There is nothing left for me but to become really and completely selfish."

Even his failure served him. Off on a wild empire chase in Egypt (1798–1799), he was not involved in the scandals that besmirched the reputation of the regime. Incredibly, he managed to carry an expeditionary force across the Mediterranean, escaping British ambush and taking Malta on the way, to defeat the fierce but anachronistic Mameluke masters of Egypt, to overwhelm most of the Turkish troops in Syria. Yet, once the French Mediterranean fleet had been annihilated in the battle of the Nile (1798), the cause was lost. All Napoleon's ruthlessness and guile could not avail before Muslim hostility, the tenacity of Turkish troops holding out in the fortress of Acre, the ravages of plague, and the British blockade which cut off succor and supplies. Within a year Napoleon was sailing back to France, leaving his army to molder beneath the pyramids and finally to surrender. Those who survived would be repatriated when Egypt was recovered by the Ottomans a few years later.

The general himself went on to better things. His return to Paris found the Directory on its last legs; successive risings of the Left and Right had been suppressed, but no regime can erect *coups d'état* into a system of government. Siéyès, one of the Directors, was looking for a safe soldier to head yet one more coup. Bonaparte seemed ideal for the purpose, amenable yet crowned with laurels. In November, 1799, the coup took place. The Directory suppressed, was replaced by a Consulate. But the First Consul was General Bonaparte, and the rule of political adventurers gave way to that of a military adventurer. First Consul in

Napoleon's Coronation, by Jacques Louis David. The self-made emperor crowns himself. Louvre, Paris.

1799, Consul for life in 1802, hereditary Emperor in 1804, Napoleon would give France a stable military dictatorship for nearly fifteen years, and modern Europe the most unsettling career of conquest that she had ever seen.

Clearly the heir of the enlightened despots, Napoleon appears as the greatest of them all. He was a creature of the Revolution, fated to affirm its gains, but no believer in its values, in the general will, in popular sovereignty, in government by assembly. Maybe he had believed in them once. But, as he said on his deathbed, "In my youth I had illusions; I got rid of them fast." He was immensely hard-working, toiling for as much as eighteen hours a day, dictating a prodigious number of orders, letters, and dispatches—some 80,000 in fifteen years of rule: an average of fifteen a day. He knew that he loved power and he knew that his going would be a relief to his subjects. "What will they say of me when I am gone? Ouf!" A voluble, lucid and captivating talker, slim, taut, little over five feet tall, dazzling when he wanted, he reveled in limitless ambition and egoism. What Napoleon believed in was competence, reason, the efficacy of an enlightened will backed by sound artillery. All this he would proceed to prove in great campaigns abroad and great decrees at home.

Finances, education, the roads, the army, all benefited by his meticulous soldier's mind. But two measures stand out among the others: the Concordat (1801) and the Civil Code (1804). Napoleon himself was indif-

130

ferent to religion, ready to use or ignore it, as it suited him. But "religion is necessary for the people"; a religion which "must be in the hands of the government." Only agreement with the Pope could secure the stability of the regime, and agreement was secured at the same time as a broad amnesty reconciled most of the *émigrés* of the previous decade. The Concordat which healed the breach between the Church and the Revolution was one of Napoleon's great victories. The sale of Catholic Church property was accepted, and religious freedom was admitted by implication when the Concordat recognized Catholicism only as "the religion of the majority of Frenchmen." Bishops became prefects in violet robes, ruled by a minister of ecclesiastical affairs; and Napoleon would be able to declare that his power was based on three forces: "My gendarmes, my prefects, and my priests."

He spoke truly, and, in due course, a catechism, taught in every French Sunday school. included a revealing passage: "What are the duties of Christians towards the princes who govern them, and what, in particular, are our duties towards Napoleon I, our Emperor?" To which the answer was: "Christians owe to the princes who govern them, and we in particular owe to Napoleon I, our Emperor, love, respect, obedience, loyalty, military service and the taxes ordered for the preservation of his Empire and throne. . . . To honor and serve our Emperor is to honor and serve God himself."* He had made peace with the Church, but made it on his own terms. When his policy called for occupation of the papal states, he did not hesitate to do it. When the Pope tried to withstand him, he ordered his arrest.

What was a triumph for Napoleon was a deep change for the Church. Gallicanism came out of the Revolution broken, the Pope's prestige enhanced by persecution, the clergy detached from the old regime tradition turned back to Rome. When Napoleon was gone, the new church would be ultramontane—that is, its eyes would be directed across the Alps, where the authority of the Vatican ruled unchallenged except by the alien hostile forces of the new age, which only made it more unyielding. At the same time, the Church would become increasingly defensive—obsessed by the past, increasingly afraid of any novelty that might bring revolution back.

Next came the Civil Code. The monarchy had long sought to submit all its subjects to uniform laws. It was Napoleon who achieved this aim. Most of. the Code he promulgated was concerned with property, which it sought to define and defend. Other provisions granted civil liberty and civil equality, except in the family, which was treated as a smaller state and just as despotically regulated. The father was master in the home, his wife (like his children) subject to his authoritarian power, unable to acquire property without his consent or, as a rule, to administer what she owned. Authoritarian, retrograde in many ways (as

* Quoted in E. E. Y. Hales, *Revolution and Papacy, 1769–1846* (London: 1960), p. 177.

with regard to the position of women), the Code reflected the ideals of a property-conscious society and the narrow morality of the Corsican upstart who ruled it. But it seems to have been ideally suited to the new century. Brief and clear, the Code firmly codified Revolutionary achievements, provided a long-needed unity of legislation, and furnished a model of civil law in the following hundred and fifty years, affecting much of Europe and America, even long after Napoleon's fall.

"What made the Revolution?" asked the new master: "Vanity. Vanity alone can put an end to it." The new regime would provide advancement, titles, even a new nobility. In the last forty years of the old regime the King had raised four hundred families to noble status, about ten a year. From 1808 to 1815, Napoleon created a new imperial nobility, often recruited from members of the old: 29 dukes, 44 counts, 1,468 barons, 1,289 knights—2,830 nobles in all, about one a day for eight years, over half of them soldiers, nearly half the remainder civil servants. Merchants, lawyers, doctors, professional men were no more recognized by the Empire than by the old regime. They would not come into their own for some time.

The furniture and decoration of this period reflected the new mood. Its shapes: solid, bulky, and four-square; its colors: dark for soberness, but with lots of gilt and rich materials from home industry; its symbols of power—eagles, thunderbolts, fasces, griffons, lions—or of victory—sphinxes, laurels, winged victories.

The symbols of victory and power were well-earned. Since his return from Egypt in 1799, Napoleon's armies had begun to inflict terrible defeats on all their enemies. But Napoleon had to go ever further to protect gains and borders to which his enemies would not resign themselves. In the end, he would go too far.

In Europe in his absence, the fortunes of war swayed back and forth across German and Italian territories. Whatever the force of France's Russian or Germanic foes, it had become clear in the process that Britain was the country to defeat. Indeed, the Egyptian enterprise itself had been intended to strike toward the main source of British wealth: India. That stroke had failed; and Napoleon, having made himself master of France, proceeded to restore the military situation on the continent. His swift strikes, his seemingly inevitable victories, achieved a brief interval of peace, first, with Austria (Treaty of Lunéville, 1801), then even with the British (Treaty of Amiens, 1802). Not peace, really, but a truce. The hero's popularity knew no bounds. But neither economically not strategically could France and Britain trust or abide each other. For Britain, Napoleon remained the man of revolution and of war, the upstart who would upset the balance of society and power. For Napoleon, the British stood in the way of his plans for European hegemony and, even more, for expansion overseas in the Americas and the Orient.

Britain was "perfidious Albion," and she seemed to prove it by being the first to reopen hostilities against France in 1803 and, then, by inciting one coalition after another to oppose Napoleon and by maintaining them with generous subsidies. Unable to strike at his unrelenting foe across the Channel, Napoleon used the troops he had assembled to invade England to defeat England's allies instead. In two years' hard, fast-moving fighting he shattered the Austro-Russian forces at Austerlitz in far-off Moravia (1805), destroyed the myth of the invincible Prussian army at Jena and Auerstedt (1806), pursued the Russians deep into East Prussia and beat them down at Friedland (1807). Then, in an interview at Tilsit on the river Niemen, he charmed Tsar Alexander into a friendly peace.

After the Treaty of Tilsit brought peace with Russia in 1807, only the stubborn British continued to hold out. Unable to defeat them, Napoleon could hope to choke off their commerce and bankrupt the state, so that it could no longer subsidize its allies. British power rested on British trade. The Royal Navy had long sought to blockade French-held Europe. To bankrupt the British and dry their source of power, Napoleon imposed his own counterblockade: the Continental System, meant to exclude British goods from European markets and to deny them the trading profits on which they ran their war.

The contest between blockading and counterblockading measures—British Orders-in-Council and Napoleonic decrees—led the British to bombard Copenhagen and seize the Danish fleet (1807), which they feared might be used against them; it led Napoleon to invade Spain in order to strike at Britain's Portuguese allies (1807). Both sides were led much further than they might have wished to go; and, while after 1808 the French became embroiled in a costly peninsular war, four years later the British would find themselves with an unwanted American war on their hands.

The meeting of Napoleon and Tsar Alexander I at Tilsit. Vanity and precaution placed the neutral no-man's-land on a raft.

H. Roger Viollet

The Continental System wreaked havoc with British trade and French privateering cut deep gaps in Britain's merchant fleet. But while Britain suffered, Europe suffered more. Smuggling flourished, prices soared, businessmen were ruined, Napoleon had to seize ever more territory in order to bring it within his system. "It is the English," he declared, "who force me to aggrandize myself unceasingly." It would be his anti-English measures, the cost of his occupation troops, the rigors of French administration and French demands, which turned his subjects and his associates against him. Spain in particular turned out a hornet's nest, providing the British with a long-awaited chance to fight the French on land as well as sea, encouraging even Francis of Austria to take up arms again—only to be swiftly and brilliantly defeated at Wagram (1809).

By 1810 Napoleon's realm stretched from Lübeck on the Baltic across the Alps to Genoa, and from the North Sea to Geneva. Europe, recast as it had not been for centuries, was gored all over by the marks of military engagements. Napoleon had littered central Europe with his victories, abolished the Holy Roman Empire (1806), reconstructed Germany and Italy, even revived a rump of Poland: the Grand Duchy of Warsaw (1807–1814).

France had despoiled all Europe of her treasures, bedecked herself with the art works and the gold of foreign palaces, drained toward her the wealth and raw materials needed for her wars, her industry, her display. Around her, a ring of satellites was ruled by the clan of Bonaparte: his brothers were kings of Westphalia, of Spain, of Holland (this last only until 1810, when it was annexed to France). His dashing brother-in-law, Murat, was king of Naples; another became Grand Duke of Tuscany; another, the Roman Prince Borghese, husband of the beautiful Pauline who has left us her image in Canova's marble statue, was prince of Guastalla. Napoleon's stepson was viceroy of Italy. There was a Bonaparte even in the papal *curia*: the Emperor's uncle, Cardinal Fesch. Beyond these territories, the hand of France lay heavy even where its garrisons did not stand guard, from the Mediterranean to the Vistula.

Having built an Empire, in 1810 Napoleon married an Emperor's daughter to secure the heir his first wife, Josephine, could not supply. Marie Louise of Austria was the conventional daughter of a conventional monarch, betrothed to the upstart who had just defeated her father—and not for the first time. Her husband's very divorce from Josephine was of dubious value, while he himself had just been excommunicated by the Pope. None of this prevented Marie Louise from doing her duty, which was to bear an heir. The heir, punctually born in 1811, was promptly styled king of Rome.

Yet the little heir found a crumbling heritage. War soon consumed what war had won. However strong they grew in Europe, the French

The Battle of Trafalgar, painting by Chambers. National Maritime Museum, Greenwich.

failed in their ventures overseas, whether they tried to carry revolution eastward to Egypt and Turkey or turned west to conquer Ireland or to attempt an English landing. Britain ruled the seas. Of this there was no doubt after the battle of the Nile and the destruction of the combined fleets of France and Spain at Trafalgar (1805). From their embattled island *entrepôt* the British watched for every opening. In the years following the French successes of 1807, they naturally lent aid to the Portuguese and Spanish opposition to the invading French.

Napoleon's own subjects began to turn against him. Dissatisfaction had been growing with the years. The imperial armies gobbled up conscripts: 60,000 a year until 1804, then over 200,000 a year, then over 250,000 every year. Desertions increased, so did self-mutilation and marriages which could exempt from military service, and grumbles from the peasants who lost the sons they needed on the land. The endless war with England, the Continental System, had proved increasingly costly. French ports lay ruined, empty, the economy dislocated, relations with allies and satellites were badly strained. Moreover, this policy hurt the middle classes in all countries, Napoleon's most obvious supporters, and persuaded them that the Corsican did not stand for enlightenment because he denied free trade, that he did not stand for equality because he set French interests above those of other countries, that—to sum things up—their interests and his did not coincide.

Except for Russia, all Europe lay in the great Emperor's thrall, but it was getting restive. Even with Russia relations were growing tense. Ruled by the grandson of the great Catherine—Alexander—Russia had followed an uncertain course. She had joined Austria against Napoleon, only to be soundly defeated with her Austrian allies at Austerlitz in 1805 and by herself at Eylau and Friedland two years later. After the Treaty of Tilsit, in 1807, on the other hand, she had changed sides and joined Napoleon against England. But the Frenchman's eastern ambitions and his Polish policies worried Alexander, while the Tsar's inability to comply with all of the blockading measures proposed against the British angered Napoleon. The Grand Duchy of Warsaw, incorporating territories Prussia and Austria had wrested from Poland, was a puppet of the French; that did not make it seem less of a threat to the Ukraine. The opening of Russian ports to neutral ships—that is, at one remove, to British goods—seemed a defiance and a challenge. Both sides prepared for war and war came in 1812. Victory in Russia would close the last gap in the Continental System, overcome the ominous giant on Europe's eastern border, open the way to the orient and to crushing stubborn Britain, all at one fell swoop.

In June, 1812, the *grande armée*, some 700,000 men, crossed the Niemen River into Russian territory. The French sought to bring the enemy to battle. The Russians avoided them, withdrawing faster than the enemy advanced, setting the towns, the crops, the countryside on fire; and what the Russians did not devastate, the horde of invaders would consume. In September, after one bloody encounter at Borodino, Napoleon was in the Kremlin. A few days later Moscow lay about him in ashes and ruins, three-quarters of it destroyed by fire. The Russian army remained elusive, French hopes of victory as usual seemed more elusive still, and the Tsar refused all of Napoleon's peace proposals. The French were in an impossible situation. With weather conditions growing worse, advance seemed impossible and retreat hazardous. Yet they must choose.

In October, winter already closing in, the retreat began. Weighed down with wounded and with loot, harassed by Cossacks and peasant guerrillas, the French were forced to move along the same route they had followed in the summer, amidst incredible devastation, in growing cold and snow, leaving behind them a long trail of arms, wagons, dead, and wounded. Soon the retreat became a rout, the rout a disaster. At the end of November, the ragged remnants of the grand army, hardly one-seventh of their original strength, reached Poland once again. Half a million men had died or been taken prisoner in the Russian plains. Space had defeated the armies no enemy had matched: space and the crushing blows of Russian winter.

The news of the defeat brought Europe up in arms. By December, rebellion was breaking out throughout the unquiet Empire. Napoleon raised fresh armies, fought new campaigns, which some consider the

Napoleon's Return from Russia, by Nicolas Charlet.

most brilliant of his whole career. But luck which had served him well and the balance of power he had so long ignored had veered against him.

At last, there were no more troops to be squeezed out of an exhausted land, the enemy whom the French had so often humbled now returned in force: the British, under Wellington, pressing up from Spain, and Russian, Prussian, and Austrian troops from the east and north. None would stand by the despot: not his wife, not his generals, not the people whom he had driven too hard. In April, 1814, the Emperor abdicated, receiving in return full sovereignty of the tiny isle of Elba, off the Italian coast.

But Elba proved too near to home: the fallen conqueror could see his victors quarreling over the spoils at Vienna, where they met in Congress in 1815; while in France the Bourbons who had been brought back in the enemy's baggage train and their *émigré* friends "who had learnt nothing and forgotten nothing" in twenty-five years of exile were stirring up old hatreds out of apathy. "I am not a man, but a historical figure," Napoleon once declared. A historical figure could not be left to molder on Elba's lava rocks. In March, 1815, with only a small detachment of his guard, he landed in the south of France. The troops sent to arrest him followed him instead. In three weeks the Emperor was back in Paris, promising peace again but awakening fears of war. For a hundred days, Europe teetered on the brink of a new batch of wars. But the Emperor had lost the magic touch, and the decisiveness of his

137

past victories. The bickering allies, restored to unity, moved against him. Enthusiasm among the French waned before new conscription for another army. At Waterloo, in Flanders, the Duke of Wellington, strenghthened at the crucial moment by Prussian support, brought him to defeat. That was the end of Napoleon and of the French attempt to dominate Europe.

This time there would be no comfortable retreat in the Mediterranean. Unable to take refuge in the United States as he had hoped, forced to surrender to a blockading British warship, Napoleon would be sent to Saint Helena, a little island off the African coast in the South Atlantic, there to write his memoirs, bicker with the Governor, decay, and finally die of stomach cancer in 1821.

He had been right. In 1814, the great sigh that greeted his disappearance had been a sound of relief. It would take six years' hard work at Saint Helena and several more after his death to elaborate the gospel of his glory and recreate the Napoleonic legend which was to echo on throughout the years. Napoleon himself had said that geniuses are meteors destined to burn up while illuminating their century. The light which he cast was tinged with red.

Nationalism Confirmed

The revolution and the Napoleonic Empire had unleashed new forces and ushered in power struggles on a vast new scale. They had to be defeated by opposition on a similar scale: the masses of Spain and Russia, the vast resources of the British thalassocracy, the immense expanse of eastern Europe. Mass against mass, the greater won.

One other force had stimulated widespread opposition to the French, turning the campaigns of 1812–1815 into wars of liberation for many who had hitherto known only dynastic conflicts. That was nationalism: a sentiment for whose growth the French themselves were chiefly responsible, for modern nationalism is the child of the French Revolution. We might best describe it as an exacerbated form of patriotism, destined to affect first all of Europe and then the remaining world.

Love of the fatherland was nothing new, of course, in the eighteenth century any more than in the fifth century before Christ. Nor was suspicion of outsiders and foreigners identified with war, fear of invasion and rapine, or the greed and passions slaked at someone else's expense. However, as the century progressed, these simple sentiments had fed on historical studies of national origins and on theories then being formulated about the origins and structure of the state. As the state grew at the expense of particular provinces, interest groups, or institutions,

EUROPE IN 1812 AT THE HEIGHT OF NAPOLEON'S POWER

French Empire
Subject to Napoleon
Nominal allies of Napoleon
Independent

——— Boundary of the Confederation
of the Rhine (1806–1813)
× Decisive battles
□ Sites of treaties

ASIA

SYRIA

Siege of Acre
1799

Jaffa

EGYPT

Cairo

Battle of the Pyramids, 1798

Alexandria

Abukir, 1799

CYPRUS

EGYPTIAN CAMPAIGN

CRETE

Athens

AEGEAN SEA

Constantinople

OTTOMAN EMPIRE

BLACK SEA

Odessa

Kiev

RUSSIAN EMPIRE

Moscow

Borodino 1812

Smolensk 1812

Riga

RUSSIAN CAMPAIGN

Vilna

OF FINLAND
(Russ. 1808)

Stockholm

SWEDEN

Göteborg

Copenhagen

DENMARK

NORWAY
(To Denmark)

BALTIC SEA

Königsberg

Tilsit

Eylau, 1807 × Friedland 1807

PRUSSIA

Berlin

Warsaw

Posen

GRAND DUCHY OF WARSAW
1806-13

Lemberg

Budapest

AUSTRIAN EMPIRE

Prague

Dresden 1813

Bautzen 1813

Leipzig 1813

Jena, 1806 × Auerstedt 1806

Hamburg

Amsterdam

Cologne

CONFED. OF THE RHINE, 1803-13

Munich

Hohenlinden 1800

Ulm

Austerlitz 1805

Wagram 1809 × Pressburg

Schönbrunn 1809 □ Vienna

Trieste

ILLYRIAN PROVINCES
1810-13

MONTENEGRO

ADRIATIC SEA

NAPLES

Naples

Palermo

SICILY

ITALY

Milan

Genoa

Marengo 1800

Savona

Toulon

ELBA

CORSICA

SARDINIA

MEDITERRANEAN SEA

MALTA

BALEARIC IS.

AFRICA

Brussels

Waterloo 1815

Paris

Valmy

Lunéville

Basel

Amiens

Boulogne

FRENCH EMPIRE

Bayonne

SCOTLAND

ENGLAND

London

IRELAND

NORTH SEA

ATLANTIC OCEAN

BAY OF BISCAY

Saragossa 1809

Madrid

SPAIN

Bailén 1808

Cádiz

Gibraltar

PORTUGAL

Lisbon

Battle of Trafalgar 1805

500 miles

the local or factional pride that people took in belonging to a city, a county, or a gild, the special loyalty and attachment which they felt for them, became overshadowed by identification with greater entities: the state, and the nation that the state represented.

This happened first, as we might expect, in those societies where state sovereignty was most advanced and whose members had good reasons for identifying with it, to gain at least a vicarious share in its successes: that is, in countries like France and England. But the notion of a common and peculiar evolution accounting for the particular nature and institutions of a society spread elsewhere. The Germans, whose empire had lost all shred of sovereignty, dreamed of reviving bygone glories; Italians—very few to start with—also recalled a glorious past, well-past, and yearned to restore it.

Meanwhile, discussions of the fatherland became involved with arguments about the conditions which should prevail in it. Classical references, which came so naturally to eighteenth-century men, suggested the role of *virtue* without which nothing availed, the role of the *citizen,* his duties and his rights. Intellectuals, seeking to understand the peculiar personality of private individuals, turned to examine their historical origins, the common roots whence their society sprang. Trying to define the nation and the state, they reached revolutionary conclusions affecting all their individual members. The nation was more, they said, than a few men who ran affairs or held the helm of politics. The nation was the people. It followed that the people, all the people, should properly have a say in national affairs. "There is no fatherland under the yoke of despotism," wrote the *Encyclopedia*; and Montesquieu, who defined virtue as love of the fatherland, added "that is to say, the love of equality." All members of the nation, shoots off a common stem, were equal by that fact. They shared a particular language, tradition, culture; they had far more in common than anything that might differentiate or divide them; and their institutions should properly reflect this.

The men of 1789 never forgot this. "The nation," wrote the Abbé Siéyès in his pamphlet, *The Third Estate,* "exists before all things and is the origin of all things . . . its will is always the supreme law." It would become evident in due course that, practically speaking, the government of the people meant, as before, the government of the few, only endowed with immensely greater moral power since they now ruled in the nation's name and spoke for it. Individuals found themselves lonely and defenseless before a government that was supposed to represent them —a magnified, better, truer image of themselves—and to oppose which would be madness—a kind of suicide. Edmund Burke was not far off the mark therefore when he saw "individuality . . . left out of their scheme of government. The state is all in all." His conclusions were ominous, and experience has not proved him wrong: "Everything is referred to the production of force; afterwards, everything is trusted to the use of it.

It is military in its principle, in its maxims, in its spirit, and in all its movements. The state has dominion and conquest for its sole objects; dominion over minds by proselytism, over bodies by arms."

To put it differently, a total world view set out to bend first society and then the world to its philosophy, revealing the totalitarian possibilities of a well-meaning creed. The state, noted the German poet Hölderlin, became a hell just because man tried so desperately to turn it into a heaven. Burke had suggested that mass democracy may turn to tyranny. The evolution of the revolutionaries bore him out. Sovereignty, which had resided in the king alone, now rested in the nation; and those who wielded it knew none of the traditional limits the monarchy had had to recognize: none but the limits of power. The logical—that is, extreme—conclusions of this attitude would in due course be drawn by German philosophers like Fichte, for whom "the individual does not exist . . . the group alone exists, and it alone must be considered as existent." But first the point of view had to be spread, and it spread through Europe close on the heels of the conquering French.

When French patriotism degenerated into nationalism, neither liberating nor respectful of the national rights of others, it set off a reaction in its own image. The French had broadcast the notion of a new kind of sovereignty resting in the people and expressed in the nation state. Many had welcomed them as harbingers of liberty. Their occupation proved that you could buy liberty too dearly and that, indeed, the national self-expression of one people might have to be accomplished at the expense of others. Ideals, as usual, had turned into policies.

As patriot risings broke out against the French and their collaborators, nationalism reaped the whirlwind it had sown. French patriots had conquered Europe. They had also taught it the acute form of patriotism that turned against them. Obviously, after Waterloo Europe was vastly different from what it had been in 1789. The revolution had ransacked it from Seville to Moscow, leaving deep traces or a light sediment of change: social, economic, administrative, intellectual. Enlightened ideas had spread, national awareness had appeared and grown, a hoard of memories had been accumulated which played their part in policies to come. For half a century, international affairs would be dominated by fear of a new general war which, in the words of Chateaubriand, would have been the ruin of the social order. It follows that, in these years, not wars but revolutions would trouble the uneasy peace.

Chapter 5

THE PEACE OF
HUMPTY DUMPTY

Congresses and Alliances

With Napoleon defeated, his victors met in the capital of counterrevolution to settle the fate of Europe. The Congress of Vienna (1815) sought to re-establish the balance of power and the principles of legitimacy, both severely shaken by the events of the past quarter-century. But it was impossible to put legitimacy together again.

The chief French envoy to the conference, the Prince of Talleyrand, was symbolic of the changes that had taken place. A married ex-bishop, an aristocrat of proudest blood who served the Revolution, the Napoleonic Empire, and the restored Bourbon monarchy, a skeptic who knew his talents as thoroughly as he understood the weaknesses of other men, Talleyrand brought to Vienna, in his words, "the sacred principle of legitimacy" his master represented. Conquest did not make right for Napoleon, he argued. No more could it justify Napoleon's victors imposing their own will upon the map of Europe. Dynastic right and general recognition by all fellow states could alone legitimize a sovereign or a regime. Without this principle, Europe must head for ruin.

Such views, which clearly served the interests of Talleyrand's Bourbon masters—strong in dynastic claims but short on power—suited others less. The Tsar, especially, who had designs on Poland, and Prussia, desiring to expand her territories, would have preferred a more liberal approach to possible expropriation of some dynastic lands. If Talleyrand's views prevailed, it may be that this was a moment in time when arguments from principle could still obtain a hearing; it may be because the restoration leaned heavily on traditionalist applause of "legitimate monarchy."

More likely, it was because the Austrian chancellor, Prince Metternich, found virtue in the Frenchman's arguments from his own point of view.

Metternich has been identified with dynastic legitimacy. He was, in fact, a man of reason and order who believed that the nationalist and liberal currents set in motion by the Revolution could only upset order, not create it. The claims of nation states could hurt his master's multinational empire as badly as the claims of liberty and equality could sap its foundations. Both must be stifled. Not that Metternich thought that they could be done away with. But they could be held in check by determinedly defending monarchy, aristocracy, and social hierarchy within each country; and by preventing international conflicts which could easily upset their hold upon the social body. If this could best be done by referring to dynastic legitimacy, or even divine right, the Austrian chancellor would appeal to them. Whatever best preserved national and international balance was good. Whatever would keep down radicals, Jacobins, who thought they could make and unmake regimes and constitutions, was better still.

In the end, the principle of legitimacy was theoretically vindicated, though only imperfectly applied. True, the Bourbons ruled in France once more, by grace of the Tsar and of Talleyrand. But old republics like Venice and Genoa never recovered their independence. The Holy Roman Empire could not be revived, nor did anybody want it back. The three clerical electorates which the French had secularized stayed so. Over three hundred German states remained in limbo. There was also talk about the balance of power; but the allies sought rather a concentration of power, first against the French whom they feared, then against the forces of revolution.

Their settlement was enshrined not at Vienna, but in the treaties of Paris (1814, 1815), whose main clauses drove France back to her borders of 1791 (thus leaving her some of the Revolution's gains) and surrounded her with guardians: the kingdom of the Netherlands, now including Belgium; Prussia, compensated on the Rhine for Polish territory incorporated in a Polish kingdom ruled by the Tsar;* Sardinia, which recovered Savoy and gained Genoa; Austria, which now dominated Italy from Lombardy and Venetia.

The Tsar made his contribution to the peace to come by drawing up a statement inspired by the "sublime truths" of religion and in which the "delegates of providence"—sovereigns by Divine Right, fathers but absolute fathers of their people—asserted their mutual support. Present-day historians, like certain observers of that day, think little of Tsar Alexander's invention. Yet it reflected and relied upon the growing attention focused on sentiment, and on a widespread international move-

---

* Her gains in north and west Germany changed the balance of Prussian population which had been one-third Slav and now became six-sevenths German, thus fitting her for a future role as leader of German nationalism.

The Congress of Vienna. Metternich stands at the left of the table with his hand apparently pointed toward Talleyrand, the third from the right behind the table, and Castlereagh, seated at the far right. Right: *Clemens von Metternich*, by Sir Thomas Lawrence.

ment that recoiled from soured politics to stress inner spiritual regeneration. Undogmatic, devotional, ecumenical, sentimental, the evangelical activities of eighteenth-century pietism had carried it from Moravia to colonial Georgia, from Britain to Russia. English Methodists had brought the Bible Society to Russia even as Napoleon was approaching Moscow; and Tsar Alexander was persuaded by them and by pietist friends around him that he was the chosen instrument of God.

It was not so farfetched to think that against the universal revolution one could lean on the pious enthusiasm of a universal "inner" church. Its romantic mysticism could appeal to vulgar commoners and sensitive aristocrats alike, spoiling both for more dangerous activities. Emotional religious commitments which, like English Methodism, did not set out to challenge the established churches, could compete with secular rationalism. Partly inspired by a vehement and eccentric missionary of the movement, the Baroness Julie de Krüdener, the Holy Alliance was a "Christian answer to the French Revolution." Its name derived from a passage in the Book of Daniel, its existence was dedicated to "the Most Holy and Indivisible Trinity." Its charter of 1815, which Metternich called a hollow and sonorous monument, and Goethe the best thing ever tried in the interest of humanity, would, in due course, be endorsed by all the sovereigns of Europe save the Pope, the king of England, and—rather naturally—the Sultan.

The essential purpose which the Holy Alliance was designed to serve—providing mutual support among heads of state against their own and others' revolutionaries—was given teeth and a machinery by the Quadruple Alliance of the victorious powers—Russia, Prussia, Austria, and Britain (1815)—whose counsels France joined in 1818. The war had been won by co-operation: only co-operation could preserve the peace. While revolution threatened, rulers did not doubt that it could be held in check as

144

A contemporary printing of the words and music to the *Marseillaise*.

long as no war diverted their attentions and their troops. To ensure great power co-operation, the signatories agreed to meet in frequent congresses where current problems could be discussed and joint action agreed upon. This was the Congress System. As long as it lasted, international peace could be accounted safe. It did not last for long.

The Revolution, uneasily buried, was far from dead. Beneath the surface of repression, police, and censorship, its believers were burrowing their shafts, meeting, talking, planning: secret societies and conspiracies flourished, especially in the backward and inefficient Mediterranean lands where the contrast between past glimpses of progress and the restored regimes seemed most striking. One such society, the *Carbonari* or charcoal burners, whose backbone seems to have consisted of anticlerical and anti-legitimist veterans of Napoleon's armies and administration, spread from Italy to France and Spain. Other societies, some of them Masonic, most of them republican-minded, grouped intellectuals, professional men, sometimes even soldiers and artisans, who believed in popular sovereignty, representative rule, and constitutions, in places as far apart as Cadiz and St. Petersburg. Power, most of them argued, was in the hands of the privileged minority. A surprise attack by a determined handful of men should be enough to topple the oppressors and open the gates of freedom. That the masses lay supine did not discourage the enthusiastic few; and indeed, their risings, when they came, showed that in an age of minority government the struggle for power was still being conducted by small minorities.

The national ideal, suspected by the statesmen of the Restoration and alien to the structures they had set up in 1815, could not be denied.

From Scandinavia to the Balkans, from the Ukraine to Ireland, men dredged the past for languages abandoned by their fathers, collected folk tales and legends, compiled chronicles and dictionaries and song books. Poets sang and painters depicted the glories of the national past, idealized national heroes, hymned liberty and self-determination. A new musical particularism made its appearance, producing not only "German" and "Russian" opera, but national anthems too, so that the *Marseillaise* would soon be matched by a *Watch on the Rhine* and *Deutschland über alles.*

And, by a natural conjunction, those who exalted the nation praised the people too, the living mass from which the nation drew its strength and its dynamic energy. Democracy, it seemed, went hand in hand with nationalism: no wonder that the men of the Restoration feared the one as much as they feared the other and that, when he compiled his *History of Freedom* in 1862, Lord Acton chose to speak of nationalism as "the most attractive of subversive ideas and richest in promise of future power." By the time Acton wrote nationalism had proved its subversive possibilities. Nor had it waited long.

We shall note that 1820 and 1821 would see revolts and revolutions in Naples and Piedmont, Spain and Portugal, Greece and South America, which tested the machinery of the Congress allies and found it wanting. True, the Italian revolutions were soon suppressed and the Iberian revolutions also in due course—that in Spain being put down by French troops in 1823. But in the meantime the allies had split. The British had refused to let "peace and order" be re-established in Spain's revolted American colonies; and, while they would not prevent the Sultan from dealing with his obstreperous Greeks, they would not countenance foreign interventions in the Balkans which would either extend Russia's sphere of influence on the pretext of protecting fellow Christians or enhance Austria's position as protector of the Sultan.

Concord and Discords

In 1822, at the Congress of Verona, called to discuss the Greek and Spanish questions, and where French intervention in Spain was decided over the protests of the British foreign secretary, Canning, Metternich had invited Rossini to attend. The Imperial Chancellor neatly argued that, since Rossini was the god of harmony, he ought to be present at a meeting where harmony was so important. The composer came and provided five cantatas in honor of the Holy Alliance, including one of that very name whose words had to be rewritten three times to please a censorship which allowed no political references, including any men-

EUROPE IN 1815
AFTER THE CONGRESS OF VIENNA

—— Boundary of the German Confederation

tion of "war" or "peace", and which could not be printed lest anybody understand anything. At a performance in the Roman arena of Verona the composer, as he tells us, conducted in fear of his life because the great statue of Concord beneath which he stood was insecure and threatened to topple over at any minute. That was the image of the Congress System.

By the following year, concord had collapsed. An alliance of great powers did not suit Britain's traditional policy of a balance of power based on national divisions. The Greek question gave Canning the opportunity to divide Russia and Austria, by arguing for intervention— which the Tsar wanted—but on lines which isolated Metternich and which led eventually to the establishmenf of Greek independence (1830) under the protection of Britain, France, and Russia. The Holy Alliance, split in 1822 by British dissidence, was shattered and international politics opened for maneuver once again. Henceforth, power groupings would reflect the difference in the evolution of the different powers: England and France faced Austria, Russia, and Prussia. This division, however, was far from constant: Austria and Russia were rivals in the Balkans, Austria and Prussia would become rivals in Germany, England and France could only co-operate as long as France accepted second place and did not let her expansionist interests challenge those of her jealous ally. Hence, England might co-operate with Russia against Austria in Greece, or with Austria against Russia when the latter's eastern ambitions grew too large; and Franco-English relations could be strained over Spain or Egypt, as they would be later over Napoleon III's Italian policies. Fundamentally, however, internal orientations affected foreign relations; and this could only be reinforced by the common fear of revolution felt by the autocratic rulers of the East.

The Restoration of France

The defeat of Napoleon was not the defeat of the Revolution, but the return of that Constitutional monarchy that had been swept away in 1792. Since Louis XVI's son and heir, Louis XVII (1793–1795), had died in prison, the throne went to the brothers of the executed king. Lazy, clever, selfish, and skeptical, Louis XVIII (1815–1824) wanted to be the king not of a party but of the whole of France. Yet, in the words of a contemporary, France housed "two peoples that differed in their memories, their habits and ideas and that could not understand each other. Two armies had fought one against the other, of which one celebrated as victories what the other deplored as defeats." The Constitutional Charter which Louis *granted* his people was meant to appease these dissensions. In some ways it heightened them. Resting on an electoral franchise determined by property qualification and by age, it added new divisions to those the Revolution had already created: not only between republicans and royalists, revolutionaries and *émigrés,* but now between supporters of a restricted franchise and those of a wider one, between young and old, rich and poor, set apart not only by wealth or age but by political definitions. A law which allowed men— provided that they paid sufficient taxes to qualify—to vote at thirty and run for office at forty, excluded the majority of grownups born after 1789, turned the political into a generational struggle with a vengeance, and went some way to explain the *mal du siècle* which affected young men avid for action and deprived of it.

All this would last not only through the reign of Louis's younger brother, Charles X (1824–1830)—a better man but a foolish ruler, a bigot rooted in a past he would not shed;* but through that of Louis Philippe (1830–1848), who only slightly altered the Charter and lowered the property qualification to double the electorate. There would be 300,000 electors in 1848, where there had been 90,000 in the 1820's, nearly 200,000 in the 1830's. An improvement, but only slightly so. There would, under Louis and Charles, be honest government, material order, and no financial finagling. There would even, at first, be relief among the young, like Lamartine and Victor Hugo, whom the heavy hand of the Emperor had stifled. But that did not last long, and disappeared entirely after the revolution of 1830, when young people were expected to know their place and innovators were accepted only when they were profitable or dead. Restlessness and growing agitation followed, at first among the propertied classes which felt they had votes but no political power, then, after 1830, when men of property came into their own, among the pettier bourgeoisie, coming up for their turn, and among the poorer classes squeezed hard by those in power. Behind it all there loomed a growing shadow, Bonapartism: the memory of Napoleon. First, in secret societies like the *Carbonari,* recruited among the students, soldiers, tradesmen, then, after 1830, becoming a kind of official cult with the return of Napoleon's remains in 1840, and an open threat (though not a serious one) with the attempted coups of the Emperor's nephew, Louis-Napoleon, in 1836 and 1840.

But Bonapartism remained for a long time only a latent force. Politics would be fought out between a Right and Left, each one divided into moderates and radicals. The King's opponents ran from the liberals— bourgeois and noble like Lafayette, future supporters of the Orléans monarchy—to Bonapartists and republicans. Among the King's supporters were the *ultras*—ultra-royalist—who referred to the arguments of Joseph de Maistre, for whom authority must finally rest on force and the executioner be acknowledged the foundation of the state, and of Bonald, for whom kings are made by God to govern men, so men must

---

* "There is only Monsieur de Lafayette and I who have not changed since 1789," he once declared.

obey kings and kings the Pope, who is God's first representative. Such extremities did not please the King or his more moderate supporters, who did not really like to hear the Archbishop of Paris refer to Christ as "the legitimate heir to the Judean throne." They felt that against the hostile bourgeoisie, the best policy was not to encourage those who wanted to re-establish a tighter parody of the old regime but to unite the ends against the middle: let the first class lean upon the last, let aristocracy gain popular support against the middle classes. This would not happen and the Revolution of 1830 was the revolt of middle classes kept out of politics against a crown which had not known how to secure the allegiance of its people.

A Restoration rests upon the revolution which it follows. Either it defines itself in contradiction to it, as the *ultras* wished, or else, as Louis proposed, it seeks to reconcile the order it represents with that evolved, evoked, by the revolution. In terms of personnel, a good few revolutionaries were integrated in the new regime.* But not enough of them and not for long. Under Charles X, the old nobility was largely in the saddle and Charles' last minister, the Duke of Polignac, believed he had been vouchsafed a special revelation from the Virgin Mary about his task. Only in 1830 did the men who had grown rich and influential after 1789 come into their own, and perhaps that is one reason why 1830 had to happen.

In terms of property a kind of settlement was managed. The question of national property—not that of the church but that seized by revolutionary governments from *émigrés*—threatened to rend the nation. Returning *émigrés* looked on their lost property as a hereditary and sacred right of which they had been deprived. Its buyers, peasants and bourgeoisie, felt that property was a social issue, defined by law and justified by labor and by action. A new capitalist class had arisen, whose fortunes were deeply involved in this matter. In Balzac's novel, old Grandet starts out as a master cooper on the eve of the Revolution, marries the daughter of a wealthy lumber merchant, uses her dowry and his savings to buy confiscated property, becomes a mayor and builds some fine roads to his farms which are assessed to pay low taxes, invests his capital in loans at usurious rates, discounts bills at frightful interest, buys a castle and the land of a local noble who has financial difficulties, puts some of his money in state annuities at 3 per cent and some in barrels, finally dies in 1827 leaving his daughter a multimillionaire. Grandet was only the image of real capitalist figures: farmers like the Thomassins of Pontoise, who under Louis XVI farmed 560 acres but owned only eight of them, who bought 185 more when national property was

---

* Chateaubriand has described Talleyrand's appearance in Louis XVIII's antechamber, when he saw "enter silently vice leaning on the arm of crime, Monsieur de Talleyrand walking supported by Monsieur Fouché; the infernal vision passed slowly before me . . ."

Liberty Leading the People, by Eugène Delacroix. For once the romantic image reflects contemporary romantic imagination.

Giraudon

being sold and 375 further acres in 1822; merchants like the Danse of Beauvais: tenant farmers in the sixteenth century, merchant dyers in the seventeenth century, important traders in the eighteenth century, ennobled magistrates under Louis XVI, great buyers of national land under the Revolution, magistrates and deputies under the July Monarchy; or, again, the Peugeots of Montbéliard, farmers in the fifteenth century, innkeepers in the seventeenth, millers in the eighteenth, who bought national goods, built a cotton mill in 1805, abandoned textiles for metal production in 1832, when they began to make swords, crinoline hoops, corset stays, and (appropriately) umbrella frames.

Such people had legally bought lands, some of which had lain neglected or ill-cultivated, and had worked them for twenty years. They were not going to let them be taken away from them and, if Louis XVIII had not guaranteed that sales of national property would be respected, he would never have been restored. However, the *émigrés* wanted compensation. National lands still left unsold were restored; but few were left and few benefited from this measure. Finally, in the 1820's, an indemnity was granted to the dispossessed—the *"milliard des émigrés"* at whose cost the Revolution was confirmed, the transfer of property accepted, and the notion that property was anything but a legal and social right (or fiction) denied forever.

But this important settlement which set property owners' minds at rest, contributed to the rising criticism of the regime. The millions of the *émigrés* was one more stick to beat the government with. Especially under Charles X, who tried to rule by principle rather than conciliation, tensions got worse. The power of the church was getting too obtrusive. Over three-quarters of the professors in royal colleges, nearly half the directors of communal schools, were in holy orders. Stringent ordinances threatened "blasphemy." Altogether, there were too many old

151

men in power, or too many men representing old ideas. Should government represent the king, or the majority in the Chamber? The crown sought to assert its supremacy over the elected representatives of the nation. In 1830, the dispute came to a head. First, Polignac's government sought to muzzle the opposition press by new laws, but they were rejected by the Chamber of Peers. Paris illuminated for joy; and an observer remarked that, however bright the illumination, it would not be enough to enlighten the ministers. He was right, and the elections of 1830 returned a liberal majority which promised trouble. On July 26, Polignac published four ordinances dissolving the newly elected Chamber and altering press and election rules to the disadvantage of the liberals. The streets filled with barricades. "Three days sufficed to overturn one throne and make all others tremble." When they were over, the Bourbons had departed never to return and France had a new king: Louis-Philippe of the junior, Orléans, branch of the royal family.

After 1830

Monarchy New Style

The Charter was revised to affirm the principle of national sovereignty; the church was placed back on Napoleonic terms defining the Catholic creed, once more, only as that "of the majority of Frenchmen"; censorship and extraordinary courts were abolished; the age of electors and candidates to office was lowered; the monarch was called king no longer *of France,* but *of the French;* the white flag was replaced with the tricolor and the royal lilies with the Gallic rooster. Monarchy henceforth was a contract, which Louis-Philippe swore he would observe.

The echoes of the July Revolution were heard far afield. Even in Stockholm there was political unrest and a slump in trade. In Germany, many like the young poet Heinrich Heine had longed for something like it: "Lafayette, the tricolor, the *Marseillaise,* it intoxicates me!" Liberals stirred and rulers were frightened into concessions, constitutions, and press laws, which they would hasten to withdraw as soon as the revolutionary danger passed. In Italy, Parma, Modena, and Rome rose up against their antediluvian rulers. The Swiss cantons replaced the reactionary administration of local aristocracies with more liberal constitutions, ensuring equality before the law, rights of free expression, and asserting popular sovereignty. Far away, in Poland, a nationalist revolt sought to free the country from its Russian masters. All Europe stirred, moved by the French example, hoping for French aid. But no aid was forthcoming. The French were eager to reassure the other powers; and Louis-Philippe stood by while the Holy Alliance reasserted its hold from the Vistula to the Tiber.

Only in Belgium did a rising sparked by the news from France achieve its end. There, the settlement of 1815 had placed the southern provinces under the king of Holland whose rule, though economically advantageous, caused serious friction—especially on religious grounds. Belgian Catholics and liberals agreed that they wanted to be free from Holland and independent. On August 30, 1830, a performance of Auber's opera, *La Muette de Portici,* with its portrayal of Neapolitans rebelling against Spanish rule, set off rioting in Brussels which grew into a war of national liberation from the Dutch. In the case of Belgium, French and British interests coincided, support was forthcoming, and before the year was over an independent monarchy had been set up. The Belgian Constitution of 1831 would prove the most liberal in Europe, founded on popular sovereignty and guaranteeing all the revolutionary freedoms which seem quite commonplace today: of press and public meeting, worship and education.

Whether in Belgium or in France, the new style monarchy, while more liberal, remained a contract between men of property (or perhaps, explicitly became one). Louis-Philippe of France has been called the last of the enlightened despots, and he was certainly enlightened in terms of the eighteenth century which had formed him, along with the Revolution in whose armies he had served. Cultivated, avaricious, opportunistic, brave, the new king set out to portray the ideal citizen ruler, a bourgeois among bourgeois, a money man among plutocrats, a manager among a managerial oligarchy.

The French National Guard was revived, so that the middle class in arms could defend the new regime. It needed defending. 1830 had scared the bourgeoisie. The years that followed scared it more. The urban masses had made the Revolution only to be cheated of its benefits. Where aristocrats had ruled, the rich now took their place. Louis-Philippe's first prime minister was a banker, Laffitte; his greatest prime minister for half his reign was François Guizot, whose advice to youth was to become rich by work and savings in order to qualify for the vote.

Guizot defined the middle class as "a class which does not live on wages, which has in its life and thought freedom and leisure, which can devote a considerable part of its time to public affairs" and which is equally removed from past privileges and "from the class dedicated to manual trades." Those who lived on wages and by manual trades objected. France was beginning to feel the impact of industrial changes. Paris was still a city of craftsmen and artisans, manufacturers and home workers, but factories were beginning to spread. By 1840, 2,000 steam engines were in use; by 1847, 5,000. By 1850, 2,000 miles of railroad track had been laid down, and railroad workers and mechanics would be noticeable on the barricades of 1848. Bread riots were being replaced by wage demands and strikes, while, behind the political publications of the middle classes, the voice of workers, of their organizations and publications, began to be heard.

The lot of industrial workers was not easy. The social dislocations and the misery that we have seen in England obtained in France as well. In the first decade of the reign the number of suicides increased 50 per cent, mostly among the poor. The number of foundlings, cared for in public institutions, had trebled between 1784 and 1830, and it continued to grow. Alcoholism was becoming a major social scourge. A long series of workers' risings speckled Paris and the provinces with blood; in eighteen years of rule there were seventeen attempts on the life of the King.

But the peasants were quiet. As long as the middle class put their trust in Louis-Philippe, the regime was safe. It had found its perfect representative in François Guizot (1787–1874), son of a protestant victim of the Terror, educated at Geneva, admirer of Bentham and Malthus and Adam Smith, translator of Gibbon and Shakespeare, cultivated, confident, austere, the very type of the *grand bourgeois* "grown rich by work and saving." Between 1840 and 1848 Guizot ruled France for the King and for his own kind, on the principle that the duty of government is to maintain social order. Tocqueville noted that the new, bourgeois rulers of France were "active, industrious, often dishonest, limited in outlook, rash at times through vanity or egoism, fearful by temperament, moderate in everything, except in a liking for prosperity and the mediocre." It looked as if that mediocrity and rule of the commonplace which Tocqueville had noted in his travels through the American democracy were spreading across the world. As for France herself, Louis-Philippe's government appeared "like a business company, all the operations of which were undertaken in view of the profit which would accrue to the shareholders."

When, in 1842, a slight electoral reform was proposed, Guizot opposed it: "All the great conquests are made, all the great interests are satisfied." Liberty had been won; order must now guarantee that liberty. Without order, there could be no freedom to act, to speak, to possess—especially to possess—when property was the ideal and reward of the age: "The goal and the reward of labor and probity, the most precious pledge of the spirit of order and stability," as the *Journal de Lille* would say on March 28, 1844. Stability was the watchword and, hence, resistance to change. This was a mistake. France's political system, as Fr. Bertier de Sauvigny has pointed out, was like a pyramid stood on its point, hence unstable. A broader base might well have reinforced it. While good times lasted the system endured. But around 1846, depression came, bad harvests, overproduction in industry, falling prices, collapse of rash railroad enterprises, a million men thrown out of work.

In their industrial struggles, the workers had learned to organize. Now

One of the national workshops under Louis Blanc. When few could read, newspapers were heard rather than scanned. But how much work was actually done there?

they were listening to political and social theories directed to their own political problems. There was François Raspail (1794–1878), a working doctor and researcher who helped found microchemistry and whom his contact with the poor persuaded that social reforms were more important than political ones; that if the rich would not help the poor, the poor must help themselves. Raspail advocated manhood suffrage, progressive taxes, and prison reform, as measures of social hygiene; and, he added, if need be, revolution too. There was Louis Blanc (1811–1882), who did not believe that self-help, the movements sponsored by Raspail, the co-operatives or collective organizations, could succeed by themselves and advocated state control of banks, railroads, insurance, and heavy industry, along with aid to labor. The best way for the state to aid the workers was by setting up co-operative social workshops. And these ideas Blanc set out in a book, *The Organization of Labor* (1839), which caught the workers' imagination. Last but not least there was Louis Auguste Blanqui (1805–1881), a professional revolutionist.* Tocqueville, when he saw him in 1848, found him to have the appearance of a moldy corpse which had passed its life in a sewer and had just left it. Blanqui was persuaded that the struggle for power between classes was unavoidable and could only be settled by an armed insurrection.

Uneasy Interlude

Belgium, Switzerland, and France apart, however, the revolutionary outbreaks of 1830 had been repressed by 1831 and the brief scare only reinforced the machinery of reaction. The crisis confirmed the fears and tightened the bonds of eastern autocrats threatened by events, and showed that the interests of autocracy were the same, whether in Warsaw or in Milan. Here was proof that Russia and Austria must stand together, confirmation for Metternich's view that their dissensions could only bring revolution in their train. But the new agreement between Rus-

* It was his pen that coined two potent concepts: Industrial Revolution and Dictatorship of the Proletariat.

sia and Austria raised the danger that they would set about solving the Turkish problem by themselves, much as the Polish problem had been solved before. What England wanted was to preserve the *status quo,* not have her continental rivals expand; and England's eastern policy would maintain this into the 1850's.

1830, said Victor Hugo, was a revolution that only went halfway. But, if the defeats or disappointments of 1830 held up the progress of revolution, they also confirmed it. To hold up is sometimes to uphold, and none could gainsay that in its crabbed and thrifty way the bourgeois monarchy of Louis Philippe fulfilled most of the dreams of 1789. So did the model constitutional government of Leopold in Belgium, a rule which soon made the Saxe-Coburg prince the mentor of constitutional-minded Europeans, not least of his English niece—Victoria.

By that time, constitutions were becoming quite familiar. Sweden had obtained one in 1809, Spain in 1812 (suppressed and re-established several times until it came to stay in the 1830's), Norway, Holland, Portugal, and a number of German states had proclaimed their own; and the 1830's would see more appear. But all representative institutions rested on a narrow franchise, and, constitution or no, the great contest of the 1830's and the forties would be between the idea that numbers are sovereign and the majority should rule, and the traditional concept of government by some kind of elite: of birth or money, property or talent. The difference between the autocratic monarchies of the east and the representative and constitutional ones of the west was immense, but it was a difference of degree. In both, political expression was legally restricted to a narrow section of society—40,000 Belgians out of 4 million, 300,000 Frenchmen out of 29 million, 620,000 Englishmen out of 16.5 million—between 1 and 3 per cent of the population. Only in the distant United States was there any approach to universal manhood suffrage. Only in Switzerland and France would this appear in 1848.

Yet these tiny groups of men who ruled by right of birth or money sought to hold the line against contenders pressing from below, and saw their problems largely in the light of squabbles with rival minority groups claiming access to political expression. Metternich knew better. Perhaps England could introduce partial change and then hold the line. No one else could afford to crack open a gate through which change was bound to rush in overwhelming force, a force the more destructive since it was more social than political. He wrote to his opposite number in France, Louis-Philippe's prime minister François Guizot, that the game of politics seemed inadequate to the needs of the time. He was right. Not political but social reforms were needed. Yet political reforms loomed so large in the mind of potential revolutionaries that when the revolution came again, in 1848, they thought of and sought for little else.

Chapter 6

THE BALANCE
OF THE POWERS

Spain

The eighteenth century was Spain's Indian summer, between the decay of the last Habsburgs and the ravages of war followed by political anarchy. Philip V (1700–1746) was no genius, but vastly superior to his Habsburg predecessors. He and his French advisers introduced Colbertian economic views and French administrative methods, fostered and protected new industries, did their best to remove at least some barriers to internal trade and some of the particularist privileges that hampered enterprise. With all their shortcomings, the first Bourbon kings gave Spain the best government since Philip II: economic recovery, industrial progress, technological innovation. Spain's population doubled to nearly 11 million, her army grew from 20,000 to 100,000, her fleet increased from 20 to 300 ships, her treasury advanced from bankruptcy to comfort. The late eighteenth century saw the American empire reach its greatest extent and prosperity, its population increasing with its riches, revenues rising sixfold in the century, while mines turned out half of the world's stock of precious metals. We should not forget that Mexico was still the major city of the western hemisphere and that Spanish San Francisco was being founded about the time when on the other coast the British colonists were asserting their independence.

Philip's eldest son, Ferdinand (1746–1759), continued his work. His reign ended on an unfortunate note when, in 1758, the death of his queen drove him from melancholy into depression. The King shut himself up, refused to shave or change his clothes, attacked the servants, tried to hang himself with the bed sheets or strangle himself with napkins, and would in his lucid intervals talk only about his illness, which was being treated with ass's milk, quinine, white decoction of Sydenham, heartshorn jelly, along with fresh vipers and cordials for strength.

In 1759 Ferdinand died and was succeeded by his younger brother, Charles III (1759–1788), the very model of an eighteenth-century ruler, great hunter and devoted administrator. Royal manufactures were founded or encouraged, roads and canals were built, trading companies allowed to be set up on the Bay of Biscay and in Catalonia; economic and patriotic societies were founded to regild the tarnished honor of productive work. The Spanish upswing came most markedly in that last third of the eighteenth century when France was in the doldrums. Catalonia, where the cotton industry employed some 80,000 workers, was second only to England in its production and exports of cotton wares. An English traveler of the 1780's found Barcelona remarkably industrialized and booming. The province was a great exporter of wine and brandy—so great that the world price of brandy was practically set in Catalonia in the eighteenth century.

Yet these political and administrative changes seem to have affected society but little. The census of 1787 found one landowner among every thirty-five peasants: the north—Basques, Navarrese, Catalans— had many farmer-owners and so had the Huerta country of Valencia, though most of them were only dwarf smallholders. But elsewhere farmers starved, stifled by tithes and dues, on vast estates, half of them lying fallow. As late as 1840, when the French writer Théophile Gautier visited Spain and found it charming, there was no sense that either bourgeoisie or working class had really grown out of a century's travail.

The crown found its servants among hidalgos—that is, the petty gentry, sometimes almost commoners. The Spanish census of 1787 gave a figure of nearly 500,000 for the hidalgo and noble population, which might be compared with some 400,000 nobles in France, a country with more than twice the Spanish population. Many hidalgos, of course, were very poor; some were not distinguishable from commoners, especially where they could be found working as weavers, masons, or cowherds, or begging in the streets. In 1773, a royal rescript announced that hidalgos could engage in crafts without derogation. In 1783 the problem was attacked from the other end, and crafts like tanner, carpenter, smith, tailor, shoemaker, and several others were specifically declared to be honorable, so that those who engaged in them could hold noble rank or be elected to municipal office.

In Spain, as in Italy or in Russia, the struggle for political change was going to take place within the nobility not against it, between aristocracy based on land and lower groups based on government service. The professional classes played only a minor role and were ill-equipped to do better. Weak and ill-respected, lacking an economic base, they were forced to take double jobs. Schoolmasters, who were quite numerous, had to earn their living as gamekeepers or public letter-writers. At the other extreme of the social scale, the grandees, though quite useless, were much in evidence. Their strength lay in the lands they owned; and in the late eighteenth century four great families owned about one-third of all the cultivable land of Spain. The vast entailed *latifundia* were owned by absentees who lived at court or in the cities, *rentiers* who seldom improved and never sold their entailed domains. With so little land coming on the market, its price would be too high for would-be peasant or capitalist buyers. Short-term leases brought in high rents, but also discouraged improvements.

Innovation Blunted

New French currents found expression in the patriotic economic societies which sprang up in the provincial towns, sponsoring schools, agricultural innovation, scientific research, and publicizing their ideas in public debates and prize-giving speeches. But men who posed as *philosophes* when traveling in France remained good Catholics and quite traditionalist in Spain. The last sorcerer was handed over by the Inquisition to the secular arm to be burnt at Seville in 1781. The Inquisition would be definitely suppressed only in 1834. Some grandees brought up their children according to the precepts of Rousseau and engaged in scientific experiments, but new influences had but a shallow hold. Society remained lethargic, formal, and dull. "I do not conceive it possible for any great city to be duller and less agreable than Madrid," wrote the British ambassador, William Eden. At the very end of the century, the Duke of Arcos had 3,000 servants, paid little or nothing, ill-lodged and ill-fed, mostly to do nothing. The Duke of Medina-Celi spent 12,000 reals a day on the upkeep of his dependents. The Duchess of Benavente hired the Italian composer Luigi Boccherini to conduct her private orchestra at a thousand reals a month, bought Goya's *Los Caprichos* in 1799 for 1,500 reals, when that same year the average daily pay of workers in the capital was six or seven reals. One pound of old beef cost twelve reals, one pound of pork cost fifteen reals, one pound of bread cost three reals, one pound of chocolate cost five reals, one pound of sugar cost four reals. A shepherd earned a maximum of 160 reals a year, supplemented by two loaves of bread a day. An Andalusian day-laborer got three to four reals a day, when he was employed. The Spanish held that "there are more days than sausages," and indeed the staple food was often bread rubbed with garlic and dipped in oil, rye pancakes, along with onions, leeks, pimentos; and the diet got more Spartan the further south one went. The peasants used woden plows, the backbreaking sickle rather than the scythe, and threshed their grain with flails on earthen floors. Blast furnaces fed on wood. Wheat from Palencia, about 150 miles from the port of

Santander, cost twice as much in Cadiz as wheat shipped from France, where better roads facilitated transport. In the royal college of Madrid, in 1745, serious examination questions invited students to consider the causes and meaning of blood showers, and asked when bells should be rung to avert storm and hail. The French ambassador to Madrid summed up the Spain of 1759 as behind all other countries by at least two centuries.

On the industrial plane, production, even expanded, was insufficient to satisfy all needs. Even handkerchiefs (some with the portrait of famous matadors) came from Manchester. This meant that the demand for goods continued to be met from outside sources, especially in the Empire overseas, whose economy was rapidly expanding, and which looked ever more to British supplies to fill needs with which the home country could not cope. Eventually, this inability to supply the Empire, along with the insistence that its markets should still be subject to mercantilist controls, would lose Latin America altogether and, with it, precious revenues. But first the enlightened political and economic ideas which affected Spain in its higher reaches had to percolate into the colonies.

The standard-bearer of enlightenment was a monk and professor of theology, Benito Gerónimo Feyjóo y Montenegro (1676–1764), whose writings, published between 1726 and 1760 introduced Spaniards to all the ideas they had so long ignored. "The works of this man," wrote a contemporary, "produced a useful fermentation, they made us begin to doubt, they made known other books very different from those that were in the country, they aroused curiosity and opened to reason the door which had been closed by indolence and false knowledge . . . for they are in the hands of everyone." Orderly thought, logical progression, suspension of judgment until evidence brought an answer, concern for truth and public utility, were the new ideas and approaches that Feyjoo preached, subject always to the restraints and discipline of Christian faith. Philip, Ferdinand, Charles, all encouraged the spread of Feyjóo's works and Ortega y Gasset insists that, as a result, the eighteenth century would be the least Spanish of Spain's history.

But the new ideas were a thin veneer. The people stayed Spanish, that is, they stayed put, opposing all change. Inertia was their sole defense against an ever-hostile world, and a French visitor of 1782 found the peasants, above all others, abiding by "the absolute principle of always doing what had been done before and in exactly the same way." The ignorant peasant, the elegant officer, the son of a noble or a bourgeois, differed in style of life but seldom in line of thought: they all shared the same submission to authority, lack of private judgment or internal life, the same credulousness, superficiality, hidebound narrow-mindedness, fed on absurd romances and almanacs.

160

He who reads Feyjóo
And he who translates the French
He who wears a frock coat
Heretic!

was a refrain still hummed in the Madrid of early nineteenth century. The enlightened *afrancesados* were un-Spanish. On one hand we have acts without ideas, on the other, ideas without acts.

The church was probably the most democratic institution in the country, the greatest employer of labor, the greatest dispenser of charity, providing also a career open to the talented, so that a charcoal-burner's son could become the primate of Spain. But it would and could accept no ideas, rejected all liberal reforms, ruined their educational plans. The Spanish paradox was that liberals were elitist and unpopular, the church popular and obscurantist. Free trade in land and goods, which reformers advocated, suited the better-off but not the peasants or the poor. The poor looked to the church, on whose doles they depended. The life and property of cathedral towns turned around it; regular priests, close to the people, were poor and respected; the hierarchy was narrow-minded but strong. There would be no anticlericalism in Spain until the 1820's, and then this would be confined largely to the towns. Over one-third of the books and pamphlets published in 1784 and 1785 dealt with religious subjects; but religion, like the world, was still viewed in medieval terms. The French Dominicans who took refuge in Spain in the 1790's and were kindly received by their Spanish fellows could not help remarking that they had stepped out of eighteenth-century France into fourteenth-century Spain.

This was the country to which Charles IV (1788–1808) fell heir, and whose dimly enlightened rulers sealed it off so tight from events beyond the Pyrenees that a French priest seeking refuge in an Aragonese town at the end of 1792 found everyone in complete ignorance of the French Revolution.

Spain and the Modern World

Peace with France in 1795 allowed the spread of the disturbing news, but with little effect beyond the colonies of foreign merchants and artisans in places like Cadiz and Barcelona. A liberal "patriot" movement developed within the narrow limits of French influence. More important, a struggle for power was shaping up between the heir to the throne, Prince Ferdinand, and Manuel Godoy (1767–1851), his parents' favorite and ruling minister. In 1808, riots organized by Ferdinand's friends chased Godoy from power and forced the King to abdicate. Ferdinand VII succeeded to the throne, which he hoped to hold with

French support. Napoleon had other plans. He wanted the Spanish throne for his brother Joseph. Ferdinand was tricked and hustled into abdicating in his turn, and French occupation troops brought a new king whom his Spanish subjects lost no time in nicknaming *Pepe Botella* ("Joe the Bottle").

The French army had no difficulty in routing Spain's regular forces. But Napoleon's miscalculation turned the loutish Ferdinand into a symbol of national resistance. Friction with French occupation troops rubbed patriotic feelings raw, exacerbated native xenophobia, and precipitated an insurrection of the most popular kind—a rising in which liberal patriots found themselves thrown together with conservatives and army generals, while fierce priests led peasant guerrillas to fight for King and Christ. Resistance was backed by British support. Relentless guerrillas, well-adapted to the land, kept the occupant stretched out and tensed beyond his capacities. Only moderately effective, the guerrilla did nevertheless encourage Spanish patriotism and ease the task of Wellington's regular soldiers. It also left a heritage of lawlessness behind, reinforced revolutionary mentality, glorified violent political action, encouraged the tendency of military men to grab for power as and when they could.

While this went on, a representative assembly had found refuge at the extremity of the peninsula, in Cadiz, where, in 1812, it wrote a constitution for Spain which would enshrine the principles of the enlightenment: national unity, national sovereignty, equality before the law, proportional taxation, property rights—the very things that Joseph was trying to impose from his uneasy Madrid throne. But that was not what Spaniards died for. As Wellington insisted later, Spain "is the only country where two and two do not make four." The war the Spaniards fought, Napoleon thought, was a war of monks: and when in 1814 Ferdinand returned, the people shouted "Long live the absolute King!" "Down with the constitution!"

Ferdinand asked no better. He put an end to liberal experiments and reintroduced the despotism of yore. Spain was bankrupt. The restoration could neither reward the victors nor conciliate the vanquished. It lacked the means for either, let alone for both, as had happened in France. So the liberals lost their places, and the soldiers were ill-paid or not paid at all. American silver could solve the problems of the state, but the Hispanic American colonies were in turmoil and the bankrupt state could not summon up the power to lay its hands on the silver without which it remained insolvent and ineffective. The discontented army, assembled to suppress rebellion in the American colonies, made the revolution of 1820, revived the constitution of 1812, but lost its chance of popular support by clashing with the church, which disapproved equally of constitutions and revolutions. The French reappeared in Spain (1823), this time to liberate Ferdinand, who was practically a

The Execution of the Rioters, May 3, 1808, by Francisco Goya. On both sides, the savagery of despair. Prado, Madrid.

prisoner in his palace. Blessed by the church and cheered by the Spanish people, they crushed the liberals and the soldiers, who stood up no better to the guns of Louis XVIII than they had to those of Napoleon.

The King now proceeded to sow the seeds of future trouble by excluding his brother and heir, Don Carlos, from the succession in favor of his daughter Isabella (1833–1868). When Ferdinand died in 1833, he left behind him a foreign widow of doubtful reputation and a three-year-old heiress whom a section of the nation, persuaded that Don Carlos was the rightful heir, would not acknowledge. This ushered in a long succession conflict.

Don Carlos drew his support from the rural provinces of the north, where the church was strongest and provincial sentiment most intense. The Carlist rebellion became the struggle of the unadapted and inadaptable against the modern world, their primitive royalism opposing the centralist liberalism of Madrid. The conflict soon turned into a struggle between liberalism and reaction. Both the Queen-Regent, Maria Christina, and Don Carlos were absolutists, but Carlos's reliance on conservative provinces forced the Queen into an alliance with the liberals and the loyalist army.

In 1836, to finance the costly struggle, church property would be nationalized, anticlericalism become identified with progressivism: monasteries became factories, ministries, prisons, or barracks, or gave way to new streets and urban improvement schemes, while church lands were bought up by rich farmers and speculators. The press was freed, generals came to dominate politics by pronunciamento, power passed into the soldiers' hands and those of local bosses, many of whom could declare, as one general did on his deathbed, that he had no enemies to forgive because he had killed them all. Pending claims to direct power,

163

the military became arbiters of politics, by providing or withholding protection for civilian governments. By 1839, Carlist guerrilla activity had collapsed into brigandage, and would continue as such into the 1860's, surviving chiefly as a loyalist, clerical, and reactionary tradition that could be revived in 1936.

Spain came out of the trial as a very inefficient but liberal and mercantile society. Entails had been abolished, the gild system abandoned in 1834, the *Mesta* in 1839; a real bourgeoisie was taking shape along with modern industry, even labor unrest was appearing in cities, along with middle-class radicalism, while Inquisition, censorship, and absolutism had passed away. Spain was still backward, still romantic, but open at last to the modern world.

Latin-American Independence

One other change that the nineteenth century brought was the loss of Spain's erstwhile empire in South America and the emancipation of most of her colonies.

Across the South Atlantic a vast empire had grown up in the two centuries since the *conquistadores,* with cities finer and wealthier by far than those of the mother countries, with presses, schools, universities, and riches which kept the finances of Spain and Portugal afloat. All this was realative, of course. Life for the whites throughout the Spanish Indies was probably better than for their counterparts in Spain; but society rested on the exploitation of native labor, made milder and more bearable only by the slackness and inefficiency of the exploiters.

Until mid-eighteenth century, neglect and fraud, corruption, petty tyranny, rapacious and unscrupulous administrators, produced backwardness and almost anarchy. Spanish officials battened on native-born *creoles,* the *creoles* on Indians and on mixed-breed *mestizos,* all of them part of a stiff dog-eat-dog heirarchy. An official report of 1749 did not mince its words: "The countries of the Indies, fertile, rich and flourishing, . . . governed by persons who often regard no interests but their own . . . are now reduced to such a condition . . . that justice has no authority and reason no power to make any stand against disorder and vice." One of the great bones of contention between France and Britain was the *asiento*—the right to supply the Spanish colonies with slaves—which Britain held until 1739 and France enjoyed on and off after the 1740's. But the Spanish government was always jealous of granting privileges which it wanted for its own Iberian subjects, and which the latter were seldom able to use properly. The colonists could not get supplies, manufactures, especially slaves, from Spanish sources; and Spain would not allow them to get them from others legally. Contraband flourished and, in the end, colonial protection collapsed under the battering of the smugglers. "Spain kept the cow, while Europe drank the milk."

Charles III tried to improve matters, appointing more efficient administrators and introducing some reforms, such as free trade among the different colonies of the Indies. As usual, the reforming measures came too late—when they were felt at all. A more efficient administration disturbed the *creoles* used to the bad old ways, and created the paradox of an absolute monarchy more liberal in some ways than the subjects it ruled—subjects who read Montesquieu and Voltaire, owned and maltreated slaves, claimed for themselves the rights they would not concede to others.

Visiting South America at the end of the eighteenth century, the German naturalist Alexander von Humboldt noted that "the most miserable European without education and without intellectual cultivation, thinks himself superior to the whites born in the new continent." As for the *creoles,* they thought of themselves as Americans, not Spaniards, and the reforms of Charles III, which included the formation of a colonial militia to improve defense, a militia in which *creoles* could satisfy ambitions frustrated elsewhere, increased their economic power and their yearning for the political rights which Spanish officials clutched so tightly. The Enlightenment was affecting both landed gentry and rising bourgeoisie; schools, periodicals, economic societies modeled after the Spanish ones, returning travelers and arriving officials, all spread ideas hostile to imperial restrictions and social humiliations. Even the economy which Empire free trade helped to flourish, created a demand for the international trade that was still prohibited.

The colonists became increasingly vocal in opposing the monopolistic policies of the old colonial system. They saw that in North America political emancipation had brought economic emancipation in its train. The thought that they too might follow the example of the northerners affected officers and landowners like the Venezuelans Francisco Miranda (1750?–1816) and Simón Bolívar (1783–1830), or the Argentine José San Martín (1778–1850), who read Rousseau, the physiocrats, and the *Encyclopedia*. In 1787, even a Brazilian whom Jefferson met in France dreamed and talked of obtaining United States support for Brazilian independence. When Charles III died in 1788, when fear of revolution hardened the heart and arteries of Spanish administration, when the old order reappeared, lethargic, venal, and oppressive, the newly awakened natives were bound to assert themselves.

All colonies depend on metropolitan—that is, home-country—arms for defense, on metropolitan goods which they cannot produce themselves or obtain elsewhere, on inertia and routine for allegiance, which will last as long as habit and lack of alternative persist. This arrangement, which had served Spain well enough, collapsed during the wars of the French Revolution. The war, beginning in 1796, cut off the colonists from the homeland, forcing the former to rely on themselves and on the foreign traders who had until then been dealt with only illegally. English and United States shipping sailed into the gap not to be dislodged again. Meanwhile, loyalty foundered before the problems which arose in Spain: should loyal Spaniards obey Ferdinand, or Joseph, or the dubious *junta* at Cadiz?

Risings and anarchy marked the years after 1808, until metropolitan rule could be restored again in 1815. But Ferdinand was paralyzed by new revolts at home and the *creoles* would not accept the restoration of the old monopolies. Brazil, whose population in 1800 equaled that of Portugal, had in 1808 welcomed the royal family fleeing before the armies of Napoleon. Rio had become a capital, in 1815 the capital of an autonomous kingdom, in 1821 that of an independent empire ruled by the son and heir of the Portuguese king. The Brazilian example proved infectious. The *creoles* too called for autonomy. They rose again in 1816, this time gaining the support of the local church which, after 1820, feared the effects of liberalism in Spain. The United States and Britain supported the insurgents, and their refusal to allow effective European intervention against them combined with Spain's own impotence meant that, by 1824, only Cuba and Puerto Rico would be left over from Spain's great American empire. Each of the several states that had sprung out of it had ports and cities to equip and build, agriculture to develop, armies to supply and train, all welcome openings to northern bankers, entrepreneurs, and shippers, first British, then French and German, at last also North Americans. A vast new market now lay open to the enterprise of the maritime trading powers.

Indeed, Spanish and Portuguese America would be the stage on which the modern variant of economic imperialism first appeared because colonial imperialism of the traditional kind would be excluded from them—at least for a long time—by the effects of President James Monroe's declaration of 1823. The American's gesture had been precipitated by specific events. The British Foreign Secretary, George Canning, at loggerheads with the Holy Allies and unwilling to see Ferdinand VII re-established in his American colonies, proposed an anti-interventionist Anglo-American declaration. President Monroe preferred to speak for the United States alone, and he was probably prompted as much by fears of Russian expansion along the north Pacific coast as by the plans of the Holy Alliance powers. His message warned all European powers against further colonial ventures in this hemisphere, and also against any attempt to interfere with the revolted Spanish colonies of the South.

Received with enthusiasm in the United States, his words fell rather flat in Europe, where the British Navy was recognized as the real deterrent to interventionism. Yet, though it meant very little until midcentury and beyond, the declaration was a momentous act. Reformulating the isolationist doctrines George Washington had first expressed, it marked the beginnings of a truly independent, American, diplomacy in the hemisphere. Behind the shield of the Royal Navy, what became known as the Monroe Doctrine allowed South Americans to fight one another almost exclusively, without having to fear the Europeans too. It also laid the ground for eventual northern domination when, late in the nineteenth century, the doctrine ceased to be used to keep Europeans out and began rather to justify United States interventions and annexations. But none of this was known in 1823; nor did George Canning suspect the future that would grow out of his initiative when he boasted to the House of Commons that he had "called the New World into existence to redress the balance of the old."

Italy

A Congeries of States

Twenty-odd dialects, a score of cities on every one of which the life of a province turned, no roads worth the name, a congeries of states, and a variety of regimes: royal in Savoy and Naples, republican in Venice, Genoa, and Lucca, papal in Rome, ducal in Tuscany and Parma, Austrian in Milan and Lombardy—such was eighteenth-century Italy, the garden of Europe, a mild, wild, sunny, fertile, poverty-stricken land of splendid decaying cities, industrious and miserable populations, lively and irrelevant cultural activity, where political divisions favored fascinating variety and petty tyranny, but scarcely any sense of Italy as such.

The economy of the peninsula was backward and fragmented, its population growing despite frequent food shortages. Agricultural productivity hovered near subsistence level; small markets and poor communications prevented real expansion. Improvement or reform on any important scale were hamstrung by the wild variety of local currencies, weights, measures, tolls, customs, civic privileges, feudal survivals, sclerotic relics of medieval practice. Smuggling, brigandage, begging, and domestic service were major industries, manufactures sluggish, illiteracy widespread. The social pyramid here too rose on a mass of peasants, many landless, some still serfs, fed on millet, maize, and beans, who could escape landless poverty in the countryside only to beg in cities or rob in the hills. Next came the turbulent but largely unproductive urban

167

population, and finally the factious, fractious, decorative nobles at the top of the pile. It was these last who stoked the fires of cultural activity, lively but with little impact on everyday life until enlightened scholars and reformers turned to improving the public weal.

Even when reforms began, mostly in the north, superstition, intolerance, and crime seem to have held their own. The papal realm recorded 13,000 murders in the 1759–69 decade; Venice executed or sent to the galleys for life 73,000 men in the years from 1741 to 1762; Milan, Austrian since 1713, was violent and crowded. An ordinance of 1762 reveals the practice of breaking on the wheel, of cutting the murderer's hand off before his head, of dragging him to death behind a horse— the executioner's fee, in this case, to include the horse which the murderer was supposed to furnish.

It was in Milan and in Florence that prosperity and progress advanced with the century. The influence of Beccaria (see p. 652) was immense. In 1769 galleys were suppressed; in 1785 the penal code reformed; in 1789 torture abolished. All this in Milan but not in Rome, where, until the French occupation, violation of a convent sanctuary, kissing a woman in the street, or possession of a pistol were all punishable by death, as was the theft of a surplice or pretending to be a priest.

Rome was the artistic center of Eruope, drawing Goethe and Mozart, Canova and David, tourists avid for antiquities, Christians craving for its churches, priests in thousands, and beggars in tens of thousands. In a way, all of Rome lived on charity. Contemporaries estimated that a quarter of the population was made up of bureaucrats, who accounted for three-quarters of the class that did not beg. Probably more. In Rome, says Sismondi the historian, everybody wears a cassock, a livery, or rags. The popes avoided all reforms which might trouble the stability and quiet of the good people used to existing abuses. In the papal states, the line between peasants and brigands was a tenuous one, while the troops preying on both were simply privileged brigands making war on brigands who were not privileged.

Travelers found the cities filthy (rainstorms, wrote a visiting Dominican friar, are the brooms of Rome) and decayed. Cows were pastured in the Forum; people relieved themselves wherever they needed and could; garbage piles awaited removal by farmers' carts or, in Venice, barges. Houses showed little furniture, few carpets, and, except in the North, fewer fireplaces. Fire, the local people told Montesquieu in 1728, is unhealthy. Visiting Sicily in 1776, Roland, the future Girondin leader, found no beds in the common people's houses, only rush mats on which the people lay without undressing, so that "their *toilette* takes no longer than that of dogs: a shake and they are ready." On the other hand, music was everywhere and one traveler compared Italy to a tuning fork, with Naples holding the octave. With its half million people, its oranges and fig trees, its oils and saffrons, its vast port in a vaster bay, the palaces of its beggared nobles and the beggars of its sunny streets—a swarm of lazzaroni (idlers), strongest support of church and king and of an arbitrary disorder—Naples was heedlessly decaying amid its beauty. Reform or revolution, its poverty and its charm seemed to remain the same. Significantly, when in 1818 King Ferdinand IV of Naples abandoned his pigtail, he was the last of European sovereigns who had worn one. Court and city took this change in hair style as a revolutionary action, and briefly wondered whether the King had become a Jacobin.

In Florence, the last grotesque heirs of the Medici died out in the first half of the eighteenth century. Cosimo, hated by his people and by his heir, had been a senile bigot who even wanted to put breeches on a crucifix. The fifty-two-year-old son, Gian-Gastone, who succeeded him in 1723, was an indolent, benevolent, and bloated drunkard who ruled for fourteen years, mostly from his bed, which he had to have bestrewed with roses to stifle the smell that arose from it. The Peace of 1735 had settled the Polish succession by giving Tuscany to Francis of Lorraine; so, after 1737 when Gian-Gastone died at last, the duchy was governed by Austrians and Lorrainers, a definite improvement over earlier regimes, especially between 1745 and 1790 under the grand duke Leopold (later Emperor), a most enlightened ruler. Leopold took council with agronomists and economists, abolished the death penalty and torture, banned the Inquisition, centralized the administration, even prepared a constitution against whose publication Joseph II advised. In 1780, Tuscany enjoyed the most enlightened legislation in the world.

But the most fascinating tourist trap was Venice, with its 400 bridges, its 200,000 inhabitants, its carnivals that began at Christmas, its powerful corporation of gondoliers, its myriad painters—Canaletto, the Guardis, the Tiepolos, and many, many others—working to please the myriad tourists, all eager to take home a remainder of its beauty. Venetian painting seems to have produced the only original school in eighteenth-century Italy. Antonio Canal, known as Canaletto (1697–1768), was probably the master of *veduti* (views) for tourists, who even translated Venetian motifs to London and to Windsor when he visited England in 1756. Francesco Guardi (1712–1793) and his brothers introduced imagination, poetry, light, and shade into the straightforward paintings of their forerunners. Pietro Longhi (1702–1785) was the master of bourgeois realism, with much ironical social description, a favorite of his fellow citizens of the middle class.

The Venetian republic, to which the Peace of Karlowitz (1699) had restored some of her great territories, lost her last holdings in the eastern Mediterranean at Passarowitz in 1718. After the Turks, she now had Austria to fear, whose new free port at Trieste was draining trade and goods away from her moldering quays. With Mediterranean trade passing into French and English hands, and Italy increasingly dominated by Austria, the republic was but the timid shadow of her former

The Ducal Palace, Venice, by Francesco Guardi. Municipal Museum, Grenoble.

self, a survivor defended only by the reciprocal determination of France and Austria to maintain a balance of power. Unlike most parts of Europe, and of Italy too, the population of the city was diminishing, infant mortality rising, the numbers of the ruling class falling particularly fast, while its spirit became increasingly reactionary and unenterprising. The wool industry and the glass works decayed, the shipyards lay idle, the 12,000 silk workers of mid-century had been reduced to 379 by the eve of the Revolution, while beggars swelled from 445 in 1586 to 19,000 in 1760 and 23,000 in 1787. One-sixth of the population were mendicants, one-tenth were servants (12,819 in 1760), 3,776 were gondoliers, who were allowed free entry to theaters. In May, 1797, occupied by the French, the republic voted its own demise; and in October its French "liberators" would hand it over to Austria, as part of a larger bargain.

Somehow theaters seem the cathedrals of eighteenth-century Italy, vast prides of their communities and just as crucial to social life, with their boxes which were but the projection of a noble salon, containing armchairs, sofas, sometimes a gaming table. Each was equipped with curtains or with shutters so that the show should not interfere with conversation, sometimes even (as at La Scala) with a kitchenette for preparing snacks. The opera or theater nearly always provided gaming rooms. For common people, entrance was cheap—about one or 1.50 lire in Venice, half the price of hire for a gondola for the day—and consumption of plays immense. Carlo Goldoni, the Venetian playwright, wrote over 200 plays, some of them in eight days. There were more than twice as many public theaters in Venice as in Paris. And it was probably the opera, with its fantastic scenery, its escape from the real world into a brighter, calmer, make-believe one, that inspired the theatrical paintings of Tiepolo.

170

The enlightenment was advancing. In 1744 the dialogues of Galileo appeared with papal license, though prefaced by the sentence of the Holy Office (see p. 372) and Galileo's own retraction of his errors. In 1757 the Holy Office permitted the publication of books which revealed the movement of the earth. The *Encyclopedia,* too, did well in Italy. There were three reprints of the French language edition: in Lucca, in Livorno (with 1,200 subscribers), and in Padua, where the seminary press was used. In 1754, the first chair of political economy had been created—at the University of Naples, where, at that time, Charles ruled who would later become Charles III of Spain. Shortly, Beccaria would be named to a similar chair in Milan. Even in distant Savoy the feudal system was being liquidated to the benefit of the crown. "Everything is coming to life," exulted a Tuscan in the 1780's, "everything is becoming beautiful. New roads, new bridges, new canals, new buildings, new lands open to cultivation . . . everywhere unmistakable signs of movement and energy.'"

The long years of peace that stretched between 1748 and the irruption of French revolutionary armies in 1796 meant prosperity: not the brilliant creativity of the Renaissance, but the steady routines of crops and harvests, the growing bustle of tourism and trade, the renovations of enlightenment. "Water, clover, cows, cheese, money and music!" noted Arthur Young in Lombardy, during the autumn of 1789. "These are the combinations that string Italian nerves to enjoyment, and give lessons of government to Northern politicians."

There were shadows, too: dependence, lack of the initiative which provided the dynamic of change beyond the Alps, the rift between a few enlightened reformers at the top and the stubborn resistance to change among the masses, the conservative church opposing the secular endeavors of enlightened despots and civil servants, the ultimate precariousness of the uneasy balance maintained throughout the Italian peninsula and ready to topple over at the first hard shove. Then, with the 1790's, the shadows darkened, reformers sheered away, once-enlightened rulers began to see a Jacobin behind every bush and to apply the label even to the mildest liberals. The poet and playwright, Vittorio Alfieri (1749–1803), who had lived in Paris until 1792 and left, disgusted and afraid, to live in Florence, found his tragedies banned by the Pope and his steps followed by spies and by police. In Naples, in 1794, a man who had desecrated a church by crying *"Vive Paris! Vive la liberté!"* was condemned to be dragged by a horse, then hung, his tongue, hand, and head cut off, and all his goods confiscated. Simple curiosity about events in France became a motive for suspicion which could easily turn into persecution. Then came the French invasion, in 1796, and this brought not just a few dilettantes but all of Italy into physical contact with the new world outside. French armies carried the Revolution with them, recasting the map of the peninsula into a series of satellite republics.

The interior of La Scala. Museo Teatrale alla Scala, Milan.

But the Italian Jacobins who welcomed the French troops represented little beyond themselves. The new regimes had little more social foundation than in Spain. As late as 1811, only three and a half per cent of the populations of Napoleon's kingdom of Italy were occupied in commerce. In Rome, remarked Mme. de Staël, only the statues were republican. What could illiterate masses in cities or in the countryside make of the new calendar, the republican rhetoric, the military occupation? They were used to repression and taxes and exactions. Now they shuddered at sacrilege which laid impious hands on the Pope and sometimes on the churches. Yet thousands got administrative experience in the new bureaucracies sponsored by the French, and thousands more saw assemblies of Italians engaging in political debate. The experience would take long to become effective; but it would not be lost.

French occupation was costly; but it brought progress too. Secondary schools opened—even one for girls at Milan, a credit and mortgage system was introduced, a road and bridge corps founded, prefects appointed, heralding new administration and new laws. Serfdom with its servitudes, feudalism with its inequalities, were abolished; civic equality and the Napoleonic Code appeared; and, when the blockade closed in on the peninsula as on the rest of Europe, local industries developed in cottons, ironware, and sugar beets.

Restoration brought Austrian domination, but many of the reforms were retained. National sentiment was still limited, and national awareness too. The risings of 1820 and 1821 sought to win reforms of a local nature, not national unity. In twenty years this would change.

Nationalism Comes to Italy

The examples of European revolution, the ferment of ideas—romantic, patriotic, Bonapartist, national—would have their effect in Italy. The revolutions of 1820 had echoed Spanish events. The new and equally unsuccessful risings of 1830 in Modena, in Parma, in Bologna, echoed the Paris Revolution of that year. From one failure to another, Italian nationalism was learning to know itself, spreading from narrow groups of soldiers, businessmen, and old public servants of Napoleon's day, from secret societies like the *Carbonari,* to reach a wider audience with the writings of men like Sylvio Pellico, whose *Prisons* (1833) told of his imprisonment by the Austrians, or Leopardi, grandiloquently recreating ancient patriotism, or Alessandro Manzoni (1785–1873), the man perhaps most responsible, with his *Betrothed* (1827), for generalizing the Tuscan form of the Italian language and the sentiment of a shared Italian past. Beneath the inefficient tyranny of sloppy despots, yearnings for reassertion, for a revival, began to stir, manipulated from abroad by the correspondence and conspiracies of Giuseppe Mazzini, a strange and fascinating figure, stern, domineering, and doctrinaire. In the 1830's, the young Mazzini had had to flee the displeasure of the Piedmontese government, first to Marseilles where he founded his Young Italy Society (1831), then to Berne where he founded another society, Young Europe, then, at last to London. His organizations were less important than his creed, which was the need to unite all the divided energies of Italy toward a common end, the building of a third and independent Rome whose mission was to inspire the making of a new and better world. Each nation had its mission in the world; this was Italy's. In its pursuit, Mazzini never ceased to fight, and to make others fight, to realize his faith.

Meanwhile, the sovereign whose police Mazzini had to flee, Charles Albert of Piedmont (1831–1849), had visions of his own. After 1815 Charles Albert's cousin, Victor Emmanuel, had set himself to recreate the old regime, complete with pigtails, feudal dues, clerical and noble privileges, antiquated court costumes. But he was the only Italian ruler whose crown did not depend on Austrian support; and the heavy taxes levied to keep up an exaggerated army also maintained an independent Piedmontese policy. Thin, pale, gloomy, an introverted solitary man, Charles Albert was yet persuaded of his mission to free Italy, a dream confirmed by a visionary nun. Charles Albert's soon-known "secret" inspired Italians everywhere as they watched him in the late 1830's promote a statistical survey of his kingdom, promulgate a new civil code, sponsor a new history of Italy, create model farms, and project railroads which would link Genoa with north European trade. Piedmont seemed to stand for the modern age: free trade in goods and in ideas, education, railroads, and technology.

Then, in 1846, another national dream—Italian union beneath the primacy of the Pope—began to take shape as Pope Gregory XVI, whose government had been a byword for obscurantism and tyranny, died and in his place arose the bland appealing figure of Pius IX. Pius began his reign with an amnesty for political prisoners and exiles, continued it by introducing gaslights, railroads, and vaccination in his states, all of which Pope Gregory had held at bay. A customs union was concluded with Tuscany and Piedmont. The papacy seemed to be taking the lead in Italian unity. Kindly and well-meaning, Pio Nono did not quite know what he was doing. As one man said, liberal ideas filtered into his head like snow blowing in around the cracks in a closed window.

And yet the Pope was neither anti-Austrian nor constitution-minded, and the king of Piedmont had neither power nor prestige enough to free Italians from the Austrian yoke. Rebellion had to start within the Austrian realm itself. And it did. Lombardy under the Austrians, was the best-governed and the best-off of all Italian states, which is not saying much but still this was a hindrance to revolt. More children went to elementary school in Lombardy (68 per cent of the boys, 42 per cent of the girls), administration was cumbrous, slow, but honest; justice was surer and milder; taxes were heavy but not overwhelming, even though in 1847 Lombardy and Venice sent to Vienna three times as much as the French occupants had managed to squeeze in their time.

Jealous memories, sanguine hopes, a temper bred of centuries catering to occupants and tourists—a mixture of servility and scorn—were factors that the occupants underrated. Most advanced, the Venetians and the Milanese could also be the most rebellious. Their resentments, like their aspirations, carried them to the van of revolt, when it came.

The Germanies

The dear old Holy Roman Reich:
How does it hold together?

sing the carousers in Goethe's *Faust*. The end of the eighteenth century would see it fall apart at last. And yet the states which it had vaguely held together—396 of them, reorganized to 39 after 1806—were still united by language, memory, and secular habit, as well as by physical circumstance. Welcome or not, German was the common language from the Baltic to the Adriatic, from the Bohemian mountains to the North Sea; and even those who would reject it in the nineteenth century still used it as a *lingua franca,* still use it so today. Gladly or not, the trade of central Europe still had to pass along North German rivers or down Austrian waters to reach a sea. And the scattering of sovereign states, though long fascinated by French culture, by the prestige and sometimes by the power of Paris, revolved in the end about one of two native poles: Austria or Prussia.

The struggle for dominion in Germany would be waged between these powers and finally decided in the 1860's. Yet, in the eighteenth

Prussian territory at the accession of
Frederick the Great, 1740

Acquired 1740–1786

Acquired 1786–1796

—— Boundary of the German Empire, 1795

RUSSIA

BLACK SEA

OTTOMAN EMPIRE

Kiev

Dniester

Danube

Nieman

EAST PRUSSIA

NEW EAST PRUSSIA

GALICIA

Königsberg

Warsaw

Vistula

SOUTH PRUSSIA

WEST PRUSSIA

Posen

SILESIA

Odor

MORAVIA

Olmutz

POMERANIA

BRANDENBURG

Berlin

SAXONY

Leipzig

Prague

BOHEMIA

A U S T R I A N   E M P I R E

Vienna

AUSTRIA

HUNGARY

Budapest

Drava

Tisza

Belgrade

BALTIC SEA

SWEDEN

Copenhagen

DENMARK

Hamburg

Elbe

BAVARIA

Munich

BAYREUTH

ANSBACH

Danube

VENETIA

Venice

Po

ADRIATIC SEA

TUSCANY

PAPAL STATES

Weser

Frankfurt

MINDEN

RAVENSBURG

EAST FRIESLAND

MARK

CLEVES

Rhine

SWITZERLAND

Zurich

PIEDMONT

Milan

Geneva

MEDITERRANEAN SEA

300 miles

NORTH SEA

Amsterdam

NETHERLANDS

AUSTRIAN NETH.

FRANCE

Seine

Paris

Rhône

Lyons

century itself, the soaring rise of Prussia was paralleled by greater Austrian interest in non-German lands. The orientation sketched out in the seventeenth century became more obvious. Tariff war with Prussia, conflicts with France, closed the North German rivers to Bohemian and Austrian trade and turned Vienna further toward south and east. Commercial treaties were signed with Poland in 1775 and with Russia in 1783, markets were developed in the Balkans and in Italy. The harbor of Trieste, which opened up in 1733, could rival Venice by 1751. The Hungarians were developing Fiume. In 1784 the first ship sailed from Vienna down the Danube to the Black Sea. Black Sea and Adriatic would be the new outlets of the Habsburg economy.

The figures who reflect the clash between Austria and Prussia are Frederick II (1740–1786) and Maria Theresa (1740–1780), whose reigns covered the crucial part of their century.

Prussia

Frederick's way had been prepared by hard-working predecessors. His father, Frederick William I (1713–1740), a stocky brute of immense girth and vast capacity for tobacco and wine, had been devoted to his barren kingdom and above all to building up an army which would affirm his realm. By 1740, the state whose population ranked twelfth in Europe maintained a peacetime army almost comparable to that of Austria and half that of the French. Nor were the soldiers wasted. In peacetime, they were employed in workshops and manufactories, producing draperies, porcelain, and glass; or back in their own village for sowing and for harvest, the men who were their officers often their lords as well.

The enlightened young dilettante, friend of philosophers and amateur musician, who had been the despair of his father, lost no time in putting this army to martial use. He had succeeded to the throne in May, 1740, determined to enlarge his territories either toward east or west. In October, the death of Emperor Charles VI decided which way he would turn. Charles' daughter, Maria Theresa, was beset with troubles. They would be his opportunity. He marched up the Oder, occupied Silesia, and, in exchange, offered Maria Theresa his support, military and political. The friend of Voltaire, the philosopher-king who had just completed a tract attacking Machiavelli and his principles, would go to any extreme to win glory for himself and respect for his kingdom.

He succeeded. Despite vigorous resistance by the Austrians, his unexpected military skill combined with the admirable army his father had forged drove Maria Theresa to come to terms. In 1742 Frederick signed peace, retaining Silesia and abandoning without compunction his French and Bavarian allies, who were left to continue fighting on their own. Soon, however, uncertain of his hold on Silesia, tempted by the possibility of further gains, he re-entered the fighting (1744), only to leave his allies in the lurch once more when, unable to conquer Bohemia, he settled for another guarantee of Silesia (1745).

When in 1748 the Peace of Aix-la-Chapelle put an end to the War of Austrian Succession, Viennese diplomats began to prepare the ground for the next round. Silesia could not be abandoned. Treaties were signed with Russia, with Saxony, and, finally, in 1756, with France, whom Frederick had brazenly abandoned in the course of the last war and which had been looking suspiciously at his negotiations with her English enemies. Frederick had only the support of the British, whom he had courted in the hope of isolating Austria. Instead he found himself almost isolated. He knew that war was coming, hostilities having already broken out overseas between France and Britain, and that it would find him at a disadvantage. Thinking a bold stroke might save him, he invaded Saxony, whose territory would usefully complete his recent Silesian acquisitions and whose army was, in any case, easiest to defeat.

As in 1740 so in 1756, his boldness was successful and the Saxons broke. But the unprovoked aggression united his enemies against him and brought Russia and Sweden into the field beside Austria and France. The following years were the most difficult period of his life. Despite brilliant generalship and glorious victories (Rossbach and Leuthen, 1757; Liegnitz, 1760), Frederick would see his territories devastated, his capital occupied by the enemy, and be reduced to the condition of king-errant, living off British subsidies and roaming with his armies up and down a ruined countryside. His resourcefulness showed at its most impressive when things were at their worst, but even superior generalship could not last long against the overwhelming odds he faced. Russia and Austria were already agreeing how to divide his realm when Frederick was saved by the death of the Russian empress and the admiring sympathy of her successor, who hastened to conclude peace with him (1762). Sweden now also left the war and the relieved Prussians were back on the offensive, soon persuading their weary enemies that nothing was to be gained by more bloodshed and Maria Theresa that hope of recovering her lost province was in vain.

Peace was concluded in 1763. It had taken seven years of further fighting to confirm the results of the War of Austrian Succession, pay for the territory seized in 1740, and assert Prussian primacy in central Europe. Still, all in all, the critic of Machiavelli had demonstrated that crime—especially given opportune miracles like the Tsarina's death—could pay—and handsomely. His wars had ruinous effects; but they secured Silesia with her industries and after 1763 Frederick put all his energy into rebuilding his war-ravaged land. Sound administration and good harvests can soon put agricultural societies on their feet. And Frederick proved himself as great a ruler as he had been a general.

Certainly, while the administration was enlightened—that is, efficient for those times—it was despotic too. The Prussian kings looked on their subjects as crucial to the state machinery, cared for their welfare much as the owner of a hog- or chicken-farm cares for the animals on which success depends. The nobles were another matter, and the originality of the Prussian monarchy—for a long time its strength—stemmed from its partnership with the nobility, for whom army commissions and the best civil service posts were kept. Many nobles were drawn into the service of the state, and this went far to hold their loyalty. Everything was done to secure their stake in Prussia. Even after the Revolution, nobles retained game and judicial rights on their estates until 1848, freedom from the land tax until 1861, police authority until 1872, church patronage until the twentieth century. Official salaries were insufficient to support their large families in style; sobriety and hard, devoted work did not always help. In 1809 the government founded credit institutions to provide the capital loans needed for noble lands, land banks which peasants would get only in 1849. Reforms, in other words, favored the noble and propertied classes, and the state's reward lay in their loyalty and in the service it could wring from them.

Even though he engaged in little fighting after 1763, Frederick's army remained the center of his policies. His realm was an inchoate jumble of provinces lying in the middle of Europe with no natural borders, no common traditions, no sense of unity except that which could be instilled by a common loyalty to the Hohenzollern dynasty, and no defenses except the army. Two-thirds of Frederick's revenue went to the army, one-sixth of the adult males served in it, many administrative reforms (like the population census) were directly related to recruiting needs.

When Frederick died in 1786, his army almost matched the French in size, although the population of his territories was only one-sixth that of France. And the two-way contract between the house of Hohenzollern and its officer corps had been solidly established, not to break until 1918. Henceforth Prussian policy would advance on the main lines Frederick had laid down: using the army to enforce an otherwise nonexistent unity and to expand whenever possible in every possible direction, and never forgetting the interests of the Junker nobility on whose loyalty both crown and army must rely.

Prussia was a highly ordered society, where a permit was needed to travel from one city to another, wages—even those of servants—were fixed by royal rescript, and the importation even of mousetraps heavily punished. Berlin grew on its sandy waste, more of a challenge to nature than ever, a garrison town with better than half its population of 140,000 in 1783 directly dependent on the service of the King, and radiating the immense prestige of its royal master.* Frederick, said Voltaire, had turned sad Sparta into brilliant Athens. In his rococo palace of *Sans-Souci,*

---

* Goethe in a Sicilian marketplace would be surrounded by curious admirers of Frederick the Great, inquiring all about him.

Frederick the Great playing the flute at Sans Souci.

chamber music, sophisticated skepticism, and philosophical conversations replaced the smoking, drinking, and swearing of Frederick William's time. Yet, in fact, as Peter Gay reminds us, Prussia remained "Sparta in a cold climate." Despite the great reputation of Berlin, its intellectual climate was not overly expansive. Lessing found it stifling and left it in 1769, writing a friend about it: "Do not talk to me about your Berlinese freedom of thought and writing. It only consists of the freedom to make as much fun as you like of religion . . . Let someone in Berlin stand up for the rights of the peasants, or protest against despotism and exploitation . . . and you will soon know by experience which country is to this day the most slavish in Europe." Not an alluring image, not an alluring reality either, but a successful one.

Austria

Frederick's rivals were less successful. Unlike Frederick William, the Habsburg Emperor Charles VI (1711–1740) had not laid the foundation of a modern state; not even, it turned out, of a secure succession. His daughter, Maria Theresa, had to fight for her crowns, and to maintain all her succession rights. Her husband, Francis, became emperor (1745–1765) and was succeeded by her sons (Joseph II, 1765–1790; Leopold II, 1790–1792). Her states, minus Silesia, were preserved. Her great service to them was to begin their administrative and linguistic reform, and to facilitate their passage from clerical, baroque, absolute principalities to a modern state, more rational, more utilitarian, more united. We do not usually list Maria Theresa among the "enlightened despots." She was pious, prudish, and thoroughly old-fashioned, she patronized the Inquisition, a formidable censorship, a cloud of police spies, and even forbade the publication of *The Index of Prohibited Books* because its list

179

Maria Theresa.

of titles could awaken curiosity for otherwise unsuspected works. Border police confiscated all works on the *Index*, even in the luggage of the most exalted persons. Thus, the Russian ambassador only regained the collected works of Voltaire on leaving the country. The ambassador of Saxony lost Montesquieu's *Persian Letters*. Confiscated works would sometimes be returned on leaving the country, but on no account could they be kept while their possessor found himself in the Habsburg states where he might lend them to the natives, thus corrupting their morals and their minds.

And yet it was under Maria Theresa's rule that her chancellor, Prince Kaunitz (1711–1794), and her son Joseph introduced one reform after another, gained control of the church and of its wealth, modernized public education, and infiltrated the civil service with partisans of efficiency and reform. By the end of the century, civil administration had become a profession with its own special training in "cameralism," the Austrian variant of bureaucracy. Almost all Austrian writers of the early nineteenth century would stem from the imperial bureaucracy which Joseph and Kaunitz founded, the only "bourgeoisie" in an empire where a true independent economic bourgeoisie appeared very late. It was the bureaucratic bourgeoisie that provided a literate and literary class, men of letters and their public both; and it was they who carried forward a Josephist ideology to 1815, 1848, and beyond.

In financial matters Joseph declared himself to be an atheist, thinking it best to act according to common sense rather than established principle. But "great things must be executed at one blow" and rashness would often get the better of common sense. Reform was painfully slow-going. Too slow for Joseph who felt that time was working against him, that the loose-knit empire which he led would dissolve if not modernized and tightened. Time was on the side of centralized monarchies.

180

Joseph II of Austria.

Austria must catch up with them, especially with Prussia, or grow ever weaker. By the time he finished, Jesuit property had been taken over and used to endow state schools at every level and in every province, where "useful, obedient and Christian citizens" should be trained. Textile and metal industries expanded. Austria won dominance in the Balkan trade. In Bohemia and in the Vienna suburbs factories almost doubled in number. State revenues, which also almost doubled in the decade after 1763, doubled again by 1788. The army was enlarged, reformed, improved, although its command remained mediocre, and thus condemned it to repeated defeats.

Joseph built hospitals, schools, orphanages, prisons, even new churches; his administration did a lot for the poor. But he cared for men as impersonal means, and men resented this. The end of the state lay not in its public works but in territorial expansion: the former were only the means of the latter. Religion, culture, economics, science, even liberty, were subordinated to power politics. It was the state that was considered sacred, Joseph its prophet and, in his mind, each civil servant cast as a missionary, living for its service. Devotion to the state was both a cult and a necessity. Files, spies, reports, and discipline were meant to bolster this sometimes lagging faith.

The two greatest problems, in Austria as everywhere, were poverty and privilege. "The peasant is miserable," reported Joseph: "the only human thing about him is his face and all he has is his bare life." In 1769, an official commission reporting on conditions in Bohemia went into greater detail. The villein labor to which peasants were constrained was tantamount to slavery. The serfs "become savage, brutish and work the lands they get only badly. They are rachitic, thin, covered with rags . . . in their rickety cabins, the parents lie on straw, the naked children on the edges of clay stoves; they never wash . . .

they have no doctor . . . whatever they own is at the mercy of their masters . . ." Savage punishments, beatings, torture, whose instruments stood on every market square or at the castle gate, kept them in check. Many serfs escaped to Prussia. The landowners chased away the Jews because they lent at smaller rates than they themselves would offer. Since taxes were paid only by serfs, the overtaxed masses could never become consumers for a market. The gentry, which could have furnished recruits for an urban class would not do so, preferring poverty to losing its noble prerogatives—freedom from taxes, from tithes, from duties. When Joseph II ordered a census and the numbering of houses, the nobles objected to this not only out of fear that it prefaced a general measure of taxation but out of sheer resentment that they and their houses could be counted on a par with common men.

Between 1765 and 1789, a series of measures seeking to transfer the fiscal burden to those who owned the land, while freeing the serfs who labored on it, set minimum limits for peasant holdings and maximum limits to what could be required of the serfs. In 1700, about 70 per cent of a serf's income went to the state, the landlords, and the church. Under the new system, with tithes abolished, 70 per cent of produce was left to the serf himself. Of the remainder, the state took 13 per cent, the landlord 17. In 1930, state taxes would take 22 per cent of a farmer's income. As this indicates, the reform projected at such an early date was too radical. The serfs welcomed it, but they could neither defend it nor adjust in time to what it meant. The landlords, faced with ruin, fought it tooth and nail. Eventually, the dogged opposition of the landowners, the central government's need for cash, and the peasant's unwillingness to rebel in his own cause, led to a land-tax settlement in 1792 which, while improving the status of the serf, really protected the interests of the proprietors. Until 1867 Bohemian nobles would continue to live off their peasants' hides.

Another reasonable scheme was to reform the government of Belgium. The Austrian Netherlands were a jungle of contradictions, confusion, administrative and legal chaos. Joseph II was prince of Brabant, Luxembourg, Limbourg, and Guelders, count of Flanders, Hainault, and Namur, suzerain of Malines, Stavelot, and Liège, governing each province separately, at least in theory. The architect of the state had his work cut out to turn this chaos toward his clear-cut ideals. But Joseph's reform attempts came down about his ears. In 1789, the Netherlands revolted. As in 1579, when they had reared at Philip II's taxes, they preferred tradition and its comforts to a more exacting efficiency, and only settled down after Joseph's death, their old ways restored. The home provinces also were in turmoil. Joseph's logic had to give in to facts.

Incapable of internal reform, Austria could not resign herself to the decline of its external power. But who could support reforms? Not the peasants, politically nonexistent; not the magnates, who resented the emancipation of serfs as an attaint against their position; not the gentry, which provided the stoutest defenders of anachronistic privileges that alone gave them a superiority over the bourgeoisie. Not the bourgeoisie, too weak, undeveloped, and heavily taxed to be of use or really friendly; not the clergy, which were disfavored, or the Protestants, who were tolerated but only just barely. No social, national, or religious groups could see the crown as its special ally, or find a particular interest in supporting its policy. Political reform should have been based on social reform. But the social structure had to evolve in time, and this is something that Joseph never gave it, nor felt he had himself. After Joseph, fear of revolution would stifle reform, as it did everywhere else, for a generation or two.

The Empire

Then, there was Germany: the Empire, a swarm of infinitesimal courts, based on anarchy abroad and oppression at home—in Westphalia, twenty-nine states within 484 square miles; in Swabia ninety states in 729 square miles. Germany, writes a noble chronicler at mid-century, "is full of dukes, three-quarters of whom are insane." They were certainly mad about hunting, as many German castles still testify today. In Württemberg, the duke boasted of the 6,500 stags and 5,000 boars that he had killed in 1737 alone. Their manners and those of their subjects were to scale: forks appeared only toward the end of the eighteenth century, drunkenness was Gargantuan, amusement vicious or childish, animal fights a favorite show, bears against bulls, wild oxen, and mastiffs, boars against hounds. Every duke, margrave, or princeling wanted a court like that of Vienna, a castle like Versailles, with a swarm of attendants like Maria Theresa's which had 700 chamberlains, or the Bavarian court with 421. Frederick the Great, who had only sixty chamberlains, mocked at a margrave who kept eight of them, lodged them in a stable and fed them on black bread.

Most of these men were irresponsible autocrats, well-described by Frederick II. They "ruined themselves by reckless extravagance, misled by the illusion of their imagined greatness . . . The younger son of the younger son of an apanaged dynasty imagines he is of the same stamp as Louis XIV. He builds his Versailles, keeps his mistresses and has an 'army' at his beck and call—perhaps strong enough to fight an imaginary battle on the stage at Verona." Many had better than stage armies: they had soldiers for hire to England or Holland or France. The Hessians of the American war cost half a million pounds for 30,000 men, of whom only 17,500 returned.

Germany was an economic jigsaw. At the beginning of the nineteenth century the twelve greatest German towns taken together could still not match the population of London or Paris; eight- or nine-tenths of the inhabitants lived on the land, the rest in small provincial cities. Agriculture, still very backward, ignored the innovations of the west, its yields about half those of similar lands in England, the peasants a wretched lot, ignorant and depressed. In a letter of 1782, Goethe compares the peasants of Weimar—where they were better off than most—to plant lice who filled themselves on rose bushes only to be sucked dry by ants: "Things have gone so far . . . that more is consumed in a day at the top than.can be produced in a day at the bottom . . ."

Voltaire had seen the rapacious and spendthrift courts, the exploited peasants, the slack and supine towns, and had predicted that Germany was doomed to eternal poverty. And it was true that those middle classes which were a source of energy and progress further west, appeared in central Europe as stagnant and submissive, very much the creatures of their petty princes. Given so little trade, a sluggish economic life (except in towns like Hamburg), the bourgeoisie were chiefly petty officials or artisans, catering to the rulers and all too dependent on their whims. Their social position reflected this and, in the early eighteenth century, the daughters of officials might well marry footmen or artisans or soldiers, while ministers of religion, physicians, or officials might marry some lady's maid, herself the daughter of a professional man. By the second half of the century, this was changing: members of the professions setting themselves off from the lower middle classes, a fact suggesting an improvement in their social—hence their economic—status.

In centers like Hamburg or Berlin, a small but prosperous and cultivated middle class welcomed the Enlightenment, furthered a cultural revival in which the Jews played an important part. Jews had long been tolerated in most of Germany, but could obtain residential rights only in exchange for heavy payments, were banned from gilds and corporations, hence from most crafts, and restricted largely to hawking, banking, or manufacture. They had to buy permits to own houses or move from town to town, paid heavy head taxes, had no political or civil rights. It might be said that orthodox Jews, in a sense, created their own ghetto: the religious observance of dietary regulations, holidays, and customs, prevented the orthodox Jew from entering military or civil service, complicated his legal affairs in which the oaths of Christian justice were unacceptable, and clashed with the laws and customs of surrounding society.

After the 1760's, a few rich bankers, intellectuals, and manufacturers left the orthodox Jewish communities and began to live like the enlightened middle class, trying to assimilate, joining reading clubs and opening their drawing rooms to a mixed, cosmopolitan, and often brilliant society. A series of governmental measures (Austria, 1782; Prussia, 1790) facilitated their assimilation; the French conquest in the 1790's and the Prussian reforms of 1812 finally vouchsafed Jews civic and political equality. The Frankfurt ghetto was abolished in 1824; restrictive regulations in the early 1830's. In return, the Jews contributed their minds and talents, their cosmopolitan inventiveness, and a loyalty which never failed the land that in the twentieth century would fail them.

Yet still the opportunities for enterprise were limited and it would seem that this bourgeoisie, teetering on the brink of some self-affirmation, found consolation in religious and cultural activities. Pietism flourished. Mystics preached an emotional faith, which Friedrich Klopstock's poetry reflected and which would reverberate in England when John Wesley was touched by the ideas of Moravian brethren. Not bourgeois only, but poor men, peasants, soldiers, wandering actors, adventurers, students, looked for salvation less in reasonable action than in chance, in luck, in miracles. As hope of social reforms waned, dreams of collective well-being turned into schemes of individual salvation, to a penchant for miraculous and catastrophic solutions that could turn Cinderellas into princesses and frogs into princes, the mentality that we call romantic and which can become revolutionary or reactionary for the sake of some heroic appeal. Coups, conspiracies, secret societies with exciting rites, or conversion to equally ritualistic and exalting religions—one way or another the new mentality abjured logical progression for gestures which would bring about some sudden change, public or private, but fundamentally unprepared. Not reforms but revolution, not work but inspiration, not thought but feeling, not Deism but illuminism, not medicine but magnetism, hypnotism, charlatanism.

Sickly, tense, nervous, ill or underfed, these people were prone to excitement and depression, fantasy and excess, their "romanticism" a hypertrophy of sensibilities sharpened by physical unbalance. Lotteries brought the rich men's gambling within the reach of all. Danzig, Moscow, Warsaw, Amsterdam, Vienna, Berlin, and St. Petersburg were fascinated by them. Get-rich-quick seemed better than get-rich-by-toil-and-saving. Love at first sight, or by a lightning revelation, better than anything. Destiny ruled. The theater provided an opportunity to play the parts which reality refused.

While the courts spoke French, read French, sponsored Parisian actors, and despised the vulgar Germans, the bourgeoisie found compensation in literary and dramatic descriptions of the vices and decadence of courts and nobility. Aristocrats were wicked, bourgeois were virtuous. Prurient fascination with noble license ran parallel with smug satisfaction that they, the bourgeois, were not like that—presumably for lack of opportunity. Plays taking this line flourished first and especially in the great bourgeois metropolis of Hamburg. The general strain of the domestic drama was personal, ethical, and private. Events and experience were seen as taking place not in the world but in the home and, better still, in the mind and heart where everyone was master. The German bourgeoisie combined a private rationalism and pietism, affirmed private morality and private life.

185

An illustration from *The Sorrows of Young Werther,* by Goethe.

Schiller's plays return over and over again to the individual's power-lessness before an unyielding society: the vain revolt in *The Robbers* (1781), the vain attempt in *Intrigue and Love* of lovers of different birth, different social status, to transcend the chasm that divides them, ending in suicide. Rebellious as a student, rebellious as a soldier, deserter from his duke's army, Friedrich von Schiller wrote his *Robbers* while chewing on potatoes that rotted in his drawer, attacked the routine and discipline that stifled all, the laws which could only hamstring real purity or greatness. Genius bred on liberty. The young men heard him. The young also shared the sense of oppression which Schiller expressed, the legacy of damping dullness, the smothering shallowness, the narrow limits of their little towns and courts and masters. They discovered nature, the world, themselves; they wandered, they rebelled; also, they waited.

How far can we see in this the protest of young men of humble birth (the philosopher Herder's parents had been very poor, the poet Klinger's mother was a washerwoman) against a society where their minds have glimpsed infinite horizons, and yet their fists beat impotently against closed doors? A rigid jigsaw of small states and minds evoked both the explosion of the *Storm and Stress* and the more lasting nostalgias of romantic escape. The German writers—some 3,000 in 1773, double that number by 1787—struggled for a public which would buy their works, and found it chiefly among the "uncorrupted middle class," for whose support they pleaded, against those alien influences and French philosophers who had been adopted by the Establishment. The *Storm and Stress* group took its name from a play of that name by Friedrich von Klinger (1775), inspired by the beginnings of the American War of Independence. For a brief moment, in the 1770's, it would represent the deliberate opposition of feeling to reason.

186

Such a philosophy had been formulated first by Johann George Hamann (1730–1788), the Magus of the North, as he was called. Man, argued Hamann, should act as a whole being, and not rely only on the reasoning part of himself. It is not reason which co-ordinates man's manifold faculties, but instinct and inspiration. The voice and will of nature are spontaneously expressed in feelings and in passions which produce not *thoughts* but *images*. Hence poetry, the most imagelike of our languages, is the most natural form of expression because it articulates these images and communicates their sense. This was the philosophy that J. G. Herder (1744–1803) would develop for his friends and disciples of the *Storm and Stress* circle, and which would provide one basis of romantic theory.

Yet *Storm and Stress* did not go very far. Its rebellious leaders grew up and did quite well in later life: Goethe became a minister, Herder a superintendent, Schiller a professor, Klinger a general in the Russian service. Meanwhile, the middle classes, which had begun by demanding freedom of thought and discussion, found that these did not necessarily bring about the acts that reasoning indicates. Reason needs an executive arm, and the French example suggested that this could be obtained only by political means. The middle classes therefore turned to political action, sought the right to take part in politics in order to carry out their ideas. Klopstock, Schiller, Goethe, welcomed the French Revolution, only to be discouraged by the Terror and to fall back on the possibilities of monarchic reforms, even if the monarchy continued absolute. Germany was not ready for a revolution. Only a very few young men, not afraid of violence, appreciated the possibilities revolution offered, and then the coming of Napoleon Bonaparte.

The Fate of the Germanies

In December, 1797, French troops occupied Mainz. Joseph von Görres (1776–1848), the future Catholic historian, considering the Empire dead, wrote its obituary: "Died at Ratisbon, on December 30, 1797 . . . aged 955 years, five months, twenty-eight days, . . . after complete exhaustion and apoplexy, fully conscious, and fortified by all the rites of the church, the Holy Roman Empire."

Görres was only a little premature. The French occupied the left bank of the Rhine, dissolved the ecclesiastical states, shared their lands and most of the free cities among the greater German princes, sixteen of whom would be grouped into the satellite Confederation of the Rhine (1806). The Empire vanished before Napoleon's will. When a German prince addressed the conqueror as if he were his peer, the self-made emperor replied "I am not your prince, I am your master!" Austria, defeated, had to contribute an archduchess to secure the master's dynasty. Prussia had decayed badly since Frederick's death. Rotten before ripe, Mirabeau had called it; and in 1806 the defeats of Jena and Auerstädt proved his point. As French troops marched into Berlin, its governor's proclamation instructed the people of the capital that "the first duty of citizens is to keep quiet."

They would not do so for long. What the romantic patriots of the 1770's and 1780's had not succeeded in doing, French occupation did. A patriotic publicist of the late eighteenth century had complained that Germans even had to swear in French because they had no adequate national oaths. In 1804 Madame de Staël had noticed that the Germans had no national spirit. This was no longer true by 1810 or so. French army boots seemed to stamp patriots out of the ground. Schiller was writing his plays about national liberation, the *Maid of Orléans* and *William Tell;* Hegel, Beethoven, Fichte, who began by welcoming French influence, now turned against it. Above all, a small group of Prussian statesmen adapted the lessons of the French Revolution, to forge a nation and instill it with a common purpose and a common civic pride.

The Treaty of Tilsit (1807) had reduced the Prussian kingdom to a third-rate power, deprived of half its territory and population, condemned to pay a crippling war indemnity. Within a few months, the King's edict of emancipation wrought a revolution from above, ending serfdom, feudal and caste privileges, granting the cities municipal self-government, even giving civil rights to Jews. Land reform turned the serfs into freeholders and, while Baron vom Stein and Karl August von Hardenberg were putting through civil reforms, generals Scharnhorst and Gneisenau were reforming the army and introducing general conscription, and Wilhelm von Humboldt forged a school system destined first to educate, then to regenerate a youth made keen and fit by the gymnastic societies sparked by Friedrich Ludwig Jahn. Gneisenau found himself wondering at the "infinite forces which slumber in the nation, undeveloped and unused." Around the University of Heidelberg, these forces were sought in folk tales, in legends, the *Nibelungen* saga was revived and adapted, the folk stirred up, the "true people of God," as Fichte called them, were taught that they could provide Europe with "a regenerating ferment." In February, 1813, the *levée en masse* would show that the French lessons had been well applied. A Prussia of five million turned out an army of 350,000, far more than Frederick had ever done.

Though it may not have been as pervasive as the patriots claimed, 1813 saw the beginnings of a really national movement in Germany. But victory was fated to bring disillusion. The landed aristocracy came back into its own, the patriotic student movements were suppressed, reform projects were stifled, local self-government suspended or abandoned, and all reforming politicians forced out of office. The French Revolution was the devil. Anything it had inspired was to be shunned—including the economic liberalism which had come in the wake of the French.

Yet, as in other lands, not everything the French did had been bad, or wasted. The Continental System, which ruined many merchants, also allowed German industrialists to develop, free for a while from English competition: cotton and woolen cloth, ironwares, sugar beet refineries, appeared and grew. The Industrial Revolution was slowly changing the face of Germany. As Theodore Hamerow has put it, the economy of stability was superseded by the economy of competition. Industry, mechanized production, began to spread across central Europe; linen, cotton, wool, silk manufactures sprang up; metallurgy grew. In the 1820's and 1830's familiar names began to appear: Krupp, Borsig, Stinnes, Mannesmann. Loans were being floated, money invested, joint-stock companies were being set up by the score. Railroads built after 1835, linked the industrial areas in the center with northern ports and created the largest railway network in Europe by 1850, which cut shipping costs by two-thirds and immensely spurred production.

The settlement of 1815 had given Prussia control of the main German coalfields in Westphalia and the Ruhr, and command of the chief commercial routes between east and west and north and south. These were the counters Prussia used, first to foster her own economic expansion by a discriminating tariff, then between 1828 and 1834 to establish her economic supremacy in north Germany by a customs union.* When Bavaria and Württemberg joined the Prussian customs union in 1834, the *Zollverein* offered a market of almost 34,000,000 people, an immense base for economic expansion and industrialization. August Hoffmann von Fallersleben, who had written *Deutschland, Deutschland über Alles,* rejoiced:

> Articles of home consumption,
> All our thanks are due to you!
> You have wrought without presumption
> What no intellect could do;
> You have made the German nation
> Stand united, hand in hand,
> More than the Confederation
> Ever did for Fatherland

Between 1815 and 1845 the German population would increase almost 40 per cent, the cities increasing nearly twice as fast as any country district. Factory workers also increased in numbers.**

---

* The great apostle of this union was Friedrich List (1789–1846), who had grown rich in the United States and returned home to preach what he had learned there: the fundamental importance of railroads and of tariffs.

** In Prussia 32,000 of them were children working up to sixteen hours a day. It was the news that the industrial districts could not meet the quota of conscripts because their physical fitness had been impaired by early work in the mills that alarmed the Prussian king and led to his order of 1839 prohibiting child labor under the age of nine and setting a work day of ten hours up to the age of sixteen. Prussia would be the first continental state to follow the English example, and this was followed in 1840 by Bavaria and Baden.

Yet factory labor accounted for scarcely 4 per cent of the population, while artisan and home industries employed three and four times as many. Hence, the decay of the old precapitalist system was sharply and widely felt. As local craft industries declined, artisan risings protesting against unemployment, hunger, and starvation wages speckled the decades between 1820 and 1848. The most famous of these was probably the 1844 insurrection in Silesia, which has been chronicled in Gerhart Hauptmann's play, *The Weavers*. The many thousands who earned their livelihoods from the linen industry were ruined by imported English yarn and cotton goods, with consequent mounting unemployment and shrinking wages. Revolt broke out against the factories, rioters sacked workshops and manufacturers' homes, subsided when looted food and wine had stilled their hunger, were crushed in blood by late-arriving troops, the ringleaders receiving heavy sentences and the survivors left worse off than before and far more bitter.

There was uneasiness on the land as well. Where the French Revolution had passed, serfs had become tenants, feudal lords had become landlords, servile obligations had been turned into rents, land became a commodity like any other. The peasants, freed from ancient servitudes, found themselves in a free economy where risks predominated over possibilities. Land hunger, loan and credit hunger, overpopulation, legislation which favored nobles over peasants, widespread dissatisfaction, boiled up in the spring of 1848 in great agrarian risings. Oppression had also meant custom and security, emancipation meant bewilderment in an unfamiliar world.

Where the lower classes yearned for better economic conditions, the middle classes longed for social and political improvements. The French Revolution suggested possibilities of emancipation, the war of liberation had caused great enthusiasm—not just against the foreigner, but for reforms which France had introduced or sparked and which the burghers approved as much as they resented French extortions and repressions. Social equality, political freedom were good, but they were lost with the Restoration. Students' clubs were nurseries of nationalism, and the professors provided fuel. Student meetings, agitation, propaganda, worried the defenders of order. Eventually a well-known writer, August von Kotzebue (1761–1819), was murdered by a student because he was an agent of the Tsar. This prompted a reaction and, by the Carlsbad Decrees of 1819, student societies were banned, professors were dismissed, and censorship tightened,* leading nationalists arrested, exiled, or, at least, closely watched. A general witch hunt drove liberalism underground.

This could not last. In 1830, Polish refugees passing through Germany stirred up enthusiasm on the way, and the sight of other nations rising for their rights encouraged Germans to think about their own.

---

* One Prussian official in the Rhineland censored an advertisement for a translation of Dante's *Divine Comedy,* arguing that divine things could not be comic.

The liberal tide began to flow again despite repression. When Jacob Burckhardt went to study in the Germany of the 1840's, he wrote back enthusiastically to his sister in Basel, thanking God that his mother-tongue was German: "What a people! What a wonderful youth! What a land— a paradise." Burckhardt would change his mind. The Germans not.

Meanwhile, more radical ideas also appeared: socialism, communism, discovered in Paris, funneled in by exiles and by publicists. The young editor of a radical newspaper forced into exile, described the revolutionary effects of capital on society and state, and prophesied the overthrow of the ruling class by workers. Marx and Engels' *Communist Manifesto* (1847) evoked as much echo as a dull thud, though brilliantly written and fated to a great future. It had little connection with conditions in Germany. As in eighteenth-century France, growing economic significance for the bourgeois paralleled political insignificance. Across the Rhine and the North Sea, bankers and manufacturers prospered and ruled. The educated middle class—lawyers, doctors, merchants—wanted as much and, to express their aspirations, they found liberalism, with its conjunction of enterprise and status, its affirmation of opportunity and its civic rewards, its rejection of the lower classes without property, its insistence on freedom of enterprise and gain. The peculiarly German concomitant to liberalism was the dream of a German union, which, it was argued, would provide the best scope for all this.

There were also radical democrats, equalitarian, calling for progressive income taxes, welfare legislation, economic and social reforms, sometimes republican, but never socialist, never communist, nothing but good bourgeois intellectuals. The Junkers and traditionalists, for their part, found a fine figurehead in the visionary King Frederick William IV, a man who, like Charles I in England, conceived the crown as the defender of the poor and weak against rapacious capital, of Christian charity and social justice against greedy immoral change. Enlightened absolutism based on the masses could win, said the romantic legitimists who gathered round him.

There was one man who knew that an alliance with the masses would not work, that the only hope of the old regime was to avoid all movement, lest it cause collapse. Klemens von Metternich (1773–1859) was the son-in-law of Kaunitz, and his heir. Born the same year as the future Louis-Philippe, speaking French better than German, Metternich was nineteen when the French invasion of his Rhineland home sent him off to Vienna to recoup his fortunes in the Habsburg service. Ambassador to Paris, then foreign minister, he promoted first Marie Louise's marriage, then the anti-Napoleonic coalitions. Just over forty and a prince in 1814, he would devote the next thirty-four years to the maintenance of that social and political peace without which his master's empire could not survive. His enemies called Metternich a butterfly; he himself preferred a comparison to spiders: "Their ugliness apart, the most charming little creatures, always busy, and arranging their houses with the greatest neatness in the world." Vain, sententious, shrewd,* and silly, certain that liberalism could lead only to Jacobinism, Metternich appears as the prototype of those conservatives who confuse moderate reformism with radical revolution, refuse all concessions, and, by sitting on the safety valve, cause the explosion which they dread.

Metternich's masters approved. "Peoples?" asked Emperor Francis of Austria: "What does that mean? I know only subjects." "The human race," declared an Austrian general, "begins with barons." Leopold II, enlightened and conciliatory, had died in 1792 after less than two years of rule. His son, Francis I (1792–1835), was a narrow reactionary, convinced of the virtues of immobility and of his right to rule by bureaucracy subjects whose only right was to obey. There was no cabinet at Vienna and, while all subjects could appeal to the Emperor directly, his decisions were never motivated, so that administrators could never tell why a project was sent back, hence did not know how it should be adjusted. Church and education were harnessed to produce high-minded religious and patriotic subjects; police and censorship were used to keep them so.

Victory in 1814 confirmed the policy and turned it into a system. When Francis died, the modern world moved into his lands. Francis had opposed railroads, industry, even (on moral grounds) the introduction of machinery. Ferdinand I (1835–1848) was a good-natured simpleton who reigned while others governed. A steamship company appeared in 1835, the first real railroad in 1839, modern industries began to be set up. Industry brought new wealth, but also new industrial problems which served to increase the force of pent-up discontents. Francis had been right. The national consciousness of the Empire's subjects was growing along with literacy and with communication. An Austrian poet summed up the situation in 1830: "The Hungarian hates the Bohemian, the Bohemian hates the German, and the Italian hates them all."

In the 1840's, inflation and hard times diminished the monolithic power which the Emperor's servants still tried to assert. Paternalistic absolutism stumbled into trouble: depression on top of oppression could only maintain itself by repression. The Prague papers, much freer than the Viennese, made great play with news of Irish miseries, which all their readers knew reflected the enslavement and the agrarian problems of Bohemia. In Austrian-dominated Italy, the scientific Congresses of patriotic societies discussed volcanoes in 1846, and the potato disease in 1847—the potato being the image of potato-eating Germans. In 1846 a Polish rising in Galicia was crushed when Vienna encouraged the Ruthenian peasants to rise against their Polish landlords. But other revolutions would not be dealt with so easily.

---

* He also proved himself a sagacious connoisseur when dividing up Europe: he kept 2 acres for himself—the vineyard of Johannisberg on the Rhine, whose vines grow the best hock in the world.

The Eastern Borderlands

Poland

The largest European country after Russia, Poland, was a republican monarchy, a democracy of the gentry, peopled by five nations—Poles and Lithuanians, Ruthenians, Jews and Germans—with as many religious beliefs. Orthodox and Catholic, Uniate and Protestant, detested one another and all despised the Jews. The land, greater than France, with only half its population, brought one-sixtieth of France's revenues. The King was poor, even though some of the magnates lived like little kings. The Lithuanian estates of a family like the Radziwills were as great as half of Ireland, the pomp and state they kept often eclipsed that of the King's court in Warsaw.

The Polish polity was in fact an anarchy, a neo-feudal arrangement in which gentry (*szlachta*) elected kings and sanctioned policy which could be vetoed by the least of its members. The Polish Diet operated on the principle of unanimity. Unanimity, real or enforced, had been the rule in most medieval assemblies. Dissenters might be threatened, shouted down, or forcibly silenced; but the ideal was maintained that a collective body (gild, corporation, chapter, or assembly) could have but one will and should act as one, with all concurring in its actions. Only with the sixteenth century did these ideals, with the consequent possibility of a veto nullifying action, give way to the vote of a majority. This may have reflected the rising individualism of the time, or the practical needs of states where legislation loomed larger than before. It certainly reflected a more differentiated view of a more obviously differentiated—hence modern—society. The principle of unanimity survived, however, in institutions like the Anglo-Saxon jury and, more particularly, where modernity itself lagged behind: in the Imperial Diet of Germany, and in Poland. If its survival reflected backwardness, it also ensured that it should continue.

Since the poor gentry were clients and cat's-paws of great magnate families, struggles between the magnates for supremacy and between foreign powers for predominance could hamstring any policy at all and usually did. "If this is liberty which one sees. here," declared the British envoy to the Polish diet of 1733, "the Lord preserve us from such liberty. Here are what they call great and little nobility which are slaves to one another by turns. All goes in confusion and disorder."

A backward economy paralleled anachronistic institutions. Peasants were enserfed, oppressed, and largely landless. The production of grain in mid-eighteenth century seems to have been about one-third of what it had been in the seventeenth. Cities were ruined by the privileges of neighboring landlords who, free of taxes, could undercut local craftsmen and, free of customs dues, could import and sell all foreign goods they wanted. Merchants became their agents. Artisans took to the land to stay alive, leaving small crafts and trades to Jews. Forbidden to till the soil, the Jews became a surrogate and much resented middle class, representatives of the gentry, whom they served as stewards, farmers, or monopoly managers, collecting dues, selling liquor or hay. There were no urban professions, there was no urban culture, there is no mention of the earth moving around the sun until 1750, there are no schools worth speaking of until mid-eighteenth century. The Catholic hierarchy, intolerant of Protestants and Orthodox, seems to have been particularly obscurantist.

The 1697–1763 period, when a Saxon dynasty ruled the land, was a time of uneasy peace, when the prosperity of a few paralleled the misery of many, when magnates lived like kings, squires like benighted tyrants, and the masses much more like wild beasts. An Englishman, William Coxe, traveling from Cracow to Warsaw in the 1770's, found scattered wooden huts with no furniture, in which men and beasts shared space, and where even the most rudimentary tools seemed lacking. Servile, humble, begging, apathetic, the Polish peasants whom he compared with their proud Swiss counterparts were also natives of a poor liberty-loving country, but utterly different. The peasants opposed any reforms attempted; their inertia was as hard to budge as the selfishness of the nobles. Cracow gave the impression of a ruined city—half of its 16,000 population Jewish—and other cities seemed to have been built to scale, a mass of ruined palaces and miserable hovels.

In 1763, the death of the last Saxon king, Augustus III, who had himself succeeded to the throne by casting out the man the Diet had elected, Stanislas Leczinski—opened a fresh succession crisis, which was solved by Russo-Prussian pressure in the accession of a protégé of Catherine II: Stanislas Poniatowski. A man of the Enlightenment, Poniatowski had been imposed on Poland in order to avoid reforms which might turn the country into an effective power. His election was followed by a near-Russian protectorate, under the pretext that Russian troops were maintaining the liberties of the Orthodox subjects of the Polish crown. Some of the most important of Stanislas's opponents were arrested and deported to Russia.

Such methods, and French intrigues as well, encouraged a section of the nobility to form the Confederation of Bar, for the defense of Catholicism and Poland, and directed chiefly against the Russians. Fighting broke out in 1768, spread into a more general war between Russia and Turkey, and ended—as far as Poland was concerned—in the first partition (1772), in which Austria and Prussia received large slices of

194

THE PARTITIONS OF POLAND

—— Boundary of Poland before 1772

To Russia
To Prussia
To Austria

300 miles

1772

1793

1795

Stanislas Poniatowski.

Polish territory in compensation for Russian gains in Turkey, while Russia herself annexed the eastern provinces of Poland, inhabited mostly by Orthodox Ukrainians. The kingdom had lost a third of its territory, but it had probably gained in homogeneity.

The crisis precipitated some much-needed reforms, both on the fiscal and the educational planes. King Stanislas placed a bust of George Washington in his study and, in 1791, while Russian and Austrian attention was directed elsewhere, a liberal constitution was proclaimed, reforming political institutions, improving the condition of the peasants, laying the basis for a modern state. The constitution, praised by men like Burke and the Emperor Leopold, appalled Russia and Prussia, who wanted Poland weak. In 1792, when Russia had once more concluded peace with Turkey and Prussian troops had turned back from Valmy, the second partition of Poland left the country with only a rump of some 4,000 square miles and just over four million population. When, under the menace of Russian and Prussian arms the partition treaty had been ratified, an insurrection broke out in the summer of 1794. Led by a butcher, a shoemaker, a Hungarian banker, above all by Thaddeus Kosciusco (1746–1817), a veteran of the American War of Independence, the Poles were crushed after a heroic struggle, and the third partition put an end to Poland as an independent state.

The coming of the French in 1806 brought a brief hope of revival, but the Grand Duchy of Warsaw which was set up from territories wrested from the Prussians turned out to be only a counter in Napoleon's games. After 1815, the Grand Duchy of Warsaw would be redivided, becoming the Grand Duchy of Posen under Prussian rule and the kingdom of Poland, which was joined to Russia by a common king. Pictures of Napoleon continued to hang in many manors, and the thought of this petty nobleman whom a military career had made immortal stirred the

196

imagination of many petty nobles in Sarmatia too.

In the 1820's, Adam Mickiewicz, a follower of Schiller and of Byron, enhanced romantic patriotism, love of fatherland, nostalgic yearnings for past greatness, and fascinated the younger generations. Joachim Lelewel began to write about Polish history and glorify the Polish nation—a great lecturer, idol of the students and horror of the Russians, who turned him out of his history chair at the University of Vilna but did not prevent his election to the Diet as a deputy. Polish musicians were investigating national folk music, with notable effects on the young Frédéric Chopin, then studying in Warsaw and about to leave Poland for the west in 1830. Secret societies were spreading, despite attempts to suppress them and to control political and cultural activities.

In November, 1830, one of the many conspiracies about to be discovered precipitated a military coup that might have petered out had it not turned into a popular uprising, which the Polish army joined. A Diet deposed Nicholas I and elected a national government. But the peasants would not join the revolution, nor did they have much reason to do so. The peasants did not like the Russians, but they saw no profit in revolt: "As we have been up to now, so we shall be afterwards. Our misery will not change . . . Indeed, it will be better for the lords when they defeat the Russians. So let them fight them." Bravery was of no avail against political and social divisions. By August, 1831, Warsaw had fallen and the last Polish forces had been defeated, had surrendered, or had taken refuge in Prussian territory. Several thousands emigrated to the west, providing a source of revolutionary ferment in Italy, Germany, and France. Galicia and Posnania too, which languished under Austrian occupation, were stirred out of inertia into patriotism, and this would flare up briefly in 1846. But Poland was crushed for good and would not regain freedom until 1918.

Hungary

To the south of Poland, the kingdom of Hungary was of course a possession of the Habsburgs. The Peace of Karlowitz (1699), transferring old Hungarian lands from Ottoman to Habsburg rule, had been a Habsburg triumph but a tragedy for the Hungarians and Transylvanians whom Turkish defeat left at the mercy of a ruler far more determined to impose his will and faith than the Turks had ever been. Religious tolerance had been the rule in principalities where Catholic and Calvinist, Uniate and Lutheran had lived side by side since the Reformation. The Emperor Leopold I was determined to impose Catholicism, and also to deprive Hungarian nobles of their age-old right to elect their kings and offer armed resistance to those who sought to break their liberties. Long years of civil warfare followed, not ended until the reign of Charles VI, when the Peace of Szatmar (1711) settled the Habsburg rule in Hungary on a basis of compromise and tolerance, respecting the Magyars' essential liberties but making sure that the kingdom of St. Stephen would not become a noble anarchy like Poland.

The country, whose sixteenth-century population stood around four million, had been devastated by Turkish occupation in subsequent wars. In 1715, the population seems to have been about 1,700,000 in Hungary proper and another 800,000 in Transylvania. Moreover, of these, the Hungarians of the plains were the least numerous, while Serbs and Croats, Slovaks and Ruthenes, were, at least relatively, reinforced. After 1715, the empty spaces filled with colonists from the more sheltered parts of the kingdom, from the Romanian provinces, and from Germany and Austria. Nobility, too, which clung tenaciously to its privileges—especially to exemption from the tax—had been decimated and was refloated by newcomers from Germany, Italy, and Spain; and also by recruits among natives of lower birth who bought vacant estates. All these, however, soon became Magyarized or left, and Magyar nobility remained strongly Hungarian, where the Bohemian nobles were always Vienna-oriented, an alien group amidst downtrodden subjects.

The Hungarian nobles were the *nation;* and they were all those men economically and physically able to carry arms. The census of 1787 showed 75,000 noble families—one out of every five or six: far more than the 20,000-odd noble families that all of Prussia counted and comparable only to the Polish situation. In the country, where the bushel of wheat cost half a florin and the florin could buy 25–30 pounds of meat, the wealth of the great magnates was extraordinary. The yearly income of Prince Esterhazy, Haydn's patron, was more than 700,000 florins and his estates ran nearly seven million acres. Other family estates topped 100,000, while quite a few varied between 20,000 and 50,000 acres. The income of Count Czobor, who died in 1741, was about a million florins a year, and many nobles, while nowhere near as wealthy, could count on 50,000 or 60,000 a year. The brilliant costume which Prince Esterhazy wore in the Diet of 1847, with its pearl seams and diamond buttons, *shed* some 30,000 dollars' worth of jewels whenever he would wear it.

The eyes of people such as these were turned increasingly to Vienna, and this by a deliberate policy of the crown. "The proud Hungarians, who on their country estates were planning schemes of liberty, have been allured to the court or to town," wrote an eighteenth-century Swiss traveler. "By the grant of dignities, titles and offers of marriage and in other ways, every opportunity has been given them of spending their money in splendor, of contracting debts and of throwing themselves on the mercy of the sovereign when their [mortgaged] estates have been sequestrated . . . There is scarcely a single prominent family in Hungary which is free from debt . . . Having thus converted the most powerful part of the Hungarian nobility into spendthrifts, *débauchés* and cowards, the court has no longer occasion to fear a revolt."

But if this was true about the powerful and the rich who sought their honors and diversions in Vienna and at the Habsburg court, the lesser gentry clung to the soil, to their old privileges, and to the old ways. The magnates themselves valued their Magyar birthright too much to sell it for a mess of Austrian pottage. Relations remained good as long as Maria Theresa's restraining hand prevented serious infringement of traditional liberties. To Joseph II, however, the process of assimilation seemed to advance too slowly to satisfy his plans for administrative and cultural unity.

In 1774 Joseph abolished Latin as the official language of Hungary, changing the *lingua franca* of its many nations to German. Latin was the preserve of nobles and of lawyers, serfs could not understand it. The Emperor argued that no nation should be governed in a language it could not understand. Many Hungarian nationalists approved, but wanted the new national language to be Magyar. The gentry, however, opposed to the modern spirit and to the enlightened absolutism which German represented, did not want to abandon Latin. "As for commoners, who speak German, Serb or Walach, they can have no voice in affairs, for supreme Providence has designated them not to regulate the country's laws and control the sovereign, but only to respect them," wrote a Hungarian noble. One interesting aspect of this rebellious attachment to Latin appeared in 1799, when a brief rebellion brought echoes of the French Revolution to Hungary. The nobility burned the Imperial registers and decrees, while singing *La Marseillaise* and the sans-culotte song: *Ça Ira,* with their lyrics translated into Latin (*hoc ibit*). An odd encounter of Rousseau and freedom with these reactionary defenders of traditional privilege who would not dream of emancipating the people, and who, when they appealed to Liberty and Nature, thought only of themselves!

Although the aristocrats revolted against Josephism and called on Voltaire and Rousseau for arguments, they were ready enough to settle for withdrawal of the liberal experiments which they resented. As for the few middle-class "Jacobins," who actually wanted a social and political reform, they got no further than the gallows in 1795. The serfs were hungry, but they were weary too; the nobles were sated and quiescent. They would not really stir until the 1820's and then, once more, a move symbolic of reform would be the Diet's abandonment of Latin—not now for German, but for the Magyar tongue. Yet with her constitution, her county assemblies, and large "noble" class, Hungary was better prepared for political action than most countries outside England and France. With one person in fourteen classed as a noble, the electoral base compared favorably with England's one voter for every twenty-four inhabitants, or even the American one in eight, let alone the proportions in countries where only nobles enjoyed political rights, like Austria (one in 353), or Bohemia (one in 828).

During the 1820's and thirties, Count Stephen Széchenyi fostered the revival of Hungarian language and Hungarian pride, built the first bridge over the Danube in the capital, started the first steamboat services on it. Offspring of a great family, wealthy and cultivated, Széchenyi had traveled through the west, especially in England, and had come home convinced that his country was a "great fallow land," the masses degraded, the masters selfish and devoid of any social sense. In 1825, he offered a year's income from his estates to found a National Academy of Sciences, whose first task would be to purify and standardize the Magyar language. Thereafter, there was no stopping the fervent young men who scandalized their elders by calling for reform on every plane, an end to economic backwardness and social oppression. To the very extent that Hungary forged ahead, the need for self-affirmation became stronger, the possibilities of bearding the Austrians more tempting. And, as the danger of confrontation increased, so did the Magyars' relations with a west represented first by Vienna, but also by Milan and Paris.

By the 1830's Széchenyi's generation was being overtaken by a new more revolutionary one, incarnated in the brilliant journalist and orator Lajos Kossuth (1802–1894), inspired by French romantic radicalism to want not only traditional liberties and material progress, but democracy too, and justice for the peasant. Despite the misgivings of more moderate liberals disturbed by his egoism and ambition, despite pointed warnings from Széchenyi who feared that exacerbated tensions would come to no good, despite imprisonment, and despite Metternich's personal offer of a government post that might domesticate him, Kossuth drove on. For his growing following, the independence of Hungary became a necessary prelude to social progress. And, as the reform movement gathered momentum through the late thirties and the forties, nationalism became its major issue. Kossuth, its prophet, bent his efforts to increasing the national consciousness of his fellow Magyars.

Russia

Peter the Great's only son, Alexei, had been murdered by him or at his orders in 1719. When Peter died in 1725, Alexei's son, Peter II (1727–1730), was only nine years old, and his brief reign was soon cut short by smallpox. The realm was ruled by women—Peter's nieces: Anna (1730–1740) and, after a brief interval, Elizabeth (1741–1762)—by favorites and palace revolutionists. Elizabeth's heir, the son of the Duke of Holstein, married another German princess, Catherine of Anhalt-

Catherine the Great, painting by Lampi. Musée Jacquemart – André, Paris.

Zerbst. Peter III (1761–1762) ruled only long enough to save Frederick the Great from destruction by withdrawing Russian troops from the Seven Years' War, and to convince his officers and courtiers that their king was mad. In 1762, a palace revolution removed him from the throne on which it placed his wife. As Catherine II, she would rule for twenty-four years.

Catherine's first object was to free herself from the praetorian power which had raised her up. Soldiers and boyars had backed her *coup d'état.* The first part of her reign would be devoted to disciplining the army and the nobles, restoring the authority of the autocratic state. One instrument in this combat would be the enlightened ideas of the time, to which she referred for arguments against noble privilege and against the serfdom on which the fortunes of the nobles rested. To counteract the political ambitions of the nobles, Catherine began to talk about a code of laws that would improve the condition of other social classes. In 1768, commissioners were appointed from the more liberal nobles, the towns, and even peasants, to revise the laws; but they made haste slowly and nothing came of the scheme except an impressive set of *Grand Instructions,* soon translated and circulated throughout the West where they enhanced the enlightened Empress's reputation.

Meanwhile, the friction between crown and gentry, and the rumors of reform, stirred up the countryside. Russian society was a juncture of nobles who owed their privileges to service to the crown and peasant serfs who served their noble masters and the state. In 1762, Peter III had issued a *Charter of the Prerogatives of the Gentry,* exempting them from the basic obligation of service to the state. News of this act aroused the peasants' expectation of a second one, which would free them from servile obligations. When none appeared, the rumor spread that the

201

gentry had conspired to suppress it; and this aroused rural unrest which, in the 1770's while Russia was deep in a Turkish war and the Empress and the nobles were at loggerheads, broke into a widespread peasant uprising whose leader, Emelyan Pugachev, claimed to be the murdered Tsar Peter III. Pugachev was captured and executed, but the social scare threw Empress and nobility together. The latter's privileges were confirmed, serfdom affirmed, and Catherine henceforth governed as the first landowner of her realm.

The realm was growing. Russian population, thirteen million in 1715, nineteen million in 1762, had practically doubled by 1800 and doubled once more by mid-nineteenth century. The birth rate was the highest in Europe; the infantile death rate twice that of France, three times that of Norway; life expectation about twenty-four. But there was land, and people bred, and moved, and bred some more. Russia's borders advanced in Asia and in Europe. The war with Turkey which ended in the Treaty of Kuchuk-Kainardji (1774), gave Russia a foothold on the Black Sea, with freedom of navigation on it and of passage through the Straits, while an obscure but useful clause gave Moscow a watching brief over the rights of the Orthodox subjects of the Porte. In 1783, Crimea and the Kuban were annexed to Russia. In 1792, the Peace of Iaşi brought all the Black Sea coast between the Bug and Dniester; * while by the partitions of Poland the Russian border came to stand on the Niemen and the Bug, far forward into Europe. It had pushed forward in the Caucasus as well, where Christian Georgia, a willing protectorate, would be annexed in 1801. During the nineteenth century, Russian expansion would take place mostly in Asia. In Europe, only three accessions were to come between Catherine's death and the reign of Stalin: Finland in 1809, Bessarabia in 1812, and Congress Poland after 1815.

The eighteenth century affirmed the rise of Russia. For the first time, in 1735, the end of the War of the Polish Succession saw a Russian army on the Neckar River. By 1815, Paris itself was occupied by Russian troops, and Alexander seemed the arbiter of all the powers. The army must have been the greatest national industry, a force which by the 1790's reached some 800,000 and gave employment to as many more. The equipment and supplies required by the army and navy, the resources which were needed to keep them up, seem to have been the central concern of the government. At Peter's death, 65 per cent of the Russian budget went to military expenses; as the economy grew more prosperous this proportion fell to 50 per cent in 1801 and 42 per cent by 1852. These remain impressive figures and they reflect the orientation of the land. They also reflect the fact, although less striking, that in this time, although the

---

* Odessa would be founded there in 1793; its population by 1814 numbered over 40,000.

ARCTIC OCEAN

0   500 miles

WHITE

URAL MOUNTAINS

SWEDEN

Nystadt
Abo

N. Dvina

KARELIA

Lake
Onega

Lake
Ladoga

Narva
ESTONIA   INGRIA   St. Petersburg

Volga

LIVONIA
Riga

*BALTIC
SEA*

W. Dvina

Moscow

Danzig
EAST
PRUSSIA

LITHUANIA

Niemen

R   U   S   S   I   A

Smolensk

Ural

POLAND

Warsaw

Chernigov

Danube

Kiev

Poltava

Don

Volga

HUNGARY

Bug

Dniester

Azov

*SEA OF
AZOV*

*CASPIAN
SEA*

OTTOMAN

Kuchuk-Kainarji

Sevastopol

BLACK   SEA

EMPIRE

RUSSIAN EXPANSION IN EUROPE IN THE EIGHTEENTH CENTURY

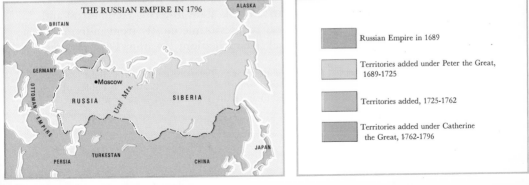

THE RUSSIAN EMPIRE IN 1796

ALASKA

BRITAIN

GERMANY

OTTOMAN
EMPIRE

Moscow

RUSSIA

Ural Mts.

SIBERIA

PERSIA

TURKESTAN

CHINA

JAPAN

     Russian Empire in 1689

     Territories added under Peter the Great,
     1689–1725

     Territories added, 1725–1762

     Territories added under Catherine
     the Great, 1762–1796

country remained backward, its wealth increased.

So did its cultural activities. The service nobility made up of foreigners and self-made men found its identity in foreign cultures, in the works published, the ideas mooted, in France, England, and Germany. The University of Moscow was founded in 1755. More books were being published, many of them translations. In 1726, just after Peter's death, seven books in all were printed in Russia. By the 1760's the annual average stood over one hundred.

Foreign trade augmented its turnover in real value four or five times between the middle and the end of the eighteenth century. Industry, still largely in the homes of peasant craftsmen catering to strictly local needs, expanded also. There had been roughly 200 or 300 factories in Peter's Russia; there would be ten times as many by 1800, 10,000 workshops by mid-nineteenth century, employing a half million workers. Around 1800, Russian iron production was probably the highest in the world. Half of the Russian work force was unfree, however, their furnaces burned charcoal and not coal, and Russian industry would lag behind the West for a good time longer.

An economist who spent some years as tutor of the future Tsar Nicholas I observed in 1815 that Russia's lack of modern manufactures must be attributed to her failure to abolish serfdom. The evidence whether free labor is really more productive, remains inconclusive. But where the man was right was that, if serfs were freed without being given land, the human capital for industry would have been made available. And it is true that industrial expansion began in Russia after the 1860's, when there were no more serfs. Until then, manufactures drew on servile labor, furnished by landlords or by the state,* which still continued to be the *primum mobile* of enterprise.

Historian Max Beloff has compared the Russian nobles to the nineteenth-century planter aristocracy of the American South: a similarly agrarian ruling class based on slave labor; prospering from the contemporary rise in prices because demand for their produce rose; facing a similar rise in labor costs—that is, the price of serfs or prime field hands—while land itself was plentiful; similarly interested in consumption, rather than efficiency or improvement; and differing only in the Russians' readiness to obey the state, to whose patronage they always looked for aid. This last applied almost as well to the manufacturing classes. For, whereas in the West, freedom was the best spur to trade and industry, in eastern countries, and very much in Russia, the spur was tyranny, with the despotic initiative of the state fostering commercial and industrial enterprise. In the West, progress came mostly from individuals and led eventually to political emancipation; in the East progress

---

* When Catherine opened a state pawnshop at St. Petersburg to furnish credit facilities to her nobles, they pawned there mostly "souls"—peasant serfs—as the nobles of the neighboring lands would have done if their credit systems had been as advanced.

tended to come from above, depended on the central power and supported its growth. This was a trend that time would but confirm, and its concomitant was the tyranny just mentioned, a tyranny less noticed for being part of a secular order of things. "In Germany or France," noted Joseph II when visiting Catherine's Russia in 1787, "we would not even dare to try the sort of thing that finds no obstacle here. The master orders and the mass of slaves obeys. They are paid ill or not at all, and they do not even dare to grumble . . . The nobility, humbled, looks on the orders of a sovereign as on laws."

Peter had superimposed the artificial symmetry of Western-style Petersburg over the organic confusion of his land. Catherine erected monumental façades before its suffering, like the Potemkin villages * which her favorite built to simulate prosperity and progress where none existed.

Talk of reform continued until fears of revolution put a stop to it, turning the aged Catherine against the innovators whom she had tolerated and even encouraged at one time. Under Paul I (1796–1801) a beginning was made in limiting serfdom and restricting noble privileges, but it did not go far under that capricious despot. Then, in 1801, the great tradition of reform by murder was revived once more. A morose, unbalanced father was replaced by his mercurial and unstable son. Alexander I (1801–1825) was romantic and cynical, mystical and erratic. His reign swung from great reforming hopes to sour reaction. Serfs were not freed, but masters were allowed to give or sell them their freedom, and, most important, a law of 1801 allowed men of all classes to own land, thus recognizing the civil rights of other social groups besides the nobles.

Yet the French wars, the news from the rest of Europe, the spread of freemasonry and of the new ideas, made the peasants' freedom and their land the focus of political concern. By 1820, Russia had a score of Masonic lodges, with 1,600 members, among them generals, ministers, and even members of the imperial family. Secret societies wove a slender net between Petersburg, Moscow, and the army camps, wherein officers and aristocrats fascinated by the revolutionary experience, resentful that the Tsar refused his aid to the Orthodox subjects of the Turks, envious of the relatively liberal institutions granted to the population of his Polish kingdom, talked about reorganizing the country and its government, if need be by a *coup d'état*. They were mostly drawing-room conspirators, their plotting (as the poet Pushkin wrote) "idle chatter between cups of champagne," their sedition "just the fruit of boredom, of idleness—the pranks of grownup boys."

* The term refers to an invention attributed to Prince Grigori Potemkin (1739–1791). It is said that in 1787, wishing to conceal the shortcomings of his administration of the Ukraine, during Catherine's progress through the newly colonized South Russian steppes, he set up the prototype of stage sets: hollow shells of thriving villages filled with fake peasant-colonists, cattle, and trappings which could be shifted from place to place along her route.

And yet, in 1825, these plots emerged briefly from officers' messes and from drawing rooms to cause the Decembrist revolution; for Alexander's death opened an unusual succession crisis. The Tsar's apparent heir, the Grand Duke Constantine, had resigned his claim to the throne, following a morganatic marriage, in favor of his brother Nicholas. Yet the new order of succession had never been made public and, when Alexander died in December, 1825, Nicholas, in charge at Petersburg and eager to avoid a possible accusation of disloyalty, hastened to make all troops and ministers take their oath to Constantine as Tsar. Confusion followed when Constantine in Warsaw, where he was governor of the Polish kingdom, absolutely refused to accept the crown and everybody had to take a new oath to Nicholas. This was the opportunity for the disaffected officers, who tried to raise some of their ignorant troops for "Constantine and the Constitution." But the insurrection was put down very quickly and several hundred conspirators imprisoned, executed, or packed off to Siberia.

The reign of Nicholas I (1825–1855) was heavily marked by its inauspicious start. Police rule was intensified, all liberalism suppressed, constitutional reform sank out of sight. "One does not die here or breathe, except by permission of Imperial authority," noted a French visitor in 1839. The universities were placed under particular watch, and interest in foreign ideas exposed one to repression, as it would do the young Fedor Dostoevski, who was sent to Siberia in 1847 for belonging to a "socialistic" group.*

Determined to restore the "police" state of Peter, Tsar Nicholas appears as a reincarnation *à la mode* of dark and violent figures from the Russian past. He was irresolute, cruel, haunted by fear, driven by duty, deluded by superstition, and ready to believe that the fire which gutted the London House of Parliament in 1834 was God's punishment for the Reform Act of 1832. Yet, even under him, the country still advanced. It advanced in the Balkans, where Turkey for a while became its protégé. It advanced internally, as witness the first systematic code of laws compiled in 1832—some seventy years after the idea had been mooted under Catherine. Railways were appearing—the first near Petersburg completed in 1838—and Whistler's father would get to know the country in 1840 as a consulting engineer on the railroad which would link Moscow to Petersburg. Peter the Great had once complained that, although he found Turennes for war, he could never find a Sully for internal government. Neither did Nicholas and, when he died, his military regime was collapsing round him. But Russia would create her own Sullys to salve the scars her rulers' narrow-mindedness inflicted.

---

* The ideas entertained by Dostoevski and his friends were actually those of the French social utopian François Fourier (see p. 657). A quarter of a century later, the writer would depict Russian Fourierists in *The Possessed* (1871).

The Ottoman Empire

The Ottoman Empire was a creature of conquest, ruled by a kind of state of siege, its military machine in decline, its administration in chaos. The Sultan was also Caliph, commander of the faithful, religious head of Muslim communities from Caucasus to Gibraltar; but even there his authority was collapsing. Russia's success at Kuchuk-Kainardji contrasted with the destruction of the Turkish fleet, the incapacity of Turkish arms, the apparent disintegration of the Empire. North Africa had long been practically independent; in Cairo the Mamelukes—Circassian slaves—ruled a quasi-autonomous province; in Arabia the Wahhabite followers of a puritan prophet preached a return to Islamic orthodoxy (no saints, no coffee, no tobacco) and refused allegiance. In 1757, the Bedouin had attacked the great annual pilgrim caravan to Mecca and slaughtered 20,000, including one of the Sultan's sisters.

Constantinople, decimated by recurrent plagues, two-thirds razed by the great fire which swept it in 1782, was still queen of the Bosphorus, the Golden Horn still concentrating the trade of East and West. But there and in the Levant European merchants secured monopolies and concessions, while most of the Empire's business was in the hands of Greek or Armenian Christians. The Empire exported raw materials, imported finished goods; but the colonies of foreign merchants in its ports worked under special treaties (capitulations) which gave them privileged status, exempt from Turkish justice and from taxes, subject chiefly to their own consuls. Soon these capitulations would be extended to the clients and protégés of foreign powers, Jews or Christians. Since Muslim law prohibited usury, there were no banks, except in alien hands. And no universities, no secular higher education, no sciences, no intellectual life except of the most conservative and sterile sort. Mustafa III (1757–1774) assumed that Frederick the Great's successes were due to his superior astrologers. The first printed books in Turkish were authorized in 1727. By 1828, eighty titles had been published: The Turkish negotiators in 1791 thought that Gibraltar was a town in England, Spain a part of Africa, the Baltic a lake unsuitable for carrying large ships.

Against the opposition of reactionary landowners and religious leaders, Selim III (1789–1807) and his nephew Mahmud II (1808–1839) tried to reform and modernize their ramshackle holdings, rationalize taxation, build warships, improve the artillery. News of the French Revolution was spreading secular ideas, but mostly among Christians, increasingly attracted by dreams of emancipation, either in the Romanian principalities which were ruled by Greek princes from Fanar, the Greek quarter of Constantinople, or in the Balkan peninsula.

Selim had been deposed and murdered for his reforming pains. Mahmud survived but he did little better. He did abolish the last remains of feudal land tenure, forced landlords and rebellious pashas to obey, destroyed the janissaries (1826) who had long been an obstacle to government or discipline, set up a ministry of war and the beginnings of a modern army with European instructors, uniforms, and arms. A medical school was founded (1827) and the first Turkish newspaper (1831); but most of these reforms got scarcely off the ground and Mahmud's wars were almost uniformly unsuccessful. The end of Mahmud's reign saw Turkey's Balkan holdings disintegrating and his sixteen-year-old successor, Abdul Mejid, become a sort of ward of European powers now watching over a corpse in which stagnation ruled.

The Ottomans were used to fighting Austria and Russia in the Balkans. The new force which appeared in the nineteenth century was that of their own Orthodox subjects, who tried to assert their presence and their independent personality, first against their Muslim masters and then against the Austrians and Muscovites who wished to exploit them. The first instance of this occurred in Serbia, where the peasants rose in 1804 under the leadership of two illiterate pig-dealers—Kara George and Miloş Obrenovitch—against the plundering oppression of janissary occupying troops. What had begun as a local insurrection against a force which the Sultan liked little more than did his Christian subjects turned into a war of liberation in which the Serbs looked for help to Russia. This they did not get, and their revolt collapsed in 1812 only to start again in 1815 and to succeed in the 1820's in securing autonomy for the Serbs. In 1829, the Treaty of Adrianople recognized Obrenovitch (who had murdered his rival in the meantime) as hereditary prince of an autonomous principality, under the loose suzerainty of the Ottomans.

A more significant revolt had broken out, however, in the 1820's. The richest and best-educated men in the Ottoman Empire were Greeks: scions of the great families of Fanar, the Fanariotes, governed the Danubian provinces of present-day Romania; Greek merchants, sailors, traders, controlled much of the Near Eastern and the Black Sea trade; Greek priests and intellectuals wove a broad cultural web from Chios to Odessa, founded a university in the Ionian Islands, revived their literary heritage and memories of their ancient empire. Late eighteenth-century interest in Greek antiquities evoked much sympathy for the cause of their independence from "the stupid Muslim," as a French traveler put it in 1782, for a war of liberation which Goethe and Schiller extolled and which the young Hölderlin in his *Hyperion* (1792) described in anticipation. The *Marseillaise* was translated and adapted into Greek; two of Napoleon's marshals, Junot and Augereau, married Greek women; and Bonaparte himself encouraged the ambitions of Greek patriots. The appearance of Russians in the Ionian islands suggested even more obvious patrons for an Orthodox crusade. Greek colonies in Odessa and Trieste, Leghorn, Alexandria, and Marseilles kept in touch with the homeland and also with the currents of Enlightenment and Revolution.

All this suggested that the time had come for ancient glories to be resurrected, ideally in a new Balkan state which would be Orthodox in faith and Greek in language and administration. This seems to have been the aim of the *Philiké Hetairia,* a secret society organized at Odessa in 1814, which hoped to gain Russian support for a revival of the Byzantine Empire. In 1821, Alexander Ypsilanti, the son of a Fanariote hospodar (prince) of Moldavia, himself a Russian general and head of the *Hetairia,* tried to begin the general rising in the Romanian principalities. The Russian support he had banked on was not forthcoming, for Tsar Alexander refused help to all revolutions. He also hoped for Romanian support, but the Romanian landlords had no love for Greeks and a Romanian peasant rising, led by Tudor Vladimirescu, seemed to conflict with Ypsilanti's interests.* Ypsilanti stupidly forfeited all Romanian sympathies by murdering Vladimirescu and, defeated, was forced to take refuge in Austrian territory where he was promptly imprisoned.

Yet Ypsilanti's abortive rising had sparked revolt in the Morea, further South, and in the Greek islands, where the Turkish garrisons were soon isolated by a general uprising. The West, all of whose culture was rooted in Greek and Latin classics, rejoiced with Shelley:

> The world's great age begins anew,
> The golden years return,
> The earth doth like a snake renew,
> Her winter weeds outworn.
> Heaven smiles, and faiths and empires gleam
> Like wrecks of a dissolving dream.

The wrecks, at first, were more apparent than the dreams. Both sides went about their business with appalling cruelty, but the Greeks had superior public relations and the Turks had greater means for murder than their unruly subjects. In 1822, Turks slaughtered over 20,000 Greeks in Chios (an event which would inspire the great painting of Delacroix), and almost recaptured control of the peninsula. But the rebels commanded the sea, and the Turks had other troubles to contend with in Syria and in Persia. In 1824, the Sultan secured the intervention of Mohammed Ali, pasha of Egypt and its undisputed ruler since his massacre of all the Mameluk beys in 1811. Before long, the Egyptian

---

* As the historian C. M. Woodhouse remarks, for the Romanians, "liberation" meant liberation *from,* not *by,* the Fanariote Greeks.

The Massacre of Chios, by Eugène Delacroix. Louvre, Paris.

army had devastated the Greek mainland and almost defeated the Greeks.

Then, in 1825, Tsar Alexander, reluctant to intervene, was replaced by Nicholas I, more interested in Balkan possibilities. Philhellene opinion was reviving under the impact of Egyptian atrocities. The Philhellenes were setting up thriving committees in Germany, England, France, and Switzerland; they were raising money, supplies, and volunteers, sending adventurers to help the rebels, and recruiting an international legion which soon saw action on Greek soil. The Greeks themselves organized a state, however anarchic. In 1827 they elected their first president, only to murder him a few years later. In 1827, too, the combined fleets of England, France, and Russia annihilated Turko-Egyptian forces in Navarino Bay. In 1828 the Egyptian troops left the country, and French troops landed to garrison the Peloponnessus and to afford a thin margin of security and order. In 1830 Greece was declared an independent kingdom, and two years later the younger son of the Bavarian king, who had been one of the most enthusiastic supporters of the Hellenic cause, was crowned as Otto I (1832–1862).

The new kingdom was very far from what Greek patriots had dreamed, or what Byron died for at Missolonghi. The history of its making reflects both the rivalries between the various subject peoples of the Ottomans, who ceased fighting the Turks only in order to fight one another, and the internal anarchy which the foundation of new states has never failed to cause. It also introduces one of the first of those irredentist problems which have plagued Europe ever since, threatening every peace arrangement with fresh attempts to win national territories remaining unredeemed.

But, however unsatisfactory its nature, it was a straw in the wind. Greek struggles were more *visible* than the Serb, and the Greeks actually achieved their independence. Further, their example stirred a new national consciousness among other subjects of the Ottomans: first the Romanians of Moldavia and Walachia, then the Bulgarians who had remained quiescent. The Treaty of Adrianople (1829) not only recognized the independence of Greece and the autonomy of Serbia, it brought the Romanian principalities into the Russian sphere. After 1821, the Romanians insisted on being ruled by native princes, not by Fanariote Greeks; and the Turks easily agreed. Between 1828 and 1834 Russian occupation of the Danubian provinces would see the elaboration of a protoconstitution there: the Organic Regulations of 1831. National consciousness was growing in Romania; and in 1835 the British Consul in Bucarest reported a rising popular desire for union under a prince who would be neither Russian nor Greek. This was not to come until thirty years later, but the process of emancipation had begun. The most underprivileged part of Europe was stirring to join the rest.

1848

Stirrings comparatively mild as yet in eastern Europe became positively eruptive once more in the west. From 1847 onward, bad harvests, famines, epidemics, all conspired to bring dissatisfactions to a head. Romantics, Socialists, Nationalists, bourgeois, workers, students, and peasants could all agree that things should change. For a brief moment the streams of discontent rush together, sweeping their disparate troops into assault against the ruling order, toppling established citadels, communing together in the feverish Mardi gras elation of revolution, only to fall apart in its chaotic aftermath. Revolutions are like carnivals, always followed by hangovers. Thus, at any rate, would 1848 appear when it was past. Only some remembered the festivities, and others the morning after.

Rising in Sicily in the first days of 1848, rebellion spread like wildfire through the Italian peninsula. The Venetians and the Milanese, when they heard the news from Sicily, made their own revolution, proclaimed their new republics, called to their aid Charles Albert and the Pope. Italy rose, the Austrians were thrown back, the country's unity seemed to have been reforged. That was in January. In February, Paris, ever the capital of revolution, exploded once again. The outbreak came, as usual, through a series of chance events. The opposition campaign for wider franchise had adopted the English method of political propaganda by banquets throughout the land. By early 1848, the government, concerned at their effect, tried to suppress them. A muddle round a last

The Revolution of 1848 in Paris.

great banquet, planned to be held in Paris in February that year, grew into a riot, the riot into an insurrection, the insurrection into the fall of Louis-Philippe and the proclamation of a Republic—second of that name.

In March, 1848, revolution struck fire in Vienna and Berlin, Prague and Budapest. In Vienna a student rising—almost a student lark—sufficed to topple the stiff, mindless regime. In Hungary, the news of revolution in Paris set off the revolution Kossuth had long nursed—a non-revolutionary revolution to begin with, which soon exceeded the constitutional limits it had first respected. The speech that Kossuth made as soon as word from the Seine had reached the Tisa's banks, turned him into an international figure.

Master of the Hungarian Diet and of public opinion, Kossuth demanded an independent administration for the Hungarian kingdom, with separate army, government, and finance, as well as constitutions for the other Habsburg provinces. The Diet voted for this and also for a free press, a national guard, the abolition of feudal rights, and the taxation of nobles. Considering that the Diet was made up of noblemen, this was not doing badly.

In Berlin, news of events in Paris also encouraged the hopes of liberals, the fever of young men and businessmen and workers who hoped that the king of Prussia would give his kingdom a constitution at last and then unite Germany around it. Anarchy and good feelings reigned in these and in the other capitals of lesser German states.* National guards were founded, liberal governments were set up, assemblies gath-

* The only reactionary revolution came in Bavaria, where it was carried out against the artistic king and his liberal mistress: Lola Montez, darling of the radical students, horror of priests and conservatives, who had interfered in politics to get higher salaries for teachers and help install a Protestant prime minister. The King abdicated, Lola went into exile and eventually died in the United States; and Bavaria went back to its beery conservatism.

ered to write constitutions and plan for the future that was opening up.

The outbreak which the Holy Allies had feared and Metternich had striven to prevent had come at last. Louis Philippe had fled to England and Metternich and Guizot also took refuge across the Channel. The king of Prussia rode through his capital with a tricolor cockade in his hat; the imbecile Austrian emperor sanctioned a constitution; so did the Pope and the king of Sardinia, acclaimed as the hopes of a new liberal Italy. Czechs and Hungarians were asserting their autonomy; Germans and Italians were clamoring for national unity. The house that Metternich held up for the past thirty-four years collapsed in all its parts. England, which had never been a part of it, remained apart, avoiding revolution once again. While Europe writhed in the grip of new convulsions, the only barricade seen in London was one which Foreign Office clerks had built in their windows with bound volumes of *The Times,* to defend themselves against the Chartist violence that never came.

Yet, as glorious spring turned to dusty summer, the victors fell to quarreling away their spoils. In Italy, Charles Albert did not want a league under the Pope, and Pius IX liked war against Catholic Austria even less than he liked the revolution. The federal solution having failed, the only alternatives left were Mazzini's republic or a union under the house of Savoy. The latter seemed crushed with the Austrian victory of Custozza in July. The former fizzled out in the siege of Rome, eventually taken by French troops in 1849. Reaction triumphed, frequently atrocious, always stifling. Piedmont, which had tried to unite the peninsula in an Italian kingdom, survived only because the French would not allow it to be eliminated. Charles Albert abdicated, but his successor, Victor Emmanuel II, could hope to persevere. The Pope, thrown back by fear and principle to the reactionary camp, the monarchy of Savoy remained the only hope of Italian patriots.

The Hungarians, who had begun by asserting their rights against their Austrian masters, ended by trying to impose them on their own subjects. While liberal for Hungarians, the new regime's nationalism made Croats, Romanians, and Germans resent its attempts to impose the rule of Budapest and of the Hungarian language. They insisted on the rights of Magyar language and education against any other; and on the right of Magyars to rule all other races in the Magyar kingdom. In the new Diet, only Hungarian was accepted; in all higher schools Hungarian had to be taught, even where the local speech was different. Vienna did not fail to encourage the resentments this aroused.

Romantic nationalism had gained Croatia too, much of it imbibed during the French occupation of Dalmatia. It fed upon the work of historians and lexicographers who plumbed the depths of time for memories of medieval greatness overlaid by habit and oblivion. The Croat language, long forgotten among the educated, was revived and Magyar domination challenged. Croatian particularism, from which Vienna had shied away during the thirties, now proved useful and the Habsburg government did not fail to invoke it against the nationalist pretensions of the rebels in Budapest. The Slovaks in the north, the Saxons and the Romanians of Transylvania, also protested against the Magyar tyranny and the decision of the Assembly in Budapest to incorporate them, unconsulted, in a realm that showed so little regard for their own national aspirations. But it would be the newly elected *Ban* (Governor) of Croatia, Colonel Joseph Jellačic, who first asserted the freedom of his province and then, after a long and weary struggle, helped Russian troops reduce Hungary to submission.

Defeat was followed by repression, a brutal military occupation, and the abolition of the country's secular autonomy. Hungary was administered by absolute bureaucrats backed by a newly recruited *gendarmerie*. Higher education was carried out in German, particularist privileges eliminated. The poorer peasants, left in possession of their freeholds, benefited; nobles and middle classes were hard-hit by loss of land and ruinous taxation. Kossuth, from exile, called for emancipation, but this, when it came in the 1860's, came not through further revolution but through conciliation.

Germany: Reaction Triumphant   The worst disillusions came in the German lands. The liberals, unexpectedly bombarded into office by the March revolution, dreamed of Parliamentary government and industrial development, of federal union opening rich vistas of political and economic freedom, careers opened to talent and not just to birth, riches available for investment. There were railroads to build, banks to found, factories to create, fortunes to be made. But could these prospects secure and keep the support of those masses whose risings had opened the gate of power, and without which the old order would sweep them out again? The hard core of those masses were artisans, and they wanted a return to just those gild regulations which the liberals opposed, and the destruction of the machines which the liberals cherished. Peasant insurrection or industrial unrest threatened the property and order that stood highest on the list of liberal principles. By April-May, the moderate liberals in power—lawyers, teachers, businessmen—had repressed any incipient revolution from below, and gathered in Frankfurt to forge a constitution in which liberty and property, opposition and order, could recently combine. While the peasants clamored for rural reform, artisans for industrial regulation, and counter-revolutionaries sulked or ranted, the liberals tried "to assure the middle class a preponderant influence over the state," formulated a declaration of rights, a federal union based on manhood suffrage and economic unity, and finally, in March, 1849, a new constitution.

Meanwhile, small farmers, small artisans, workers without work, peasants without land, gildsmen without gilds, strove only to survive. Ideology meant nothing to them; food, work, security meant all. The

The opening of the Frankfurt Parliament, May 18, 1848.

philosophical debates, the political struggles were of little interest to them except insofar as they advanced their cause, a cause which they hoped the old authorities would take to heart, then the liberals, then the patriarchal authoritarians of Bismarck's ilk. The men of Frankfurt had lost touch with their political supporters: dissatisfied artisans and handicraftsmen were rejected for the sake of free enterprise which they bitterly opposed, rustic support alienated by refusing to violate proprietary rights on behalf of the peasants.

During this time, reaction regained lost ground. The conservatives extolled particularism against federalism, men against machines, crafts against industrial anarchy and the money power, romantic loyalties against the liberal ideology. While the debate went on in Frankfurt, Vienna and Prague had been subdued by Austrian arms, Berlin had slunk back to obedience, one prince after another had recovered power either by force or, as in Prussia, by deals in which the peasants and the urban artisans got some of the things they wanted, like credit institutions and gild regulations in return for their support.

In March, 1848, Kossuth had called on "our beloved archduke Francis-Joseph," the Emperor's eighteen-year-old nephew, to support the aspirations of a free people. By December, while bitter war raged in Hungary, the Emperor Ferdinand abdicated in favor of Francis-Joseph, who would retain the throne until 1916. The new emperor's regard for a free people's aspirations was mirrored in the policies of the soldiers around him. The assembly was dissolved and the constitution abrogated. And still the Frankfurt Assembly talked on. By the time Parliament offered the imperial dignity to Frederick William IV, the king of Prussia was ready to reject what he called "the crown from the gutter." The Frankfurt Parliament melted away. A few scattered republican risings found little support and were quickly put down. The German

215

Confederation was restored and reaction triumphed, along with Austrian influence.

In 1848, says A. J. P. Taylor, "German history reached its turning point and failed to turn." Yet signposts for the new road had been laid down, the Germanies had been brought into the nineteenth-century world, the political problems raised in 1848 would be dealt with in the 1850's, and, even though German political developments took a different course than those that we can observe further west, their social and intellectual coloring would henceforth be the same.

France: The Most Singular Insurrection   In France, the King had fallen because he had served interests too narrow to afford a solid base, ignored the call for electoral reform which would have broadened it, and the demands for social reforms which were becoming louder. Political dissatisfaction and social distress combined in a familiar mixture and exploded as we might expect, but as no one at that particular time expected. Once the explosion had taken place, the tensions which had caused it still remained. Slavery was at last abolished in French overseas territories, and also flogging in the navy; public libraries were set up, agricultural schools in the countryside, even a university course for women, and government grants kept the theaters going by distributing free tickets to the poor. But, when it came down to essentials, there would be manhood suffrage, but there would not be work. There was little the Republic could do about this during a depression and less that contemporary economic ideas predisposed it to do. The middle class got the vote,* the workers were refused the right to work, and the vast majority of Frenchmen approved. So, in June, barricades arose for the second time that year, and the workers, thoroughly isolated both from their erstwhile middle-class allies and from a disapproving nation, fought alone, and lost, and were massacred. "It was not," Tocqueville recorded, "a political struggle, but a struggle of class against class, a sort of Servile War . . . the revolt of one whole section of the population against another;" and it was something new: "The most singular insurrection . . . in our history," a harbinger of things to come.

Americans in Europe at the time, who consistently rejoiced at popular successes and criticized the miserable conditions which lower classes at home in America escaped, doubted whether the revolutions could come to port with class divisions as intense and leaders as impractical as they were. European society was affected by a sickness that *America felix* had escaped. The Austrian assembly abolished the feudal system almost absent-mindedly before moving on to other things. The Germans, gathered in Frankfurt, talked more of unity than of reform. Mazzini told

* The Constitution of the Second Republic would amend manhood suffrage by requiring three years' residence in the same place, thus specifically excluding workers and the poor, who often changed their lodgings. Note that the formula "universal suffrage" gave no thought to women.

the tailors of Milan to wait when they asked for better pay and relief from Sunday work. In France, the republicans aggravated provincials and peasants by raising taxes partly intended to keep the workers quiet, but refused any hearing to the workers themselves. Meanwhile, the newly self-conscious nationalists were clashing with one another.

The theorists of nationalism had seen it as the foundation of widespread harmony and peace. Patriotism, wrote the French historian Jules Michelet, "is the necessary initiation for universal brotherhood." Mankind, cried Mazzini, dedicated apostle of Italian nationalism, "is an alliance of all nations to carry out their mission on earth in peace and love." But competing aspirations, however high-minded, foundered on the rocks of intransigence. Nationalism turned out to breed less harmony than divisions. In place after place, as Metternich had predicted, the veil which liberalism had cast over political revolts was torn down by radicalism in action.

Revolution had been defeated once again, partly by the dissensions that action had revealed, partly by the indifference or hostility of the majority toward a "revolution of the intellectuals," but largely by the surviving backbone of the Holy Alliance: the Tsar, the Emperor, and their armies, which, in the end, acted the part allotted to them in 1815. Reaction triumphed in Germany, in Italy, in Hungary, wherever Russia and Austria held sway. Hangings, whippings, stifling repression, marked the restoration of legitimate order. Police kept watch over the loyalty of teachers and civil servants everywhere. Even Froebel's *kindergarten* were suppressed as dangerous centers of socialism and atheism. Of those voices that could still be heard, only that of the British Foreign Secretary rose to condemn the brutality of military repression and to describe the Austrian troops as "the greatest brutes that ever called themselves by the undeserved name of civilized men."

The spate of revolutions which culminated in 1848 seemed to have had little effect on Europe, little indeed on the map of it: Serbia and Greece had come into existence, Spain and Portugal had lost great territories overseas, but, though in each case this stemmed out of rebellion, it had been achieved only as a result of intervention by some greater power. Not popular but power politics still reigned. Not revolutions but power struggles on traditional lines recast the map of Europe in the years following 1848. The next thirty years showed that not newfangled revolutions but old-fashioned wars would forge new Europe much in the image of that antiquated one it liked to reject as obsolete.

Withal, the revolutions had not failed as badly as it might appear. Russia and Turkey apart, the feudal autocracies which rode out the storms of 1789 did not survive the convulsions of 1848. The feudal system was dead, even in the most reactionary states which came out of the torment modernized: with forms of suffrage and assembly, new judicial, tax, and administrative structures. Social legislation had been used

217

in Austria and in Prussia to splinter the revolutions and detach peasants, workers, or artisans from the political liberals. This legislation endured when the liberals had been defeated. Vast land reforms had been carried through, serfdom and legal servitude abolished, the conquests of 1789 carried forward to the rest of Europe. 1848, writes the French historian, Charles Pouthas, "brought about the end of a world, exhausted the ideology of 1789 by fulfilling it."

That *liberty* which had been one of the great slogans of 1789—one of those words that have more value, apparently, than sense—had been won; by some. The revolutionary Buonarotti derided it as no more than "the unlimited faculty to acquire." But many thinking men accepted the definition and thought that it was good. This was the point of view of those "higher and middling orders" which Macaulay, the historian, regarded as "the natural representatives of the human race" and which between 1830 and 1850 were finally taking over from the old regime.

Whether we attribute it to the political revolution or to the apolitical —industrial—revolution, the change cannot be ignored. This was when the black coat, symbol of bourgeois values, became the accepted garb of polite society despite original protests against men turning up in drawing rooms wearing "working dress." This was when the morality of Franklin's *Poor Richard,* with its respect for social utility and private enterprise, triumphed throughout the West. This was when moral values began to acquire a quantitative air reminiscent of industrial accountancy: a man's time is money, a man's word is as good as gold, a man's worth is evaluated in cash or credit, a man's happiness becomes the sum of an equation between pain and pleasure. The new society wanted to count, to measure, to know everything. Statistics, inquiries, reports, blue books of royal or parliamentary commissions, cascaded upon the century and upon an avid public. Unquiet, self-conscious, public opinion demanded them and fed its anxieties upon them. Curiosity, interest, replaced fear and suspicion of the census, of statistics, and inquiries. Facts, quantitative proofs, furnished the arguments of politicians and the color of the novels that the public read.

These people believed in progress: the progress which their predecessors promised and their heirs enjoyed. The "age of revolution" was the "age of improvement" too. About 1820 we find Walter Scott referring to the "improvement of national taste and delicacy." In 1848, Macaulay's *History of England* delighted in the fact that its story would fill all patriots with hope when they see how the history of England since 1688 "is eminently the story of physical, of moral, and of intellectual improvement." Even the least pleasing aspects of the new men stemmed from improving motives. Bourgeois snobbery was the new arrivals' desperate attempt to fit into the old society whose structures were still standing; hypocrisy insisted on some standards of morality and behavior; prudishness attempted to supplant the laxness and brutality of the older world; temperance campaigned against the plague of drunkenness which raised impassable barriers to social and political progress; "respectability" tried to attain and spread a new civilization, rather unrefined, better nevertheless than the gross brutality which ruled among the masses and especially over women, whom the new views protected with a kind of cosseting despotism; the gospel of earnestness and labor sought to make the most of new opportunities. The results could not be ignored: "Europe is racing towards democracy . . ." wrote Chateaubriand in 1834. "France and England like two enormous battering rams beat again and again upon the crumbling ramparts of the old society."

True, dreams of the future are sometimes an uneasy haven from present torments, as Condorcet indicated when he concluded his *Sketch for a Historical Picture of the Human Mind* (1794) with the admission that to contemplate the prospects of continuous improvement "is for him an asylum, in which the memory of his persecutors cannot pursue him." But there were concrete achievements to show, where there had been only dreams before. In 1816 Robert Owen could boast that in his mills at New Lanark 2,000 employees produced as much as the whole population of Scotland would have done sixty years before. "Wealth and speed are the things the world most admires . . ." wrote Goethe in a letter of 1825; "this is the century of clever minds, of practical men who grasp things easily . . ." What such minds and men achieved, no one has said better than two of their most typical representatives, the authors of the *Communist Manifesto,* writing in 1847.

[The bourgeoisie] has been the first to show what man's activity can bring about. It has accomplished wonders far surpassing Egyptian pyramids, Roman aqueducts and Gothic cathedrals: it has conducted expeditions that put in the shade all former Exoduses of nations and crusades. . . . The bourgeoisie, by the rapid improvement of all instruments of production, by the immensely facilitated means of communication, draws all, even the most barbarian, nations into civilization. . . . It creates a world after its own image. . . . It has created enormous cities, has greatly increased the urban population . . . and has thus rescued a considerable part of the population from the idiocy of rural life. . . . It has agglomerated population, centralized means of production, and has concentrated property in a few hands. . . . Political centralization [means] one nation, with one government, one code of laws, one national class interest, one frontier and one tariff.

The bourgeoisie, during its rule of scarce one hundred years, has created more massive and more colossal productive forces than have all preceding generations together. Subjection of Nature's forces to man, machinery, application of chemistry to industry and agriculture, steam navigation, railways, electric telegraphs, clearing of whole continents for cultivation, canalization of rivers, whole populations conjured out of the ground— what earlier centuries had even a presentiment that such productive forces slumbered in the lap of social labor?

Chapter 7

SENSE AND SENSIBILITY: THE ENLIGHTENMENT

Eighteenth-Century Science

The Applications of Science: Technology

"This is the enlightened century of philosophy . . . the age of enlightened reason . . . the philosophic century . . ." exulted the academicians of Tuscany in mid-eighteenth century.

Enlightenment meant knowledge and knowledge meant science, enthusiasm for the natural sciences especially, for experiments private and public, for courses which fashionable ladies and gentlemen crowded out, all cultivated people studying the mysteries of natural philosophy and worshiping at the shrine of scientists like Buffon or Franklin. Such widespread favor could be superficial, and often was, as when Joseph Addison praised the new science in the *Spectator* (No. 262 of 1711) because "it draws men's minds off from the bitterness of party and furnishes them with subjects of discourse that may be treated without warmth or passion . . ." The air pump, the quadrant, the barometer, could be "innocent amusements" diverting busy spirits from more disturbing activities.

That may have been a reason why many rulers sponsored the setting up of such a spate of scientific academies (Berlin, 1700; Uppsala, 1710; St. Petersburg, 1724; Stockholm, 1739; Copenhagen, 1743); but hardly the chief one. For the academies, once the select club and refuge of a cultivated elite, now turned to stimulate intellectual activity among the greatest possible number, to serving state and society and encouraging unity between them, to elaborating but also spreading knowledge. The sciences, explained an erudite Tuscan, were meant "not to exhibit ingenuity with useless pomp, but to be of service to navigation and manufacturing." Scientists had to be useful; techniques and application, once excluded from intellectual concern, became one of their primary interests: science had to be *applied*. The general laws of nature of the seventeenth century were brought to bear not only on the world as it was, but as it could be made to be: man could manipulate them for his benefit. He need not only admire his world—he could master and remake it.

Navigation and cartography offered a crucial instance of the truth of this. The problem of establishing longitudes still plagued the sailors. In 1750, Dutch and British maps placed the Newfoundland coast nine degrees from its true site; in 1741 Admiral Anson had wandered for a month looking for the island of Juan Fernández in the Pacific while eighty of his men died of scurvy; in 1763 a French ship bound for the Cape of Good Hope ended in Brazil; in 1775 a British ship bound for Gibraltar thought it was off Cape Finistère at the time when it was running aground near La Rochelle. In 1714 the British Parliament had offered £20,000 to anyone who could provide a solution to the longitude problem. By the 1760's and the seventies a chronometer helped provide one, and its inventor received at least half the prize money. If the device did not come into general use for one or two decades, that was no fault of the scientists bustling about their useful tasks.

This alliance between social and scientific progress comes out very clearly in the famous Lunar Society whose members began meeting around 1766 at Soho, in Birmingham, where Matthew Boulton's works provided the center for their original scientific-technological interests. Among the members were Boulton and James Watt, Samuel Galton, a manufacturer and chemist interested in optics and a fellow of the Royal Society, Dr. Joseph Priestley (1733–1804), the Unitarian minister who discovered oxygen and its role in supporting combustion. They would often by joined by John Wilkinson, the ironmaster who married Priestley's sister, by Josiah Wedgwood, whose work in chemistry revolutionized pottery techniques and glazing, and by the famous Dr. Erasmus Darwin living in nearby Lichfield. These men and their friends conducted experiments, reported on their findings, and their discussions of scientific topics soon moved on to the wider social and political questions that arose from them.

Men such as these moved easily and naturally between scientific inquiry, technological improvement, and civic affairs. For instance, with the population of Birmingham doubling between 1760 and 1800, radical problems of social hygiene arose. It was the Unitarian friends of Priestley and of Boulton who founded the municipal hospitals in Manchester

221

and Birmingham, advanced projects for smoke abatement, town planning, and education. A man like the Liverpool banker William Roscoe, author of a then-famous *Life of Lorenzo de Medici* (1795), tried to turn Liverpool into the Venice of the north, founded its Society for the Encouragement of the Arts of Painting and Design (1773), organized the first public exhibition of paintings in the English provinces, fought for the abolition of the Test Acts and of slavery. As late as 1809, when the Lunar Society was no more, its radical membership blown apart by the storms of the French Revolution which most of them had welcomed, a visitor to Soho found that its influence survived "in a spirit of scientific curiosity and free inquiry, which even yet makes some stand against the combined forces of Methodism, Toryism and the love of gain."

We might look upon practical applications as a minor branch of scientific inquiry, in which curiosity and inventiveness used some possibilities suggested by research with sometimes quite remarkable results, but which stemmed rather from ingenuity than from creative thinking. In this category should probably be placed the balloons which thrilled late eighteenth-century crowds, beginning with the one the Montgolfier brothers sent up in 1783, by harnessing the properties of hydrogen. The first manned flight took place in the same year; then, in 1785, an American and a Frenchman flew across the Channel from west to east. The armies of the revolution would be equipped with balloon companies which they used for military observation. However, the great problem remained that of steering, and this was not solved until the late nineteenth century by the German, Ferdinand von Zeppelin. More practical, perhaps, was the visual semaphore system first introduced in France by Claude Chappe (1763–1805), who persuaded the revolutionary Committee of Public Safety to introduce his telegraph towers. These brought messages back to Paris in a fraction of the time that news had previously taken, and they remained in use well into mid-nineteenth century, until superseded by the electric telegraph.*

This latter probably came into existence to serve the spreading railroads' need for a warning system. The German astronomer and mathematical genius K. F. Gauss (1777–1855), who had at the age of ten worked out on his slate the principle of arithmetical progression, and who later became famous for his work on magnetism and optics, devised an electric wire which could carry coded messages between his observatory at Göttingen and his physics laboratory. Rejected by the German railways, Gauss's invention was taken up by the English, whence it would spread to other railway systems, was endowed with a code alphabet by Samuel Morse, and opened to public use in the late 1840's. By

---

* The Chappe telegraph took three minutes to convey a message from Paris to Calais (170 miles, 33 stations), eight minutes from Paris to Brest (375 miles, 54 stations), and twenty minutes from Paris to Toulon (667 miles, 100 stations).

R. B. Fleming

Experience Areostatique faite a Versailles le 19 Sept.^{tre} 1783. en presence
de leurs Majestes et de la famille Royale par M. de Montgolfier avec un
Balon de 52 pieds d'hauteur sur 41 de Diametres, Cette Superbe machine a fond
d'asur avec le Chiffre du Roi pesant 900 livres. Ce balon a été enlevé avec
toutes l'applaudissement de tout les Spectateurs et a tombé dans le Bois de Vaucresson
Carrefour Marechal.

Montgolfier's balloon rises from the courtyard at Versailles, September 19, 1783.

1848, Siemens engineers were trying out a submarine cable in Kiel Harbor; and the following year news of the Frankfurt Parliament electing Frederick William IV as emperor of Germany was sent to Berlin by the first long-range electric telegraph wire in less than one hour.

There were numerous other inventions which contributed to changing our lives, like the first gaslights which appeared in London in 1803; the arc-lamp devised by Humphrey Davy in 1801; the canning method which Nicolas Appert provided to preserve the food for Napoleon's military and naval needs; the stethoscope invented by another Frenchman, the great physician René Laënnec, and first used in 1817; the printing presses capable of turning out 1,100 sheets an hour in 1814 and 8,000 by 1846, when the rotary press introduced a completely new dimension into printing; the sewing machine invented in France and perfected in the United States, which revolutionized clothes manufacture, making ready-made clothes possible and also the sweatshops; and the kindred American machine for the mass production of boots; not least, the humble sulfur match, which, invented in 1809, would come into general use in the 1820's and 30's.

Great advances were also made in medicine, greatest of them the innoculation against smallpox which Edward Jenner (1749–1823) perfected by a vaccine made from cowpox serum. Vaccinations began to be administered in the 1790's, were offered free of charge in France beginning with Napoleon, in England after 1840 (where they only became compulsory for infants in 1853), were gradually accepted everywhere, though some suggested that they went against destiny and Divine omnipotence. In the 1750's, Dr. James Lind had discovered the use of citrus juices (lime, lemon, orange) in preventing scurvy. His methods were introduced in the British Navy in the 1790's with staggering re-

223

The Academy of Sciences at St. Petersburg, founded in 1724.

sults, cutting the casualty rate from sickness almost by three-quarters. Most interesting perhaps was the new enlightened interest in physical exercise and games, doctors and patriots both agreeing that gymnastics could build better bodies, train better soldiers, make better citizens.*

Last but not least, the harnessing of steam would provide a mobile and effective moving force to replace unreliable wind and water. The steam engine was invented in the 1680's or 1690's by Denis Papin (1647–1712?), a French Huguenot refugee, assistant to the Dutch scientist Christian Huyghens, who was fascinated by the possibility of propelling a boat by steam. It was improved, as we have noted earlier, by Thomas Savery and Thomas Newcomen of England, who at the turn of the seventeenth into the eighteenth century applied it to mine drainage pumps; and finally perfected by James Watt, a Scot who in the 1760's applied it to industrial use. A steam truck had been developed in France in 1770, but locomotives were first developed in England around 1800. A steam and paddle steamer was demonstrated at Lyons in 1783, but it would be in England and the United States that the new invention was successfully applied. We can do no better than quote Erasmus Darwin's ecstatic paean of 1789 to the steam engine's possibilities:

> Soon shall thy arm, *unconquer'd steam!* afar
> Drag the slow barge, or drive the rapid car;
> Or on wide-waving wings expanded bear
> The flying chariot through the fields of air.
> —Fair crews triumphant, leaning from above,
> Shall wave their handkerchiefs as they move;
> Or warrior bands alarm the gaping crowd,
> And armies shrink beneath the shadowy cloud.

* The relation between hygiene and enlightenment was sometimes very close: Botot, inventor of the mouthwash, was secretary to the revolutionary Director, Barras.

224

Philosophical Aspects of Science

However crucial, this technological branch was but a secondary aspect of the scientific revolution of the time. Science made little direct contribution to technology, beyond its point of view. It suggested system, order, method, logic. It contributed agronomy to agriculture and interchangeable parts to industry: precision, machine tools, accuracy of construction and production. But modern science was really something else. It was the heritage of the seventeenth century, when teleology had been displaced by mechanism, when the view that developments are to be traced to their ends was replaced by a relation to causes, and empirical observations were generalized into formal laws suggesting a general structure which could be checked by experiment and modified by fresh observation.

Modern science was power, and power was the understanding and control of motion. Newton had sought the force that moved planets according to Kepler's model, and had concluded that this force must be for each planet proportional to its size and in inverse proportion to the square of its distance from the sun. This attraction was exercised not only by the sun on its planets, but by all planets on those bodies that came within their own spheres—satellites like the moon, or simple objects. Here was the theory of universal gravitation, worked out with the help of a new mathematics, the infinitesimal calculus. This had been developed by Newton and by Leibniz, each working separately to find a way of simultaneously expressing a given state and how such a state varied in direction and intensity, that is, a method which would enable them to analyze continuous movement rather than stable states. Eighteenth-century mathematicians improved this method, while by mid-century astronomers verified Newton's findings. The researches and discov-

An early eighteenth-century laboratory.

eries that this set off may be said to culminate with the publication of Laplace's *Exposition of the System of the World* (1796), in which a vast and changing universe appears in continuous evolution, full of galaxies, of suns, of stars, all of which take shape, burn, die, vanish, over an immense space and time.

Meanwhile, the search for power was the search for heat, for sources of kinetic energy and for its control. First, heat had to be measured. Galileo had invented the first primitive thermometer and Robert Boyle improved it. Fahrenheit, a meteorological instrument-maker from Danzig, worked out a scale for it (1724); Celsius, professor of Astronomy at Uppsala, built a more conventional one (1742), known as the centigrade; others were formulated. By 1780, nineteen scales were in use. The thermometer enabled Joseph Black (1728–1799), professor at Glasgow University, to differentiate between quantity and intensity of heat, between the latent heat of bodies and the specific heat of different bodies, and hence to infer the possibilities of their fusion and to control the steam arising out of this. And Black's labors permitted James Watt to perfect his engine.

But that was a side product. The main subject and object of these labors was really electricity. The possibility of producing quantities of electricity and storing it in condensers such as the Leyden jar (a glass bottle coated with tin foil), provided a marvelous toy, a source of canned lightning whose demonstration never ceased to fascinate. Louis XV roared with laughter to see a mile-long line of monks, all holding hands, leap up as one at being administered an electric shock. John Wesley was a confirmed believer in the curative power of such shocks. In 1748, Franklin and his friends killed a turkey by electric shock, roasted it on an electric spit over a fire lit by using the resources of the Leyden jar, and ate it while drinking the health of all famous electricians in electrified glasses, to the sound of the discharge of an electrical battery. "Electricity is universally allowed to be a very entertaining and surprising phenomenon," wrote Charles Burney in 1771, "but it has frequently been lamented that it has never yet, with much certainty, been applied to any useful purpose."

Burney was wrong. In 1752, Benjamin Franklin had drawn electricity from clouds by his famous kite and invented a lightning rod which George III would soon set up on Buckingham House. The first lightning rod in London appeared in 1762, in Italy in 1776, in Paris in 1782. By that year, Philadelphia had 400. The seventeenth-century philosopher Boileau had thought that thunder was the voice of God. Now lightning was explained and neutralized: divine ire had to find other means of expression. Then, in the 1780's, Luigi Galvani (1737–1798), professor of anatomy at Bologna, conducted experiments on frogs which convinced him that the animal's body was an organic Leyden jar: a holder and conductor of electricity. And Alessandro Volta (1745–1827), pro-

226

An illustration of Galvani's experiment on frogs.

fessor of physics at Como, found that electricity could affect the nerves, invented the electrical battery—an artificial producer of current—with which in 1800 water would be decomposed into its elements.

The new electrical current provided the means of analyzing bodies into their component parts; and chemistry in turn suggested that electricity might be measured, its quantity proportional to the mass of elements it isolates. In Copenhagen, Oerstedt discovered that magnets are activated by electricity too. The study of electromagnetics (on which the electrical telegraph would be based) was developed by Ampère and Faraday (the latter's work also permitting the conception of the dynamo), and its measurement suggested by the German, Gauss. This meant that electricity was now incorporated in mechanics, as astronomy had been the century before, and that it came within the empire of mathematics.

Soon, the same would happen to the universe. George Louis Leclerc, Count de Buffon (1707–1788), was himself something of a force of nature, with his love of pleasure, of money, of food, his speculations and his business enterprises, his peacock enjoyment of adulation in the *salons*. Yet he found time to publish thirty-two volumes of *Natural History* (1749–89), from which all spiritual activity was excluded and where natural history became simply the study of matter in motion: a system of laws of universal and necessary relations between observed facts. In 1749, Buffon's *Theory of the Earth,* and again in 1778 his *Ages of Nature,* outlined a theory in which the earth and other planets were parts of the sun's incandescent matter, torn off perhaps in some collision and progressively cooling while the sun (because of its mass) continued to burn. Buffon suggested the stages through which the earth had passed, the appearance of physical and animal life on it, the origin of fossils. He estimated the earth's age—some twelve times longer than that then approved by theology—and guessed the time it would take (93,000 years) before further cooling would again extinguish life on earth. Here was an audacious pattern, suggestive of evolution, based on geological and chemical experiments, and harbinger of modern geology and history— quite at variance with accepted dogmas and highly attractive to the educated reader, the more so because of the author's brilliant style.

Since it went counter to Genesis, *The Theory of the Earth* was condemned. Buffon submitted in word and persevered in deed, going on to suggest, at least by implication, that complex animals had developed from simpler organisms, which, in due course, became the organs of an evolving whole. This was the beginning of transformist doctrines—which Jean Baptiste Lamarck (1744–1829), tutor of Buffon's son, would formulate early in the nineteenth century.

The Swedish biologist Linnaeus, had classed man with the primates. Buffon had resigned himself to treating him as one of the animal species. In 1809, Lamarck's *Zoological Philosophy* suggested a theory of the evolution of species, the species varying according to the physical challenges they encounter and to which they respond or die. Here was the long-accepted notion of fixed, divinely created species challenged; and the debate this produced rose to a high point in 1830, so that Johann Peter Eckermann, expecting to find his friend Goethe preoccupied by news of the revolution in France, discovered him instead fascinated by "a far graver debate" going on there. Goethe was right: Lamarck's views may not have been correct, but they were far more revolutionary than their political counterparts. Nature, he said, is *the* great plastic force that makes, unmakes, remakes, animals and species. The physical environment changes; so do needs, so does behavior by willful action, and this becomes habit which eventually will affect the relevant organ, the whole organism, and ecology itself. Here was a voluntaristic and relativistic doctrine, appropriate, as we shall see, to the romantic age.

Already, Marie-Jean Condorcet in his *Historical Outline of the Progress of the Human Mind* (1794) had drawn his own conclusions from the science of his time and produced a theory of progress which sees man as indefinitely perfectible, confined only by the physical limitations of evolution. Condorcet's essay, completed on the run and on the brink of death, was an act of faith rather than a scientific argument; but it would link science and history with the romanticism of those who came after him.

In physics and also in chemistry—where it is hard for a layman to quite understand the dividing line—crucial developments were taking place. Here, too, the English seem to have held the experimental lead, while Frenchmen were the theoretical masters of their time.* Henry Cavendish (1731–1810) discovered inflammable air—that is, hydrogen; Joseph Priestley isolated and recognized seven new gases, among them oxygen and ammonia; while Daniel Rutherford (1749–1819) isolated "noxious air," or nitrogen. The experiments of Antoine Laurent Lavoisier (1743–1794) showed that air, fire, and water, which had been held

---

* Frenchmen published the first dictionary of chemistry in 1766, and the first dictionary of physics in 1781. The excellence of French chemists ensured that their side enjoyed the best gunpowder both in the American War of Independence and in the Revolutionary and Napoleonic Wars.

to be the basic elements, were actually compounds of other constituents: air being for instance a mixture of oxygen and nitrogen, water of hydrogen and oxygen. In 1789 Lavoisier's *Elementary Treatise of Chemistry* would do for that science what Newton's *Principia* had done for physics: provide the foundations for its study as a science, listing the elements, formulating the law of the indestructibility of matter. In 1791 Lavoisier could announce "the revolution in chemistry is accomplished." Three years later the other revolution, still advancing, would claim his head.

The revolution had taken place in more than chemistry. We have seen that for a great many people before 1800 science had been little more than a pastime or diversion. Now scientists became professionals, producing systematic treatises, instructing students, building a whole structure of teaching and communication which today we take for granted but which had never existed before. Experiment now became a structured procedure, conducted in established laboratories, with results reported in specialized periodicals. The French *Ecole Polytechnique*, founded in 1794, would, after 1806, be imitated throughout Germany, Switzerland, and Bohemia in *Technische Hochschulen* or technological institutes. When, in May, 1827, after twenty-five years of residence, Alexander von Humboldt left Paris for Berlin, it was an indication that the leadership in science and scientific research was shifting to Germany, where young men who had studied in Paris were now setting up their own laboratories and seminars, colleges, and specialized publications.

Science was no longer the preserve of a small elite. It had become a public concern. As scientific activity everywhere increased, discoveries would become cumulative and the progression which Malthus observed with so much dismay in the human race would be observed with mounting excitement in the scientific race: hopefully, the one making up for the other.

A contemporary illustration of the apparatus used by Lavoisier for the decomposition of air.

The Enlightenment and the *Philosophes*

At the end of the seventeenth century the first dictionary of the French Academy defined *philosophe* as one or all of these things: a student of the sciences, a wise man who lives a quiet life, a man who by free thought puts himself above the ordinary duties and obligations of civil life. The first of these definitions applies quite well to the protagonists of modern thought in eighteenth-century France, and the last applies in part, for *philosophes* though often emancipated, had a strong social conscience. The second definition, however, does not apply at all. Whether the philosophers were wise or not, they never lived or sought a quiet life.

What, then, were the *philosophes,* torchbearers of the eighteenth-century enlightenment? Many and different things but, chiefly, it would seem, rationalists determined to assess and teach the rights and powers of human intelligence. Pierre de Marivaux (1688–1763), the exquisite playwright of their age, has left us a working definition of what his generation meant by this. To philosophize, he says, is to render reason all its dignity, restore it to its rights, shake off the yoke of opinion and authority. This squares with the definition which Peter Gay, the most sympathetic American historian of the movement, has advanced in his book, *The Party of Humanity*: "The commitment to criticism, to humanity, to passion; the respect for the classical past coupled with a healthy self-confidence; stoic courage in the face of suffering; and irreverent humor . . ."

Decisive factors in shaping the doctrine of the *philosophes* were the science of Newton and the psychology of Locke. Newton taught that all nature is founded in universal law and can be mastered by the

Montesquieu, engraving by B. L. Henri-
quez. Opposite: Among the *philosophes*
seated at the dining table are Voltaire
with his hand raised, looking at d'Alembert
in the left foreground. Diderot is seated on
the left of Voltaire. Condorcet sits with his
back to the reader in the center foreground.
La Harpe is seated on Voltaire's immediate
right.

human mind. Locke taught that "the faculty of reasoning seldom or
never deceives those who trust in it"; and that men are reasonable beings,
capable of using their own knowledge and intelligence for the promotion of their own happiness. So the *philosophes* believed that if you
want to make men happy and perfect, all you had to do was to enlighten
them. Enlighten about what? About themselves. "Sole judge of truth,
in endless error hurled/The glory, jest and riddle of the world," men
had to know themselves above all as social animals, understand the
laws by which society lived and they in society, become historians and
sociologists to know how they could live most fully and most reasonably.
History was to provide the data for this, sociology interpret it, abstract reason analyze and conclude, argument persuade the world of the
conclusions.

History as Sociology

Giovanni Battista Vico (1668–1744), who spent all of his life in his
native Naples, appears as one of the founding fathers of sociology.
His *New Science* (1725) explains how, within the human species, there
are different societies, nations, formed according to peculiar circumstances, all of which must be studied in detail. Religion, law, government, ways of life and thought change under their own influence and
that of other circumstances but, above all, according to superior cycli-
cal laws which rule these evolutions. Among societies, peculiarities and
uniformities may be found—statics and dynamics in social evolution, a
sovereign law of eternal return. Appreciated only by a few friends, Vico
himself was little known in his time; but a French traveler in Italy
would read him and, through Charles de Secondat, Baron de Montesquieu (1689–1755), Vico affected the century.

In Montesquieu, sociology became the handmaiden of history—that is, of philosophy. The Frenchman observed, described, advanced from facts to laws and, thence, to principles. Examining the structure of societies, he would reveal their *laws*, that is, the principles on which they grow and work. His first and most popular book, *The Persian Letters* (1721), an ironic commentary on French society as seen through the eyes of two visiting Persians, placed all apparently fixed and unquestioned things, including monarchy, religion, and social values, in a relative and debatable light by comparing them with the institutions of Persia and Islam. His *Considerations on the Greatness of the Romans and on Their Decay* (1734) presented history as a tale of change, in which laws, institutions, and political power can be related to physical and economic circumstances and to social changes. At last, in 1748, his *Spirit of the Laws* sought to interpret the infinite diversity of laws and customs by which men ruled themselves; it deduced the principles of political institutions from their foundation in nature and historical circumstance and suggested the social implications of his conclusion that institutions were relative to circumstances and determined by them. Awareness of such determined laws would permit man, acting in consequence, adapting his social structures to their lessons, to move as freely in the social as in the physical world whose laws he had uncovered.

Liberty, said Montesquieu, is doing not what you want but what you ought to, and not being forced to do what you ought not. Liberty means freedom from arbitrary interference, from pressures that go contrary to the natural law which operates in a society just as it does in nature. But social laws, unlike their physical counterparts, differ from place to place. Some institutions are better suited here and others there, and laws should take this into consideration. Above all, though, laws must be not only good—that is, appropriate—but clear, and known, and properly applied, not subject to the arbitrary caprice of some prince.

This would become one of the first aims of the philosophers: "The finest right of humanity is to depend on the laws alone and not on the caprices of men," wrote Voltaire. "Liberty consists of depending on the laws alone. On this basis, a man is free today in Sweden, England, Holland, Switzerland, Geneva, Hamburg . . . A citizen of Amsterdam is a man; a citizen several degrees of longitude from there is a beast of burden." In this connection, it was important to limit the power of men, or groups of men, to interfere with laws. And Montesquieu's solution for control of power was that the legislative, executive, and judicial should never be concentrated in the same hands, but balanced one against the other as he thought was the case in England, social stability being based on continuous compromise and balance between competing interests.

Time was to show that Montesquieu's views had been too optimistic

CENTERS OF THE ENLIGHTENMENT

■ Cities with academies (with dates of founding)
● Birthplaces of writers and musicians

NORWAY

HOLBERG

St. Petersburg
(Sci. 1725)

Upsala
(Sci. 1728)

Stockholm
(Sci. 1741)

SWEDEN

NORTH
SEA

DENMARK

Copenhagen
(Sci. 1743)

BALTIC SEA

KANT

HERDER

RUSSIA

SCOTLAND

SMITH
Edinburgh
(Sci. 1731)
BURNS HUME

IRELAND

Dublin
(Sci. 1739)
BURKE
SWIFT

Hamburg

Warsaw

RICHARDSON
Liverpool

NETHERLANDS

HARTLEY PAINE

ENGLAND

London
(Lit. and Arts
1766)

FIELDING LOCKE

BENTHAM
BLACKSTONE
DEFOE
GIBBON
HOGARTH
POPE

Amsterdam
MANDEVILLE

Antwerp

Brussels

HOLBACH

BEETHOVEN

CONDORCET

D'ALEMBERT
HELVETIUS
QUESNAY
TURGOT
VOLTAIRE

Paris

DIDEROT

Berlin (Sci. 1700,
Lit. and Arts 1703)

Göttingen (Sci. 1750)

HANDEL

HOLY

BACH

ROMAN

GOETHE

EMPIRE

SCHILLER

LESSING

Erfurt (Sci. 1754)

GLUCK

AUSTRIA

Munich
(Sci. 1730)

MOZART

POLAND

Cracow

HAYDN

Vienna
(Lit. and Arts 1704)

HUNGARY

ATLANTIC

OCEAN

FRANCE

SWITZ.

Dijon
(Sci. 1740)
BUFFON

Lyons Geneva
ROUSSEAU

Milan
BECCARIA

Verona
(Sci. 1780)

Venice

ADRIATIC SEA

Bordeaux
MONTESQUIEU

Turin
(Sci. 1760)

Genoa

Toulouse
(Sci. 1746)

Marseilles

Bologna
(Sci. 1712)

ITALY

FEYJÓO

Madrid
(Lit. and Arts 1713)

Barcelona

CORSICA

Rome

Naples
VICO

SARDINIA

PORTUGAL

Lisbon
(Sci. 1790)

SPAIN

Palermo

SICILY

Seville

MEDITERRANEAN

SEA

and his impression of the English system wrong. But his ideas, rational and progressive, suited the tendencies of a buoyant age and would provide not only the base of the politics of his fellow *philosophes* but the fundamental inspiration of the American Constitution of 1787, the French Constitutions of 1791 and 1795, and of the Prussian Law Code of 1792. Above all, though, there was the long-range influence of the historical image he presented. History drew attention to changes which had occurred in the past, suggested that the present was also subject to change, a part of history in which change comes about because of what men do. Change is inevitable, but men are the actors in it. What was true of the past must also be true of the present; and society, whose institutions and ideas had been shown to evolve with changing conditions, was also subject to the laws of change. From a mere chronicle of change, history thus became its inspiration.

The relativism of Montesquieu had to be reconciled with the ruling humanist tradition, which saw men and societies obeying the same universally valid laws. This was first attempted by those who argued, in the classic vein, that diversity and incoherence were only apparent. Alexander Pope, the English poet, advanced the argument in his *Essay on Man* (1732–1734):

> All Nature is but Art, unknown to thee;
> All Chance, Direction, which thou canst not see;
> All Discord, Harmony not understood;
> All partial Evil, universal Good;
> And, spite of Pride, in erring Reason's spite,
> One truth is clear, *Whatever is* is *right.*

Such a confident attitude—which so irritated Voltaire, whose *Candide* is directed against "the mania for pretending that all is well when all is ill"—saw universal harmony not only in nature, but in society too where "God and Nature link'd the gen'ral frame,/and bade Self-love and Social be the same." The great morality tale of this point of view was to be found in Bernard Mandeville's *Fable of the Bees* (1714), with its argument that even private vices become public benefits, that each bee pursuing her selfish interest contributed to the well-being of the hive, and that the introduction of moral notions could lead only to decline and ruin. "Luxury," wrote Mandeville

> Employed a million of the poor,
> And odious pride a million more.
> Envy itself, and vanity
> Were ministers of industry;
> Their darling folly, fickleness,
> In diet, furniture and dress,
> That strange ridiculous vice, was made
> The wiry wheel that turned the trade.

Montesquieu approved the argument and so did Voltaire, though many others, moved by the puritan sentiments that often accompany progressive views, disapproved of conspicuous consumption. It was Rousseau who formulated this latter view. Luxury, he said, feeds a hundred poor in our towns and kills one hundred thousand in the countryside. But

Voltaire dictating even as he gets out of bed, by Huber. Musée Carnavalet, Paris.

Rousseau was no *philosophe* and, for the moment, we should turn rather to the *philosophes'* greatest and most typical representative, Voltaire (1694–1778).

Voltaire

Conservative in his liberalism, critical in his acceptance of situations which could and should always be improved, Voltaire sought to repair the social structure, not destroy it; and to repair it before its faults led it to destroy itself. A creature of "fire and fickleness," as Byron described him, Voltaire was also a man of sense, and this proved at least as dangerous as his passion. Whenever Voltaire turned his mind to accepted ideas, the effects tended to be disintegrating: "The art of government consists in taking the greatest amount of money possible from a large portion of the citizenry to hand it over to another portion." "History is nothing more than the record of those who have availed themselves of the property of others." "Faith consists of believing what our reason cannot believe." Voltaire respected not battles and soldiers, but men and works who "prepared pure and lasting pleasures for men yet to be born. . . . *I call great men all those who have excelled in creating what is useful or agreeable.* The plunderers of provinces are merely heroes."

His was a modern mind, utilitarian, practical, concrete, preferring canals to courts and a beautiful painting to military glory, opportunistic in reformism as in private life. His program, like that of the *philosophes*

235

in general, was secular, cosmopolitan, and humanitarian. *Candide,* which charges ruthlessly against the kind of optimistic world view that seems tantamount to resignation, is a vigorous and pessimistically cheerful work. The best way to put up with life, it says, is by practical action, not resignation or metaphysics. Cultivate your garden: positive action within your accessible ken is the best kind, and the one most likely to make the world work a little better. All this, told with great verve, set in the midst of improbable yet very concrete events, sparkled its way to immortality.

Yet Voltaire's works were not mere literary exercises or diversions, they were political pamphlets and "military machines" in a long campaign against social injustice and, above all, against the *Infâme,* the infamous fanaticisms and superstitions that helped perpetuate the existing mess. If these campaigns were bitter, we must remember the atmosphere of repression and constraint within which Voltaire and his fellows labored, the occasional violences which stood out the more in the midst of enlightenment and relative tolerance. In 1720 England, Voltaire could not get over the freedom of conscience that Englishmen enjoyed: "An Englishman, as freeman, goes to heaven by the road he likes." In France this was not so. Protestants were not officially tolerated there until 1787. Huguenot assemblies were dispersed, men sent to the galleys, women to life imprisonment, pastors to the gallows, as late as 1762. That was the year when the Calvinist Jean Calas was broken on the wheel at Toulouse, accused of having murdered his son (who had actually committed suicide) to keep him from turning Catholic. This was the origin of a great campaign, led by Voltaire, which three years later secured acknowledgment of the judicial crime committed against Calas and compensation for his family. Then, in 1766, an eighteen-year-old nobleman, the Chevalier de la Barre, was convicted of disrespectful behavior toward the Holy Sacrament and condemned to have his tongue cut out, his head cut off, and his remains burnt by the public executioner, together with Voltaire's *Philosophical Dictionary* (1764), which had contributed to his sacrilegious mood.

Repression and Subversion

Such were the kinds of thing that hung over the heads of *philosophes* and of all those who might express their skepticism in public. Their books were burnt by the public hangman as contrary to true religion and good morals, or simply condemned and banned. They risked imprisonment, sometimes brief, sometimes less so (Diderot spent four years in jail, another man died in prison); or exile, like Voltaire, who had to escape repeatedly. Many of their works could circulate only secretly and could be confiscated by police. Louis Mercier's *Sketches of Paris Life,* published in Amsterdam during the 1780's, leaves the impression of an atmosphere prefiguring certain twentieth-century regimes: "It is eleven at night or five in the morning; there is a knock on the door, the servant opens, your room fills with a squad of *myrmidons, . . .* resistance is superfluous; everything that you might use as a weapon is kept away from you and the ensign, who will not fail to brag about his bravery, takes even your inkstand for a pistol. Next day a neighbor, who has heard a noise about the house, asks what it could have been:—Nothing, just a man that the police arrested.—What has he done?—We do not know; he may have committed murder or sold a suspected pamphlet.—But, Sir, there is some difference between the two offenses.—That is possible; but he has been arrested." No wonder the writers of the age opposed political and religious tyranny alike, the *lettres de cachet* or the equally arbitrary condemnations on moral, theological, or political grounds of Sorbonne, Parlement, or royal censorship.

No wonder, too, that their exhortations sapped at the foundations of the established order. Criticism and irreverence chipped away at notions and institutions long accepted without question, rationalism and humanism proposed plausible alternatives to authorities and beliefs now every day denounced as arbitrary or superstitious. The *philosophes* were more than men of letters: they were embattled propagandists. Their ideas, widely publicized, flew across the world to spark or articulate devastating notions in the British and Spanish colonies of America as well as throughout Europe. The *Encyclopedia* they turned out was being read on the banks of the Vistula and of the Mississippi: Voltaire, Diderot, and lesser men as well, were honored guests even at royal courts. Despots like Frederick or Catherine, who were far from practicing what was preached in Paris, nevertheless realized the value of *philosophes* as publicity agents and the use that could be made of the rational approach which they proposed. *Philosophes* staffed the new academies of eastern Europe, supplied tutors for princes, and professors for distant universities. Their publications and their correspondence cast a wide web over the western world; and foreign visitors, converted in the salons of Paris, carried their message back to Milan and Naples and Madrid, to Philadelphia, Warsaw, Petersburg, and Stockholm. Not since the Reformation had so few men exerted so much influence so far in space and time.

"The fewer superstitions, the less fanaticism," declared Voltaire; "and the less fanaticism, the fewer calamities." It was true that religion, apparently, had spilled less blood than politics, but its crimes appeared more glaring because religion itself had been meant to curb them. The *philosophes* were not against religion as such, but they considered that it should be a private matter. A few were atheist or agnostic, but most of them were *deists* who believed that no church was necessary to worship God. Men had from primitive times worshiped God in a great many

The title page from the first edition of Diderot's *Encyclopedia,* 1751. Opposite: an illustration from Diderot's *Encyclopedia,* depicting the manufacture of buttons.

ways, and out of this basic awareness and awe, this *natural religion,* all religions, including Christendom, had sprung. That being so, the claims of any one religion to exclusive truth or rights were quite unjustified, let alone any claims for state support or for the right to persecute those of a different mind. What the *philosophes* fought was therefore not religion but the "enthusiasm" which it seemed to sponsor, a kind of madness which they traced to fears or frustrations, and which they felt endangered the balance of a society or mind; and those organized institutions —church, Jesuits, Sorbonne—which appealed to such enthusiasm and to the ruling powers in order to stifle free discussion and reform.

For ages man lived in a state of bondage, the slave of an impossible and capricious nature and of his ignorance. Now material conditions appeared to lend themselves to his emancipation from institutional and spiritual bonds. Society was rapidly acquiring power over nature. It could acquire more. The church stood in the way. Of course, the whole of the eighteenth century was not passionately anti-Christian. Lutheran pietists, full of simple faith, ignored theology and found strength in God. Johann Sebastian Bach, who died in 1750, headed all his pages "S.D.G.": *Soli Deo Gloria* (To the Glory of the only God). Handel, in England, declared: "I should like to die on a Good Friday, in the hope of joining the good God, my sweet Lord and Savior on the day of his resurrection." His prayers were almost answered, and he died on Easter Saturday, 1759. But if pietism persisted and Methodism flourished, the liveliest representatives of their time justify the description of anti-Christian.

It may have been weariness of the high religious tension of the seventeenth century. It may have been an effect of the mood reflected in

Spinoza's attempt to quantify the moral universe (see p. 405). It may have been disgust at the excesses of religious mania—the persecutions, tortures, burnings, endless quibbles. It probably was in part the effect of the revocation of the Edict of Nantes, bringing all this home to the most industrious and articulate of communities, spreading it abroad by their exile and propaganda, or inoculating indifference on the heels of the conversions which it forced. Indifference could stem from the shock and horror of religious treason, of the forced abandonment of a faith for a conformism. Indifference, or hostility. There lay the seeds of a new attitude toward religion.

It was necessary to "change the general way of thinking," as Diderot hoped the *Encyclopedia* would do, to light up the great darkness that still obscured the world, to reveal reality and the possibilities that lay before man. The god of the deists was a constitutional god obeying his own natural laws, the principle of the nature that he himself had structured, forerunner of constitutional kings ruling according to the charters they vouchsafed or accepted. God or king, religion or legislation, their purpose was as self-evident as our forefathers proclaimed: the happiness of man, of a mankind most properly engaged in its pursuit.

Thus *la philosophie des lumières*—the philosophy of enlightenment—exalted light against obscurity, work against idleness, will against supineness, energy against indolence. But not all the enemies of the *philosophes* were indolent or supine; some of them were very active indeed! So, when the *philosophes* campaigned against error, against superstition, against the great pools of shadow which these evils cast around them and over the popular masses, they saw themselves battling the party of darkness, of obscurantism, of outworn and stupid but sturdy prejudice.

The Encyclopedia *and the* Salon

The heaviest gun of the Enlightenment was the *Encyclopedia* (1751–1780), whose thirty-odd volumes were turned out by 130 contributors under the editorship of Denis Diderot (1713–1784) and Jean d'Alembert (1717?–1783). The *Encyclopedia* could have taken as its slogan Francis Bacon's belief that knowledge is power. Rationalist, utilitarian, matter-of-fact, it sought to present the evidence of every subject treated, referred to experience, analyzed facts in terms of cause and effect, undermined old ideas and suggested new ones. The *Encyclopedia,* soon paralleled by the Edinburgh publication of the *Encyclopaedia Britannica* (1768–1771), offered its readers an immense survey of existing knowledge and, by its very existence, suggested more to come. But, despite its formidable influence,* revolution—Voltaire pointed out—could not be made by folio volumes selling at high prices. A vast propaganda machine was needed: newspapers, periodicals, and small cheap books, academies, philosophical societies, clubs, masonic lodges, even drawing rooms were launched, enlisted, mobilized to spread the light.

The eighteenth century is the century of the *salon,* the drawing room where taste and opinion are made by conversation, where reputations are established by word and wit. The cultural dominance of the court was passing to more intimate circles, the reign of wit replacing that of hierarchy and form. *Esprit* or wit, as Voltaire defined it, was simply ingenious reason operating in society, implying always more than it would say, using words as much to suggest as to articulate a feeling, a thought, a possibility. A social virtue, an art or pastime which needs a public more than most, relying on its echo in the partner's eyes to amplify and fulfill it, wit is superficial, evanescent, made for small company, light minds, quick hearts. Wit is not a guffaw but a smile; it is charm; it is a discreet sensuality and a convivial pleasure. Of the few.

In the salons we find an eloquence adapted to the age of Mozart and to the host of influential women who helped to make opinion and spread it abroad, women like Julie de Lespinasse, or Horace Walpole's friend, Madame du Deffand; or Necker's wife, in whose salon her daughter, the future Madame de Staël, sharpened her wits and her European education; or, greatest of all, Madame Geoffrin, whom Stanislas II of Poland called "Maman," the friend of Joseph II and of Catherine the Great, of whom it was said that she was one of the three empresses ruling Europe in the 1760's. In Madame Geoffrin's salon one could meet ambassadors like Kaunitz, Maria Theresa's future chancellor, artists and writers and foreign visitors: Hume, Wilkes, Beccaria, Garrick. It was a European institution, one of the most effective bases from which enlightened ideas spread.

Freemasonry

Another base, less charming but more widespread, was in the Masonic lodges which began to migrate from England in the 1720's, expounding and conveying their creed of humanity, brotherhood, and progress.

---

* La Tour's portrait of Madame de Pompadour shows the *Encyclopédie* and Montesquieu's *Esprit des Lois* beside her.

Reading at the Home of Madame Geoffrin, by Lemonnier. Musée des Beaux Arts.

The ideals of medieval Masonic corporations, adapted to eighteenth-century needs and seasoned by secrecy and symbolic rituals, caught the imagination of nobles and intellectuals all over Europe. Lodges appeared in Belgium (1721), Paris (1726), America and Russia (1731), Rome and Lisbon (1735), Copenhagen (1743). Montesquieu was introduced to the order in 1730 by Lord Chesterfield; the Prince of Wales, the future emperor—Francis of Lorraine, and Frederick II were all Masons. In 1738 the movement which bound members in a common fraternity, regardless of class or creed, was condemned by the Pope. But, although suspect, it was tolerated everywhere so that it grew and spread.

We have seen the influence of freemasonry in the 1825 Decembrist revolution in Russia. But the advance and effects of the Masons were most marked in France. By the 1770's lodges had been set up in army regiments and in the provinces; the movement which had begun as an aristocratic fantasy became an inspiration of the middle classes, fascinated by its social opportunities and its liberal, humanitarian philosophy, as well as by the ritual and hierarchy that created a parallel knighthood to that which survived from old. The Duc d'Orléans was its Grand Master, nobles and bourgeois mingled in its assemblies along with men like the Abbé Siéyès and the future Marshal Masséna. Many came, attracted by hope of witchcraft, magic, or occult wisdom; others in pursuit of virtue or of useful social connections. In the Paris lodge of the *Nine Sisters* one could find Voltaire, Franklin, the Dr. Guillotin, the sculptor Houdon, the painters Vernet and Greuze, John Paul Jones, and the future tutor of Tsar Alexander, the Swiss La Harpe. But elsewhere membership was more modest, including small rural bourgeoisie, non-commissioned officers of the army, lawyers, farmers, and even artisans. Masonry was equalitarian and, equally important, it got its adepts used to a structure of meetings, elections, and debates, which would provide good training for the maneuvers, discussions, and activities of the political assemblies of the new age.* The same was true of other societies, academies, lecture or reading groups—all of what Augustin Cochin, their historian, has described as *sociétés de pensée*.

Hostile to the official clerical establishment which disapproved of them and of their ideas, the Masons promoted secular schooling and devoted much attention to the educational questions which also preoccupied the *philosophes*. Enlightenment, after all, was largely a didactic campaign, predicated on the belief that men are rational beings capable of ever-greater advances to perfection, and that their minds can be formed by education. The mind, John Locke had written in his *Essay Concerning Human Understanding* (1690), which begins as a kind of blank, void of ideas, is furnished by experience. Experience contributes simple ideas, which the understanding learns to associate into more complex ones. Knowledge is founded in sensations, the action of external objects on the senses; man's mind is formed by his experiences, and these could be deliberately ordered and manipulated by education.

"Of all the men we meet with, nine parts of ten are what they are, good or evil, useful or not, by their education," wrote Locke in 1706. "I imagine the minds of children as easily turned this or that way, as water itself." Such statements implied equality, given an equal opportunity for training: "Men's happiness or misery is most part of their own making." When Shakespeare's Caesar had said as much, it had been *hubris*—undue pride; when Locke said it, it was common sense, which Helvétius echoed in 1758: "Goodness and humanity are not the work of nature, but only of education."

In 1749, David Hartley's *Observations On Man* carried the implications of Locke's sensationalism (the belief that nothing can appear in the mind which has not been channeled there by the senses) a step further. Ideas, Hartley said, arising from outside stimuli, tend to become associated in the mind. This means, on the one hand, the need to learn the laws governing such associations of ideas—that is, the psychological laws affecting the working of the mind—and, on the other, the need to manipulate the experience and education of children in order to provide the right impressions in the right order. At the time when the prevailing view still held that man was born with certain

---

* Of fifty-three future members of the National Assembly who took part in various deputations to the court in January and February, 1789, thirty-one were Masons. Among the deputies to the Estates General, half of the Third Estate, a third of the nobles, 10 per cent of the clergy are said to have been Masons. In many places the proportion of Masons among elected deputies was quite impressive: in one town of the Loire, four out of six.

innate ideas and instincts, the new doctrines insisted, as we can see, on habit and the acquired behavior, intellectually developed, inculcated by an education to which all men were open.

The point was further elaborated by Claude Adrian Helvétius (1715–1771) in his book *On the Mind* (1758). Children's qualities and thinking were made by education, argued Helvétius. Ultimately all children are much the same. How they evolve depends on the teacher who is responsible for developing their intellectual and their public spirit. Men are moved by self-love; the important thing is to use and direct their passions to the advantage of society and their own. Helvétius advocated teaching civics and social science. Society could be reformed by education but, clearly, education would only be reformed by a society that wanted such reforms. The Masons stood for the enlightenment that would facilitate reform and bring further enlightenment in its wake. The Jacobins were to take this up, along with Helvétius' pleas for practical training that might build up not only citizens but productive men.

Utilitarianism

This brings us to utilitarianism, the fundamental motive which seems to have inspired most of the philosophers of this age. Their analyses of man, of mind, of society, all aimed not at gratuitous enlightenment but at *use,* toward which all their efforts tended. Even the grandfather of the sect, old Bernard de Fontenelle (1657–1757)—the prettiest pedant in the world, as an enemy once called him—who had made his name with his *Entretiens* (conversations), in which a gallant astronomer initiates a charming marquise into the plurality of worlds (1686), while strolling in a starlit garden—even Fontenelle had devoted a whole treatise to happiness and concluded that happiness is "only a question of calculation."

Enlightened utilitarianism would even be reflected in the work of some eighteenth-century architects who strove to put up functional structures, eliminate ornaments which had lost their structural use, adapt furniture to the human body, and sometimes tried to express a building's purpose in its shape and decoration. This last led to some fascinating but awkward essays in expressive architecture, in which salt works were ornamented with stalactites of salt, offices for a river overseer planned in a kind of cylindrical funnel through which the river ran as through a turbine, and a monument to Newton was projected as a vast sphere speckled with tiny holes: stars lighting up the heavenly vault above the great man's tomb.

Literature, too, had its exaggerations. Thus, Julien de La Mettrie (1709–1751), a brilliant and eccentric doctor whom Frederick made a member of his Berlin Academy, published his *Man a Machine* in 1747. Man, argued La Mettrie, is nothing but an animal, made up of a number of springs, all set in motion by one another. This was the fictional figure of Hobbes carried to its logical conclusion. Ultimately, "man is a machine"—a modification of matter. Nature has created him to be happy, to do what comes naturally. Virtue is self-love; morality is self-interest; crime should be cured, not punished, by adjusting the mechanism. Helvétius said as much in greater detail, but turned self-love into a social purpose. Since "pleasure and pain are and will always be the only principle of human action," laws should take this into consideration and try to serve the needs of public utility—the interest of the greatest number.

Another philosopher, Baron d'Holbach (1723–1789), agreed: the end of society is utility, social utility must be gaged on the happiness of its members, and virtue is the furtherance of this end. The conclusion could only be that society should be organized for the welfare not of particular groups but of the greatest number of its individual members.

The first concrete results of such views came in the realm of law and law reform. The prevailing contemporary use of law was that it should be as terrifying as it was often ineffective. In progressive England alone, acts of 1722 and 1758 added some 350 capital offenses to the Statute Book. The law was not designed to deter from crime, but to avenge as harshly as it could those crimes which the forces of order were too ineffective to prevent. In 1764, Cesare Bonesana, Marquis of Beccaria, born in Milan in 1733 and educated in a Paris Jesuit college, a passionate reader of Montesquieu and of the other *philosophes,* would bring out a short analysis of the relation between crime and punishment: *Dei deletti e delle pene.* Soon translated into French, the little book caused a furor and inspired, first in intellectual circles and later everywhere, important penal reforms.

Beccaria's main idea was that, as in Gilbert and Sullivan, the punishment should fit the crime, and that it should not be exercised for vengeance's sake, to inflict suffering, but to prevent new crimes against society. "It is better to prevent crimes than to punish them. This is the fundamental principle of good legislation, which is the art of conducting men to the maximum of happiness and to the minimum of misery, if we may apply this mathematical expression to the good and evil of life." The object of legislation was "the greatest happiness of the greatest number." Society has an interest in keeping crime to a minimum, and "the true measure of an offense is the damage inflicted on society." If the criminal can be redeemed, so much the better; in any case "unnecessary and barbarous torments"—torture—are bad. As for punishments, they should be public so as to discourage others, prompt so that

A N

I N Q U I R · Y

INTO THE

Nature and Caufes

OF THE

WEALTH OF NATIONS.

By ADAM SMITH, LL. D. and F. R. S.
Formerly Profeſſor of Moral Philoſophy in the Univerſity of GLASGOW.

IN TWO VOLUMES.

V O L. I.

LONDON:

PRINTED FOR W. STRAHAN; AND T. CADELL, IN THE STRAND.
MDCCLXXVI.

The title page from Adam Smith's
The Wealth of Nations.

the connection between crime and punishment is obvious, the lightest possible appropriate in the circumstances, proportionate to the crime, and fixed by law. Each of these commonplaces was a revolutionary demand in its time, and would reverberate through Europe as first Voltaire, then Jeremy Bentham, took them up.

In legal as in other matters we may take the *philosophe's* ideal, as Holbach voiced it, to be liberty, property, and security. Liberty to pursue one's own happiness without injuring others. Property being the advantages that each man could gain by his own labor and talent. Security to enjoy these in peace, under laws which prevented others from depriving one of them by using force or privilege. Such views would find fulfillment in the ideology of the young United States, of the Girondins in the National Assembly, and of the Orléanists who ruled in France after 1830. But the true heirs of the *philosophes* were the English utilitarians. And the seminal work in this tradition is Adam Smith's *Wealth of Nations* (1776), dedicated to developing Pope's remark that "true self-love and social are the same," by proving the harmony of economic interests in situations where free competition rules and where demand and supply are allowed to find their own levels.

Smith said many things in his essay which would be translated into French, German, Italian, Spanish, and Danish before 1800. He held that labor was the real standard of the value of a product, that the price of objects should be the price of the labor that had gone into them, and that this reward should go to the worker—the producer. He perceived that when a capitalist owns the instruments of production he lets the workers use them while keeping for himself a portion of the price; and that capitalist and worker struggle, each to appropriate a greater part of this price, thus giving rise to a class struggle. Smith admired all producers and refused to take sides in the struggle between classes, unlike some of his later readers, like the young Karl Marx. But most of those who read him paid little attention to such side issues. What they retained from Adam Smith was that wherever nature is left to herself, natural order must assert itself. Man will follow his tendency to improve his condition and, since every man is the best judge of his private interest, the conjunction of private interests was bound to tend toward the public good. *Laissez-faire, laissez passer:* an invisible hand guided the economy to equilibrium. Men should be left free, merely apprised of their dependence upon other men in the vast web of producers and consumers. Nature would do the rest.

This was exactly what progressive men wanted to hear and, in its implication, what the physiocrats were saying to the French (see p. 425). Freedom brought progress. But the argument could be conducted from another base, just as attractive to the modern mind: that of calculation; and this is what Bentham insisted on. The thing to remember about Jeremy Bentham (1748–1832) is that he was an eighteenth-century man, bred on a philosophical diet, fascinated by the reigning spirit of discovery, improvement, and exploration; persuaded that "knowledge is rapidly advancing towards perfection." Bentham would take the utilitarian principles of the *philosophes* for granted. The measure of right and wrong, his first work published in 1776 announces, is the greatest happiness of the greatest number. In 1779, his *Introduction to the Principles of Morals and Legislation* drew the appropriate conclusion: "Nature has placed mankind under the governance of two sovereign masters, *pain* and *pleasure*. It is for them alone to point out what we ought to do, as well as to determine what we shall do."

Laws, institutions, political and educational systems, were to reflect this search for satisfaction and for use. If God's will is eliminated from the political equation, only man's interest could be left, and that suggested a majoritarian calculus in which the satisfaction of the majority had to be the ultimate consideration. Should the majority have what they think they want—bread and circuses—or should they be taught what they ought to want, if need be by terror? There was the conundrum. One answer was provided by the argument that only those capable of rational thought should count in the political equation, and this was the utilitarian position in nineteenth-century England, and that of the Orléanists in France. The chief spokesman of the utilitarians, James Mill (1773–1836), tried to turn the closed society of merchants, landlords, and hereditary oligarchs into one open to those better qualified to govern in the general interest, that is, to the middle class—"that portion of our people to whom everything that is good among us may with certainty be traced." Here were the chosen people of utilitarianism: frugal, educated, enterprising, and productive. The problem was to secure them popular backing; and this, Mill suggested, might be done by education and universal suffrage. Bentham and Mill looked forward to a time when men would learn to connect social and selfish interests, so that they could act spontaneously as if the two coincided. Only the right education and the right political regime could bring this about and make the greatest-happiness principle an automatic reference point.

Meanwhile, social conditions were persuading some people that the best interests of *all* were not necessarily identical, that workers' interests were not necessarily the same as those of their employers and that, indeed, the very existence of a good many people was contrary to the interests of society as a whole. Before the eighteenth century closed, Thomas Malthus's *Essay on the Principle of Population* (1798) argued that—but for the intervention of famine, or disease, or war—population was bound to multiply beyond the means of subsistence. While mankind must increase in geometrical progression, the means of subsistence lag behind, increasing only in arithmetical progression. Misery is fatal and only ruthless countermeasures could prevent catastrophe. Education might intervene to restrict population growth. Unnecessary mouths, said Malthus, must be allowed no claim "to the smallest portion of food." They have no business to be here at all: "At nature's mighty feast there is no vacant cover for [them]."

That was the kind of view which made Coleridge fear the likelihood of being governed "by a contemptible democratical oligarchy of glib economists compared to which the worst form of aristocracy would be a blessing." But it also led Charles Darwin to his theory of natural selection, after reading the book of Malthus in 1838.

Since the 1790's were times of trouble and distress, Malthusian arguments caught on. The first national censuses, taken in 1801 and 1810, bore Malthus out by showing the population of England and Wales growing by a million and a quarter in ten years; experience suggested that industry could not use, or the fields feed, such masses. The radical political philosopher William Godwin (1756–1836) answered that misery was due not to overpopulation but to poor distribution of wealth, which was concentrated into few hands. In due course, Marx and Engels would also argue that this kind of theory treated the workers as just other animals. Actually, the masses were fed into the factories to turn out yarn, and more were being imported from Ireland to labor even at cheaper rates building thousands of miles of canals, roads, and docks, laying tracks and rails for railroads; and this, too, provided arguments against Malthusian strictures, which the workers themselves did not fail to take up.

By the second decade of the nineteenth century the great debate was on, and the workers joined in it, arguing against utilitarian economists and Scotch philosophers. The more poor there were—they argued—the fewer consumers there would be. Better wages would create more buyers, greater demand, further employment. Less child labor must mean more work for adults; shorter hours would allow less unemployment. Collectivism argued against competition, and competition won. In any case, reasoned their opponents, "scarcity . . . promotes industry." The worker "who can subsist on three days' work will be idle and drunken the remainder of the week . . . A reduction of wages . . . would be a national blessing." As early as 1771 we find Arthur Young declaring: "Everyone but an idiot knows that the lower classes must be kept poor, or that they will never be industrious."

The great thing about Robert Owen (1771–1858) is that he proved that humane methods did not reduce profit. Himself a graduate of the looms, Owen became the manager of textile mills at New Lanark in Scotland and braved bitter opposition to raise wages there and to reduce working hours from sixteen to ten and a half a day, abolishing all child labor under ten and making his factory village a model with decent quarters and free education. To everyone's surprise, productivity and profit went up, and his reform proposals could now expect a hearing. In his writings, Owen condemned child labor and the tendency to care more for inanimate machines than for human ones. Uncontrolled economic growth was creating a society where more and more people were being alienated or destroyed. Yet, like the utilitarians, Owen believed that if only ignorance were banished a society could exist where crime and poverty were cast out and health, intelligence, and happiness improved. "Train any population rationally and they will be rational," he argued.

Owen's pleas failed to impress the statesmen whom he tackled in 1818, at the Congress of Aix-La-Chapelle, but they had enough effect on Robert Peel to produce England's first Factory Act in 1819. They also inspired a long series of experiments designed to set up communities that we now call utopian, where property would be held in common and where the good life in co-operation would replace the catch-as-catch-can morals which presently ruled the world.

In 1825, Owen himself tried to set up a community in the United States at New Harmony, Indiana, which could serve as a showplace for his ideas, but, like most other such experiments, New Harmony collapsed. The division of labor and its reward caused too many problems, the strain of existence under a state of siege from society outside was too much to bear. But where utopia failed, compromise in the real world would work better. Owenism in England appealed to old traditions of mutual support and co-operation among working men in trades clubs, benefit and friendly societies. The English trade unionists referred to Owen and to an Owenite or Jeffersonian vision of a co-operative society of craftsmen and small holders. The Chartists (see

Robert Owen's textile mills at New Lanark.

p. 306) sought manhood suffrage, because through it manhood could be rehabilitated and workers gain some control over their own lives and labor. The idea that co-operation was better than competition, mutual aid superior to the profit motive, was a medieval notion not so far removed from what English workers still believed. It was tried out in practice, beginning on a small scale with the exchange of services among the members of voluntary associations, then going on to the marketing of their products, and it worked. By 1832, there were 500 co-operative associations in England, with 20,000 members; a hundred years later they would be a hundred times as numerous.

Strangely enough, this practical idealist is generally classed together with his French contemporaries, Fourier and Saint-Simon, partly because all three sought ways of creating a more harmonious social order and of integrating the oppressed into the world, not only of production, but of enjoyment too. Yet the two Frenchmen seem more in the utilitarian tradition of calculating the root of the good life, rather than building it. Charles Fourier (1772–1837) for one—who had directed the statistical office at Lyons during Napoleon's Hundred Days—was a true mathematical visionary, his writings full of figures, where evil was an equation, and so was good.

Fourier felt that the French Revolution had failed because, while plutocracy had taken the place of aristocracy, private interests still clashed with common interests, while general misery increased along with national wealth. The only remedy lay in *association*—a planned co-operation of people gathered in *phalansteries* where all would find something to do and all would be assured a basic minimum. Producers, said Fourier, are also consumers, and in *phalansteries* all members would be doing work suited to their abilities and inclination. Their education there would aim at developing their personality, not cast it in a set mold; and women, whom nurseries and other collective facilities would free from drudgery, could also work at what they pleased.

249

More influential in the long run was the thinking of Claude-Henri, Comte de Saint-Simon (1760–1825), a strange, brilliant eccentric who set out to formulate a philosophy appropriate to the new age which he could see beginning, and who proposed the reorganization of humanity not on the hit-or-miss basis which caused all revolutions and reforms to fail, but resting on a *positive science*—not on conjecture, but on verified facts.

Saint-Simon's attention turned increasingly toward industry, which alone could ensure universal peace and harmony when the government of men would have given place to the administration of things. He even edited a journal, *Industry,* which, financed by the banker Laffitte, bore as its slogan "All by industry, all for industry."

Modern society has one object only: production, industry. "A nation," says Saint-Simon, "is nothing but a great industrial enterprise." This means that it should be run not by useless politicians but by engineers, technicians, and scientists. The modern religion is labor. Wealth must go to ability, all producers must be reconciled in a rational, industrial order. After Saint-Simon's death, his disciples enshrined the doctrine in a manifesto that launched the well-known phrase: "From each according to his abilities, to each according to his needs! "

Soon, this would be described as *socialism,* a word already in current use in English Owenite publications. And, while many Saint-Simonians went on to apply their respect for industry by becoming rich and successful in the banking, business, and railroad enterprises of the 1850's and 60's, others, like Pierre Leroux, harked back to Jacobin memories of Gracchus Babeuf, who had called for community of property and for a society "where there should be neither rich nor poor," and who had lost his head for it in 1797. In 1847, Leroux's *League of the Just* would change its name to the *Communist League.* The future challenge to utilitarian liberalism had sprung from its very bosom.

Opposite: a design for a Phalanstery. The central portion was planned for public rooms; the wings were to house various workshops, with the noisiest placed at the extreme ends. Residents would live on the upper floors. Right: Le Comte de Saint-Simon.

The Metaphysical Philosophers

Liberalism, as we have seen, was based on a rationalist tradition according to which adjustment was possible between man and society, society and nature, on lines which could be rationally calculated or (in another view) expected to work out for the best. The link between man and the world was provided by the senses. Locke had furnished a plausible materialistic philosophy for an increasingly materialistic world. Yet, while Locke's sensationalism continued to be accepted, consciously or not, as the basis of most current arguments, it was being torn to shreds in the works of David Hume (1711–1776), who argued that, although ideas are born of sense impressions, our senses are very fallible instruments. The ideas which senses may convey often turn out to be phantoms risen out of error, or put together from figments of experience oddly juxtaposed by a fertile imagination. We could never know more than the appearance of things, said Hume, for that was all our mind was capable of grasping; causality is illusion, faith cannot be proved by reason. The only tenable position is one of skeptical relativism.

All this suggested that the "truths" and "rights" on which society rested, or might be made to rest, were no more than conventions, explicable by some prior development, but valid if at all only because society found them generally convenient, or chose to think them so. Man makes his own world, then he believes in it.

This idea would be carried further by Immanuel Kant (1724–1804). Our mind, the Königsberg professor argued in his *Critique of Pure Reason* (1781) and the *Critique of Practical Reason* (1788), does not re-

251

Immanuel Kant.

flect the image of things about it, as Locke and the sensationalists pretend. It molds its image of what may come its way on the basis of a kind of Platonic reality which it can never really know, but which has an existence in the mind before experience comes knocking at the door. Ideas, perhaps innate, perhaps conveyed by the society about us, color and shape every experience, every sensation, even our self-consciousness. We cannot know the world as it is, nor things as they are: we only know them through the deforming mirror of our understanding. Hence, science working with concrete realities is practically useful but cannot be harnessed in the service of metaphysics, of higher truths, whose scientific conception is impossible since reality is not equivalent to truth.

Kant claimed to have wrought a Copernican revolution of his own, by shifting the focus of philosophical inquiry from the traditional search for a truth to be found beyond a kind of existential veil to the relation between knowledge and man's mind—that is, the limits and possibilities of the latter, when tackling the mysteries of the world about us. The mind, as Kant conceived it, is a kind of explorer, testing the bounds and possibilities of perception, and pressing forward to the limits of perception in order to chart what can be known or practically inferred from what is known already. Yet, this must leave a vast margin of uncertainty. In the midst of a world which runs in terms of causalities and contingencies that we ignore, man can and must act *as if* he were free; and he is free because he thinks—as long as he thinks—that he is free.

But he is not alone. Man is surrounded by many other men, all at least endowed with the capacity to decide freely, and when he acts he takes them into consideration by acting only on such principles which he would be willing to turn into universal laws. The important thing is our estimate of the situation, and of the right way to act in it. No matter the nature or the results of our act, provided we honestly regard the act as right. If we think it is right, then it is right. Good will, said Kant, is innate; and reason shows how it might be applied.

252

Murder is bad; the murder of a tyrant, for example, is morally bad if undertaken in order to gain something, morally good if undertaken because considered just and right; and this is valid even if the murder should prove an error. This is the *categorical imperative* of Kant: to act on a maxim which you can wish to see become a universal law. The important thing is that men should act so that the free use of their will can coexist with that of other wills, according to a general law.

From utter relativism Kant was deducing the basis of new absolutes; creating an equalitarian assertion of a new freedom born of necessity, whereby each man must forge his law, a law which could be valid for every man just as Rousseau's General Will is taken to be. Here was a philosophical formula for translating thought to action, a bridge between speculation and practice, a shift from metaphysics toward the empirical fulfillment of self-made ideals which would mark the century to come.

Kant's work lies at the base of all the philosophical trends of the nineteenth century, and of a good deal in the twentieth century too. His relativism, which seemed to place decisions in the hands of every individual, could just as well reinforce the authority of the society whose partial product the individual was. This process can be seen in the evolution of Johann Gottlieb Fichte (1762–1814), who had begun as a democratic individualist, finding the source of all values in the conscience, refusing to accept social privileges or institutional rights which might prescribe morals or legislation. Such views led to Fichte's dismissal from his chair at the University of Jena, after which he moved to the Prussian capital, at Berlin. There, his thought turned from individual self-expression to those conditions which would permit it. The ideal state, which he described in *The Closed Commercial State* (1800), was one in which planning ensured the right to work, controls ensured fair shares for all, and tariffs stabilized the market, creating self-sufficiency. The humiliation of occupation by the French evoked his *Address to the German Nation,* a series of lectures delivered in the winter of 1807–1808, in which the philosopher fell back on ancient traditions whose inspiration could revive German self-confidence and create the kind of national spirit without which no social or political recovery was possible.

The extreme individualist ended as an extreme statist. Society was a unity and should be organized to function efficiently as a unified whole. Only the state could undertake such a task, which suggests among other things that individual life has no reality outside the transcendent meaning imparted to it by the agency of the state. There is no more sympathy for *laissez-faire* liberalism revolting against the autocratic state, but a very popular ideal of a paternalistic state devoted to the good of society as a whole and ruling its subjects with this good in mind—which necessarily meant the subjects' good as well—even if private property or interests had to give way before the general interest determined by the state.

Greater than Fichte, Georg Wilhelm Friedrich Hegel (1770–1831) would build his whole philosophy on contradicting Kant, in whom he found his source. Reality is not inaccessbile to our perception, argued Hegel; our own ideas forge reality. It is the movement of ideas that creates, that *is* reality. The ceaseless clash and combination of opposite ideas embodied in societies and institutions makes man progress beyond the possibilities of his present stage into one more advanced. The idea is the only thing that has a reality of its own; it is the absolute, which fulfills itself by the agency of the state—that state which alone can blend liberty and authority, the two poles and essentials of political life. Man is an abstraction which exists truly only in society, and society expresses itself truly only in the state: a state which embodies history— the worldly expression of God—and is therefore completely sovereign and also the only vehicle of liberty for its subjects.

Hegel's state was not, like that of Adam Smith, a structure which had been devised to protect the property and activities of men. It was an organic growth whose roots went deeper than classes or individuals, whose rights rode higher than those of its members, whose purpose was defined by history and to whose self-affirmation private interest or morality were irrelevant. The state was self-defining, sovereign, morally autonomous; its subjects existed through and by it, and its history alone could judge it.

But if the state, as Hegel saw it, is history in action, the history is largely one that has already taken place. The basis of Hegel's teaching seems to have been a sense that the era of great deeds was over, the time of meditation and interpretation had been reached—a time of philosophy which comes into her own when a civilization has grown old and an epoch is drawing to a close. This inclination to set an end to the historical development which he had sketched, to the rich dialectical process in which opposing forces ceaselessly resolve into new advances, in its turn evoked the criticism of Karl Marx.

Georg Wilhelm Hegel lecturing in 1828.

Karl Marx.

Marx (1818–1883) proceeded to take over Hegel's dialectic method in order to account for a reality which changes by encountering opposite ideas, and turned Hegelian idealism into a materialism which could explain social relations in terms of man's changing needs and means. It is not man's consciousness that determines his way of life, said Marx, but his way of life that determines his consciousness. Man creates God, ideas, ideals, to match his needs or, more correctly, the needs of the economically dominant class at a given time. Since in all ages different social groups struggle for the possession of the means of production, history is a record of their struggles—of class war. The latest act in this drama has been the conflict between the feudal and the bourgeois class. Now the latter, having won not only the political but the economic struggle, has to face the very creation of its economy, the proletariat which can only free itself by destroying the class and the economic structure that enslave it. Destroy capitalism, said Marx; destroy the state that serves it (as it must always serve the master class), free the proletariat, allow mankind at last to blossom out in a classless society.

Marx had gone far beyond the limits of Hegel's argument. He had suggested a rich and diversified interpretation of historical change, only to end like Hegel in a static situation. The interesting thing is that, for him as for his master, the basic fiction on which their philosophy stands comes not at the beginning (as with the mythical concept of a state of nature) but at the end. Here was a new teleology, reflecting an age that believed in progress. Out of the skeptical criticism of existing laws, new laws had come to be deduced, new necessities asserted; out of the relativism which tried to come to terms with its own limitations in a private morality for each individual man, great thinkers had built

255

new massive systems which justified the authority of collective bodies: classes, states. With wry historical irony, skepticism drifted into dogmatism and laws built on relativity turned out as constraining as the divine or natural precepts they had replaced.

The Traditionalists

Amidst these critical currents, tradition and religion retained their votaries. Indeed, while fascinated by highly articulate philosophies and systems which would become so influential in our time, we are liable to forget that most men remained religious, most men did not think to question the habits and beliefs on which their lives were based, and that—whether affirmative or critical—conservative theories too were being formulated which still subsist in our own day.

The eighteenth century had shaken religion badly. The upper classes had lost their religious faith and kept up only the forms of religion, for the sake of social convenience and perhaps also, as Voltaire implied, of order. But they missed something to believe in, and sought it avidly in mesmerism and occultism, and masonic lodges, and in the tear-drenched sentimentalism associated with Rousseau. A religion of humanity replaced the religions of God, a religion of humanity which in the last analysis turned into a religion of self. Worse still, in respectable eyes, such beliefs implied that man must be the measure of all things, and opened the door to egalitarian reforms which, as the Revolution proved, could threaten the very existence of their upper-class believers.

By that time it was becoming evident that philosophy and science—Kant and Laplace—produced an interpretation of the universe which explained its order in purely physical terms. Without meaning to, Galileo had begun to replace God with nature and Descartes to turn him into mathematics or, rather, into the creator of those mathematical possibilities Descartes enjoyed so much; so that, as Bertrand Russell has put it: "No God, no geometry; but geometry is delicious, therefore God must exist." But if, for Descartes, God—in whom he profoundly believed—was simply the creator of matter and motion, once given which everything else follows; if, for Newton, God was just the designer and maintenance man of the universal clockwork—the "intelligent agent . . . very well skilled in mechanics and geometry"; then an explanation of how matter and motion could have come about might render Him inessential, especially in the particular guise which organized religion offered. Deists remained, but their deism, just like religious ritual, would seem increasingly irrelevant to the functioning of the mechanical universe.

Although it took time for this to be acknowledged, the new alternatives were both subjective ones: faith or denial. And yet it seemed, as Napoleon said, that society could not exist without religion. When we have made this world unbearable to men, the least that we can do is promise them another. The early nineteenth century saw the revival of religious faith and of religious institutions. Sentiment found solace in the aesthetic qualities, the beauties of religious worship, so that with Chauteaubriand men wept and they believed. Hope found fulfillment in the pietism of enthusiasts like Madame de Krüdener, who prayed with Tsar Alexander in his tent and promised that regeneration would surely come through repentance. The poor found exaltation or escape in revivalist meetings, the well-intentioned found in the Christian spirit a vital inspiration of practical reform, lastly the men of order saw in the church—in all the churches—a strong support of order that they could not do without.

This last was put most forcefully by the philosophers of the Restoration, a term probably suggested by *The Restoration of Political Science*, which the Bernese patrician Karl Ludwig von Haller published in 1816, advocating a return to feudal and corporatist traditions, and to religion as the only trustworthy basis and instrument of political power.* But Haller was only one, one of the less important, among the many who sought order, stability, rest, after twenty years of agitation and disorder. Such men aspired to stability in the midst of change, and became prophets of the past in an age which yearned toward the future. Instead of a renaissance, they offered a restoration. They rejected their time or, at least, tried to freeze it, rejected the city, suspected social mobility, fell back on rural reality, on the soil, the family, on stable property, a stiff hierarchy in home and state.

To secure this last on the most enduring possible foundation they brought in God, enlisting religion in the service of conservatism. We have seen how Methodism in England turned its devotees from public to personal reform. German Pietists, likewise, damned the Enlightenment and considered the French Revolution to be the Beast of the Apocalypse. But Protestantism, however orthodox, nursed a spirit of free inquiry that threatened established values. Only the Catholic Church offered serious guarantees of authority without which there could be no enduring order. A romantic Frenchman, Félicité de Lamennais (1782–1854), condemned the spirit of free inquiry that had inspired Luther. "There can be no peace for the mind," he wrote in 1817, "except when it is sure of possessing the truth." Not individual opinions but the theocratic authority of the Middle Ages restored could furnish such assurance, only the Catholic religion could ensure it. In Belgium and Austria, in Prussia and Bavaria, theocratic ideas, theological justifications for legitimacy, obedience and hierarchy, led to conversions and religious activity.

* Haller himself converted to Catholicism in 1820 for political reasons.

But the clearest formulation of such views was found in France.

In 1820, Louis de Bonald (1754–1840) would see his work as showing the intimate alliance of religion and political truths. Even superstition, said Joseph de Maistre (1753–1821), was but a vanguard of religion. And when, in 1832, the French university curriculum enjoined professors of philosophy to teach the existence of God and the immortality of the soul, people such as these protested against the introduction of rational argument, of any argument at all, where only authority should reign. There should be no debate; not even the seeds of one. Proving the existence of God, declared Bonald, was to abolish faith.

Yet, though the Catholic Church, like most of the other churches, firmly ranged itself on the side of reaction, it would be split by a liberal minority that called for the freedom of conscience which the Vatican denounced. The oppression of Catholic Irishmen by Protestant Englishmen, the complaints of Catholic Belgians against the Calvinist Dutch, above all the Polish rising of 1830, reminded Catholics that some tyrannies denied the liberties of the church as well as many others. In France especially a liberal group arose. Lamennais's romantic radicalism could lead as easily to populism as to reaction. His newspaper, *Avenir*, founded in 1830, argued for freedom of education, of press and association, for more elections and a broader electorate, for the separation of church and state. In 1832 the encyclical *Mirari Vos*, condemning freedom of conscience and of the press, crushed his incipient crusade. At the same time a papal brief addressed to the Polish bishops implicitly condemned the rising of Catholic Poles against their Orthodox Russian masters. Yet Lamennais's friend, the Count of Montalembert, translated Mickiewicz's passionate plea to God to save Poland from her Orthodox oppressors (1833), and this in turn inspired Lamennais to write his *Words of a Believer* (1834), which preached radical social ideas in biblical language, and which the Pope condemned, unwilling to accept a distinction between spiritual obedience and temporal freedom.

Lamennais had begun by looking to the church for salvation from the state; he would end by turning to the people for salvation from both. Condemned by the Pope, Lamennais would in turn condemn him and leave the church to devote the rest of his life to social struggles. Within a few years, his *Modern Slavery* (1839) outlined the antagonism between proletarian workers and masters of capital and denounced the latter. The foundations of Christian socialism were being laid.

Religion could evidently be turned against the existing order as well as to its support. The most reliable philosopher of conservatism would not be drawn from the ranks of the religious faithful, but from eighteenth-century rationalism. Edmund Burke (1729–1797), who had justified revolution in America because men have the right to resist oppression, condemned it in France for a similar reason: because it did not bring liberty for all, but the supremacy of a group which, brutally setting history aside, upset the delicate balance of society. Burke's *Reflections on the Revolution in France,* translated into French by Louis XVI himself, earned him a medal from the king of Poland, the praise of his own king, and the hatred of the Whigs whom he had helped lead during the American conflict and whom he now abandoned in revulsion against the anarchy across the Channel.

To Burke, all society was a historical product: a partnership between the dead, the living, and those yet to be born, the result of long evolution and experience, its laws and institutions forged by trial and error and not to be lightly—let alone violently—altered. In the American Revolution, as in 1688, historical evolution had used force to press ahead on its established path. In 1789 it had been thrust aside by men who would ignore it for some theoretical scheme which they were ready to impose by force at great cost to society. Burke's anger was an honorable one: he hated suffering in India or in Ireland, as much as he did in France. But, as Thomas Paine reminded his readers in the *Rights of Man,* Burke pitied the plumage and forgot the dying bird. Against Burke, Paine "contended for the rights of the living" against "the manuscript-assumed authority of the dead." Each generation could redefine its rights, reform its government. Not government by precedent but government by people—by the people—that is, by the majority "framing their own laws," as Wordsworth sang in 1793, was what the new recipe recommended.

Yet such a doctrine introduced a principle of endless instability that no society, Burke contended, could accept and survive. There is virtue in lasting institutions, in social constraints which avoid a far worse anarchy, in religion as a great social institution and supporter of traditional values, even in prejudice, which, Burke explained, "renders a man's virtue his habit." What Burke did not like about radical agitation was that it removed the Emperor's clothes and showed him naked, shivering and imperfect: "all the decent drapery of life . . . rudely torn off." This is just what radicals have always found so exhilarating. A great truth—the rights of men, of nations, of workers—once revealed had set them free, first to shout and then to hit out. And that is just what made bystanders uneasy—even those whom the radicals proposed to emancipate—and drove them to agree with Burke and rush to replace all that decent drapery without which life, presumably, would be just too awful to bear, too fearful to behold.

But Burke could offer more: he could suggest a way to reconcile history—that is, change—with stability by insisting that past advances removed the need for serious future ones. Above all, his argument that political institutions should conform to the political traditions of their particular society combined relativism and tradition in a pragmatic way which would provide the basis of modern conservatism.

Chapter 8

SENSE AND SENSIBILITY: THE ROMANTIC REACTION

It is practically impossible to define romanticism, while the attitude which we currently describe as "romantic" is a part of human make-up scarcely confined to any given time. Yet, since the romantic movement played a crucial part throughout the nineteenth century, it is essential to give an account of it. Germaine de Staël (1766–1817), whose book *On Germany* (1810) revealed romantic art to the international public, thought its "originality" lay in being "modern, national, popular, grown from the soil, from religion and the prevailing social institutions." This puts its finger on some crucial characteristics—the predominance of the particular over the universal, the popular over the elitist, the sentimental over the rational, the original over the conventional, the modern over the classical—and it suggests that, in effect, romanticism is the diametrical opposite of the classical spirit, the culmination of a revolt against classicism, but also against the enlightened rationalism which reigned over the eighteenth century.

The more or less enlightened society of the old regime could be both charming and revolting. It was an urbane world which, much of the

The Swing, by J.-H. Fragonard. Wallace Collection, London.

time, seems to have been dedicated to keeping life at bay, excluding pain and age by refusing to admit them, arming against the slings and arrows of outrageous fortune in a gilded carapace of amenity: courteous and cool. Enthusiasm was excluded. An eighteenth-century gravestone praising the virtue of the deceased tells us that she had been "pious without passion." Of course, passion survived; indeed all the passions, but harnessed by manners, by a conscious effort to put on a good face. This made a gracious life for those who could afford it, and leaves behind a glow of charm and taste. It also carried risks: artifice can become habit, coolness degenerate into callousness, hollow formality come to fill all life. Keeping the heart out of things, behind the fence of manners, would lead in due course to wearing the heart on the sleeve, an attitude more trivial and less dignified. One thing is striking: when these men and women do not charm, they chill. And those they chilled rejected them as and when they could, them and their manners and their values, their taste and their approach to life. Herein, as we shall see in due course, lies one important aspect of romanticism.

But there was more to it. To the great rationalistic current which culminates in the Enlightenment, the great search for order and efficiency which plays such a large part in modern history, there is a parallel tradition—and one as strong although not always evident—which from ancient days has championed Dionysius against Apollo, passion and inspiration against method and discipline, content and color against form and line. We have seen this expressed in the mysticism of the Counter-Reformation and in the wild flamboyance of some of the baroque. We meet it again under different aspects in rococo and in romanticism. And, if the Enlightenment was first a French creation, it might be said that romanticism was English—perhaps German: the reaction of rival cultures against the predominance of the French.

Paris in the eighteenth century, and to some extent in the nineteenth, was the cultural center of Europe; and even movements which opposed it tended to advance only when taken up by the metropolis. It is in the eighteenth century that the French language takes the place of Latin for good, as the international idiom all cultured people understand. Voltaire, arriving in Berlin in 1750, heard not a word of German spoken at the Court of Frederick the Great. A Scot traveling through Germany twenty years later found French the only language of fashionable people, whose children learned it before their mother tongue. The transactions and the publications of the academies of Berlin and Petersburg appeared in French, Frederick the Great, Catherine, Leibniz wrote in that tongue, Gibbon published his first work in the French language even though in London (*Essais sur l'Etude de la Littérature,* 1761). Many other books by Dutch, Italian, German, or English authors were first published in French in order to reach a wider public, many ideas and fashions, even Anglomania were spread by such French writers as would take them up, and English or Italian works were often translated into other languages from French translations of their originals. "Europe is a state composed of several provinces," had noted Montesquieu; a state whose capital was in Paris. And it would be in France, in the early years of the eighteenth century, that the rococo style was born, a native reaction against the rigors of an older day.

Rococo

The death of Louis XIV in 1715 ushered in a revolt which had long been brewing against the stateliness and the restraints of the previous reign. With the Regency, and even more under Louis XV, imagination, grace, and comfort took over, attempting to create a world upon which crude life impinged as little as it could. Furniture grew softer and less massive, Turkish sofas appeared that one could lounge upon discarding earlier stiffness in the bearing, lightness and gaiety brightened ladies' dresses and even the fripperies of fashionable men. Ponderous grandeur was no longer admired. Humor, elegance, brightness, intimacy,

Designs for three chairs, by Thomas Chippendale.

were what the new fashions sought. The pupils of François Boucher (1703–1770), who was the favorite painter of Madame de Pompadour, are said to have thrown bread pellets at paintings of the days of Louis XIV; and if the story is apocryphal it is certainly in character, for lack of reverence was still another feature of the moment.

If baroque aimed to astonish and impress, then rococo was meant to delight and charm. How well it succeeded one may tell by looking at the paintings, furnishings, decorations produced in France and Italy roughly between the twenties and the sixties of the eighteenth century and culminating in the days of Madame de Pompadour. Enchanted wistfulness with Watteau, enchanted exuberance with Boucher, enchanted theater in Tiepolo, enchanted mirages in the Guardis, enchanted flippancy in Fragonard: always enchantment, color, freedom, and delight.

Rococo and romanticism are closely connected, appropriately enough in gardens, where so much of the activity of both seems to have taken place. The word *romantic* was first used in England, early in the eighteenth century, to describe new style gardens, picturesque places that favored reveries and rambles, unlike the orderly alleys of the French style that seemed more like open-air drawing rooms. Shadow and mystery had been excluded from the straight beds and disciplined concourse of classical parks, like those around Versailles. Now, whimsical twists, irregularities, the unexpected, would be reintroduced—partly by way of a growing fad for exotic things. *Chinoiseries* and *Turqueries* marked the first fashionable appearance of that taste for the outlandish so characteristic of the romantic age. Rococo was fanciful. The news that in the imperial gardens of Peking there "reigns a fine disorder, an antisymmetry" reinforced this. The vaporous, apparently frivolous lines of Eastern art fitted the contemporary protest against old formality, lent themselves to bizarre illusions on porcelain and fans and screens and garden walks.

"Gaiety, magnificence, the rude Gothic or the Chinese unmeaning style, are the study of our modern architects, while Grecian and Roman

263

Jean-Jacques Rousseau, by La Tour.

purity and simplicity are neglected," complained an English architect in 1755. The effect of this could be seen in the tremendously popular designs of "household furniture in the Gothic-Chinese and modern taste" of Thomas Chippendale (1754), where lacquer, gilt, and caprice blended Chinese and gothic in fantastically decorative ways. Pagodas now sprang up beside Grecian templets. Fragile asymmetrical constructions replaced the straight and solid lines of classicism. "Without doors, from the seats of our dukes to the shops of our haberdashers, all is Chinese," wrote the London *World* in December, 1756. "And in most places within . . . Raphael and Titian give place to the more pleasing masters of Surat and Japan."

It was on these artificial props that the rococo fed its pretty fancies. But fancy could find nourishment nearer home. The *philosophes* cherished not only reason but nature, not only thought but feeling. They were convinced that the source of wholesome, vigorous sense lay in sentiment; and this could easily degenerate into sentimentality. Thus, Diderot's plea to painters: "Touch me, thrill me, startle me, make me cry and shudder"; and his admiration for Greuze's soapy attempts to sentimentalize and moralize painting.

Rousseau

The master of this trend came from one of those borderlands which characteristically felt the full impact of French cultural dominance and yet reacted against it. Jean-Jacques Rousseau (1712–1778) came from Geneva, most French of un-French cities, to Paris of which he disapproved and which he exploited to the full. The opening words of his novel *Émile* reflect the conclusion which he drew from this: "Nature has created man happy and good, but society depraves him and makes him miserable." Against the dangers of a corrupt and corrupting world the only refuge is to be found in nature, the only hope in the common people. Rousseau alone had criticized Mandeville's *Fable of the Bees,* and the educator who brings up Émile would exhort his charge: "Respect your species, remember that it is composed essentially of the masses of common people and that, if all the kings and philosophers were taken away, they would not be missed and things would go on just the same." Against the reefs of a tormented and tormenting world, the only refuge is in our feelings, in our hearts: "We are small as far as our lights go, but we are great through our feelings." "True worship is worship of the heart." And though our hearts may be corrupt already, it is still possible to put our hopes in those of children, if 'they are well brought up. So Rousseau wrote the great educational novel of the eighteenth century, *Émile.*

The educational ideas that *Émile* expressed were quite revolutionary: that child psychology is different from that of adults and that a child's view of the external world differs from his teacher's; that children's minds develop through various stages and that educational experiences should accommodate themselves to this; that experience is better than books and that children must learn to think for themselves, not be stuffed with other people's precepts; that education is for living not for profession or vocation. In all these points *Émile* became; in the words of a Danish philosopher, the Magna Carta of all children, the inspiration of the great educational reformers like Pestalozzi, Montessori, and Froebel. More immediately, it was taken as a treatise on the original goodness of human nature.

If *Émile* offered a recipe for man, the *Social Contract,* also published in 1762, offered one for man in society, a counter-political science in contrast to that expounded by contemporary *philosophes,* based on a counter-psychology of man and nature. For Rousseau, the state of nature knew no laws and no morality, no notions of good and evil. Original man was happy and perhaps even good because he did not know what being happy or good meant; he followed his instincts in the solitary, unthinking life he led. Society turned man from a beast following its appetites into a more or less reasoning being, but one depraved because society was depraved and because the values he could learn from it were not only unnatural but deformed. Nature endows man with the capacity to be good, but *men* live in society, and society will not permit them to be good. Hence men are miserable and nasty. The problem is to reconcile them with society, and Rousseau approached this by suggesting not how men should be improved but how society should be mended: a revolutionary difference between him and many others, and which would turn him into the great denouncer of social evils, an antisociologist whose *Social Contract* submitted a recipe for the abolition of social conflict in the unanimity of the general will.

Montesquieu had already observed that a man's freedom does not consist of license to do all he wants, but of not being subject to another's will. In a society of social contract, each individual giving up his independence becomes subject not to any other individual but to that impersonal entity, the community, whose will he can obey quite freely because in doing so he obeys simply a general will as impersonal as a law of nature. You can submit to the law of gravity without a particular feeling of constraint; you can accept the general will in the same way, as you would the impositions of your own body. Having given up the capacity to satisfy physical appetites with no regard for anybody else, you are emancipated from the animal impulses which you once obeyed, and you become a civic, thinking being, free to enjoy the higher freedom of moral liberty as a member of the collective body you have joined, a member of the sovereign people—whose will carried out by the state is really the true higher will of each.

It is fairly clear that such an argument reflects profound alienation and a desperate attempt to resolve it. But Rousseau's success—especially with contemporaries—suggests that his case was not an isolated one. As the traditional social order broke up and familiar bonds, the accepted framework of life, were loosened, as society shifted toward anonymity and mass, the question began to pose itself: when is a mass of individuals more than a mere mass—a real, political, and social entity? This was the question Rousseau asked, the question of the modern world in which social disintegration, personal disquiet, social alienation, suggest an emphasis of roots, of nature, of some kind of organic belonging. With Rousseau, the unbalanced modern individual enters the lists of history: sensitive, anguished, raw, and self-pitying, fascinated by his own quirks and feelings, and ready to exhibit them to all; seeking escape from this exacerbated self-obsessed individualism in some kind of *whole,* the lost limb redeemed in organic salvation.

Political philosophers had long attempted to find a balance between private and public, man and state. Rousseau looked not for balance but for integration. In his vision the clash between individual and society is abolished as the individual merges with all others, surrenders his rights to the community, where all is one and one is all. When the self becomes collective, freedom becomes the will of all, a supreme law which none dare to gainsay without challenging their own self, transcended in the community. Whoever refuses to obey "shall be forced by all the body, which only means that he will be forced to be free." One more vindication of tyranny in the name of freedom, of terror in the name of love, pleas which the human mind has been so fertile in devising. In 1793, when the liberal ideas of emancipation seemed to have run their course, the Revolution could turn to this for arguments why the general must always have precedence over the particular and, if need be, even exterminate it. A mystic, an exile, and a neurotic, unwittingly provided the recipes for the totalitarian, organic, integral nationalism of the nineteenth and twentieth centuries.

The Precursors

If Rousseau carried his views to the most logical and hence most extreme conclusions, the tendencies that he expressed were, on a more moderate level, those of his age. Reason and sentiment, the return to nature, the cult of simplicity, touched all contemporary society as they touched the arts. The intertwined currents of rationality and sentimentalism preaching a return to nature can be noticed in contemporary music. Franz Joseph Haydn (1732–1809), probably the inventor of the modern symphony, produced one called *The Philosopher* (No. 22 in E flat major of 1764). In his string quartets Goethe could recognize the intelligible "conversation of four sensible people." But Christoph Willibald Glück's *Orfeo* (1762) has arias like popular ballads which delighted Herder, the folklorist, and many other operas of the time eschewed the grandeur of the lyrical tragedies that Louis XIV admired. The tradition of Lully and Rameau was forsaken for harmony and melody and simple tunes reminiscent of folk songs. The subjects of operas also changed. If Mozart's apparently frivolous works (1756–1791) still mirror noble society in never-never land, Pergolesi's *La Serva Padrona* and Rousseau's own *Devin du Village* are about the doings of simple people in places far removed from the drawing rooms that furnished their audience.

It may well be, of course, that this was only another form of exoticism, a game of leaving one's own element, like the fake farms and stables with which Marie Antoinette played, like the pet lambs which ladies in bright satins led about on ribbons. And the exotic existed in time as well as space. Early eighteenth-century England discovered the titillating possibilities of historical ruins as well as history. Edward Young's formidably successful *Night Thoughts on Life, Death and Immortality* was

Horace Walpole's country house at Strawberry Hill. Built in 1747, it was redesigned and altered to its master's taste beginning in 1750 to become a model of gothic eclecticism.

written in the 1740's; but in 1726 already another English poet, David Mallet, could make great play with tombs and ruins, skulls and bones, moss and solitude:

> All is dread Silence here, and undisturb'd
> Save what the Wind sighs and the wailing Owl
> Screams solitary to the mournful Moon
> Glimmering her western Ray through yonder Isle,
> Where the sad Spirit walks with shadowy Foot
> His wonted Round or lingers o'er this grave.

What Kenneth Clark describes as a love for dramatized decay would affect first literature, then painting. By 1739, an English traveler at the Grande Chartreuse was writing of cliffs, precipices, torrents, as "pregnant with religion and poetry." Then, in 1764, Horace Walpole published *The Castle of Otranto: A Gothic Story,* which matched contemporary romanticism and set off a whole wave of gothic romances. From graveyards to dungeons, gloom, mystery, and horror thrilled the readers, but also stimulated imagination and, perhaps, chivalry. The Gothic Middle Ages became fashionable, and so did all their trappings: churches and houses began to be built in the gothic style, and Horace Walpole again led the field when he remodeled his country house at Strawberry Hill in the 1750's.* By 1772, young Goethe would expatiate on Strasbourg Cathedral: "It rises like a most sublime wide-arching Tree of God which, with a thousand boughs, a million twigs, tells forth to the neighborhood the glory of God." God, nature, and the Middle Ages, all at one. And the aesthetic medievalism which led to the building of fake cloisters like Fonthill Abbey (1796) also brought recruits into the Catholic fold, beginning with the herald of French romanticism, René de Chateaubriand.

The taste for medievalism could go a long way. But the way was generally eclectic, for lovers of the bizarre sought it in all quarters. Thus in the 1780's a Duke of Württemberg built a dream castle for his favorite in whose park there stood a temple of Flora, a temple of Vesta, a large pyramid, a funerary monument dedicated to Nero, and an ancient prison. His mistress could wander past sham ruins of arches and broken columns, leading a lamb on a ribbon. The park was filled with evocative scenes: a monk tolling a bell, prisoners rattling their chains in dungeons, shepherds sounding their horns, a hermit praying before the empty tomb destined for the Duke himself. In 1793, while revolution raged across the Rhine, the Margrave of Hesse-Cassel built the first *château troubadour* in his park of Wilhelmshöhe. Nor did the revolution bring only ill to England. In the 1790's the Duke of Bridgewater was one of the most

---

* When the houses of Parliament burned down in 1834, nothing seemed more natural than to lodge the defenders of "our old Gothic constitution" beneath arches suitable to a free people.

The Oath of the Horatii, by J. L. David. Louvre, Paris.

generous hosts to emigrant French ecclesiastics. Several score of monks were put up on his country estate, where chapels and lodgings were built in the gothic style, with the sole obligation that on certain days a bell tolled and all had to walk around in the habit of their order, breviary in hand, to create a suggestive sight that the Duke could point out to his guests. Much more picturesque, their host would remark, than sheep or deer! Medievalism was in the air, and even the Cadiz *cortes* of 1812 argued the case of a constitution inspired by the Enlightenment and by revolutionary France by referring to medieval Spanish precedents.

The ancient world, too, about which so much contemporary education turned, was being brought back to life. Herculaneum was excavated in 1738 and Pompeii discovered ten years later, although excavations there did not begin until the 1760's. These and other ruins were being illustrated in books and lithographs that caught the public fancy. One of their most important generators was a Venetian architect who had settled in Rome—Giambattista Piranesi (1720–1778), whose etchings of Roman antiquities exercized vast influence, not only by popularizing Roman sights but by their romantic quality. The romantic inspiration is particularly evident in his series *The Prisons*—which, though imaginary, actually inspired some real jails, like London's Newgate Prison, built in the 1770's. In 1764, J. J. Winckelmann (1717–1768), son of a German cobbler, fascinated by antiquity, published the first *History of Ancient Art,* which treated the subject in the context of the social and religious life of the societies that had produced it. Winckelmann idealized and glorified the "noble simplicity" and "calm grandeur" of the Greeks. This fitted the preoccupations of contemporary *philosophes,* and it became proper to condemn those arts that spurred moral decay, titillated

An etching by Piranesi. Collection of
Mr. and Mrs. Barry S. Brook.

the senses, and undermined the vigor of society. Luxury, it seemed, led to
moral decline and art was one of the corrupting agents. It could equally
well be an agent of revival, and, by mid-eighteenth century, Diderot and
his friends were appealing to painters and sculptors to turn their hand
to nobler themes that would elevate the soul and inspire the mind.

There is a paradoxical quality about the fact that, just when the early
stirring of romanticism began to assert subjectivity, sentiment, and relativism, the classical revival seemed to affirm the opposite: a fundamental
external reality, independent of man or history, and which the artist
sought to express in the great Palladian structures of early eighteenth-
century England, or the neoclassic style of the century's second half. The
fact is that Greece and Rome inspired the romantics as much as the
Middle Ages would; and the mingled inspiration is very obvious in the
engraving of Piranesi or the paintings of Hubert Robert, where ancient
grandeur is always qualified by a strong dash of the picturesque. The
prints that revealed the ruins made the most of local color—ivy, natives,
camels (when appropriate—for instance in Palmyra), and stage effects that
fall just short of the theatrical. Then, around 1775 simplicity and purity
would triumph briefly, and romanticism was sent back to gardens, there
to bide its time while Rome and Greece preached moral virtue, service
to the state, and devotion to duty. Louis XVI bought David's *Oath of the
Horatii*—the great painting success of the decade—a trade trend which
the stirring revolutionary years and the imperial ambitions of Napoleon
would only stimulate.

Yet sensibility also marched on. Suicides and swoons became increasingly fashionable; deep feelings were indispensable. "Alas!" sighed
Madame de Staël's nine-year-old daughter, "they think me happy and I
have abysses in my heart!" And a lady who had just seen a horror play:
"What a pretty show! I was taken ill three times!" Tears were ever on

the verge of welling, and that prose was deemed best that brought them most. Napoleon, whose favorite poet was Ossian—that "mist of the imagination" as Lamartine described him—confessed that he could never read a minor trashy book, *The Trials of Sentiment,* without crying.

The truth is that these people were eclectic, like their age. But the taste for sentiment and sensibility, the attention paid to personal character and psychological analysis, led to re-emphasis of the individual, insistence on individual faces, on portraits, on intimacy. From the nostalgic reverie of gardens there was but a step into the evocative alleys of romantic parks where one could find at will the melancholy, unquiet echoes of inner unease or the inner peace to be derived from nature.

Here, in the new role of nature and its new importance, we find another herald of romanticism. As the eighteenth century ended, men talked less about clocks and more about trees. Mechanics became less important than organic ideas. Rousseau had called for man in his natural genuineness. Rousseau's influence produced a radical change in taste, a novel appreciation of natural beauty, wildness, forests, fields. To seventeenth-century travelers the Alps had been "huge monstrous excrescences of nature." In mid-eighteenth century, Voltaire's niece had shunned his charming but rather isolated château of Cirey in Lorraine as "a lonely place terrifying to humanity . . . in a country where there is nothing to see but mountains and uncultivated lands." Half a century later, mountains and uncultivated lands had become a landscape which cultured people had learned to see and like, so that even the author of *An Essay on the Management of Hogs* could turn away from a field of turnips to expatiate on the beauty of a distant prospect. The same was true of those humble themes in which, as Wordsworth had it, "the passions of men are incorporated with the beautiful and permanent forms of nature."

Romanticism

All these tendencies—to nature, naturalness, simpler or humbler themes, to mystery, history, and sentiment, to a rejection of the rules and order more generally accepted all around—would come together first in Germany in the wake of Lessing, of Herder, and of Kant. The first, a playwright and dramatic critic, insisted in his *Laocoön* (1776) that the task of art was not to copy from some classic model but to create, to add a new world to the real one from which it starts. The second, an unclerical Lutheran minister, spoke much like Rousseau of "human feelings flowing from a full heart." The artist, said Herder, tries to communicate "the obscure and ineffable forces" in his soul. For Kant, beauty was subjective, an ideal each man must devise for himself. There could be no more universal standards, no more academic art with its set rules.

Of course, none of this meant that standards and rules disappeared. It did mean that they would be challenged in the name of values more indefinite but no less strongly held. *Subjective* values—a term that first appears in dictionaries about 1812—now faced, clashed, and competed with the objective world. And out of this romanticism was born.

Born out of battle, there hangs about romanticism an aura of rebellion which is very strong: Byron, Shelley, Schiller turn with great violence against the world, against society and values which they will not accept. Schiller's play, *The Robbers* (1781) contrasts two brothers: the calculating and conformist representative of existing society, and the decent, generous youth driven to outlawry by dint of being honest. Goethe's *The Sorrows of Young Werther* (1774) which so marked the age were due at least in part to Werther's rejection by, and of, unjust society. And the group which first embodied so many of these values has gone down in history under the label *Sturm und Drang*, meaning storm and stress. We have already seen (pp. 186–187) the role it played, if briefly, in Germany's political awakening.

There is, or there should be, a kind of psychopathology of romanticism. The stress and fever that sear so many works must have affected artists quite literally, burnt up many among them: Novalis, Shelley, Keats, Bonington, died before thirty; Schubert at thirty-one; Bellini and Géricault at thirty-three; Hölderlin, Lenau, Schumann, Poe went mad. Lermontov, Pushkin, Évariste Galois were killed in duels; Kleist, Chatterton, Nerval committed suicide. Others died of hunger, of consumption, of strange, peculiar illnesses and accidents. The crisis of a changing world seems to have been reflected in these stormy lives, in consciousness tormented by, revolting against the present, yearning for vanished Edens, golden ages, or the lost imaginary innocence of childhood. If the essence of classicism lies in stability, repose to be found in order, romanticism is movement, yearning, the endless search for what is not to be.

This is how the German romantic Friedrich Schlegel (1772–1829) describes himself: "An aimless love burnt in him and consumed him . . . without aim and without occupation, he roamed midst men and things . . . all could attract him, nothing could satisfy him. . . . His unsatisfied desire made him ever more savage; despairing of the spiritual, he became sensual, began to do foolish things to challenge destiny. He could well see the precipice before him, but felt it wasn't worth it to slow down . . ." It does not seem surprising that such men turned to death or to a suicide which forced the pace of death, supreme escape from the world with which they could not cope.

But not all died, of course; and then escape had to be found elsewhere: in the theater, for example, where the artificial world of illusion could

ARTS AND LETTERS
DURING THE LATE EIGHTEENTH
AND NINETEENTH CENTURIES
▲Birthplaces of leading figures

BLACK SEA

OTTOMAN EMPIRE

GREECE

SERBIA

AUSTRIA–HUNGARY

POLAND

▲DOSTOIEVSKI
• Moscow

▲TOLSTOY

• St. Petersburg

▲MICKIEWITZ

▲KANT
▲HERDER
Warsaw ▲CHOPIN

Danzig •

BALTIC SEA

Stockholm •

SWEDEN

NORWAY

Oslo •

NORTH SEA

DENMARK

▲KIERKEGAARD
Copenhagen •

▲WEBER

Hamburg •
▲BRAHMS
▲MENDELSSOHN
Berlin •
▲WAGNER
▲F. SCHLEGEL
▲LESSING
▲FICHTE
▲NIETZSCHE
▲HEINE
▲BEETHOVEN
Frankfurt • ▲GOETHE
▲SCHILLER
▲HEGEL
R. SCHUMANN ▲
▲DVORÁK

GERMANY

Vienna •
▲SCHUBERT
▲J. STRAUSS
▲LISZT
Budapest •

Munich •

▲BURCKHARDT
SWITZ.
▲ROUSSEAU
Geneva •
Milan •
▲MANZONE

ADRIATIC SEA

ITALY
▲LEOPARDI
▲D'ANNUNZIO
▲ROSSINI
▲PUCCINI
▲VERDI
▲MAZZINI

Rome •

Naples •

Palermo •
SICILY

SARDINIA

MEDITERRANEAN

NETHERLANDS
Amsterdam •
Brussels •
BELGIUM

▲FOURIER
▲HUGO
▲PROUDHON
▲COURBET
▲BERLIOZ
▲STENDHAL
▲DAUMIER
Marseilles •

FRANCE

▲FLAUBERT
Paris •
▲LAMARTINE
Lyons •
▲INGRES
▲COMTE
Barcelona •

BAUDELAIRE
DELACROIX
DE STAEL
GERICAULT
ST. SIMON
SAND

▲BALZAC

Bordeaux •

SCOTLAND
Edinburgh •
▲W. SCOTT
▲CARLYLE
▲WORDSWORTH
Liverpool •
▲MACAULAY
▲OWEN
ENGLAND
▲COLERIDGE
▲DICKENS
London •

CONSTABLE
▲BYRON
▲KEATS
▲SHELLEY
▲TURNER

NORTH SEA

IRELAND
Dublin •

ATLANTIC OCEAN

Saragossa •
▲GOYA

Madrid •

SPAIN

PORTUGAL

Lisbon •

Frederic Chopin, by Eugène Delacroix. Louvre, Paris.

make up for everyday disillusion, where a *coup de théâtre,* an unexpected twist, could always unravel impossible situations. In space which steam was laying open, broadening the horizons of travel but also of fantasy: the golden east, the misty isles, the frozen somber north, different worlds and climates, especially those like the Spanish or the Arab lands that still lived in the past, all the mysterious and prestigious places on which romantic reveries could feed. In time, especially times that seemed most picturesque, spiritually alive, nationally—hence personally—significant. "Night of the Middle Ages, maybe!" wrote Schlegel: "but it was a night resplendent with stars!" Above all, in music, which alone can express the inexpressible, carry vast passions on its slender wings.

Music becomes a kind of poem, a kind of painting, evoking nature and feeling as no other art can do. In Karl Maria von Weber's *Freischütz* (1820) the forces of nature become symbols of good and evil, the music seeks to capture the sound and soul of the landscape, the sighing of the wind, the murmuring of forest trees. Ten years later, Felix Mendelssohn's *Fingal's Cave* would be greeted as landscape painting in sound. The tone poem is a romantic invention, and the tone painting too. Before the painters learned to catch the moment in a dab of color, the composers learned to ride with it through time, stirring emotions which otherwise would be crushed under the weight of words: anguish or reverie in Chopin, introspection in Schumann, explosive lyricism in Berlioz, heroic exaltation in Weber and in Wagner; and always, always color, brimming over into the other arts which music can inspire and musical terms—analogies—supply.

Music had remained one of the least prestigious arts until the first representatives of romanticism became concerned with expressing feeling and dream rather than action and thought. "All music which depicts nothing is nothing but noise," d'Alembert had said, and his contemporaries found the art diverting when it did not try to do more than that. What music can do supremely well, however, is to express those things words cannot express, passions and sentiments that can hardly be depicted in rational terms. These were the very things romantics cared about, for whom rational activities could neither plumb nor express essentials, and for whom music—the limitless language of the unconscious and the unknown—was the idiom above all others.

The nineteenth century—especially its beginning—would be the age of the *virtuoso,* musical incarnation of romantic individualism, whose self-expression was facilitated by the piano's triumph over the more tinkly clavichord. There were virtuosos of the violin, like Kreutzer for whom Beethoven wrote the *Kreutzer Sonata* (and who never condescended to play it), or Paganini; and even virtuosos of brass instruments, like Sax, inventor of the saxophone. But the greatest lions were pianist-composers like Chopin and Liszt who, when they performed, evoked shrieks, faints, hysteria among their admirers, fits which Heinrich Heine attributed to "musical cantharides." The heroine of one of Stendhal's novels, living in a provincial town, missed only one thing from Paris: the music "which had the power of increasing in surprising fashion the intensity of her spells of reverie." A generation later, the wife of a Paris publisher spoke in a similar vein: "It is a terrible thing to hear Chopin: bourgeois life seems pretty tedious on the morrow . . . the ideal discourages real life."

Perhaps that was the intention. Certainly, as Baudelaire explained, the romantic artist set out to "create a suggestive magic, containing at the same time object and subject, the world outside the artist and the artist himself." If romanticism is a way of feeling, romantic art is the communication of that feeling as forcefully and as directly as it can be done. That was one reason why the theater of men like Victor Hugo and Alfred de Musset rebelled against the bulbous, convoluted "noble" style whose pompous monuments in prose and verse were turning early-nineteenth-century literature and theater into elusive puzzles.* Now, poetry on stage and page became, as Hugo called it, "a sonorous echo" of its author and of his sentiments, an echo that everyone could hear and feel.

Painting underwent a similar evolution. The art historian Marcel Brion has pointed out that an age of revolutions and great wars developed a new, more dramatic vision, new ways of feeling and of communicating feelings, a new interest in the tragic and unusual aspects of life, in tension, suffering, madness, darkness, death—as can be found in the paintings and engravings of Francisco Goya (1746–1828) or in the work of a much younger man, the Frenchman Théodore Géricault (1791–1824)

---

* Thus, in the poetry of a much-appreciated author of that day—Jacques Delille (1738–1813), an umbrella would be apostrophized: "Precious and supple structure of that ilk/That joins the arts of whalebones and of silk!" while a pig became "Cold celibate ill-suited for pleasure/Unwilling martyr to a table's measure."

The Raft of the Medusa, by Théodore Géricault. Louvre, Paris.

whose painting *The Raft of the Medusa* was based on interviews with survivors from a shipwreck and endless sketches of sickness and of corpses.

Since the Renaissance, painting had operated in the realm of measurable things and conformed to the rules of measure, with perspective, proportion, and form to govern its compositions. Now it would quit this ponderable ground for the realm of suggestion and suggestiveness, where what counts are moods and sentiments, not visible things but the intimate, the secret, the sensed. Not form but color, not realism but imagination, not tranquility but movement, would henceforth dominate; and the romantic artist led the way in the great nineteenth-century break out of reality into fantasy. It had been possible, the classic artists thought, to reproduce things objectively. Romantics disagreed. And were it possible, they said, it would not be nearly so interesting as the poetic vision of one given man—provided that he has a vision to impart.

Goethe contrasted and sought to reconcile *Dichtung und Wahrheit*—Truth and Poetry—implying that they are two different things. Art is a dream or, rather, its evocation, the resonance of a secret vision which hopes to evoke an echo in some beholder's soul. The images which the artist handles reach out to pluck the senses, not the mind. The painter pursuing "the suggestive magic" tries to combine color, light, and shade in such a way "that they go straight to the heart." These are the words of Eugène Delacroix (1798–1863), and one can see them come to life in the man's paintings. The work of Delacroix mirrors most of the concerns and passions of his time: the romantic fascination with suggestive heroes like Dr. Faustus or Hamlet and with Byronic characters, with the Middle Ages in his historical paintings, with the exotic and colorful and wild in his Moroccan and his hunting scenes, with philhellenism in his *Massacre of Chios,* with revolution in the famous *Liberty Leading the People* and *The Barricade,* finally the characteristic romantic yearning for the impossible in his last great fresco of Jacob's struggle with the angel. Movement, color, passion, vivid intensity and tragic vision, made Delacroix the greatest painter of his time.

The tide of fantasy and of imagination which we can see at its flood in Delacroix must not make us overlook a parallel directness and simplicity. The romantics looked around them with their eyes wide open; and their revolt stemmed from the things they saw: hypocrisy, injustice, ugliness, against which they fulminated—shouting so loud because most people would not lend an ear. Southey denounced the way in which "men and beasts are considered mainly as machines;" and Coleridge pointed out that "national wealth . . . is national only in statistical tables," and asked that "even for patriotic purposes no person should be treated as a thing." Hugo described "that people which works and suffers" and which no one, after his *Misérables,* could any more ignore. The growing interest in historical sources, in sagas, folk songs, ballads, spawned the historical novels of Walter Scott and the historical chronicles of Augustin Thierry (at one time personal secretary of Saint-Simon).

Colorful, heroic, lyrical, resurrecting a romantic version of the national past, such works could not fail to draw attention to the people, the folk, fount of national energy, generous, laborious, pure, from whose depths alone regeneration was to be expected, and yet oppressed, degraded, driven to destruction by forces which, in weakening the people, weakened the nation too. In 1820, Augustin Thierry had called for a history not of kings and heroes but of citizens and subjects: of the people. In 1837 Thomas Carlyle's *French Revolution* provided such a book, where events in street and workshops and before the hearth were in the foreground of the action. At last, in 1846, Jules Michelet's *The People* raised a paean to their essential role.

One can refer to a romantic populism, deeply connected with their interest in the nation and in national sources; or a romantic nationalism, arising out of their historical self-consciousness. It may not be far-fetched to see in this a logical outcome of that relativism which the eighteenth century did not exactly discover but at least made public. The great romantic exercise is history, the chronicle of change and its continuous proof, vulgar or academic, vicariously exciting and frequently unsettling—in opera, in painting, in literature, even in philosophy where, for Kant and Hegel, consciousness develops in time. History is, like music, the art of time and change. It now became the great exponent of those diversities of experience which lie behind the variety they stress: variety of regions and of nations, languages and traditions, folklores and laws, justifying not only present differences but future change as well, a promise to some and a threat to others.

New Public and New Culture

Education

By the eighteenth century, the traditional seats of learning had become quiet harbors for fossils of a former age. Despite occasional flashes of life, the older German and Italian universities were decaying; the Sorbonne in Paris was the Gibraltar of anachronism; Oxford and Cambridge, the homes of "ignorance in stilts" as Cowper, the poet, called it. Gibbon records his recollection of mid-eighteenth-century Oxford: "I spent fourteen months at Magdalen College; they proved the fourteen months the most idle and unprofitable of my whole life." The Fellows were "decent easy men, who supinely enjoyed the gifts of the founders . . . From the toil of reading, or thinking, or writing, they had absolved their consciences."

True, while the old universities decayed, new colleges were being founded in America and new universities in Europe, designed to carry forward the spirit of Enlightenment: Yale (1701), Göttingen (1734), St. Petersburg (1747), Moscow (1755); while at Halle and Leipzig teaching methods were reformed under the influence of a disciple of Leibniz, Christian Wolff (1679–1754), professor of mathematics and physics, which were the typical sciences of the modern age. The new curricula, still strongly based in classics, now also emphasized mathematics and philosophy, learning by thinking as well as by mere rote. But change came only slowly. Göttingen provided understanding and a home for scientific studies, but it remained exceptional for quite a while. At Innsbruck, in 1740, the university refused to set up a professorship in botany and chemistry, which could be studied quite well in apothecary shops; at Erlangen the professor of chemistry had to set up his own laboratory at home, in order to provide the practical instruction his university spurned.

At last, in 1810, the Leibniz-Wolff tradition would find embodiment in the University of Berlin, whose courses were designed not just to pass on knowledge but to develop the student's mind, train him for life, prepare a grounding from which he could develop any specialization he might later need. Above all, Berlin held out the ideal of a school where students were free to pursue learning and teachers to impart it as they thought best. Unfortunately, this was easier said than done; especially since the university was dependent on the state and on its vagaries.

Meanwhile, through most of the eighteenth century, men interested in the new ideas were pursuing them in academies, clubs, and coffeehouses,

278

rather than in schools. In Britain, while universities ossified and the upper classes turned to the local vicar or to private tutors, the middle classes found the most useful education in the Dissenting Academies founded in the provinces to train nonconformist ministers and to give laymen "some knowledge . . . in the more useful branches of literature, and to lead them to an early acquaintance with and just concern for the true principles of religion and liberty." Clearly, religious and political dissent were bound to combine. It was in the Dissenting Academies in the 1760's that history and English literature were first treated as regular academic disciplines, along with natural history, science, and living languages. The Scottish universities also, close-linked with civic life, heeded the changing world which the richly endowed colleges of Oxford and Cambridge could afford to ignore. Professors applied their knowledge to worldly needs, sought to solve the problems of the linen industry or, like Adam Smith, professor of moral philosophy in the University of Glasgow, analyzed industrial civilization, labor, and production in lectures which would furnish the basis for his *Wealth of Nations.*

At last, in 1828, the influence of Scotland, of Berlin, of Jefferson's new University of Virginia (1819), which offered a wide curriculum and a liberal education, led to the foundation of University College, London, designed to serve "the middling rich," as its sponsors (Bentham, Priestley, Mill—himself an Edinburgh graduate), put it, who were aspiring to a more modern world and a more modern education.* Opposed by the establishment as the "Godless college," part of the philosophical radicals' campaign to "overthrow altar and throne," University College was only officially recognized in 1846 as part of the new University of London, alongside King's College, which had been founded in opposition to it

* Indeed, aspiring to be educated at all; for Jews, Catholics, and Dissenters were still at this time excluded from Oxford and Cambridge.

University College, London, as it appeared in the early nineteenth century.

279

by friends of King and church. Meanwhile, Durham University had also been founded, and a college for Wales as well—St. David's, Lampeter.

At lower levels, too, changes had taken place. The lower schools had long concentrated on inculcating knowledge by rote learning. Since children were held to be weak in judgment, it was thought best to fill them with facts rather than understanding until they went to college. In the late sixteenth and in the seventeenth century, a number of educational reformers had moved away from this insistence on memory and appealed to the students' intelligence. Jesuit educators and Protestant grammarians came to think that learning was best related to reality, lectures enlivened by example and anecdote, rules placed in the context of their application, with examples drawn from literature and life. Texts were still learned by heart, but they were also explained; classical authors were still parsed but they were also illuminated by connecting them with the experience of the students; mathematics and natural sciences were considered increasingly relevant.

The eighteenth century brought further reforms. If, as the philosophers thought, man is what he makes of his experience, the way to make him better is to expose him to better experiences. *Émile* had argued that children should be allowed to develop freely, and learn as much as possible from experience. A Swiss teacher, Johann Heinrich Pestalozzi (1746–1827), set up an experimental school to apply these theories, educate children for life rather than pump them full of knowledge, turn out not trained puppets and regurgitators of set formulae but good citizens, whose freedom from constraint would also free them from the rebelliousness arising from repression. In 1837 an admirer of Pestalozzi, the Prussian Friedrich Froebel (1782–1852), would pioneer the education of smaller children, and found the first Kindergarten. A German follower of Rousseau, Johann Basedow (1724?–1790), attempted to put his views in practice in the 1770's in an experimental college founded at Dessau. His *Philantropinum* was coeducational, residential, and progressive, abandoning wigs and awkward clothes for sensible garb and country walks and river bathing, trying to teach *real* things—languages, sciences, skills—in lively fashion. *Realschulen* spread through Germany as far as Russia and, leaving their mark on German upper schools whose excellence the nineteenth century admired, helped to make Germany "the classic land of barracks and of schools."

All this, of course, served only the upper classes and "the middling rich." Enlightened men, who talked a great deal about education, were chiefly interested in universities and secondary schools. Voltaire, who wanted education to enlarge the middle class, did not wish it to change the common people who, if educated, would not want to carry out the difficult and unpleasant labors that someone must perform. Napoleon created a grandiose public education system, but one which stressed discipline and higher education—the lower classes being better off without much learning. By 1814 France boasted 36 *lycées* with 9,000 inmates, largely the sons of middle- and upper-class families, whose day began and ended to the sound of a drum. But there were fewer village schools than under the old regime. The career open to all talents was evidently still some way off. The Austrian Empire had free and compulsory education, with probably the worst-paid teachers anywhere but nevertheless providing a great opportunity for bright farmers' sons in lands where, to get married, men had to show an elementary-school certificate; and high schools took the better elementary graduates tuition-free, letting the parents pay their board in kind. Many students at Vienna University, too, were poor and attended free, living on a pittance. The nobles had tutors at home or went to a special nobles' academy for the army and the diplomatic corps called the *Theresianum*.

But, really, outside a few countries like Austria and Denmark, the problem of the illiterate masses was hardly being touched. In France a royal ordinance of 1816 enjoined every commune to educate all children. But it did not work. In 1821 France boasted 28,000 primary schools, in 1829, 30,000; but of the 39,000 communes in the country nearly half had no primary school at all and of a hundred conscripts only forty-two were found able to read; among twenty-five million adults fifteen million could not read. Nevertheless, the number of those who could read and write was steadily increasing. In the hundred years before the Revolution, it had grown by 18 per cent for men and 13 per cent for women; and it would grow better than twice as fast in the three-score years that followed. Education had always been the concern of Christian churches, and where these existed, priests, monks, and nuns continued to furnish a majority of teachers. But teachers were scarce, perhaps because they were so ill-paid, and various schemes attempted to make up for it: in Sunday schools, launched in the eighteenth century by Robert Raikes of Gloucester; or in the monitorial system devised by Joseph Lancaster (1778–1838), which used more advanced students to drill the younger ones in the rudiments of reading, writing, and arithmetic, thus enabling large numbers to be trained in economical fashion.

But education for the poor was looked on with suspicion. The Sunday School Union, founded in 1785, argued that Sunday schools would produce "orderly and decent comportment." Their critics rejoined that education would refine and innervate, disqualifying its recipients "for the duties of a humble station." Pioneers like Hannah More, the "Bishop in petticoats" of the Clapham Sect (see p. 498), had to reassure themselves and the propertied classes that their little charges were not being brought up to be Jacobins. They certainly ran little risk of it under Miss More's tutelage where, as she wrote in 1801, "they learn on weekdays such coarse work as may fit them to be servants. I allow of no writing for the poor."

Actually, education would have advanced faster if it had not got caught up in endless and bitter religious arguments. In England the Royal Lancasterian Association of 1810 had to be matched by a National Society for the Education of the Poor in the Principles of the Established Church in 1811. In other countries, too, clergy and anticlericals, church and chapel, tugged at the schools and students until learning itself fell out.

Yet, even so, more poor learned how to read. In the 1780's and 90's already, corresponding societies were gathering together artisans, laborers, small tradesmen, who wanted to spread knowledge among their own kind: "To enlighten the people, to show the people the reason, the ground of all their complaints and sufferings." The workers taught themselves in their own adult and infant Sunday schools, which taught not only reading and writing, but also hatred "of our corrupt and tyrannical rulers." They taught themselves at home, using nearly 120,000 copies of Cobbett's *Grammar of the English Language* between 1818 and 1833. Many remained ignorant, like the arrested English rebels who thought a provisional government was one to give them more provisions, or the pitmen who thought universal suffrage meant a kind of suffering in common. Nevertheless, some two out of three workingmen in England could read in some fashion, although fewer could write. Many bought and more read pamphlets and papers like Cobbett's *Twopenny Register,* which sold 40- to 60,000 copies a week, or the *Black Dwarf,* which sold 12- or 13,000. By 1840 French workers had their own newspaper, written and run by workmen like themselves and called *The Workshop.* A broader literate public was appearing. True, literacy and education, advancing fast among the middle classes and skilled artisans, were forging ahead more slowly in the lower classes, painfully slowly in the countryside; but the scale of the new reading public was incomparably greater than it had ever been, and this reflected on the trades which provided its supplies.

The Writing Trade

Traditionally writers, like artists, had always depended on the support of patrons drawn from the church, the court, or the nobility. Art by itself did not nourish its man, unless a patron helped him. Ben Jonson had complained that poetry beggared him, and many could say as much. By mid-seventeenth century opportunities appeared to gain security by entering public service. John Milton was Latin Secretary under the Commonwealth, Andrew Marvel gave up a post as private tutor to become Milton's assistant, Dryden was secretary of Cromwell's chamberlain, Pepys entered the civil service before the Restoration and continued in it until 1688. Thereafter, English literary men did even better: Matthew Prior was appointed ambassador; Addison became secretary of state and married the dowager Countess of Warwick; Steele became a member of

Parliament, and so did Sheridan and a dozen others. Pope of course held court at Twickenham:

> Above a patron, though I condescend
> Sometimes to call a minister my friend.

In eighteenth-century France, as we may guess, the prestige of literary figures was also growing. Ocean-going ships were being named for Rousseau, Voltaire, and d'Alembert; and a contemporary observer could declare that three qualifications were needed for social success: birth, wealth, and literary talent. The second qualification was new enough as a social factor; the third was a revolutionary novelty. Yet, probably, the estimate of literary talent was not unconnected with whatever wealth its success could bring.

With illiteracy shrinking, the reading public grew and so did the size of editions of new books. Authors gradually freed themselves from private patronage, first in England, where successful authors could earn really large sums, then in France, and slowly gained economic independence. Milton received £10 for *Paradise Lost;* Matthew Prior, who died fifty years after Milton, got 4,000 guineas for his collected poems. The revenues of most continued to be modest, and men like Diderot still depended on help from generous patrons like Catherine the Great, while Rousseau who tried his best to stay independent by copying sheets of music or herborizing, had to accept the aid of his well-meaning friends.

Part of the problem lay in pirated editions, which made money for publishers but brought the authors nothing. This did not come to an end in· France until the Revolution, which, in 1793, brought a Conventional decree vesting control of all writings, compositions, and works of art in their creators for their lifetime. The property of playwrights in their plays, which had been pirated just as often, had been established in 1791 by the Constituent Assembly.

Another difficulty was simply that books were costly, and many people got theirs from lending libraries and reading rooms which flourished everywhere. We have a picture of such a library in Paris of the 1780's, whose author sensibly observes that the most worn books are those in greatest demand: "Those works which describe the manners, which are simple, naïve, and touching, which are not affected or arrogant and use no academic jargon, these are the ones that people come to get from all quarters of the town . . ." And "there are works which cause such a ferment that the book dealer is forced to cut the volume in three to answer the eagerness of the numerous readers; and then you pay not by the day, but by the hour . . ." In Germany around 1780 circulating libraries catered to craftsmen and soldiers, as well as to the better-off. By 1806, a German journalist noted that reading, once the preserve of scholars, had become a general habit, "even of the lower classes, not only in the towns but in the country too."

Among the things found in reading rooms were papers and periodicals, whose number also increased so that they, and the works of reference and popularization now in great demand, furnished an important source of income to struggling authors. Dictionaries, encyclopedias, grammars, would pay the rent; reviews and articles in a journal could bring in something too; but popular fame could be acquired most quickly with a successful play. The broadening interest in literature, the greater numbers of the literate, were reflected in the theater-going public. After mid-eighteenth century this grew to include not only the cultivated middle class—lawyers and school-masters, writers and members of the liberal professions—but footmen and barbers, porters and shop assistants, the livelier representatives of the lower classes who had presumably picked up a taste for plays and literature in their employers' houses and in reading rooms.

Hack work of every kind could still be supplemented by pensions, sinecures, and grants from official sources. But the strongest support for professional writers, their best source of employment, came from the growing press. Newspapers and periodicals seem to arise from old-fashioned almanacs and calendars, which became biannual in the sixteenth century, for sale at fairs, and then monthly or even weekly in the seventeenth century, as numerous cities began to publish bulletins of news. Such publications appeared first in the great Italian cities of the sixteenth century, where professional newsmen provided selected subscribers with regular newsletters based on information gathered in local inns, banks, and antechambers.

From a subscription business, the bulletins became an open trade, beginning to be sold in the city streets. In Rome their producers were called *novellanti* (newsmen) or *menanti* (drivers or leaders) because, as the Venetian ambassador explained, "They lead opinion." They were already attacked for being liars with no respect for the authorities or God, and in 1629 Ben Jonson's play *The Staple of News* satirized their exploitation of public credulity. By that date the press had aroused two of its constant concomitants: official repression on the part of governments suspicious or resentful of its influence, official patronage from similar sources eager to gain publicity for their ends.

Where the Inquisition did not undertake the task, the state controlled booksellers and printers (often the same men), trying to limit their numbers in order to facilitate surveillance. In mid-seventeenth-century France, salaried royal censors were appointed to carry this out independent of the Sorbonne and parlements. A century later there were four-score of them and by 1789 they numbered 178. Between 1667 and 1676, the number of printer-booksellers in Paris fell from 84 to 36: still more than the 20 printers authorized in London. There, after 1660, rigid censorship had been re-established and only one government

An ad appearing in the first issue of the *Illustrated London News,* May 14, 1842.

news-sheet was allowed to appear. Any other, as the editor of the government publication explained, "makes the multitude too familiar with the actions and councils of their superiors."

This remained the crux of the matter even when censorship disappeared in the 1690's and England joined those rare lands like Holland where the press was relatively free. The problem of keeping the news from the multitude was solved by stamp duties which raised prices, kept circulation low, and made the press dependent on handouts and subsidies. These the political parties and especially the government managed either directly or indirectly by taking out advertisements in friendly papers or buying large numbers of their copies for free distribution.

Daily papers were beginning to appear: the first in London in 1702. Paris and Philadelphia followed in 1777 and 1783 respectively. But daily newspapers depended on a concentrated buying public which only some big cities could provide, and on possibilities of regular distribution, and these were not available throughout most of Europe until postal services improved with the nineteenth century. Periodicals were more successful, like Defoe's *Review* (in which *Robinson Crusoe* provided the first serial novel) or Addison and Steele's *Tatler* (1709) and *Spectator* (1711), or the *Mercure de France* (1798), providing literary, political, and social comments; or then, again, like the *Monthly Gentlemen's Magazine* (1731), accounts of Parliamentary debates disguised as reports from Lilliput. Beside these, a myriad of pamphlets and flysheets would spring up written for plain folk who could read and pay their penny, and out of which many a workman's child would be taught to read. Despite all the attempts to muzzle it, the English press enjoyed increasing freedom. This would come on the continent but slowly, even the Revolution opening the gates only briefly before Napoleon slammed them shut again, not to reopen for several decades.

But even while the free press languished, the popular press grew, enjoying the advantages of new technology. Paper from rags was dear and growing scarcer. In the late eighteenth century, its manufacture from wood pulp had been proved possible and large-scale manufacture

285

began by the time of the Restoration. Printing processes were revolutionized when, in 1814, the London *Times* introduced printing machines—
devised by a German, Koenig—which printed 1,100 sheets an hour,
eventually increased to 7,000. Koenig's machines were soon installed in
Paris and Berlin. Other technical advances permitted the publication of
illustrated papers (the *Illustrated London News* in 1842, *l'Illustration*
of Paris in 1843), which appealed to many families not interested in the
political, literary, commercial, or society news of the regular periodicals.
Illustrations could also mean satire and caricature, which were much in
vogue in the 1830's and 1840's; especially the political and social satire
of weeklies like *Charivari* founded in 1832 and much in demand for the
drawings of Daumier and Gavarni, of *Punch* founded in 1841, or the
Fliegende Blätter (1844).

The French electoral law of 1831 doubled the number of electors;
the British reform of 1832 introduced the petty bourgeoisie to political
life; primary schools were spreading skills and disciplines in Prussia
and Switzerland, England and France. A new reading public was growing, which the press attempted to attract. But taxes and production
costs still put the papers beyond the reach of poorer men. In the late
1830's, Émile de Girardin cut the cost in half by relying on publicity;
and the 38,000 subscribers of his *Siècle* almost equaled the combined
sales of all the London dailies, which came to 40,000 in 1829. In 1833
the *New York Sun* had launched the daily at two cents, which gave it
by 1835 greater sales than the London *Times*. That year Gordon Bennett published the *Morning Herald,* triumph of popular sensationalism,
which printed 33,000 copies in 1849. Freed of stifling duties only in the
1850's, the London press would take longer to grow. The penny press
was born in 1855 with the *Daily Telegraph,* selling at the equivalent
of the *Sun's* two cents or the *Siècle's* subscription price. By 1855, the
Times, which printed 17,000 twenty years before, was selling 60,000.

Interestingly, the attraction of popular papers differed in different
lands. In France, sales went up through serials on whose adventures the
public hung. Balzac, George Sand, Alexandre Dumas, brought thousands
of subscribers to the papers; above all was Eugène Sue, whose serials
were devoured by tens of thousands. His *Mysteries of Paris* would be
translated and then copied by many German papers eager to attract new
readers, to such an extent that thirty-six varieties of *Mysteries* were published in Germany in 1844 alone. Indifferent to politics, the European
reader could be caught by love and adventure stories. The Americans
cared little for literature, even of the most vulgar kind. The *Sun* or
Herald offered a diet of human interest stories, "true facts," crimes, city
news, and family tragedies. With all their differences, newspapers now
appealed no longer to a small elite but to all those who could read.
The unrefined public which they tapped was wooed with rough, attrac-

tive fare fitted for simple minds and simple people; and this is what it has remained since then.

Publicity is to business what steam is to machines, said Lord Macaulay. It certainly was that to newspapers, which had to provide ever more pages at an ever smaller price. Production costs could not be covered by income from sales without increasing the price and thus reducing sales; the answer to this was found in advertising income, which could cover the deficits. And advertising became one of the great forces which maintained and influenced the press.

Better roads, then better railroads, meant that newspapers could be carried and sold over a wider area. They also meant, along with the new electric telegraph, that news could travel further and faster. In November, 1847, Queen Victoria's speech at the opening of Parliament was telegraphed in full. The great newspapers set up correspondents and messenger services all over the world. News agencies were founded, first in Paris by Garnier and Charles Havas in 1832,* then by Julius Reuter, who settled in London in 1851 having learned his trade with Havas, and by Bernhard Wolff in Berlin.

Men still contended that all this paper was only devoted to telling public lies in private causes. Many felt what a Balzac character expressed: "All newspapers are cowardly, hypocritical, infamous, lying, murderous; they will kill ideas, systems, men, and flourish on it." Perhaps. But the same could have been said just as easily about mankind. For better or for worse, a great new social force had taken shape.

The Public Arts

The interaction between a changing public and its purveyors which is so evident in the written word also appears in other fields. Despite a diversity of tastes that henceforth increased diversity of forms up to the eclecticism of the twentieth century, music—like painting, literature, and architecture—proceeded to reflect the subordination of classical lines to the pictorial element, the anecdote or the subjective feeling dear to the romantics. To begin with, opera particularly, with its vast productions, remained in the eighteenth century a luxury of the rich, especially of the courts and narrow cultivated circles of refined connoisseurs for whose expert delight servant-composers labored. Public performances appear more like leftovers from the royal board, unless they are organized for some special festivity or religious occasion, such as the concerts of religious music that one could hear at Christmas or in Lent. As the eighteenth century drew on, however, more and more cities set up permanent

---

* In 1840, Havas scooped the news market by organizing a carrier-pigeon service between Paris, London, and Brussels. America got its first news agency when the Associated Press was set up in New York in 1856.

287

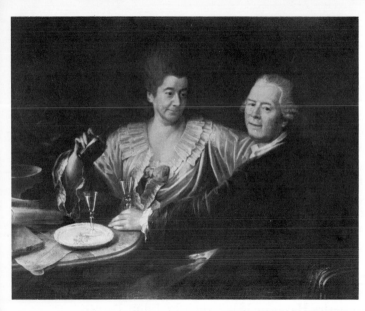

C. W. Gluck and His Wife. Historisches Museum der Stadt Wien.

music societies with concert halls of their own, and musicians found that they had a choice between hiring themselves out to private patrons or to a less-exalted public and one whose expectations were quite different.

Both Johann Sebastian Bach (1685–1750) and George Frederick Handel (1685–1759) may be said to have written music for the select, their tonal architecture directly related to emotional, philosophical, and mystical values, their musical dramas full of psychological characterization expressed in melody. This, along with a lot of picturesque ornament and design and an architectural magnificence dear to their age, made for a rich kind of stateliness that can be compared with the dresses, the wigs, and buildings of their day. Then, in middle life, Handel turned from writing operas for the entertainment of his royal and aristocratic patrons to oratorios for a soulful and unsubtle middle class: "What the English like is something they can beat time to," Handel told Gluck. He gave them the vigorous, unsubtle, and often-rollicking oratorios which many could sing and all, even Philistines, can still enjoy. Frivolous or mythological themes had been abandoned for Biblical ones; a rich, capricious public for a sober, solid one. The same might be said of Franz Joseph Haydn, whose sparkling classsicism in the service of the great magnate family of Esterhazy shifted into a more accessible, less rigorous key in the London symphonies he wrote in the 1780's.

In the second half of the eighteenth century, the rococo which had begun in exuberance and fantasy was drying into vulgar sentimentalism. The change can be seen in painting between Boucher and Greuze. In music, the same drift from frivolity to simplicity meant that more complex earlier forms were abandoned for melodic effects that would please a less refined public, more interested in melody and tonal color than in structural elegance.

However, the eighteenth century was also the age of enlightened philosophers who were, as we know, much interested in music, in its reform, in its return (like society's) to "nature" under the example of antiquity. Their great musical ally and exponent was C. W. Gluck (1714–1787), who had begun by writing operas in the Italian manner, or smaller ones full of rococo charm. In 1762, with *Orfeus and Eurydice,* Gluck abandoned this ornamented manner for a more sober style aimed at the sort of antique purity which Lessing's *Laocoön* had recommended. His clarity and logic, the correspondence of words and sounds in the tunes he wrote, reflected the philosophy of the encyclopedists and the plastic ideals of Greek art. Maria Luigi Cherubini (1760–1842) continued the heroic opera style of Gluck, which he adapted to the revolutionary spirit of the 1790's. Cherubini dealt realistically with people—with *the* people—now being taken seriously for the first time, with violent death, and fear, and rescue from danger, and relief at escaping them, along with the concomitant joy.

As the Revolution habituated people to crowd participation in hymns and ceremonies, often propagandistic, opera too became increasingly grand. Soon, the emotional expressionism which Gluck played down, the use of instrumental tone color, the adaptation of heroism to patriotic rather than classical themes, would appear in the operas of Karl Maria von Weber (1786–1826), whose *Freischütz* in 1820 revealed the triumph of national sentiment along with the possibilities of romantic opera.* Weber was the director of the "German" opera at Dresden, in which Wagner's adoptive father sang the tenor roles; and when in 1844 Weber's body was brought back from London where he had died to be reinterred at Dresden, it would be Richard Wagner (1813–1883), then the conductor of the city opera, who composed the funeral march for the occasion. By that time Wagner, who scored his first successes with *Rienzi* (1842) and *The Flying Dutchman* (1843), was refusing to make any concessions to the public taste; and his *Tannhäuser* (1845), with its long recitatives, was not very well received. Increasingly disgusted with the Philistines who did not appreciate the complex web of sound in which he tried to weave the heretofore-distinct elements of the operatic pattern, Wagner drifted into radical politics, ended up on the barricades of 1849, and had to flee Dresden to exile and to fame.

We notice here how quickly the artist working for a patron had become first a caterer to the public and then a creator looking to himself alone, if need be at odds with conservative music publishers and slow-moving public taste. Beethoven had already seen himself not as a mere

---

* Similar patriotic concerns, combined with respect for the national past, led to the rediscovery of idioms quite different from the composers' own. It was romantic musicologists who revived the works of Palestrina, Protestant church music, and old Dutch music; it would be Felix Mendelssohn who discovered and first performed in Berlin (1829) Bach's *St. Matthew Passion.*

entertainer, but as the priest and officiant of a new cult (especially in the *Ninth Symphony,* first performed in 1824), whose ideas music carried better than words could do. The late quartets of Beethoven or the songs of Schubert were the beginning of a new tradition, which Gustav Mahler articulated at a later time when claiming that he composed not for his contemporaries but for posterity.

And yet, of course, no artist however stubborn can escape his time. Some do not wish to do so. Thus, Rossini's *William Tell,* first produced at the Paris Opera in August, 1829, was a deliberate appeal to current nationalistic ideas, a fact which nowise affected Rossini's credit at the Court of Charles X. In the next few years, the inclusion of his opera in the repertory of other European theaters posed significant problems: in Milan, the Austrian censorship had the Swiss patriot turned into a Scotsman—William Wallace—and Austrians to Englishmen. In Rome, papal censorship turned William Tell into Rudolph of Sterling and filled the lyrics with pious references. In Prussia, William Tell became Andreas Hoffer, a hero of the Tyrolean insurrection against Napoleon's French; in Russia, he became Charles the Bold of Burgundy. In Vienna alone of all reactionary capitals Rossini's libretto was left unmauled, the public shouting "Long live the Habsburgs!" after every performance, thus reassuring a lenient government. Yet, even Rossini, who lived for nearly two-score years after *William Tell* had triumphed, wrote scarcely anything thereafter, a strange self-censorship which may be explained by the words he wrote a friend shortly before his death: "This art of music which is based solely on sentiment and ideals, cannot escape the influence of the times we live in, and the sentiment and ideals of the present day are wholly concerned with steam, rapine and barricades."

The story of the theater is somewhat similar. Much seventeenth-century drama had been either stilted and unreal, or else licentious: abetting cynicism, adultery, and deception to such an extent that in 1719 a reforming chaplain conclusively demonstrated that the plays of his time offended a minimum of 1,400 Bible texts. Then came John Gay's *Beggar's Opera* (1728) and George Lillo's *London Merchant,* which ushered real life onto the distant stage. Gay's play took London by storm, running for sixty-three days—a record at the time. Everyone assumed that Gay's rogue-hero, MacHeath, was a portrait of Walpole and delighted in a social satire whose protagonists were footpads, fences, and prostitutes. Lillo's play allowed a middle-class hero—and an apprentice at that—to glory in the kind of tragic ending which had hitherto been reserved exclusively for nobles. Both represented "vulgar" subjects with humor and vitality, using a language which sounded forceful—at least by its novelty.

All this time stage lighting, scenery, stage effects, were improving: dividing the stage from the audience more effectively and thus perfecting the possibilities of illusion, allowing the theater to become more realistic and, in a sense, less theatrical. This lent itself increasingly to social satire,

The first page of *The Beggar's Opera,* by John Gay.

such as the comedies which Sheridan or Beaumarchais provided, or to plays of manners which paralleled the novels of the time. Since sober people still abstained from the theater during most of the eighteenth century, or were deprived of its pleasures by lack of means, the latter mode was more apparent in books than in plays and it is there that we most clearly see the change in mood that marks the 1740's. Frivolousness and cynicism retreated; virtue and sentiment, prudence and morality, must now serve the sentiments, the conscience, the prurience of a new kind of public.

It was for these people who suspected elegance, distrusted the other classes, and indulged their own emotions that Samuel Richardson (1689–1761), a printer's devil who eventually married his master's widow, began to write the model letters from which readers could learn style and manners. By 1740, the letter-writing manual had become *Pamela, Or Virtue Rewarded,* the prototype of a thousand romances in which the prudent poor girl gets the seducer in the end. Then, after *Pamela,* came *Clarissa Harlowe,* which Alfred de Musset considered the first novel in the world and which was avidly read by men like Goethe and Diderot. After that, there was no stopping the cult of broken hearts, of pathos, and moralizing.

But *Pamela* evoked a counterblast in *Shamela,* where Henry Fielding (1707–1754) exposed those hypocrisies that Richardson glorified. Fielding abandoned the rather primitive letter-writing convention for a straightforward and exuberant narrative that makes him the real father of the English novel. Fortunately, his technical skill was complemented by wit and by sympathetic knowledge of human nature. In works like *Joseph Andrews* (1742) and *Tom Jones* (1749), Fielding's shrewd and forthright humor sketched out a world whose humanity goes far beyond the platitudes of Richardson, and proved that self-delusion need not necessarily set the pattern of modern fiction.

The plastic arts, too, underwent similar changes, built up new structures adapted to different social conditions, adopted themes suited to new attitudes, and methods devised to reach a broader public. There had been no museums, no galleries, no exhibitions, before the seventeenth century. To see real paintings, usually, one had to gain admittance to private collections; to sell them one had to hang them in a tavern or attract buyers to one's home—a more likely method of getting an order from a rich patron. In France alone there existed since Louis XIV the Academy of Fine Arts with its drawing school, its scholarships for study abroad, its annual exhibition: the *salon*. In England, the first public exhibition dates back only to 1760, the Royal Academy of Art to 1768.

The growing prosperity of the middle classes meant a new art public, unversed or uninterested in mythological themes but rather, like the seventeenth-century Dutch, in more familiar subjects. And so, perhaps by way of England, the great materialistic tradition of the Dutch came back into its own, the intimacy of everyday scenes, the pleasures of family life, the solid quality of humble objects, lived again in the canvases of Pietro Longhi, of Sir Henry Raeburn and of Sir Joshua Reynolds, above all in the work of Jean Baptiste Chardin (1699–1779), the most concrete and dignified observer of reality. Yet intimate realism could drift into sentimentalism, as it did with Greuze, or into academicism, which preached the use of ideal forms to express moral sentiments. Thus, Reynolds painted *The Triumph of Truth* (1774), in which a professor refutes Hume, Gibbon, and Voltaire, and other edifying painters limned every sort of virtue to the edification of respectable art patrons. The man who built a bridge between the solemn and expensive horrors committed in academies and cheaper but equally moralistic products for a more general public was William Hogarth (1697–1764).

Hogarth appealed to middle-class tastes and pockets against the tyranny of aristocratic patrons and connoisseurs. He turned his paintings into prints, put the prints up for subscription and lottery, demonstrated that artists, like writers, could find an alternative source of income, found that engravings could be pirated in a way that paintings were unlikely to be, and, to defend his property, fought for and obtained legal protection for the result of artistic invention—a copyright law, Hogarth's Act. Against the tyranny of fashionable taste, Hogarth set out to prove that pictures can be legible, reviving a cartoon technique that anyone could follow without classical references; and the crudeness which put

Marriage à la Mode: The Contract, by William Hogarth. National Gallery, London.

off the elegant attracted the common people, who gaped and commented at his works exhibited in shop windows.

Hogarth's work inspired many of the great English novelists—especially Fielding—and it has left us with the richest picture book of his age. Thereafter, images multiplied, first by the invention of lithography in Germany (1798), which greatly simplified reproduction and permitted the illustration of books, periodicals, and the printing of separate pictures like Daumier's; and then in 1839 by the photograph, soon to be perfected by two Frenchmen—Niepce and Daguerre. The arrival of color and decoration for walls which had for centuries stayed bare might well have outweighed the shoddy wares they spread.

True, the appearance of a new mass public meant on the whole the triumph of the senses over the mind, of vulgarity over refinement, of show over taste. It was just because Paris had a large theater-and opera-going public that its plays and operas were so often third-rate, seeking the level of that larger public to which they must appeal, that Dumas triumphed on the boulevards and Donizetti, Bellini, Auber on the musical stage, that Rossini was preferred to Mozart and Meyerbeer to Berlioz, that Wagner was laughed off the stage for refusing to place a ballet where dandies late from dinner could enjoy it. Music like art was an amusement, a decoration.

Yet other things became available. There was, increasingly a *choice*— a choice for more and more people. The theater based on box office remained sporadic or uncertain, the literature grew florid and diffuse, painting conformist and all too often dreary. Yet the vogue of amateur theatricals, like that of chamber music, like that of water colors, could spread to bourgeois homes. Once the preserve and practice of the very few, the arts were becoming public before they became popular.

With few exceptions, the seventeenth-century art public had still been restricted to the court and church, the very noble or the very rich. By the nineteenth century, municipal theaters, opera houses, and museums were making art available to the middling classes: first steps in a process leading from Molière's *Bourgeois Gentilhomme* to H. G. Wells' Mr. Kipps, the little clerk avid for culture, which he considers a part and perhaps a path of social promotion.

As the nineteenth century opened, most poets, artists, writers, stemmed from upper reaches of society. The age of private enterprise was also the age of private incomes and, in their shade, creativeness—which sometimes wilted—also put forth astonishing blooms. Ingres and Delacroix, at logger-heads about the way to paint, were free to wield their brushes as they pleased: both greatly. Gustave Flaubert (1821–1880) would never have developed his literary talent without the solid family fortune on which he lived. Nor would Charles Baudelaire (1821–1867), whom we shall meet again, who bore his poems while squandering his father's legacy.

Yet, by the 1840's already, many aspiring artists were of humbler extraction: offspring of tanners, artisans, small shopkeepers, minor employees. Henri Murger (1822–1861), who in 1845 began to sketch their world in his *Scenes of Bohemian Life,* was the son of a janitor who doubled as a tailor; the father of Champfleury, founder of the realist school in French literature, was a provincial town-hall clerk; Courbet, the painter, was of peasant origin. A private income was no longer a necessity. In the arts, as in contemporary commerce, a greater public, a wider market, afforded more variety and greater options: in style, but in content too; for the buyer, but for the purveyor as well, free(r) to pursue inspiration, fantasy, or profit, to react against fashions and conditions or to accept them. And all of this reflected a diversified world where opportunity and insecurity went hand in hand.

PART II

The Age of Masses

1848 to the Present

EUROPE · 1848 to 1914

POPULATION INCREASES
BY PERCENTAGE, 1850–1910

5–10
10–25
25–50
50–75
75–100

URBAN POPULATIONS
IN THOUSANDS OF PERSONS

1870   1914

50–100
100–250
250–500
500–750
750–1 million
1–2 million
2–4 million
More than 4 million

Revolutions of 1848

Boundary of the German
Confederation, 1848

BLACK SEA

OTTOMAN EMPIRE

AEGEAN SEA

CYPRUS

CRETE

GREECE

ADRIATIC SEA

MONTENEGRO

MEDITERRANEAN SEA

TRIPOLI

TUNISIA

ALGERIA

MOROCCO

St. Petersburg

Riga

Kiev

RUSSIA

Warsaw

Łódź

POLAND

Danzig

PRUSSIA

Berlin

Dresden

Chemnitz

Leipzig

Nürnberg

Prague

BOHEMIA

Budapest

Vienna

AUSTRIA–HUNGARY

Stockholm

SWEDEN

NORWAY

Oslo

Copenhagen

DENMARK

BALTIC SEA

NORTH SEA

Hamburg

Hanover

Cologne

Frankfurt

BAVARIA

Munich

Stuttgart

LUX.

NETH.

Amsterdam

Rotterdam

Antwerp

Brussels

BELG.

SWITZ.

TYROL

PIEDMONT

Turin

Milan

Venice

TUSCANY

PAPAL STATES

Rome

Naples

KINGDOM OF THE TWO SICILIES

SICILY

Palermo

SARDINIA

CORSICA

Paris

FRANCE

Lyons

Marseilles

Bordeaux

Barcelona

SPAIN

Madrid

PORTUGAL

Lisbon

ENGLAND

London

Birmingham

Nottingham

Stoke

Manchester

Sheffield

Liverpool

Leeds

Burnley

Newcastle

Rhondda

Bristol

Portsmouth

SCOTLAND

Glasgow

Edinburgh

IRELAND

Belfast

ATLANTIC OCEAN

500 miles

0

The End of European Hegemony

No PERIOD, certainly none in the six centuries or so covered by this book, shows a more impressive internal coherence than the interval between the revolutions of 1848 and the aftermath of the Second World War. There is something of Greek tragedy about this hundred years: the rise of the tragic hero, his self-confidence and pride akin to the *hubris* the Greeks always warned against, the prophecies of doom ignored, the lengthy catalog of errors, the final crash, and the humiliation leading to some extent to self-exposure and, perhaps, to greater understanding. There is even a sequel, a *coda* of fresh liveliness which marks the end but also a beginning—just of what it is hard as yet to say.

The hero of all this is Europe: a smallish peninsula at the western end of Asia whose power, wealth, and historical significance we have watched increasing since the fourteenth century, an increase whose internal dynamic became greater all the time but never at the pace or on the scale that the late nineteenth century witnessed. As the century closed, Europe dominated the world: its wealth, its science, and its guns ruled it from end to end. Where they did not, those of its offspring did. Yet already, at the peak of its power, signs of an ebb were showing. Confusion grew. Values and self-confidence, which had seemed like the motor and mirror of its dynamism, crumbled away. There was mounting awareness of mighty challenges sprung out of its own energies in semi-European powers: Russia, the United States. All this brought talk of decadence. There was no decadence; but it would come and would accelerate, as the forces Europe had made and which made Europe in their turn—national states, democracy, industrial and military power—having reforged the world, turned in upon themselves, devouring one another. The process culminates in the weary, murderous, thirty years' war that began in 1914; and Germany—itself a creation of the late nineteenth century—incarnated Europe's *hubris*. To reassert Europe once more, Germany united it by conquest and sought to claim that world power which all felt to be slipping out of Europe's hands. Then Germany fell, and Europe conquered (or liberated) by American and Russian arms, fell with it. Whatever the eventual recovery—and it would be impressive—the age of European supremacy was ended.

Here, then, is one of the great themes of the coming pages: world dominion briefly achieved and lost. But there are others. Foremost, the phenomena to which the title of this part refers: the unprecedented growth of population, the increasing concentration of people in cities, and the involvement of more and more of them in national affairs.

Between 1850 and 1950 roughly a quarter of the world's population lived in Europe. But, if the proportion stayed about the same, absolute numbers rose from 266 million in 1850 to 400 million in 1900 and nearly 600 million in the 1950's. The problems and possibilities such numbers represented were crucial in Europe's dominant world role and also in the struggles waged for supremacy in Europe. We shall see in Chapter XVI how Europe's human resources changed the face of the world. The great migrations, the great invasions of the fourth century which toppled the Roman Empire and altered the face of the West, involved a few hundred thousand souls. Between 1846 and 1924 some sixty million Europeans left Europe. They—and those who stayed behind—would write the history of the world.

Meanwhile, the changing demographic picture within Europe itself altered the balance of power which generally inclines, like God, to the side of the big battalions. And battalions had to get bigger as war came to consume not thousands but millions and its accounting grew ever more costly. The older European powers—England and France—would be challenged by more populous Germany; and Germany would be overborne in turn by still more populous nations cast on continental scales.

Other millions moved about within Europe, from country to country, or from country to town, reflecting the human concentration in large cities, which by 1900 would shelter a majority of the population of industrial nations. And cities spawned more cities; for, paradoxically, the flight of urban dwellers out of the great centers in search of relief created new resorts destined for urban development in their turn: Brighton, Nice, Miami, Chamonix, or Darjeeling. Chapter XX will show the social developments all this evoked, the way people lived and thought in their new circumstances.

The concentration, the new weight and altered conditions of great masses, affected ideology too, and politics. Despite their failures, the movements and the revolutions of 1848 affirmed or confirmed the importance of new classes and, above all others, of the *bourgeoisie*. Except for Russia, 1848 was the last of the great string of political revolutions which, since the 1780's, had put an end to the privileged order of the old regime. Now that the old hierarchies were abolished, advancing industrial revolution would create new social classes based on fresh kinds of wealth and different functions. The middle of the nineteenth century saw the triumphant assertion of this process which culminated as the twentieth century began. Here too, however, forebodings were in order. Just as European expansion created the competitors who brought it to an end, so the industrial base of bourgeois supremacy created the economic and social groups which challenged its power and slowly wore it down: the men and women who dug its mines, ran its factories, drove its ships and trains and trucks, staffed its offices and shops, increasingly diversified, increasingly ready to claim a share of the wealth that bourgeois initiative had engendered but workers' sweat had watered.

The revolutions of 1848 shed a crude light on the new class conflicts and men were not slow to draw conclusions: as the *bourgeoisie* had wrested power from the old orders, so workers would have to win it in their turn. What happened was rather different: more and more workers came to live like bourgeois and to think like them, the vague term "middle classes" (usually in the plural) came to describe an increasing proportion of modern societies, and political action—no longer the preserve of a narrow group—eventually exhausted the bourgeois monopoly of wealth and hence of power.

This did not happen without difficulty. Most men regard the change of existing conditions as catastrophic; and those who liked things as they were put up a stout resistance against those who did not. The great battles in this struggle were fought out (to the west of Russia) in the quarter-century preceding 1914. Some of the most striking achievements were won in the 1930's. But the embourgeoization ·of the proletariat, and the narrowing gap in income and living standards between the poorest wage earner and the best paid, were not achieved on a mass basis until after the Second World War. By then, bourgeois supremacy was no more; nor could one clearly say what a bourgeois was or was not. The term had lost its meaning and it is doubtful whether the class definitions of the nineteenth century apply to its grandchildren of the mid-twentieth. Certainly the close relation between personal wealth and power, or even social status, so characteristic of the bourgeois age, has been worn down if not eliminated now that power in its various aspects lies in the hands of managers rather than of owners.

Which brings us to another crucial change. An important aspect of the century after 1848 is the predominance of politics, that is, the public discussion of affairs of state or of society; and of politicians, men whose lives are devoted to this task. With few exceptions, politics had been the preserve of very small social groups, carrying on most debates or disputes in private, over what amounted to personal opinions or interests. There had been moments when, as in the Wilkes affair or the French Revolution, the debate was carried to a wider public and an attempt made to enlist broad sections of society in support of a cause no longer essentially private. But not until 1848 do we see such attempts sustained in time and progressively elaborated toward the kind of political action with which we are familiar, because not until 1848 did really large sections of the public have a say in politics.

After 1848 the masses entered politics and politicians adjusted their activities to the new situation, elaborating parties, doctrines, national networks, permanent organizations, public meetings, a whole new strategy suited to an increasingly numerous and self-assertive electorate. In England there were 650,000 electors after 1832, over 4.5 million after 1884. In France, 241,000 in 1847, 10 million in 1852. In the Prussian lands after 1867, in all of Germany after 1871, universal male suffrage obtained. Gradually, as the old century ended, as a new one began, other countries followed suit. But the machinery of representative government had been devised for a restricted public, educated, reasonable, able to debate or consider arguments concerning its interests. Adjustment to the immensely vaster scale of manhood—let alone universal—suffrage inevitably meant maladjustment. The need to mobilize the greatest possible number of votes from a disparate public meant that political platforms would be as general as possible, avoiding concrete issues as far as could be done and the most awkward most of all, appealing whenever they could to sentiment and passion rather than to mind. Such methods, inherent in the machinery which democracy had inherited from oligarchy, were soon recognized as manipulative and dishonest, a fragile front for the old-fashioned pursuit of interest and power. Politicians were denounced and political institutions pilloried for their failures; but would-be reformers tinkered with the mechanism instead of replacing it.

The war of 1914 and its after-effects accented the failure of representative institutions. When national survival was at stake, public and politicians placed their policies in the hands of providential leaders at the head of governments and armies; of managers who could operate vast supply, planning, or financial services. Then, as the free market economy of the 1920's (what was left of it) disintegrated, so did free market politics. The Soviet government in Russia, the Fascists in Italy, and the Nazis in Germany, experimented with new structures of representative government. All, in different ways, tried to cope with the mass nature of politics by getting closer to the groundroots in soviets, or gilds, or corporations, by "educating" and indoctrinating the citizenry to issues and necessities that faced them, by treating the masses *as* masses rather than as collections of many separate and rational individuals.

While none of these experiments proved successful, they did underscore the disintegration of traditional democratic politics. And, while the defeat of fascism left Europe apparently divided between contending political structures, these now look upon government less as the embodiment of an ideal program or doctrine than as administration and management. Political contests which once opposed different philosophies of how life should be lived and how things should be done now take place between rival teams of managers and efficiency experts, each claiming that they can achieve the common end faster or more economically. The problem of scale and effect—of making people feel that they really have more than a consumer's share of what is being done to them or planned for them—remains unsolved. Lincoln's well-known formula reflected the aspirations of the political age, even to its totalitarian climax which tried to reconcile the sovereignty of the general will with that of a national state. Apparently it failed. Government of the people by some people, even if it is for far more people, remains the rule.

Another thing that failed was the sovereign national state operating in a world of sovereign national states; a magnified reflection of the other nineteenth-century political ideal, the free individual operating in a world of free individuals. There have never been completely sovereign national states or completely free individuals, but both existed as ideal concepts and as legal notions most forcefully expressed during this period. Both were seen to be impractical at the time of their greatest apparent success. The free individual was nibbled away by society; the sovereign state triumphed in 1918 only to reveal its insufficiencies. The outbreak of the Second World War was the ransom of its failures, its ending an indication that something else was taking shape. Quite what, we do not know.

To sum up, then, the story that unfolds after mid-nineteenth century is one of affirmation and disintegration: a class structure in which the bourgeoisie plays the predominant role develops and exhausts itself, a political structure designed for a restrictive leadership is stretched to fit a mass electorate and collapses, democracy is realized on a scale that turns it toward technocracy or totalitarianism, modern states affirm their independence only to learn that it is an illusion. Even the most extreme affirmation of the notion of national independence, war with another state, stresses interdependence. What A. J. P. Taylor has called "the struggle for mastery in Europe" had to be settled by two world wars. One thing that both wars had in common was that, beginning as conflicts over fairly clear issues, they ended in utterly unexpected ways: the first changing the map of Europe, and the second its place in the world.

Chapter 9

INTERNATIONAL PERSPECTIVES

The Age of Steam and Gold

Beneath the surface of the conventional account that lists wars, revolutions, governments and laws, a current runs (closer and closer to the surface in modern times) which is that of economic life; a current whose flux affects moods, attitudes, and actions. Just as the economic recessions of the fifteenth century stirred up the disquiet of the "waning middle ages," so the economic expansion of mid-eighteenth century spurred the sanguine enlightenment, and the fresh recession of 1817–1852 played its part in the romantic pessimisms and the social troubles of those years. The economic fluctuations of the period may similarly be reflected in the optimism of 1850–1880, the self-doubt of the so-called *fin-de-siècle,* the aggressive recovery of the decade before 1914, and the tense tone of the postwar years. This is a rough and superficial index. It can easily lead one into error, for prosperous periods knew momentary setbacks and some countries advanced while others experienced recessions or marked time. Furthermore, periods of recession like the 1880's and the 1890's brought comfort to certain classes and dismay to others. A general survey can register only the most general trends and, generally speaking, the economic curve that we can follow until 1914 is an ascendant one.

"Railroads and gold mines are the two secrets of Europe's commercial and industrial prosperity," wrote a French review in 1865. Certainly the transport revolution of the 1850's and 60's played a major part not only in the economic but in the political history of Europe. Between 1850 and 1914 railroads multiplied thirty times, European mileage increasing from 35,000 to one million kilometers. There was a close relation between prosperity and the density of the rail network: Britain, Germany and France averaging about 13 kilometers of rail per 100 square kilometers of territory, while Austria showed 8, Italy 6, Spain less than 3, and Russia—despite heroic efforts in building 74,000 kilometers—only 0.32. Railroads were the first expression of the mass age and its first great agents as well, shifting greater numbers and quantities than any means of locomotion before them, facilitating the mobility of persons and of goods, eventually their mobilization too. In 1880 French railroads carried 18 million persons and 4.5 million tons of goods; by 1913 they were carrying 547 million persons and 173 million tons of goods. By that time, 6 billion travelers a year were journeying on the railways of Germany, Britain, and France. The economies of such countries received an extraordinary impetus, their social structures were affected by the armies of employees enlisted in the upkeep and administration of great networks, their national administration expanded to keep up with new needs, their armies learned to take advantage of new possibilities.

Railroads integrated nations as nothing else had done, linking distant provinces, developing truly national economies where there had been parochial ones, orienting the flow of travelers and goods along their line of passage, stamping new cities out of the ground (as along the great American and Siberian railways), or animating old ones.* Railroad networks imposed the primacy of the capital where they began and ended, advanced cohesion in newly forming nations, breathed new life into continental areas heretofore cut off from economic activity. Before rails advanced into the great land masses of the world, power which went with the riches of trade, of productivity depending on easy access to raw materials and to shipping points, accompanied maritime activity. Wealth and power nested on the shores of the Mediterranean, the Atlantic, or the Baltic Sea. Continental countries—central and eastern Eur-

---

* While French population grew 9 per cent in fifty years, that of towns along the Paris-Nice railway line doubled.

302

Opposite: a complex
London railroad
crossing in the 1860s.
Right: digging for
gold in South Africa.

ope, even the United States—found it hard to compete with the wealth
and enterprise of the maritime powers. Railroads permitted the settlement, equipment, and exploitation of vast continental zones in North
and South America, Russia, Africa, and China. Thus, a great European invention which began by affirming and expanding European supremacy, would end by strengthening other continents against Europe.

Before the twentieth century made this evident, the advantages of
steam were there for the reaping. Europe was following England into
the "cotton millenium" and steam power, in George Eliot's words,
had "driven on every wheel double pace and the wheel of fortune along
with them." But coal alone was not enough to stoke the fires of fortune.
Another fuel was needed: gold. And gold was running short, hampering exchanges, trade, expansion; its dearth contributing to the hunger
of the hungry forties.

Between 1848 and 1851, gold discoveries in California and Australia
provided (as the London *Times* put it) "an electric impulse to our entire business world," and moved the future Lord Shaftesbury to wonder
in his diary whether this was not "God's chosen way to fulfill his com-
mandment and replenish the earth." In twenty years, between 1850
and 1870, as much gold was added to the world's stocks as in the previous 350 years, stimulating the economy, raising prices and production,
quadrupling profits between 1851 and 1873. In the late 1890's fresh
supplies from South Africa and western Canada ended the recession of
the 1870's and 80's by pumping more resources into the economy. More
gold, more paper money backed by it, more money circulating, higher
prices, consumers buying more, producers and merchants making, stock-
ing, and selling more, employing more workers, willing to grant higher
wages, stimulating greater buying power. This was (and still remains)
the mechanism of expansion and inflation. By 1904 the world gold stock
was four times greater than it had been in 1885. Its index figure, taking
the year 1500 as 1, stood at 45 in 1800, 1,000 in 1860, 2,800 in 1914.

His way eased by gold and steam, modern industrial man began to install himself in the climate of change and mobility which the previous half century had ushered in. Change became a part of life and of experience in politics, in society, in economic activity. The world adjusted to this too: legislation took note of industrial workers and their needs; municipal government organized or reorganized the great encampments of transient slum dwellers (transient largely between land and death) into something more stable and even more comfortable in its dreariness; some of the rising prosperity began to spill over into the working classes, improving their standards of living and their expectation of life.

We shall see that the improvements were relative. Surveys taken in England early in the twentieth century showed one-third to a quarter of the population still miserably poor, depending on earnings "insufficient to obtain the minimum necessities for the maintenance of mere physical efficiency." By this definition over one-third of the people of London, over one-quarter of the people of York, lived in poverty. One Englishman in five died in a workhouse and was buried in a pauper's grave. One baby out of every six born in the working classes died before a year, one out of every two grew up underfed, underdeveloped, sickly, and poor. That was the richest country in the world.

Yet this must be seen in the perspective of a mid-twentieth century where the richest country in the world admits that one-fifth of its population still lives at or below the margin of subsistence. And certainly a fitter image of the period may be found in the great London International Exhibition of 1851 that ushered it in, and in the Crystal Palace that symbolized its excitement and ingenuity. One million square feet of glass, 33,000 columns, 2,300 girders, all prefabricated and most interchangeable, 100,000 exhibits by 14,000 exhibitors, 6 million visitors, proclaimed the triumphs and the expectations of the age. The bad old days before 1848 were left behind, part of another era. The Crystal Palace proposed "a new starting point, from which all nations will be able to direct their further exertions."

And, true enough, Europe now forged itself anew. Railroads, roads, utilities, machinery, spread and multiplied throughout the West, even in North Italy and northwestern Spain. Then, in a second phase, beginning in the 1870's, western Europe, having built itself, set out to equip and develop the rest of the world and also the more backward parts of its own continent. Mines, oil wells, plantations, bridges, canals, power plants, port installations, tramways, banks, lighthouses and docks, gasworks and sewers, carried European industrial civilization throughout the world, to Constantinople and Nagasaki, Romanian oil fields, Bolivian mines, and Asian estates. Between 1870 and 1914 British foreign investment tripled; between 1880 and 1914 French foreign investment followed suit. From the 1840's to the eve of war the value of

THE GROWTH OF RAILROADS
IN EUROPE · 1850–1914

——— Representative railroads in 1850

——— Increases to 1914

Trackage per square kilometer (1914)

0–2 kilometers	2–4 kilometers	4–10 kilometers	More than ten kilometers

- - - - Boundaries in 1914

500 miles

BLACK SEA

OTTOMAN EMPIRE

Moscow

RUSSIA

Kiev

St. Petersburg

AEGEAN SEA

Athens

GREECE

Bucharest

RUMANIA

BULGARIA

Sofia

SERBIA

Belgrade

MONTENEGRO

ALBANIA

Warsaw

Stockholm

SWEDEN

BALTIC SEA

AUSTRIA-HUNGARY

Budapest

Vienna

Berlin

GERMANY

Copenhagen

DENMARK

Oslo

NORWAY

ADRIATIC SEA

ITALY

Rome

SWITZ.

Milan

NORTH SEA

NETH.

Amsterdam

BELG.

Brussels

LUX.

Paris

FRANCE

CORSICA

SARDINIA

SICILY

MEDITERRANEAN SEA

Marseilles

Barcelona

London

ENGLAND

SCOTLAND

Glasgow

Dublin

IRELAND

SPAIN

Madrid

PORTUGAL

Lisbon

ATLANTIC OCEAN

Constantinople

The Crystal Palace at the
London International Exhibition of 1851.

world trade increased thirteen or fourteen times and Europe carved
out a major share of it. England, of course, remained the greatest trader
in Europe and the world but, significantly, by 1913 Germany replaced France in second place, her 13 per cent of world trade challenging the 17 per cent of Britain.

Such competitive jockeying reminds us that national rivalries were reflected in economic competition, and that the latter had its share in
egging nations one against the other. Economic liberalism had set out
to free economic life from political motives. By the late nineteenth century it had enlisted politics to serve particular interests. Soon, political
interests would come to manipulate economic activities, to the limits
of control, planning, and economic autarchy. Political and economic
liberalism crumbled together, the proponents of the one being often the
first to pick at the other. Yet capital was international. Coal and iron
companies operated across the Franco-German, Franco-Belgian, Bel-
gian-German borders, owned mines and factories in all countries. Russia's Putilov works were dependent on German companies like Krupp
and French ones like Schneider, which, like England's Vickers, sold their
arms to everybody; Belgian capital helped to build the Paris subway;
two-thirds of the hotels on the French Riviera were owned by foreign
capital.

The dominant trend of the prewar years was toward exchange not
autarchy, expansion not retrenchment. Europe overflowed with people,
capital, goods, techniques, ideas, ways of thought and action. These
poured into the other continents and in due course trickled back, bringing subtle alterations in thought and taste, obvious contributions to the
table and warehouse and treasury of the West. The captive world en-
meshed its captors in a network of political and economic interests, the
industries of one dependent on the materials of another, the markets of

306

one swallowing the products of another, the profits or labor of one depending on the prosperity and activities of another. By 1914, Britain, France, and Germany among them accounted for seven-tenths of the world's productive capacity, for 83 per cent of all the world's foreign investments (compared with 5 per cent for the United States). They were the center of world economy, of its money market and international trade. The east European countries were their economic colonies, so were most countries overseas. Russia, Britain, and France ruled over half the world, over one-third of mankind. The foreign territories owned by Britain were one hundred and forty times greater than the home country, France's twenty times greater, Belgium's eighty times greater, Holland's sixty times greater.

Yet hindsight points out some crucial indices of relative decline. Europe accounted for 75 per cent of the world's trade in 1800, 66 per cent in 1900, 58 per cent in 1913. By 1938 this had become 52 per cent. Her share of goods produced throughout the world was also falling, and some began to look uneasily at a trend whose acceleration they forecast as continents and countries that Europe had equipped began to claim a part of the profits and possibilities of trade.

Politics for the Masses

Never has the world known such a political age—such widespread politicization—as in the last hundred years or so. The notion of political debate had arisen in the ancient Greek city states, when rulers and restricted ruling groups based on traditional authorities were replaced by oligarchic factions that sought wider support in their disputes. It only reappeared when similar circumstances made it relevant in the urban politics that flourished between the thirteenth and the sixteenth centuries, to wane again before the reappearance of patrician or monarchic rule. With few exceptions like the Netherlands, it was not until the nineteenth century that the notion revived that social and economic life offers alternatives, that one can *choose* among different courses, among different kinds of institutions, that debate directed to such objects is more than academic. As long as the appointed round of life had seemed everlasting and the structure within which it unfolded perpetual (for memories were short and alterations were soon regarded as part of an unchanging destiny), the realm of choice was limited and petty. Men (a very few) disputed over *interests* far more than *policies,* issues of finite scope within the ineluctable infinity of fate.

Only new men—individuals who carried their destinies in their hands not in their birth—could challenge such a view. Part of the rise of the bourgeoisie was its belief that the structure and course of society could be changed. Men are not fixed once and for all. They are not only free to choose, they are condemned to have to choose. Whether they choose or not, they are still choosing—the *status quo* or an alternative—even if they are only choosing not to choose. As men claimed power or a say in it not by some immemorial and unchallenged right, but by argument (which goes with choice) and reasoning (which goes with argument) and force (if only the force of numbers, often brought in to settle arguments), the shape of modern politics was rounded out by theoretical constructs which placed immediate issues in a broader context, defined or rationalized the values in whose name men strove, proposed new models of reality against the old that were being rejected or at least contested.

The tensions that these arguments and struggles generated brought ever more men within the scope of politics. Even the "revolutionary" politics of early nineteenth century had been played out among restricted numbers. By mid-century this began to change, echoes of the restricted contest awoke new batches of contenders, the scale of politics spread out to include all members of the nation, the issues and effects of political disputes were seen to be so vast that one ignored them only at one's peril. Masses acquired political relevancy, and politics became a struggle relevant to every one of their members.

But if the politics of masses affected nations, the beliefs that lent them inspiration cut across national boundaries. Liberalism, socialism, or reaction could unite men whom the accidents of birth or geography divided, persuading them that class, conviction, or historical neccessity gave them more in common than a passport could. And this, in turn, provided a significant factor in the history of the time; for the political attitudes of ordinary men and women began to weigh on national and international affairs.

Basic political attitudes can be found in Plato's Athens, where conservatives stood for a social order rooted in hereditary privileges and castes, in agriculture, frugality, and the simple life, suspecting trade, novelties, foreigners, and everything that might be responsible for change. Opposed to them, the partisans of change and movement rejected anachronisms, inclined to democracy or tyranny, welcomed modern life, favored the merchants, developed the fleet, relied on foreign trade to increase the private and public riches. Before such widespread contrasting attitudes can be made meaningful to the modern world, the shape that they took needs more definition.

Liberalism

The first partisans of movement in more recent times were the liberals—description less of a party than of a point of view, a climate of opinion. The term "liberal" had long been used with reference to education or

John Stuart Mill.

else to generosity. Its political application began in Spain, during the revolutions of the 1820's, and took some time to live down the pejorative connotations that attached to it as they had done to words like "Whig" or "Tory." Then it came to mean a political attitude associated with national assertion, free institutions, constitutions, individualism; an economic doctrine that said the state should keep out of economic activities, leaving them to free enterprise; and a philosophical position supporting freedom of thought and of expression, humanity and tolerance. In places such as England, Germany, and Belgium, Liberal parties also appeared whose programs included some, though not all of these propositions, parties that represented a middle-class elite competing with landowning interests and with the aristocracy of the old regime, but as opposed to the masses as they were to the restrictions and the privileges of birth.

The finest expression of liberal ideals at mid-century is to be found in John Stuart Mill's essay *On Liberty* (1859). Mill's idea of liberty was that men should be free to make of themselves what they want and can, live their own life, do as they please, as long as they do not interfere with others, develop their personalities to the fullest extent compatible with the interests and development of their fellow men. The idea was excellent. Its fulfillment posed almost every social problem men had faced over the ages. Just as an example, advocates of *laissez faire* objected to public education on the grounds that men were responsible for the upbringing of their children, not those of others; refused public subsidies to cultural activities since art, an industry like any other, should learn to make a profit; opposed conscription because soldiers should be hired at the going market rate like other laborers; and argued that any limitation of working hours or conditions interfered with the personal liberty of the worker. One man's freedom was another man's restriction, one man's logic another man's poison.

All this lent weight to conservative criticisms of bourgeois liberals with their pious economic slogans and their selfish political restrictions.

It was individualistic liberalism, said the conservatives, whose *laissez faire* created the proletariat, introduced change, questioned religion and hence destroyed resignation, creating social unrest. Materialist motives must be replaced by old-fashioned charity, human relations restored to the personal plane, change banished by stability, discipline, patience, and hope of a better world not in the realm of reform or science fiction but of God.

Yet the liberal logic that could lead to illiberal conclusions was equally capable of radical developments, witness the work published in the same year as the essay *On Liberty*: Samuel Smiles' *Self Help*. In less than half a century *Self Help* would sell a quarter of a million copies, more than the sales of the great novels of its time; it would be translated into French, German, Dutch and Danish, Italian and Japanese, Turkish, Arabic, and several Indian languages; while quotations from it were inscribed on the walls of the Khedive's palace in Cairo. Its creed, that God helps those that help themselves, was appropriate to a mobile, dynamic society where it was no longer a crime to educate a child beyond his station, and where every man could hope to rise by his own perseverance.

Interestingly enough, Smiles had started as a radical in the 1840's and his lectures, from which the book was put together, were directed at the working class whose education and social promotion were very near his heart. What he preached was self-improvement through education and work, thrift and determination, a recipe that made sense in times when prosperity created opportunities for all and inflation did not whittle savings. It reflected an awareness (strong in the nineteenth century, weak in ours) that the ultimate radicalism is not expressed in a combination of dependence and interference, but in individualism. As Richard Cobden, the free-trader, wrote to Smiles in 1853: "Depend upon it, there is a spice of despotism at the bottom of all this intervention by combined bodies in the concerns of individuals . . ." There was and is, and most societies seem to oscillate between despotism and interference at one extreme, injustice and inequality at another. This was the quandary that Mill faced but could not overcome in his essay *On Liberty*.

Yet, as Smiles grew old, his advice grew less relevant. Industry was getting larger and less competitive; social promotion came to depend more on the education received in youth than on initiative and self-help when adult. Thrift itself began to be attacked by economists who argued that savings made for underemployment and checked economic development. Finally, the wheel came full circle. Smiles had come to self-help when radical experience convinced him that collective action could only fumble in the dark as long as individuals rotted in poverty and ignorance. By the 1870's men like Mill himself had qualified their view of liberty. Men could not become or be themselves without the opportunities that society alone was able to provide. Real individualism and self-fulfillment needed a collective springboard. Samuel Smiles was turned upon his head. "The social problem of the future," noted Mill in his *Autobiography* (1873), "we considered to be, how to unite the greatest individual liberty of action, with a common ownership of the raw materials of the globe, and an equal participation in all the benefits of combined labor."

An answer to this question would be formulated by T. H. Green (and other "Oxford idealists") in his *Lectures on the Principles of Political Obligation* (1879–1880): "Human development in its richest diversity" can only exist if the state provides the opportunities for it. The freedom of the individual can be endangered if economic evolution is allowed to act without hindrance. The common good may be served by state intervention to free the individual, by providing him education, sanitation, housing, credit, opportunities to work, security in illness or old age. In 1881, Gladstone's Land Act provided security and opportunity for Irish farmers. After 1883 Bismarck's insurance acts provided greater security for German workers. As theoretical liberalism turned into social liberalism, the last two decades of the nineteenth century would see a spate of social legislation all over Europe, the beginning of the welfare state.

Old-fashioned liberal entrepreneurs, like the Scotch-American ironmaster and millionaire Andrew Carnegie, still regarded the world as an unregulated free-for-all and rich men like themselves as benevolent oligarchs, responsible for improving their community. Yet when Carnegie's *Gospel of Wealth* appeared in 1889, liberalism had undergone a sea change. Mill, Green, and the Fabian group that derived from them articulated the change of mind and heart that led liberals from individualism (asserted against privileged oppression of one kind) to collectivism (asserted against privileged exclusivism of another kind). The evolution in the way they viewed the situation was reflected in their doctrines. The long gradual infiltration that brought about capitalist supremacy in the developed world would now be followed, said the Fabians, by socialism: transforming capitalism by stages into something that conforms still better with the requirements of the new economic and industrial order.

The social liberals and the Fabians were not alone in their perception that the world had changed. Both Bismarck and Louis Napoleon believed that prosperity could replace liberty, that strong government could reconcile economic and social antagonisms, educate and discipline both entrepreneurs and wage earners. For Louis Napoleon "The day of class rule is over, the day of mass rule has begun. The masses must be organized so that they can formulate their will, and disciplined so that they can be instructed and enlightened as to their own interests." This splendid formulation of democratic authoritarianism had only one weakness: its aims would be achieved not by authoritarians but by their opponents —the socialists. At least until the twentieth century.

The political debate which had been reserved largely to the educated, the wealthy, and wellborn, was being taken up (as we have seen) by interlocutors representing portions of society which had little voice and less say until that time; above all by the urban workers. This meant that the factors in debate would change, its tone would rise, and its implications would become more serious for all participants. The terms of the debate still reflected the two dominant views of earlier days. The evolutionary, moving with the times and relying on the changes time would bring; and the revolutionary, rejecting any possibility of adjustment, putting its trust only in violent change. But the participants altered. Gradually, Liberal parties attained most of their ends and lost their sense of purpose, declining into sectarianism or concern with preserving what they had won. They became conservative in fact if not in name, and conservative sentiments now preserved or developed many achievements of the liberal era. The new parties of change were those of labor or of nationalism, less revolutionary to the extent that reform anticipated discontent, more so to the extent that force sought to suppress it. All were more conscious of divisions—national or social—than their predecessors who believed in unity; all paid more attention to struggle than to reconciliation, which had been their predecessors' hope. In these ways, too, they seem to have reflected the modern character of their age, the more so since of the two major movements of the Left one amplified the individualistic tendencies of waning liberalism and the other the scientific obsessions of the day. And the seminal thinkers behind each, P. J. Proudhon (1809–1865) and Karl Marx (1818–1883) hailed respectively from France and Germany.

Anarchism

The anarchism that we associate with Proudhon's name was almost a logical projection of Samuel Smiles' *Self Help*. Printer by trade, Proudhon believed that workmen of his kind could count only on themselves, on their own efforts and associations to improve their lot, gain a just return for their labor, demolish economic inequalities, abolish the private property which, he said, is nothing but theft—the appropriation by one man of the plus-value created by the work of others.* The universal suffrage dear to democrats cannot provide a true reflection of a country's nature, for all democracy leads to centralism and authoritarian government. Only the removal of all the things that trammel individual liberty can lead to freedom and this can never be done from above. State,

---

* The French novelist, Anatole France, makes one of his characters, Monsieur Bergeret, ponder that the essence of social justice rests on the fact that while theft is wicked, its gains are sacred.

P. J. Proudhon, by Gustave Courbet. Petit Palais, Florence

army, police are all part of the repressive organism set up to protect the property of the few who exploit the efforts of the many. Whoever controls this machinery, the exploitation will continue even though the hands switching the levers of power may change. So, said Proudhon, only their destruction—dismantling the governmental machinery, suppressing the state—can emancipate the society of the future so that there could be a loose federation of small, free communities working under no constraint. Democracy—the rule of the people—shall be replaced by *demopedy*—education of the people. Politically anarchist, organizationally Proudhon was a syndicalist, advocating the independent action of workmen grouped in their professional associations, uninvolved with politicians who always in the end will let them down and sell out to some new oppressive government. Ultimately, Proudhon was a moralist, aiming at a *just* society, one where the collapse of bourgeois injustice would permit the evolution of a "new man," no longer exploited, asserting his dignity in Saint-Simonian terms as worker and producer.

Proudhon's disciples followed similar lines. Their criticism—not only of society, but of the tendency reformers have to become oppressors in their turn—is cogent. Mikhail Bakunin (1814–1876), a volcanic dinosaur of a man, appears as a survivor from another age, the seeming embodiment of anarchism. Liberty was the be-all and end-all of Bakunin's philosophy, but a liberty admitting neither property nor competition, neither exploitation nor *laissez faire*. Opposed to any society based on coercion, insisting on free groups where no coercive authority balks the individual or thwarts the associations he may freely join, Bakunin's revolutionary gospel looked forward not to the capture of the state but to its abolition. Not revolutionary organization, but the revolutionary instincts of workers and peasants voluntarily grouped in *ad hoc* associations, would overthrow the old society and recreate a new.

313

The important thing was to get on with it; for as Bakunin saw it, there was no time to lose. Unless anarchism were established right away, the industrial revolution would come and prevent it.

Bakunin—who had fled his aristocratic Russian home, fought in the revolutions of 1848, survived long years of jail and of Siberian exile to escape and fight again—moved through the Europe of the 1860's as an incarnation of revolt, founding secret societies wherever he went, preaching and plotting revolution and helping to found the First International Workingmen's Association in 1864. A greater theorist, Prince Peter Kropotkin (1842–1921), agreed with him that we could dispense with the coercive armor of society and state because men's social nature produces social behavior spontaneously. Men, argued Kropotkin, himself a distinguished geographer and ethnologist, incline to work together without being forced to it. They will do so in pursuit of common aims, like other animals and savages. Civilized men are as naturally bent to cooperation and gregariousness as they are to struggle and competition. Society should reflect not the survival of the fittest but "mutual aid," which was the title of his major study published in 1902.

The arguments of anarchism, superficially so attractive, collapsed before the contact of reality. Its social and psychological criticisms were forceful, but they denied the possibility of any organization that would carry them out. The anarchists' ideals made their political action ineffective. Ready to blast society to pieces, they could envisage no workable alternative to the order they found wanting. They faced their greatest problems in more advanced industrial societies in which the limited local structures and voluntary associations that anarchism recognized were overlaid by means of transport and production which only wider organization and co-ordination could keep up. An Andalusian or a Calabrian peasant need not care about railroads or power stations; an English, French, or German worker did. And the more economically developed countries showed relatively little interest in anarchism.

In these latter countries, anarchism was also adversely affected by growing trade union and labor organizations whose scale and practices went counter to its views but which achieved evident gains for labor. In countries like Russia and Spain, where governments kept the social opposition from expression, it was more effective. In others, like France and Italy, where unions were backward and fragmented and the revolutionary tradition strong, a compromise anarchism took shape, incorporating some of its techniques, like direct action and the general strike, in *syndicalism:* separate unions, ignoring politics and parliament, carrying on their fight on purely professional grounds by sheer industrial warfare. Generally though, where anarchism did not somehow compromise with political socialism, its most forceful expression came in isolated acts of violence. Direct action translated into terrorism brought a long string of murders and attempted murders: attempts to kill the Kaiser, the kings of Italy and Spain, assassination of two American presidents (Garfield in 1881, McKinley, 1901), of an emperor (Alexander II of Russia, 1881), an empress (Elizabeth of Austria, 1898), a king (Umberto of Italy, 1900), a president of the French Republic (Carnot, 1894), and countless other political figures.

When in 1910 Kropotkin wrote the article on anarchism for the eleventh edition of the *Encyclopaedia Britannica,* he pointedly denied that such "propaganda by the deed" was its inseparable essence. Everybody uses violence, he wrote, "in proportion as their open action is obstructed by repression and exceptional laws render them outlaws." There was much truth in that. But it was equally true that, in proportion as their appeal was slipping in freer societies like France, the anarchists also used the means which Alfred Nobel's invention of dynamite (1868) had put to hand. The year 1892 alone would see over a thousand dynamitings in Europe, over five hundred in the United States. France, in the 1890's one of the freest societies in Europe, was harshly struck by anarchist outrages directed as often against cafés as against banks or the Chamber of Deputies. Desperation can stem as much from depression as from repression. The anarchists were losing ground, and knew it, not to oppression but to the modern world. When in 1898 an international governmental conference met at Rome to concert means of combating them, most of the special measures there envisaged were actually directed against a more serious threat to the established order and to anarchism alike: the growing power of the socialists.

Socialism

As all discussions of anarchism start with Proudhon, so all discussions of modern socialism begin, perhaps unfairly, with Karl Marx. Where Proudhon insists on the particular, Marx looks to the general. Proudhon was a moralist who believed in justice for the individual. Marx was a moralist who believed in scientific laws, sought their expression in human society and economy, described a historical mechanism which explained the rise and predicted the fall of capitalist society.

The model Marx proposes is a sociology based on economics, that is, on the belief that the structure of production, the economic structure of society, is the basis of its legal and political institutions, of its culture, of its morals, of its self-consciousness. "The means of production of material life determines in general the social, political and intellectual process of life." Hence Marx's studies of the framework of production on which different classes rise, dominate, and challenge one another; and his theory of class struggle—not a new invention, but now presented as part of a process of historical evolution in which the latest victor, the bourgeois, was meeting a new challenger, the industrial proletarian, whom present exploitation only steeled for victory to come. Since the class structure at any given time changes with the forces and structure of economic production, the class struggle of modern industrial society was bound to end in the victory of the proletariat and in its dictatorship, which (since no other class would be left to contend for power in its turn) would usher in a classless society in which class struggle was impossible for lack of classes and the repressive state edifice therefore could be dispensed with.

There is greatness in Marx's historical models, and a splendid instrument of social analysis: a structure of hypothesis into which almost every historical phenomenon can be fitted. But in the end his utopia is not very different from that of Proudhon, whom he detested. The really important thing about Marx (apart from the lessons historians have learned from him) is his contribution in persuading the workers that they had a collective personality, and in holding out the "scientifically demonstrated" hope of a better world based on the fact that the very economic forces on which the capitalist world was thriving were working against that world and against its capitalist masters. Professor Tawney once remarked that he did not need Marx to tell him that capitalists exploited workers. Yet Marx provided more than an economic explanation: a trumpet call, the text for a thousand sermons and the inspiration for effective action.

One might say at once that Marxist thought took time to make its way. The *Communist Manifesto,* ignored in 1848, remained a rare pamphlet for connoisseurs until reprinted in 1872, and became a best seller only in the 1890's with the rise of social democratic parties in the West. The first volume of *Das Kapital* appeared in 1867. A Russian translation was published in 1872 and did quite well since the censors did not think it worth suppressing.* As late as 1879, when the English wife of the heir to the German throne read it and inquired about the author, she was informed that "it will not be he who, whether he wishes it or not, will turn the world upside down."

The Princess's informant was mistaken, not only because Marx's theories fitted important needs of a rising class but because they fitted the preconceptions of the modern mind. Marxist relativism attacked belief in absolute values. Values, said Marx, are relative to their time and place. Slavery, serfdom, capitalism were all progressive innovations in their time and could only be criticized when they became obsolete

---

* The censors had suppressed a Russian translation of the *Communist Manifesto* in the 1860's. Its first English translation dates from 1886. *Kapital* was translated into French in 1875 and into English in 1887. A new Russian version of the *Manifesto,* with an introduction by Marx, appeared in 1882, a year before his death. The 1870's had convinced him that there was no hope of early revolution in the West; now he was finding more followers in Russia and beginning to think that perhaps conditions for social revolution there were better than elsewhere.

and hampered further development. That was why Marx and Engels *
attacked capitalism, not because it was absolutely or inherently bad, but
because in turn it had become corrupted. Such relativism came close to
the evolving scientific attitudes of the day which regarded all truths as
only approximate at best, all involving contradictions to be revealed and
resolved in time. Hence Marx and Engels' scientific theories appealed to
scientists. Their dialectic analyzed history and social development in
terms not of abstract *ideas* but of events and *things,* used concepts like
force and motion familiar to the natural sciences, which, Engels pointed
out, were naturally dialectical because they studied the movement and
the interaction of bodies no more static or independent than men and
societies. Dialectics, too, was a science: "the science," Engels said, "of
the general laws of motion and development of nature, human society
and thought."

This coincidence in approach and language was as important to the
fortunes of Marxism as the coincidence of liberalism and the Enlightenment had been a century before. Intellectuals are the clergy of modern
times: during the eighteenth century and much of the nineteenth their
values and perceptions coincided with those of the bourgeoisie.
Through most of the twentieth they would largely coincide not with
those of the working class but with its interpreters, first and foremost
Karl Marx.

As has been said already, socialism progressed slowly, Marxism even
more so. After 1848, "political reaction and economic recovery advanced
hand in hand to destroy what was left of the revolutionary movement
in the leading countries." ** When the first Socialist International was
set up in London in 1864, as the International Workingmen's Association, its founders were British and French trade unionists joined by a
number of exiles like Marx, Engels, Mazzini, and Bakunin. The followers
of Owen, Proudhon, Blanqui, and Marx could join behind the slogan
"Proletarians of all lands, unite!" They did not stay united long and the
history of the First International is a long account of feuds, intrigues,
and scissions.

The first workers' mass movement appeared in Germany in the
1860's, the work of a brilliant, dynamic Silesian Jew, Ferdinand Lassalle
(1825–1864). Before he died in a duel at the age of thirty-nine, Lassalle
had founded a vast organization whose first demand was for manhood
suffrage. Where Marxists tended to side with the progressive sections
of the middle class against the aristocratic and autocratic state, arguing
that they would turn against the bourgeoisie when this had performed

* Friedrich Engels (1820–1895): Marx's closest collaborator, son of a prosperous German manufacturer and himself manager of one of his father's mills, in Manchester,
until he retired at forty-nine to devote himself to writing, study, and the criticism of
the class of men he represented.
** G. D. H. Cole, *A History of Socialist Thought,* vol 2.(London: 1953), p. 3.

its historic task of displacing its anachronistic rivals, Lassallians preferred a workers' alliance with the state against the bourgeoisie, and Lassalle himself put much faith in Bismarck. The state (as Fichte had preached) should be the instrument of the people's good. Once workers had the vote, the state's policy would reflect their wishes. They would be given credit to set up their own enterprises and, free of their capitalist employers, would henceforth enjoy all the benefits of their productivity, not just the tiny share they now received in wages.

As a matter of fact, Bismarck seems to have borrowed some of Lassalle's ideas when he introduced manhood suffrage first in the North German Confederation (1867), then in the German Reich (1871). But he borrowed them only to nullify them and, when this was realized, the Lassallians merged with the Marxist Social Democrats (1875) led by Wilhelm Liebknecht (1826–1900) and August Bebel (1840–1913). By that time the French working-class movement had been destroyed in the hopeless Paris Commune (1871), which left the leadership of Western socialism to the Germans. German Social Democracy thus became the model and ideological leader of the string of Marxist parties about to be set up.* Its Marxism became orthodox doctrine throughout the renascent labor movement and the accepted doctrine of the Second International which the Socialist parties joined (1889–1914) and which asserted its reviving influence by the international demonstrations of May 1, 1890: the first labor day.

The Second International was an altogether more visible body than the First and its member parties soon won a significant place in the political structure of their countries. With the beginning of the twentieth century, French Socialists were playing an important role in various governmental coalitions, the young British Labor Party began to reveal itself as an electoral force, new franchise laws in Austria enabled Austrian Social Democrats to elect 87 delegates to the *Reichsrat.*** On the eve of the First World War, Italian Socialists had 79 deputies in the Chamber, French Socialists 103, the Germans—with over a third of the votes cast—were the most numerous party in the *Reichstag.* Even in the United States the Socialist Eugene Debs who had garnered 100,000 votes in the presidential election of 1900, could win ten times as many in the election of 1912.

All this had been achieved by hard organizational work; and the organization that spelled success, also (as the Anarchists predicted) spelled eventual decay. Mass movements are the modern answer to the weakness of individual men facing the power of rich and influential adversaries. But, born to serve as armies of democracy, they often developed undemocratic traits inherent in their structure. It was a pioneer student of Ger-

---

* Denmark and Spain, 1879; France, 1882; Britain, 1884; Belgium, 1885; Norway, 1887; Austria and Switzerland, 1888; Holland and Sweden, 1889; Italy, 1892.
** Their anti-semitic Christian Socialist opponents had 96 seats.

man Social Democracy, Robert Michels, who pointed out as early as 1910 that "the masses" are the weakest members of society, that they can be effective only when organized, and that organization generates its own conservatism, its own oligarchic power structure, which subjects the membership to a new authority the better to fight the old. The bigger the organization, the bigger its leaders' power and the less the democracy in whose name it was built. These perceptions of 1910 were verified first in the history of Social Democratic parties and of the bigger trade unions, then in that of Communist and Fascist parties, eventually in the better organized political parties everywhere.

Leaving aside the undemocratic tendencies of mass movements, their very need to triumph on the electoral plane—that is, to attract a majority of voters—meant that they had to bend principle for the sake of practice, devise a compromise that would satisfy their militants' beliefs without frightening off potential supporters. For Socialists began to realize that a workers' party could not gain majority power by workers' support alone. The number of industrial workers was growing, but the proportion of white-collar workers was increasing too: in 1866 France counted ten commercial employees to 240 other workers, by 1914, 120 to 240: the proportion had changed from 1:24 to 1:2. It would change even more after the war. G. D. H. Cole contrasts the acuteness with which Marx observed capitalist developments around mid-nineteenth century against the lack of realism with which he appraised events thereafter. The creation of a new petty bourgeoisie recruited among managerial and administrative employees, the growth of a new middle class consisting not only of *rentiers* but of technicians and managers, the new labor skills taking the place of disappearing ones, the improving standard of living of more and more workers, the growing number of small investors, all contradicted Marx's predictions that petty capitalists would be superseded by large-scale production.

The Socialists, as one of their leaders put it in the *Social Democratic Catechism* of 1893, were "a revolutionary party, but not a party that makes revolutions." They would gain power by legal means, win a majority of the popular vote, a majority of seats in parliament, then change society by passing laws. Class warfare would be organized, it would be peaceful, it would be less and less class-conscious or warlike. Like extras in a chorus line, the Socialists sang "We march! We march!" and never moved beyond the footlights. They tried to reconcile revolutionary language and reformist activities, the former camouflaging the latter and confusing issues: preventing co-operation with natural allies among middle-class reformists, giving the increasingly conservative Social Democratic movements a good radical conscience and permitting them to evade real issues like the supremacy of Junkers and soldiers in Germany, or the lack of mass support in Germany or France for any real revolutionary policy.

319

Here was a sit-tight policy that became increasingly apparent and from which different people drew different conclusions: some, like the Frenchman Georges Sorel, whose *Crisis of Socialism* appeared in 1898, tried to enlist revolutionary syndicalism in a revision of Marxist theory which would revive the revolutionary tenor of the movement. The necessity of a revolution, not just to improve existing conditions, but to destroy the existing order and replace it with a better one, was being lost from sight. Reformists and temporizers were forwarding the corruption of the very class from which salvation could still come. They believed that the proletariat could be integrated in a society that was rotten to the core. They accepted the scientist optimism of the bourgeoisie and the pragmatism that Sorel denounced as "the last stage of bourgeois thought": a philosophy for *parvenus* in a cynical world.

Attacking *The Illusions of Progress* (1908), Sorel argued that the working class must build its own civilization *against* existing society, assert its values against the parliamentary reformists who sought to integrate it in a decaying world. Here was a morality and a world-view strongly affected by Proudhon.

An essay published the same year, entitled *Reflections on Violence,* reiterated and developed the theme. The proletariat, if it chose to, could act upon the world around it rather than let the world mold it to its will. The proletariat could be shaken out of the lethargy into which reformist sops had cast it by the effect of *myths,* which Sorel defined as "the constructions of an indeterminate future in time," and which, he said, could provide a means of acting on the present, hence of preparing a revolution, if they incorporated the strongest tendencies (albeit unconscious) of the people, party, or class they were destined to affect. Here was one reflection of an age increasingly aware that dreams are relevant, and that dreams held in common are a tremendous lever in shaping, hastening, or simply revealing the future. And the dream—the revolutionary myth Sorel proposed, his great remedy against apathy and reformism—was the general strike, a method much discussed in the mid-nineteenth century as a way of stopping war by paralyzing the society. In the 1890's the notion was revived as a weapon of social war, paralyzing bourgeois society, leading to civil war and revolution. Strikes, even general strikes, argued Sorel, might not get far. But, even if they failed, they would stir up political consciousness among the previously apathetic masses, make both workers and bourgeois aware of their divisions and rival interests, heighten the revolutionary tension between them. As it turned out, the general strike was used rather to fight political battles * than to exacerbate the social situation.

A diametrically different, far more important theory was the revision-

---

* By the Belgians and the Swedes to win manhood suffrage or by Dutch labor to oppose a Strike Law, in the Russian Revolution of 1905, and in Germany to put down the Kapp putsch of 1920.

ism of Eduard Bernstein (1850–1932), who attacked the catastrophic views of more orthodox Marxists. Bernstein, who had been much influenced by the Fabians, noted that Social Democracy was progressing not (as Marx predicted) in the midst of worsening misery but within growing prosperity, which made the bourgeoisie itself more amenable to ethical arguments of social justice. Prosperity and democracy together could reform the social order without revolution. As for the Socialists, they should bend their efforts not toward an impossible and improbable revolutionary ideal, but toward obtaining greater parliamentary representation, strengthening the unions, furthering public ownership at the local level (municipal socialism, quite advanced in Britain, was forging ahead in Germany and Austria), enlisting bourgeois support for progressive reforms leading toward more efficient and just social organization. Bernstein's book, *Evolutionary Socialism* (1899), argued that socialism would come as the result of piecemeal changes, not in gigantic reforms initiated only after the attainment of political power. If Socialists took advantage of opportunities for action as they came along, socialism could gradually evolve out of a capitalist society. Such Fabian views of cumulative change, though close to the practice of French and English Socialists, were unacceptable to orthodox Marxists. Bernstein was made to toe the line and continental Socialism, following the Germans, continued to puff up in splendidly ineffective isolation.

The Catastrophic Heroes

The isolation of Socialists refers, of course, to potential friends; rivals they had enough. The origin of these rival forces, like that of Socialism itself, is to be found in the nineteenth century, when optimistic doctrines of progress founded on reason were met by counter doctrines inspired by unreason, or, by values to which reason bore little relevance. Among the representatives of these views Thomas Carlyle is often mentioned ("a Lear who never came in from the storm," an English reviewer once called him): prophet of will, forcefulness, and heroic genius, always insisting that instinct and imagination would provide the answers which his contemporaries sought in logical progression. But the great prophet of this camp was Friedrich Nietzsche (1844–1900), a German intellectual whose aphoristic philosophy would deeply mark the generations of the twentieth century.

Profoundly moral in an amoral world, Nietzsche had to recreate a structure of morality. Deeply religious in a godless world, he had to become God. Obsessed by death, he had to create an immortality of his own. The undertaking drove him to madness, which he himself described as "the mask of a deadly and too self-assured wisdom." "It is not doubt," he wrote, "but certainty that makes us mad." Of course, his certainties were answering the pressure of his doubts.

Friedrich Nietzsche.

Like all philosophers but more than most Nietzsche has lent himself to misinterpretation. The briefest account of what he had to say risks being misleading. What is said here reflects at most the kind of notions that contemporaries derived from reading his works (which they began to do around 1890) and even more from echoes caught at second hand from those who had read them.

Nietzsche reacted against the ruling determinism (which Darwin and Marx accepted and bolstered further) by asserting the primacy of human will over rational intelligence too apt to be affected by ambient pressures. Rejecting the human anthills piled up by modern industry and education, he insisted on the suppression of a mythical equality, the need for self-differentiation, "the creation of all powerful beings." What the world needed was not fat conformists but creative individuals superior to their circumstances, whose will and vision could transcend existing values and forge new ones. This insistence on personality and will in an age of growing conformity fascinated not only intellectuals—Gabriele D'Annunzio, the poet, George Bernard Shaw, Thomas Mann, and Richard Strauss—but popular publicists for whom the vulgarized version of Superman became a convenient theme.

The dramatic tension of works oscillating between dream and nightmare was enhanced because they expressed the fundamental instability and the insecurities of a fast-changing *fin de siècle* world in catastrophic terms. Many appreciated Nietzsche's criticism of the pretentious, false, and stodgy bourgeois values which he lashed with inspired moralism. Many responded to his appeal for vital and heroic living. One may well ask how far the sentimental and brutal world that Nietzsche tore apart was from the brutal sentimentalism of his admirers; one can point out that the false wings of his Superman, the pretentious philosophy of his followers, the inflated rhetoric of his *Thus Spake Zarathustra* were very close to those they excoriated. The fact remains that in the "era of the common man" most leading figures in thought and literature were in the opposition, arguing for Superman with Nietzsche and with Shaw, for the elite with Lenin, for detached, heroic individuals with Malraux, Mann, and H. G. Wells, André Breton, T. S. Eliot, D'Annunzio, Proust, Yeats, and Marinetti.

The new interest in nobility of character may have been an attempt to compensate for the disappearance of nobility of birth, fulfilling society's need to replace a lost authority by another whose ethical pretentions did not prevent its being modeled on an ideal image of the knightly nobleman. Knights, heroes, and heroics were a constant theme and inspiration to an age whose standards of behavior, rapidly changing, gave an impression that values were declining, creating a sense of need for new codes and orders, preferably reassuring new editions of the old. Besides, democracy itself called for outstanding individuals.* The modern hero is himself the product of a mass society, all of whose members are small, inconsequential, and eager to surpass their mediocrity by projecting their image of an ideal on one man after another. Aristocracies have few heroes, and those are often designated by birth or function. In democracies heroes are a necessity. Nietzsche articulated this need at a high level. Some of his disciples expressed it on a considerably lower plane.

It was the paradoxical fate of Nietzschean ideas to be devalued and demeaned by adaptation to the very mass conditions he detested. Proud elitists of the ending nineteenth century came to the conclusion that they could best be themselves as part of the particular society in which they had their roots, their land, and their dead. They fled the mass and came full circle back into the nation, affirming which (they said) they best affirmed themselves. We can see now that at a time when old authorities were waning and decaying, when even God was discovered to be dead (Nietzsche announced it in 1882), the nation could appear a living authority, its history and tradition endowing patriots with the sense of identity they felt was missing, and faith in it providing a religion that tapped new sources of social energy for national revival and self-assertion.

In 1846, the French historian Jules Michelet had penned one of the fundamental expressions of the populist nationalism of those days, his essay *The People*. The people, said Michelet, embodies the momentous myth of the spontaneous dynamic force of a historical creation naturally oriented to justice and collective freedom. Men are good. The People is good. There is no need to fear it. A nation revives its strength by plunging back into its refreshing, revivifying waves. The mass age would find a creed to its measure by learning to worship itself. Here were spirits with which one communed by instinct, not by reason. Here was an

* This is what President Grévy of France did not understand when he visited the annual painting exhibition during the 1880's. "No great painting this year," said the Director of the exhibition to him, "but a good average." "A good average—just what a democracy ought to have!" answered Grévy. Quoted in Gordon Wright, *France in Modern Times* (Chicago: 1960), p. 297.

inspiration that one expressed less in words than in primeval gestures, in violence, in action. Here, too, at last, was a political idiom that one could oppose to effete democracy, corrupting Socialism, all the socially divisive policies of reason.

Against Socialist notions of class struggle, Nationalists asserted the organic unity of the nation. For the rest, the most radical among them could sound remarkably like Socialists, opposing the decadent, hypocritical bourgeoisie, big business and big labor for their soullessness, the money powers that exploited the defenseless poor, calling for a social and a spiritual revolution that would regenerate and purify the whole community. The major difference between the nationalism that flourished in the early 1800's and that which revived as political force at the century's end, was that the latter had shed its liberalism and, while retaining certain leftist aspects as can be seen above, was also shedding its leftist associations.

Populist but antidemocratic, authoritarian, activist, and generally young, the new Nationalists applied current notions about the survival of the fittest (which the Marxists interpreted in terms of class) to the struggle between nations, consciously or unconsciously refocusing aggressions on the external plane. They also enlisted romanticism in the service of their cause, developing what would become two principal traits of mass politics in the twentieth century: the organization of paramilitary bands of toughs to sell their newspapers, terrorize opponents, and dominate the streets; and the paranoid style of politics (as Raymond Carr has called it). The latter, which saw society threatened by secret, subtle, and powerful conspiracies among its "foreign" elements—atheists, Masons, Protestants (or Catholics), Jews, Marxists, or even intellectual ·eggheads—had long been a specialty of conservatives and reactionaries. Now it became a political staple, particularly effective among the half-educated and those (increasingly numerous) who felt their way of life threatened in some respect.

One cannot tell to what extent the nationalist leaders were sincere in the fears they professed for national welfare threatened by subterranean enemies. One thing is sure: obsession with alien conspiracies deflected their sights from social problems which also, they claimed, concerned them. And the greatest of these derivatives was anti-Semitism: the Socialism of fools as it has been called.

Anti-Semitism: An Aberration

The Jewish lot in Europe has always been affected by paranoid visions. The intolerance manifested against the Jews—rising, at least in theory, from their guilt for the death of Jesus and their constant refusal to recognize his divinity—was basically connected with a tendency men show everywhere to suspect outsiders, particularly in times of strain when everyone seeks a scapegoat for his troubles. The strangers in our midst become obscurely and mysteriously connected with all the evil coming from outside, whether invasion, drought, or epidemic. In societies like the Christian, where social identification was closely connected with religious practice, the Jews were the most obvious, the most identifiable, and omnipresent aliens. When they did not conform to the society they lived in, they were considered unassimilable and possibly ill-intentioned. They must be kept at a distance, relegated to functions others would not undertake. When they turned in upon themselves, in their ghettoes or conventicles, they became even more suspect; when they converted, on the other hand, they must denounce their sometime-fellows and put flesh on the horrid skeleton of popular fancy to prove their own good faith.

In the course of the nineteenth century, the secular restrictions directed against Jews and stemming from religious prejudice were gradually removed. The emancipations witnessed in the major Western countries before 1848 followed more tardily elsewhere. Jews were confined to ghettoes in Piedmont until 1848, in Rome until 1870, excluded from Spain until 1869, lived only on sufferance in several Swiss cantons until the 1860's. By then, however, such holdouts were exceptional in the West. Given equal rights, Jewish communities prospered remarkably, took advantage of opportunities for education and enterprise, produced some considerable intellectuals, financiers, and entrepreneurs— notably the Rothschilds of Frankfurt, the Saint-Simonian Péreire brothers in Paris, or Bismarck's banker, Gerson Bleichröder, "the Rothschild of Berlin" and the first Prussian Jew to become a hereditary nobleman without conversion. They would soon figure prominently in political life, providing Britain with a Prime Minister in Benjamin Disraeli, France with a number of distinguished figures, and Socialist movements everywhere with an important section of their leadership.

In 1860, leading Jewish personalities had founded the *Alliance Israélite Universelle,* to protect and advance the interests of their people —as they did, for instance, soon after its founding by securing Napoleon III's intervention to improve the lot of Jews in the Romanian principalities. Jewish numbers also were increasing. Some three million around 1830, they stood around seven million forty years later. Between two-thirds and three-quarters of these lived in the so-called *Pale* of Russia and Poland, once, long ago, a refuge from persecutions elsewhere but now an immense ghetto stretching along the western borders of the Russian Empire. There Jews lived in separate Yiddish-speaking communities, subject to medieval restrictions and victims of destructive pogroms, in which popular dissatisfaction could be vented not against the government and the great but against more helpless objects.

Eager to escape their onerous condition and settle where opportunities and freedom were both greater, thousands of Jews left the Russian Pale, hundreds of thousands in the second half of the century, especially after the unsuccessful Polish rising against Russia in 1863 and 1864, and again after a great spate of pogroms that followed the Tsar's murder in 1881. Those who could made their way toward the Western countries or America. But most settled in the first freer lands they reached: Germany, Romania, the territories of the Habsburg Empire. Their coming in great numbers revived or emphasized the old prejudices against aliens, while blending with resentments of a more modern kind. In a time of change which many feared and resented, Jews appeared as the most visible agents of change: bankers, traders, journalists, carriers of a cosmopolitan culture and market economy. "Down with Rothschild! Down with Jews!" wrote a French nationalist leader, Maurice Barrès in 1890: "It's the formula which summarizes the resentments of those who have not enough against those who have too much."

Poor Jews frightened the rich and competed with the native workers; wealthy Jews competed with the native rich and were resented by the poor; successful Jews were thought to have succeeded at the expense of natives; unsuccessful Jews were resented when they cost money for relief; assimilated Jews were identified with their fellows of more recent coming who dressed, spoke, and behaved so strangely. All became the object of bitter, anti-Semitic campaigns that spread from the more backward Eastern countries—Russia, Romania, Hungary, Austria, Germany—in the 1870's as far as France in the late 1880's. Christian Social parties trying to build up a clientele among the peasants, the laborers, the lower middle classes of central Europe, found anti-Semitism a useful talking point directing social tensions not toward property owners but against the ill-assimilated immigrants. Above all, the new Nationalists saw them as the principal source of national weakness, an alien host exploiting and corrupting the race in whose midst it settled.

Contemporary fascination with the notion of "races," identified with "Peoples," directed Nationalist attention to racial purity in which they saw a factor of national strength. The Jews, they argued, marrying only among themselves, were the purest of European peoples and hence most likely to dominate all others; and they unveiled a vast conspiracy (shaped only in their minds) whereby the "Jewish race" engaged in a ruthless struggle against other races, kept itself pure while using every means at its disposal—the ruin wrought by its financiers, the social disruption of the political movements it manipulated, the moral and intellectual pressures of democratic or Marxist doctrines, the blood pollution of mixed marriages—to weaken its opponents. No matter what Jews did it could be held against them for they were judged guilty before trial began. At the turn of the century, a French liberal pacifist like Romain Rolland could persuade himself that Jews were "a national danger": at worst because they destroyed the Fatherland, at best in wanting to replace it by a wider community.

Notions such as these enabled Nationalists to ignore the real nature of social evils which they criticized and to concentrate their fire upon irrelevancies. Just as medieval epidemics were blamed on spirits, witches, or the Devil rather than on hunger, dirt or rats, so now real social evils were blamed on fantasies which the Jew embodied. While this prevented the identification of real evils, let alone their cure, it also maintained the notion of basic national unity, so that German or French exploiters were merely misguided tools, German or French Socialist workers ill-advised followers of conspirators outside the national body.

Such ideas were far more socially disruptive than the fantastic conspiracies that they pretended to reveal. Sensible men rejected them and they did not make a serious impact except where societies at the end of their tether adhered to them as a last resort.* They would come into their own with the Great War and the new conditions war created.

Europe and the World Overseas

Europe Explodes

Not coal or oil but men are the basic fuel of history, the energizing and explosive factor of its movement. No part of the world has tapped so much of this human fuel as Europe in the past two centuries; none had the resources Europe seemed to have. In the Stone Age, about 10,000 years ago, the total population of the world did not come up to 20 million. In 1800 it probably topped 900 million, which more than doubled by 1930 and trebled by 1960. Until quite recently, Europeans and their descendants led in this accelerated race to increase and multiply. Between 1800 and 1930 "whites" or "Caucasians" increased in number from 200 to 700 million: that is, from one-fifth to over one-third of mankind.** The great reservoir of manpower lay in Europe, whose population increased by 30 million between 1850 and 1870 and by another 100 million between 1870 and 1900, at which time it numbered some 400 million: about a quarter of mankind.

Between 1851 and 1960, about 60 million people left Europe for Siberia, other parts of Asia, or other countries overseas. Over a third of these went between 1870 and 1900, the flow increasing thereafter until it reached its peak before the First World War when, between 1909 and 1914, about a million and a half immigrants were spilling out of Europe

* Or, one might add, as in Russia, where governments in similar straits appealed to them to excuse their bungling.
** By 1960, with 860 or 870 million, their proportion of the world's 2,700 million population would once again be lower.

every year.* By 1900, Europeans had settled the Americas, Australia, New Zealand, Siberia, the Caucasus, and South Africa. More thinly and less solidly in some cases than in others, but in every case sufficiently to generate further expansion from the settlements themselves. Population seemed to grow at compound interest: the 10,000-odd French people who had first settled Canada in the seventeenth century had, by the twentieth, become five million (not all, of course, descendants of the original settlers); the new self-governing colony of Victoria in Australia boasted a population of 97,000 in 1850, a million in 1875—Melbourne alone, its capital, was a great city of over half a million when Queen Victoria died. European languages had penetrated everywhere, taken over the Americas and the Pacific, provided the major means of communication between myriad peoples in Africa and India, or the base of new mixed languages chiefly derived from English (*pidgin*), while new mixed religions inspired by Christian variants sprang up from China to Haiti, from Congo to Brazil.

Europeans had always traveled, traded, conquered, settled. The nineteenth-century acceleration of this process came when steam helped them to push up river valleys, repeating rifles gave them a murderous superiority over opponents, modern medicine provided immunity against tropical fevers. The natural obstacles and diseases which had once held them back were being eliminated. So, to a great extent, were the human ones. In 1849 Carlyle eulogized the law of force and cunning in *The Nigger Question.*** A little later, the English prophet of muscular Christianity, Charles Kingsley, asked whether Christian values applied to "beasts" like the Dyaks of Borneo. "Sacrifice of human life?" he asked their intercessors: "First prove that it is *human* life." Such feelings were widespread among invaders to whom superior technological equipment suggested a kind of righteous racism soon reinforced by Darwin's theories.

The white invaders shot or poisoned natives who hampered them, particularly in the Americas and the Pacific. In California as late as the 1870's Sunday shooting parties were organized against the Indians; and American atrocities are said by experts to compare only with the brutality which Russians exhibited in Siberia and Alaska. More murderous than weapons were the diseases which invaders carried, against which they themselves were immunized by habit, but which burned like wildfire through peoples unprepared for them. By 1876 the native population of Tasmania was extinct, the number of U.S. Indians diminished by three-fourths, that of New Zealand Maoris by four-fifths, and the aborigines of Australia, hunted like wild beasts, seemed to be dying out.

This was about to change. Much of the destruction, wrought un-

---

* The flow thinned to less than half that figure in the 1920's and to about 130,000 a year in the 1930's; it would rise again to half a million a year in 1946–1960.
** Soon answered by J. S. Mill's *The Negro Question* in 1850.

The Last of England, by Ford Madox Brown. The City Museum and Art Gallery, Birmingham, England.

wittingly, was a by-product of individual enterprise careless of anything except immediate profits or private satisfaction, changing the ecology of great regions, destroying native ways of life when they did not decimate the natives.* In due course, as in the industrial revolution, the more destructive aspects of private enterprise would incite the public conscience to intervene, while its more stimulating aspects benefited survivors or descendants of the sufferers themselves.

Bare figures tell the tale of a world in which the touch of Europe both opened scars and healed them. Epidemics were harnessed, famines circumscribed, food circulated farther, health improved. Today, the Maoris of New Zealand, the Indians of South America, have recovered their numbers of preinvasion days. The 800 million inhabitants of Asia in 1914 do not equal the population of today's China alone. This is some indication of our role in breaking the natural balance between soil and water on one hand and the number of mouths to feed on the other. Most suggestive is the case of Egypt, which probably supported some 7 million people in the days of its ancient greatness. By Napoleon's day this had shrunk to less than 3 million. It then began to rise: 5 million in 1850, over twice as many in 1900, about 30 million in the 1960's, it holds out the fearsome prospect of coming close to 75 million in the

*As we can find in *Moby Dick,* the mid-nineteenth century saw whales disappear from the Northern Hemisphere and whalers turning toward the Antarctic. By 1900 the buffalo, basis of the economy and livelihood of the American Plains Indians, was practically exterminated thanks to the repeating rifle. Buffalo would survive thereafter only in zoos and game preserves. Men exploited the whole world and whole species disappeared, hunted to extinction for a moment's profit before game preserves or artificial breeding (seals, ostriches) intervened.

year 2000 with no idea of how such numbers will find nourishment and livelihood.

Imperialism

Demography and technology provide the concrete background of modern imperialism, a reflection of the dynamics affecting European peoples and their offspring for several centuries and culminating as the nineteenth century ended in the vastest colonial expansion that the world has seen. During the two score years before 1914 the Western nations took to themselves the greatest part of the remaining world.* Much has been said and written about the economic factors behind this process which Lenin described as part of the final—monopoly—stage of capitalism. In fact, economic motives, which had their share in white expansion, need not have led to modern colonialism. As recent experience shows, capital could achieve its ends more profitably under different conditions. Egypt, before the French and British took it over, was already (in a British statesman's words) "an earthly paradise for all who had money to lend at usurious rates of interest or third-rate goods of which they wished to dispose at first-rate prices."

Throughout the colonial period, the economic involvement of imperial countries in their own empires was and remained relatively small. In 1914 Britain had not quite 13 per cent of its total foreign investments in its own colonial empire; France had less than 5 per cent; the Germans less than that. There was more German money invested in British colonies than in their own. To many, as to Benjamin Disraeli, the "wretched colonies" remained "a millstone around our necks." In 1913, German colonial trade amounted to half of 1 per cent of German total trade, while colonial deficits cost German taxpayers over a billion marks. Investors much preferred developed areas to backward ones, which meant that most Western capital stayed at home or went—like 70 per cent of Britain's foreign investments—to independent countries in temperate climates.

Industrial nations are always one another's best customers. The French put their money in Europe and in the Ottoman Empire, the British placed more loans in the United States than in any other country, the United States invested more in Canada than Britons did. Companies existed which made vast profits from colonial enterprises, but they never had sufficient influence or power seriously to affect national policy. This was achieved in part by national vanity and excess energy, in part by demagogues and dreamers who reflected these, providing them with purpose and direction. The true imperialist was really a dreamer, burning to

---

* As an example, in 1875 Europeans held 11 per cent of Africa; in 1902 they held 90 per cent. During that time one-tenth of the world's population and one-fifth of its land had come under their rule.

turn the fiction of today into the reality of tomorrow, to conquer Egypt or China, tame the Sahara, plumb the mysteries of the Congo, join Berlin to Baghdad or the Cape to Cairo, link the Mediterranean and the Indian Ocean. Before they lay on the green baize tables of diplomatic conferences or financial board rooms, the maps of men like these had sprung from the *Thousand and One Nights*. It is significant that the many-faceted movement of expansion remains embodied in what has been called the scramble for Africa, poorest and least profitable of the continents, yet redolent with challenges which sparked their own response.

Africa　　We have already seen that antislavery forces played an important role in encouraging African trade. There would be as many missionaries in Africa, Asia, and the Pacific as there were soldiers, most of the time and, until 1900, probably more. Trade was closely bound with missionary fervor, a fervor both cultural and Christian, both religious and secular. There was a great task of exploration, which mapped most of Africa between the 1840's and the 1880's,* but also of "alleviating human suffering" by bringing medicine, hospitals and popular education to the natives, as David Livingstone (1813–1873) insisted.

The hope that the explorer Speke expressed in 1855 "of raising his fellow men in the scale of civilization" was explicitly voiced by David Livingstone in his account of *Missionary Travels and Researches in South Africa* (London: 1857). Livingstone expected that, by promoting commerce, Europeans would end the slave trade,** "introduce the Negro family into the body of corporate nations," and bring "a much larger diffusion of the blessings of civilization." He was right in thinking that the economic activity would be more effective than "efforts exclusively spiritual and educational"; but he did not make enough allowance for exploitation and for greed, nor for the sheer destruction wrought by the appearance of this tougher civilization in the midst of traditional societies which it would smash to smithereens. Self-satisfied dynamism, viewing the values it brought as supreme, spared little thought for those which it displaced. What counted—as King Leopold II, one of the greatest colonial entrepreneurs, told the International Colonial Conference meeting at Berlin in 1885—was that "the most intelligent of our youth demand wider horizons on which to expend their abounding energy, our working population will derive from the virgin regions of Africa new sources of energy and render more in exchange."

By then the scramble for territories had already started, set rolling by adventurers fascinated by the possibilities of lands which they surveyed. It acquired momentum under the pressure of public opinion

---

* The sources of the Nile were found in the 1850's and 60's, and the Congo Basin mapped in the 1870's, Mount Kenya and Kilimanjaro discovered in the 80's.
** In East Africa, largely in Arab hands.

dazzled by vainglorious chauvinism. National pride prompted governments to seek compensation for one anothers' advances, national interest furnished them with arguments—the strongest of these being that territories acquired by others were lost to national trade. When the powers began to back their traders and investors, commerce turned into territorial claims and these spread from the coasts over the interior like great patches of oil. Shortly they would find, as a British prime minister put it, that the appetite had grown with eating. The division of Africa was manufactured in Europe and decided as if the land were empty, open to the decisions of European diplomats who projected upon it the ambitions and the bargains of another continent. Africa itself was still little known, the maps inaccurate, the frontiers often traced along lines of latitude and longitude for lack of more detailed information, their reality slight on the ground and long meaningless to peoples whose destinies had been bandied about European Cabinets and Conferences.

It is well to remember that the alternative to colonial expansion by one power was not freedom for a territory (whatever that might mean), but colonial expansion by another power. The undeveloped, unorganized parts of the world were going to be developed, organized, exploited, and dominated by some nation that would take advantage of the opportunities, respond to the challenges, they offered. The only question was which nation it was to be. The dynamic of imperialism was negative: trade may or may not have followed the flag (more often it was the other way around), but where one flag went the trade of others was largely excluded. So, dreams and pride were followed and borne on by policy and interest. But behind it all lay the burning vision of a few men like Pierre Savorgnan de Brazza or like Cecil Rhodes, the notorious King of Diamonds whom a French diplomat described as "a force cast in an idea." "One is facing more than a business man, an instrument of government or of a company; here is the passionate, violent, audacious, indefatigable agent of British expansion . . . ," manifest destiny personified in a heroic figure who complained that he could not reach the stars, declaring "I would annex the planets if I could."

For men like Rhodes, or the French General Lyautey who pacified Morocco, the joy lay less in acquisition than in action. In Africa, Siberia, or Southeast Asia, the great proconsuls of the time found a kind of *tabula rasa* on which their will and character could leave its mark. Perhaps that was the loudest call of empire for men who fulfilled themselves by pushing ever further without a direct object for their deeds. They managed to communicate their will and vision, appropriate to an expansive age, to a large part of the general public which gained not profits but vicarious satisfaction from what they did and from seeing maps on which the national possessions loomed increasingly large. Imperialists like these could have cited Cromwell: "He goeth furthest who knows not whither he is going." The costs of colonial

COLONIZATION IN AFRICA
TO 1914

Dependent states:

British

French

Belgian

Portuguese

Spanish

Italian

German

Independent states

AZORES (Port.)
EUROPE
0   1000 miles
ASIA
MEDITERRANEAN SEA
Tangier ER-RIFF 1912
MADEIRA IS. (Port.)
Tunis
TUNISIA 1881
FRENCH MOROCCO 1912
ALGERIA 1830, 1902
Tripoli
IFNI Agadir
CANARY IS. (Spain)
LIBYA 1912
Alexandria Cairo
RIO DE ORO
EGYPT 1914
Nile
MAURITANIA
FRENCH WEST AFRICA 1889, 1912
CAPE VERDE IS. (Port.)
Senegal
Timbuktu
Agades
Omdurman
Khartum
ERITREA 1885
Adowa
Dakar
Niger
Lake Chad
ANGLO-EGYPTIAN
FR. SOMALILAND 1881
GAMBIA 1843, 1888
Shari
EQUATORIAL AFRICA
SUDAN 1883, 1898
Fashoda
Addis Ababa
BR. SOMALILAND 1864
PORT. GUINEA 1490
Benue
NIGERIA 1886, 1912
ITALIAN SOMALILAND 1889
Freetown
SIERRA LEONE 1787
LIBERIA
IVORY COAST
GOLD COAST 1871, 1896
TOGO
DAHOMEY
Lagos
ETHIOPIA
Accra
CAMEROON 1920
Ubangi
Uele
L. Rudolph
Libreville
SP. GUINEA
Congo
L. Albert
UGANDA 1890
BRITISH EAST AFRICA 1895
EQUATOR
ATLANTIC OCEAN
Ogowe FRENCH
Stanleyville
Lake Victoria
Nairobi
EQUATOR
Brazzaville
Kasai
BELGIAN CONGO 1885
Tabora
Mombasa
CABINDA
Léopoldville
Lake Tanganyika
GERMAN EAST AFRICA 1885, 1890
ZANZIBAR 1890
INDIAN
Loanda
Kilwa
OCEAN
ANGOLA 1891
Elizabethville
L. Mweru
Benguela
Kubango
Zambesi
NORTH RHODESIA 1889
L. Nyasa
Blantyre
Mozambique
Mossamedes
Salisbury
NYASALAND
MOZAMBIQUE 1500
Tamatave
SOUTH RHODESIA 1889
Bulawago
Beira
Tananarive
GERMAN SOUTHWEST AFRICA 1884 (To Union of South Africa, 1920)
BECHUANALAND (PROTECT.)
MADAGASCAR 1643, 1896
Swakopmund
WALVIS BAY
TRANSVAAL
Johannesburg Pretoria
Limpopo
Fort Dauphin
Luderitz
Vaal
SWAZILAND 1903
Orange
UNION OF
ORANGE FREE STATE
NATAL
Kimberley
BASUTOLAND 1884
Durban
SOUTH AFRICA 1806, 1910
Cape Town
Cape of Good Hope
Port Elizabeth
RED SEA

enterprise were larger than the profits: in 1885 a French politician pointed out that for every Frenchman then settled in Algeria four men had died and two soldiers stood on guard. Why, asked Lord Kimberley, who had found both a fortune and a title in the goldfields of South Africa, why dispute for "barren deserts of places where white men cannot live, dotted with thinly scattered tribes who cannot be made to work." Nevertheless, as Beatrice Webb noted in her *Diary*, imperialist sentiment was "in the air!—all classes drunk with sight-seeing and hysterical loyalty."

If the material profits were dubious, the psychic revenue seems to

333

THE RHODES COLOSSUS
STRIDING FROM CAPE TOWN TO CAIRO.

Cecil Rhodes. Left: a contemporary cartoon from *Punch*.

have weighted the balance. Frenchmen, Belgians, Germans, Britishers, argued that their "conquest of virgin nature and heathen races" was a "peaceful crusade," bringing millions "into the Empire of civilization" helping them to "raise themselves bit by bit towards our level." Western superiority implied a moral responsibility to

> Take up the white man's burden
> Send forth the best ye breed—
> Go bind your sons to exile
> To serve your captive's need;
> To wait in heavy harness
> On fluttered folk and wild—
> Your new-caught, sullen peoples,
> Half devil and half child. . . .

The white man's burden, as Kipling formulated it, was heavy. On the other hand, willingness to shoulder it could be construed as evidence of superiority, avoidance of the responsibility as a sign of weakness, perhaps of decadence. "All great nations in the fullness of their strength have desired to set their mark upon barbarian lands . . ." argued the German historian Treitschke in 1887. "Those who take no share in this great rivalry will play a pitiable part in time to come. The colonizing impulse has become a vital question for a great nation." Conversely, the very act of self-assertion might be expected to improve a nation's forces and morale. To many French nationalists before 1914 North African expansion was an important factor of the Nationalist revival they wished to bring about, Moroccan territory—often described as

334

le Far West of France—would be the cradle of a new race of energetic self-confident patriots, the source of soldiers whose aid would be essential in struggles yet to come.*

Not only social energies but also social peace could be expected from the imperial harvest: social and demographic pressures would be eased by emigration, without the nation being impoverished by the loss of its men settling in foreign lands. The passions of the working classes might be directed toward common enterprises that would contribute employment, opportunities, and benefits more difficult to wrest from the possessing classes at home. "If you want to avoid civil war," argued Cecil Rhodes, "you must become Imperialists." Many were convinced like those Italian politicians who, in the 1890's, beset by public scandals and frightened by social agitation, thought to find a diversion in colonial enterprise . . . and found only defeat.

Others did far better. Thus, in the 1870's, the exploration of the Congo Basin was undertaken by an international association sponsored by Leopold II of Belgium and devoted to opening the Dark Continent to civilization. In 1885, a Congo Free State was recognized as independent, under the sovereignty of Leopold who undertook to suppress the slave trade, protect missionaries and explorers, and open his territories to international commerce. In fact, while the Arab slave trade was indeed suppressed, the Congolese were chained to more efficient slavery by being forced to labor on land and in the mines.** Their tribal lands were taken and all resistance was brutally suppressed. What had begun as a progressive enterprise turned into a ferocious pursuit of minerals, ivory, and rubber in which the worst atrocities were lost from sight before the indifference or ignorance of the public.

A few of those who knew tried to tell the world. In 1899 the Polish-born Joseph Conrad wrote *Heart of Darkness* to denounce (he told his publisher) the "criminality of inefficiency and pure selfishness when tackling the civilizing work in Africa." In Conrad's pages, even the hero —a once-liberal, progressive scholar, preparing a thesis on the eradication of barbaric customs—ended by scrawling his conclusion across it: "Exterminate the brutes." Perhaps it took a Pole to sympathize with the paradox of civilized people surrounded by barbarism, of subjects oppressed by superior power. In 1904, at last, the revelation of Congolese abuses set off an international agitation which ended in 1908 with the transfer of the Free State to Belgium, whose colony it became.

By then the Boer War (1899–1902) had brought the whole imperial issue into question by opposing a seventeenth-century farmers' republic founded on slavery and small enterprise to the twentieth-century

---

* Other Nationalists, on the contrary, condemned colonial enterprises as dangerous distractions from the "blue line of the Vosges" where the main task of *Revanche* against the Germans awaited patriots.

** The people of Mozambique still, apparently, maintain that monkeys refuse to speak for fear that if they do they will be put to work.

imperialist dreams of Rhodes, founded on mining interests and economic progress. The Dutch-descended Boers had fled the Cape to remain independent from the British. The modern age caught up with them when gold and diamonds were discovered on their ranches. Now the rural society for which they stood, reactionary and static, had to withstand far less the imperial ambitions of Great Britain than the demands of industrial society and capital. Kruger, the Boers' leader, was a puritan farmer who thought the world was flat and all worthwhile knowledge lay in the Bible. Rhodes was a visionary millionaire who pursued money for the power it brought and power for the great things that could be done with it—especially controlling the world through an Anglo-American union. Both inspired utter loyalty in their followers, for there was meaning as well as meanness in their visions. Inevitably (or so it seemed), anachronistic Transvaal succumbed before the British Empire. Less inevitably, it only did so after a long and desperate resistance in which the British troops suffered serious reverses and the British ego far more serious ones. The Boer War showed the British how isolated they were, and suggested an alteration of their diplomacy which led first to the Japanese Alliance and later to Entente with France and Russia. Equally important, it spurred soul-searching almost as profound as that which their defeat by the American colonies had suggested and accelerated important changes in the imperial structure.

For over half a century the stated goal of Britain's colonial policy had been responsible self-government for its component parts. Australia had been granted this in the 1850's, the British North America Act of 1867 set up a united Dominion of Canada with its own federal government and legislatures, the Cape colony was founded in 1872 and New Zealand in 1876. All, it will be noted, were white settler colonies where home rule was meant to prevent the disaffection which lost the American empire. In 1907, within a few years of the Boers' defeat, these colonies became dominions, and were joined within two years by a self-governing South Africa. A few men perceived that emancipation of white settlers would prevent that of native peoples—especially of Africans whose safeguard had prompted so much of nineteenth-century colonial enterprise. A look at Irish policies and problems would have shown what later decolonization would make obvious: that one man's freedom was to be achieved at another's expense. But comparative judgments of this sort did not begin to be made until mid-twentieth century.

India   The great showcase in which the possibilities and failures of colonial government were displayed was India, since the late eighteenth century crux of the British Empire. There the East India Company subjected to increasing parliamentary control lost first its monopoly of trade, then its commercial functions, and, finally, its governing power. This

An illustration from a contemporary book, *Campaign in India,* depicting an attack by the Bengal Lancers on the mutineers of 1857–58.

final change occurred in 1857, when the great Indian mutiny burst out of the varied discontents of change, caste and religious grievances, peasant dissatisfaction with foreign innovations, to shake the very core of British power. Reforms and interventions—abolition of suttee, in which a widow would throw herself on her husband's funeral pyre, and infanticide, efforts to emancipate women, disregard of the caste system, missionary challenges to Hindu religion, educational threats to Hindu and Muslim orthodoxy—provoked revolt directed less against the foreign presence than against the accelerated westernization of the past few years. If the trouble first broke out in the army, it was because there alone were Indians organized in any numbers. Beginning in 1857, fighting raged over North and Central India; European men, women, and children were massacred, battles were fought in temperatures as high as 110° in the shade, and more combatants on both sides died of sickness and heat than were killed in battle. By 1859 the mutiny had been put down largely with the help of loyal Indian units, the East India Company abolished, and reform accelerated to allow for the participation of more Indians in the magistracy, the executive, and the legislative branch of a government of India now run from London and controlled by the British Parliament.

In many respects, the sources of the great rebellion misnamed a mutiny may be found in the inevitable consequences of alien rule, however well-meaning. Yet Jawaharlal Nehru has drawn attention to the fact that one of the Hindustani words which soon became a part of the English language was "loot." Continued trade which was the origin of the British presence meant that, when the native administration failed, the

337

British must step in. The Moguls were no more than an expensive sham. They finally disappeared in 1856. Meanwhile, the peninsula was governed, administered, taxed, defended by the British. Indian economy was subordinated to British interests and British policy in turn was deeply affected by India's needs. India's security dictated the British orientation toward Russia, Persia, and Afghanistan, toward China, Burma, and Southeast Asia; it suggested the necessity of Egypt—finally occupied in 1882—and the significance of the Cape; dictated the occupation of coaling stations for the steam-driven iron ships which in the late nineteenth century came to defend the Empire.

Under British rule, religious murders were gradually suppressed, bandits thinned out and outlaws hunted down, telegraphs and railroads built, irrigation sponsored so that there were fewer famines.* Public works and public administration meant an educated class trained in Western ways. How could the British, asked Lord Macaulay, subsidize education according to native beliefs, use public funds to teach children an astronomy that would throw an English girls' school into fits of laughter, a history of kings 30 feet tall and reigns 30,000 years long, a geography where seas ran with treacle? A new Western-educated class grew up which absorbed English values to the point of reacting against England from which it had learned nationalism and a sense of its own tradition. Nineteenth-century Europeans had discovered Indian culture, Sanskrit literature, Buddhism, and the historical achievements of the Hindus. The westernized Indian, torn between his school and home, between fascination with the British Raj and frustration at the lack of opportunity to use his education, clutched at European admiration of his country's past for a tradition that he could take pride in, and on whose basis he could assert himself.

Crushed, the rebellion of 1857 left an enduring legacy of bitterness, enlarged the gulf between Indians and their occupiers, making the latter feel more insecure and the former more resentful. Attempts to govern India in an Indian way were now abandoned. The British were trustees whom providence set over the continent, not answerable to the people's will as in Australia or in Canada but only to their own sense of right and wrong. The Indians should have freedom too, like others, but only when they were fit for it. That time seemed far off, as the coronation of Queen Victoria in 1876 as Empress of India indicated.

The Indians would, of course, be ruled for their own welfare. As things turned out, they would see little reason to believe this. The British were concerned more with stability than with development, more with order than with reform. They concentrated on good administration and honest justice—which benefited most those who could afford it; on sanitation—which helped the population soar beyond the economic

---

* By 1940 nearly 33 million acres, one-fifth of the peninsula's cultivable area, were under irrigation.

potential of the country; on cash crops like tea or jute—which enriched planters, not the natives. Over one-third of the Indian peasants had no land; all were deep in debts whose interests (as high as 100–200 per cent) might take up four-fifths of a family's annual income. Old handicrafts and village industries collapsed before the influx of machine-made goods, and native industry was very slow in making an appearance. When it did start it produced the familiar horrors of industrial revolution magnified by the extreme poverty of the land. Child mortality among the working classes of Bombay was more than one in two. Life expectation, twenty-three years in 1911, would rise to twenty-seven years in 1931 and thirty-two years in 1955.

Still, the growth of local representative institutions continued, leading to demands for provincial and national self-government. In 1885 the Indian National Congress (established with official sponsorship) provided a forum in which the native middle classes could militate against the occupants. But, having succeeded in creating an Anglicized upper and middle class, the British now refused the moderate reforms these classes were demanding. The British, said the Viceroy in 1905, must govern the peninsula "as if . . . forever."

The Far East   We have noted the tendency for Europe to form and inspire the men and societies that would, in due course, become its challengers and competitors. Nowhere was this as true as in one Asian country which never lost its independence: Japan. For two centuries the islands had kept themselves tightly secluded against disturbing influence from the outside. This isolation collapsed before the guns of American warships appearing before Yedo (modern Tokyo) in 1853. Within ten years Japan shed her feudal garments and set out to oppose Western power by learning its secrets and adapting them to her needs. "Rich country, strong army," became the slogan of modernization, of the awareness that only productivity can finance military strength, that only military strength can defend riches, and that both—at that time—depended on skills and knowledge that could only be garnered from the West.

In 1868 the Emperor's "Charter oath" declared that "Knowledge shall be sought all over the world." It was; and it was put to use. Teacher training colleges were established in 1872. By 1886, 46 per cent, by 1896, 61 per cent, by 1906, 95 per cent of school-age children were receiving an elementary education. An industrial structure was built up. Cheap and shoddy foreign manufactures were countered by cheap and shoddy Japanese goods which the Japanese could turn out as shoddily and more cheaply than anybody else until it became good business to improve quality, when they demonstrated that they could do that too. But there was nothing cheap or shoddy about the military equipment or the military training in which they invested much of their resources and their

Prisoners of the Boxer Rebellion being held in Tientsin.

energy. Within a lifetime of 1853 the results of their will and enterprise would be seen in the defeat of a European power by the new might of modernized Japan.

The greatest of Asian powers, China, had also secluded herself from outside intrusion. But her masters lacked the Japanese capacity for decisive action. Except for Macao, which had been granted to the Portuguese in 1557 for services they rendered against pirates, foreign trade had been confined to the port of Canton alone. The foreign merchants trading at Canton operated under onerous restrictions, but their business was too profitable for them not to accept the rules set by the Chinese. Trouble came only in 1839 as a result of friction between the local Chinese authorities and the British. The latter wanted to sell their Indian opium; the former tried to enforce the imperial ban against it and quash all contraband. The right of Indian opium to the Chinese market was enforced by British battleships. In 1842 the Treaty of Nanking marked China's inability to withstand them and opened a long period of national disintegration before Western encroachments. Through the door which the British blasted open came other foreigners: French, Germans, Americans, and Russians, extorting more and more concessions, settlements, bases, extraterritorial rights, and picking off the frontier provinces of the Empire.

As the weakness of the imperial government became more evident, revolutionary movements and societies began to organize, some seeking national salvation in reaction and others in Japanese-style westernization. There were sporadic insurrections, but the imperial government maintained itself—partly with foreign help. In 1894 a crisis occurred when China stumbled into war over Korea not with a Western power but with her smaller neighbors in Japan, only to be disgracefully defeated. The shame of this defeat intensified the debate between westernizers and traditionalists. It also persuaded the imperial government to modernize the country's structure and these timid beginnings of reform stirred up a wild reaction, rising to fanatical heights in the Boxer Rebellion of 1900, which had to be put down by foreign intervention.* China became a kind of common colony of the foreign powers which controlled her ports, her customs authorities, almost her government. More and more students who wanted to learn how to reassert national independence against the foreigner went to Japan to study.

It would be Japan, as we shall shortly see, which reasserted Asia's will to independence and to imperial power.

The Intrepid Americans

The United States is a good if exceptional example of a colonial country which freed itself first from foreign rule, then from dependence on foreign capital, to become in turn a colonial and imperial power.**

When the constitution had been signed, the United States owed European creditors some 60 million dollars. From such small beginnings American borrowers made their country the world's greatest debtor by 1914, owing 6.5 billion dollars to a variety of European investors.† By that time the Union was a great world power. It had eliminated the native enemy and competitor of the invading settlers by killing the Indians, pushing them across its borders and herding the rest into reservations. It had broken the economic power of the slave-owning aristocracy in a great civil war (1860–1865) which liberated the slaves, opened the continent to settlement and speculation, and freed American industry of a conservative rival.

Encouraged by the vast demands created by the equipment of a continent with a growing population, protected by tariffs which the defeated South would not have let grow so high, fed by the cheap labor hordes of immigrants provided, industry grew apace. By 1889 the Eiffel Tower in Paris would be equipped with American elevators. By 1900 the United States claimed the industrial leadership of the world, which it would lead into a second Industrial Revolution that would be sped no longer by steam, but by oil and electric power.

Meanwhile, advancing across the continent which they would make their own, Americans expropriated or bought out not only their old British masters and other colonial powers like France, Spain, and Russia, not only the native Indians, but also neighbors like the Mexicans.

* The "Boxers" were members of village militias and patriotic societies organized to defend the country against foreigners. "Righteous Harmony Bands (or Fists)," they believed themselves invulnerable to bullets, murdered Christians and missionaries, and beseiged the foreigners in Peking until defeated by an international relief force.

** Such an evolution, far from being unusual, frequently appears in history. The story of ancient Rome, of the Parthian Empire, or of early medieval England may serve as examples of it, no less than those of sixteenth-seventeenth-century Sweden or of Russia. But such comparisons may appear less relevant than modern instances of similar developments in Australia or South Africa.

† Even the 11 million dollars needed to buy Louisiana from Napoleon had been advanced largely by English, Dutch, and French bankers.

Between 1850 and 1900 the population more than trebled, rising from 23 to 76 million, exports grew tenfold; one-third of the world's industrial power, 41 per cent of its railway mileage, lay within the borders of the United States. It was time, men like Cecil Rhodes insisted, that the United States shoulder the white man's burden; and it was to them that Kipling directed his appeal to that effect. Mark Twain answered Kipling in a little note the New York *Herald* printed on December 30, 1900, and which purported to be a salutation from the nineteenth century to the twentieth: "I bring you the stately matron named Christendom, returning bedraggled, besmirched and dishonored from pirate raids in Kiao-chou, Manchuria, South Africa and the Philippines, with her soul full of meanness, her pocket full of boodle and her mouth full of pious hypocrisies. Give her soap and a towel, but hide the looking glass."

In 1898 U.S. imperialism would cut its teeth on a suitably dilapidated foe: Spain. When the war ended, the United States found herself with a colonial empire on her hands: the Philippines, which were to be granted independence at the earliest possible moment and got it in 1946; Puerto Rico, which was annexed as a dependency in 1899; and Cuba. The Cubans had fought hard for independence and this they officially secured in 1902, when American troops evacuated the island. But the United States kept a base at Guantánamo (on a ninety-nine-year lease) and retained intervention rights which they exercised when circumstances appeared to call for it. The revolutionary ideal of a free, democratic republic foundered on the alliance of Cuban oligarchs and American interests. Cuba subjected its economy to a single crop—sugar, its sovereignty to American oversight, and its domestic politics to a succession of strong men.

The North Americans were taking the lead in inter-American affairs where Spain and later Britain had held sway. The Monroe Doctrine would be interpreted not only to keep others out, but to force or insinuate Americans in. Since 1889 Pan-American conferences held out prospects of close friendly relations which were belied by U.S. policies and by South American realities and desires. Most South Americans were closer in sympathy and culture to western Europe than to the Protestant power to the north. Many on the east coast found Europe more accessible than their own neighbors, let alone than the United States. In any case, Pan-Americanism was regarded as an instrument of political and economic penetration wielded by the superior power whose activities did little to belie the thought.

To face its new imperial responsibilities in both Atlantic and Pacific, the United States took a strong interest in plans for joining the two oceans by a canal that would allow its fleet to pass at will from one ocean to the other. The most convenient place for the canal was across the Isthmus of Panama, in Colombian territory. But Colombia was uncooperative in conceding what the Americans felt were safeguards necessary for the security of their canal. In 1903, revolt conveniently broke out in Panama province. United States forces intervened to restore order while preventing the Colombians from doing the job themselves. A Republic of Panama was swiftly organized, and hastened to sign a treaty recognizing U.S. sovereignty over the Canal Zone itself.

It soon appeared that the demands of the Monroe Doctrine called for armed intervention and occupation (to forestall European interference) whenever the United States judged fit: in Cuba in 1906–1909, in Nicaragua in 1912–1933, in Mexico in 1914 and 1916, in Haiti in 1915–1934, in San Domingo in 1916–1924. Clear indication that, with the best intentions, no great power can abandon its interest in the economic and political space it dominates.

The Uneasy Balance: Europe 1848–1914

It was against this background that diplomats and politicians went through their complicated motions, any account of which is bound to be schematic and selective. Historians have interpreted the events of this period as the fulfillment of a historical trend toward national unity and independence, progressively advancing through the events of 1859 (Italy's war for unity), 1866 (Austro-Prussian War), 1871 (Franco-Prussian War), all the way to 1918. Or, again, in terms of England's steadfast attempt to maintain a balance of power in Europe, and that of other countries to incline the balance in their favor. They have talked about the rivalry of Germany and France as a secular enmity rising to a climax between 1870 and 1940; or, more convincingly, about the progressive narrowing of the possibilities for international maneuver as Europe's debatable lands, which had long served as a kind of safety valve for great power ambitions (in the manner of the American frontier), were pared down by the appearance of new sovereign states, first in the center and then in the east of Europe. Every one of these theories provides some foundation for a general interpretation. But it is possible to include them in an argument which divides the time since 1848 into a short spell of twenty years or less dominated by France, followed by a longer period of German hegemony ending in 1944 or 1945. During this time Germany exhibited the same aggressiveness that her predecessors—Spain and France—had shown in the days of their ascendancy.

One can relate Germany's new energy to demographic changes by which France, still except for Russia the most populous country in the Europe of 1851, was soon outstripped by Germany as her population tripled in the course of the nineteenth century. About equivalent to French population in 1871, it would be 55 per cent greater in 1914.

POPULATION IN MILLIONS, 1851-1951

	BRITAIN *w/out Ireland*	*GERMANY*	*FRANCE*	*ITALY*	*RUSSIA* *w/out Asia*
1851	22.6	35.9	35.7	25	57.2
1901	38.7	56.3	38.9	32.4	103.4
1951	50.6	68	42	46.5	150

And, while there were more Germans, they were also younger, hence more active and more readily available for productive work or military service. By the eve of the First World War persons over sixty numbered 126 per 1,000 in France, only 78 per 1,000 in Germany. By 1940 the same age group accounted for 127 Germans in every 1,000, but for 135 English and 150 French per 1,000.

War in Crimea

At any rate, before the unification of Germany, France continued to be the most populous advanced country in Europe, and its policy, in the hands of the great Napoleon's nephew, Louis Napoleon (1848–1870), was dedicated to undoing the verdicts of 1815: reaffirming French supremacy, furthering the national aspirations which the victors of 1815 had scotched, dividing the Holy Alliance which Russian intervention in 1849 had reasserted. The first opportunity to carry out these intentions came when Russian ambitions in the Black Sea area began to alarm both Austria—fearful of her rival's expansion in the Balkans—and Britain, concerned for the security of India and its Middle Eastern approaches. Ottoman attempts to reform their ramshackle empire disturbed both their Christian subjects and Russian hopes for an early Ottoman collapse. In 1853, a Russian ultimatum demanded a watching brief over the interests of all non-Latin Christians in the Sultan's lands. When this was refused, Russian troops occupied Moldavia and Walachia, and the Russian navy moved toward the Bosphorus, destroying a Turkish fleet and convincing Britain that only intervention could keep Russia out of Constantinople. The clash of two obscurantist empires became a struggle between the interests of Western liberalism and the autocratic imperialism of the Tsar. "In this instance," noted Karl Marx, "the interest of revolutionary democracy and England go hand in hand." Indeed, only a few years after 1848 and 1849, many who cared little for the balance of power which Russian actions threatened, looked on the Tsar as a tyrant, and on his power as the chief obstacle to European freedom.

Thus, when war broke out in 1854, Russia was isolated. While Britain and France sought to put their naval power to use by besieging Sebastopol in the Crimea, Russia's main naval base in the Black Sea,

Interior of fortress guarding Sebastopol after evacuation by Russians.

Austria—but recently saved by tsarist intervention in Hungary—maintained a hostile neutrality. Piedmont, eager to curry Franco-British favor, provided an expeditionary corps in 1855. Only Prussia showed sympathy for a neighbor whose friendship she might someday need. For two years the Crimean War dragged on: messy, costly, and largely inconclusive in a military sense. Short of equipment, supplies, and food; led by brave, squabbling, incompetent generals; the troops on all sides suffered incredibly from cold, dysentery, cholera, and typhus. Characteristically, what we remember of the Crimean War are the charge of the Light Brigade—a body of British cavalry sent by a series of mistakes to attack impregnable Russian guns and destroyed in the process; and the work of the British nurse, Florence Nightingale, to ease the lot of the sick and wounded. Over 10 per cent of the French troops, over one-third of the British, perhaps half a million Russians, died—far more from sickness than in battle.

All sides were glad to conclude peace in 1856 after Sebastopol had fallen. The treaty signed in Paris in that year gave the Ottomans a respite from Russian pressure, transferred Bessarabia from Russia to Moldavia, replaced the Romanian principalities under Turkish suzerainty and neutralized the Black Sea: a humiliation Russia cast off in 1871. The great loser of the war would be Austria. The house that Metternich had built had finally collapsed. The failure of the Austro-Russian entente born in Napoleon's time opened the way to the advance of Prussia, which could take place only at Habsburg expense. It also opened the way to Italian unification, likewise achievable only against Vienna's interest.

The Habsburgs Humbled

With Russia eliminated for a generation, Austria weakened by Russian hostility, Britain more interested in peace and overseas affairs, Napoleon

III seemed to become the arbiter of Europe. The Treaty of Paris had been signed with a quill torn from an eagle in the Tuileries Gardens. For the next decade he would use his power to implement the nationalist ideas of his youth, when he had dreamed of "tyranny dethroned" and nations free at last to give themselves the institutions they desired.

Under the impulse of their ambitious premier, Camillo Cavour (1810–1861), the Piedmontese had joined in the Crimean War chiefly to assert their existence and their future claims to Anglo-French support. They would be the first to benefit from Napoleon's tendency to enlist his good intentions to the greater glory of France. In the summer of 1858 Cavour and the French emperor met at Plombières, a spa in eastern France, and there agreed how to provoke a war with Austria which would advance the course of Italian unity. It was, however, less the plot hatched by the two conspirators than Austrian blunders in threatening Piedmont that led to the outbreak of the war they wanted in April, 1859.

The Austrians' timid generalship led to their defeat in a series of engagements—greatest among them the battles of Magenta and Solferino, both fought in June—and their total loss of Lombardy. Soon after this, Napoleon III, appalled by the carnage of the battles he had witnessed, entered into secret negotiations with the Austrians, concluding in the Armistice of Villafranca (July, 1859), prologue of a compromise peace that threatened to cheat Cavour of the gains he banked on. Yet, Villafranca proved unenforceable and Austrian defeat permitted the Piedmontese to annex not only Lombardy but other states that had risen to the call of national liberation: Tuscany, Parma, Modena, and Emilia.

In the end, neither Cavour nor Napoleon got quite what he had hoped for. The former was disappointed of Venice, left in Austrian hands. The latter had not expected his Italian enterprise to snowball as it did when, in 1860, spurred by Garibaldi's expedition, the double annexation of Naples and the papal states created a Kingdom of Italy up to the gates of Rome. He consoled himself with Savoy and Nice, which Piedmont ceded to France in exchange for her support of Cavour's enterprises.

French diplomacy also promoted the Romanian cause. In 1856, the Peace of Paris had stripped Russia of the right to interfere in the Danubian principalities, and returned these to the Ottoman realm with a promise of "independent and national administration" within it. Before three years had passed, Napoleon's support enabled Moldavia and Walachia to unite under a common ruler. By 1862 the two principalities had merged into a new political entity: Romania. By 1866 they had acquired a prince of the house of Hohenzollern: Carol I, who brought them independence in 1877 and the consecration of a royal crown in 1881.

Napoleon had humbled the Habsburgs; he had advanced the interests of the Prussian Hohenzollerns, Vienna's traditional opponents, generally regarded as representatives of nationalism and progress in Germany. He would have liked to aid the Poles when they rose against their Russian masters in 1863, but neither Britain nor Prussia would co-operate. The British saw no reason to advance French power which had become too great already; the Prussians—aware of their own Polish subjects—were sympathetic to the Russians. In any case, they had better fish to fry: German national aspirations were expressed in 1864 at the expense of the Danes. Austrian and Prussian troops campaigned together to wrest the Duchies of Schleswig and Holstein from the Danish crown and Napoleon, peeved by British coolness over Poland, refused in turn to support their gestures on the Danes' behalf.

But Prussian ambitions went far beyond limited enterprises. Since 1862 Prussia's first minister had been Otto von Bismarck, a Prussian patriot and brilliant opportunist. Differences over the newly occupied duchies furnished the pretext for a break with Austria, skillful diplomacy afforded the opportunity to challenge her on favorable terms. Napoleon was sympathetic, so were the Russians. An alliance with Italy which was promised Venetia forced a split in Austria's forces; and English sympathies for Italy ensured Britain's benevolent neutrality. Above all, the Prussian army and the Prussian railroads brought swift victory. Helmuth von Moltke (1800–1891), Chief of the General Staff, who had already distinguished himself in the war against the Danes, used his country's new railroad network to concentrate his troops against the lumbering, ill-equipped, Austrians. In July, 1866, the battle of Sadowa (Königgrätz) in Bohemia foreshadowed the shape of the century to come, altering not only the map of Europe but its balance of power. After Sadowa, Austria was excluded from Germany. Prussia, her own territories vastly increased, forced most of her partners of the Zollverein into political federation too.

Prussia now dominated a North German confederation whose resources in man- and industrial-power matched those of France. The achievement of complete unity, by incorporating those German states like Bavaria which still maintained their independence, was only a matter of time. It was precipitated by Napoleon III's desperate attempt to rescue something from the ruins of his policy. He could not stand by while a dangerous rival rose without trying to obtain some gain that would serve French interests or at least salve their pride. Belgium, Luxembourg, the Rhineland, were all considered as possible consolation prizes. But Bismarck refused to co-operate, and other European powers were indifferent or hostile. French diplomacy sought allies, but Austria was suspicious and undecided; the Italian friendship foundered on the rock of Rome, which Catholic opinion obliged Napoleon to defend for the Pope against the Italian will to regain the nation's obvious capital. "Rather the Prussians in Paris than the Italians in Rome," declared Empress Eugénie, ignoring that the one would open the way to the others.

Franco-German tension grew, both sides increasingly persuaded that a showdown was inevitable. It came in 1870, when the Spaniards, desperately seeking a candidate for the throne from which they had removed a queen, persuaded a Hohenzollern prince (brother of the one ruling in Romania) to accept it. It came, too, during the summertime, when all who could were taking waters at some fashionable spa. The permanent secretary of the British Foreign Office had just remarked that he had never known such a lull in foreign affairs. The French prime minister, speaking in the Chamber, found that the peace of Europe had never been so stable. Then, the news of a Hohenzollern prince about to become king of Spain revived the Habsburg situation of long ago, the possibility of a two-front war for France, the certainty of a new diplomatic humiliation. Tempers boiled and did not simmer down even when the Hohenzollern renounced his candidacy.

Paris might have remained content with a diplomatic success. The war party, encouraged by Empress Eugénie, sought more. The king of Prussia, head of the Hohenzollern clan, must make amends to salve French tempers. Approached by the French Ambassador while holidaying at Ems and asked for an assurance that the Hohenzollern candidature would never be renewed, the old gentleman refused to entertain the suggestion. The cable he sent to Bismarck, with an account of his courteous refusal to discuss the matter further, was edited by his chancellor in such a way as to turn the defeat of Bismarck's policy into a snub inflicted on the French. Broadcast in the Prussian press, then in the French, sensationalized, exaggerated, the Ems telegram inflamed tempers in both countries to the point where all reason was abandoned. Belligerent Paris mobs abetted by a belligerent Chamber carried France to the war Bismarck later claimed he had always wanted in order to realize "the construction of a united Germany."

The Franco-Prussian War

In 1854 already, British public opinion had driven a divided government into hostilities with Russia "in defence of the right," and welcomed with Tennyson "the blood-red blossom of war with a heart of fire." Now, French public opinion—or what passed for it—would do the same for France, and with direr results. And so the French, the Spanish issue determined in their favor, nevertheless went to war with Prussia (July, 1870)—went to war and lost.

The first result of war declared was that the states of southern Germany, long suspicious of Prussian aggrandizement, joined their fellow Germans against the aggressive French. The next was that the superiority of Prussian staff work under Moltke's direction, and the greater efficiency of Prussian mobilization, railroads, and supply system, enabled them to concentrate long before French reservists could rejoin their units.

Outnumbered by nearly two to one on the battleground, outgeneraled, outfought, the French were pressed back in Lorraine, their main armies divided, their chief force under Marshal MacMahon surrounded at Sedan near the Belgian border, and shelled into surrender.

Within seven weeks of the declaration of war, the Emperor—who had accompanied MacMahon—was a captive in German hands (September 2), the Empire was no more (September 4). Another three weeks and Paris was besieged, to starve throughout the winter until an armistice (January, 1871) opened talks of peace. In May, 1871, the Treaty of Frankfurt showed that French supremacy in Europe was at an end. The French would pay a war indemnity calculated to match that which Napoleon had imposed on Prussia in 1807, and German troops would occupy eastern France until the indemnity had been paid. More important, France lost Alsace and much of the neighboring province of Lorraine to the new German Empire which had been proclaimed during the siege of Paris in the Hall of Mirrors at Versailles. The war had achieved the unity of Germany, north and south. It had been the king of Bavaria who, at Bismarck's urging* had hailed William I of Prussia as first emperor of the new German Reich.

A German Empire then; and a French Republic—third of the name— confirmed the great reversal begun in 1866. The greatest significance of the war, however, lay in the issue of Alsace-Lorraine which it raised between Germany and France and which, in Woodrow Wilson's judgment, "unsettled the peace of the world for fifty years." The defeat of the second empire need not have sowed lasting hostility between Germany and the French Republic. Loss of national territory was bound to turn occasional conflict into historical enmity, persuade both countries that the other was its "secular" foe, and create the preconditions for further conflict. Bismarck probably felt that Alsace-Lorraine would be the cement of German unity. For the present, he was not far wrong, but in the long run he built on quicksand.

Bismarck's Europe

Within a ridiculously short space of time and through three swift, successful wars, Bismarck's dream had been achieved and Germany, now Prussia's Empire, rose over Europe, a mass over 40 million strong. The problem now, as Bismarck saw it, was to stabilize the situation. Germany was sated and wanted no further change. Henceforth, Bismarck's great abilities were bent on preventing change in Europe, for any major conflict could result in a modification of Germany's favorable situation. His first concern was the isolation of France, so that the new republic could not pursue her plans of revenge. His second, rising out of this, would

---

* And his promises of Prussian subsidies for the Bavarian's vast artistic and architectural projects in and around Munich.

be to keep Russia and Austria from clashing over the Balkan spoils of decaying Turkey. The danger of this happening was stressed in the mid-seventies when a Bosnian rebellion against the Turks was followed by the intervention of Serbia and Montenegro and then in 1877 by that of Romania and the Russians. Hard fighting in Bulgaria and the trans-Caucasus ended in Russian victory by 1878. But the treaty which the victors imposed on Turkey suited neither Austria nor Britain, and a new settlement had to be negotiated at Berlin while Bismarck acted as arbitrator between the contending parties. Russia recovered Bessarabia; Serbia, Montenegro, and Romania were recognized as independent kingdoms; Bulgaria—considered too much under Russia's thumb—remained a vassal principality of the Turks.* Last but not least, great power balance was maintained when Austrian troops received the right to occupy Bosnia and Herzegovina, where the revolt had started three years before.

There is no good reason why so much fuss was made over the Balkans, except that the area provided the last debatable land in Europe. Bismarck, who held that they weren't worth the sacrifice of even one Prussian grenadier, had the right idea; but he could not persuade the Austrian soldiers or the foreign investors or the international meddlers to keep out of the thieves' kitchen. Neither Balkan wars nor Turkish collapse need have proved an international tragedy if the powers could have divided their loot amiably as they had done with Poland, instead of grudging everyone else's gains except their own. There was nothing wrong, there was nothing new, about international anarchy until it became rigid. Bismarck's purpose was to keep it fluid. Lord Salisbury described Bismarck's diplomacy as "employing his neighbors to pull out each other's teeth." It would seem rather as if he bent his energies on persuading them to sheath their claws or at least, if not, to use their teeth and claws on lesser antagonists whose straits would not precipitate a European war.

The base of his diplomacy would be the Austrian alliance. Once they had been excluded from Germany, it was in Prussia's interest to keep the Habsburgs friendly and to moderate Balkan ambitions which their defeat in Germany was bound to spur but which, if pressed too far, risked upsetting the uneasy balance. To do this, Bismarck calculated, he would make Vienna feel secure by German guarantees of her existence. In 1879, the Dual Alliance assured the Habsburgs of German support in case of a Russian attack. The treaty, concluded for five years but regularly renewed until both partners' collapse in 1918, became the keystone of German diplomacy. Yet Russian friendship had to be maintained. So Bismarck encouraged Russia to turn eastward, where her ambitions would not challenge those of Austria and where, furthermore, her expansionist policies would make Britain uneasy, thus hopefully moving that power to rely increasingly on German support. Italy, too,

---

* The southern part would only join the north in 1886. The country became an independent kingdom in 1908.

had to be prevented from disturbing Austria. This was done by encouraging her to join the Austro-German camp in what became the Triple Alliance of 1882, and to spend her energy in Africa where she would clash with France. France, lastly, must have her eyes diverted from Alsace-Lorraine. She was encouraged to seek compensation overseas, where, in her turn, she clashed with Britain and with Italy, powers which otherwise might be too amical toward her.

All this worked well enough while Bismarck, at the helm of the state, steered it through the shoals of trouble. By 1890, when a young emperor, William II, decided to "drop the pilot," it was beginning to fail, less under political than under economic pressures. The free trade policies which much of western Europe had adopted during the prosperous sixties succumbed to criticism from sectional interests when times got worse in the mid-seventies. Developing industries demanded protection; so did the farmers threatened by a flood of grain from Russia and the New World. In the United States alone 400 million acres were brought under cultivation between 1860 and 1900. Yet it was not so much new lands being put to plow, as the new railroads, which, in the United States were tapping the wheat fields of the Great Plains and in Russia bringing grain to the Black Sea and Baltic ports. Their effect had been delayed first by the Crimean War interrupting Russian trade during the fifties, then by the American Civil War interfering with United States exports in the sixties. But then, in the seventies and eighties, reduced transport costs more than halved the price of grain shipped to European ports. As a result, tariffs began to rise in the United States and Russia, Germany and France. Between 1879 and 1893 every Western country except Britain, Holland, and Belgium built ever higher walls around itself. With tariffs there went friction, and one such issue hammered in the wedge between Russia and Germany, the latter's agricultural producers doing all they could to keep out cheap grain from Russia's Polish and Ukrainian wheat fields.

Economic differences between Germany and Russia were compounded by renewed friction over Russia's Balkan activities. In 1886 and 1887 Bulgaria provided the occasion of new strains which almost led to war. They were resolved, but in the process, as part of German pressure on St. Petersburg, Russian bonds had been excluded from the Berlin stock market. Russia could not develop her resources or maintain great power status without capital. Hard put for this and unlikely to get what she wanted in hostile London, she turned to France, which had money to lend and every interest in lending it if, by doing so, she could detach Russia from her German friendship. Within a few years (1891–1894), the two countries were allies, though odd ones for the Russians remained friendly to Germany and hostile chiefly to Austria and Turkey, while the French (holding most of the Turkish state debt) were cool to Russia's Balkan plans and hostile to Germany. Russia and France

Bismarck.

could agree only on common enmity to England, whose overseas enterprises clashed with the ambitions entertained in Paris and Moscow, and this posed no threat to German interests as yet.

Yet Bismarck's ingenious structure was not at the end of its troubles. For, encouraged by hints from Berlin, the French had been pressing forward in Africa, where Franco-British rivalry in a dozen places climaxed at Fashoda in 1898, when a British army pushing up the Nile met a small French mission installed there after a year-long 3,000-mile march to claim the upper Nile for France. The soldiers faced one another while the diplomatic crisis spun itself out in Europe. It soon became clear that France could not fight a power which, unassailable in its island, could use her fleet to pick off French colonies one by one. She not only gave in on Fashoda but, drawing the conclusions of her failure, decided that understanding would be more profitable than contest. The outstanding issue between Britain and France was Egypt, which Britain had taken over by default but very much to French chagrin.* France, which held Algeria and Tunis, coveted Morocco. Perhaps the French could concede the British rights to a country that did not belong to them but which they already held, if Britain looked with favor on the idea of France acquiring a country which did not belong to her but that she would like to hold. In 1902, the German ambassador in London reported a long conversation between the French ambassador and a leading British minister of which he overheard two words: "Morocco" and "Egypt." His government reassured him. It was as unlikely that France and Britain would draw together as that Britain and

* Egypt, still formally a Turkish dominion until 1914, gained strategic significance after the opening of the Suez Canal in 1869 gave it control of a crucial route to India and the Far East. Though the Canal had been a French enterprise, Britain acquired a controlling portion of the shares in 1875 and followed this up seven years later with military occupation of the country—a *temporary* measure which ended only in 1956. The Canal and the Middle Eastern base Egypt provided remained the crux of Franco-British rivalry for over a generation following the 1870's.

Russia would resolve their differences. Two years later the *Entente Cordiale* had come into being; three years more and the differences between Britain and Russia had been resolved as well.

Bismarck's successes were coming home to roost. Launched on a course of eastward expansion, the Russians were not doing things by halves: in Persia, in central Asia, in China, Manchuria, and Korea, they pushed forward, threatening British interests in the Middle East, in India, and in the Far East too.

A short story by Rudyard Kipling, written in 1891, features an unpleasant Russian cavalryman visiting a British regiment in India, all of whose officers, like their Russian guest, are convinced that there would soon be an Anglo-Russian war for India.* There is no understanding turn-of-the-century politics without remembering this widely held assumption.

The British became increasingly uncomfortable. They had reveled in their splendid isolation: now they found it lonely and looked for support. The only power that could effectively aid them was Germany. But Germany, as Bismarck said, had no intention of pulling British chestnuts out of the fire. Moreover—staunchly though Bismarck had resisted the notion of colonial expansion—business and shipping interests and above all the impetus and vainglory of national pride, had propelled him into the colonial field as well, and his successors looked upon the British as rivals. They, like the French, had drawn the moral of Fashoda and decided that a colonial empire needed a fleet to protect it—a fleet which could hurt its probable rival badly even if it could not hope to match it. In building such a fleet the Germans posed a serious threat to British security and even more to British pockets; for, faced with the German naval building program, the British had to keep ahead whatever the cost. This did not help the fraying friendship between English and Germans or calm British nerves.

Only one power at the beginning of the twentieth century felt just as threatened by Russia's advance as Britain, and this was an unknown quantity, risen out of limbo to dubious prominence: Japan. Japan, too, looked for support in Berlin against Russia, and failed to get it. In 1902 Britain and Japan gambled on each other's support. Clearly, the treaty they signed that year was directed against Russia; but there was danger that Russia's ally—France—might be dragged in somehow. And it was partly to forestall this eventuality that the Franco-British *Entente* of 1904 was concluded at the time when Japan, her flank secured, set about liquidating the Russian danger. A sudden night attack sank a good

---

* The opening of Kipling's tale is particularly interesting: "Let it be clearly understood that the Russian is a delightful person till he tucks in his shirt. As an Oriental, he is charming. It is only when he insists upon being treated as the most easterly of western peoples instead of the most westerly of easterns, that he becomes a racial anomaly, extremely difficult to handle. . ."

Theodore Roosevelt at Portsmouth with (*left to right*) Witte, Rosen, Komura, and Takahira.

part of the Russian Far East fleet moored in Port Arthur, a sudden land invasion rolled the Russian armies back through Manchuria, and the heavy fighting that dragged through 1904 and 1905 only confirmed these first defeats. By 1905 a Russian relief fleet had been annihilated in its turn, and the naval fortress at Port Arthur forced to surrender. The peace, eventually signed in 1906 at Portsmouth, New Hampshire, under the aegis of President Theodore Roosevelt, settled Russian evacuation of Manchuria, transferred Russian leases of Chinese territory (especially Port Arthur) to Japan, and determined Japanese preponderance in Korea. Russia would advance no farther in the Far East, where the sun of a new power was arising. Soon, Russian diplomatic interests swung back to their other pole: the Balkans. Not before, however, they had settled their differences with England in an agreement of 1907 which focused on Persia but intimated more. After 1907 the Triple Alliance faced a Triple Entente joining France, Russia, and Britain.

Triple Alliance and Triple Entente

Yet both these groupings were exceedingly fragile. England's chief concern was to keep out of war. France's rival was Germany: she had no quarrel with Austria. Russia's rival was Austria: she had no quarrel with Germany. Germany felt threatened by France and made Britain feel threatened. Austria's interests lay southeastward. As for Italian interests, they lay in Austria; and, indeed, Italy detached herself progressively from her allies, once she had resolved her conflicts with France by an agreement in which the French recognized Italian interests in Libya (then a Turkish possession) in return for Italian recognition of French interests in Morocco (then a more or less independent state).

Africa and the Balkans would be the two weak points of European peace, the focus of the long series of prewar crises whose cumulation

354

built up a situation in which the outbreak of war came to be taken for granted and only its occasion remained in question. While the powers jockeyed for place, international tensions magnified the growing sense of insecurity that marked the opening years of our century—an insecurity even stronger on the social and intellectual than on the military plane— turning people toward symbols of stability and lasting order: armies, navies, flags, and discipline. The multicolored elegance of uniforms at a time when gold braid, plumed helmets, and garb of every hue and shade were still the norm delighted the crowd. So did military tattoos and torchlight processions reinstituted shortly before the war to catch civilian fancy. So did the massive self-confidence of officer corps in which many could see the last surviving instance of traditional authority.

But there was more to armies than braid and pretty fancies. After 1866 and 1870, conscription, universal military service, militarized Europe from Belgium to the Balkans. War was seen to depend as much on transport as on armaments, especially on railroad networks able to move troops and matériel swiftly from one point to another. Strategic railways added a costly burden to national budgets, and one which does not usually appear in armaments statistics. But modern war was also waged with modern weapons, their range ten times greater under Napoleon III than in his uncle's day, forty times greater in 1900 than in 1800, vastly more deadly and vastly more efficient. When the American Civil War broke out, Colt had given mankind his repeater revolver. Soon Doctor Gatling produced his "labor-saving device for warfare," capable of firing first two hundred then twelve hundred rounds a minute. By 1889 the modern machine gun was perfected, capable of incredibly murderous rates of fire. But these and other martial splendors involved crippling costs, the higher because modern war materials have a rapid rate of obsolescence. Between 1875 and 1914 armament expenses doubled in France, tripled in Germany and Britain. One-third of Russia's budget went into armaments. In France, 1.5 billion was allotted to the army and navy compared to 330 millions for educational purposes. Every shell of a battleship cost the yearly salary of a public employee. This at a time when, unlike any previous period, the state had also to face the costs of burgeoning public education, social security, and social welfare.

For the age of mass production replaced highly trained professional soldiers by mass armies which were like the mass products of industry— cheaper and more numerous but, like machine-made goods, not quite the same as in professional days. Mass armies meant educational and medical services for the masses that would serve in them, to make them fitter, more literate, more technically efficient and also more uniform. If all members of the population were subject to conscription it mattered that they should be fit, that they should be loyal, that they should speak and understand one and the same language. This played a major role in the social revolution of our time. But, having so to speak nationalized the masses, the politicians found they had to count with them, heed the resentments, the prejudices, and antagonisms which they had helped create by education and by propaganda. Doctor Frankenstein had made public opinion and public opinion henceforth was a monster to take into account.

Public opinion fed on crises and was exacerbated by them. There was a host of minor incidents, border troubles, and flare-ups which heightened tension, filled the air with threats and counterthreats, sharpened the sense of insecurity and mutual suspicion. The British had given the French a free hand in Morocco in return for French recognition of their position in Egypt. Now, as France edged forward, the Germans also sought a *quid pro quo.* Their heavy-handed methods created serious crises in 1905 (Tangier) and 1911 (Agadir), gained them little, but persuaded the French that Germany was bent on war. She was not: she was only clumsy. Balkan affairs would show that she was not alone in this respect.

In the Balkans, the national aspirations of small newborn states threatened what was left of Turkey's realm in Europe. They also endangered the multinational empire of the Habsburgs. In 1908, the imprudent schemes of a Russian foreign minister with an eye on Constantinople failed, but enabled Austria to annex the provinces of Bosnia and Herzegovina which Austrian troops had occupied since 1878. This proved a serious setback to Russian prestige; one whose repetition St. Petersburg would not permit. But Serbia, remembering the increase that wise alliances and fortunate campaigns had brought Piedmont, still dreamed of a great South Slav kingdom; and her ambitions cast a shadow over the newly annexed provinces, and over Croatia too. The stronger Serbia became, the greater her attraction for the Slav subjects of Austrians and Magyars. In 1912 and 1913 this danger grew acute, through a conjunction of African and Balkan issues.

The French, determined to secure North Africa from Tunis to the Atlantic, had promised compensation not only to the British, but to the Italians too. As usual, it was to be carved out of somebody else's territories: in this case, those of the Ottomans. When, in 1911, France openly declared her protectorate over Morocco, Italy was free to raise her claims: Italian troops attacked the Turks in Libya and occupied Tripoli. The Turks resisted with determination and the fighting drew out. Meanwhile, Turkish problems provided a chance which the Balkan Christians were quick to seize. They had several times—but unsuccessfully—tried to defeat the Ottomans and deliver those Orthodox Christians still remaining under Turkish rule. In 1912—with the main Ottoman forces fighting the Italians—Serbia, Bulgaria, Greece, and Montenegro attacked and defeated their old Muslim masters. But their troubles were only just beginning. Bulgaria also saw visions of a great South Slav kingdom, only led by her; and in this she was encouraged

THE BALKAN WARS

- Independent Balkan states
- Ottoman Empire

1913

1 To Greece, 1913
2 Annexed by Austria–Hungary, 1909
3 New State, 1912
4 To Italy, 1912
5 To Montenegro, 1913
6 To Serbia, 1913
7 To Bulgaria, 1913
8 To Rumania, 1913
9 To Greece, 1908

RUSSIA
Odessa
MOLDAVIA
Bucharest
ROMANIA
TRANSYLVANIA
WALLACHIA
Danube
AUSTRIA–HUNGARY
Budapest
BULGARIA
Sofia
Belgrade
SERBIA
BOSNIA-HERZEGOVINA
Sarajevo
CROATIA
DALMATIA
MONTENEGRO
Cetinje
ALBANIA
MACEDONIA
Constantinople
Adrianople
Gallipoli
OTTOMAN EMPIRE
MYTILENE
CHIOS
EUBOEA
Athens
GREECE
DODECANESE
RHODES
CRETE

1900

Vienna
RUSSIA
MOLDAVIA
Bucharest
RUMANIA
TRANSYLVANIA
WALLACHIA
Danube
AUSTRIA–HUNGARY
Budapest
BULGARIA
(Autonomous tributaries of Ottoman Empire, 1878)
EASTERN RUMELIA
(To Bulgaria, 1885)
Sofia
Belgrade
SERBIA
BOSNIA-HERZEGOVINA
(Occupied by Austria–Hungary, 1876)
Sarajevo
CROATIA
DALMATIA
MONTENEGRO
Cetinje
MACEDONIA
OTTOMAN EMPIRE
Constantinople
Adrianople
Gallipoli
MYTILENE
CHIOS
EUBOEA
Athens
GREECE
DODECANESE
RHODES
CRETE

0   200 miles

by the Austrians who wished to balance the growing influence of Belgrade. By 1913, the victors had fallen out over the spoils. Serbs, Greeks, and Montenegrins, joined by Romania, fell upon the Bulgarians whose ambitions threatened all of them. Thus, by the end of 1913, not just the Turks but the Bulgarians also, became the losers of the Second Balkan War. And these remote conflicts involved great interests: for Serbia's victory redounded to the prestige of her patron, Russia, and increased the insecurity felt in Vienna.

There, some politicians and many soldiers were becoming persuaded that the national agitation and the anti-Habsburg conspiracies which grew in intensity with the excitement of the Balkan Wars were a serious danger to the security of the monarchy. They could only be suppressed by suppressing Serbia and turning her into a province or a satellite of the Habsburg empire. Such an undertaking must mean war. And an Austrian attack on Serbia would not take place in a vacuum. The Russians could not stand by and see their Slav brethren beaten down. If they intervened to defend them, they would set in motion the machinery of rival alliances, with Germany bound to aid Austria and France Russia. Yet—whatever speculations might be pursued in Vienna—Austria was in no position to start a major war. For one thing, the Magyars had no wish to incorporate still more Slavs into a realm where they were already too numerous for their taste. Budapest opposed a warlike policy. More important, the Germans held their Austrian allies on a leash, and only when they slipped it did war become a threat.

In any case, Austro-Serbian friction was only one of many conflicts that diplomacy and compromise had settled in the past. Why should they fail this time? As it turned out, it seems that war came when enough men believed that it would come and, most particularly, when certain men in Germany became convinced that the sooner it came the better.

Discussions of the war of 1914 and of the lesser conflicts that preceded it have tended to attribute them to imperial rivalries and economic interests. But the first never led to full-scale conflict between European powers (which preferred weaker prey), and the second operated on the whole *against* a settlement by arms (peace is more profitable than war). True, wars raise prices, create profitable scarcities, make fortunes for brokers negotiating loans and manufacturers selling supplies. But economic arguments against war went deeper. Russia was Germany's greatest source of supplies, Britain was Germany's best customer. The French were more interested in trade with Austria than in fighting her. British financial circles were strongly opposed to any intervention in continental conflicts. War increased taxes for the rich and took the peasants' sons for military service, it disrupted business, it hurt government credit, it strengthened the military whom the workers detested and the middle class distrusted. The arguments for war, therefore,

Archduke Francis Fer-
dinand and his wife
shortly before they
were assassinated.

found more solid ground in sentiments of national pride, concern for
the safety of the nation's soil, love of excitement and of sensation,
even calculations that defeat might open the gates of revolution. All
these were reinforced by recurrent crises, by the mounting uncertainty
that hurt trade and fretted tempers, by a growing feeling that, if there
was to be war, it had better come and be done with.

But arguments and even feelings do not make war or unmake it. Men
decide, who have the power to decide and the means to act. When, in
June, 1914, Archduke Francis Ferdinand—heir of the old Emperor Francis Joseph—and his wife were clumsily murdered in Bosnian Sarajevo
and Austrian resentments against Belgrade where the murder had been
prepared welled into bitter hatred, there was nothing that made war
inevitable except the will of those who wanted it to take place. These
men now sat in Vienna and Berlin.

The constant threat that Serbia's existence and ambitions posed to the
fissile Empire seemed to have materialized at Sarajevo. Vienna was determined that the Serbs should be brought to heel, their challenge eliminated once and for all. Encouragement came from the leaders of the
German General Staff and from the Kaiser himself. The Austrians felt
their position getting ever weaker as nationalism threatened the monarchy with disintegration. The Germans felt at the peak of military
preparedness. In a few years their competitors might gain on them or
even, if Russia ever marshaled its latent strength, overtake them. But
soldiers, in those days, did not decide on wars; they only fought them.
The trouble was that Germany lacked other effective institutions with
power to decide. The German people spoke with many contradictory
voices: it had a representative assembly—the Reichstag—but the assembly had neither authority nor effective powers. Since 1890, the
Chancellor had been a creature of the Emperor; since 1908, when he
had disgraced himself in an interview to an English paper, the Em-

peror had lost much of his own political authority. Hence crucial decisions were made by action rather than deliberation; gestures and intrigues committed the German Empire to its course, and the actors found themselves in charge by default, writing their script as they went along.

The Germans promised to back Austria to the hilt against the Serbs. The Austrians sent the Serbs an impossible ultimatum which the Serbs all but accepted to everyone's surprise. The Austrians, set on war, seized on one slight demur to declare it. The Russians, unable to stand by and see their protégés destroyed, mobilized against Austria, were told that this would bring Germany into war against them on Austria's side, and nevertheless went on. The Germans set their own war plans in motion. The French, who still hoped they might escape a war, had to be forced to fight; for German war plans envisaged a two-front war beginning with a knockout blow at France, after which the giant in the east could be dispatched at leisure. The essence of the plan was an attack on France, passing through (neutral) Belgium. This was one act England would not condone. Her ultimatum, demanding German evacuation of Belgian territory, referring to the little kingdom's neutrality guaranteed by Germany since 1839, exasperated the German chancellor: "Just for a scrap of paper, Great Britain is going to make war upon a kindred nation," he remarked bitterly to the British Ambassador. So, having hesitated to help France, Britain came in to help itself by helping Belgium. And in London, while crowds cheered around Buckingham Palace, the Foreign Secretary, Sir Edward Grey, looking out of a window at the gas lights being lit in the street below, remarked to a friend: "The lamps are going out all over Europe; we shall not see them lit again in our lifetime."

By August 4, 1914, a great part of Europe had gone to war. One thing which had played little part in it was the alliance structure. The Austro-German Alliance, designed to hold Austria in check, had actually dragged Berlin into a Balkan quarrel, not so much by the workings of the treaty as by the unconsidered gestures of Berlin. Russia had no obligation to intervene on Serbia's side, France hoped to escape her obligation to join Russia, England felt no obligation at all to fight for Serbia,* and, as for Italy, the Triple Alliance bothered her not at all.

Thus all the participants joined in with· a perfectly good conscience, each able to tell himself he had never wanted war. Both Austria and Serbia believed that they were fighting for survival; the Russians believed that honor and Slav solidarity commanded their intervention on Serbia's behalf, which only German meddling had turned into gen-

---

* Just before war broke out London's *Punch* commented:
  Well, if I must, I shall have to fight
  For the love of a bounding Balkanite;
  But O what a tactless choice of time,
  When the bathing season is at its prime!
  And how I should hate to miss my chance
  Of wallowing off the coast of France!

EUROPE ON THE EVE OF WORLD WAR I

Nations of the Triple Entente

Nations of the Triple Alliance

eral war. The Germans, sharply aware of the hostility their clumsy aggressiveness had itself created, feared encirclement and the isolation that an Austrian defeat would bring. The French felt they had been forced to fight and fought in a good cause, for national integrity and for Alsace-Lorraine. The British, whatever triggered their intervention, followed a secular policy: "We have always fought for the balance of power," wrote the *Times* of August 4. "We are fighting for it today."

War 1914–1918

Between 1871 and 1914 there had been no national wars in Europe outside the restricted cockpit of the Balkans. For over forty years the West had enjoyed peace and growing prosperity, a period of time to which the twentieth century would wistfully look back and which it would invest with all the charms of a lost golden age. How true this was for people living then we shall see in later chapters. Yet peace itself, undoubtedly maintained, was shaken constantly by crises which never allowed fears of war to fade. Peace did not mean peacefulness, and those who grew up in the last third of the nineteenth century never felt that war was far away. Then, with the new century, tensions increased. Crisis followed crisis, inuring public opinion to the thought of war, sharpening national tempers and the expectation of an inevitable clash. Many young men, ignorant of warfare, longed for its thrills and glories. Many older men saw in it an opportunity for fulfillment or revenge. The social and political conflicts, sharpened by the rise of workers' parties or by nationalist claims, were setting nerves on edge and suggesting to some that the consensus which a war could bring would solve insoluble problems, to others that war might accelerate the fulfillment of their revolutionary hopes.

The outbreak of war pricked the growing tensions and brought relief from political and social struggles. All could express themselves now, if only briefly, by turning their hostilities against external foes. The German chancellor rejoiced about "this wonderful spirit, which welds the hearts of the German people into an unprecedented unity . . . As if by magic, the barriers have fallen which . . . separated the sectors of the people from each other . . . It is a liberation and a blessing that at last all this trash has been swept away, that only the individual person counts, one equal to the other, one stretching his hand to the other for a single, holy goal." This temper would pass, but the memory of it survived: the memory of exaltation, of fraternity, and of what could be done with people in such a mood.

Indeed, for a good many men—especially those employed in offices and shops, in dead-end, unexciting jobs—the war must have appeared as a relief from a pointless round, a holiday from routine, a doorway to excitement and usefulness. Military service can bring not only release from responsibility, but a sense of purpose which the whole apparatus of organized opinion labors to maintain. All this imparted an extraordinary glow to the war's beginning, an enthusiasm soon lost, forgotten, as Europe floundered forward in its blood but which is worth remembering as part of the explanation of many modern wars.

Young Frenchmen in red trousers and blue coats attacked in close formation behind their white-gloved officers with drawn swords and fluttering plumes and banners. Germans went forward with military bands playing immediately behind the fighting troops. All fell like flies. "I adore war" wrote Julian Grenfell to the *Times.* "I have never been so well and so happy . . . the fighting excitement vitalizes everything . . . ." "It is all a terrible tragedy," Rupert Brooke, the poet, wrote home, "and yet in its details it is great fun. And—apart from the tragedy— I've never felt happier or better." The tragedy itself could be transcended: a twenty-six-year-old lieutenant wrote to his parents about what he called the happiest moment of his life, under heavy shelling, surrounded by wounded men: "We were all just on the brink of the next world. Suddenly everything seemed to become clear, and one no longer saw through a glass darkly; one felt certain about what one hardly understood at all. And fear and nerves and egoism all vanished in the joy of just being there. I am not mad, and I will one day try to explain it to you." He did not live to do so; and the mood itself withered away as "the fresh and joyous" war of August dragged out into the weary misery of winter.

Strategy and Slaughter

For the swift war everyone expected soon turned into something else, and the conflict which had begun with four months of movement ended in four static years of trench warfare. As we have seen, the German plan hinged on a hard drive through Belgium, violating her neutrality for the sake of a break through the French flank which would roll up the French armies in short order and enable German divisions to turn about and defeat the slow-moving Russians. Burning and destroying, the German Right Wing swung through Belgium, brutally discouraging opposition, ravaging villages, executing civilian hostages, reducing cities like Louvain with its unique medieval library, to flames, massacring 678 civilians at Dinant—including a three-week old child.

But the great German blow against France was held just short of Paris on the Marne, in early September: a long, confused struggle through the fog of broken-down communications, in which divisions marched toward the sound of the cannon, and which saw the first tactical use of motorized infantry when a brigade rushed out of Paris in requisitioned taxicabs and buses, to reinforce the hard-pressed French.

Having held the first German attack, the French and British counter-attacked with no decisive results; and the fighting turned into a series of attempts to outflank each other, moving progressively closer to the Channel coast: a race for the coast whose prize would be the Channel ports by which British reinforcements and supplies could enter France. Marching and countermarching for days on end, with only three or four hours' sleep in twenty-four, the soldiers of both armies staggered along in a daze, seeing mirages, and sometimes dropping in their tracks, fast asleep. Retreating troops were sometimes forced through sheer fatigue to stand and fight, as the British did at Le Cateau (they won). Supplies ran out, especially those of the advancing Germans, buoyed by a sense of victory but often hungry and frequently slowed down for want of silly things like horseshoe nails that could immobilize whole cavalry and artillery divisions. But courage and enthusiasm, in these early days, never flagged. In October, 1914, the first battle of Ypres caused such losses in the German reserve divisions—almost all young students—that the Germans dubbed it "the massacre of the innocents": *der Kindermord von Ypern.* Despite such sacrifices, the Germans lost the race though they stabilized their lines across a good part of northern France and most of Belgium. By November, 1914, the two sides faced one another from parallel lines of trenches and fortifications running from the Swiss border to the English Channel.

If the Allies had managed to contain the German thrust, it was in part thanks to the Russians whose desperate offensives had drawn off German reserves at the height of battle. Ill-armed and ill-prepared for modern war, Russia relied on manpower. By 1917, one Russian in three would be called up to be thrust into battle, sometimes without a weapon, often without ammunition, and generally without serious artillery support. Where the war in the west turned static, that in eastern Europe surged over immense distances, while great infantry battles, now forgotten, were won or lost in hand-to-hand fighting where bayonets counted more than firepower. Things had changed little since Napoleon had passed through the plains and marshes of Poland and the Ukraine. Roads were few, dusty and choking in summer, quagmires in the rain, traps for wheeled transport, misery for marching men. The Russians, under pressure from their allies to attack while still unready, suffered heavy losses—nearly four million men in the first year alone—replaced by untrained and often unarmed draftees, expected to pick up experience, like a rifle, on the front itself.

Such sacrifices, effective enough against the Austrian armies, availed little against the modern equipment and superior generalship of the Germans, but probably saved the French and British from irresistible pressures. And, while the Russians grimly fought on despite immense

500 miles

U.S.A.
(APR 6, 1917)

NORWAY

SWEDEN

DENMARK
Copenhagen
Kiel

Hamburg

Berlin

GERMANY
(AUG 1, 1914)

Munich

SWITZ.

Geneva

SCOTLAND

IRELAND

GREAT BRITAIN
(AUG 4, 1914)

ENGLAND
London

NETHERLANDS
The Hague
Brussels
BELGIUM
(AUG 4, 1914)
LUXEMBOURG
(AUG 4, 1914)

Paris

FRANCE
(AUG 3, 1914)

Bordeaux

Marseilles

PORTUGAL
(MAR 9,
1916)

Lisbon

Madrid

SPAIN

Barcelona

MOROCCO

ALGERIA

CORSICA

SARDINIA

ITALY
(MAY 23,
1915)

Rome

Milan

SICILY
Palermo

TRIPOLI

EGYPT

ST. PETERSBURG

Helsingfors

Riga

Vilna

Minsk

RUSSIA
(AUG 1, 1914)

Moscow

Kazan

Astrakhan

CASPIAN
SEA

Tiflis

Tabriz

Baghdad

Erzerum

Erzingan

Poti

Trebizond

Aleppo

Damascus

SYRIA

CYPRUS

OTTOMAN EMPIRE
(NOV 2, 1914)

Angora

Constantinople

Gallipoli

Athens

CRETE

AEGEAN SEA

BLACK SEA

Odessa

Kiev

Kharkov

Rostov

Lublin

Brest-Litovsk

Warsaw

POLAND

Danzig

Prague

Vienna

Budapest

AUSTRIA-HUNGARY
(JULY 28, 1914)

Sarajevo

Belgrade

SERBIA
(JULY 28,
1914)

MONTENEGRO
(AUG 5,
1915)

ALBANIA

Salonika

GREECE
(OCT 18,
1916)

ROMANIA
(AUG 27, 1916)

Bucharest

BULGARIA
(OCT 14, 1915)

Sofia

BALTIC SEA

NORTH SEA

ATLANTIC OCEAN

MEDITERRANEAN SEA

ADRIATIC SEA

SEA

WORLD WAR I • 1914-1918

Allied Powers

Central Powers

Neutral states

(AUG 1, 1914) Date of entry into the war

——— Farthest advance of Central Powers

- - - - Front on eve of Russian Revolution

Intensive trench warfare, 1914–1917

·········· Brest-Litovsk line

——— Armistice lines, east and west

——— Farthest Russian advance

——— Boundaries in 1914

Trench warfare.

costs in life and territory, the war of movement in the west became a gigantic slugging match. Machine guns and barbed wire turned it into mutual siege and, under siege conditions, old methods and primitive armories were revived: bayonets cut into saws or taped to broom handles turned into spears, coshes, knuckle-dusters, jam-tin bombs, mines and countermines, mortars, grenades, flame throwers, finally armor and helmets.* Stretching for some 450 miles, the western front was a lunar expanse scarred with trenches, with their smell of stagnant mud, latrine buckets, rotting sandbags, disinfectant, lime, and stale sweat, stretching amidst muddy fields and tangles of barbed wire, flooded in rain, freezing in winter, ceaselessly shelled and sniped and raided, treeless, birdless, and with no wildlife besides rats, lice, and fleas, where the thick square ration bisquits were often used for fuel, where soldiers were expected to last four or five months, sergeants and junior officers half that time, and where men who considered themselves under suspended sentence of death prayed for the flesh wounds that would save their lives.

Even within this great sausage machine—as its own victims called it because it was firmly screwed into place while one fed living beings in at one end, to have them churned out as corpses at the other— even there none of these horrors could hide the fact that, as a combatant reported home, "the most terrible part of war is still man." Yet individual man was most likely to be lost from sight behind the plans, the maps, and statistics of those who used him. The best military thought on the eve of war insisted on the superiority of moral over material factors, of quality over quantity, of movement over firepower, of bayonets and the offensive spirit. This nonsense would be shattered in the charges of the first few weeks; but its victims did not live to point out the fact, and so the generals kept their prestige and the power to send more masses to their slaughter.

With very few exceptions, the military leaders on all sides (Haig

* Envy of the Germans, first to be equipped with capacious steel helmets, led to their being dubbed "jerries."

366

leading the English, Moltke and Falkenhayn the Germans, Joffre, Pétain, and Foch the French) showed an extraordinary lack of imagination and enterprise. Strategy gave way to tactics, and this last seems to have consisted largely of massive blows in which even surprise was soon sacrificed to vast artillery bombardments and what counted was the weight of matériel and men. Ingenuity was contributed by civilians like the First Lord of the British Admiralty, Winston Churchill, who suggested combined operations to outflank the Germans in Belgium or open the Dardanelles; but such suggestions were only reluctantly taken up by the soldiers and steadfastly bungled.* What counted was steadiness under fire, which generals like Joffre and Pétain had in plenty.

With the western front settling into siege conditions, the strategy of the Central Powers should have been to hold there while trying to knock Russia out of the fight. Two great generals, Hindenburg and Ludendorff, had already inflicted serious defeats upon them. Instead, both the Germans and the Allies continued to feed hundreds of thousands into offensives which netted little except corpses. "Corpses, corpses, corpses," noted a German writer serving in Flanders: "streams of wounded . . . everything becomes senseless, a lunacy . . . a negation of all civilization, killing all belief in the capacity of mankind and men for progress . . ." The greatest of these holocausts took place at Verdun, which the Germans planned to use as a vast slaughterhouse that "would bleed France white of all able-bodied men," and where the fighting raged murderously from February to December, 1916, slaying over 600,000 evenly divided between the two sides. The French, under General Pétain, held their own and the German commander Falkenhayn was replaced by the Ludendorff-Hindenburg team which for the next two years commanded not only the German army but increasingly Germany as a whole. Meanwhile, on the river Somme, a great Allied offensive proved even costlier than Verdun, especially for the British who lost 400,000 men —twice as many as the Germans who gave practically no ground. Both Verdun and the Somme were important more for their symbolic value than for their results: the one proving the French nation's will to fight, the other that of the British, whom German propaganda accused of fighting only to the last Frenchman. But they were costly tokens of determination, and if they improved home-front morale, they did not do so well for the morale of troops increasingly skeptical about the uses of such slaughter.

Deadlocked in the west but unwilling to admit it, both sides also tried to divert the enemy's resources and to increase their own by opening other fronts or drawing other combatants into war: Turkey (1914) and Bulgaria (1915) on the German side; Italy (1915) and Romania

---

* Thus, in 1915, Allied attack on the Black Sea straits foundered at Gallipoli, while Turks honed their martial ardor by massacring three-quarters of a million Armenians, and the poet Rupert Brooke, yearning to sail to Constantinople with the conquering British fleet, died of blood poisoning on the Greek island of Skiros.

Supplies backing up the last German offensive at the Somme Front, April 1918.

(1916—just in time to ease the pressure on Verdun) on the Allied side.* The Allies missed their chance of active Greek support because the Russians feared Greek designs on Constantinople, which they wanted for themselves. Thus, Greek willingness to join in the war against Turkey was rejected in 1915 on the direct intervention of the Tsar. Thereafter, the Greeks lost interest in a conflict from which they could expect no clear gains. Hard pressed to abandon neutrality for commitment on the Allied side, they were gradually forced into belligerence by 1917, especially after Russia left the war.

The superior mobility of British sea power brought little direct profit when combined operations against the Belgian coast or the Dardanelles ended in failure. It did permit German colonies to be picked off and to establish a blockade of the Central Powers, while ensuring massive shipments of food and supplies from overseas, especially from the United States.

The Eastern Front

The first decisive break appeared in the east, where fortunes had fluctuated from the first in the far more mobile fighting. For three years, the Russian armies, abominably equipped though they were, put up a solid show, did well against the Austrians, less well against the Germans, gave ground but still held their own. Then, in 1917, riots that began with the sacking of bakers' shops turned into revolution. By the autumn the Russian front had dissolved, the soldiers "voting with

* One might add Portugal, on whom Germany declared war in 1916 for seizure of German ships in Lisbon harbor, and which sent a small expeditionary force to the western front.

their feet" against continuation of the war. A great deal has now been written about the Russian Revolution and the Allied opposition to it. It is important to realize that even while a revolution in March, 1917, forced the Tsar's abdication and another in November brought the Bolsheviks to power, the "Ten Days That Shook the World" really did not. The world had its eyes fixed elsewhere: on the long stretch of mud, shell holes, and barbed wire across northern France where the Allies faced the Germans; on the gray-green waters of the North Atlantic which had become the graveyard of thousands of sailors and hundreds of thousands of tons of shipping; on the banks, factories, and training camps of the United States; on the great struggle between the Western powers and Germany. In this context, what happened in Russia was a distraction, relevant only in terms of the effect it could have on the war, and Allied hostility to Bolsheviks stemmed less from fear of their revolution than from the belief that it was "made in Germany," that Lenin & Co. were German agents, and that their power in Russia must be destroyed as part of the war effort.

We know that they were not destroyed. But if the Allies were mistaken in some of their judgments they were right in considering Bolshevik victory a disaster for their side. Russia's new masters, determined to end hostilities, accepted German conditions at Brest-Litovsk. The Romanians, driven into a corner, their capital occupied, also sued for peace. It seemed as if the Central Powers might win the war; and the treaties of Bucharest and Brest-Litovsk, imposed in the spring of 1918, provided an indication of the kind of peace which they had in mind. Romania, Poland, the Ukraine, and the Baltic states became satellites of Germany. Russia lost 26 per cent of her population, 27 per cent of her arable land, a quarter of her railroad mileage, a third of her textile and three-quarters of her iron industries, and had to pay a large war indemnity to her victorious foes. None could know that all this would come to nothing. For six tense months, Romanian grain and oil, Ukrainian wheat and coal, replenished the resources of the Germans, while divisions withdrawn from the eastern front stiffened their potential in the west. After four years of blockade and war, the German army on the western front was twice the size it had been in 1914.

The Bitter End

The Allies, on the contrary, were weakening. While German supplies improved, theirs fell, along with the means to buy more of them from the United States. The winter of 1916–17 was the worst Europe had known since 1880. At the end of April 1917, Senegalese infantry on the western front were so numb with cold that their French officers had to load their rifles for them. And 1917 as a whole was the most bitter time that the Allies had to endure. A devastating German submarine campaign briefly faced Britain with starvation; the Italian front came dangerously near collapse; French troops mutinied all along the line, refusing to go uselessly to slaughter. Drastic steps were taken to cope with the situation, reinforcements rushed to Italy, the Allied commander-in-chief, Joffre, replaced by the more aggressive Foch, command on the western front entrusted to Pétain who had made his name at Verdun and who now enhanced it by husbanding the lives of troops under his command. Cold, methodical and taciturn, he was a defensive fighter, sparing of his men and sparing in his moods. The English Cabinet had been restructured in 1916 under a strong popular liberal, David Lloyd George. Now an old Jacobin took the helm of France: Georges Clemenceau, who, said Keynes, "had one illusion—France; and one disillusion—mankind, including Frenchmen." Clemenceau remembered France's defeat in 1871 and was determined that it should not recur.

Equally important, Germany's submarine campaign at last brought the United States into war on the Allied side where ideology and investments already ranged them.* While American troops would be of little help until 1918, American factories and banks were better than the Ukraine. In spring 1918, when the Germans launched their last offensive, seven million soldiers faced one another in Flanders and northern France, about equally divided between the two sides. Under the leadership of Foch, the Allied lines strained, cracked, but held. By summer 1918, the Allies had taken the offensive. The long siege had ended. Turkey and Austro-Hungary were breaking, Allied troops moved forward on every front, the German military leaders, defeated, asked for an armistice. The war was over.

* A tremendous propaganda campaign had been waged to win U.S. support. In New England, a contemporary remembers attending a great meeting sponsored by the local church during the winter of 1916–17: "A speaker demanded that the Kaiser, when captured, be boiled in oil, and the entire audience stood on chairs to scream its hysterical approval."

Imperial War Museum

Signing the Brest-Litovsk Treaty, the German representative, von Kühlmann, on the left, and the Austrian, Count Czernin, on the right, March 3, 1918.

Chapter 10

NATIONAL COUNTERPOINT: INTERNAL AFFAIRS, 1848-1918

The thoughtful traveler who crosses the swift border between France and Spain, or flies from the brisk atmosphere of Stockholm into the strangely preserved anachronisms of Leningrad, knows that the changed environment is both contemporary and alien. Even when he does not have to adjust his watch, the world he walks into lives on a different time: its smells, its food, its rate of movement, its scale of values, its code of behavior, its processes and practices have a life of their own, similar to others across national borders and yet true to some distinctive experience. Even if all such factors cannot be noticed here, some of them must be, for they illuminate national characteristics and national history. Different national traditions, conditions, institutions, produced men and societies which—while sharing the common fate of other Europeans—lived out their lives each in specific ways.

A general treatment of the great lines of history leaves little room for particulars. The impact of industrial and technological advances, the development of political institutions, the evolution and expression of ideological currents, differ from place to place, and such differences are best understood in terms of more limited traditions. A general account of industrial changes that turns on England and on France casts little light on the peculiar fate of countries that industrialization affected less or later. The effects of the First World War, cataclysmic in central Europe, were felt quite differently and less in England, hardly at all in neutral countries like Spain. The ideas of socialism took on different shapes, created different institutions, in Germany, England, or France.

The following sections illustrate how the general trends we have been examining worked themselves out in particular terms, how movements and events already sketched above affected different members of the patchwork: Europe.

In some respects the same events seem to recur in country after country; but with a difference. What matters is this modified framework, the diverse circumstances, creating in the end dissimilar situations, so that industrialization (for example) proceeds in Germany with a distinct tempo and evokes quite different effects than in France or England. Each story told below, then, is a tale apart, yet part of a greater whole as well. Each provides the counterpoint of the great central theme and interweaves with tales of other parts, each emphasizing some particular aspect of the *ensemble*.

One fact should become clear as one reads on: that events which had great effect on one country passed others by, so that wars, especially wars —great favorites for beginning or ending chapters—made little impact beyond belligerent lands. Thus, during the Crimean War, Russia continued to pay interest on its foreign loans to enemies as well as to neutrals; and the war of 1870–1871, crucial for Germany and France mattered far less in London, Moscow, Vienna. Even in France, people lived on as they had done before, as most would still do after 1914. In other words, great political crises may be no more than marginal to the economic trends, to the everyday realities, more direly affected by inflation in the early twenties, by Depression after 1929, than by victory in war or even by defeat. True, after the holocaust of 1914–1918, the lives of the defeated were altered more radically than those of men and women on the winning side but probably not as thoroughly or to the same extent as they were to be in the 1940's.

At any rate, what counts in all these sections is not a country's international role but her internal travail and evolution; the latter hopefully casting some light on the former that we already know. Nevertheless, given the long sweep of time each of these sections covers, one remark may be in order. This volume is predicated on the belief that the years between 1848 and 1945 have a particular unity that overrides the different crises cutting across it like great crevasses in the 1890's, in 1917–1920, or again after 1929. Despite the fact that the national histories that follow run only to the First World War—1917, 1918, or 1920—it is well to remember that this is a matter of convenience. From 1848 to 1945, continuity matters more than particular changes. And some changes came, or failed to come, with little regard for climactic dates. "It was in 1915," wrote D. H. Lawrence, "the old world ended." But Lawrence himself retained a maid much longer than that, suggesting that some essential aspects of the old world persisted.

Britain

Seen from the present the history of the United Kingdom is one of comfortable decline. For an observer of 1850 it could look like a spectacular rise, at least up to a point. It may be possible to reconcile these views with the suggestion that relative decline set in around the end of the nineteenth century and that it became absolute in the 1930's with the rise of much greater powers. Certainly the last part of the nineteenth century would see the highest point of British influence. "With steam and Bible," as a historian of the great exhibition of 1851 put it, the British covered the world. The country's shipping tonnage, which doubled in the quarter century before 1850, increased five times in the next score years. By that time—1870—two-thirds of the world's ocean-going tonnage flew the British flag. Britain led the world in coal and iron, trade, and investments overseas; and it led Europe in real income, which grew 30 per cent between 1851 and 1878 and somewhat less thereafter until the end of the century, despite a continued increase in the population, which also rose at an unheard-of rate.

But Britain's economic supremacy shrank back eventually before the changes that her own investments and inventions wrought elsewhere. Her share of world trade, one-fifth in 1880, had fallen to 14 per cent by the eve of war. Yet she remained the largest trading nation and the London money market reigned supreme, still clearing deals half a world away. In 1894, Peking's war indemnity to Tokyo was paid through the Bank of England; a generation later, London still acted as the chief banker of her European allies.Yet, by 1914, British industry, though outwardly thriving, was slipping behind its competitors because it failed to modernize. Reluctance to try new things, to sacrifice textile machinery working well enough for the more efficient sort installed by American firms, to introduce modern equipment in mines and mills and foundries relying on plentiful cheap labor, was a kind of prodigality for which modern nations have to pay in the end. In the decade after 1900 the Germans doubled their steel output, the Americans increased theirs 150 per cent, the British only 20 per cent. In chemicals and dyestuffs Britain was far behind the Germans, in the electrical industry behind the Germans and Americans, in the automobile industry behind America and France. The reckoning would come during the First World War and after. Until then, the exuberance of expansion persuaded most Britons of their superiority. They were, as Thomas Arnold put it, "one of the chosen peoples of history," carrying out—explained Charles Kingsley— "the glorious work which God seems to have laid on the English race, to replenish the earth and subdue it."

Britain (whose safety, thought Lord Shaftesbury, was "the special care of Providence") dominated the world as it ruled the waves; the world whose clearinghouse it had become, its greatest shipper and carrier, banker and supplier:

> Pride in their port, defiance in their eye,
> We see the Lords of humankind go by.

The Lords of humankind believed in free trade and self-help, smugly ignoring those who were not free to help themselves. They also believed in representative institutions like their own.

> Where freedom broadens slowly down
> From precedent to precedent,

especially by rational debate based on a common moral code. Truth was "a question of the reconciling and combining of opposites." It was to be attained, argued John Stuart Mill's essay *On Liberty,* "Only by the collision of adverse opinions." Yet, Asa Briggs remarks, debate of this kind was only possible because very few people joined in it. Free interchange of ideas took place, but its scope was limited to agreed bounds, to restricted circles, and to private rather than public circumstances.

A system such as this carried no further than the limits of the deferential society that practiced it. Its own reforms reduced its potential by introducing more participants in the debate and whittling down the possibility that particular decisions would meet with general acceptance. The second Reform Bill of 1867 gave the vote to urban laborers; the third Reform Bill (1884) to most of the rural laboring classes, with Conservative majorities passing both.* But, even after 1885, residential, economic, or educational qualifications gave half a million Englishmen more than one vote, so that a university graduate who also ran a business in the City of London voted three times: once at home, once for his university, and once in the city. Democracy was a relative term; deference—the habit which takes respect for social superiors for granted— toward the upper classes still lived on. In the most advanced industrial country in the world the badge of the ruling class continued to be the ownership of land, as long as it was owned in great quantities. In 1873, four-fifths of the United Kingdom was owned by less than 7,000 persons and, though the wealth of the landed classes in relation to the

---

* It is interesting that the strongest opposition to electoral reform came not from the aristocracy or even from the rich but from intellectuals who opposed mass rule in the name of education and intelligence.

other classes was declining, the aristocracy—based on land—increased in strength and confidence at least until the 1880's.

Withal, Britain in mid-century was a middle-class nation and, though the term is impossible to define except as what the society itself considered middle-classness, it would appear that the category numbered about 3 millions in 1851 (one-tenth of the population) and over 5 million in 1867. Along with the "upper classes," almost a quarter of the nation lived in a way that was not that of the "lower classes," thinking of itself as "gentle" and "respectable." This group was obviously growing, prospering, abandoning the thrift and sobriety on which it had risen for conspicuous and competitive consumption which publicized their rise and announced another age.

The major moral values of this dominant class were drawn from religious belief. An evangelical conscience survived the Evangelical movement: keen awareness of rewards and punishments in the hereafter, bearing them in mind in prayer and church attendance, basic honesty (also good for trade), and self-improvement. This waned very slowly.* Far into the twentieth century inertia maintained what conscience once imposed, and sometimes for the better. The social aspects of the evangelical conscience were bolstered by the spread of education. The Reform Bill of 1867 persuaded the politicians that "now we must educate our masters"; and free compulsory elementary education was the result of this. At another level, the new civil service built up by reformers rested on probity even more than business did, and the new English public (that is, private) schools tried to turn out decent, loyal, upright men. The mores of the English were to be those of gentlemen, their values those of the public schools; and useless gentlemen, gradually excluded from the public service as patronage gave way to selective recruitment, were to be replaced by useful gentlemen in every aspect of national life. Greater moral and political awareness (however relative) played its part in further political reforms: the secret ballot introduced in 1872 and the Corrupt Practices Act of 1883, which, limiting election costs, made possible really representative government not based on influence or bribery.

The Crown and the Parties

As suggested by its lasting label, the spirit of Victorian England found an appropriate symbol in its monarch's personality. Emotional, loyal, obstinate, endowed with little intelligence but much common sense and many good intentions, Queen Victoria (1837–1901) was once de-

* The worst horrors of the English Sunday began to give way at the turn of the century, under the impact of the Prince of Wales's weekend parties and Sunday festivities. But the religious orientation had already veered. In 1870 there were more than twice as many books on religion published in England as works of fiction; sixteen years later novels far outnumbered religious works.

Queen Victoria (1) surrounded by her royal relatives. They are (2) her daughter Victoria, wife of the German Kaiser Frederick III, (3) her grandson, Wilhelm II, (4) Czar Nicholas II, and (5) his wife, Alexandra, (6) her son, the Prince of Wales and future King Edward VII of England, (7) the Crown Princess, and (9) her son, Duke Alfred of Coburg.

scribed by Bismarck as "a jolly little body." But Bismarck also added: "What a woman! One could do business with her!" Her most Victorian aspects grew under the influence of the short-lived husband (1840–1861) whom she never ceased to worship: Prince Albert of Saxe-Coburg-Gotha, an earnest, conscientious German intellectual of liberal leanings, devoted to music, art, and progress, endowed with statesmanlike abilities. The Crown, however, had very limited powers. With the appearance of party government, executive duties had fallen into the hands of the Cabinet. By 1867, when Walter Bagehot published his popular account of the English Constitution, the rights of the sovereign could accurately be defined as "the right to be consulted, the right to encourage and the right to warn." Within a system in which until today the monarch has a say in who the prime minister should be, the influence of the Crown never disappeared. But the real power henceforth lay with the political parties, characteristically in this period born from clubs: the Conservative Carlton Club founded in 1832, the National Union of Conservative and Unionist Associations (1867), the Liberal Reform Club founded in 1836, and the National Liberal Federation (1877), finally and much later the Labour Party founded in 1900.

During the last half of the nineteenth century the political scene would be dominated by their leaders, chief among them Benjamin Disraeli (1804–1881): the brilliant, charming, resourceful son of a Jewish man of letters, for thirty-three years Conservative leader in the House of Commons, and who died Lord Beaconsfield; and William Ewart Gladstone (1809–1898): the formidable son of a Liverpool merchant, who held his first government office at twenty-five and would be four times

William Gladstone. Right: Benjamin Disraeli.

Liberal prime minister between 1868 and 1894 for a total of almost fourteen years.

The rivalry between Conservatives and Liberals was incarnated in the emulation of their two great parliamentary leaders, both of them reformers and both in a sense trying to see who could initiate more reforms. The Electoral Reform Bill of 1867 was due to Disraeli's determination to "dish the Whigs"; Gladstone's Franchise Bill of 1884 extended the franchise practically to manhood suffrage; Disraeli's administrations were responsible for legislation on public health, artisan dwellings, conditions in the merchant navy; Gladstone's for educational and civil service reform, army reorganization, and the first measures to fix employers' liability in industrial accidents. Yet Disraeli's name would remain attached above all to Britain's new imperial policy, facilitated by his acquisition of a controlling interest in the Suez Canal (1875) and the assumption by Queen Victoria of the title of Empress of India (1876). And Gladstone's reputation would be colored, as we shall shortly see, by his Irish policy and his insistence on Irish Home Rule, which would break up his party by driving some of the liveliest Liberals into the dissidence of Unionism.

This long excursion should not be taken to mean that Conservatism and Liberalism were the only political movements; simply the most important. Social and political reform found its champions rather outside these parties. Radicalism was embodied in Charles Bradlaugh (1833–1891): a convinced republican, atheist, and Malthusian, who fought against the established Church, against the blasphemy laws, against the requirement to take oaths on the Bible, and against restrictions on birth control propaganda.* Social idealism found advocates in men like

* This last with Annie Besant (1847–1933), later a Fabian leader. Elected to the House of Commons in 1881, Bradlaugh refused to take the oath necessary for being seated, was expelled, was re-elected and expelled again in 1881, 1882, 1884, and 1885, finally winning his point and being allowed to *affirm* instead of swearing. In 1888 a law to this effect made affirmation legal in the courts.

John Ruskin (1819–1900) and William Morris (1834–1896), who were less radicals than reactionaries on aesthetic and moralistic grounds. In *Unto This Last* (1862), Ruskin denounced the selfishness of current economic views and the decay of popular arts and artistic feelings. Men should be reintegrated into society, purpose and execution reintegrated into things they made, as they had been joined (thought Ruskin) during the Middle Ages. The good life could be restored by curing the alienation caused by industrial production, turning the worker back into a craftsman, re-establishing social and creative identity. Morris, the younger man, carried these views further.

Artist, craftsman, and poet, William Morris was shocked by the drudgery and wretchedness of most workers, not only poor but condemned to toil at jobs which provided no satisfaction, no pride, no pleasure. Eliminate exploitation and profit-making, give people a chance to serve ideals not masters, educate them to the point where this becomes a real possibility: Morris disliked the depersonalization of producers and of objects in mass production. They should be "a joy to make and joy to the user." Social equality, social fellowship, social craftsmanship could bring social salvation. How they were to come about (except by education) Morris did not say, though he did say it should not be by violence. That was his Socialism, close to Anarchism, hoping that, once men had found a better way of life, the state would wither away of its own accord.

In 1883, Morris joined the Democratic Federation founded by Henry Hyndman (1842–1921), who called for public ownership of land and capital.* But, though their ideas found an eager audience, the movements of Morris, Hyndman, and even the Independent Labor Party (ILP) founded in 1893, never pulled much weight. Much greater influence would be exercised by the Fabian Society, founded in 1884 by middle-class intellectuals committed to Socialism but also to its achievement in a gradual manner, as their label—furnished by the name of the great Roman temporizer—implied. The founders of the Society were mostly in their twenties—George Bernard Shaw (1856–1950), Sidney Webb (1859–1947), Beatrice Webb (1858–1943), Graham Wallas

* The two men soon split, the one setting up his own Socialist league, the other a Marxist Social Democratic Federation.

Warder Collection

Intellectuals in politics: Sidney and Beatrice Webb.

(1858–1932), H. G. Wells (1866–1946)—and they had many years in which to leave their mark on England. But the *Fabian Essays in Socialism* that they published in 1889 showed their philosophy to be in the classical English tradition: not Marxist but utilitarian, not revolutionary but evolutionist. They all believed that economic developments rendered Socialism inevitable (though what was Socialism each one defined in his own way). But it would come by an evolution which was already well advanced and which democratic pressure would push further. Someone had to show the electorate how to accelerate the process, how they could manage their own affairs dispensing with their capitalist masters, and this was the purpose of the Fabians. The intellectual power of the little group, its activity and its wide connections, ensured that British reform would, in effect, take place on the lines they advocated, that British Labor would be not Marxist but revisionist, that the political coloring of all the British parties in years to come would be tempered by the Fabian outlook.

In another sense the Fabian philosophy was simply the reflection of a tradition which rendered revolution irrelevant. Reform, often sluggish, never quite ceased after 1832. It received an unexpected boost from the Crimean War, which, said Nathaniel Hawthorne, gave England "a vast impulse toward democracy." The mess of the war splashed off on its leaders: soldiers were brave enough but officers were incompetent, administrators chaotic and ineffective. Roused public opinion suggested that great administrators and contractors, men who managed factories, railroads, and shipping lines, might do better than politicians. Charles Dickens wrote *Little Dorrit* (1857), lampooning the Circumlocution Office and the useless breed of Barnacles in it. Associations sprang up throughout the country calling for military and administrative reform. A bill was introduced opening the Civil Service to competitive examinations. None of this brought concrete changes for over a decade, but the agitation helped clear the atmosphere.

The third quarter of the century was in any case a time of social progress advancing on a flood of prosperity. Then, when recession and unemployment in the 1880's made economic progress seem less infinite, a wave of trade union agitation and the concurrent rise of labor movements shifted the radicals from liberalism to socialism, and the workers from support of Liberals to support of a party of their own: Labour. Between 1885 and 1890 union membership tripled, no longer restricted to the aristocracy of skilled workers but drawing on poorer, less skilled groups who needed bargaining agents. A ferment of working-class activity began, expressed in strikes and industrial unrest. The greatest social troubles come not when the poor are very very poor but when their condition is improving, and when a little luck can help to accelerate the trend.* At least, this was what happened in England where

* The improvement, like everything else, was relative: in 1912 there were 280,000 inmates in workhouses and, by Salvation Army estimates, some 10 per cent of Britain's population lived on the brink of starvation or actually died of it. Shaw's *Major Barbara* (1905) is predicated on this.

the prewar years saw a spate of social legislation inspired by Fabian reports, sponsored by Liberal governments, and copied from Bismarck's measures of the 1880's.

With all their shortcomings, the Housing and Town Planning Act of 1909 and the National Insurance Act of 1911 were the prelude of English legislation in these realms. A flamboyant Welsh lawyer, David Lloyd George (1863–1945), fought to get the money for these limited measures and, in the process, abridged the power of the House of Lords. Meanwhile, Britain was prey to a general political and ideological ferment. All repressed groups—workers, women, and colonial peoples—were astir. Militant suffragism harried ministers and destroyed property; militant labor created industrial unrest; worst of all, in Ireland, Catholics and Protestants seemed on the brink of civil war.

Ireland

> Ireland never was contented
> Say ye so, ye are demented . . .

So runs the song; and it seems an accurate account of conditions since 1848 or, indeed, before then. The island colony had recovered slowly from the great famine and losses of mid-century. In 1858 a secret society called the Fenian Brotherhood (from the Gaelic *Fianna:* soldiers) was founded there and in the United States to organize rebellion in Ireland and an attack on Canada from the United States. In 1865 a wave of arrests broke the organization's back in Ireland and the rising, when it came in 1867 along with action in England where jails were attacked and prisoners released, was soon put down. Marx had hoped that an Irish insurrection might help spark a wider social revolution. As it happened, it sparked soul-searching and eventual rebellion within the English Liberal Party.

The Liberal leader William Gladstone saw the pacification of Ireland as his mission, tried unsuccessfully to achieve it by compromises between what he thought was good for the Irish and what Parliament could be persuaded to vote, split his party on the issue of Home Rule for Ireland (1886), and sent the Liberal unionists into co-operation with the Conservatives. Gladstone finally carried Irish Home Rule in 1893, and this was followed by a lull really broken only by new home rule disputes after 1912. The trouble now came less from the Catholic Irish than from Protestant Ulstermen in the North, who feared that they would be submerged by Catholic majorities in a self-governing island. A bitter struggle raged around this issue until it was overtaken by the war and the disputed measure suspended *sine die.* In 1916 an Irish Republican rebellion broke out in Dublin and was put

English troops raiding a Sinn Fein party printing office in Dublin during the Irish Rebellion.

down. A more serious rising occurred in 1919, and Irish "troubles" unfolded like a prototype of later colonial wars of liberation in which terror, murder, and guerrilla warfare conducted by an activist minority eventually wears down the alien occupiers already doubtful of their moral right and even more of the profit involved in hanging on. In 1921–22 the nagging sore was settled by partition. An Anglo-Irish Treaty separated six northern Protestant counties from the rest, giving home rule to the Irish Free State, which became a dominion of the Commonwealth,* and making Ulster a largely self-governing part of the United Kingdom of Great Britain and Northern Ireland. Ireland would pose no more internal problems until the 1970's.** But there were enough other problems to keep the British busy.

France

If England suggests that too much stability and too little friction may be a problem, France presents the alternative: a society constant in its instability, fervent in its divisions, whose members look upon their compatriots as their fiercest competitors, where perhaps men hate their neighbors even more than they hate themselves, where—as if deliberately —a great nation applies itself to proving Rousseau wrong and Hobbes correct.

The history of France since the great Revolution had marked the

* "The settlement was followed by southern civil war between the intransigent supporters of United Ireland and the moderates content with what they had. In 1932 under Eamon de Valera, Eire proclaimed itself a republic, whose independence Britain recognized in 1937, as it did in 1948 its independence from the Commonwealth.
** Even when the late 1960's saw Ulster resume the civil conflicts that once ripped all Ireland apart, these troubles no longer affected English politics directly.

381

A contemporary drawing of Napoleon III on horseback.

failure of every attempt to reconcile the nation to any one regime. Lacking the English notion of a loyal opposition and gradual reform, the French viewed politics as sheer struggle for power, defeat in which could mean exclusion (or self-exclusion) from national affairs. There was little in their experience to suggest other solutions. The legacy of 1848, like that of previous revolutions, was bitter. The rebels of June had been blasted out of their barricades—2,000 or 3,000 killed, 12,000 arrested, the Republic made safe for property, and class hatred established on solid foundations of mutual fear. General Cavaignac, the hero of the bourgeoisie, became military dictator. There would be no more national workshops, no more social reform. A new constitution balanced legislative and executive power—a parliament and a president, both popularly elected—but did not say how they could be reconciled. The first president would solve the problem. In the presidential election of December, 1848, the poet Lamartine received 17,000 votes, Cavaignac a million and a half, and Louis Napoleon (1808–1873) five and a half million.

A New Napoleon

The new president was forty years old. Son of Louis Bonaparte, king of Holland, and of Josephine's daughter, Hortense, he had grown up in Bavaria and in Switzerland with a Jacobin tutor who was the son of one of Robespierre's most devoted friends. In 1830, Louis joined in the Italian struggles for liberty and narrowly escaped being arrested. In 1832, Napoleon's son, the duke of Reichstadt, died in Vienna and Louis became his uncle's political heir. Two unsuccessful attempts to claim his heritage had netted an imprisonment for six years in a lonely fortress, escape from which in 1846 took him to America and then to

382

London, where he remained until the revolution of 1848 allowed him to return home legally.

Louis's character was a mass of contradictions, a little like a many-faceted stone that sparkles differently according to the light. Sensitive and taciturn, kindhearted and ruthless, idealistic and skeptical, apathetic and dynamic, a loyal friend, a cynical intriguer, this was the mass of apparent contradictions who came to be known as Napoleon III. For the moment he was only the president of France's Second Republic, although elected by almost three-fourths of the votes that had been cast. Louis had campaigned as representative of order and security to reassure the respectable, promising amnesty to Socialists, freedom of schooling to Catholics, "revival of credit, resurrection of labor, protection of religion, family and property." But it had been his name which brought in the votes. "The Napoleonic cause," he once said, "goes to the soul." Presumably, he knew the soul was a more effective political motor than the mind. Veterans whose ears and noses had frozen in Russia, peasants who hung the Emperor's image on their cottage walls, men who recognized this name when they knew no other, followed the magic of a memory.

Now, Louis Napoleon faced the competition of a legislature dominated by conservative interests and remembered that in 1852 his term would end and the Constitution did not permit his re-election. In his first years he played along with the legislature, signing their bills to reform education in a Catholic direction, to restrict the suffrage and deprive one-third of Frenchmen of a vote, to whittle down freedom of the press and of political assembly. Perhaps he hoped that, in return, the Constitution would be revised allowing him to succeed himself; perhaps he was only giving the legislators rope to hang themselves in the public's eyes. At last, in December, 1851, when it was clear that he would get nothing legally, he seized power by a military coup, imprisoned his opponents, dissolved the Assembly, restored universal suffrage, and had his actions ratified by a plebiscite in which 7.5 million voted *yes* and 650,000 *no*. The country was weary of instability, the wealthy feared unrest, the workers detested the bourgeois who had put them down in 1848 more than they did Louis Napoleon, the peasants wanted security for their harvests. A new constitution made him chief of state with a legislative assembly subject to him. Within a year, nearly 8 million people voted *yes* in one more plebiscite (only 250,000 voted *no*). He was now Emperor Napoleon III.

The French historian and economist Ernest Labrousse suggests that Napoleon came to power because nineteenth-century men faced with twentieth-century problems of moving from agricultural to industrial conditions while living in an eighteenth-century society panicked, and looked for a providential man. They certainly found a very twentieth-century solution which enlisted nationalism, socialism, and a widespread sense of insecurity, in the service of personal power.

Napoleon dreamt of a state both authoritarian and socialistic, which would take over from the incompetent bourgeois regime disintegrating around him—the faster for his help. He had no precise political orientation. His team grouped Orleanists like his half brother, Charles de Morny,* who looked on the masses with a kind of utilitarian paternalism, well-intentioned but suspicious of them; and democratic socialists like his cousin, Prince Jerome Napoleon. As he once expressed it: "The Empress is legitimist, my Cousin is republican, Morny is Orleanist, I am a socialist; the only Bonapartist is Persigny and he is mad." **

But if Napoleon III was no Bonapartist, he was certainly heir of other doctrines, not least those of Saint-Simon (see p. 658). Throughout Louis Philippe's reign the Saint-Simonians had repeated that, having come to power in alliance with the people, the middle classes must meet their allies' material needs by developing education, credit, means of communication, and opportunities for employment, or lose their power. The middle classes failed to heed this. The years 1848 and after proved that the Saint-Simonians had been right. Louis Napoleon profited by the lesson. He has been called a Saint-Simon on horseback and, in effect, his regime was a great time for producers and speculators, entrepreneurs, engineers, and financiers, many of Jewish or Protestant origin and many of them disciples of Saint-Simon, graduates of the Polytechnic School, adepts of industrial civilization. The regime fulfilled their creed. This was when the French industrial revolution really got its start in industry and coal mining, the rise of department stores and credit enterprises whose chronicles we can find in the novels of Émile Zola. Even the free-trade treaty signed with England in 1860 reflected the personal initiative of the Emperor, convinced by Saint-Simonian arguments; and the alliance of competence and money was sanctioned by the influential philosopher, Ernest Renan, suggesting an elite ruling by its skill and reason; and by the founding of a school to train this elite: the School of Moral and Political Sciences created by a Saint-Simonian, Boutmy.

Between 1847 and 1867 foreign trade trebled, urban population grew from a quarter to a third of the country's total, ironworks like Le Creusot which turned out 18,000 tons a year in 1847 were producing seven times as much twenty years later. The French economy passed from the artisan to the industrial plane, although new factories still lived side by side with workshops and home industries. The value of industrial production doubled, that of trade quadrupled, so did the number of workshops using steam engines, while the horsepower in them grew fivefold. New

---

* "A consummate politician with all the daring of a gambler," Morny (1811–1865) was an aristocratic adventurer with flair for profit, talent for political maneuver, and incredible lust for pleasure. He burned himself out too soon to help Napoleon III in the difficult years of transition to a liberal Empire, dying just in time to be regretted by all, "even by his wife."

** Persigny was Napoleon's devoted friend and minister.

A contemporary en-
graving showing the re-
construction of Paris.

banks mobilized capital, pulling small savings into investment and speculation. The railroad network grew from 3,600 to 18,000 kilometers and
railroad personnel from about 30,000 to about 140,000. Living standards
improved and the Second Empire would see consumption of wheat rising
20 per cent, sugar 50 per cent, potatoes 80 per cent, wine 200 per cent,
coffee 300 per cent.

Great public works helped spread prosperity. The greatest of them
all, the reconstruction of Paris under the leadership of an Alsatian Prefect, G. E. Haussmann (1809–1891), produced the fortune of many a
speculator and also the city that we know today with its impressive
vistas, its wealth of squares and parks, adequate water supply, and
sanitary sewers. Haussmann and his aides did not only seek to increase
security, lessen the chance of revolution and of barricades; they appreciated the majesty of straight, broad avenues, the disappearance of the
maze of alleys where crime and insurrection bred or sheltered, the new
physical barriers that amplified and clarified social ones. Poorer people
who could not afford high rents in the new central quarters migrated
into suburbs. The distance between bourgeoisie and workers, who
once had lived in the same buildings and the same parts of town, grew;
and one effect was that both parties began to nourish fantastic or exaggerated notions about the other's way of life. Thus even the best intentions could have unexpected results and the ambiguous nature of the
regime appeared in everything it did.

Napoleon III sought to reconcile the revolutionary appeal to universal suffrage with the stability of hereditary succession, the Napoleonic
tradition of expansion with support of national self-determination, populist sympathies and economic development, political power and liberal
tendencies. This worked well enough for a while. Universal suffrage
provided the dynasty with a solid base of peasant loyalty, successful campaigns brought glory and a feeling of achievement, economic expansion

gave prosperity to the *bourgeoisie* and left some over for the working class, a subtle political game gave all parties something that would please them. Then, in the late 1860's, things began to go wrong. The workers were stirring. The discipline that factories imposed reduced working hours but also the absenteeism that had lightened the workers' load. *Saint Monday,* which many workers worshipped by staying away from work lost its faithful; and even the "shorter" twelve-hour working day often drew out to fourteen, when one counted meals and machine cleaning. There were worse restrictions on the workers' freedom: all employees had to carry the *livret,* a certificate which marked dates and places of employment, along with possible comments, introduced in 1746, suppressed in 1791, re-established by Napoleon in 1803, somewhat forgotten during the July Monarchy, to be reaffirmed by a law of 1854 and only abolished in 1890. Even the workers' better pay was only relative, for, while real wages rose by about 28 per cent between 1850 and 1870, employers' profits increased fourfold.

Artisans, doing badly as their crafts declined, hollered for help; skilled workers did well, but wanted to do better. A French miner's pay went up 30 per cent between 1852 and 1870; the dividends paid to owners of mining stock tripled. Workers' housing in the industrial north was as bad in the 60's as it had been in the 40's. Even the new houses lacked light, sanitation, let alone adequate space. Pregnant girls were unable to tell magistrates whether their father or their brother had put them in the family way. And while far more salaries at the end of the Empire allowed a decent life provided the wage earner was childless, the employers' growing fortunes ostentatiously stressed the contrast between them and the poor wages of their personnel.

Napoleon had confiscated most of the property of the Orléans family, allotting the considerable proceeds to credit unions, mortgage banks, workers' housing, and a retirement fund for destitute parish priests. Honest government pawnshops had replaced usurers; earnest attempts had been made to curb alcoholism; Sunday rest had been introduced in government offices and enterprises. After an early period of repression, workers' self-help received much encouragement, co-operatives were subsidized and supported; and it was Napoleon's initiative in sending a large worker delegation to the London Exhibition of 1851 that led to the foundation of the First International. But the attempt to reconcile the workers failed. Strikes, legalized after 1864, were still looked upon by employers as rebellion, and government officials often protected blacklegs as well as property, prefects and judges being less impressed by the distress of the strikers than by the ingratitude they showed to their employers. When freedom of assembly and of the press were granted in 1868, they released a flood of criticism and opposition. Concessions only spurred demands for more concessions. In the plebiscite of 1870, while seven and a half million approved the liberal orientation of the Empire, one and a half million showed their opposition not to liberalism but to its inefficiency: the urban workers had passed into the opposition camp.

Yet many had reason to be satisfied. France was growing richer and its wealth was being more widely distributed. Without the tax burden being raised, revenue from taxes increased from 42 to 57 francs per inhabitant between 1851 and 1861. In 1849, 730,000 persons had 97 million francs in savings bank deposits; in 1869, 2.5 million had eight times as much.* Investments grew and turned increasingly from land to stocks, to the kind of deals best carried out with someone else's money, until (in the words of a novelist) the Stock Exchange became for this generation what the cathedral had been for the Middle Ages, and the habit of investment or speculation spread to the lowest classes—with Ferdinand de Lesseps of the Suez Company being told by a cab driver: "I am one of your stockholders." To have money invested in stocks and a *rente*—a yearly income from them—became the crux of comfort and every Frenchman's aim: what an estate or office had been under the old regime. In 1800 the sum of annuity interest paid out in the country was 713 million francs; in 1870 it was 12 billion, and 36 billion in 1895. In this last year, state bonds alone accounted for 80 billion owned by 3 million bondholders, while almost 9 million persons had savings accounts totaling over 4,000 billion francs.

The history of the French middle class in the nineteenth century will not be written or its economics understood until we have a history of that crucial figure: the *rentier*. The *rentier* was not always retired on his savings. Ideally he or she had never had to work. The hero of Flaubert's *Sentimental Education* (1869) is such a person. Frédéric Moreau had dreamed great dreams of conquering Paris before he found out the figure of his yearly income—the equivalent of a paltry 600 dollars (far more than an industrial worker or servant earned). On this, he could only envisage vegetating in his provincial home, going to Church with his mother, playing cards, brooding on his frustrations. Then he inherited a fortune from an uncle,** revived, returned to Paris expecting to become at least a minister, and, finally, ended up as the coupon-clipper he had started. Never in all his ups and downs, however, did Frédéric envisage taking a job and really working at it. The rewards of labor were too small to justify the effort when one could stay alive by other means: and this perpetuated a situation in which millions were immobilized by private revenues. For some like Manet, Degas, Proust, or the young Léon Blum, this meant that they were free to direct their creative talents as they pleased, and literature, art, politics, scholarship all benefited

* This would remain a French characteristic, at least until the First World War: 13 per cent of the national revenue was salted away in savings under the Second Empire, nearly as much in 1910.

** Not merely a literary device, inheritance was a major factor in the aspirations and the realities of nineteenth-century life, when very few indeed could envisage comfort on what they earned alone.

from it. But for the few set free to do something creative, there was a mass of useless consumers living in cautious comfort, contributing to the country's stability but hardly to her wealth.

The End of French Supremacy

The security of such people would be only briefly shaken by the collapse of Napoleon's foreign policy. The Emperor had re-established a kind of French supremacy in Europe. Wars in the Crimea (1854–1856) and in Italy (1859) had affirmed the power of French arms, humbled first Russia and then Austria. But Napoleon had to spare the feelings of the Catholic party and he was forced to do this by protecting the Pope's hold on Rome at the expense of Italian friendship. Then, business and conservative interests plunged France into a weary conflict overseas. In Mexico, intense unrest had risen to chaotic proportions. In the thirty years after 1827, executive office changed hands forty-seven times. In the mid-50's revolt by the reformist forces eventually resulted in a civil war, with the Liberals led by the Zapotec Indian, Benito Juárez (1806–1872), opposed by conservatives and by the Catholic Church. In 1861, Britain, Spain, and France sent troops to Vera Cruz to extort payment of the sums which the bankrupt Mexican Republic owed to its European creditors. Mexican conservatives welcomed the intervention, which they hoped would help restore their interests. The United States, engaged in civil war, was unable to assert the Monroe Doctrine but did its best to discourage the powers' trespassing on what she regarded as her domain. The British and the Spaniards finally withdrew, but the French were persuaded to stay on. To many Mexicans their help was the only hope of countering U.S. pressure which had been far more costly over the years than any European interference. Egged on by his empress, Napoleon now hatched the dream of a Mexican Empire which would defend the Catholic Latin cause against Anglo-Saxon Protestantism and persuaded a brother of the Austrian emperor, Archduke Maximilian, to accept its crown (1836–1866). But nothing availed against the Republican forces of Juárez, nor was there time to wear them down. In 1865 the United States was free again to aid Juárez. In 1866 the French expeditionary corps had to be withdrawn under this pressure and that of events in Europe. Maximilian's ramshackle realm collapsed and Maximilian, who refused to flee, was captured and executed at Querétaro.

Worse than the Mexican debacle: Napoleon's German schemes were going wrong. He had hoped to keep Germany divided, while providing all possible satisfaction to German national sentiments. After 1866 a new and dangerous power had to be taken into account, partly as a result of his miscalculation; and in 1870 the crisis came to a head. By that time, more than a third of French foreign investments were concentrated in Spain. When the Spaniards offered their throne to a German prince, the prospect of a Hohenzollern on the Spanish throne compounded the economic and political danger.

Meanwhile, the Empire seemed threatened from within—partly by the political tremors which the regime's liberalization started, partly by the failing power of Louis Napoleon, ever more frequently disabled by the dreadful pains of the gallstones which would finally kill him in 1873. Historians have spoken of growing disaffection. This is true: in the elections of 1869 opposition candidates attracted almost 45 per cent of the votes cast. Yet in the plebiscite of May, 1870, better than seven Frenchmen out of every nine endorsed the Empire's policies. Twenty years' rule had made no dent in the support Napoleon could count on. Not the opposition but the Court threatened the dynasty. As the Emperor weakened, the influence of Empress Eugénie (1826–1920) grew. The beautiful, pious daughter of a Frenchified Spanish grandee, Eugénie was cosmopolitan, haughty, supremely elegant, a dyed-in-the-wool reactionary worshiping at the shrine of Marie Antoinette. Her enemies who had begun by finding the marriage futile, ended by considering it fatal to the Empire. That is what it proved.

Eugénie and her friends had pressed to keep French troops in Rome and send others to Mexico. Now, their obstinacy turned a quest for diplomatic success into military disaster. In July, 1870, the Hohenzollern candidature to the Spanish throne became a handle to the humiliation of Prussia. Under French pressure, William of Prussia intervened to make his Hohenzollern nephew withdraw his acceptance of the Spanish crown, but the war party in the Tuileries were not content with that. When the old Prussian king refused to be pressed too far, Eugénie's bellicose friends steered France into a war for which the country was ill-prepared and which, to the world's surprise, her generals quickly bungled. In a few weeks, the superior generalship of the Germans defeated the main armies of the French and, on September 2, 1870, Napoleon III was a prisoner at Sedan. Two days later a Third Republic had been proclaimed in Paris and Eugénie, deserted by all but her American dentist, was on her way to England.

The Third Republic

But the new Republican government had to admit defeat in its turn. The hastily organized levies could not long withstand the well-trained German armies and Paris, after a nineteen-weeks' siege during which it was reduced to near starvation, had to capitulate. Peace talks had prepared an armistice in January, 1871, but Bismarck would conclude peace only with a properly elected government. In February, with German troops occupying a large part of the country, elections were held, turning largely on the issue of peace or war. Sentiment for peace worked against the

Leader of the Third Republic, Adolphe Thiers (hand outstretched), and his Council of Ministers, 1872.

Republicans who, under the leadership of Léon Gambetta (1838–1882), favored continued resistance. The war was blamed on the Bonapartists, its continuation on Gambetta, who had escaped beleaguered Paris in a balloon to organize resistance in the provinces. The new Assembly counted 400 Monarchists, mostly provincial gentlemen who had kept away from the discredited Empire, and only 150 Republicans. It was this conservative and pacific majority, under the leadership of a seventy-four-year-old survivor of the July Monarchy, Adolphe Thiers (1797–1877), which ratified the German peace terms: loss of Alsace-Lorraine, a war indemnity of 5 billion francs, and German occupation of eastern France pending the payment. It would soon face a serious internal crisis.

Paris with its host of workers, artisans, students, drifters, and assorted intellectuals, had always been a radical powder keg. The siege bore hard on its population and, at one time, a radical and socialist rising to set up a Commune in the tradition of 1792 had been put down by force. Nerves frayed by suffering and tension were wound to fury by the peace terms. It is hard to tell whether the loss of Alsace-Lorraine caused greater indignation than the brief Prussian occupation of the capital. Then came the news that the reactionary Assembly, gathered at Bordeaux, had decided it would not return to Paris but settle at Versailles, where it would be out of reach of the disturbances the city mob might breed. Along with this came a decree that rents and bills, on which a moratorium had been placed during the siege, must be paid at once. Unable to meet overdue bills at short notice, many shopkeepers and householders were faced with ruin. The city seethed with anger, while many of the wealthier citizens who had left the city in search of better air, diet, or security as soon as the siege was lifted, were missing to counterbalance the rebellious mood. At this point, in mid-March, 1871, a government attempt to seize the artillery of the National Guard (bought by public subscription) set off an insurrection. While Thiers withdrew his troops and government to Versailles, the Commune ruled in Paris during ten further weeks of siege, and social war raged between the insurrectionists and the Versaillese, who only recaptured the city at the end of May.

Between March and May, the *Communards* barked loudly but bit little. They talked of decentralization, separation of Church and State, abolition of the standing army to be replaced by the National Guard, but had no clear-cut program beyond their pent-up frustrations. There was no unity among the Commune's leaders—most of them very young —who ranged from Jacobins to followers of Proudhon or Blanqui or Marx, some of them manual workers, some journalists or soldiers, but almost all, whatever their doctrine, earnest humanitarians.

While the Versaillese shot rebel prisoners out of hand, the Commune hardly killed a prisoner or hostage until the end, when, in the midst of chaos, individuals took the law into their own hands. Marx, watching from London, would criticize the Communards for doing little to destroy the fundamental institutions of the order which they challenged. Indeed, their most radical measures were to prohibit night work in the bakeries and, under the guidance of Courbet, the painter, to topple over the great column in the Place Vendôme on which the first Napoleon's statue stood. The financial executives of the Commune respected the deposits in the Bank of France, kept scrupulous accounts, and maintained an orthodox financial policy. None of this moderation stood them in good stead when they were beaten. Humiliated by the Prussians, the upper classes took out their terrors and resentments on revolutionary Paris, carrying fire and sword through its streets, executing 20,000 and deporting more, turning an unsuccessful popular rising into a lasting symbol and a memory. The actual performance of the Commune came to be less significant than the myth it left to later propagandists of a first attempt to set up a Communist state.

Thiers and the Assembly were now free to make France safe for conservatism. The country was liberated from the Germans when, in 1873, Thiers paid off the war indemnity eighteen months ahead of schedule and did it without increasing taxes, preferring to have recourse to loans. It

Hostages put to death during the Paris Commune.

Staatsbibliothek. Berlin

A contemporary engraving of Paris burning during the Commune.

could not be freed as easily of the democratic danger. Manhood suffrage could not be abandoned, but the Chamber of Deputies which it selected was balanced by a Senate designed as the Grand Council of the country's communes, made up by indirect election from electoral colleges where every municipality—whether Paris with its millions or a large village with only a few hundred—had an equal vote. The highly conservative Senate served as a check on the direct democracy of the Chamber; and this became important when in a few years the Monarchist hopes of 1871 were ruined and the Republicans forged ahead once more.

The Monarchist majority was actually divided between supporters of the Bourbons and those of the Orléans. Each side preferred a Republic to the triumph of its rivals until a settlement was reached by which the Comte de Chambord, Charles X's grandson, was recognized by his Orléanist cousins as Henry V (1820–1883) and he, having no children, tacitly accepted the Orléans princes as his heirs. Royalist hopes were raised and, in 1875, France was endowed with a Republican constitution that could be adapted to a monarchy by giving the head of state powers greater than those of many European kings, and which, as it was to turn out, would not be used by the eleven presidents that spanned the course of the Third Republic. In 1873 Thiers was replaced by one of Napoleon III's better soldiers: Marshal MacMahon, who was expected to cede his place to the Bourbon pretender at the first opportunity. But restoration plans foundered on Henry V's refusal to accept the tricolor flag and, by 1877, MacMahon had to contend with a Republican majority in the Chamber. His unsuccessful attempt to go against them, by dissolving the Chamber he did not like, failed and ensured that no other president would dissolve an elected assembly and that, in other words, the legislative power would be predominant over the executive.

After 1879, when MacMahon resigned in disgust, France was governed by moderate Republicans; but memories of every other political allegiance survived so that the nation was endlessly divided by rival creeds. While things went well and the economy remained prosperous, this did not matter much. Under strain, the usual recriminations of political parties were colored by the tendency to question fundamental institutions, to recognize as good Frenchmen only those who held the right political views, and to exclude all others from the national community. France had known so many constitutions, so many dynasties, so many loyalties and political doctrines in less than a hundred years, that no political institution seemed stable or enduring. Even the most patriotic Frenchmen kept their strongest loyalties for the family and for the abstract concept of a fatherland with which the state or government were identified but little. Hence the paradoxical contrast of an unusually stable society with equally unstable politics.*

The Heart and the Pocketbook

Despite serious recessions, the years to 1914 were quite prosperous. The great depression that affected Europe in the late 70's, the 80's, and the early 90's, hit France far less than more developed and hence more vulnerable countries. The serious difficulties of agriculture were largely remedied by protective tariffs which permitted farmers to vegetate without fear of competition. But the static penalties of protection were lost from sight behind its advantages. Between 1870 and 1914 industrial output tripled, the national income doubled, real wages in industry went up 50 per cent. In 1870 a third of the peasantry was still illiterate. By 1914 illiteracy had been wiped out. Schools, trains, bicycles, newspapers, all spread political awareness through the land. France was a country of small men content to be independent on small profits and a German proverb described the good life as living like God in France.

Population shifted from agriculture to industry, but it did so more slowly than in neighboring countries. In 1914, 44 per cent of the population still made a living out of agriculture. Many of these consumed a good part of their produce, bought as little as they could, kept out of the market economy as far as they were able, putting little money into circulation and investing their savings in safe quarters: mainly state bonds, foreign or French, least productive from the viewpoint of capital expansion.

Industry lagged, partly for lack of capital, partly from lack of raw materials—above all, coal. French coal deposits were few, awkwardly situated, costly to exploit. A ton of coal cost about one-third more in France than in Germany or England. Furthermore, in the territories lost to Germany in 1870, the Republic had also forfeited her main iron-ore deposits. Developed in 1878, the Gilchrist-Thomas process of turning mineral ore to steel made available Lorraine deposits which were too mixed with phosphorus to have been used in earlier converters. Great ironworks arose in French Lorraine, but none were so important as those developed on the German side. In any case, the coal for their furnaces

* The Third Republic enjoyed forty-two different governments between 1881 and 1914, forty-odd more between the wars.

came mostly from the Rhineland and the Saar. French heavy industry, dependent on German fuel, was tied to German industry and limited by it.

Given the role of coal (and steel) in modern war, industrial inferiority was translated into political weakness whose effects continued evident as late as the defeat of 1940. Its economic effects were felt more quickly, for a modern economy depends on the heavy sector whose relative backwardness and high production costs slowed down the pace of French economic progress until mid-twentieth century.

Another fuel was also in short supply: industrial manpower. New arrivals from the land preferred small businesses to factories. Between 1866 and 1906, the number of industrial workers increased by a quarter, that of tradesmen by two-thirds. It was France which now became a nation of shopkeepers. "The Frenchmen work for the few, but we for the millions," declared an English manufacturer. French industry was caught in its tradition of catering for luxury trades. Buyers of perfumes and dresses, glass or leatherware, jewelry and fine wines were more constant in their means and even in their tastes than the new popular buying public, which was tempting in its possibilities but frightening in its capricious changes and in the fluctuations of its revenues.

More important, perhaps, were the Frenchman's reluctance to invest money in industry when he could get equal or greater revenues from state loans, and his historical tendency to retire from business, withdrawing his capital when he could no longer personally control it and placing it in *rentes*, in real estate, or, simply, in the coffers of some bank. Between 1850 and 1914 a third or a half of French savings were lent or invested abroad—even more than Britain's. French loans and investments in Russia amounted to 16 billion francs in the thirty years before the war. There and elsewhere French investors would lose a large part of their money in 1918. Reluctance to invest in industry made for a leisurely pace of life but had unfortunate consequences. Some of the century's great discoveries in medicine, physics, hydroelectrics, and cinema were made in France, but their use was slight and slow. It was the work of French engineers that brought the first cargo of refrigerated Argentine meat to Le Havre in 1878, but French investors would not provide the capital to follow up the success and the inventors turned to Britain. In 1914, of nine great dyestuff factories in France, five were German, one Swiss, and 87 per cent of colorants used in France came from Germany, which boasted 30,000 chemists, fifteen times more than France. Inventive enough, France lagged in industrial application and its productivity lagged behind that of other powers.

So did its population. At the beginning of the eighteenth century more than one-third of Europeans were subjects of Louis XIV. Toward 1850 the French accounted for 14 per cent of the continent's population, by 1913 only for 9 per cent. The rate of population increase, probably the weakest in Europe, was six or seven times less than that of France's nearest neighbors. For every four children born in the 1860's there would be only three on the eve of war. By then, the annual excess of births over deaths for every 10,000 inhabitants was about two. It had been 67 under Charles X. If the nation's numbers were stagnating, its body, too, was getting older, with all the immobilism, retrenchment, and defensiveness that this implies. In 1851, for every 1,000 people 361 had been under 20; in 1911 only 126. By 1945 there would be two old people for every seven adults, twice the proportion found in contemporary Russia . . . or in eighteenth-century France! While Britain, Germany, Italy poured out emigrants, France now became an immigrant's haven drawing the surplus of Spain, Italy, and eastern Europe: by 1881 a million foreigners, by 1914 three million, were taking up the slack in her population.

All this had repercussions on the political scene. The early years of the Republic had been marked by struggles between Conservatives and Progressives, which, by the 1880's, the latter won. The educational opportunities that they now created brought all the middle classes into political life, giving them every chance to assert themselves at the political level. The proportion of the population in the professional classes and in public service was growing faster than any other class except the tradesmen and, hence, more and more people felt that they had a stake in society. But the society they liked and wanted to keep expanded only slowly and could ill afford to find resources that would improve the lot of those who did not get a fair share of its benefits. The farmers, shopkeepers, small tradesmen, doctors, lawyers, *rentiers,* who formed the backbone of the political Left so long as this concerned itself with issues like secular education or the separation of Church and State (finally achieved in 1905), turned Rightward when the issues became social; and unions, labor laws, income tax, threatened their pockets. If the hearts of the great French middle classes remained on the Left, their pocketbook was on the Right and the politics of the past century reflect the tension between these two poles. The tension would be resolved in a swing which, by the 1930's, had shifted a majority of the population to the Right. They remained radical in theory but security-minded in practice, patriotic in spirit but pacific in fact, appreciative of revolutionary-sounding rhetoric but favoring revolutionary leaders who proposed to lead them backwards, out of danger and especially away from the threat of change.

The threat of change was represented by the working-class movements beginning to revive during the 1880's,* a constellation of contending factions that mirrored every kind of tendency. By the end of the century France harbored six Socialist parties, two major union organizations,

* The Communard prisoners were amnestied in 1880; the first Marxist-Socialist party founded by Jules Guesde in 1882, the unions given legal status in 1884.

and several anarchist groups. Compared with the German Socialists all were puny: five out of six workers were not unionized, the political parties were small, and relations between them and the unions were made more difficult by the philosophy of syndicalism. This rejected politics because they split workers into factions and favored industrial action by trade unions, which would be the instruments first of social struggle and then of management by the producers themselves. In 1895, partly out of labor exchanges which the syndicalists had established to help themselves, a confederation of labor (CGT) was finally organized and, a few years later, in 1905, under pressure from the Socialist International, a unified socialist party was also founded (SFIO).

The SFIO's leader, until his murder in 1914, would be Jean Jaurès. Orator, humanist, statesman, Jaurès had started out as a professor of philosophy. He ended as the conscience and the inspiration of the movement he sought to organize. Jaurès saw that, having overthrown the hierarchies and the faith which gave cohesion to the old regime, his generation had to find fresh social cement, a new inspiration, which, he proposed, lay in social justice and equality. "You have stilled the old song which had lulled mankind," he told the Chamber. In its stead Jaurès offered not a lullaby but a march. He knew that in a country where the middle classes were growing fast while the industrial proletariat hardly increased at all, no social revolution could succeed without middle-class support. For a moment, he believed that this would come out of the Dreyfus Affair.

Right, Left, and the Dreyfus Affair

In 1894 a Jewish officer, Captain Alfred Dreyfus, had been accused of selling military secrets to the Germans and condemned by a court martial to life imprisonment on Devil's Island, off the South American coast. By 1897 a growing number of people, alerted by Dreyfus' family and his few friends, had become aware that the court had judged on the basis of secret evidence, some of which turned out to have been forged. They called for a review of the case. The army leaders refused to admit that an error could have been committed, eventually arguing that even an injustice could not warrant the harm done to their authority by the revisionist campaign. By 1898 the case had become an affair, had turned from a particular issue of alleged injustice to a contest between national security (the honor of the army) and individual freedom.

One of the most interesting things about the Dreyfus affair is the thought that it would be so utterly unlikely to occur today: not because there are no possibilities of injustice, but because they make so much less of a stir. What mattered in France, however, was that the case polarized the fissiparous country into two political camps: on one side the partisans of order and tradition, the Church, the army, nationalists, and

Captain Alfred Dreyfus.

conservatives *; on the other the radical middle class and the workers, who had drifted apart on economic issues, now reunited by a principle that radicals like Clemenceau and socialists like Jaurès could both agree on: justice.

In 1899, Dreyfus, found guilty for a second time "with mitigating circumstances," was pardoned by the President of the Republic after France had briefly edged on civil war. No one had really won; and the disillusion of idealists on either side increased the national inclination to political skepticism. But the affair had precipitated an important change. The Left, especially the left-wing intelligentsia, which for a century had maintained the Jacobin nationalism of revolutionary tradition, had spent several years fighting the general staff, the army, militarism, and nationalism. It now jettisoned its Jacobin heritage for the internationalism, antimilitarism, and pacifism of socialism, while the Right, which had been pacifistic and rather internationalist through most of the century turned toward nationalism. Instead of providing a bridge between the workers and the middle class, the Dreyfus affair and its consequences thus built one on which the "radical" but patriotic middle classes could join the conservatives: a common nationalism beneath whose shield their opposition to social reform henceforth sheltered.

The right-wing radicalism of new style nationalism had been developing partly in connection with demagogic calls for anti-German *revanche,* partly in reaction against the corruption and incapacity of Parliament. In 1888 and 1889 it had been incarnated briefly in the figure of a handsome officer on a black charger who became the darling of the radical masses for his patriotism and populism. But General Boulanger was a flash in the pan. Triumphantly elected to Parliament from Paris in January, 1889, he already had his future behind him. Instead of seizing power, as his friends expected, he temporized, missed his chance,

---

* These categories are general. There were, of course, conservatives, Catholics, and even soldiers on the Dreyfus side and plenty of the middle class against him.

and fled the country. It was revealed that he had bid for Radical support and received subsidies from the Monarchists. The alliance of the ends against the middle, of those dissatisfied with Parliament and those who rejected the Republic, proved popular and electorally effective. It might have worked but for Republican determination to wreck it by all available means. Boulanger was convicted of a treason he had never dreamed, his movement's electoral progress stopped, and the general committed suicide shortly afterward. Boulanger's legacy was the antiparliamentary, populist, and authoritarian language which his youngest and most idealistic supporters inherited and which Maurice Barrès forged into the doctrine of a new nationalism. This blossomed forth during the Dreyfus affair and played a great part during the prewar years in persuading France that a conflict was inevitable. One of its offshoots would be a refurbished monarchism, whose prophet, Charles Maurras, argued that France could only be herself under a king and that true nationalism and royalism were one. Another was a school of military thinking which insisted on the offensive spirit, believed that the coming war would be won not by matériel but by bravery, and sent many thousands to unnecessary death charging machine guns with swords and bayonets in the opening weeks of fighting.

The men who believed that democratic and parliamentary institutions could not carry France through danger were proved wrong in the war. It was the steadiness of her conscripts in the trenches and the determination of an old Jacobin radical—Georges Clemenceau (1841–1929) —that enabled her to win it. But they would get their chance when the war was over.

Germany

In Germany, the years before 1864 or 1866 were, according to Bismarck, "a time when nothing happened." Enough happened, however, to make possible the events of 1866, a first fulfillment of the unitary aspirations that had gone down to failure in 1849. The most important of these happenings were in Prussia.

Prussia's king, Frederick William IV (1840–1861), was a vain, romantic addlepate. Loyal to the Habsburgs for traditional reasons and to Prussia for dynastic reasons, he could not accept the sovereignty of the people, nor any paper constitution coming between his country and the purposes of the Almighty embodied in himself. Fascinated by possibilities of greatness, Frederick William could not grasp them when they came to him from the hands of "bakers and butchers." He refused the German crown the liberal Assembly of Frankfurt proffered, while yearning for one from his fellow princes. His disappointment in this expectation, like the liberals' disappointment in their expectations of him, put an end to the dreams of 1848. Liberals and radicals were emigrating, conservatism and provincialism spread over the land.

A brief attempt by Prussian conservatives to assert Prussian supremacy in a union of states in North and Central Germany was soon defeated by the superior diplomacy of the Austrians. In 1850, the agreement of Olmütz, in which the former recognized the primacy of the latter, sealed Prussia's humiliation. The German Confederation carried on in the invertebrate terms of 1815. Yet Austria took no advantage of her opportunities, remaining outside the *Zollverein,* which Prussia continued to dominate. While German industry forged forward, Austrian economic development suffered from the Crimean and Italian wars. Investment, speculation, profits, took people's minds off 1848. "The German nation is sick of principles and doctrines," wrote the educator Julius Froebel in 1859: "What it wants is Power, Power, Power!"

This would be given it at last by Prussia. Frederick William's unbalanced mind had given way to madness and his sixty-one-year-old brother William ruled as regent (1857–1861) and then as king (1861–1888). Frugal, direct, hard-working, William I had, as his brother said, all the characteristics of a sergeant major. Among them was an overwhelming devotion to the Prussian army. It was the Prussian Diet's unwillingness to provide credits for the army reforms which he contemplated that brought about a constitutional crisis in 1862 and set William looking for a man who could put the reforms through against the Diet. He found him in Otto von Bismarck (1815–1898). Son of a middle-class mother and a Junker, Bismarck combined the intelligence of the one and the self-assurance of the other. They must have been difficult to reconcile, for Bismarck was throughout his life doubt-ridden and neurotic, facts he concealed behind a massive facade of confidence and increasingly imperious authority.

The new prime minister stated his point of view at once, before the finance committee of the Liberal-dominated Diet: "The great questions of our time will not be decided by speeches and majorities—that was the error of 1848—but by blood and iron." He forthwith demonstrated his determination by ignoring the Diet's votes, putting through the contested military reforms despite it, collecting taxes and duties which the Diet had refused to sanction, and managing quite well since times were prosperous and the yield of tax revenue was rising. The Diet had no legal means to prevent his actions and it was powerless to oppose him. But Bismarck knew that the first sign of failure would mean perdition. He operated, so to speak, on short-term credit. He had to show successes fast or else his king and, not least, he himself would be in serious trouble.

THE UNIFICATION OF GERMANY

Prussia before 1866

German lands, 1866–1867

German Empire in 1871

Boundary of German
Confederation, 1815

And he meant to show successes very fast, above all in defeating Austria and fulfilling the national dreams of the Liberals.

Bismarck gained Russian friendship by supporting her against her Polish rebels in 1863. Then a controversy over the succession to the Duchies of Schleswig and Holstein and over Schleswig's union with Denmark led to war with Denmark in 1864, Schleswig and Holstein's incorporation in Germany, and their occupation by Austro-Prussian forces. Bismarck's policy now aimed at eliminating Austria from North Ger-

Kaiser William I.

many and annexing the two duchies. When Austria proved unwilling, he concluded a military alliance with Italy, which was promised Venetia, and nonplussed the Liberals by supporting a new constitution based on universal suffrage for North Germany. A three-week summer war in 1866 sufficed to defeat Austria and exclude her from the rest of Germany, annex Hanover, Hesse, Frankfurt, and Schleswig-Holstein to Prussia, and form the North German Confederation. Then, four years later, the Franco-Prussian war, this time six months long (1870–1871), completed the unity which Bismarck many years before had described contemptuously as "the German swindle," and capped it with an Imperial constitution that at first sight fulfilled the liberals' dearest dreams, and yet maintained the supremacy of Prussia for which Bismarck labored.

A German Character?

In 1871 no country in Europe had a lower house elected by manhood suffrage as the new Reich did. But its Reichstag could not initiate legislation, could not enforce its will, and had no control over government policy. It was, a Socialist once described it, the fig leaf of absolutism. Real power lay in the hands of the chancellor, who was also prime minister of Prussia, and in the old emperor-army alliance—the emperor appointing all imperial officials including the chancellor, and the army supporting him unhesitatingly as long as the interests of the landed officer corps were defended by him. They were defended well: by 1906, all of the Guard regiments counted only one officer of bourgeois origin and he would be transferred to the General Staff in 1907. Until the war,

401

officers remained the very cream of society: "After God the Father comes the cavalry officer, then his mount, then nothing, nothing, still nothing, then the infantry officer. Very far behind come the civilians: first the reserve officers and at last . . . the remainder."

Officer was almost identical with Junker, by now symbolic figure of a ruling military caste of feudal landowners whose estates, originally conquered from other races, had been more recently wrested from the peasants at whose expense they had been put together. During the nineteenth century, while many peasants became landless laborers, the Junkers' power increased, especially in East Prussia, where farms over 250 acres took up almost half the arable land—four or five times as much as in the rest of Germany. Most Junkers were small and medium landowners, lacking the metropolitan and national experience which made greater aristocrats aware of the new world of coal and steam and iron, lacking the margin, too, which could make greater men envisage compromise—the sacrifice of something to save something else. The Junkers felt they could not afford to abandon anything: poor, they scrabbled for more; fearful, they stonewalled against all change except that which might profit them; short of capital, they could not modernize, increase productivity and profits. They were caught in a vicious circle from which they expected the state to save them by protection, subsidies, or both. Their pressure groups supported governments which supported them, opposed and upset those that did not. Since they furnished the greater part of high administrators and army officers, their influence, which went far beyond mere votes, lay heavy on the Wilhelmian Reich before 1914 and on the Weimar Republic after 1918.* This was the class that furnished the backbone of the army and thus fulfilled an indispensable role.

As it had been for Prussia, the army was the bond of the disparate new empire. The vicarious pride it instilled, the order it ensured, the industrial profits it secured, all helped toward social and national unity. So did universal military service. The conscript learned to be faithful, brave, obedient, his standards of duty and honor focused not just on one dynasty but upon Germany as a whole. He also developed a readiness to accept blows from above and pass them on below when the occasion offered, a sadomasochism which would become a latent national characteristic prompt to reveal itself.

As for the Liberals, territorial unification and economic expansion meant that the content of their creed ran out as fast as the profits were raked in. The essence of German liberalism had been unification. When it was offered to them on a plate in 1866, Liberals quickly abandoned parliamentary principles and constitutional quibbles, gave Bismarck the indemnity bill he requested for having collected taxes without

* Twenty-one out of thirty-five Prussian district presidents before 1914 were titled; 90 per cent or more of upper ranks in the services were so too.

parliamentary sanction, legalized all the transgressions they heretofore condemned, and conceded that not they but the government should henceforth make German policy.

All this had momentous effects on the German people. One has to ponder that the new German empire covered over 200,000 square miles in the center of Europe, bound by more iron rails than any of its neighbors and turning out more coal than France and Belgium together, eventually more iron and steel than the United Kingdom. It was ridiculous, William II said in 1911 when told that Germany wanted to dominate central Europe: "We simply *are* central Europe . . ." Here was the sense of destiny and power that audiences found in the works of Wagner, all rooted in the notion of a chosen people, a young, pure Germany imposing her will on herself and others, carrier of a heavy fate, fulfiller of a mission. Yet German unity had in all a very short existence: seventy-four years, forty-seven of them in the Empire, fifteen under the Weimar Constitution, twelve in the Third Reich. There was an exaltation about such temporality, but also restlessness and fever. Unlike some nations that need think little about their being, the Germans never settled down or took themselves for granted. Anguished, self-questioning, uneasy, the German self was torn between mountebanks and nihilists.

Bismarck's successes rehearsed the same tale as those of Frederick the Great. They seemed to prove that discipline and determination could work miracles, achieve the apparently impossible. Will, courage, toughness, and self-sacrifice became the German ideals: qualities which, while valuable, demand a great deal of tension and repression, accompanied by fear of failure which must be compensated by rigor and overacting. The German was no more brutal or ruthless or brave than anybody else; but, being taught that he had to be all these things, he became a prey to conflicts and rigidities that other Europeans did not have to suffer, part of a mental climate whose price would be paid in the twentieth century. Other-directed and seeking security in discipline and obedience, the German tends equally to be self-absorbed to the point of ignoring any other point of view. His lack of self-confidence is counterbalanced by a strong wish to have his own way.

In 1862, when Bismarck refused to respect the Constitution and talked about blood and iron, one Liberal lawyer warned him to remember what he presented as a fundamental German characteristic: "the belief in a firm moral and legal order as the last and decisive factor in the history of states." If this belief prevailed in 1862, after Bismarck it would be no more. As long as the country had been poor and weak, it put its trust in principles. What else could it do? Success taught it other values, as it had done the French in their days of power. But so did failure: failure before Bismarck's strength, which convinced many Germans that he was justified in asserting that might is right and that "whoever has the power . . . acts according to his views." Bismarck's autocracy relegated the middle classes into economic rather than political activity, broke the beginnings of their self-reliance, and, at the same time, by a familiar process, encouraged them to identify with the triumphant autocratic state. Parliament was no place for men to shine: the ambitious went into business, the independent into lonely rebellion and angry sulks, the masses were left to apolitical loyalty, Philistinism and conformity.

The Political Spectrum

These are generalities. Politics are more specific and Bismarck was a politician above all. The king of Prussia and his army were patriots for Prussia and for the Hohenzollern dynasty. If they envisaged German unity it was as an accretion or conquest around Prussian territories, not as the middle-class revolutionaries of 1848 had hoped to establish it, regardless of the dynasties or of Prussia. Bismarck produced a German empire which gave the Liberals unity and the Prussians dominion; and based it on the alliance of these two forces, which worked well enough as long as he was there to manage it. But middle-class Nationalists and Prussian patriots had more differences than they had things in common. The first were liberal, the others authoritarian and conservative. Nationalists were opposed to particularists. Against them there arose first the Center Party, chiefly Catholic but grouping all opponents of the new regime—priests opposed to Prussian Protestantism, aristocrats who preferred Vienna to Berlin, provincial opponents of Hohenzollern centralism like the Hanoverians annexed in 1866, workers and peasants —especially Catholic and Polish ones—ranged against the big business supporters of the Empire, all of whom opposed Bismarck's middle-class allies; and the Social Democratic labor movement, growing rapidly in the 1870's. Bismarck managed to play Catholics and Socialists against each other, while keeping his original allies in hand.

The Catholics were not only by definition opponents of the Protestant Prussians, they were predestined allies for Catholic Austria and France, Germany's defeated enemies and chief rivals. Against them one could muster both Prussian Conservatives as Prussian patriots and the liberal middle class as German Nationalists. In 1871, Bismarck began the so-called *Kulturkampf*, restricting the political activities of the clergy, their supervision of schools, and their authority over Catholic laymen, banning first the Jesuits, then foreign or foreign-educated clerics, and finally most of the religious orders. By 1876, every Prussian bishop was in prison or in exile. This lasted until 1878, when need for support against Social Democrats and Liberals led to a gradual relaxation of the siege. Relations with Vienna had solidly turned to fair, the

Third Republic in France was becoming increasingly anticlerical, the Church itself was militantly opposed to socialism. A *rapprochement* with the Catholics took place at the expense of Social Democrats, who now received the brunt of the Chancellor's fire. Beginning in 1878 a series of anti-Socialist laws dissolved the party and the structure of Social Democracy and kept them underground, even though individual Socialist candidates continued to be elected to the Reichstag. Between 1878 and 1890 Germany had no Socialist party. The only antibourgeois movements left in the open were Christian Social ones, which moved even further to the right as Socialist competition revived after 1890.

While he muzzled the workers with one hand, Bismarck tried to content them with another. Between 1884 and 1889 gigantic welfare schemes, the first of their kind in the modern world, provided health, accident, and disability insurance, pensions for widows, orphans, and the aged, giving workers greater security and better living conditions. Germany could afford it. She was undergoing an economic explosion from which she emerged by the turn of the century as Europe's most advanced industrial economy, challenging England's primacy with a more modern and enterprising industry and a far superior educational system. Between 1870 and 1914 German population grew from 40 to almost 70 million; national income rose faster than that of other European powers, and so did living standards. The new generations consumed twice as much meat and beer, three times as much sugar, ten times as much rice, fifty times as much cocoa and tropical fruits, a hundred times as much coffee (all per head) as in mid-nineteenth century.

At that time, agriculture had still been the major occupation. In the early 1890's the number of persons employed in industry passed that of those employed in agriculture. By 1907 industry employed nearly twice as many as did farming, and the scale of industry grew like the small steel business that Alfred Krupp had founded with four workers in 1826 and which in 1887 counted 20,000. In heavy industry, chemicals, dyestuffs, and electrical products, Germany stood supreme. Native tradition suggested the planned use of relatively meager resources and state support for industrial enterprise—but also for education and for culture. Around 1900, Germany was the musical center of the world, boasting some 120 opera houses, scores of symphony orchestras, hundreds of choral and chamber music societies. None could gainsay the prestige of her schools and laboratories, her music and her art, her scholars and her soldiers, her *Kultur* and her superior technology and methods. Her

The Krupp steel mills in 1876.

Kaiser William II on the far left, and Archduke Francis Ferdinand, center foreground, with other members of a hunting party.

material primacy in Europe could be compared with that of France a hundred years before: her army intake was double that of the French Republic, her population, her productivity, her resources could not be matched. It was Germany's turn to grasp for European mastery as France had done, and her struggle for this would not end until 1945.

Yet behind all this there lay a serious lack of balance. The German middle classes never developed the self-confidence, the values, the capacity for criticism and self-criticism which would permit them to seize political power or, when entrusted with it, to exercise it. They accepted the ideals of the establishment which kept them out, they bowed to the values in the name of which they were excluded from power. This was reflected even in literature and art, whose outstanding task, declared the Kaiser, was "to foster the ideal." In the 70's and 80's, when English, French, and Scandinavian writers explored society and current spiritual problems, the Germans continued to write in a conventional way, detached from the surrounding world, idealistic, romantic, and conformist. When in the 1890's rebellion in art and music did appear, it tended to combine social and apocalyptic notes, as if no other conjunction could bring change. Anguished and messianic, the German art of the turn of the century reflected the despair of men imprisoned in structures so rigid that thoughts of escape turned from concrete possibilities to fantasy, a foretaste of the tendencies exhibited by the existentialism of Husserl between the wars: the more cosmic for being less concrete.

This lack of balance was reflected also in the personality of the new Kaiser, William II (1888–1918). Born in 1859, the same year as the *Origin of Species,* a withered arm gave the Emperor a lack of balance more evident in character than in physique. William invited adjectives and seems to have justified them all: restless, impulsive, vain, abstemious and flamboyant, humorous and magniloquent, given to playacting and to fantasies, he embodied some of the best and the worst traits of his race. His typically truculent mustaches just as typically

"Dropping the Pilot," a cartoon in *Punch* at the time of Bismarck's resignation.

masked the sensitive features in front of which they raised their aggressive points. Torn between his admiration for England and his pride in Prussia, affected by ancestral insanities and by modern tensions, he strove to live up to a grandiose image for which he lacked the stature and the means.

"The Kaiser," muttered Bismarck, "is like a balloon. If you don't hold fast to the string, you never know where he'll be off." The first to be off, in the circumstances, was Bismarck himself, nagged into resignation by 1890. The great chancellor retired to the hotel near Hamburg that he had turned into a country house, carting along with him his collection of 13,000 bottles.* German foreign policy passed into the hands of Friedrich von Holstein, whose name survives in the veal cutlet which he was first to surmount with a fried egg; and of a series of chancellors the best of whom, Bernhard von Bülow (1849–1929), has been described as "nothing but plaster beneath the shiny paint."

The political spectrum was no more promising: everywhere a little scratch revealed the plaster close beneath the paint. German Liberals were not liberal, they were capitalists: industrialists, bankers, big businessmen. They were against the landowning interests that constituted the backbone of Prussian policy and against agricultural protection, but for Prussia's aggressive imperialism, for expansion and colonialism and militarism, not any kind of parliamentary liberalism or democracy that the term evokes.

Liberal democracy, with all the humanism and all the indecision this implies, became the preserve of Social Democrats. We have seen already that the revolutionary slogans of the Socialists masked a reformist spirit. Their theories which relegated revolution to the morrow of electoral victory also prevented them from exploiting the reformism which they practiced. Dazzled by numbers, fascinated by their organization, fuddled by their own verbiage, the Social Democrats made the worst of all

* All full.

worlds in imperial Germany, as they would do after 1919 in Weimar. Allowed to operate freely after Bismarck's fall, they won ever greater proportions of the Reichstag vote: 20 per cent in 1890, 30 per cent in 1903, one-third of all votes cast in 1912, nearly twice as many as the next strongest party, the Catholic Center. Such gains made them overoptimistic. Their power was illusion; their impotence was real. For one thing, they had not fought for their successes but cashed in like all others on the gifts of Bismarck. They had never, like the French, the Belgians, or the British, struggled to obtain the suffrage or social legislation. With no tradition of combat, they could as easily lose what they had easily gained. For another thing, only a coalition could produce a majority in the Reichstag and, while coalitions sometimes helped win elections, their occasional allies of the National Liberal Party tended to back away toward the Conservative alliance that they much preferred. The professional men, shopkeepers, and salaried employees who might be briefly persuaded to co-operate with Socialists always sheered off as soon as they heard the bugle calls of imperialism.

Just as patriotic as other Germans, the Socialists were hampered by their internationalist and pacifistic doctrine. Nationalism was a realm in which they could not match the competition; and nationalism in Germany was trumps. In the 1890's, a Pan-German League had been founded to assert the rights of the Master Race to colonies, and gather in all sons of the German race. They talked a plausible line. Between 1871 and 1881, 800,000 Germans left their country. Far more had left over the century as a whole. The population was growing, and patriots felt that if Germany had colonies for her men to settle there would also be greater demand for her goods, and hence more jobs to keep prospective immigrants home. In 1842 the king of Prussia had refused an offer to buy California from Mexico. A little later a chance to settle independent Texas had been missed when Texas joined the United States. Most Germans did not want colonies—their attentions were engaged nearer home. Bismarck agreed. Overseas trade could be advanced without costly acquisitions or the internal and international friction that went with them. A brief change of mind in the 1880's led to the annexation of territories in Africa and the Pacific, but they were largely leftovers, arid, disappointing, and, by 1914, held no more than 25,000 Germans including officials and troops. Still, the shipping interests, the banks and iron industry that fed them, and the navy too, supported a policy whose rewards must have been more psychic than concrete.

The Pan-German League was a middle-class organization of teachers, businessmen, and lawyers out to forget their pettiness in their country's greatness, their personal frustrations in Germany's success. Action, vigor, determination, regardless of anyone who stood in the way (including Germany's own real interests), was what they wanted. While they always remained a lunatic fringe, their rabid national chauvinism inevitably affected the mind of Germany, the more so since even more

Solid citizens for pride and profit: a meeting of the *Deutsche Gesellschaft,* businessmen affiliated with the Pan-German League.

moderate men spoke in similar accents. For the sociologist, Max Weber, Germany could have done without unification "if it was to be the end and not the beginning of a policy of German world power." And in 1897, Friedrich Naumann, a leader of the Progressive Liberal party which sometimes allied with the Social Democrats, published his *National-Social Catechism,* in which nationalism was defined as the effort of the German people to spread their influence over the whole globe.

Lastly, the Reichstag had only limited powers.* It could not dismiss unrepresentative ministries any more than the Prussian Diet could in 1862, or control policy. This went to such lengths that in 1914 the Reichstag had no knowledge of how diplomatic negotiations were progressing between the murder of Archduke Francis Ferdinand and the outbreak of war. Parliament and party leaders kept up with events by reading the papers. There was no parliamentary system, as we know it, in Germany before 1918. Nor did the Reichstag have a say in the internal affairs of the separate states, each with its own kind of representative assembly. In Prussia, greatest of German states, representatives to the Diet were elected by a cumbrous indirect voting system heavily weighted in the Junkers' favor. In Saxony in 1896, where a much wider franchise had obtained until then, a system similar to Prussia's was introduced especially to thwart the Social Democrats. The peaceful conquest of political power became less likely every year. The Social Demo-

---

* Just how limited would appear from the incidents that took place at Saverne in Alsace during the winter of 1913. There, friction between locals and officers of the garrison culminated in demonstrations against the officers' behavior. The garrison commander, feeling the civilian authorities were not carrying out their functions, ordered his soldiers to seize a number of the demonstrators and shut them up in the barracks, a move far exceeding his powers and suggesting that high-handed military action could always trample on civilian rights. In the Reichstag debates where this scandal was brought up, the army defended its own, the government stuck by the army, and, while a large majority condemned the government position (293 to 54), a court martial held immediately after vindicated the colonel responsible and showed that the Reichstag and the majority of the nation were powerless against the officer corps and the Prussian system.

crats would never admit this. But their demands for truly representative government and a fair franchise at all levels remained unfulfilled until 1918.

From Bismarck's day to 1914 no German government had a secure majority in the Reichstag. All had to rely on a series of coalitions and combinations with anti-Socialist parties. The Social Democrats, strongest of the parties, could have used this situation to achieve measures they favored by opportunistic alliances with opposition parties, most of which also wanted more constitutional government, ministerial responsibility, and the liberalization of state machinery. But Social Democrats were wedded to the view that they must not co-operate with bourgeois parties but wait for their collapse, never adding to the power of the state (for example, by nationalization) until they themselves could take it over. Thus, while urban and working classes grew, the legal framework of society did not alter. Now that the middle classes had accepted the political order along with prosperity, it was the turn of the workers to be antimilitarist, critical, and internationalist. Concessions could have won their support for the established order, but neither the privileged aristocracy nor the profit-making employers would really make concessions, and those who did propose them were powerless. Germany stuck in a political deadlock, where the executive would not introduce the legislation the Reichstag wanted and the Reichstag, unable to initiate legislation of its own, would not accept that of the executive.

Then, in 1908, the London *Daily Telegraph* published an interview in which the Kaiser protested his friendship with England while revealing alleged sympathies for her during the Boer War. This caused a tremendous uproar in Germany and a serious political crisis from which the Kaiser came out much diminished, having promised in future to respect his "constitutional obligations." Since these remained as unclear as ever, the effect of the incident was to remove yet one more source of authority, however imperfect, and leave Germany more than ever in constitutional chaos.

After 1908, the Kaiser had no real authority, nor did the chancellors who existed through him, nor did the parties which had no effective avenue of expression, nor did the Reichstag which had no hold on power. Not even the services were of one mind: the sailors opposed England, the soldiers opposed France, and their pacifist or progressive opponents opposed Russia. Policy oscillated according to the chance of events and, in the end, Germany stumbled into war less because she knew what she wanted than because she did not know what that was.

The Nemesis of Power

The Germans, the best of whom could carry out a particular task supremely well, were incapable of deciding on a direction or a context; and this also prevented them from agreeing on precise war aims. The soldiers who, by default, had brought them into war were allowed to continue fighting (which they did very well) without precise direction, aim, or limit to their endeavors. The vacancy of authority which permitted the drift to war prolonged the drifting through it.

On the home front, things got steadily worse. Enthusiasm or resignation among virtually all sectors of the population made light of deprivations that for the poorer classes came close to famine. And only the soldiers' decision that they could do no more put an end to the fighting and presented the civilians with a revolution ready-made. In 1918 authority changed hands largely by default. The Kaiser abdicated. A republic was proclaimed. But even when the autocracy was revealed as an empty suit of armor, the reins of power were not grasped by conscious claimants, as in Russia, but gingerly placed into civilian hands by soldiers concerned to cut the army's losses. Once again, German institutions and German liberties increased without exertion, as a gift from above.

There had been mutiny at the end of October, 1918, when the fleet at Kiel had received orders to put to sea for a last forlorn battle, and there had been voices raised calling for the Emperor's abdication. Revolt had spread and "Soviets" had been founded here and there, while in Bavaria, always autonomist, an independent Republic under a Socialist, Kurt Eisner, was proclaimed. During the war, while the unions and the Social Democratic party fully supported the war effort, a very small opposition movement on the party's extreme Left had gradually grown under the leadership of Karl Liebknecht (1871–1919) and Rosa Luxemburg, sturdily antimilitarist, pacifist, and unwilling to exchange their revolutionary ends for patriotic ones as most of their fellow Social Democrats had done. Liebknecht and Luxemburg believed that workers should organize for revolt not collaboration, and that they held a stout weapon in the general strike which should be used to overthrow the existing order. In other words, they held to the original party doctrine; and in this they were at odds with the moderate leaders of Social Democracy.

In 1917, stimulated by revolution in Russia, by growing famine among the poor at home, and by disgust with the continuing, increasingly useless slaughter, this group left the party and set up the Spartacus League, named after the leader of the greatest Roman slave rebellion, which called for a revolution to end the war and seize power for the workers. The year 1918 gave them the chance to put their views in practice, views which were shared by revolutionary groups in other parts of the country. It soon became clear, however, that the extreme Left had a very small following even among the workers, most of whom supported the majority Social Democrats when they did not prefer the Catholic Center. It also became clear that Germany was not ready for revolution, that the Socialist-Center coalition which ran the first republican government under Friedrich Ebert (1871–1925), who had led the pro-war Socialists in the Reichstag, refused to countenance disorder, and that the army would not stand for it.

The Prussian military aristocracy which had run the army had largely been mowed down on the battlefields. But the power of the army and the professionals that managed it endured. It had been General Erich Ludendorff (1865–1937) who forced the Kaiser into abdication and permitted the proclamation of a republic; and Friedrich Ebert had greeted the troops returning from the front with the assurance that they remained undefeated. Ebert understood quite well that, without the army, extremists might take over. He kept in close communication with the Chief of Staff, while encouraging the formation of auxiliary "Free Corps" of national veterans and students which would be free to operate where the regular army was checked by the victorious allies. When the Spartacists, hoping to drag a reluctant people into revolution, rose in Berlin, they were crushed and their leaders murdered. Other Communist risings —such as that in Bavaria—were similarly·dealt with. The new regime, like past ones, would be founded on an alliance between the army and the state, the former tolerating the activities of the latter as long as its interests and its existence were preserved.

Italy

Eight different states, a score of dialects unintelligible to outsiders, local traditions ranging from the French-oriented culture of Piedmont and the progressive tendencies of Lombardy to the clerical corruption of the papal states and the backward feudalism of Sicily: such was the Italian peninsula in 1849. Charles Albert of Sardinia-Piedmont had disgraced himself in Lombardy, the Pope's wonted liberalism had turned to despotism under the guard of a French expeditionary force, municipal rivalries had proved stronger than national sentiments. Charles Albert had declared: *"Italia farà da sé."* In fact, she could not go it alone. Charles Albert having abdicated, his son Victor Emmanuel II returned to a conservative policy and to entente with Austria (until one with France could be obtained). Even defeated, his country remained the symbol of Italian hopes, the only state preserving the red, white, and green flag and a vestige of constitutional government. In the capable hands of Massimo d'Azeglio and Camillo Cavour, rationalism, anticlericalism, and cautious reforms marked its government.

Piedmont and Unity

Son of a nobleman who had married a Swiss Protestant, strongly influenced by English parliamentary ideas and by the moderate liberalism

412

Camillo Cavour. Right: Victor Emmanuel II, known for various motives as "the father of his people."

of Louis Philippe's bourgeois monarchy in France, tireless improver and modernizer, Cavour became the motor of Italian unification. The Agricultural Societies, banks, railroads that he promoted, the newspaper he published—*Il Risorgimento* (The Resurgence), even the Whist Club that he founded in Turin, endowed Piedmont with the framework of a modern state. All became pillars of nationalist activity. As Victor Emmanuel's premier from 1852 to his death in 1861, Cavour reorganized finance, spurred railroad construction, encouraged agrarian credit and co-operatives, improved the army and his country's standing in the world. Shrewd, moderate, persevering, aware of the disproportion between the ends that he pursued and Piedmont's means, Cavour had to contend with patriots less patient than himself, with the republican followers of Mazzini whose ideas of Italian unity did not include the Crown, and, above all, with the brave and bellicose Giuseppe Garibaldi (1807–1882), a charismatic and uncontrollable leader who had learned the trade of arms as soldier of fortune in South America. After twelve years of guerrilla warfare in Brazil and Uruguay, Garibaldi returned to his native Nice in 1848.* Thereafter, he would act as a patriotic firebrand, his rashness often landing him in trouble and sometimes cutting across Cavour's more deliberate plans.

Each in his way, Cavour the schemer and statesman, Garibaldi the impassioned demagogue, contributed to the rise and unification of their land. But it was not Piedmont's slowly recovered strength that made Italian unity. French support brought it Lombardy in 1859, British support allowed Central Italy to choose annexation to it in 1860, and, that same year, Garibaldi's genius and initiative contributed Naples, Sicily, and the opportunity to annex most of the Papal states. The first *Italian* parliament met in Turin in 1861 and Cavour, whose diplomacy

* French at the time of his birth, Nice was part of the Kingdom of Piedmont from 1815 to 1860, when it was returned to France together with Savoy after a plebiscite to which Piedmont consented in return for Napoleon III's acceptance of the accession of the central Italian states to Victor Emmanuel's crown.

413

Giuseppe Garibaldi.

had been behind the lightning expansion, died·six months later. But there was more to come. In 1866 the Prussian victory at Sadowa brought the lands of Venice. In 1870, the French troops guarding Rome for the Pope were withdrawn at last and Victor Emmanuel's men marched into their longed-for capital. Italy stood united, when twelve years before she had still been a geographical expression of the textbooks: but united neither by the popular initiative that Mazzini hoped for, nor by the valor of its own arms, and, still, united only in the most formal sense.

The long peninsula was quartered by the Apennines and broken up into further segments by its hills. What nature had put asunder railways bound together again: but at the price of debts and taxes. The sovereign states now became *prefectures,* too often governed by officials from Piedmont so that their inhabitants sometimes felt less free when ruled by fellow Italians than when the Austrians had been there. Southerners especially exchanged their retrograde and inefficient Bourbon kings for an oppressive colonial administration that taxed peasants more heavily than the Bourbons had and drove them to desperate rebellion in the 60's and to chronic banditry for a long time after.

From the nineteenth century into the twentieth two nations endured side by side. In both there was unemployment, underemployment, hunger, and malnutrition; but the southern part was poorer, worse fed and housed, more illiterate, more malarial, more *African.* In Sicily and Calabria the feudal world survived on great estates and among brutalized peasants who sometimes rose like storms out of despair.

Divided We Stand

Rent by regional, historical, and cultural differences—between north and south, country and town, growing industry and small-scale produc-

414

tion, between Anarchists, Socialists, Syndicalists, Republicans, Mazzinians, Monarchists, Liberals, and Conservatives—the kingdom was hurt by one division, still more profound. For threescore years after 1870 the Pope refused to accept the occupation of his city, Rome, or recognize the existence of the Italian state. Regarding himself a prisoner in the Vatican, he rejected the overtures of the government and in a firm decree (*Non Expedit*) forbade all Catholics to vote in elections or take a part in national affairs. The government reacted: if the Pope rejected Cavour's principle of a free Church in a free state, the state would apply it unilaterally—the freer for the political absence of the Catholics. Inevitably, official policy became more anticlerical than it would have been. Tithes were abolished; Church charities were taken over by the state, thus shifting the influence that came from the control of alms and doles from priests and friars to secular officials; secular education spread and inculcated the anticlerical views of the regime.

Still, Italy remained a very Catholic country. Even anticlericals were often married in Church and had their children baptized there. Soon disendowed foundations were endowed once more and, in the last twenty years of the nineteenth century, the number of monks and friars increased, while that of nuns almost doubled. By 1904 the Catholics were back in politics to support moderate policies against the Socialists and, the following year, a Papal encyclical withdrew the *Non Expedit* of 1871. Meanwhile, however, the combination of a kind of administrative colonialism in large parts of the country and of the internal emigration of the Catholics had dug a ditch between the popular masses and a government nominally representative, but viewed most often as an alien and oppressive power wielded by men somehow unrelated to those who paid for their caprices.

In fact, part of the heavy taxes went for necessities of a modern state which were not evident to a great many people and yet essential for its growth, like communications. When the Kingdom of Naples had become part of Italy, 1,621 of its 1,848 villages had no roads at all. Until roads were built they would never, even in the slightest way, become a part of the new national and economic unit being forged around them. The opening of the Suez Canal, coinciding with unification, improved the economic situation by placing the peninsula on the now reopened trade routes to the East. Rice, sugarbeets, and orchards prospered in the north where the possibilities of hydroelectric power began to be put to use. But roads, and rails, and power projects cost money; so did schools and teachers, however pitifully few; so did the army.* And there was little basis for a sense that most of those who paid for all these things had any share in them. Until 1882, while total population stood over

---

* Between 1901 and 1921 about 2.4 per cent of the country's budget was devoted to education and fine arts; between 20 and 30 per cent to the army and navy.

28 million, about half a million men had votes. Then, until 1912, by which time the population had grown to 35 million, there were 2 million voters. The franchise was kept narrow by tax and literacy requirements. It was only in 1912 that most workers and peasants got the vote; and the first elections under manhood suffrage were held in 1913. Thus politics remained the plaything of a limited class, rather alike to that which profited from the July Monarchy in France from which Cavour had drawn his inspiration, while the industrial workers and, in some parts, the rural proletariat struggled for better conditions and greater legal rights.

Ultimately, the country's problems arose out of economic imbalance. Italy lacked the natural resources on which Britain, Germany, and France built their industries. Where at the turn of the century one Frenchman in three, one Englishman in twelve, got his living from the land, three out of every five Italians drew their living from it, a few more than in Japan at the same time. Even in 1921 more than twice as many Italians worked in agriculture as in industry; and this continued to be true until the mid-1950's. The development of Italian industry was much slower than that of other countries to which industrial expansion also came late: Sweden, or Russia, or Japan. The country developed labor and revolutionary organizations even before the industrial substructure was productive enough to furnish some of the things that labor asked for; and labor unrest probably held back some of the developments that could have taken place. Industrial expansion bogged down in wrangling and strife, while the invertebrate character of Italian politics prevented both effective reforms (as in Britain) and effective repression (as in Russia or Japan).

The country's economy crept forward where its neighbors' rushed. Wages never caught up with prices. The condition of laboring people improved, but so slowly that they fell ever farther behind their contemporaries in other Western countries. This relative stagnation and the resentments born of fear, want, and insecurity meant chronic turmoil. Prolonged, violent, and generally futile labor struggles created a climate in which the classes watched one another like cats and dogs, in which no moderate unions could survive, and labor identified with the politics of revolution, while industrialists and landowners placed their hopes in repressive reaction.

In the 1890's a Socialist party was organized, not unconnected with the popular unrest and the irrelevance of parliamentary cliques. Nationalist groups sprang up in the early years of the twentieth century, and a Nationalist party was formed in 1910. But while the Socialists hoped to solve the country's problems by revolution, the Nationalists tended to look for relief in overseas expansion, colonial settlements that could ease the population problem and help the economy—quite how, they did not say. The African wars this brought were marked by humiliating failures, the worst being the defeat Italian troops suffered in 1896 at Adowa, at Ethiopian hands. Labor opposition, violence, disorder had now become endemic. In 1900 an anarchist workman (who had returned from America) killed King Umberto I (1878–1900). His heir, Victor Emmanuel III (1900–1946), promised reform, permitted unions to operate legally, but only precipitated a wave of strikes and walkouts accompanied by shootings and violence. There was too much pent-up misery for peaceful evolution, the trumpery parliament helped little, and a contemporary recession worsened economic conflicts.

The negative experiences of this time inspired a number of reactions: the historical idealism which Benedetto Croce formulated against the materialism and the self-satisfaction of the bourgeoisie; the romantic Nietzschean rebellions of poets like D'Annunzio and Marinetti disgusted with the sham and mediocrity they witnessed all around; the elitist political theories of social philosophers like Gaetano Mosca and Vilfredo Pareto cutting through the cant of pretended democracy and the pretenses of political hypocrisy. On the political stage, meanwhile, Socialist militancy grew more intense as the government entered the Libyan war; and their antimilitarist campaigns popularized the youngest and most dynamic among Socialist leaders: Benito Mussolini—son of a Socialist blacksmith and of an elementary-school teacher—named for the father of Mexican independence, Benito Juárez, himself teacher and journalist, fiery, erratic, grandiloquent, and forceful.

Every military campaign consumed resources the country could ill afford, to very little profit. This seemed particularly true when European war broke out in 1914 with Italy happily neutral. Neutrality was what most Italians wanted to maintain, but there were also cries for intervention. France and Britain played on irredentist sentiment for the still-unredeemed territories in Habsburg hands, in the Trento to the north of Venice and at the head of the Adriatic, around Trieste. Mussolini now emerged as a leading advocate of intervention, breaking with his Socialist comrades and founding a Nationalist newspaper, probably with Allied funds. While propaganda tried to rouse the martial ardor of a pacific country, behind the scenes frenzied bargaining went on: the Italians were demanding exorbitant compensation from the Austrians for Austria's expansion at Serbian expense. The Germans, eager to keep Italy neutral, urged their Austrian allies to give in. The Western allies, on the other hand, were ready to offer more for Italian intervention, since none of it would be at their own expense; and they needed her help. But Vienna made up its mind too slowly: a few days before it accepted Italy's demands, the secret treaty of London had been signed, promising Italy, among other territories, Trentino, Trieste, and much of the Dalmatian coast. In May, 1915, Italy had been maneuvered into war. She would have done better had she remained neutral.

Spain

The political reality of a country where universal suffrage had been imposed on a backward society, where electors were ignorant and apathetic, where local patriotism had more meaning than national and national issues no meaning at all, was *caciquismo*—the feudal regime of local bosses protecting their clients and their particular regions and "delivering" them in turn at the polls. "Politics ran like an express train, through the desolate townships and villages of Spain, stopping only at election times."* The rest of the time it was a case of charity and jobbery.

Of course, elections counted little. With a small electorate, nearly half of it made up of state and municipal employees or pensioners, electoral fraud was standard and the opposition often abstained from the machine-dominated polls, leaving elections in the hands of governmental parties and showing them up for the mockery they were. What really counted was the occasional intervention of the army: ill-paid when paid and recurrently discontented. Privates regarded service as a kind of serfdom, the junior ranks as ill-rewarded drudgery. "Nothing is more common," reported the London *Times* in August, 1847, "than to see Spanish officers . . . begging alms in the streets of Madrid after having in vain tried to earn a livelihood as servants in hotels." An officer's only hope of comfort lay in a rank or a political prebend to be achieved by insurrectionary gestures that shook things up and propelled him faster than the endless promotion schedule would have done. So politics was permanent sedition in which the discontent of the military joined with that of a faction out of power to make a pronunciamento—that is, a rebellion by mutiny. Yet political power achieved by insurrection invited further mutinies which could bring others into power in their turn; settling political issues by rebellion made rebellion the key issue of politics and other working compromises the less likely.

For the past century and more, every Spanish regime has lived and died in function of the army: created, tolerated, or upset by it. Republics or monarchies, *juntas, cortés,* and cabinets rose and fell, came and went; rebellions broke out, pronunciamentos were attempted; the constant fact remained that without the army nothing could keep going or be done. Under the surface of political chaos constantly brooded the fear or hope of social and political revolution. The rebellious tendencies of the Carlists clinging fiercely to tradition and church, the millenial dreams of Anarchists, republicanism under the Monarchy, monarchism under the Republic: stability was the rarest commodity in Spain.** As for the

* Raymond Carr, *Spain 1808–1939* (Oxford: 1966), p. 369.
** The two most relatively stable periods have been 1874–1898 and the years since 1939.

simple people, they projected their yearnings and their hopes to escape poverty on bandits, bullfighters, and generals risen from the ranks. But primitive rebellions paralleled loyalties and conservatism just as primitive and just as fierce. Latent or active, revolution and reaction were the two poles of Spanish politics.

There was a third factor in the political game: the Court, which tried to hold the balance between. political machines and the army. The Court meant Ferdinand's widow Maria Christina, and then her daughter Isabella (1833–1868), declared of age in 1843 when she was only thirteen years old. Maria Christina had secretly married a shopkeeper's son and had as much trouble concealing her repeated pregnancies as her speculations and ventures into the Cuban slave trade. Isabella, an obese, devout, ill-educated girl, was also torn between her sexual proclivities and her religious guilt, eventually succumbing to scandal and political failure like her mother, after a reign marked by reactionary laws and bloody insurrections.

In 1868 one more such insurrection presided over by General Prim deposed Isabella, established manhood suffrage and constitutional government, and began the search for a new monarch which would set off the Franco-Prussian War. The brief reign of Amadeo, son of the king of Italy (1870–1873), ended in abdication and was succeeded by a republic also of two years' duration, which enjoyed four presidents—one of them a Socialist who held office for one day. Prim had been murdered in 1870 and, in the absence of any dominant figure, the Republic was a spell of civil war between Carlists, Anarchists, assorted Republicans and the supporters of Isabella or, rather, of her son Alfonso XII (1874–1885). In the last days of 1874, the latter (who had just come of age) was proclaimed king by a generals' *junta*. The suffrage was limited once again but, on the whole, Alfonso's ten-year reign enjoyed prosperity. When Alfonso died in 1885 the country once again had an infant king, Alfonso XIII (1886–1931), who reigned under his mother's regency. This time the politicians avoided instability by a tacit agreement to share power in alternating liberal and conservative governments. In 1890, a liberal cabinet reintroduced manhood suffrage, which merely reinforced the *cacique* system of electoral management, now master of rigging lists and intimidating voters.

By that time, economic development in the northern cities was beginning to create labor unrest. Representative government was evidently a farce, the parliamentary system discredited, and the underprivileged were driven to violent extremes—particularly anarchism, which, in the rural regions, meant chiefly land redistribution but which appeared everywhere as a violent idealistic reaction against a confused, unjust disorder perpetuating itself by corruption and force. Since the Catholic Church was allied with the possessing classes, the opposition parties became violently anticlerical and none more so than the Republicans and

Spanish and Belgian Royal Families. Standing, from left to right, are Prince Leopold of Belgium, King Albert of Belgium, Alfonso XIII of Spain, and Prince Charles of Belgium. Seated in front are Queen Beatrice of Spain and Queen Elizabeth of Belgium.

Anarchists. Anticlericalism was almost a precondition of liberalism in countries where the Church appeared an obstacle to every kind of progress. But it saddled progressive parties not only with a stubborn foe but with a dangerous canker; for it became an easy substitute for reform, driving other issues from the center of progressive preoccupations. Time was to show that persecuting priests and burning churches was no substitute for concrete social measures, although it often proved (like anti-Semitism elsewhere) a convenient way of channeling popular passions.

While radicals concentrated their energies on the clergy, conservatives were looking overseas. In Cuba, a ten-year long revolt had been ended in 1878 by a convention in which the mother country promised liberal reforms. Some such reforms were partly initiated. Notably, slavery was finally abolished in 1886. But Spain these days was incapable of fair administration. Unrest broke out again, encouraged by the United States, which looked upon the island with economic and strategic interest. By 1897, when a liberal government offered the Cubans something like autonomy, the Cuban leaders had decided that they would only be satisfied with independence. Unwilling to abandon an island it could not afford to keep, jingo opinion called for war at first against the Cubans and then against the United States (1898), whose own jingoes succeeded in forcing a conflict which most sensible men hoped to avoid. The war went disastrously for Spain. She was decisively defeated, losing not only her last American dominions (San Domingo, Cuba, and Puerto Rico) but also the Philippines. It was no consolation to the Spanish that defeat rid them of a colonial drain with which the United States would now be saddled. In any case, soldiers and jingoes would seek no less costly compensation in the colonial possessions that were left, especially in nearby Morocco, which became the particular preserve of the army and the chief terrain where promotion might be gained or mutiny hatched.

Spain remained caught in a familiar dilemma, her economy typical of backward lands whose population grows faster than their productivity. As long as the vast majority of Spanish people, living on the land, remained in misery, purchasing power was lacking to back industrial expansion on any serious scale. As late as 1936 more than half the Spaniards still wrung their living from agriculture; in 1956, 47 per cent.* Economic and political backwardness could be overcome only with resources that progress and reform could bring, but progress and reform would affect powerful interests vested in keeping things as they were. Additional revenues could be found only by estate and income taxes, which the political situation and the ruling mentality rendered out of the question; and the imperial ambitions of the military meant an army and a navy ** too big for available means, yet useless for any purpose except employing several tens of thousands and cowing the rest.

Spain was still a congeries of provinces uneasily held together with little sense of a national or cultural community. In 1904, when the aspiring young Pablo Picasso left Barcelona to affirm himself on a broader canvas, it was not to Madrid that he went but to Paris. By then, though two-thirds of the population over seven was still illiterate, a limited cultural renaissance was going on. In 1870, no Spanish scientist had known how to use a microscope. About that time a group of professors expelled from their chairs for their liberal ideas set up the Free Institute of Education, which became the center of secular education and of an intellectual revival. Inevitably the effects of the Institute were as limited in scope as those of the enlightened *afrancesados* a century earlier. But it helped breed the "generation of 1898"—social critics and enlighteners like Miguel de Unamuno, José Ortega y Gasset, and Ramiro de Maeztu, who tried to regenerate society by a heroic appeal to cultural patriotism (*Hispanidad*). Strongly affected by Nietzsche and George Bernard Shaw, these men rejected the crude materialism of the ruling bourgeoisie along with the vulgar masses and the shabbiness of democratic politics against which they affirmed their impossibly exalted ideas. But the shabbiness of Spanish politics, like the sobriety of the Spanish people, stemmed not from taste but from necessity. Policy and apathy had made a poor country even poorer. Food, quarters, equipment were comparable to what existed in southern Italy or the Balkans; the countryside hardly saw a bicycle before the 1930's; motor cars belonged only to the few and rich.

The Spanish death rate had been nearly twice the European average. With the end of the nineteenth century this was curtailed. By 1940 life expectancy for those who lived beyond the age of one was fifty-two

---

* In 1956, 42 per cent of the national income came from agriculture compared with 66 per cent in 1913. This figure should be compared to India's 50 per cent, and contrasted to 10 per cent in France or 17 per cent in Italy in 1960.
** After 1898 Spain was left with over a hundred admirals and no capital ships.

José Ortega y Gasset.

for men and fifty-nine for women: about the same as half a century before in France. Population grew from 18 to 24 million by 1930, faster thereafter. Those who could went to the cities or to America. Twentieth-century towns became what their nineteenth-century counterparts had been in France and England: vast refugee camps, half their population made up of laborers who had left the land to find casual work or unemployment in the city. Needs outran possibilities in a manner characteristic of such situations, outskirts turning to slums, electricity lighting populations which still got their water from inadequate pumps. Municipal government continued to be primitive and wretched. As late as the 1920's Madrid could collect only one-third of the town's refuse, leaving the rest to scavengers and the sewerless outer suburbs to death rates double those elsewhere.

Trotsky once pointed out that workers are fashioned by their masters and masters get the kind of workers they deserve. The violence of a country's social struggles mirrors the violence of the oppression out of which they grow. In Spain, the attempts of industrial workers and rural laborers to set up unions and associations were looked upon as insults to employers, somewhat akin to servile revolts, and were repressed as such. This attitude on the part of employers and officials tended to produce the revolts it had been meant to stifle. There ensued a dialogue of repression and reprisal in which each side felt certain that *it* stood for right and its opponents for wrong and provocation.

Social unrest was intensified by particularist stirrings in the Basque provinces of the northwest and in Catalonia. After 1893 a powerful Catalan nationalist movement sprang up, particularly important not only for reflecting a traditional resentment of Castilian rule but because Catalonia was Spain's richest and most advanced province and Barcelona the country's economic capital. In 1909 serious defeats in Morocco forced the government to find reinforcements by calling up the Catalan reserv-

422

ists. This set off a general strike in Barcelona, followed by bloody riots in which convents were set on fire, monks and priests were killed in what had become part of the ritual of Spanish insurrections. Following this "bloody week" a well-known anticlerical radical, Francisco Ferrer (1859–1909), was arrested, tried, and shot. Ferrer had been in England at the time of the rising and bore no responsibility for the massacres that marked it. But he was the founder of the "modern school" movement and a leading rationalist. His secular enterprises threatened the educational monopoly of the Catholic Church and aroused its violent hostility, while the schools he launched threatened the political monopoly of the ruling classes. A brief liberal reaction that followed Ferrer's death soon crumbled before the opposition of the King, and Spain was left to traverse the war years once more in conservative hands.

Russia

"A strange superstition prevails among the Russians," wrote the American minister to St. Petersburg in 1853, "that they are destined to conquer the world." Less than a century later, the idea seemed far from strange. It is the purpose of this section to span the interval between the time when it appeared humorous and that when to many it became a frightening likelihood.

Up to 1917, Russia remained formally the same monarchy that Catherine the Great had ruled. The Tsar was the father of his people, an irresponsible autocrat. Ministers answered to him alone and none—at least in theory—could gainsay his will. Mid-nineteenth century found Russia under the rule of the same Nicholas I (1825–1855) who smothered the Decembrists. It was under his rule that a French traveler compared the Empire to a military camp living in a state of siege, that Marx gained his impression of a looming barbaric power whose reactionary masters, allied with equally reactionary Prussia, threatened to overwhelm the progressive West. But Nicholas died under the impact of defeat in the Crimea, and for a while the threat discerned by Marx hung fire. Nicholas had three successors: Alexander II (1855–1881), oscillating not unlike his namesake between good intentions and disillusioned failure, was finally murdered after fifteen years of unsuccessful attempts on his life; Alexander III (1881–1894), more reactionary than his predecessor, a conscientious autocrat devoid of ability or imagination; and Nicholas II (1894–1917), stubborn, weak, and foolish, a naïve traditionalist without capacity or decisiveness to maintain the autocracy he stood for.

The accession of Alexander II seemed to usher in a liberal period. Rigid censorship regulations were relaxed, education was reformed, a new enlightened generation trained in new model schools, above all a beginning made in the burning question of "baptized property": the peasants. In 1861 private serfdom was abolished, some 20 million serfs granted civil rights. They could own property, move about, engage in business, marry or go to court as free persons, which was a great advance. Great but limited, for all kinds of legal, economic, and social discriminations remained, or were now raised against them. Thus, the reform raised serious problems, for relative freedom which did not carry with it the means to stay alive was bound to cause more troubles than it solved. The new free men lost part of the land which they had tilled as serfs and had to pay for that which they could keep. The sense of grievance arising out of this erupted in widespread agrarian troubles in the 60's and the disillusion of 1861 marked Russian politics until 1917. Conspiracy and agitation never ceased again.

Still, Alexander's reign saw quite material changes: local government assemblies (*Zemstvos*) were set up; a new judicial system was introduced, based on a surprisingly independent judiciary operating in open courts, frequently with juries * ; the army was reformed and based on universal military service; vast areas of land changed hands. About a third of noble lands passed into the hands of capitalists or richer peasants more interested in production for the market; perhaps as much was bought from the poorer peasants affected by taxation and by their need of cash to redeem themselves from serfdom.

None of this altered a basic situation of very limited liberties and even more limited facilities for leading a decent life. For the *mujik,* so went the proverb, God was too high and the Tsar too far. Judging by the mortality rate, said to have risen from about 24 per 1,000 at the beginning of the century to 35 per 1,000 in 1880 (though in Russia such statistics are even less reliable than elsewhere), emancipation did not improve the lot of most. As the 1870's ended, about half the peasantry owned enough land to keep body and soul together. As population kept growing,** more of the peasantry fell below the subsistence level. Even well-to-do farmers like Leon Trotsky's parents lost four out of eight children, used few candles and less soap. Lesser people found even tea a luxury.† Famines remained current until late nineteenth century; malnutrition, degeneracy, and illiteracy were commonplace. In 1894, school attendance figures were 24 per 1,000 in Russia as compared to 140 per 1,000 in Sweden or 172 per 1,000 in Germany. After the turn of the century, while some peasants—the *kulaks*—grew

---

* In 1878 a young girl, Vera Zasulich, shot the governor general of St. Petersburg in reprisal for the corporal punishment of a political prisoner, and was tried and acquitted by a jury. As a result the government abolished jury trial in political cases.

** Despite heavy mortality it grew over 50 per cent between 1860 and 1897, when it stood around 125 million, one-third of these landless poor.

† The Russian word for "tip" is "for tea."

more prosperous, the immense majority continued poor and deep in debt. Even the not so poor carried a heavy burden of debt and taxes which forced them to sell all the grain they could, grain which they would otherwise have consumed themselves, thus providing the exports that made Russia the granary of Europe, a granary where most denizens never ate their fill, but which did give Russia a favorable trade balance, kept the ruble steady and allowed high interest payments on foreign debts.

Reform and Revolution

On the political side, after hopes of more reforms had died in the middle sixties politically minded Russians had to be revolutionaries, for they had no other form of action left. Even expressing their thoughts was a revolutionary act, thus ensuring that few Russians would be politically active, but that those who were would be revolutionary. They had to operate underground, in a kind of vacuum, and were driven to extreme ideas and activities. The only hope of ever changing a system far harsher than the mitigated autocracies of Habsburg and Hohenzollern lay in revolution. The choice lay between a policy of immediate revolution and its preparation for a more distant future by social and educational propaganda. Both these avenues were treated by the state as equally subversive.

Three major tendencies can be noticed among the small, but determined and often violent, opposition groups. The first might by styled Populists, in that they followed Alexander Herzen's advice of 1861, "Go to the people" (*Narod*), seeking both strength and purpose among the peasant masses. Their prophet was Nikolai Chernyshevsky (1828–1889), who believed that Russia could avoid the industrial capitalism that was defacing the West and create a free, democratic society based on peasant producers. Translations of the social novel he had written in prison, *What Is To Be Done?* (1862), influenced opponents of industrialism and centralization all over Europe, inspired *Narodniks* to shy away from politics and parties toward the wretched, oppressed, illiterate bulk of the nation who had to be civilized and led to the point where they could help themselves. But the masses they wanted to help were indifferent or hostile. Populism, like socialism in one revolutionary's words, "bounced off the people like peas from a wall." Reformers could establish no contact with the masses of the Russian people, whom they so desperately wished to help. The young idealists who "went to the people" evoked no response except suspicion and resentment. The government had no difficulty in rousing the dross of cities and countryside against Jews, as against those forces of change the Jews were made to symbolize. Pogroms diverted resentments, frustrations, hatreds from the system to the scapegoat. Russians, like everybody else, found no difficulty in believing that people who were pursued and persecuted must be guilty of *something*. For awhile the threatening revolution would, as Plehve—the minister who permitted the greatest pogroms—put it, be drowned in Jewish blood.

The Populists, caught in a cruel dilemma of ends and means, reacted to these experiences with a contemptuous determination that ignorant men would have to be forced to be free; or else with utopian visions in which the state, captured and transformed, became the protector of the masses, shepherding them to liberty and self-realization. In due course, they organized themselves into the Social Revolutionary Party. This stood for land reform, more land for peasants, co-operative enterprises, village revival, and believed that such things could only follow political revolution.

Meanwhile, many disillusioned or impatient Narodniks had turned toward the less peaceable alternative of nihilism, a term spread by another novel of 1862: Turgenev's *Fathers and Sons,* one of whose characters—the revolutionary Bazarov—rejected all existing social values *in order to think them out afresh.* Many of Bazarov's admirers (most of them students) went only as far as the rejection. Individual emancipation, they believed, could only be achieved by exploding all the values of society, destroying bourgeois morality and the institutions that perpetuated it. Social nihilism soon turned to politics. Violence, terror, would blast the way through to peace and order, humanity and tolerance. "History is terribly slow," said one, "it must be pushed forward." In 1881 it was, with the murder of Alexander II, one among the many of their terrorist enterprises.

The third revolutionary formation was the Social Democrats, whose principal figure was Georgy Plekhanov (1857–1918), chief interpreter of Marxism to the Russians and of Russian Social Democracy to the West. The Marxists, as we might expect, placed their hopes in the development of urban industries and of an industrial proletariat rapidly growing toward the end of the nineteenth century. They were the least important of revolutionary groups and significant only in view of their later effect on Russia and the world. We have seen already that, in 1903, Russian Social Democracy split on the issue of who should join and who should lead the party. Lenin wanted a tight, disciplined group made up of dedicated militants, ruled from the center, and one in which the intellectuals, who dominated the Social Democrats as they did every other Russian movement, would be balanced by proletarians and subject to "proletarian discipline." Lenin's opponents envisaged a mass party, open to anyone it could attract, watering down its program if need be for the sake of inclusiveness and unity. The clash between elitism and mass, between centralism and compromise, was resolved when Lenin got his way in the party Congress and his opponents broke off to form a new party—the Menshevik or minority faction of the Social Democrats —leaving the original organization to the majority Bolsheviks.

Alexander III invested the energies of the state equally in economic development and in political repression. Aided by his old tutor, the Procurator of the Holy Synod, K. P. Pobyedonostzev, an antediluvian strong man devoted to the Middle Ages, the Tsar ran a tight ship. Religion, police, censorship, Russification policies for minorities, anti-Semitism to furnish do-it-yourself circuses for lack of bread, marked a regime sustained by foreign loans, ravaged by famines, seared by land hunger, misery, and painful adjustments to incipient industrial revolution.

Russia's great problem (and one well known to developing countries in mid-twentieth century) was that her rapid population growth was not matched by any comparable expansion of agricultural productivity or of alternative openings in industry. Rural poverty limited the domestic market and offered no outlets to industry; without outlets, industry could not grow and absorb the surplus rural population; the peasants remained underemployed, •industrial progress slow. Beginning in the 1880's—and especially after the accession of Nicholas II—desperate attempts were made under the aegis of two vigorous ministers—Sergei Witte (1849–1915) and Piotr Stolypin (1863–1911)—to foster economic development, force-feeding industry and mobilizing peasants by putting agriculture on a money basis and encouraging the farmers to own their land or leave it for settlement in colonial Siberia and the Caucasus, or for the towns. Rural credit for the one alternative, foreign capital for the other would, it was hoped, raise the country into the modern age. For the moment it only threw it into worse confusion. To the cacophony of political grievances and calls for reform, economic and social arguments were added and the relative success of Witte's industrial policy and Stolypin's land reforms increased the stresses and the maladjustments . . . or simply awareness of them.

The sound of axes chopping down the cherry orchards was advancing.* Railroads pushed their steel tentacles in all directions: 1,000 miles in 1860, they stretched 14,000 miles in 1880, twice that in 1900, almost doubling again by the eve of war. To feed them, coal, iron, and steel production rose vertiginously; so did exploitation of the men, women, and children recruited to turn them out.** The number of urban workers doubled and doubled again between 1865 and 1900, growing faster than the population of the country or even that of the expanding cities. In other words, the worker proportion of the urban popula-

---

* "The time has come, an avalanche is descending upon us, a great wholesome storm is brewing, approaching, almost here, about to sweep idleness, indifference, prejudice against work and foul *ennui* out of our society. I shall work, and 25 or 30 years from now, everyone will be working too." Chekhov, *The Three Sisters*, 1900.

** The Donetz steel industry began in 1869, with blast furnaces built by English and Welsh steel workers led by John Hughes whose name lived on until 1940, when the city of Hughesovska (Yusovska) became Stalino. In 1903, two brothers from Lancashire brought the cotton industry to Moscow. One of them would also found the first Russian football team, the Morozovtsi, who retained the national championship until 1914.

tion was increasing and their place in cities becoming established, as the floating casual workers of yore—just up from the land and likely to drift back to it—became the hereditary factory hands of the new industrial landscape.

The average monthly salary of a male industrial worker was 14–15 rubles a month, that of a woman about 10 rubles. While skilled workers could hope to take home two or three times as much, sums such as these compared badly with the pay of a lady's maid, who could expect 15 rubles a month* in addition to her clothes and keep: some 180 rubles a year, compared to the 600–700 rubles a year of a ballerina, or the 700–800 rubles of a second lieutenant in the army. Hardly up from serfdom, Russia's industrial proletariat were merely serfs of a different sort, re-enacting the sufferings and tragedies of Western industrial revolution but with fewer traditional defenses than existed further west: no unions, no right to organize or strike, no parliaments to intercede for them, no respectable public opinion to which they could appeal.

"A Short, Victorious War"

Then, in 1900 industrial growth, which had been advancing at a great rate during the past decade, ran out of breath. Depression aggravated the workers' lot and that of the people in the countryside who had to pay heavier taxes—that is, hand over a larger share of their crops so that the government could pay for railways, imports, and equipment just at the time when their growing numbers asked for food. The government, ever in fear of insurrection, banked on "a short victorious war that would stem the tide of revolution." The venue for it would be the Far East, where the Treaty of Peking (1860) had consolidated Russia's position on the Pacific shore. Since then her influence, spreading in Manchuria, had been strengthened by the acquisition of Port Arthur in North Korea

* Same as the price of a box for one show at the Bolshoi Theatre. We might remember that the pay of a ballerina at the same theater was 50–60 rubles a month, that of a priest 60 rubles a *year,* that of police spies 20–50 rubles a month.

Warder Collection

The locomotive of a Trans-Siberian railroad train laden with tourists during the early 20th century.

and the building of the great Trans-Siberian railway, finished in 1903. Now she met opposition from Britain, whose interests in central Asia she imperiled, and from Japan whose ambitions in Korea rivaled hers. Instead of coming to terms with them at China's expense, Russia blundered forward to a clash with Japan, hoping that war would dam the revolutionary pressures rising at home. The war (1904–1905) was uniformly disastrous and culminated in the brisk destruction of Russia's Baltic fleet, which had sailed round the world to founder at Tsushima (1905).* It discredited the regime and set the tide of revolution, which it had been meant to stem, running even faster.

Revolution rose in the end directly from another government initiative designed to deflect it. The new industrial proletariat had sporadically organized itself to improve its lot. A spate of strikes in the last years of the nineteenth century had precipitated passage of a Factory Act (largely unenforced) limiting the workday to eleven and a half hours. Police and government were not especially sympathetic to employers, most of whom represented foreign investors, many of whom favored constitutional reform, and whose interests often clashed with those of Tsarist autocracy. But they did want to control the explosive forces of the workers. So, the police inspired "tame" unions, which were allowed to voice some real grievance provided they did not come under Socialist or revolutionary control and which sparked great industrial strikes in 1902. In 1903, the mildly liberal policy of Witte was abandoned for the reactionary plans of Viacheslav Plehve, who tried to divert unrest into anti-Semitic channels and, finally, into war.**

Under the impact of defeats suffered in the war with Japan, the feeling grew among sections of the population which revolutionary propaganda had not touched before that drastic reforms were needed. Conscription, taxes, the economic and social dislocation, first of war itself, then of defeat in it, widened the unrest. One Sunday in January, 1905, some 150,000 persons led by a priest, Gapon, whose labor union had been subsidized by the St. Petersburg police, marched to the Winter Palace singing hymns and carrying icons and pictures of Nicholas II, to whom they wanted to present a petition asking for constitutional reform, land settlement, and redress of economic grievances. The great, unarmed crowd, full of women and children, was met with gunfire and there were hundreds of casualties. The Grand Duke Sergius, governor of Moscow, would be assassinated shortly after in partial retribution. Meanwhile, great strikes broke out in Petersburg and spread to other cities, venting the grievances which the massacre of "bloody Sunday" exacerbated

* On its way to Korea, the Baltic fleet took some English fishing vessels encountered in the North Sea for Japanese destroyers and opened fire with dire results. The future King George V would comment: "All I can say is they must have been drunk or else their nerves must be in such a state that they are not fit to go to sea in Men of War." He was probably right on both counts.

** Plehve died in 1904, murdered in a plot stage-managed by a Jewish agent whom his own police had planted in the Social Revolutionary terrorist organization.

Bloody Sunday, January 22, 1905.

and the general opposition to the war.

The agitation which had begun among the poor soon gained the middle classes. Liberal elements had long struggled for a hearing in the *zemstvos,* the local government bodies, in rural areas, where certain landowners, officials, and economists argued in favor of agrarian changes, credit banks, and assistance to the more prosperous and enterprising peasants. Now these formed a party—the Constitutional Democrats or *Cadets* led by Pavel Milyukov (1859–1943)—calling for constitutional government and greater power for local government bodies like the *zemstvos.* Middle-class agitation relayed rural and industrial troubles from Warsaw to Baku, a naval mutiny at Odessa in which the conscript crew of the battleship *Potemkin* mutinied in sympathy with the local strikers, and fresh pogroms encouraged by the police and carried out by the reactionary *Black Hundreds.* The Social Revolutionaries led the peasants in attacking landlords, the Social Democrats (while squabbling between Bolsheviks and Mensheviks) tried to work with the Soviets. These had grown up as strike committees grouping union and factory representatives, which became local executive authorities and spurred industrial revolt in the cities. The army could not be trusted.

In October, 1905, the Tsar, who had been ready to flee, promised constitutional government, a legislative assembly—the Duma—and franchise for peasants and middle classes. This split the middle-class reformers while the revolutionary movement was wearing thin. Strikes began to die down, fresh military and naval mutinies were crushed, the Soviets were put down, sometimes after heavy fighting. By December, 1905, reaction was back in the saddle. The promised reforms were watered down, indirect elections gave preponderance to the landlords and the rich, there would be no ministerial responsibility, the Duma's decisions were subject to the Tsar's approval. Even so, the strongest party in the Duma remained the liberal Cadets, not the reactionaries. In mid-1906 the new assembly had to be dissolved and the more repressive regime took up where it had left off in 1905. Governmental agrarian reform and a large French loan bolstering finances improved the situation of the regime even while courts-martial terrorized the revolution underground. Despite this, a new Duma in 1906 turned out even more radical than its predecessor, but just as hopeless. Dissolved, its leading radicals arrested or hunted into exile, it was succeeded by a third assembly, elected on a franchise revised to ensure reactionary success and which became a government rubber stamp. Jew-baiting revived. Land reform went ahead. Foreign investment in industry, reassured by restored stability, grew. Where 1905 had counted about three million strikers, by 1909 only 64,000 dared to take such a step. By that time the number of active underground revolutionaries stood around 10,000—less than a tenth of what it had been in the revolutionary year. Revolution had been beaten down.

It seemed that Russia had turned the cape of her troubles. A prosperous peasant class was taking shape, agricultural productivity increasing and diversifying, industry speeding up again—by 1914 per capita income was comparable to that in Italy. Social mobility was greater than anything in living memory. So was the middle class. Urban population had trebled in the past fifty years to some twenty million, one-sixth of it industrial workers now. Important industrial concentrations had risen in the Ukraine, around the two capitals and on the oil-rich Caspian shores at and near Baku. The horsepower of steam engines had soared, the educational budget had increased sixfold between 1894 and 1914.

Russia was still very backward when compared to the West: there were two and a half times as many wooden plows as iron ones, fifty times as many wooden harrows as iron ones. One-third of the peasants had no land, one-third of the farms had neither cattle nor farming instruments, average yields per acre were half those in France, a third those in Germany or Denmark. Rents and taxes were heavy and growing heavier. In all essentials of industrialization Russia was an underdeveloped land, its production of iron (per head of population) one-seventh of Germany's, one-eleventh of the United States'; of coal one-fourteenth of Germany's, one-twenty-sixth of the United States'. Even the expanded armaments industry could only turn out a little over three million rifles between 1914 and 1917 for the fifteen million men in uniform. Still, Russia could take pride in its advance. Then came 1914, and war again.

Russian policies in the Balkans continued tendencies at least as old as Peter the Great. But the slow, opportunistic moves of earlier Tsars had been rationalized into a new nationalism for popular consumption. In the last third of the nineteenth century, Pan-Slav doctrines had adapted current Darwinism to the needs of the Russian struggle less for existence than for supremacy. In 1871, Nicholas Danilevski's *Russia and Europe* argued Russia's mission to unite all Slavs whatever their creed or nationality, if need be by force. The struggle for existence raged among nations as it did among species. Russia could only survive by delivering her fellow Slavs from the foreign yoke, founding a Slav empire which, free of Western influences, would "overthrow decadent Roman-German civilization." Pan-Slav literature looked beyond Eastern Europe to Constantinople and the Near East. Constantinople—Tsarigrad—was a constant aim and symbol of the struggle it postulated. War was envisaged not only with Turkey but with Austria—Russia's rival for Turkey's spoils and the oppressor of other fellow Slavs: Czechs, Poles, and Serbs. The echo of such ideas drove Russia into war with Turkey in 1877. It kept up constant pressure, especially on behalf of the Southern Slavs. It would have been very difficult—especially after the humiliation of Japanese defeat—for Russia to stand by in 1914 and see the Serbs annihilated by Austria. And so it went to war.

The End of the Tsars

Ill-prepared and inefficient, Russian armies nevertheless played a major role in war. Their first offensive in 1914 probably saved the Marne and Paris; another in 1916 played a similar role at the time of Verdun and helped bring Romania into the war. But the costs were immense. The first year's fighting alone saw four million casualties. The troubles of a half-industrialized country fighting a modern war against a great industrial power were magnified by corruption, profiteering, disaffection, and incompetence. Men died, went barefoot or unarmed, so that some contractor should make millions; Petrograd (the capital's name had been Russified in 1914) went hungry while the court jeweler, Fabergé, boasted that business had never been so good. The winter of 1915–1916 was outstanding for casualties, diamonds, and extraordinary ladies' gowns. Men went about muttering that "everybody steals, and Christ himself would steal if his hands were not nailed to the cross." Industrial wages almost doubled, but prices nearly tripled, while essentials rose even more: bread 500 per cent, butter 830 per cent, shoes and clothes 400–600 per cent. By January, 1917, the cost of living was seven times what it had been when the war broke out.

Not even this would have brought disaster had there been a Peter or a Catherine at the helm. But the Tsar, Nicholas II, as the Kaiser once told a British foreign secretary, was only fit to live in a country house and raise turnips; while most of his family of grand dukes knew little besides how to make the fortune of champagne merchants. For a long time, Sir Bernard Pares has written, "the Russian ministers were selected by an ignorant, blind and hysterical woman on the test of their subservience to an ignorant, fantastic and debauched adventurer."

Grigori Rasputin, an illiterate, licentious, self-styled holy man from Siberia, had managed—probably by hypnotic power—to stem the Tsarevitch's deadly hemophilia and thus gained vast influence at court, where the Empress regarded him as her family's "holy friend." His influence and that of allegedly pro-German ministers led to talk of treason in high places, eventually to his assassination in an aristocratic plot in the

Tsar Nicholas II and
his family.

last days of 1916. The war was going badly, morale was very low, and
it is possible that a palace revolution would have broken out had not
strikes, riots, and mutinies in the capital forestalled it in March, 1917.
Within a week the Tsar had abdicated and formal authority passed
into the hands of the Provisional Government, headed by Prince Lvov
(head of the liberal *Zemstvo* Union) and joined by men like the Cadet
leader Milyukov and the Socialist Alexander Kerensky.

Pending the election of a Constituent Assembly, the Provisional Government tried to carry on the military operations, promulgate social reforms and civil liberties, manage a major revolution in the midst of a
major war. It could not be done. The great mass of the Russian people
looked for two things from the revolution: peace and land. Most of the
middle class, the intellectuals and officers, considered these popular aims
secondary to the pursuit of war, fulfillment of Russia's obligations to
her allies and the eventual conquests (especially of Constantinople) to
be reaped from victory. The two points of view could not be reconciled
and this was proclaimed widely in the Soviets, which had been set up
in the wake of revolution according to the example of 1905.

Representing the soldiers and workers who had made the revolution,
elected and controlled by factories and army units, the Soviets had much
more effective and immediate influence than the government, whose
authority rested on very little. But the rivalry between Soviets and Provisional Government did not mean that the former wished to overthrow
the latter. They only wanted to goad it forward. In the view of the Socialists and the Social Revolutionaries who led most Soviets, the government representing the Duma and the upper middle classes should
carry through the revolution, just as its French forebears of 1789 had
done. Unless this happened and the capitalist revolution was achieved,
the proletarian revolution would have no base to rise on according to the
historical analogies they accepted. There followed a brief paradoxical

433

struggle between the bourgeois moderates, whom the Soviets cast for revolutionary roles but who rejected this, and the Socialists, including the Bolsheviks, determined if need be to make the revolution for the *bourgeoisie,* then settle down to wait until capitalist developments opened the further way to socialism. This changed only when in April, thanks to German funds and German permission to cross their territory on his way home, Lenin steamed into Petrograd's Finland Station.

The sealed railway car in which the German government permitted Lenin and his Bolshevik companions to return home from their Swiss exile, has become the modern equivalent of the Trojan horse. There can be little doubt that such an unusual gesture was sparked by hope that revolutionary activity in Russia would redound to Germany's benefit. As for Lenin, he was quite prepared to take advantage of any opportunity to hasten the march of a revolution which was getting bogged down in theoretical considerations and revisionism.

Lenin had seen at once that the theoretical process could be accelerated, the bourgeois revolution skipped, if workers, peasants, and soldiers could carry out a socialist revolution of their own and establish the dictatorship of the proletariat without further ado. The analytical theory of Marx was adapted to the "objective situation" of the moment in a new kind of revolutionary strategy we now call Leninism: one which Lenin had found in Marx himself. One of the last things Marx had written was a preface for the new Russian translation of the *Communist Manifesto,* published in 1882; and, there, the old contemner of that barbarous land changed sides. Impressed by the immense changes that had taken place in Russia since 1848 when the Tsar was the chief reactionary of Europe, impressed by the rapid advance of industrialization and capitalism, Marx wondered if Russia might avoid some of the stages of capitalist development that western Europe had known and make her revolution, achieve a socialist structure, on the basis of "Russian peasant communism." Half the Russian land was already held in common in village communes. "Russia constitutes the advance guard of the European revolutionary movement . . . If the Russian revolution becomes a signal for the working class revolution in the West, so that the two revolutions complement each other, the existing communal property in Russia can become the starting point for a communistic evolution."

Lenin now grasped that economic backwardness and political anarchy could be used as springboards to propel his tiny group to power. He admitted that Russia was not ready for socialism; but Europe beyond it was. War had made Europe ripe for revolution. The Russians, having given the example of overthrowing a rotten old regime and grasping power, could hope that proletarians of other countries would soon follow their lead. When this happened, socialist governments in industrially advanced countries—particularly Germany—would provide the base and motor

Lenin addressing Moscow crowds. Trotsky stands to the right of the platform.

of true Marxist revolution and the possibility of carrying it out in Russia itself. Using these arguments and grasping every opportunity to apply them, Lenin raised the Bolsheviks in a few months from a few thousand underground conspirators to become first the masters of the Soviet network and then the rulers of some 150,000,000 people, no more than a quarter of whom endorsed them in elections to the Constitutional Assembly at the end of 1917—the last free elections to take place in Russia.

Lenin's first move was to reverse the previous policy of his fellows by calling for "all power to the Soviets." This meant in effect that the Soviets, which already controlled far more effective strength than the Provisional Government, should be given formal power too. He then advanced a program calling for an immediate end to war, immediate seizure of land by peasants, immediate control of industry by workers. While the Soviets argued about this (with Lenin strongly supported by Trotsky, who had arrived from America in May), the government and the Duma argued over war aims. A last Russian offensive collapsed in June, precipitating another workers' rising in Petrograd, which the government suppressed, arresting a great many Soviet and Bolshevik leaders, including Trotsky. Lenin went into hiding to escape arrest.

Nevertheless, Soviet pressure had driven the Provisional Government steadily to the Left. Partisans of patriotic war to the end, like Milyukov, had left the government in May. Now, in July, 1917, Prince Lvov resigned and the moderate Socialist Kerensky became prime minister, holding the fort against the peace for which the country yearned. But Kerensky's position depended on the support of officers who rejected all the ideals he stood for. In September one of these, General Kornilov, under the pretext of liberating the government from Soviet pressure, advanced on Petrograd. The incipient counterrevolution was broken only when Kerensky enlisted the support of the Soviets (advised by Trotsky from his prison cell); and now the Bolsheviks were on the move

435

Russian soldiers join Bolsheviks in front of the Winter Palace during the 1917 Revolution in Russia.

again. Within a few weeks they felt strong enough to remove Kerensky. Their leaders released or returned from hiding, they established their headquarters in a girls' academy whence they began world revolution by overthrowing the Provisional Government on November 6 (October 24) 1917.* Kerensky fled and subsequently went into exile. The Girondist phase of the revolution had passed. The Mountain was in power.

The following day the Second All-Russian Congress of Soviets opened in Petrograd and attendants cheered the newly elected president of the new Council of People's Commissars, Vladimir Lenin. An American enthusiast has left us a description of Lenin on this occasion: "A short, stocky figure, with a big head set down in his shoulders, bald and bulging. Little eyes, a snubbish nose, wide generous mouth and heavy chin . . . Dressed in shabby clothes, his trousers much too long for him. Unimpressive to be the idol of the mob, loved and revered as perhaps few leaders in history have been . . ." ** Within three weeks, elections for a constitutional assembly brought less than half the country's 90 million electors to the polls. Over half of those who voted, voted for the Social Revolutionary heirs of the Populists, a party chiefly identified with the rural population. Bolsheviks got about a quarter of the votes cast and half as many deputies as the Social Revolutionaries. The Constituent Assembly met in January, 1918, and was dispersed at once. The Bolshevik government brooked no opposition. By then, opposition was rife all around it.

The first thing Lenin's government did was to open negotiations with the Germans for a peace "without annexations or reparations." The peace they were finally forced to sign at Brest-Litovsk abandoned one-third

* Russia having retained the Julian Calendar when most of Europe adopted the new Gregorian style, its dates were thirteen days behind those of the West until 1918, when the Soviet government abandoned the old style for the new.

* John Reed, *Ten Days that Shook the World* (New York: 1960 edition), p. 170.

of Russia's arable land and population, four-fifths of its coal, one-half of its industry. Nor was anyone sure that the Bolshevik government could retain the rest. "White" opponents supported by the Allies, allied expeditionary forces—British, French, American, Japanese, and even a Czech contingent—, eventually when Germany collapsed German, Polish, Ukrainian, Finnish, and Baltic armies, operated in every corner of the Russian Empire. In July, 1918, the imperial family were murdered *en masse* in the cellar of a house far away in the Urals and their bodies burned. Their deaths did not end White resistance. By August, 1918, about twenty governments were operating on Russian soil, and none could have predicted which one of them would last.

The Habsburg Empire

The Austrian Lands

After 1848, as after 1815, the major concern of the Habsburgs was that they should last. The symbol of survival was Francis Joseph (1848–1916), who once described himself to Theodore Roosevelt as the last European monarch of the old school. Sober, austere, pious, and conscientious, he went meticulously through his long, ceremonious life. Francis Joseph lacked all spark of originality or brilliance and he was probably not very intelligent; but his characteristics were well suited to keeping his uneasy crown from being upset.* In retrospect his reign appears in a tragic light: his son committing suicide, his next heir murdered, his Empress going mad and being murdered too, his brother executed in Mexico, his wars all lost, his power in decline. But in a reign that spanned sixty-eight years, itself part of a dynastic history ten times longer, these were but sorry incidents of a vast design.

It may have looked at first as if the power of the Crown could be reestablished. The Liberal Constitution of March, 1848, was revoked in 1851. Four years later, a concordat assigned great privileges and powers to the Catholic Church, restoring its property and its hold on education. Most of the peasants were satisfied by their emancipation, which weakened the nobility but not the Crown; Germans and Czechs found opportunities in the growing bureaucracy of the Empire; the Poles were pleased with what amounted to home rule in Galicia; the army en-

---

* That this devoted man repressed something all his life appears in his one impulsive act, his marriage to his cousin of Bavaria. Empress Elizabeth seems to have been a kind of elf, tall for the part but beautiful and dreamy, who stifled in the stuffy, conventional Vienna court, loved the livelier Hungarians (who loved her in return), and who broke down after her eldest son's death in 1889. Her madness ended in absurd assassination by an Italian Anarchist in 1898.

sured order. 1848 had shown that the Habsburg realm rested on its army. "Austria reposes in your camp," the poet Grillparzer told Field Marshal Radetzky: "We are but scattered fragments." The army was the base and cement of monarchy; and when the army lost the monarchy was shaken. First after 1859, then after 1866, constitutional government advanced through the gaps which defeat had torn in the absolutist structure. Concessions had to be made, especially in Hungary; and the *Ausgleich* (compromise) of 1867 brought a settlement which lasted fifty years.

Hungary became once more an independent kingdom, its crown joined to Austria's by the common monarch. Except for military, financial, and foreign affairs, each state had separate governments and separate citizenship as well. Each was a medley of many nations.* During the discussions of 1867, the Austrian premier had told the Hungarians: "You look after your barbarians and we'll look after ours." By 1914, of the 51 million subjects of the dual monarchy 30 million lived under Austrian rule. Of these only one-third were Germans, almost one-fourth Czech and Slovak, some 17 per cent were Poles, and there were sizable minorities of Ruthenians, Slovenes, Croats, and Italians. Most of these lived on the land, working on large estates or drawing a meager living from dwarf holdings. In the 1870's, agricultural workers whose wages had doubled since 1848 labored from dawn till dusk for 12–18 cents a day and women for less. Conditions gradually grew better, but they never approached those further west.

After her defeat by Prussia in 1866, Austria set out to modernize her institutions and, above all, the army. Universal military service was introduced, compulsory elementary education was decreed on paper, jury trial became common in the courts, freedom of religious belief and unbelief was at last established, and the last legal restrictions on Jews were removed. During the 1880's and the 90's electoral reforms broadened the franchise to include Jews, peasants, urban middle classes, and even many members of the working class. Almost inevitably, the more liberal orientation, however relative, brought friction with the Church. In 1870, when the doctrine of papal infallibility was promulgated, the Concordat of 1855 was denounced and state policy turned back to Josephism. The Catholic Church of Austria, a foreigner explained in 1915, is less a state church than an ecclesiastical state department, working like the army, the police, or the civil service to support the government's interests.

But if the Church became a kind of state department, Catholic influence played a major part in politics where Christian Socialist movements

* In 1880 Austro-Hungary counted 9 million Germans, 6 million Magyars, 17 or 18 million Slavs, 3.5 million Romanians and Italians. In 1910: 12 million Germans, 10 million Magyars, 8.5 million Czechs and Slovaks, 7 million South Slavs, 5 million Poles, 4 million Ukrainians and Ruthenians, 3 million Romanians, three-quarters of a million Italians.

among the poor rivaled the Socialists and spread a potent anti-Semitic miasma· particularly among the peasants and the petty bourgeoisie. The great protagonist of Christian Socialism would be Karl Lueger, who, as mayor of Vienna from 1896 until his death in 1910, made the capital "the best administered city" of his time and "the most socialized," with all transport and utilities in municipal hands and stringent control over city planning. Hitler, who lived in Vienna at this time, learned his lessons from Lueger's party, which was both national and social and which skillfully used anti-Semitism to channel the more radical instincts and resentments of its followers toward a select, "alien" group, thus protecting fundamental conservative interests by equating big business only with the Jews.

Nationalisms vs. Unity   Lueger hoped to preserve Austrian cohesion, but, while phenomenally successful, he could not fight against the nationalisms which strained against the Empire. The Austrian Germans felt no more attachment to the Habsburgs than the other nations did. Many looked forward to national fulfillment in a greater Germany; many accepted the Empire only as a matter of custom and convenience; but at least they knew they were the ruling race. The Czechs on the other hand had no such consolation. Industrially they were the most advanced of the Habsburg peoples. The Czech aristocracy had every interest in upholding the union with Austria on which their own privileges were based but, as the century ended, industrial and economic development created middle and working classes which formed the base of a more widespread and militant nationalism than that which had been crushed in 1848. After 1868 Emil Skoda's ironworks at Pilsen had grown into a vast metallurgical complex; while in Moravia Thomas Bata used American manufacturing methods to build the largest shoe and leather works in Europe. By the end of the nineteenth century, with nearly half the monarchy's railroad mileage, Bohemia was its industrial center, providing half its textiles, beer, and sugar, one-third of its paper, and one-fourth of Austria's revenues.

The nationalism of 1848 had not been really popular or democratic; but in the 1880's a liberal democratic Young Czech movement sprang up, recruited among intellectuals and the middle classes. It demanded home rule similar to that which the Hungarians enjoyed, and soon came to dominate Czech politics. Its leader, Thomas Masaryk (1850–1937), had worked his way through the University of Vienna and been appointed professor of philosophy at Prague, where he opposed French and English thought to German influence but also stressed the rich native tradition to which the majesty of the Bohemian capital bore a living witness. A national theater opened in 1881, could draw on the works of native poets like Jan Neruda and composers like Bedřich Smetana (1824–1884), Anton Dvořák (1841–1904), and Leoš Janáček (1854–1928),

Thomas Masaryk, father of modern Czechoslovakia.

all inspired by national history, folk poetry, and folk music. What counted even more was the *Sokol* athletic movement, combining gymnastics and patriotism as Jahn had done in Germany in Napoleon's time. By 1914 the Sokols had over 130,000 members: the militants and cadres of Czech patriotism.

The Southern Slavs were more backward in national awareness. The Croats were subjects of the Hungarian Crown but in Bosnia, occupied since 1878, the Austrians too ruled a sizable Slav population. The Bosnians did well under Austrian rule. Between 1878 and 1906 their numbers grew by half, industry, roads, and railroads were created, schooling and order improved, revenues rose. Yet nearly half of the population followed rather their orthodox faith than their interests and looked to Serbia not Austria for fulfillment. It would be the growth of Pan-Serbian agitation that helped to decide Austria's annexation of Bosnia and Herzegovina in 1908. But this only envenomed the situation and led, as we know, to war.

In 1906 and 1907, the reverberations of Russian revolution persuaded the government in Vienna to grant manhood suffrage or something very close. Part of the purpose of the reform was to enlist a large body of new uninstructed voters and thus upset the pressures of the privileged classes which were becoming increasingly critical of the regime. In fact, the Franchise Law was so structured that it emphasized the national separateness of Habsburg subjects at the expense of unitary parties like Liberals or Socialists. There was no escaping the effects of nationalism. Even the Jewish community, whose important social and economic functions made it the scapegoat of Christian Socialism, was inspired by its difficult position to a nationalism of its own. It was a Viennese journalist, Theodor Herzl, who, having tried and rejected both assimilation and socialism, formulated a political Zionism aiming at a Jewish homeland in Turkish Palestine.* By 1907, four Zionists sat in the Austrian Parliament. The same tendencies can be seen at work in the Socialist Party. Founded in the 1880's by the Viennese psychiatrist, Dr. Victor Adler (1852–1918),

* *The Jewish State* (1896).

the Socialist Party called itself the Little International, for it reflected current nationalist strains, each major national group insisting on its own organization, more national than socialist much of the time.

Twilight in Vienna   The sense of disintegration all this created was echoed in the works produced in Austria at this time, brilliant, vivid, subtle, and ironic, but haunted by transience and melancholy, as in the plays of Arthur Schnitzler (1862–1931) and Hugo von Hofmannsthal (1874–1929).* Like life, art insisted on the combination of irony and pathos: poetic and grotesque experience went together. The Emperor asserted a tranquil genius for mediocrity, the Court and government remained oases of talentless stuffiness amidst the talent crowded in a brilliant city. Yet if the results of official nullity were serious they were never grave; for gravity was not an Austrian characteristic, let alone a Viennese, and the surface splendors of the Empire concealed its feebleness.

Nothing could be further from the dreary grandeur of the imperial court than the liveliness of the imperial capital, handsome with new avenues and buildings, fat with pastries and cookshops, gay with the light wine of its hillsides, lounging in its cafés, twirling to the waltzes of its garden-orchestras, bursting with intellectual and artistic activity. The schools and thinking-shops of Vienna were the focus of southeastern Europe; the medical work done there was world famous and, in their shadow, disapproved by the professional establishment, Sigmund Freud (1856–1939) spun the analytical system which, by the eve of war, was beginning to affect European thought.

Some of the great Viennese composers reflected their awareness of Freud's discoveries and also of the crisis within which they lived. The tormented, contradictory music of Gustav Mahler (1860–1911), who directed the Vienna Opera from 1897 to 1907, reflects a consciousness of internal anguish, confessing the failure of modern man, compensating external decline by private greatness affirmed in works of gigantic scope, a last romantic attempt to escape from civilization to nature, god, and self-destruction. A cooler expression of similar sentiments appears in the works of Arnold Schönberg (1874–1951), expressionist like the German painters of his time, dissolving classical forms in harsher, unfamiliar tonalities. In 1911 Schönberg dedicated his revolutionary *Treatise on Harmony* to Mahler, in whom he recognized the most audacious and modern of German musicians. Schönberg's *Pierrot Lunaire* (1912), now a classic of the twelve-tone scale, followed upon other compositions that have been described as "musical psychoanalysis . . . in an unreal world of morbidity and hysteria." Here was one reaction of sensitive spirits to a Vienna where the end of a century foreshadowed the end of

---

* Schnitzler is best known in the West for his sardonic *La Ronde;* Hofmannsthal for *Everyman* and the wistfully brilliant libretto he wrote for Richard Strauss's *Rosenkavalier.*

a whole way of life.

But the music of Schönberg was appreciated by only a small circle, and even that of Mahler was less well known than the waltzes and operettas of Johann Strauss or the clever scores of his namesake, Richard Strauss, whose *Rosenkavalier* triumphed in 1911. The typical Viennese *genre* was the operetta, dedicated to the glorification of wine, women and song, like Franz Lehar's *Merry Widow* (1905). Its light music, bubbly humor, frothy plots, unreal, erotic, evanescent situations that bankers and shop assistants could enjoy together set the hallmark of those halcyon days, "the very breath of it transforming facts and the bludgeonings of fate into something light as eiderdown, as thought itself." Robert Musil, the author of these words, used them to describe another aspect of the Viennese character. His *Man Without Qualities*, written in the 1930's, recaptured the dominant mood of imperial Vienna: live while you can, gently, pleasurably, aware that the sun is setting and that, while the afterglow is golden, night may fall at any time.

However, in the declining empire, the light was as yet far from gone. Against the fissile tendencies of its different peoples and the forebodings of its intellectuals there stood tradition, habit, inertia, dynastic loyalty, fear of alternatives; but also more positive reasons. The Empire was the largest free trade area in Europe after Russia, more advanced, more economically integrated, better administered, better equipped with industrial and commercial facilities than its eastern neighbor. Dynastic patriotism and material reasons were the twin pillars of the Habsburg realm. But the first was fragile and the second could, if circumstances changed, turn against the Empire's preservation. In 1918, defeat meant disintegration. The Emperor Charles I (1916–1918) abdicated on Armistice Day. The Polish, Czech, Hungarian, and South Slav provinces split apart and German Austria was left, the unwieldy rump of a once great empire, forbidden to join the German Republic as most Austrians wanted and forced to learn to live uneasily by itself.

The Hungarian Lands

The Magyar revolution of 1848 aroused immense enthusiasm but also vast dissensions; not only Croats and Romanians but many Magyars too objected to the brand of democratic nationalism put forward by their leader: Lajos Kossuth. In the end, Kossuth was brought down not just by Russian troops but by the opposition of an aristocracy that preferred foreign rule to native democracy, and of the Romanians and Slavs who preferred Habsburgs to Hungarians. After the defeat of 1849, Hungarians, deprived of their autonomous institutions, were governed by imperial bureaucrats. Then, by the *Ausgleich* of 1867, they recovered their historical rights and more: the Habsburgs, emperors in Vienna, were kings in Budapest. The army of the monarchy was federal, but Hungary had its own territorial forces, its own parliament and government and budget, an electoral system even more backward than that in Austria, and its own subject peoples.

The kingdom of Hungary included Slovakia, Carpatho-Ruthenia, Transylvania, Croatia, and Slavonia. Ten million Magyars, three million Romanians and as many Slavs, two and one-half million Slovaks and Ruthenians, two million Germans. Over these lands in which they constituted less than half the population, Magyars ruled. Croatians had home rule since 1848 but, aside from them, 95 per cent of the deputies in the Hungarian Parliament were Magyars. This was achieved in part by electoral manipulation designed to ensure Magyar supremacy over the crazy quilt of their subject nations, in part by a determined program of Magyarization, which, applied in all schools beginning with kindergarten, affected almost all the middle class. Budapest, which had been largely a German city in 1848, was four-fifths Magyar by 1900. Anyone could become a Magyar by assimilation and many twentieth-century Hungarian nationalists were of German, Slav, Jewish, or even Armenian descent.

In a country where four-fifths of the rural population was illiterate, electoral arrangements based on property and educational qualifications meant that about 6 per cent of the population was eligible to vote. The lower classes could never challenge their masters effectively, either on national or on social issues. The latter were gaining importance as industry developed. By 1900, 13 per cent of the active population was in mines or in industry, in conditions better than those on land but nevertheless quite shocking.* Like the enlightened Nationalities Act of 1868, with the extensive rights it promised to minorities, most labor legislation remained a dead letter. When in the 1890's unions (legalized in 1872) sought to better hours and wages, a so-called "slavery law" (1898) suppressed all strikes and labor agitation, while making rural workers subject to compulsory labor. Here as in Austria, to fight the growth of socialism and radical agitation, Social Catholic parties used anti-Semitism to channel the hostility of the poor against the Jews.

By 1900 the Jewish population, less than 1 per cent a hundred years before, had grown to some 5 per cent of Hungary's population. Concentrated in the towns, their wealth and influence appeared out of all proportion to their numbers. In Budapest, where about a quarter of the residents were Jewish, nearly half the doctors, over 45 per cent of lawyers, over 42 per cent of journalists, over one-fourth of those engaged in "literature and arts," better than 1 in 10 of teachers and professors were Jews. So were a large proportion of radical and Social Democratic leaders. The Jews, of all Hungarians, had been most enthusiastic in accepting Magyar culture and their contribution to it was extremely high. For that very reason, so were the resentments they accumulated, just as they did

---

* The first Factory Laws in 1872 had fixed the maximum work day at 16 hours. Samuel Gompers, the American labor leader, visiting Budapest in 1909, found skilled workers earning less than 80 cents a day, women less than 40 cents, miners who worked 21 hours a day 60 cents.

in the German lands to the west and north. Resentments founded on competition and on prejudice were fed by a constant influx from the East, which took the inhabitants of the Russian *Pale* in stages first to Romania, Bohemia, Bukovina, and Hungary, then on to Vienna, Berlin, and cities further west, the more acclimated, skilled, or enterprising leading the migration westward, constantly replaced by unadapted migrants. This process, which has not yet been studied, probably played an important role in the anti-Semitism of east and central European countries, where culturally assimilated Jews were constantly identified with numerous unassimilated aliens who presented an easy target for their enemies' calumnies.

Yet even anti-semitic parties shared in the rising radical mood that marked the beginning of the twentieth century when the news of the Russian Revolution of 1905 disturbed all eastern Europe, causing widespread agrarian uprisings from the Black Sea to the Baltic and setting off fresh agitation for reform. But the electoral reforms that Francis Joseph granted in his Austrian dominions would have upset Magyar supremacy in the Hungarian lands. Even the radical nationalists opposed them on this ground and nothing came of successive efforts to introduce manhood suffrage bills but growing agitation, disturbances, and friction between various nationalities. Francis Joseph, at loggerheads with Budapest over the federal army, for which he wanted more Hungarian recruits and in which the Hungarians wanted to substitute their language for German, exploited the suffrage issue to get his way and, while the Empire finally got a stronger common army, its Hungarian part never got the vote. Many of its people were not going to get it until after the Second World War.

Eastern Europe

The lands of the great belt between Germany and Russia have much in common. From Black Sea and Aegean to the Baltic lay agricultural countries, most of the peasants farming for subsistence only, living on plots too small for comfort let alone for profit, constantly subdivided, using primitive cultivation methods, bowed down under a burden of debt (for they had no credit) and taxation (left mostly to them by the wealthier classes). Except in Poland and Romania, where large estates exported their crops, only a few regions produced cash crops like pigs or tobacco. Except in Romania where oil was discovered in the 1850's and exploited after 1900, industry was negligible: mostly handicrafts. In Poland, by the 1920's, only some 10 per cent of the population would be employed in mining, factories, or transport; no more in other countries, generally less. Everywhere living standards were low, illiteracy astronomic, underemployment maintained by meager industrial development, and industrial wages depressed by the endless supply of unskilled labor drifting to the towns. Emigration appeared as the poor peasants' only hope.

Avenues for social promotion existed. The sons of wealthier peasants could rise in the world if they went to school, found a career in the armed forces, state administration, law, teaching, or politics, eventually joining the middle class. This was more true in Greece, Serbia, or Bulgaria, where peasants owned their land, than in Poland or Romania, where a landed aristocracy created greater problems. But everywhere the dearth of opportunities meant that underemployment on the land would be reflected in an underemployed middle class, desperately scrambling for a limited number of places and leaving a residue of disgruntled men who placed their hopes in political preferment or political change, while their social position and their education made them more interested in national self-assertion than in social change.

Above all this there loomed the antagonism of Slav and German, continued hostility to Turkey in the south, and the political rivalries of the contending nations. Most of the inhabitants of the area were Slavs. But while patriots in Slovakia or Croatia were enthralled by the maps in nineteenth-century ethnographic studies which showed how far Slavdom spread, the Slav world was divided among four religions, a dozen nationalities, and even more ambitions. Slovaks and Czechs, Croats and Serbs, Serbs and Bulgarians, Russians and Poles, Poles and Ukrainians, Ukrainians and Russians: their aspirations clashed. To the Poles the Russians were Asiatics, the Ukrainians serfs; to the Croats the Serbs were barbarians; to the Serbs the Bulgars were brutish enemies. These were the basic facts upon which the politics of the region would be founded.

North of the Carpathians, national aspirations had to contend with foreign domination. Bohemia was ruled from Vienna, Slovakia and Transylvania governed from Budapest, the Baltic lands from St. Petersburg. The ancient Polish kingdom had become the restive colony of its greater neighbors: in the south, Galicia was a Habsburg province, Posen or Posnania in the west had been annexed by Prussia, the kingdom of Poland and Lithuania lay under Russian rule. After the abortive Galician rising of 1846 Poland lay quiescent. The fireworks of 1848 attracted attention but raised no effective echo. Partition was creating different conditions in the different portions of the land. The Galician Poles probably did best, since after 1867 they were left to rule the Ruthenian masses in exchange for political support in the Vienna *Reichsrat*. The Prussians tried to Germanize their subjects and settle German farmers on Posnanian lands. But the Russians were the most successful in their policy of destroying Polish linguistic and cultural consciousness.

In 1863 as in 1830 a national insurrection failed, less because of Russian might than because of internal factions and the deep divisions between aristocrats and peasants. Fighting between "Red" Poles and "Whites" (those who wanted and those who opposed social and land reform) killed more people than the returning Russians would execute. In 1864 the Tsar's decree rewarded the peasants for remaining quiet by freeing them from serfdom, thus giving them what the White wing of Polish nationalists had refused. The emancipation of the serfs reduced the power of the nobles and eased the economic way of peasant farmers, who could advance themselves if they abandoned Polish for Russian and co-operated with the occupants.

Not everybody was attracted by the prospect. Thousands of political refugees were followed in the decades to come by nearly two million Polish migrants to the United States, Canada, Brazil (where in the state of Paraná in 1900 a quarter of the population was Polish), and Germany, where wages in Silesia and Westphalia were 50 per cent higher than at home. It was not the exiles or the rebels who kept up the hopes and the unity of their land despite police censorship and hostile officials, but the poets. Poets, novelists, intellectuals in the universities, nursed memories of past greatness and hopes of recovering independence. As the nineteenth century ended, Mickiewicz found an heir in Henryk Sienkiewicz, preaching the hopeful faith of early Christians in adversity (*Quo Vadis?*) and the eventual triumph of Polish knighthood in works like *Pan Wolodyjowski*. But Polish nationalism had to contend with the attractions of the occupiers, with opposition between democrats and the reactionaries who dreamed of a restored Poland ruling its subject races, and with divisions between Russian, Prussian, and Austrian Poles, each of whom looked to another power as sponsor of their plans.

The southern peoples were, in some ways, more fortunate—at least politically. Ottoman rule was easier to shake off. Greece achieved independence in 1830. Serbia had enjoyed autonomy since 1829. In 1878, the Congress of Berlin recognized her independence and that of Romania whose principalities—Moldavia and Walachia—emancipated from Russia by the Crimean War, had managed to unite in a Romanian state (1861). Bulgaria, her autonomy accepted after 1878, followed the same course as Romania, growing under Russia's aegis before it emancipated itself from their protectorate. By the 1880's "the Balkans"—a cultural label rather than a geographical term—had achieved independence, even though Bulgaria only acquired it formally in 1908 and though, in practice, all were the client states of greater powers.

All would be ruled by men who started out as revolutionaries to attain a national independence decree and, in some cases social changes too; and who, once they gained their end, became in their turn oppressors. In Romania, union, then independence, had been achieved by the landowner class and it was they and their urban allies who ran affairs under a liberal constitution (1866) which covered a multitude of sins. Rack renting—squeezing everything the farmers would bear and then some—and ruthless taxation kept the mass of peasants poor and backward. The beginnings of industrialization only increased the gap between their misery and rising prices, their subsistence economy and the rising productivity of the large estates, the isolation of the villagers and the Western-oriented culture of the educated. Only taxpayers voted and the poorest taxpayers were vouchsafed little in direct representation. After 1905 echoes of Russian and Polish risings articulated grievances, set off first a spate of pogroms, then a tide of peasant risings in 1907 which were crushed in blood, leaving behind them the memory of 10,000 dead.

Social unrest, however, could often be shuffled off into external conflicts: irredentist campaigns against Hungary in Romania, against Austria in Serbia, against the Turks in Bulgaria and Greece, clamored that the redemption of national minorities under a foreign yoke would somehow solve the problems of the miserable masses at home. War in 1912 and 1913 brought defeat first to Turkey, then to the Bulgarians who had turned upon their Christian allies, and territorial gains to Greeks, Serbians, and Romanians. Success made it harder to control the passions of nationalists whose greed grew with success or of politicians in Vienna who feared that a greater Serbia would eventually challenge their hold on the Southern Slavs. This combination of alarm and ambition exploded in 1914 when preventive war arose out of Austrian apprehension of the Serbs and other countries followed their greed, fear, or hatred into hostilities.

Turkey

Perhaps the people of this area which proved most successful in negotiating the transition to modern nationhood was that from which such advances could be least expected. As every schoolbook tells us, the Ottoman Empire of the nineteenth century was the sick man of Europe—sicker by far than Austrians or Russians, for it was caught in an impossible quandary. To match their rivals, the Ottomans had to reform their institutions. But, while standing pat meant that their power crumbled and fell a little lower all the time, reform could lead to its disintegration and the cure might kill the sickness and the sick man both.

Islamic tradition counseled against change: "The worst things," went a saying attributed to the Prophet, "are those that are novelties. Every novelty is an innovation, every innovation is an error, and every error leads to hell fire." The Ottomans had always borrowed from the West things fitting their needs—at first mostly for war, like guns and ships, then for peace as well (such as a fire brigade, first organized in Istanbul by a French convert in 1720). But the basic sense of superiority over barbarian unbelievers, reinforced by the successes of the past and ossified into stubborn indifference, continued until the French Revolution provided ideas untainted by Christian associations, secular notions that Mohammedans could consider without danger to their religious beliefs. As the nineteenth century advanced, Western material culture, Western political and social ideas, affected the society, the politics, the aspirations of Islam in new and revolutionary ways. They sapped old authorities and suggested new ones in government, society, and law, introducing a long struggle to reorganize and reform, sowing dragon's teeth of nationalism and rationalism in the exhausted fields of Islam. The power of the West which Ottomans were learning at their increasing cost seemed somehow associated with western constitutions and parliamentary institutions, with Western patriotic and liberal ideas. If the West where such ideas and institutions ruled was strong, perhaps the Ottoman state could profit by their adoption.

The first to be adopted were the most obvious things in areas where the Empire was immediately deficient. Mahmud II (1808–1839) tried to build a modern professional army, but never perceived the need for corresponding modernization in the economic and social spheres to help bear the costs. Over the years, other novelties were introduced. In 1831 the first newspaper in Turkish had been founded. By midcentury this official gazette was supplemented by private newspapers and also by official censorship, prohibiting all mention of troublesome or touchy subjects.* A postal system was founded in 1834 and became the chief factor in the building of a post-road network. In 1855, during the Crimean War, the French and British laid the first telegraph lines that would become a powerful instrument of central government. The first railroad appeared in 1856 and, while as late as 1913 the Ottoman Empire still had a smaller mileage than Belgium, the first train from Vienna reached Constantinople in 1888. All this immeasurably strengthened administrative centralization.

But the institution most closely identified with Westernization and reform remained the army. It had been in its realm that the deficiencies of the traditional structure were felt most sharply. It would be from its ranks that impulses for further change would come. The new model regular army of the nineteenth century was the embodiment of the "new order." It would be its harbinger as the century advanced. All innovations were connected with military needs: either directly with equipment and training, or indirectly with the administrative structure without which there could be no adequate revenue, conscription, or control. New educational institutions were meant to prepare competent officers: a medical school opened at Istanbul in 1827 trained doctors for the army while civilian ones were still turned out by traditional institutions; an imperial music school (1831), boasting Donizetti Pasha (brother of the composer) among its instructors, provided bandsmen for the army;

---

* Thus, regicide could never be reported; so that the Empress Elizabeth of Austria died of pneumonia, President Sadi-Carnot of France of apoplexy, President McKinley of anthrax, and, when the King and Queen of Serbia were murdered in 1903, Turkish readers were told they had both died of indigestion.

a school of military sciences (1834) was modeled after the French military academy of Saint Cyr; finally, after 1838, very slowly, grammar schools appeared to supply a modernized civil service. But the crux of training for government and public affairs lay in the young men who, beginning in the 1830's, were sent to receive their education or improve it abroad, learn Western languages and acquire Western ideas, chiefly in Paris but also in other Western capitals.

Among these men the kernel of reformist opposition began to take shape. Inspired by Western experience and especially by the positivism of Auguste Comte, they opposed constructive Turkish virtues to the anarchic fanaticism of Arabs, and proposed to merge the disparate nations of the Empire into one common fatherland. This "Young Turk" opposition came to the fore during the reign of Abdul-Hamid II (1876–1909), who did his best to keep the Empire afloat—though only barely—by playing on the divisions of the great powers. To crush unrest among his Christian subjects, Abdul Hamid attempted to revive Muslim religious passions, stifling Bulgarian, Cretan, and Armenian insurrections by mass murder and extraordinary atrocities unmatched in scale until the 1940's. The Young Turks, who had placed the Comtean slogan "Order and Progress" on the masthead of their clandestine publication and chosen for themselves the title "Union and Progress," * were distressed to see the country so barbarous, but more distressed still at Hamid's policy of retrenchment, police rule, censorship, and not the slightest hint of any real reform that might compensate for the brutality of police repression. Their propaganda spread among the administration and the army. In 1908 it triumphed. Many army officers were disgusted with the inefficiency of a government that kept them from using the skills it had taught them, and, worse still, starved the army of credits, equipment, and pay. The government seemed to reject Ottoman traditions but offered nothing in their place. The Young Turk officers rebelled in the name of modernity: national patriotism, political freedom, constitutional government. Their mutiny quickly spread, the Sultan was forced to yield, and constitutional government dominated by the Committee of Union and Progress was installed.

But the constitutional revolution and the nationalist regime were badly hit by losses in territory and prestige as Bulgaria declared its independence, Austria annexed Bosnia and Herzegovina, Crete joined Greece, and home conditions failed to improve. Ottoman nationalists, the new men tried, as the British Ambassador put it, a policy of "pounding the non-Turkish elements in a Turkish mortar." It did not work. Nor did their increasingly terroristic government. As rebels became oppressors they sparked new rebels where they themselves had risen: in the army. In 1912, the impact of the Italian war brought a new officer rebellion. The Committee of Union and Progress could only maintain itself in power by a virtual military dictatorship which ruled until 1918.

*The Union and Progress Committee included a Christian and a Jew.

Chapter 11

THE WORLD

FROM WAR TO WAR

Peace?

When the Great World War was ended, all agreed that there had been
—there could be—no other like it. The world could never again bear
such a toll. Over 8 million Europeans, perhaps 10 million people in all,
had died on the battlefields *: 2 or 3 million Russians, 2 million Germans, 1.5 million Frenchmen, three-quarters of a million from the United
Kingdom. Germany and France had each sacrificed some 16 per cent of
their male population. The 300,000 Serb dead were 9 per cent of the
country's population, a loss whose equivalent in terms of the present
American population would come to some 15 million of this country's
adult males. The figures are uncertain, yet so astronomical that several
hundred thousand seem irrelevant. Of 74 million men who had been
mobilized during the war, about 10 million died in battle; almost as
many were taken prisoner, of whom some 10 per cent died in captivity;
millions more—perhaps three times the number of the dead—were
wounded, many of them crippled for life. Finally, in 1918–19, a vast
influenza epidemic swept through a cold, hungry, weakened world,
killing about twice as many people as the war had done.

Such immense exploits cost money: England alone had spent 44 billion dollars on the war—more than all British capital invested in all the
industrial and financial undertakings of the United Kingdom. War costs
swallowed 22 per cent of Germany's national wealth, 26 per cent of that
of Italy, 30 per cent of that of the French. France had lost half its gold
reserves, Italy six-sevenths of the gold it had.

* C. R. Cruttwell, *A History of the Great War* (London, 1934), p. 630, puts the number killed at about 13 million.

Here was the ransom of the mass national wars whose ideology the French revolutionaries had been first to conceive. Since then, the inventions and industrial achievements of the nineteenth century had amplified all possibilities and these meant not only objects and facilities in unprecedented quantities, but techniques too: logistics, the modern version of the ancient art of getting there firstest with the mostest. The American Civil War had been the first modern war. Between 1860 and 1870 soldiers had learned to mobilize great masses of matériel and men in contests where victory depended on superior industry and communications. War, Clausewitz had long before explained, was "an act of violence pushed to its furthest limits." There was no way of winning such a war "without great bloodshed." Modern warfare would be "absolute"—that is, total. But Clausewitz's readers never envisaged the war into which they blundered: one in which all human and technical resources were enlisted in the fighting and affected by it, in which the scale of the contest dwarfed the contenders and its needs obscured all other considerations.*

Such tremendous efforts could only be kept up by involving the whole nation morally and emotionally in the struggle. War aims formulated in economic or political terms, a piece of land, a diplomatic success, could not warrant the sacrifices demanded. A moral cause alone could hope to justify the senseless immorality of extended murder. God, Justice, Right, became the prize of war and tremendous efforts were made to persuade each side that it was right and just, the others wrong and wicked. War was thus turned from concrete aims into a trial by combat; public opinion was persuaded by the miseries and propaganda of four years to look upon the enemy as guilty, upon victory as an opportunity not only for material gains but for meting out punishment.

When the war was over, the first great cry was that the guilty men be punished, the Kaiser hanged, the enemy be made to pay for the destruction which he inflicted, "squeezed until the pips squeaked," as one English politician put it. Northern France and parts of Belgium lay in

---

* When asked why he wanted to annex so much Baltic territory, Hindenburg replied: "For the maneuvering of my left wing in the next war."

Northern France in ruins.

ruins. The former alone counted 300,000 houses, 8,000 factories and mines, 52,000 kilometers of roads, 6,000 kilometers of rails destroyed, over 7,-000,000 acres of arable land ravaged and lost to cultivation. Nor could it be forgotten that (whoever had begun the war) the Germans would never consent to end it and to make a peace "with no annexations or indemnities." The kind of peace they favored had been demonstrated at Bucharest and Brest-Litovsk. It is in this perspective that the treaties which the Allies imposed on their defeated foes * have to be considered.

Seeds of Trouble

The victors received their rewards: France in the return of Alsace and Lorraine; Belgium in two small chunks of German territory; Britain in the destruction of the German fleet; Italy in the recovery of the still-unredeemed *irredenta* in the Austrian Trentino, and portions of the Adriatic's eastern shores; France, Britain, and Italy in shares of the German and Turkish empires overseas. Serbia became the center of new-born Yugoslavia—the greater South Slav kingdom of her dreams. Romania doubled in size, acquiring Transylvania from Hungary, Bessarabia from Russia, and portions of Austrian and Bulgarian territory. New republics sprang up in Czechoslovakia, Poland, and four Baltic states. Only the United States got nothing. Crucial in victory, dominant in peacemaking, Americans thought to achieve justice and reaped muddle and disillusion. President Wilson, the high pontiff of Versailles debates, preserved the Rhineland for Germany by offering to guarantee French security jointly with the British; attempted to reconcile Yugoslav and Italian demands in the Adriatic; tried to defend and apply the principle of nationalities and self-determination; above all, sought to establish the noble notion of a League of Nations which would preserve peace, apply a juster and more effective international law, train lions to lie down with lambs and lambs to operate as full-blown sheep. Such excellent intentions did not prevent a failure which must be attributed first and foremost to the circumstances in which the treaties of peace were formulated by the victors, imposed on the vanquished, and finally applied on a catch-as-catch-can basis.

"We had to let this war occur," Max Weber, German sociologist and patriot, explained in 1914, "in order to have our say in deciding the future of the earth." The future of the earth looked glum indeed in 1918, with Soviet republics rising or threatening in Budapest, in Munich, and, briefly, in Berlin; with revolutions or nationalist wars flaring in every borderland from Finland to Asia Minor. Even in Switzerland, where Lenin's Zurich exile had left its mark on local Socialists, a general strike

---

* The German treaty signed at Versailles in June, 1919, the treaty with Austria signed at Saint Germain in September, 1919, the treaty of Neuilly with Bulgaria in November, 1919, and that with Hungary at Trianon in June, 1920.

EUROPE AFTER THE
TREATY OF VERSAILLES

–·–·– 1914 boundaries

New independent nations

Zone of Allied occupation

——— 1926 boundaries

*WHITE
SEA*

Murmansk

FINLAND

NORWAY

SWEDEN

Oslo

Stockholm

Helsinki

Petrograd

ESTONIA

*NORTH
SEA*

BALTIC SEA

LATVIA

LITHUANIA

Moscow

DENMARK

Copenhagen

DANZIG
(Free state)

Danzig

Memel

U. S. S. R.

GREAT
BRITAIN

London

The Hague

NETHERLANDS

Hamburg

Berlin

(GERMANY)

BELGIUM

Brussels

GERMANY

Warsaw

Brest–Litovsk

Kiev

LUX.

SAAR

POLAND

Versailles

Paris

Prague

Cracow

Lemberg

FRANCE

ALSACE–
LORRAINE

CZECHOSLOVAKIA

Munich

Vienna

BESSARABIA

Lyons

SWITZERLAND

AUSTRIA

Budapest

MOLDAVIA

Geneva

Milan

HUNGARY

ROMANIA

Trieste

Venice

Fiume

Marseilles

SPAIN

Barcelona

CORSICA

ITALY

Rome

ADRIATIC SEA

YUGOSLAVIA

Sarajevo

Belgrade

WALLACHIA

Bucharest

*BLACK
SEA*

BULGARIA

Sofia

Naples

SARDINIA

ALBANIA

Constantinople

GREECE

*AEGEAN
SEA*

TURKEY

Algiers

MEDITERRANEAN

SICILY

Athens

Tunis

MALTA
(Br.)

SEA

CRETE

ALGERIA

TUNISIA

0   500 miles

in November, 1918, was meant as a preliminary to social revolution. This was the background of the peace conference which one member of the British delegation described as a "riot in a parrot house", and Winston Churchill as "a turbulent collision of embarrassed demagogues." All those present looked anxiously over their shoulders at the reactions of the home electorate, of the press, and of political opponents ready to exploit any apparent weakness on their part.

Whatever the final treaty may have been, one thing is certain: it was democratic, with all the rancor, the shortsightedness, and the incoherence but also the good intentions and high hopes that tend to color popular politics. The treaty has been criticized for its harshness, for its weakness, for its unrealism, for its lack of idealism. Yet it was a fair compromise and might have worked had statesmanship made it work. The real point about it, as about any treaty, is that it was a compromise whose virtues or weaknesses would come out in its application. And it was to be the latter that triumphed. "Peace," quipped Clemenceau, "is only war pursued by other means."

We must remember that, on the whole, the peace largely confirmed the results of war and could have done otherwise only at the cost of further war. Nothing else could have deprived Poles, Czechs, Romanians, and Serbs of the territories they had occupied from their fallen foes and, clearly, having proclaimed that national self-determination was one of their first aims, neither France nor Britain, let alone the United States, would fight to prevent its expression. Beyond Alsace-Lorraine restored to France and the territories wrested from Poland in the eighteenth century, Germany herself lost very little: some chunks of land to provide the Poles with access to the sea and some more in Upper Silesia to assuage their hunger for industry and coal. The Saar was placed under French administration for fifteen years, the produce of its coal mines to count as partial repayment of French losses, but a plebiscite would then determine what its future was to be and few doubted that this future would be German. Germany had, of course, been deprived of her territories overseas, but it is hard to tell whether this was a blow to national interests or merely national pride.

The great losers lay in the east, where a string of newborn or newgrown nations marked the disintegration of three multinational empires. From Finland to Bessarabia, the borderlands Russia had gained since Peter the Great detached themselves; Austria and Hungary became small independent states, poorer, weaker, and less populous than the new Czechoslovakia, Romania, and Yugoslavia that rose around them; Turkey, which suffered few further losses in Europe, was shorn of its Arabian Empire now shared between the British and the French. From the ethnic point of view, the new arrangements were less unjust and more consistent than those which they replaced. Yet we shall see that they were not just or consistent enough to last; and perhaps it was in the nature of things that they could never be so.

Now German, Russian, and Ukrainian minorities lay under Polish rule; German and Hungarian under Czech; Hungarian, Ukrainian, German, and Bulgarian under Romanian; Hungarian and Bulgarian under Yugoslav; German and Slav under Italian. The national triumph was a lopsided one. Over a third of the population in Czechoslovakia, a little less than a third in Poland, a quarter in Romania, were minorities; and for a long time better than half the population of Yugoslavia was in the same situation while Serbs lorded it over Croats and Slovenes. Multinational empires were now succeeded by multinational states almost as checkered, almost as uneasy, but far less powerful and hence less able to maintain themselves. The obvious means of doing so was by the victors closing ranks against the nations which they had despoiled. But a consistent policy on these lines was prevented by the contentions of the victor states themselves. Poland was at loggerheads with Czechs and Lithuanians, Italy with Yugoslavs and Greeks. The aftermath of war was marked by squabbling and crises between former allies whose future security depended on co-operation. Most publicized among these was the friction between Yugoslavia and Italy over Austro-Hungarian lands along the Adriatic, where the old city ports were Italian-speaking, the countryside was Slav. The port of Fiume, chief bone of contention at this time, was occupied for a year by the black-shirted bands of a romantic and highly demagogic Italian poet and war hero, Gabriele D'Annunzio, and finally left to Italy (while the hinterland went to Yugoslavia), not without an enduring rift between the two countries.

Italian claims, indeed, were as vast as their war record had been meager.* Perhaps as compensation for a dispiriting war which they had entered in answer to Allied entreaties and survived only thanks to Allied aid, Italian policy sought a hegemony over southeastern Europe and the eastern Mediterranean which the country's resources scarcely justified. Disappointment over ambitions gone sour made the Italians the first revisionists of the treaties to which they had put their signature, and led them to support Hungarian and Bulgarian claims against their Balkan neighbors.

Perhaps more important than some of the things done at Paris were certain things that were left undone. Thus, Russia, ignored in all the treaties, still figured there somewhat like Banquo's ghost, its ominous revolution which all dreaded inspiring an attempt to build along its borders an "isolation belt" that would prevent its spreading. But there were still the Germans, some 60 million of them, to whom the principle of self-determination was denied when the small Austrian rump of the old Habsburg Empire was not allowed to join the new German Republic risen from defeat, when 3 million Austrian Germans in Bohemia were incorporated in the new Czech state, when the German city of Danzig

* However, they had held a difficult mountainous front and suffered heavy casualties.

was forced to be Free rather than German in order to serve the interests of the Poles. Had these groups joined Germany, as great majorities among them wished, the country would have come out of the war stronger by far than it had entered it. Even so, Germany lay in the midst of Europe, greater and more populous than any of its neighbors, apt at any time to try to reverse the verdict of defeat. The French, who had only two-thirds of Germany's population, were well aware of the danger this presented—first of all to Germany's eastern neighbors, eventually to themselves—and tried to diminish it, particularly by detaching the highly developed Rhineland and making it autonomous. This France's allies did not permit to happen, nor in all likelihood did the Rhinelanders want it to. Instead, the treaty's terms demilitarized the Rhineland, giving the French a margin of security on their border where Germany could neither build fortifications nor station troops; and imposed stringent disarmament conditions on the beaten Germans, cutting down their forces to where they presented no serious threat to their neighbors.

War Debts and Reparations

The British, of course, as soon as the war was ended and their own safety ensured by the elimination of the German fleet, approached European problems in terms of a balance that did not want France too strong or Germany too weakened. But the deciding voice through 1919 was that of the United States, or rather of its president, Woodrow Wilson, a man whose high ideals deeply affected the making of the peace. American intervention had probably saved the Allies from defeat, American help had certainly won the war. During the cold, hungry, miserable postwar period, some 35 million tons of American supplies, freely distributed, brought relief to many parts of Europe. The Allies knew that they owed not only gratitude, but some 10 billion dollars: weighty arguments on the American side. What counted even more than the wealth and power which Wilson represented were the hopes he bore of a just settlement followed by a reconciliation and a lasting peace, hopes which millions throughout Europe shared. Yet justice looked far different according to one's stance: Italians and Yugoslavs, Germans, Poles, or Frenchmen, Romanians and Hungarians, differed fundamentally on what justice was. The statesmen who thrashed things out in Paris—Wilson among them—could only compromise between ideals and interests. The peace they put together was imperfect. Its only hope of lasting even as it stood (and many thought imperfect peace better than a war) was that Americans who had contributed to its making should help maintain it. They did not.

Americans, inclined by historical experience and the vocabulary of their politics to see complex questions in the simplest terms, had been encouraged to believe that power and good will could straighten out a

PEOPLES OF EUROPE
AFTER WORLD WAR I

Celts
English
Scandinavians
Dutch, Flemish
Germans
French, Walloons
Spanish, Portuguese
Italians
Rumanians
Greeks, Albanians
Finns, Esthonians
Hungarians
Turks
Latvians, Lithuanians
Poles
Russians, Ukranians
Czechs, Slovaks
Serbs, Croats
Bulgarians

——— 1926 boundaries

ASIA

AFRICA

ATLANTIC OCEAN

NORTH SEA

BALTIC SEA

BLACK SEA

AEGEAN SEA

ADRIATIC SEA

MEDITERRANEAN SEA

BAY OF BISCAY

ENGLISH CHANNEL

500 miles

IRELAND
ULSTER
SCOTLAND
WALES
ENGLAND

NORWAY
SWEDEN
FINLAND
DENMARK
ESTHONIA
LATVIA
LITHUANIA
(GER.)
DANZIG

NETHERLANDS
BELGIUM
LUXEMBOURG
ALSACE LORRAINE
FRANCE
SPAIN
PORTUGAL

GERMANY
POLAND
U.S.S.R.

CZECHOSLOVAKIA
SWITZ.
TYROL
TRENTINO
AUSTRIA
HUNGARY
ITALY
CORSICA
SARDINIA
BALEARIC ISLANDS
SICILY

TRANSYLVANIA
BESSARABIA
ROMANIA
YUGOSLAVIA
ALBANIA
BULGARIA
GREECE
TURKEY

CRETE
RHODES
CYPRUS

web entangled through the centuries. Wilson's influence at Versailles prevented power politics from running riot, but failed to write utopia into treaty terms. Meanwhile, internal political developments discredited even what had been achieved, defeated Wilson's policies, withdrew the United States from a Europe which failed to carry out their hopes and had instead confirmed secular prejudices against a bad old world that most Americans or their ancestors had fled and left behind. The United States had joined the war to make the world safe for democracy and to protect their investments. The world refused the former and threatened the latter. Americans cast off from the world or tried to do so, and their first step was to reject the peace. Having elicited great concessions from their allies, partly by military guarantees such as the one Wilson and the British offered to the French, the United States flounced out of their undertakings, leaving Europeans to pick up the pieces and retaining mostly the right to criticize. The League of Nations which Wilson had conceived and that the United States never joined was left to operate as best it could. The British refused to stand by France alone when the United States no longer acknowledged the guarantees Wilson had shortly promised. France was left to look after her own security. which she could only ensure (or so her leaders thought) by keeping Germany down. "This isn't peace," commented Marshal Foch. "It is an armistice for twenty years."

There was one thing the United States retained and that was the power of the purse. A major issue at Versailles had been the reparations that Germany should pay her victors, particularly to Belgium and to France, large parts of whose territories had been devastated, often deliberately, by German acts. The sum of reparation payments was finally fixed not in terms of concrete possibilities but of political pressures in the victor countries, at the astronomical figure of $32,500,000,000, a bill expected to be paid in forty-two annuities between 1921 and 1963, pending whose payment portions of German territory would remain under Allied occupation and other portions (like the coal-producing Ruhr) subject to it in case of default. The reparation issue proved a long canker eating through the twenties, clear evidence to many of rancorous injustice—especially on the part of the French who pressed it furthest. Yet France was spending half her yearly budget on reconstruction and war pensions. No wonder she was intent on reparations and bitter about her war debts. Moreover, deprived of their allies' support and faced with a renascent giant—one of whose first acts, they feared, would be to threaten them—some French could see salvation (however temporary) only in a nagging policy that drained Germany of resources, slowed her recovery, and maintained it weak. This policy was abandoned in the later twenties, though not before creating vast resentment in Germany, where the government, ready to cut off its nose to spite its face, precipitated ruinous inflation in the postwar years, threatening the foundations of society and the state for the sake of its anti-French measures.

There was one broader problem that better relations themselves were not enough to solve. For the crux of reparations lay in the war debts which the Allies had contracted to the United States. As long as they were held to payments on these, the Allies could not afford to do without payments to them from Germany. Nor did it seem just that the defeated Germans, who were responsible for the war, should have their debts remitted while the winners were condemned to pay theirs to their own rich ally. The matter was extremely complicated, with the French and many other European countries owing Britain almost as much as Britain owed the United States; and Britain repeatedly proposed the general remission of all war debts among allies, along with serious scaling down of German reparations, suggestions which the United States would not entertain. Instead, complicated arrangements were made whereby the German war debt was indeed scaled down (Dawes Plan, 1924); and American banks lent money to Germany which, in a sense, was used to pay reparations to America's European allies who could then pay their United States creditors. There must have been simpler ways of doing it.*

The Twenty Years' Armistice

War, Trotsky once said, is the locomotive of history. The war of 1914–1918 had pulled Europe and the rest of the world a long way from their starting place. One of the greatest changes which had taken place was that in the role and position of the state. Gradual advance, gradual increase in the functions that the state performed has been a constant part of modern trends, particularly so in the quarter century before 1914 when large numbers of people brandishing new votes made politics hinge on satisfying mass demands. Now, this process took on a new and faster pace.

The state had already been called in to police safety, not only against crime but against undue exploitation. Factory laws appeared in the 1830's and 1840's. By mid-century Britain enforced its regulations by inspection. The first state inspectors appeared in Prussia in the 1850's, in the United States after 1866, in France in 1883. Meanwhile, the greatest mass of workers on land, in shops and offices, domestic servants or outworkers, were not yet touched by new regulations. Universal male

* Between 1924 and 1929 Germany paid 8 billion gold marks—2 billion dollars—half of it to France, one-fifth to Britain. In 1930 the Young Plan revised reparation debts to a new lower figure payable in fifty-nine installments ending in 1988. The plan went into operation in 1930 when the Depression was about to make it meaningless and Germany paid very little after that, while the last Allied occupation troops left Germany in June of 1930.

suffrage, established or approximated in France, Germany, and Switzerland in the 1870's, in Britain in the 1880's, in Belgium, Holland, and Norway in the 1890's, eventually in Sweden (1907), Austria (1907), Italy (1912), gradually created a new political clientele increasingly concerned with government services and placing an ever heavier burden on them.

Budgets, once kept as low as possible, began to expand in answer to the masses' demand for security. Workers' insurance schemes were introduced almost everywhere in the last twenty years of the nineteenth century. In 1909 a young English politician could sum up democratic politics in the word "insurance." Whether the result of social pressures or of government attempts to head them off, the first steps toward the collectivist spending policies which marked twentieth-century economics were being taken. The state was intervening in everybody's private life and activities, regulating industry and conditions of labor, fixing minimum wage rates, running public utilities, supervising sanitation and education, controlling wealth and redistributing it by graduated income and capital taxes and death duties.

But planning, social security, a fairer distribution of incomes, preventive medicine and national health policies, social services, all made the greatest advances during the war, when all states needed to elicit collective sacrifices by promising collective gains. Nor was collective compensation the only motive force. Even more important were the demands of a struggle which one could survive only by harnessing all energy and resources to its pursuit. Production and distribution had to be planned, supplies rationed, prices controlled, manpower directed, the whole economy co-ordinated. This was achieved first in Germany, where businessmen like Walther Rathenau (who had learned economic generalship in his father's giant electrical corporation) ran the country's economy, and the General Staff ran the country: its officers distinguishing themselves not as heroes but as experts and managers in uniform, owing their places less to privilege than to competence and intellectual achievement, masters of planning and of calculation, manipulating men, machines, transport, propaganda, and espionage in a manner and on a scale unknown by earlier soldiers. Soon, warfare came to be regarded less as a collision between armies than as a contest between collective economies. Most belligerent countries set up ministries of armaments and munitions, shipping and labor. Those that did not do so collapsed, like the Russians, or came very near it, like Italy. And, while most of these structures would be dismantled after the war, they would soon be revived piecemeal.

Structured or not, however, there was no going back on the swelling attributions of the state. The British, most reluctant to encroach on the prerogatives of privacy, reflected the glacier-like inevitability of the trend. In 1850, the British government spent 12 per cent of the gross national product and only 3 per cent more than that half a century later. In 1914, despite a new social legislation and heavy expenditure on defense costs, Britishers spent more on drink than on *all* their government expenditures. By 1918, this had changed. The government had become a dominant force of national economy, spending over half the national income. By 1944, a generation later, it spent nearly three-quarters of it and controlled two-thirds of Britain's labor force.

Big government and big industry went hand in hand or, rather, side by side. As industry developed, so did its need for capital. Beginning in the 1850's and the 60's, joint stock companies and limited liability mobilized investment by encouraging anonymous and irresponsible shareholders who left management to others. In the 1860's the cotton crisis set off by the American Civil War hit small manufacturers, forced bigger ones to install costly new machinery (such as for Indian cotton), led to a concentration of the textile industry throughout the West, just as the effects of the Zollverein in Germany and of the Franco-British Free Trade Treaty of 1860 worked in the same direction. The concentration of industry also meant concentration of industrial labor, growing class consciousness and organization; and in France, for instance, the *Comité des Forges*, grouping the largest iron and steel masters, was set up in the same year, 1864, as the International Workers' Association. The recession of the 1880's saw the further elimination of smaller enterprises and the growth of trusts set up to monopolize production or distribution,* cartels set up to control associated and subsidiary industries catering to a group of firms, and *agreements* between rival producers to share out the market and fix prices or fares or freight rates affecting their products. "The day of combination is here to stay," mused John D. Rockefeller. "Individualism is gone never to return."

Competition in action tended to kill competition in fact, and those whom this hurt appealed to the state for help. Government intervention, government control were invoked by the very advocates of the free trade which free competition restricted. In the United States, the Sherman Anti-Trust Act of 1890 enforced competition by law and penalized its logical conclusions. The state would regulate enterprise and lay down rules as to how business could properly be conducted.

Up to a point. "The thrusts," opined Mr. Dooley, "are heejous monsthers—on wan hand I would stamp them under fut; on th'other hand, not so fast." A few years before the war, 1 per cent of American enterprises employed a third of the labor force and turned out 43 per cent of all manufactured products. At the same time in Germany 1 per cent of enterprises employed two-fifths of the labor force and used three-fourths of the power. This concentration of industry and labor continued after the war, unions continued to grow, the largest trusts in

* The first trust was Rockefeller's Standard Oil Corporation in 1882; the first international trust was Nobel's Dynamite Trust in 1886.

Germany were formed in these years, and large-scale concentration pressed even further in countries like Italy and Russia. Here was the firm base and the raw material of the new economic order in which industrial capitalism became state capitalism; in which, indeed, business and industry on one side, public administration on the other, vied with each other, the former regarding the latter not only as a source of costly interference in its affairs, its production, and labor expenses, but also as a dangerous competitor for lawyers, administrators, accountants, and experts, raising their wages or tempting them with holidays, greater security, or more relaxed conditions of work.

Planned economies stemmed not from socialist ideas but out of the great industrial concentrations which first planned and regulated production and trade on a vast scale. From trusts that controlled an immense proportion of a country's manufacturing capital, to the assistance lent them by government, to the shift of economic planning from private to public offices, the transition took place almost insensibly, speeded up by the industrial mobilization of the war and precipitated by the crises of the 1930's and the forties, to be dealt with in the following pages. From control by a few capitalists to control by a few bureaucrats there was but a step, once business and politics had interpenetrated. When national and international economic structures broke down, there would be no withstanding the demand for deliberate planning to replace the free self-adjusting ideas of the nineteenth century. Politics were called into play to redress the balance of economics.

By that time, experience was beginning to suggest that economy was manipulable, like men, not ruled by unchangeable natural laws with which one could not tamper. Government, like economics, was seen less as a free market than as an organized structure that was best run by experts. In 1942 the economist Joseph Schumpeter concluded that controlled planning was the least evil for coping with our problems. In the same year James Burnham's *Managerial Revolution* predicted the decline of the liberal economy and its replacement by state capitalism managed by technicians and technocrats. A second great war had precipitated the conclusions of the first.

The End of Liberalism

All this would be confirmed by the catastrophic tremors and quakes that rocked the economy of the world in the 1920's and thirties to bring much of it crashing down. However traumatic the war itself had been, millions had gone through it as through an incident, had preserved their way of life with only a few scars, and meant to treat it as a parenthesis after which things could be taken up where they had been left off. Young men, like Max Ernst, the painter, "died on the first of August 1914 and returned to life on the 11th of November 1918." And it is true that, whereas for some countries the war brought radical change, in others it could be viewed as a passing disturbance whose end permitted life to go on as before—permitted, that is, a conscious attempt such as we find in Aldous Huxley's early novels to recapture and recreate the past, not move with the times.

This sleeping-beauty view of life was bound to go awry. Thomas Mann was more correct when, in his 1924 foreword to *The Magic Mountain,* he spoke of the novel's taking place "in the long ago, in the old days, the days of the world before the Great War . . ." That this was long ago and far away would seem much clearer to a central European than to a Westerner. All combatants had financed war costs largely out of loans, all had to pay for it when war came to an end in higher prices (they had, for instance, risen 250 per cent in France and Italy between 1913 and 1920) and inflated currency. In France, where reconstruction was also financed by loans (supposed to be repaid from reparations) and where the public debt was nine times larger in 1921 than in 1914, the franc, five to the dollar defore the war fell as low as fifty in 1926. Soon thereafter it was stabilized at twenty-five, a fifth of its prewar value. This was a hard blow for savers, *rentiers,* creditors, pensioners, small businessmen having to replenish stocks at ever higher costs, and wage earners wearily pursuing mounting prices.

Much worse was the plight of the defeated countries whose currencies practically collapsed or had the hard task of adjusting to new borders, and where productivity proved highest among the printers grinding out new and worthless bills. In Austria prices rose to 4,000 times their prewar level, in Hungary they multiplied 23,000 times, in Poland 2,500,000 times, in Russia 4,000,000,000 times, in Germany a thousand *billion* times. Housewives took baskets of money to market and returned with small loaves of bread. In November, 1923, the German mark stood 4,200,000,000,000 to the dollar and when the Poles introduced their new currency, the zloty, in 1924, it was exchanged for nearly 2,000,000 of the paper marks that were in use till then. Before currencies had been stabilized—in Austria 1922, in Germany 1923, in Hungary 1924, in Britain 1925 (idiotically at prewar parity with the dollar, thus sacrificing industry and employment to banking interests), in France 1926 (more wisely, well below the prewar level, thus facilitating exports and eventually delaying the effects of the world slump), in Italy 1927—millions had been ruined. Not merely hurt, as in France or England, but ruined utterly, their way of life smashed and with it much of the old stability of which they, with their small savings and possessions, were an essential part.

Something else and something more profound had also passed away.

463

The industrial center of gravity of the world, long settled on the Atlantic's eastern shores, had shifted to North America. By 1913, the United States produced one-third of the world's manufactures: almost as much as Germany, France, and Britain together. Fifteen years later she would produce two-fifths. The war encouraged further industrial development in the United States and also in countries like India and Japan which had been cut off from their normal sources and had learned to shift for themselves. Meanwhile, European economy had been focused on profitless murder, capital equipment worn or destroyed, currency disorganized, foreign assets much reduced. European countries, once creditors, were now debtors of the United States, which had become in turn the greatest creditor in the world.

Not only industry expanded during the war. Production of foodstuffs and raw materials, too, had advanced all over the world—even in regions where production costs were normally too high for a competitive market. Once the war was over, once shortages had been filled and European production recovered, capacity exceeded demand, surpluses began to accumulate, and agricultural producers found themselves in difficulties. Farmers had contracted debts in good years which they couldn't settle in the bad. Coal mines found themselves in similar difficulties as new sources of power were developed (gas, hydroelectricity) and consumers learned to economize on solid fuel. Producers caught in wage/price squeezes tried to increase their output only to depress prices further. Industry, which expanded capacity and increased output by 20 per cent in the decade since 1914, was in a quandary. Industrial production increased more rapidly than the production of raw materials and basic foodstuffs, but the population of the areas producing raw materials increased more rapidly than that of industrial areas, while the wealth of the latter grew faster. Industrial producers required relatively smaller quantities of foodstuffs, primary producers wanted more industrial products but could only pay for them if the industrial areas bought more of their stuffs, which they did not, or did only at reduced prices. Between 1919 and 1928 the price of wheat fell by half, of corn by four-fifths, of rice by three-eighths, of cotton by two-fifths. In 1927 the revenue of American farmers, a quarter of the country's population, was half that of 1919. So the countries and peoples that wanted to buy available goods could not afford to do so, demand for them fell and cut even further the purchases that primary producers could afford to make, until the demand for industrial goods began to fall in turn. One man's difficulties created others: the farmers' problems meant fewer buyers, less demand, a further shrinking market. Sporadic unemployment had been part of the business cycle that went from boom to slump throughout the nineteenth century. Now unemployment became endemic. After 1921 there were never less than one million unemployed in Britain, twice as many in the United States. At the height of renewed prosperity in 1927 and 1928 Germany had one and a half million unemployed. Costly to city or

Inflation in postwar Germany. Small firms prepare to meet payrolls with bags containing 4½ million marks each.

state, unemployment would be a demoralizing experience for workers and work-seekers, an increasing number of whom never found a regular job at all.

This was the vicious spiral behind the spurious upswing of the latter twenties when, with agriculture in difficulties and industrial profits falling, stocks continued to advance perhaps because there was no other direction left for loose money to take. The precarious structure of international credit, founded on receding realities, needed only a push to topple over. In October, 1929, the great stock market crash on Wall Street removed the credit with which American investors had propped up the finances of central Europe. In 1931 attempts to shore up the German and the Austrian economy in an Austro-German Customs Union collapsed before Franco-British opposition and, with them, the greatest of Austrian banks went into bankruptcy, dragging down a long train of other banks and institutions. The United States proposed a year's moratorium on all international debt payments while the financial situation straightened out. But solvency was no greater in 1932 when, as a matter of fact, the crisis reached its peak. Since 1929, industrial production in the United States and Germany had been halved, and wholesale prices had fallen 37 per cent in the United States, 28 per cent in the United Kingdom. Worst hit were those countries whose economy rested on primary products. In January, 1933, rubber prices were 13 per cent of what they had been three years before, silk 28 per cent, wool 22 per cent, copper 29 per cent, cotton 34 per cent, coffee and rice 41 per cent, wheat 42 per cent, sugar 50 per cent, timber 55 per cent. In other words, the rubber planter got 13 cents where he had got a dollar a few years before, and the farmer 42 cents.

Catastrophe for primary producers spelled some mitigation for those who fed these raw materials through their factories, such as the English whose real incomes fell relatively little.* Even so, unemployment soared:

* Indeed, the incidence of the Depression was uneven. Britain, though hard hit, benefited from low raw material prices. France, less industrially advanced than her neighbors, enjoyed a balanced economy and the advantages of a cheap currency at least for

465

in March, 1932, nearly 3 million Britishers, 5.5 million Germans, 13.5 million Americans, were out of work. The hope that international payments might resume when the year's moratorium ended proved vain. America's debtors proposed abolishing reparations altogether in return for a settlement with their creditors; but the Americans would not accept. With Germany freed of her obligations, the debtors now refused to be held to theirs, and defaulted on their debts. Reparations were at an end, and so were normal financial relations between the powers.

Men had become persuaded that free competition and free markets would not work. The economy had to be regulated in peace just as in war. Economic liberalism was being jettisoned even in its American fortress. In 1931 the Harriman Committee of the United States Chamber of Commerce called for "a national program of production and distribution" and for a national council to co-ordinate the country's economic problems. In 1932 a German "moderate" declared that the "times of laissez-faire, laissez-passer and unlimited individualism" were past. It was time now for the state to intervene by deflationary measures to restrict credit, control prices and wages, regulate or nationalize private enterprise, devalue currency, control exchange and supplies, subsidize crucial enterprises or undertake new ones, reabsorb the unemployed or keep them on the dole, regulate independent economic activity, investment, and production, secure recovery on autarchic lines of national self-sufficiency. Abandoned internally, the free market with its jungle laws of survival was acknowledged only in the international free-for-all wherein every country sought to save itself by every means at hand.

The notion of property as an absolute right, freedom of contract, integrity of salaries, had all been shaken during the century. Now society's right to interfere with owner and employer was generally acknowledged. Municipal or state governments henceforth fixed rents, wages, prices, arbitrated settlements, set wages no longer governed by considerations of supply and demand alone, and supplemented them by allowances, insurances, and pensions. "Money," which had been looked on as a basic value, was now recognized as "nothing more than a means of facilitating the production and exchange of goods and services." Of course, people had always known this, but they had preferred what-

---

a while. The French counted 10,000 unemployed in 1929—equivalent to nothing—and still welcomed immigrant labor. By 1932 the unemployment figure had tripled but was still one-thousandth of the unemployment rate across the Channel. Hundreds of thousands of foreign workers had been expelled to protect the welfare of French labor. By 1935 France acknowledged half a million unemployed and, although this receded only slowly, French unemployment figures were never as high as elsewhere. In the United States, certain financiers did not suffer as much as others. Andrew Mellon acquired twenty-one paintings from the Hermitage Museum in St. Petersburg for about 7 million dollars in 1930—indicating Russia's shortage of exchange but also the capacity of *some* American millionaires to raise a lot of cash in the depths of the Depression.

ever served as money to have some intrinsic value and had acted as if the gold and silver coins they used really had such value. When coins were replaced with paper, gold reserves were kept as backing for the currency. By the 1920's and 30's, however, men realized that what really counted was the possibility of exchanging currency for something of the value it was supposed to represent, of having it accepted as "money"—that is, a token of exchange at its face value—and that what counted in maintaining this possibility was not the gold reserve but confidence that fair exchange was a real possibility.

The sacred international gold standard, which assumed that currency was convertible into gold and that credit and debit balances in international trade could be settled out of national gold stocks, was suspended and exchange rates were now arbitrarily set at artificial levels. Finally, the brilliant English economist J. M. Keynes eased the survival of. a capitalism adjusted to changed challenges and conditions by arguing that attention must shift from distribution to production, from private to public scales, from shortage of consumption and demand to means of reviving them by coaxing savings into investment, by increasing the money in circulation, redistributing revenues, creating fresh demands, and breathing new life into the economy.

The first to adopt means similar to those Keynes suggested were the societies in direst straits. Russia, Germany, Italy, Japan tried to secure outlets for their products by means of bilateral agreements negotiated by state agencies which were in a good position to deal for vast quantities and exact the most favorable conditions, especially from the small producers of eastern Europe and Latin America, taking a vast proportion of their exports and, in the process, turning them into economic satellites. The most explicit in this policy and the most successful were the Germans. Between 1934 and 1938 the German exports to Bulgaria rose from 22 to 58 per cent, to Yugoslavia from 16 to 50 per cent, to Turkey from 15 to 51 per cent, to Hungary from 20 to 48 per cent; and these countries' exports to Germany from 30 to 63 per cent for Bulgaria, from 8 to 50 per cent for Yugoslavia, from 13 to 48 per cent for Turkey, from 12 to 50 per cent for Hungary. In other words, over half these countries' foreign trade came to be with Germany alone.

We have already seen how industrial concentration facilitated the exercise of state power. The latter almost presupposed still more concentration, which the Depression furthered by sending the weaker to the wall. In the United States in 1929 out of half a million companies, 500 made half the total profits, 20,000 companies accounted for nearly nine-tenths of profits. Now necessity accelerated developments which had already taken place in the world's leading producer—the United States. By 1935, eighteen great firms controlled two-thirds of British iron and steel production, and great trusts controlled the chemical, tobacco, and auto industries. In Italy fewer than 1 per cent of the country's enterprises owned more than half of the industrial capital. In Japan fourteen trusts controlled two-thirds of the investment capital and three-fourths of the bank deposits. In Germany less than 200 firms owned two-thirds of the investment capital.

Under the pressure of necessity, technical efficiency also increased. In 1938, the industrial output per man hours was half as great again in England than in 1913, twice as great in the United States. Thus, even as recovery began, new hands were joining the labor pool while industry had learned how to raise the volume of production with fewer employees. In those countries where the economy was least organized and activity still free, chronic unemployment survived to the end of peace, a constant factor of uneasiness and social guilt. Recovery was relative in any case. By 1936 international trade stood well below its level of 1929. Two years later European trade figures were still only 40 per cent of those of 1929.

Even so, most people in the West were better off on the eve of the Second World War than they had been on the eve of the First. They would have been better still had not many countries organized for war rather than for prosperity. War production did, however, mean that national economic structures had less to change in shifting from a peace to a war economy in 1939, particularly in Russia, Germany, Italy, and Japan, but also in other countries where planning and intervention during the thirties simplified rationing and control during the forties. This was the economic background against which the film of the twenty years' armistice unrolled, the setting for the rise of great pseudoreligions offering panaceas for Europe's worldly ills.

A Revolutionary Left: Communism

The first and perhaps greatest of twentieth-century creeds was an offshoot of late-nineteenth-century Socialism. It would be formulated by Vladimir Ilyich Ulyanov (1870–1924), better known as Lenin. Born at Simbirsk on the Volga, the son of a college principal who later became the director of elementary education throughout the province and whose position made him a member of the nobility, Lenin grew up in the subversive atmosphere that teachers' families notoriously generate. All of the Ulyanov children were revolutionary and in 1887 the eldest son, involved in an abortive plot to kill the Tsar, was executed. Vladimir himself, expelled from the university for his political activities, was finally permitted to secure a law degree and practiced law and Marxism side by side until he was arrested and exiled to Siberia. Released in 1900, he escaped to Geneva and founded a periodical: *Iskra* (The Spark), which, printed on cigarette paper, was smuggled into Russia to spread the Marxist gospel there.

Lenin's Russian experience gave him little sympathy for revisionism or for conventional mass movements, both of whose possibilities he doubted. In a long pamphlet of 1902, entitled *What Is To Be Done?* he gave his recipe for political action based on "a small, compact core consisting of reliable, experienced and hardened workers . . . connected by all the rules of strict secrecy with the organizations of revolutionaries." Though the recipe was given in a tactical context, its implications went against the democratic bent and tradition of the International, rejoining certain subversive arguments which had been heard among reactionaries and anarchists, doubting the capacity of majorities to help themselves and even to see clearly what would help them.

When in the last third of the nineteenth century revolutionaries discovered that universal suffrage was less a weapon for radical reform than a tool of autocracy and reaction (as Napoleon III and Bismarck knew), they began to think that only a conscious minority could be trusted to advance the cause of revolution, carrying the masses along. Representative democracy traded on the votes of fools. Utilitarian liberals had long thought so. Lenin agreed with them. In 1903, the second Russian Social Democratic Congress agreed on the necessity of socialist revolution and of the dictatorship of the proletariat, but divided over the nature of the party which would bring these about. Was it to be a mass party patterned on the West, or the disciplined, dedicated elite of professional revolutionaries that Lenin thought fitted Russian conditions better? Lenin's argument won the day, the tiny party split into majoritarians (Bolshevik) and minoritarians (Menshevik), and Trotsky, who belonged to neither faction, predicted what Lenin's model of revolutionary militancy implied: the party would be dominated by its organization, the organization by its central committee, and the central committee in the end by a dictator.

For the moment, none of this mattered very much and few paid great attention to the disputes of a small and exotic party. Yet Lenin's chance would shortly arise out of the war the Socialists had not been able to prevent despite repeated invocations. It would come because, when Russia collapsed into revolution, Lenin alone saw how the transition from autocracy to socialism could be telescoped by Bolshevik revolution. But also because social democracy had discredited itself during the war, almost all its leaders unable or unwilling to stand up either for peace or for revolution, their patriotism greater in the end than their revolutionary principles.

The victory of Bolshevism in Russia, enthusing millions of Socialists abroad, posed an awkward challenge to Socialist leaders. Communist centralism was incompatible with the parliamentary socialism of most

Western parties accustomed to working with a mass electorate interested in local questions and immediate gains, and utterly unready to give up the gains achieved over a generation of parliamentary action in order to pursue a will-o'-the-wisp of revolution in the Russians' wake. The Russians, on the other hand, followed Lenin in demanding that fellow parties shed their parliamentary-style leaders and policies, and acknowledge the supremacy of the Third International which they had set up in Moscow (1919).

After 1921, Socialist parties everywhere split on this issue between national-reformists ready to collaborate with other political parties on gradual reforms and democratic government and Communists dedicated to the pure, hard line of class war and revolution. This meant, in effect, that the Left was weakened afresh by its divisions: the Communists long remaining small though dynamic groups, never strong enough to make their revolution and heavily dependent on Moscow aid; the Socialists fated to ineffective compromises unlikely to secure the reforms they hoped for. From France to Scandinavia (and in Italy too, until suppressed in 1926), Socialist or Labor parties made a strong showing in elections, but never strong enough to let them take office unhampered by bourgeois allies.

Socialist parties were showing signs of staleness. Their leaders seemed conformist and increasingly aged—especially when compared to those of their revolutionary competitors. Their membership—increasingly middle-aged as the young, impatient, took their energy elsewhere—became more middle-class, as the industrial workers drifted into Communist ranks to be replaced by teachers, white-collar workers, and other partisans of moderate reform. Participation in governmental coalitions gave Socialists "governmental" habits of compromise, designed less to achieve particular measures than to remain in power. They were then further compromised by failure to answer the challenge of depression.

In moments of crisis when sacrifices are in order the essence of power is the capacity to impose these sacrifices on others than oneself and one's friends. This is the stake of the political game—a very important stake, as politics of the 1930's would show—and one which the Socialists lost when they proved unable to initiate any original measure that would not hurt the poorest citizens first. Caught in the maelstrom of the Great Depression, Labor and Socialist parties never managed to rethink their programs, foundered to disgrace along with other parties, or were suppressed as in eastern and central Europe. The only Socialist party which applied original methods was the Swedish, which, after 1932, went in for deficit spending, public works, and major investments in ways similar to those recommended by Keynes and thus curtailed unemployment, setting off economic recovery.

Rare were the labor leaders who formulated other possibilities. Some tried to reconcile autarchic retrenchment and economic revival, socialism with ambient nationalism: among them Oswald Mosley in England and Henri de Man in Belgium. The latter's *Beyond Marxism* (1927) voiced conclusions suggested by the experience of the Germans whom he had learned to know: the force of national feelings, the use of state machinery in controlling the capitalism of trusts and monopolies, to give workers a chance to build a stake in society, own property in it, become bourgeois too. Nationalization—part of the basic program of Socialist parties—was necessary only in crucial sectors like banking, transport, heavy industry; for the remainder, state *control* would be as effective as state *ownership*. De Man's ideas, which made their way into France during the thirties, were first applied by Fascists and by Nazis, before becoming the general practice of Western capitalism. Tarred with the Fascist brush, however, they horrified Socialists as did various attempts to blend socialism and nationalism. Socialist parties clung to the good old doctrine as they had done before the First World War and persuaded all who looked for fresh answers to their pressing problems that they would have to look elsewhere.

Increasingly, such people looked to Communism, less for its similar doctrines than for its certitudes. Socialism had taken on too much of the pessimistic, timid coloring of the society to which it had adjusted. Zealous, active, fanatically persuaded that their cause was right, Communists attracted a good many people who were dissatisfied with things as they were and more interested in change and action than in the precise nature of either, so that a number of them eventually turned to Nazism or to Fascism. True that in Russia—showplace of the creed—the dictatorship of the proletariat soon turned into dictatorship over the proletariat. The ruling Bolshevik Party, vanguard of working-class revolution, was a centralized authoritarian organization, a cross between teacher and policeman, a more efficient, more technocratic, more bureaucratized version of its heavily organized predecessors. But Russia was only a beginning, one could reason. Besides, it was far away and more impressive as a distant beacon of hope than as actual fact, while all around the tide of reaction rose.

Reaction reared against machines, against individualism, against science and alienating rationalism, against the technological advances causing unemployment, against the class struggle, against mechanization and mass production (glorifying gilds, artisans, and peasants). The optimist philosophy of progress was jettisoned all along the line. Those who did not like this had almost no choice but to join the Marxist camp. Once again, the intellectual appeal of a hopeful creed of change mobilized intellectuals increasingly convinced that the social order responsible for so much misery and injustice could not be maintained.

Socialism, as all could see, hampered the functioning of the profit system without doing anything to change it. Communism, even if unable to replace it with a better system, at least promised its destruction. Intel-

471

lectuals and artists who had engaged in anarchic and detached rebellions during the postwar years—W. H. Auden, John Dos Passos, Louis Aragon, André Malraux, Fernand Léger, Pablo Picasso, and many others—went over to commitment. In the Soviet Union, wrote Malraux in 1935, the writer was no longer alienated from industrial society; Soviet writers were one with their civilization. No wonder Westerners sought to follow suit! The economic interpretation was as one-sided and as unconvincing as any other creed. But it was psychologically satisfying. It provided the key to the impenetrable confusions of history, a plausible, clear, well-structured pattern of interpretation, suited to the materialistic mentality of our age. A materialistic idealism: what more could one ask? It need not be true, only convincing: simple, certain, prophetic. Besides, it seemed to offer the only hope in a world increasingly dominated by other, darker forces and ideologies.

A Radical Right: Fascism

We have traced to late nineteenth century the ominous rise of notions that can be described as catastrophic in more ways than one. Insecurity and discontent would help them soar from insignificant beginnings to overwhelming force, especially as they provided an alternative to hopes (or dangers) on the Left.

War introduced habits and practices that we today associate with social revolution: regimentation, propaganda, state control of vast sectors of economy and life, rule by decree, the fixing of prices and wages, requisition or confiscation of certain private property or even people, limitless expenditure and limitless waste, the argument that money and property must be at the service of a society many of whose members were laying down their lives for it, the implied rights of fighters and workers whose sacrifices must be repaid by recognition, a heroic or dramatic approach to public affairs increasingly viewed in totalitarian fashion so that the sacrifice of private opposition or private values to a public consensus became the acme of morality, faith in the tonic value of action—forceful and prompt rather than appropriate or even effective. Men had been told that criticism was treason, had learned that patriotism justified the end and, with it, the means. The infallibility of leaders pounded into nations to improve morale gave followers a good conscience and the vast relief of sharing in a righteous but risky game played recklessly. The dictatorial figures of the next decades had only to perfect what their predecessors had begun.

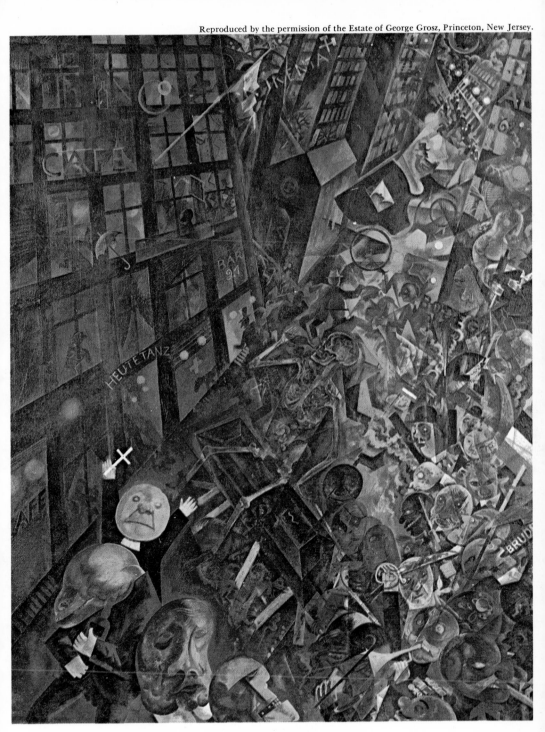

Leichenbegängnis, by George Grosz. Staatsgalerie, Stuttgart.

This was one kind of change. But there were others. Fortune or ruin, death or survival, were now seen once again (after the brief interval of a century or so when man had thought himself the master of his future) as the result of chance. The strongest and most skillful were not necessarily those who survived the fighting. The thriftiest did not come through inflation better than the shiftless kind. Men who had worked and saved all their lives saw their income (from pensions, stocks, or bonds) fall or disappear. No wonder the following generations lost interest in saving, even when they had the chance. Consumption was better than loss or devaluation; immediate gratification safer than any deferred prospects.

A major effect of this, thought a sensitive observer, was "loss of all confidence in justice as one of the principles which regulate the course of human life." Once belief in causality was replaced by faith in Providence, reward and retribution, cause and effect, became anachronistic concepts. One expression of this trend was the reliance on chance and random experience that we find in much contemporary art and literature. Another was a tremendous loss of faith in previously respected authorities: age, public bodies, political institutions, tainted with the lies which they had told, with wartime propaganda,* and, above all, with failure. Rulers of defeated countries paid for their failure by being overthrown; but the institutions of the victors were just as compromised.

The parliamentary system had long been under fire from reactionary quarters. As the nineteenth century ended, other critics began to express themselves. Universal suffrage, remarked Tolstoy, was no more than a method whereby prisoners elect their prison guards. Its representatives had, as the title of a book expressed it, "the cult of incompetence and the horror of responsibility"; and parliaments were only a haven for a multitude of parties and politicians squabbling over access to the public trough. This was what the dreams of 1848 had come to by 1900, the snows of hope melting to grubby slush in the light of experience. After the war, men who had experienced the lies and hypocrisies of their governments, had seen parliamentarians betraying their ideals and profiteers prospering by it while their fellows died,** retained no faith in what a young French Socialist convert to communism described as "the uncertain regime of the popular will surprised every four years in its sleep."

The opportunity for revolutions of the Right and Left was excellent and, facing the critics of the radical Left, a radical Right arose, reformulating the nationalist aspirations of the prewar years in the more favorable circumstances of the 1920's. Nationalists had two advantages which they had lacked before: the revolutionary menace now embodied into

---

* The French called it brain-stuffing (*bourrage de crâne*).
** As in the famous *Punch* cartoon that shows a small boy inquiring of his porcine parent: "Father, who did you do in the Great War?"

actual practice, which predisposed many sensible people to back the most forceful opponents of communism, and the aftermath of war and economic depression, which turned many more individuals into potential recruits. Many demobilized soldiers missed the comradeship of the trenches and looked for some alternative to the struggles of civilian life. Workmen torn out of their regular routines, women and adolescents mobilized for war service and being ordered back to shop or scullery or school, yearned for a stronger purpose. Finally, crisis—apparent or real—shook the enduring structures of established order and persuaded a good many people that salvation lay in action—even if only action for action's sake. Apart from communism, which many of them rejected, existing political movements offered little choice: the Liberals ever less liberal, the Radicals ever less radical, Conservatives merely conserving, and Socialists ever more the party of the middle-aged middle class.

This was the opportunity and source of fascism, which combined (in theory at least) the methods and appeals of national and social action, proposing to replace democratic and parliamentary institutions by a dictatorial one-party state and the free economy of liberal competition by one organized and planned on *corporative* lines: the virulent fulfillment of modern nationalism. Beginning as small bands of loud-mouthed hooligans, the Fascists gained in appeal and numbers in those societies where the relation between political power and the expression of the popular will was either absent or seemed least evident, and where belief in the capacity of individuals to express their interests or opinions was most restricted. Out of the Italian turmoil of the early 1920's the first of fascist movements grasped at power under the leadership of Benito Mussolini. It concealed, even from many followers, a fumbling kind of conventional politics beneath the guise of radical-seeming gestures, in the service of a disciplined mass movement (no more alienation) endowed with a supreme leader who claimed exclusive possession of political truth (no more individual responsibility), and exclusive power to assert it (no more squabbling parties).* Here was a new kind of security, a new kind of fulfillment, that would be expressed most fully in the national socialism of Adolf Hitler (1889–1945). Where Mussolini practiced action for action's sake, Hitler preached action for the sake of doctrine. The fascism of Mussolini was a brutally pragmatic opportunism. Hitler's Nazism attempted to play out a gigantic fantasy that proved as enthralling to millions as it proved murderous to more. Hitler's fantasy was racist. It used possibilities inherent in nationalism but which need not necessarily be developed, as the Italian experience showed, where racism was only a foreign and ill-accepted import. For

---

* Fascists did not attract hooligans only, but idealists too, interested in developing the collectivistic and populist aspects of its romantic nationalism. In Italy and elsewhere, fascist-type movements often recruited in circles similar to those of the radical left: disaffected syndicalists, students eager for action, intellectuals searching for a faith still undiscredited.

Hitler and Mussolini parade through the Brandenburg Gate in Berlin, 1937.

Hitler racism was essential: scheme of a giant combat between good and evil, the former embodied by the Germans—core of the blond Aryan race—the latter by the Jews, incarnation of dark Semites. Baseless in fact, this myth which Hitler and many followers accepted as Holy Writ served a moral and dynamic purpose: the one enabling the Nazi Party to justify all means by the inspiring end, the other by furnishing ideological impetus and unifying force.

In Hitler, turn-of-the-century nationalism reached a logical conclusion, before it foundered on the blood of millions sacrificed on the altars of a maniac faith. But we may remember that many other trends were accomplished in his one-party state. There was the dominant power of the state itself, whose powers, we have noted, had been growing all along and paradoxically so under the impact of democracy. Once the state became truly democratic (and liberal reforms seemed to hold out such a prospect), then there was no further need to restrict its powers. If only large-scale intervention could increase efficiency and improve society (as T. H. Green believed), then state bureaucracy was more important than laissez-faire tradition; if patriotism overrode particular loyalties, then the national state could claim far greater rights than the older oligarchic and particularistic structure. In any case, new nations, formed, as Karl Marx put it, "by the simple addition of like entities, much as a sack of potatoes consists of a lot of potatoes huddled into a sack," lent themselves to little else. The political opinions and influence of such people, whose identities are unexpressed and not clearly perceived, tend to operate in favor of some executive which runs society from above—democracy making for autocracy. Already in the seventeenth century Hobbes had spoken of the state as a "mortall God." The twentieth century would prove both terms where earlier times applied only the latter.

THE GROWTH OF THE
NAZI AND FASCIST POWERS

Areas of Axis control, August 1939

The trend toward the rule by experts, the talk about "a conscious minority" manipulating the levers of power was a part of this. Talk of the good society in progressive circles at the turn of the century suggested not only Nietzschean supermen like those half humorously set forth in some of the plays of George Bernard Shaw, or H. G. Wells's dedicated samurai, half boy scouts and half knights, but also eugenics, selective breeding, euthanasia, the elimination of weak, useless, or criminal elements from society. All these Hitler carried out or tried to, though with a heavier hand than Shaw or Wells would have liked to see.

Finally, Hitler's politics were as popular with his people as those of democratic politicians and perhaps more so: a kind of fulfillment of popular representation. If Michelet's version of "the people" showed it sane and just, other observers sang another tune. The people, wrote the Intendant of Marseilles to Colbert in 1667, is "a hundred-headed beast that wants to be led without knowing where it is going." Two centuries later the first analytical observer of the masses, the French sociologist Gustave Le Bon found that the *crowd* was worse in character and conduct, more violent, less reasonable, less decent certainly, than its average member. The character of a crowd is set by its lowest common denominator. So, often, is that of modern mass society. Swayed by rumors, catchwords, appeals which would leave the average individual cold or revolted, the crowd turns into a mob, doing or condoning things that no sensible individual by himself would accept.

Such crowds had existed in other ages. But now they had become a political factor, an electoral mob, endowed with sovereignty and armed with votes, capable of letting their crowdlike proclivities run riot or having them enlisted for witch hunts and wars presented by some showman as a great crusade. José Ortega y Gasset's *Revolt of the Masses,* published in 1930, noted not only the essential novelty of the mass age itself, but its tendency to treat violence—the direct action of Syndicalists, Anarchists, Sorelians, Fascists, and Nazis—as the supreme means of action and expression. It is easier to understand this when we remember that the vocabulary of politics changes as interlocutors change. Separate individuals speak the language of reason. Individuals in the mass are most effectively swayed by primeval noises, react most readily in terms of their common animality. That most people are not so most of the time is a tribute to the immense changes that have taken place not only in society but in human character since the Stone Age. But the voices of sanity, proportion, decency, and restraint whisper in public while others bellow coarser appeals. Hitler rightly sensed this and used his perception with masterly force to ride the whirlwind which he conjured up to its—and his—appointed doom.

The Day of the Dictators

We have seen that the Bolshevik revolution almost reversed the course of the First World War and, for some years thereafter, appeared to threaten the rest of Europe with social war. The determination of Bolshevik leaders to leave the war brought allied support for their political enemies: the White or anti-Bolshevik forces. This continued even when the German war was ended, for by that time all powers in the West felt their stability and their interests threatened not only by Bolshevik policies inside Russia but by "red" revolutionary propaganda outside. There seemed to be no possible compromise between a regime convinced that its survival depended on the cause of world revolution and regimes at whose expense such revolution had to be achieved.

In any case, Russia was difficult of access and the news that trickled out made its experience sound less like that of 1789 or 1793 than like that of the Congo or Indonesia today. Bolsheviks were criminals at home, subversives abroad, best represented by the image of the man with a knife between his teeth. Not surprisingly, their neighbors feared their contagion and the Western powers lent support to White forces which for several years attempted to resist and defeat the Red revolution. This was also why the peace treaties excluded the Russians whose public image placed them outside the counsels of the civilized world—hopefully, as a temporary aberration. Clemenceau refused to let Soviet representatives set foot on French territory. Wilson and Lloyd George, who would have liked to deal with the Soviets as a *de facto* government, could convince neither their allies nor majority opinion in their own countries. Between 1917 and 1920 the tides of undecided warfare that surged along the confines of central Europe, the spate of revolutions and revolutionary strikes that broke out from the Arctic to the Mediterranean, sharpened awareness of the Bolshevik danger.*

At first, the real barrier against Bolshevism was envisaged in the long string of succession states between the Baltic and the Black Sea that were supposed to provide a so-called *cordon sanitaire,* or quarantine belt, which—since the new Russia could not be stifled—would contain and seclude it. Time proved the barrier to be a flimsy one, too dependent on the support of its Western patrons and on the acquiescence of the Germans. As this became increasingly apparent, the diplomacy

* Arno F. Mayer, *Politics and Diplomacy of Peacemaking: Containment and Counterrevolution at Versailles, 1918–1919* (1968), argues convincingly that the main unstated object of the peacemakers was not to establish self-determination and to make the world safe for democracy, or even to humble Germany, but to preserve the world from Bolshevism and to isolate Red Russia.

of the Western countries tended to look to Germany as the only really reliable barrier against Bolshevism, a fact which greatly restricted the Westerners' possibilities of diplomatic maneuver. This worked in favor of the Germans, suggesting an argument destined for a long run: that undue harshness shown to the Germans would throw them into the arms of Bolshevism. The German peace treaties were somewhat mitigated by this consideration and so was their application, especially as regards reparations. "Ordinary common prudence," explained Lloyd George in 1922, "demands that Germany should be treated decently in order to save her from Communism."

To begin with, however, the most striking aspect of postwar diplomacy was the disunion of the victors concerning how Germany should be treated: the French taking a hard line toward their impenitent neighbors, the British showing a more conciliatory attitude. Hoping to construct a rampart against both Germany and Russia, France turned to the successor states of eastern Europe—Poland, Czechoslovakia, Romania, Yugoslavia—equally aware of the dangers that a resurgence of the defeated camp could represent. Soon, a series of alliances linked these countries with one another and with France. Unfortunately, while France depended on her allies to strengthen her position, they in turn relied on her to affirm theirs, creating not a real force but a conjunction of weaknesses destined to give way before serious pressure. On the other hand, Russia and Germany, determined to make up lost ground, drifted together. In 1922, an international economic conference held at Genoa and designed to lighten the burden of reparations offered an opportunity for representatives of Russia and Germany to meet in nearby Rapallo, settle their economic differences, and sign a pact of friendship that shocked the other powers and ensured the collapse of the larger conference.

Britain and France reacted in opposite ways to the Treaty of Rapallo. The French, angered by German defiance, became more insistent on Germany's fulfillment of her obligations. When in 1923 Berlin defaulted on the schedule of its reparation payments, French troops were sent to occupy the Ruhr, vital center of German mining and industry. The occupation was answered by a general strike and this in turn brought about the collapse of German economy: there was soaring inflation, political confusion, social disruption on a vast scale as millions lost their savings and investments. The international repercussions of this crisis which soon affected the economies of other countries persuaded even the French to make concessions. The British, whom Rapallo had strengthened in the resolve that only kindness could keep Berlin and Moscow from moving even closer together, were glad to help mend the German predicament. In 1924, reparation schedules were revised and foreign loans provided by an international commission headed by an American banker, Charles Dawes; and this was followed in 1925 by a political agreement that guaranteed existing boundaries in the west.

The Treaty of Locarno, which settled outstanding disputes between Germany and her western neighbors, enlisting Britain and Italy as guarantors, seemed to open a more peaceful era of collaboration between the powers whose quarrels had marked the last six years. In 1926, Germany entered the League of Nations; in 1928 twenty-three nations signed a pact in Paris abjuring the use of aggressive war; in 1929 reparations were further scaled down by another commission headed by yet another American financier, Owen D. Young; and the last Allied occupation troops left German soil the following year. But Locarno settled some disputes only to let others fester: notably the question of Germany's eastern frontiers, deliberately left out of account because unacceptable to Berlin as they stood. The possibility of raising this issue (although one that, according to the treaty's terms, could only be settled by peaceful means) provided a potential threat to the French alliance system, but also an expression of the—tacit—hope that German expansion, should it begin once more, would be directed eastwards, reinforcing her assigned role as champion of Europe against Bolshevism.

Thus, to a great extent, European relations between the wars were affected by fear of Soviet Russia; and this raises the question how such fear can be explained. Why these precautions? What was the challenge of this revolution that stirred and alarmed great countries and great masses of people?

Louis Fischer, who went to Europe as a very young free-lance reporter just after the war, describes Bolshevism both as a protest and a hope: a protest against the old world and the old men who had made the war and spoiled the peace; a hope, as he put it, not of a better present but of a brighter future. Even when they merely presented old appeals dressed up in fresh slogans, this promise of a brighter future proved terribly important against the background of a dreary present. The Communists could point to a promised land which really existed, and this gave their talk of reshaping Europe a special power and effectiveness. Especially since, as Fischer points out, if Europe had needed no reshaping, it would not have been so worried.

That was the crux of the matter. The war had plunged Europe into a revolutionary situation. It revealed the incapacity, the impotence of the existing system and of the men who ran it to deal with the problems that they themselves created. It is possible that there would have been revolutionary outbreaks even without the Russian example. But the Russian example was there to act as an inspiration and the revolutionary situation created by war, economic collapse, and political confusion was compounded by the revolutionary lead of Moscow. Thus, those who feared the overthrow of their established order and the subversion of their way of life were justified in dreading the new revolutionary power arising in the east and doing everything to hamper or to tame it. Not because they disapproved of Soviet terror and dictatorship, but because they disapproved of the ends to which these methods were directed.

That fear of Bolshevism was more than suspicion and condemnation of the dictatorship and loss of political liberties in Russia can be seen from the fact that the democracies found dictatorship and its implications easier to accept when this respected property and used its force to maintain the familiar order rather than upset it. Between the wars, as David Thomson put it, "It seemed that democracy had merely made the world safe for dictatorship." In 1918 four empires fell, and all but the German fell to pieces. All had been dynastic, oligarchic, multinational, authoritarian structures. All were succeeded by very different entities—national republics or monarchies (except for the federated Soviet Union), popular or populist at least in outer guise, yet soon to evolve more toward authoritarian government. With the single exception of Czechoslovakia, the succession states were backward societies, largely illiterate, politically inexperienced, ignoring how to make multiparty government work when suddenly endowed with universal suffrage.

Representative party government in the West was the creation of small, self-conscious groups that ruled somewhat inert apathetic masses until these last developed a political consciousness. In most of the new countries (or in old ones like Portugal, Spain, and Turkey) where little political consciousness and less experience in democratic politics existed, a mass electorate and an authoritarian-minded political class could only coexist by dint of manipulation, which critics called corruption and, finally, by forcefully imposing the dictatorial rule of a man or faction. Thus, very soon, for widely differing reasons. countries as far divided in their tendencies as Hungary and Russia, Turkey and Italy, rejected liberal government for dictatorship: Hungary in 1919, Turkey 1920, Spain 1923, Italy 1925, Portugal, Poland, and Lithuania 1926, Yugoslavia 1929, Germany, Austria, and Estonia 1933, Bulgaria and Latvia in 1934, Greece in 1936 or earlier, Romania in 1938. This does not in all probability exhaust the list but gives an idea of its variety. The only thing all dictatorships had in common was a determined anticommunism. Some, as in Romania, were royal dictatorships of an old-fashioned authoritarian kind or, as in Hungary, almost the same thing without a king. Some, as in Spain during the 1920's, reflected a strong man's rule using personal prestige and military power to impose the will of one faction and exclude all others. Such regimes did not abolish parliament or representative institutions but rather circumvented them and pulled their teeth. More determinedly reactionary regimes appeared in Portugal and Austria, where dictatorships based on the Catholic Church, the army, and the police attempted to launch "new states" firmly antiparliamentary and antidemocratic.

482

Mussolini

The most original dictatorship, however, established itself in Italy between 1922 and 1925 when the King backed the government of a former Socialist leader turned nationalist—Benito Mussolini—and the one-party rule which he imposed. Mussolini's Fascists had grown out of the national resentments of Versailles and the social fears of postwar readjustments. Yet they were more than mere reactionary bands. Pretending to defend society against "Red revolution" they also touted a revolution of their own against the dreary and corrupt established order, its exploitation and its compromises, its worn old men and its corrupting ways. Nationalist and populist, they used revolutionary language against the revolutionaries, attractive to those who wanted change (especially the young) but also to those who feared the greater change that the Reds might wreak. To the young they promised action, to the old, order; to the exploited they promised justice, to investors, stability; to the restless they spoke of change, to the replete and fearful, of tradition; to the ambitious they offered an avenue of social promotion, to the patriotic they hymned national greatness and unity. This last, indeed, was their most specific disagreement with the Left, to whose concept of class struggle they opposed one of class reconciliation and common interests within the organic body of the nation. Spottily formulated, slowly articulated, capable of being most things to most men, Fascism crudely joined the two great concerns of modern times—the national and the social—in a social nationalism whose influence carried far.

When this motif has been perfected in the national socialism of Adolf Hitler, and after Hitler had come to power in Germany in 1933, variants of what we might call fascism appeared in every country's politics, though nowhere as luxuriantly as in Italy and Germany. Fascist-type parties appeared in every land from Finland to Switzerland and Britain. They would grow strongest where government was weak, social and economic problems great, the traditional structures of society threatened or collapsing. Where an effective conservative or authoritarian government maintained itself in power, as in Hungary, fascism got no grip. Where social and economic problems did not overwhelm the system, as in France or England, or where they were solved with a will, as in the United States, the Fascist movements remained embryonic, often competing with more conventional reactionary or conservative groups. Where, as in Germany, the foundations of life seemed to give way beneath the feet of millions who lost their jobs, their savings, and their self-respect, coming to feel that anything was better than the present, the revolutionary and millenial note of Fascist politics could reach the masses, their violent language and methods promised forceful ac-

483

tion, while all the time their reference to nation and tradition conciliated the ruling classes.

Just as anti-Bolshevism reconciled the victors of 1918 to spare and humor Germany, so it prompted the partisans of established order to spare and humor fascism, and then to favor it. In each of these cases things eventually went wrong, for fascism proved both revolutionary and destructive. At first, however, it merely seemed the most forceful and efficient of the modern creeds, a useful ally against Bolshevism and most impressive in the apparent order and unity it created by eliminating those opportunities for free expression which tend to make democratic societies such a jumble of contending voices.

Fascist dictatorships also made an impressive show of force. Their rulers knew what they wanted and went about it with a dramatic will. Among the first to adopt the doctrines of economic relativity and control, they were the first outside Soviet Russia to absorb the suppurating unemployment that dragged down morale as much as prosperity. Before the apparent "triumph of. their will" the democracies seemed limp and decadent. In a sense they were, for the advanced democracies were also most advanced in the decline of that demographic curve whose rise in past centuries had marked their own rise in the world. The twenties and especially the thirties saw birth rates falling in all countries, particularly in northern and western Europe where, despite a compensating fall in death rates, the population growth slowed down from 12 per cent in England of the 1890's to 4.5 per cent forty years later, from 13 per cent in Switzerland to 4 per cent, from 2 per cent in France to less than 1 per cent, whereas in Germany the fall over the same period went only from 14 to 9 per cent and in Italy from 10 to 9 per cent.

The Malthusian tendency of attributing unemployment to overpopulation and favoring birth control was oddly rare outside Britain. Other countries were more concerned about the gun and factory fodder they were losing, and staged campaigns to raise the birth rate by family allowances, loans, preferential treatment for large families; and none was more successful than the Italian Fascists and the German Nazis, both of whom succeeded in raising birth rates far above what they had been at their accession. In France and England meanwhile, the proportion of older people in the population increased. In England, where in 1901 32 per cent had been below fourteen and 20 per cent had been over forty, by 1940 21 per cent were below fourteen and 32 per cent over forty. France of the 1930's was the country where there were more old and fewer young people than anywhere else in the world. This kind of shift implied adjustments in economic structure which aging populations are ill fitted to make, and suggested that the growing number of aged would have to be maintained by a shrinking active population. In the military sphere a deficiency of manpower meant a reluctance

The tunnels of the
Maginot Line.

to engage it, well reflected in the defensive strategy whose massive symbol stretched from the Swiss to the Belgian border in the gun-bristling fortifications of the Maginot Line. Determined to husband her diminishing manpower, France entrenched herself behind a long wall of concrete which, expected to ensure her safety, merely certified her impotence. Military immobility meant diplomatic inertia. The fortifications became a ghetto from which the French watched the destruction of their eastern allies before they permitted their own.

The greater proportion of older people also hinted at growing conservatism, failure of initiative, slow and hesitant reactions, fumbling policies. Those conditions which had made for dynamism in the eighteenth and nineteenth centuries were now to be found in the Fascist and Communist dictatorships, which assumed the aggressive stance given up by their aging rivals; and the politics of the 1930's reflect this change.

Hitler

Although he impressed his contemporaries—not least Hitler—Mussolini was not in a good position to make a mark on the world. The country which he ruled did not afford him a sufficient base. Only a great power could provide that and Italy never had the resources to become one.

485

Germany did. In Adolf Hitler she found a maniac leader who combined incoherent vulgarity and delusive obsessions with insights that cut through the conventions of national politics like a hot knife through butter. Hitler meant to reverse the verdict of 1918, redeem Germany's honor, and establish her unchallenged dominance over all of Europe, perhaps all the world. He proclaimed not only his mission but also his intentions in far greater detail than any politician before or since; and reaped the profits of his candor in the enthusiasm of his followers and the skeptical disbelief of foreigners unable to accept the scale or implications of what he ingenuously proposed. Yet Hitler achieved much of what he set out to do, partly because many of the gains he sought on the international plane were at the points where the peacemakers at Versailles had failed to reconcile principle and practice, leaving their heirs a strong feeling of guilt.

Hitler's demand that Germans be allowed to join their homeland and German territories be reunited to the Reich sounded plausible—the more plausible perhaps for the thought that Germany satisfied would rally to the cause of peace, that German claims denied would lead to war, a war in which either Germany won anyway or else she fell and, with her, the last solid barrier against Bolshevism. This was the rationale of appeasement which in practice, writes A. J. P. Taylor, "meant endorsing the claims of the stronger and then making out that these claims were just." It also meant throwing your friends to the wolves in the hope that the wolves would be sated before they got to you. Evidently, governments based on popular approval found it harder to face the prospect of war than those who could force their decisions on their subjects. At the same time, not only the "democracies" but the "Fascists" too based their policies on a wide range of popular approval. We might note that—more than ever before and perhaps since—the foreign policies of Britain, France, and Germany between the wars mirrored the opinions and the wishes of majorities. Democratic politics got the representatives and the results that they deserved.

Thus, Europe labored out of the Depression years into hard times of recurrent crisis on the political stage, a half decade of anarchy which partly reflected the post-operative shock of the Great Depression. "There never was a war in all history easier to prevent by timely action . . . without the firing of a single shot . . ." Churchill would recollect in 1946. "But no one would listen and one by one we were all sucked into the awful world war."

The first sort of timely action envisaged by the politicians of the West had been the enlistment of Mussolini in a common anti-German front. This might have worked (whether it *should* have worked is another matter) had not the British public in 1935 refused to sacrifice principle to policy. Mussolini wanted Ethiopia as an imperial sop. Aggression was immoral; no more immoral, though, than the aggressions whose results created the French and British empires. Yet, public opinion would not stand for it and the politicians who heeded their public fell between two stools: unwilling to use force against Italian aggression, they let it happen while making ineffective gestures to prevent it, thus ensuring their own inefficacy while driving Mussolini into Hitler's arms.

The Axis and the Allies

In May, 1936, Italian troops occupied Addis Ababa. A few weeks before, something far more important had occurred, as crucial as the battle of Sadowa seventy years before: German troops had reoccupied the Rhineland, a territory which they were bound not only by the Versailles Treaty but by freely signed agreements (Locarno, 1925) to leave demilitarized. It had been Clemenceau who pointed out that as long as the Rhineland remained demilitarized Germany could not move against the Czechs' Bohemian bastion. Once allowed to fortify it, she was free to challenge all European arrangements. Clemenceau was right. The year 1936 liberated Hitler from fear of a French invasion should he become obstreperous. Now he could turn against his eastern neighbors—who were also France's allies—without fear that French retaliation might overrun a rich, unfortified portion of his land. Nor did he need to fear any Italian demonstration on his flank, for Italy was now his ally as a direct result of the Ethiopian war, which had left Mussolini with no alternative allies. Announced on November 1, 1936, the Rome-Berlin Axis sharply challenged the sleepy London-Paris tandem.

Another war, this one a civil war in Spain, would tie the Axis allies even closer. Spain had been a republic since 1931, oscillating between left- and right-wing government, prey to repeated risings and disorders, teetering on the brink of worse disorders still. Early in 1936, general elections returned a coalition of left-wing parties combined in a Popular Front whose policies encouraged military revolt that summer. Spain had a long tradition of pronunciamentos and that of 1936 might have been one more had not determined resistance by workers and students turned the half-successful military coup into prolonged struggle. This soon took on the coloring of social war, with Europe's Catholic and right-wing forces supporting the military insurgents under General Francisco Franco, and the Left, from liberals to Communists, supporting Spain's legal government. The latter's obvious support would come from France and Britain, democratic countries, in the first of which moreover a similar Popular Front also ruled. Its fate was sealed when, determined to keep out of trouble, the British government put pressure on the French to deny the Spanish government their aid. Instead, the two democracies bravely launched a policy of nonintervention which prevented aid from reaching the republican camp while placing no obstacle in the way of German and Italian help to Franco's "nationalists."

As a result of such democratic self-denial, the levers of governmental power in Spain gradually passed to the most determined anti-Fascists, mostly Communists; and Soviet aid convinced conservatives in the democracies that they were right in favoring the nationalist cause. The civil war dragged on to 1939, focusing most of the feelings and sympathies of the liberal public on both sides of the Atlantic. It seemed symbolic that in this first confrontation between Fascism and what appeared to be the forces of freedom or, at least, of popular government, the latter should be left to fight and lose alone while governments in which the liberal world set its hopes withdrew their skirts from danger. In fact the situation was deceptive, for neither side really stood for freedom; and Franco, who readily accepted Fascist help, was not himself a Fascist but an authoritarian conservative of ancient stamp. This did not alter the fact that, while the Fascist powers effectively helped their friends, the democracies let theirs down.

Nothing went so far to reinforce this view as the events of 1938, when the defeat of the Republicans in Spain became a foregone conclusion and when Nazi aggression was carried out with impunity with Italy's aid and British benediction. Italy had helped maintain Austria's independence. Now that Italy was Hitler's friend, Austria became Hitler's prey. In the spring of 1938 he plucked it. Few could gainsay the right of a German population to join their brethren in the German Reich. The more so since Austrians, by and large, welcomed *Anschluss* (that is, union with Germany), and many, at their worst, outdistanced German Nazis in their fanaticism. And, Vienna taken, the argument of national self-determination would be used to claim back some three million Germans, onetime Austrians or Saxons, who lived within the borders of Bohemia.

Czechoslovakia was France's ally: a solid, stable country, a real democracy, whose army, behind strong fortifications supplied by the gigantic Skoda armament works, could offer serious resistance to the Germans, especially if backed by fellow democracies in the West. But France's government was most reluctant, and any readiness on its part to back the Czechs was sapped by British pressure. Britain was bound—as much by interest as by treaty—to help the French in case of war, and Neville Chamberlain, the British prime minister, was utterly unwilling to lay down British lives "because of a quarrel in a far away country between people of whom we know nothing." Then there was Russia. Hitler's pretext for marching into the Rhineland in 1936 had been a Franco-Soviet Pact which seemed to revive the Franco-Russian Alliance of 1894. Now, Russia offered help to Czechoslovakia in the name of collective security. But she had no more common border with the Czechs than had the

A contemporary French cartoon satirizing the Munich agreement. Right: Mussolini and Hitler leave the building where the Munich Conference was held. Behind Hitler, Mussolini's son-in-law, Count Ciano. To Ciano's left, Goering.

French; and Czechoslovakia's neighbors were more concerned about their own security from Russia than about facilitating any aid to the Czechs. In any case, the thought of help from Russia, if not underrated, was quite enough to spur Chamberlain and the French foreign secretary, Georges Bonnet, even further in seeking to accommodate Hitler without war. If Chamberlain had no heart for war, Bonnet did not have guts for it; while Daladier, the French prime minister, a veteran of the trenches and an old schoolteacher, shared the shamefaced reluctance of his fellow Frenchmen to face the horror of warfare once again.

The predicament was solved at a quadripartite meeting called at Mussolini's behest and held in Munich in September, 1938. There, Daladier and Chamberlain conceded on behalf of the Czechs all Hitler's claims to the Bohemian borderland. The Russians had been totally and significantly ignored, the Czechs treated as objects in a trade, whose fate mattered but little. Hitler and his acolytes triumphed once again. The vainglorious vulgarity that we perceive so well in retrospect about the Nazis only sets in relief the weak, vapid, well-meaning mediocrity of Western leadership, whose bad faith concealed both cowardice and guilt. Hitler considered his Western interlocutors nonentities, and Daladier must have agreed with him when the Paris crowds greeted him on his return from Munich not with rotten vegetables but with flowers. Chamberlain had no such doubts. He knew that his abdication represented, as A. J. P. Taylor recently wrote with a straight face "a triumph

489

for all that was best and most enlightened in British life." So did the crowds that gave him a hero's welcome on his return from Munich.

Chamberlain would awake when, within six months of Munich and of Hitler's declaration to him that the Sudetenland was his last territorial demand in Europe, Nazi troops occupied the rump of the country he had helped dispatch, leaving some pickings to Poland and Hungary, glad at this time to act as jackals to the German wolf. It appears that Chamberlain honestly hoped that a fair settlement on ethnic lines would still Hitler's appetite. If so, it seems strange that, riled by Hitler's breaking his personal word to him, Chamberlain chose to deny the Germans the right to Danzig, and to certain territories within the Polish border to which they had as good a right as to the Sudeten regions. But he did, and reacted to German occupation of Bohemia by guaranteeing all Polish territory against attack. This created several problems. In the first place, the French were as reluctant to go to war for Danzig as the British had been to fight for the Czechs. In the second place, the Franco-German border now consisted of two giant lines of fortifications which made any effective intervention from the west most doubtful, and suggested that help for Poland could only come from the east. But the Poles, remembering past experience, rejected Russian help. As arrogantly confident as they were ill prepared, the colonels who ruled Poland thought they could hold the Germans by themselves.

The French and British made somewhat half-hearted efforts to persuade them to accept Russian aid, and equally half-hearted efforts to negotiate a pact with Russia. They only succeeded in persuading Stalin that Russian security lay in a pact with Hitler. It seemed as if the Western powers, equally afraid of Communists and of Nazis, wished the two to fight each other. Certainly some Western newspapers hinted as much. But the Russians would not pull capitalist chestnuts out of the fire. They could make a more profitable deal with the Germans, dividing the lands between them rather than fighting over them. In August, 1939, with a Nazi propaganda storm over Danzig at its height, the news of the German-Soviet Pact burst on the world. It seemed as if, once again, Hitler would achieve his aim without war. Who could withstand him now? Who would? "Our enemies are little worms," he told his generals on August 26, 1939. "I saw them at Munich." He had good reason for his judgment. And it seemed borne out by a letter which the London *Daily Telegraph* carried on September 1, 1939, from Lord Alfred Douglas, delighted that Britain could avoid "the odious predicament" of alliance with Russia now that Russia and Germany had allied instead, and relieved that "there would be no war."

The first of September was the day the Germans invaded Poland. Forty-eight hours later Europe was at war. The worm had turned at last. Awkwardly, reluctantly, not knowing quite what to do, perhaps at the wrong moment, perhaps in the wrong cause, it had perceived that it must stand and fight for it had no choice. There is something ironic about the way in which those men whom we describe as statesmen will disavow the most reasonable statements of their predecessors. Bismarck had declared that the Balkans were not worth the bones of a single Pomeranian grenadier and his successors staked the empire Bismarck built upon a Balkan issue. In 1925 the British foreign secretary, Austen Chamberlain, deliberately echoed Bismarck: "For the Polish Corridor no British government ever will or ever can risk the bones of a British grenadier." His younger brother was to prove him wrong—though right in the event, like Bismarck.

The Second World War

Defeat in Europe

German troops attacked Poland on September 1, 1939. Britain declared war on Germany at noon on September 3 and France followed suit a few hours later. But the action, unlike a quarter of a century before, was in the east. Impotent and circumspect behind the Maginot Line, the Western allies watched Poland overrun by Germans, invaded by the Rus-

German tanks sweep into Poland. Warder Collection

sians, and, before the month had ended, partitioned for a fourth time between its greater neighbors. In mid-September Harold Nicolson dined with a conservative minister and noted in his diary: "At heart he is longing to get out of it . . . any reference to Russian assistance makes him wince and at one moment he sighed deeply and said, 'You see, whether we win or lose, it will be the end of everything we stand for.' By 'we' he means obviously the capitalist classes."

Quite a few men in France as much as Britain felt that their countries were at war with the wrong enemy. They suffered, one might say, from a counter-idealism so acute that they forgot where their national interests lay, remembering only their deep prejudices against Bolshevism. That Germany threatened their national existence seemed less significant than the danger which the Soviets constituted for a world order they confused with their personal interest. It would take a dyed-in-the-wool Tory like Churchill to see his country's immediate interest clearly, detached from personal predilections, and to understand, as some great predecessors had, that one concludes alliances to serve not taste but interest and that one makes war to win. But before Churchill came to power, Britain and her ally indulged a mealier mood. The war along the western front trod water while Hitler bade his time and, further east the Russians sought to enlarge their defensive *glacis*. Having advanced up to the Curzon Line in September,* during October they secured military privileges in the Baltic states,** and in November sought to obtain similar rights from Finland. When the Finns refused, war broke out— a war which at once aroused the enthusiasm of the Western world and offered it an opportunity to escape the uneasy situation which the French called *la drôle de guerre* (the phony war). Unable to make real war against the Germans, the French and British now proposed to make war against the Russians too. Some may have hoped that before long they and the Germans could be reconciled against the predestined enemy. They were disappointed when March, 1940, brought a Russo-Finnish treaty that gave the Soviets more than they had asked at first—specifically more ground between their second city, Leningrad, and the border.

Thereafter, events moved fast. In April, 1940, German forces invaded Denmark and Norway, making short shrift of the local armies and of the improvised expeditions that France and Britain sent to help. In May they struck at France through Holland and Belgium, turning the flank

* Suggested in 1920 by the then British foreign secretary as a means of settling the Russo-Polish conflict, the Curzon Line left the Ukrainian provinces east of the Bug River in Soviet territory. Though ignored by the Poles, this line provided a rough border between Orthodox Ukrainian peoples and the Catholic Polish-speaking population further west.

** Estonia, Latvia, and Lithuania would be occupied in June of 1940.

A street scene during the bombing of London.

of the Maginot Line, using their aviation to clear the way for armored columns which broke through all opposition. Four days from the attack's beginning the Dutch army had capitulated; the Belgians held out for sixteen. Swiftly, mercilessly, the British Expeditionary Force in France, cut off from its allies, its flank exposed by the Belgians' fall, was forced on to the coast. The first days of June saw an extraordinary feat: 215,000 British and 120,000 French troops evacuated from the Channel beaches, chiefly near Dunkirk. Meanwhile, the Germans raced on. They were in Paris on June 13. The fleeing French reconstituted their government, placing at its head Henri Philippe Pétain, the hero of Verdun, who asked the Germans for an armistice (June 16). The armistice was signed on June 22 at Compiègne, in the same railroad carriage where twenty-two years before the Germans, too, had signed armistice terms. Forty-two days had passed since the campaign's beginning. Hitler could think that the war was over.

So did most of the French. Meeting at Vichy, the parliament of the Third Republic handed full powers to Pétain as head of a state more than half of which lay under German occupation. The capital of the unoccupied zone was in Vichy itself, a spa for sufferers from liver ailments. The ancient enmity for Britain reappeared, fed by deep resentment when—fearful that the French fleet would end in German hands—the British attempted its destruction and the subversion of French colonies. Men like Pierre Laval, an astute parliamentary figure, felt that France's hope lay in developing better relations with the Nazis. The war,

Pierre Laval with Hitler. Right: Laval defending himself while on trial as a war criminal.

he thought, would soon be over and favorable terms could only be secured if France collaborated with her occupants. Few dissented: among them an unknown brigadier, Charles de Gaulle, whom the British helped to set up a national committee of Free French in London to continue the fight against the Germans. Britain's new prime minister also disagreed. For Winston Churchill, who had succeeded Chamberlain in May, following the Norwegian fiasco and on the eve of the German offensive in the west, Britain "had only begun to fight."

Most of Britain's military equipment had been left behind at Dunkirk. Fresh arms and supplies were secured from the United States, naval and air bases in Britain's Atlantic possessions exchanged for American destroyers to patrol the sea lanes. The Royal Air Force, however, had been saved and, while Britain rearmed, it beat off the constant air strikes which were supposed to usher in German invasion. Between August and October, 1940, many British cities had been torn and burned, civilian casualties stood at tens of thousands, 14,000 had died in London alone. But nearly 2,400 German planes had been brought down against only a third that many lost to the R.A.F. The courage of the latter's fighter pilots, the spirit of the British people, and the radar network which provided early warning of the enemy's approach, had won the Battle of Britain: in General von Rundstedt's opinion, the crucial battle of the war. By October, 1940, the direct German threat had been fought down; but very heavy raids continued on every part of the country, and particularly on London, until May, 1941, when the German air force had to turn its face toward the east. The Battle of Britain was the first German defeat: as in the 1800's the conquerors of the Continent could not cross the Channel and finally turned eastward to seek a solution to their perplexity. As in those years but more so, the unconquered island remained a lonely fortress base at the enemy's rear from which the final assault against him could be mounted. As in those years too, the overweening conqueror would break his teeth on Russia, the stubborn resistance of her peoples, and the no less stubborn immensity of her space.

While Germany was conquering the west, Russia had recovered the territories lost by the Tsarist empire in the Baltic, Poland, and Bessarabia. Her demand for this last from Romania—whose rulers had counted on a French alliance rendered quite worthless by the French defeat—set off a spree of claims on the territories that country had acquired from Bulgaria in 1913 and Hungary in 1919. Cut down in size by almost half, Romania gave herself a military dictator and joined the Axis in search of self-protection. So did her Hungarian and Bulgarian enemies.

Yet Germany's Balkan flank floundered in a situation that Mussolini had created out of sheer folly. When war had started in 1939, Italy had not been prepared to join it. Both sides were glad to see her neutral: the Allies to have one less enemy, the Germans for the supplies that could be channeled through her. In June, 1940, however, Mussolini could not resist the spoils of France then being overrun. He declared war on the Allies and Italian troops did miserably in the Alps before the French fighting ended. That same autumn, with German power spreading through the Balkans, Mussolini sought compensation against Greece. He had no reason to attack that country except the desire to gain some cheap glory while Germany was triumphing all along the line; but he found that his troops did no better there than against the French. Across the Mediterranean, in Africa, the British overran his colonies. No attack on Russia could begin without the Balkan flank secured. The Germans intervened, which meant that first they must subdue the Yugoslavs who refused them passage into Greece. Within a few weeks the Balkans had been won. By the end of April, 1941, German writ ran to the Aegean Sea. It would have run still further had not the British managed to secure Iraq and to prevent the Vichy French governors of Syria and Lebanon from handing their air bases over to the Germans.

Now Germany was free to attack Russia, despite frantic attempts on Stalin's part to avoid a showdown. And when, in June 1941, German, Finnish, Hungarian, Italian, and Romanian troops opened hostilities on a front that ran 2,000 miles, Churchill at last found a reluctant ally, but one that would fight ruthlessly to the end.

A blow-by-blow account of a great war would be impossible in this context. Slowly, what had begun as a European contest drew in the remaining world. Russia had attempted to stay outside it and could not. The United States, increasingly aware that British defeat menaced her own survival, was drawn into taking a more active part in the defense of sea lanes which were the island's lifeline. American forces landed in Danish Greenland, Dutch Guiana, and in Iceland. America, too, however, sought to avoid open warfare and might have done so had not Japan, Germany's ally but careful for her part to avoid war with Russia, tried to use the opportunity to gain dominion over the Pacific.

The World at War

The Japanese had waged war since 1931 to win and keep control of China. After the fall of France they had obtained the right to occupy Indochina and they controlled Thailand as well. They coveted the resources which lay in the colonial territories of the other powers that Germany had defeated, but knew the United States would not stand by and see them taken. They must annihilate America's power to withstand them, and they went far toward doing so when, on December 7, 1941, they unexpectedly attacked Hawaii and the Philippines, destroying much of the U.S. Pacific fleet in Pearl Harbor. Within six months, the Japanese tide had swelled as far as India's borders and the Aleutians, engulfing British, Dutch, French, and American territories in its wake.

Now the lines were drawn: on one side aggressor powers which had conquered immense areas of the world and meant to conquer more; on the other Britain, the United States, and Russia with their allies, a disparate group forced to hang together if only to avoid hanging separately.* War spread its wings over all continents: a new kind of war, not only in its scale but in its limitless implications. For, if Japan and Italy visualized gigantic gains from their aggressions, Germany hoped that hers would bring her dominion of the world.* * Considering the means that the twentieth century could furnish for control and conquest, the

---

* Hindsight suggests that, once the United States had been drawn in, the war's result was a foregone conclusion. Not counting the areas occupied by their enemies, the Allies had over three times the national income, almost four times the industrial power, almost double the population of the three Axis countries.

** As the SS song went:

> If the whole world lies in ruins
> What the devil do we care?
> We march on still,
> For today Germany is ours
> And tomorrow the whole world!

WORLD WAR II
1942–1945

Allied advances

Maximum extent of Axis control

Areas controlled by Vichy France

FINLAND

NORWAY

SWEDEN

Oslo

Stockholm

BALTIC SEA

NORTH SEA

ATLANTIC OCEAN

IRELAND

GREAT BRITAIN

London

NETHERLANDS

BELGIUM

LUXEMBOURG

Antwerp 1944

Arnhem?

Caen

NORMANDY INVASION 1944

Loire

Paris

FRANCE

Vichy

St. Nazaire

Bordeaux

Toulon

Barcelona

SPAIN

Madrid

PORTUGAL

Lisbon

Leningrad

ESTONIA

LATVIA

LITHUANIA

EAST PRUSSIA

Danzig

Moscow

U. S. S. R.

Don

Volga

Stalingrad

Dnieper

Kiev

1943

1943

1945

1944

Vistula

Warsaw

POLAND

CZECHOSLOVAKIA

Elbe

Hamburg

Bremen

Berlin

Potsdam

Cologne

Remagen

Rhine

Leipzig

GERMANY

Prague

Nuremberg

Munich

1945

1945

1945

1945

1944

Vienna

AUSTRIA

SWITZ.

HUNGARY

Budapest

1945

1945

Belgrade

YUGOSLAVIA

ALBANIA

ROMANIA

Bucharest

Danube

1944

BULGARIA

Sofia

Odessa

BLACK SEA

Istanbul

TURKEY

GREECE

Athens

CRETE

ADRIATIC SEA

Milan

Salò

ITALY

Florence

CORSICA

SARDINIA

Rome

Cassino

Anzio

Naples

1944

MEDITERRANEAN SEA

Palermo

SICILY

1943

MALTA

Tunis

TUNISIA

1943

1943

ALGERIA

Algiers

Oran

1942

1942

MOROCCO

1942

1942

500 miles

0

CASPIAN SEA

IRAN

IRAQ

SAUDI ARABIA

SYRIA

TRANS-JORDAN

LEBANON

PALESTINE

CYPRUS

EGYPT

El Alamein

1942

Tobruk

1942

Benghasi

LIBYA

1942

proposition was a tenable one, and no price too great for its achievement.

The really dreadful thing about such a conquest was that not only its process but also its achievement promised only slavery, terror, and destruction for millions and scores of millions. More consciously and deliberately than any previous conqueror, and even than their own allies, the Germans meant to establish the supremacy of their master race and sacrifice all other nations to their needs, exterminating some peoples, condemning others to lingering destruction, ruling and exploiting all, the basic differences among non-Germans ranging from servants through cattle, to even lower beings like the Jews or Gypsies, whose extermination was to cleanse the world.

War was again transformed into trial by combat, but its implications were sometimes worse for noncombatants than for the men at arms. From Java to the Japanese concentration camps of California and to central Europe, civilians of every age and sex were penned up, humiliated, treated as potential enemies or burdens that were expendable at best. Everywhere, great herds of prisoners were driven to more or less forced labor for their conquerors.* But the Germans added to this a refinement which only monomania could suggest: torture and murder for millions, on which an important part of their resources and organization were lavished to the extent of diverting them from the war effort itself. Much of all this went on in darkness—in night and fog as the Germans characteristically dubbed their extermination plans. At the front of the stage, in the fierce light of battle, lay the tides and eddies of a war in which the Axis powers that grasped at victory in 1941, were slowly pressed back thereafter as their enemies marshaled and organized their strength.

Allied Victory

The tide of battle turned in 1942 when the Americans began to leap-frog forward through the Pacific islands; an Anglo-American force invaded French North Africa clearing that continent of Germans and Italians, providing the base of the Free French state and a jumping-off ground for invading Europe; and Russia held the Germans on the Volga before forcing them back in 1943. The year 1943 opened with the great victory of Stalingrad which marked the turn of the Russian tide, when twenty-two German divisions cut off in the ruins of that Volga city were forced to capitulate. Then, as the Russians rolled slowly westward, the Allies began advancing north through the Italian peninsula. Mussolini fell, escaping to head a make-believe Fascist state in the shadow of

---

* German forced labor policies provided resistance movements in occupied countries with recruits, most of whom would have preferred to stay at home but who, after 1942, preferred outlawry to slave labor in heavily bombed German factories.

the Alps, while Italy signed an armistice and became a battleground in her turn. All over Europe partisan bands went into action, often led and organized by Communists but armed and supplied by the Allies whose air bombardments were pounding German cities into ruins, preparing the ground for invasion in the west.

This came on D-Day: June 6, 1944. The greatest amphibious operation of all time, commanded by General Dwight D. Eisenhower, brought into play all the experience and planning skill the Allied Command had gained in North Africa, Italy, and in scattered landing operations on the European coast. Ten thousand planes, 4,000 ships to ferry troops and supplies, 80 warships to guard the armada and use their heavy guns to flatten a way for the assault, artificial harbors to provide port facilities, eventually an underwater pipeline from England to the coast of France, contributed to success. Within a week of D-Day, over 300,000 British, Canadian, and U.S. troops had landed on Normandy beaches. By mid-August their numbers stood well over 2 million, backed up by 4 million tons of supplies carried in nearly half a million vehicles. By the end of August Paris had been freed. By September Allied forces stood on the Rhine. They would not cross it until March, 1945, and would face some of their bitterest fighting in the interval. But the war was being won.

In the east the Russians, having delivered their own country, pursued the Germans into Hungary, Romania, and the Balkans. The Germans fought desperately, the more so since Nazi propaganda made the most of the Allied demand for an unconditional surrender. Russian, American, and British troops converged through lunar landscapes that merciless retaliation bombing had brought about, made more dramatic by the progressive liberation of German death and torture camps. The last

The D-Day invasion of France as seen from an Allied landing craft.

Warder Collection

few months of war brought the Götterdämmerung, the twilight of the Nazi gods, which Hitler, the Wagnerian, always envisaged as the only alternative to victory.* Hitler and some of his close lieutenants committed suicide just before final defeat which unconditional surrender acknowledged on May 7, 1945. Their country lay in ruins all about them. Three hundred and fifteen tons of explosives had been dropped on Germany for every ton she had dropped on Britain. Over three million Germans were dead, more than twice as many maimed. Around Germany, all of Europe lay crippled and devastated by her mad grab for power and by the consequences it had brought about.

Japan, too, was being fast defeated. In July, 1945, the Allied leaders meeting at Potsdam to decide the fate of Germany and the future conduct of the war invited the Mikado to surrender. There was no reply. On August 6, the port of Hiroshima and three days later that of Nagasaki were destroyed by atomic bombs. Within a few days Japan followed her late allies to surrender.

There has been much discussion about the decision to use the atom bomb at all. But six years of desperate destruction had forged a mentality and attitudes difficult to recapture in a time of relative peace. From the Caspian to Glasgow, from Sidney to the Aleutians, men had learned the language of terror, had yearned for retaliation, had come to think of the enemy as purely evil—which he often was. In the kingdom of war destruction was coin of the realm, destruction sometimes for destruction's sake, as when England's cathedral cities were ruined or when, in one night of February, 1945, one of Europe's most beautiful old cities—Dresden—was wiped out by Allied bombardment from the air and at least 120,000 people with it (possibly twice as many): more victims than would die at Hiroshima. In winter and spring of 1945, as tens of thousands died in Germany's blazing townships, the British and their allies had reason to fear that murderous German rockets falling on their cities would soon be equipped with atomic warheads which the enemy would not hesitate to use. Japan, too, even before the 200,000 dead of the atomic raids, had suffered considerable civilian losses and stood to suffer more. The accountancy of horror becomes meaningless: enough to note that fear, suffering, hatred had made men brutes. Europe appeared "a rubble heap, a charnel house, a breeding

---

* All possibility of any other end was defeated by the failure of a desperate plot to murder Hitler at his headquarters on July 20, 1944. Hitler escaped with a light concussion and almost all conspirators were brutally executed. Most of them had been Christian Conservatives and German patriots, senior officers or civil servants, diplomats or clergymen, who envisaged a compromise peace that would allow Germany to keep some of Hitler's conquests without Hitler. Their success might have allowed Germany to collapse in the Italian fashion. Their failure meant that she would fight to the finish.

Few buildings stand in Hiroshima after the atomic bomb.

ground of pestilence and hate," as Churchill still described her two years later. Nor was there any hope as there had been in 1918; and that proved an advantage, for there were no illusions this time to embitter men. Hope rose like a mist over the ruins, and men scarcely spared a glance for it.

"The end of the war is simply the end of this war," noted Jean-Paul Sartre in 1945. "The future is not committed: we don't believe anymore in the end of wars . . . but one has to bet. The dying war leaves man naked, without illusions, abandoned to his own forces, having learned at last that he can count only on himself."

Chapter 12

NATIONAL COUNTERPOINT: INTERNAL AFFAIRS SINCE 1918

The internal affairs of the individual countries unfolded at different rates and in different ways. We return now to look at each of the countries, taking them up in the aftermath of the First World War and carrying them to the present day. In all this, 1945 stands as a great watershed. The quarter century since 1945, during which particular national developments are less significant than *European* politics as such and Europe itself can be treated adequately only as part of the wider world, will be surveyed in Chapter 21.

If the march-past begins this time with Russia—perhaps least European or representative of the great powers—this is in order to establish from the start *the* great event of the twentieth century: a revolution of world consequence yet of peculiarly Russian coloring; a movement that saw itself as the fulfillment of a long tradition which placed 1917 after 1776, 1789, 1848, and 1871, yet that unraveled in a quite different way; finally, an event (and the society it created) in terms of which the men and politics of our century have largely defined themselves.

Germany follows. If Russian history stays stubbornly marginal to common European experience, that of Germany is central and, in this period, crucial. Where England and France dominated the culture and politics of Europe during previous centuries, Germany grasps the lead late in the nineteenth century, grimly maintains it despite her setbacks, becomes the last power to assert (or attempt asserting) European supremacy in a wider world.

Italy, too, makes a brief gesture in the same direction, rasher but just as catastrophic in its ending. Like Germany, Italy is a newcomer among the *nations*, born in the nineteenth century out of diplomatic maneuvers and a few swift wars, a heterogeneous coagulation of states, each boasting a tradition older and more enduring than that of the new nation-state, united by the will of a minority, kept united by determined dreams as much as by interest or habit. Like Germany, too, Italy feels at a disadvantage for having entered the world scene too late as a unified nation, and tries to make up for it by acting in haste. Impatient and sometimes violent self-assertion marks its international stance; patchy, sporadic, and uneven activity provides the hallmark of internal policies.

None of these three nations—Russia, Germany, Italy—has a tradition of liberal institutions developing in time. All represent first the authoritarian, then the totalitarian forms that would be one European answer to the problems of mass democracy.

France and Britain follow: older nations that had led the field in the nineteenth century, almost imperceptibly giving way thereafter until the trend accelerates and the Second World War, at last, reveals decline in the most brutal light. Different as they are, the atmosphere and institutions of the United Kingdom and of France represent another possible response to the emancipation of the masses, while, on the other hand, their political fortunes illustrate the connection (more evident, more urgent today than it has ever been before) between productivity and power.

The other countries that are mentioned had their hour of glory some time before, or never had it at all. They struggle not for dominion but simply for survival or for recognition. Their significance is incidental, like Spain's—arena of a civil war transformed into the first armed encounter between Fascists and their foes; like Austria—rump of the Habsburg empire whose clumsy attempts at self-preservation set off the First World War; like the vast and varied area from Baltic to Aegean that furnished the last debatable lands of Europe and its unfailing powderkeg. Most of the time such countries do not decide, they just endure. At certain moments, though, some desperate or foolhardy gesture may turn a pawn into a pivotal figure—as in 1914 and again in 1939.

The second great war of the century precipitated the ruin which the first began, putting an end not only to an epoch but to a way of life. As with the swordsman who thought his opponent's blow had missed him until he shook his head,* the world supremacy of Europe, the

* It fell off.

social supremacy of the upper classes, the commercial or diplomatic initiative of heretofore sovereign exchanges and marketplaces, all collapsed at once.

Each of the following sections sketches not only the collapse but the recovery that followed. The interesting aspect of the post-1945 years, however, is that what was done in them was done no longer in terms of European initiatives, models, aspirations, but of foreign ones. Economic recovery, the shaping of new alliances, the abandoning of colonial aspirations, the patching up of political and financial crises, allowed for an extra-European factor. This was new.

So was the mass fulfillment of what, until that time, had been premonitions: mass politics, mass markets, mass education, mass access to culture (and concomitant mass indifference to it). Hitler had failed to conquer Europe. But he succeeded in pushing her over the brink of a nineteenth century that had persisted beyond its time. Those institutions that continued to subsist did so under suspended sentence. And we shall see in Chapter 21 that even the greatest political invention of the modern age, the national state, was to be called in question.

Russia

In the midst of chaos the Bolsheviks had hammered together an administrative structure, while the ruthless leadership of Leon Trotsky forged a Red Army more successful than the tsarist one. They had not only to reconquer but to re-educate a whole nation, as their French predecessors had had to do; and they accepted the precept Saint-Just had formulated that "what makes a republic is the total destruction of those opposed to it." In 1920, one of the Commissars, Zinoviev, admitted that he and his fellows had never expected they would have "to resort to so much terror or find our hands so bloodstained." Terror was supplemented by conscription of wealth, direction of labor, food levies, wages paid in kind when money lost all value. For three years the Bolsheviks fought for dear life over a ravaged country where men stumbled through famine and terror, not knowing whence their death would come.* War communism was a disaster, but it pulled them through. By 1920 Russia turned out 5 per cent of the steel, 6 per cent of the textiles, about half of the grain produced before the war. Transport had broken down, consumer goods were impossible to find, 7 million had died since 1917, 5 million or more would die of famine in the Great

---

* In 1918 the Suprematist painter Ivan Puni (Jean Pougny) glued an empty plate to a canvas—the first provocative statement of hunger at a time when war and revolution made hunger a matter of fact.

EUROPE AFTER WORLD WAR II

ZONES OF OCCUPATION:

British | American
French | Russian

BERLIN

CITY LIMITS

SOVIET SECTOR

FRENCH SECTOR

BRITISH SECTOR

BRANDENBURG GATE

TEMPLEHOF AIRPORT

AMERICAN SECTOR

10 miles

Potsdam

Moscow

U.S.S.R.

Leningrad

FINLAND

BALTIC SEA

Stockholm

SWEDEN

Oslo

NORWAY

Copenhagen

DENMARK

Hamburg

Bremen

NETHERLANDS

Amsterdam

The Hague

Brussels

BELGIUM

LUX.

Bonn

GERMANY

Berlin

Potsdam (See inset)

Leipzig

Dresden

Frankfurt

Nuremberg

Zurich

SWITZERLAND

Geneva

Danzig

Warsaw

POLAND

Cracow

CZECHOSLOVAKIA

Prague

Vienna

AUSTRIA

Budapest

HUNGARY

Belgrade

YUGOSLAVIA

ROMANIA

Bucharest

BULGARIA

Sofia

ALBANIA

GREECE

Athens

Trieste

ADRIATIC SEA

ITALY

Rome

Milan

CORSICA

SARDINIA

SICILY

MEDITERRANEAN SEA

Marseilles

FRANCE

Paris

GREAT BRITAIN

London

NORTH SEA

ATLANTIC OCEAN

500 miles

SPAIN

Madrid

PORTUGAL

Lisbon

BLACK SEA

TURKEY

Ankara

Yalta

CYPRUS

Drought of 1921 and the following winter. Seven years of chaos since 1914 had taken some 28 million lives. But Bolshevism was firmly in the saddle. In 1920 the last serious threat to the new regime—a Polish attempt to conquer the Ukraine—had been repulsed to the gates of Warsaw; and, though that penetration was followed by defeat, an armistice with Poland was concluded in the fall. The last White forces were ousted before the year had ended. Peace returned: a peace of exhaustion.

The Bolshevik revolution had succeeded at first because it promised what an immense majority of Russians wanted: peace and land; then, because the tightly organized and well-directed Bolsheviks faced no real institutional opposition and their enemies never really united against them; lastly because in the civil war the peasantry was on their side. But now the peasantry was restive and the sympathetic revolutions the Bolsheviks had hoped for in other lands were burned out or crushed. Soviet Russia, devastated by civil war, was left to make its way alone. Then, in March, 1921, the sailors of the naval base at Kronstadt, outside Petrograd, who had helped the Bolsheviks into power, took arms against them calling for "a third revolution," for Soviets not dominated exclusively by Bolsheviks—the kind of Soviets the October Revolution had envisaged, without dictatorship, coercion, or bureaucracy. The mutiny was put down but it forced the Communist Party (as the Bolsheviks had renamed themselves in 1918) to a new course designed to provide the country with a respite and the party dictatorship with a safety valve of wan prosperity.

The New Economic Policy (NEP, 1921–1927) sponsored by Lenin was in the economic sphere a kind of Bolshevik Thermidor, only self-executed, nearly suspending the advance of revolution by temporary concessions to what Marx had once described as rural idiocy. To reconcile the peasants and encourage them to provide more food for the starving towns, grain levies and requisitions were replaced by a limited grain tax, inspiring farmers to plant more and make a profit, re-creating a class of *kulaks*—richer and more productive peasants—and ending in a general upswing that affected both industry and trade. Within a year or two, three-fourths of the country's retail trade was in private hands. While the strategic heights of the economy continued to be controlled by the state, NEP men played an increasingly important role as middlemen, traders, retailers, and even manufacturers of consumer goods.

Determined attempts were also made to re-establish relations with other countries, attract capital and technicians from outside, revive exchanges without which the Russian economy panted for oxygen. Russia's greatest hope in this direction lay in German resentment of Versailles and Germany's readiness to grasp at any straw to further her revenge. In 1922, the Treaty of Rapallo, settling outstanding differences between Germany and Russia, marked the co-operation of the two "pariah nations" as Lloyd George called them. But this itself harked back to earlier trade relations, to a common hostility to Poland, and to certain secret agreements concluded in 1921 whereby German armament factories were set up in Russia, German advisers helped to train the Red Army, and German credit speeded the country's industrialization.

Behind the relatively liberal façade of NEP, party power grew. The more concessions the Bolsheviks made, the less criticism they tolerated, for the more criticism was likely to be effective. This was the period when the tolerated remnants of open opposition—Social Revolutionaries or Mensheviks—were finally "liquidated": a term which, in those days, meant that they were forced into the Communist Party, into exile, into silence. This was also when the Soviet system was finally structured into two parallel hierarchies. On the one hand, the Soviets, their All-Russian Congress, its Central Executive Committee, and the small, ultimately effective Council of Peoples' Commissars. On the other hand, the great structure of the Communist Party whose members staffed most government posts, a state within the state, with its own professional party men—the *apparatchiki*. As we have seen happen in other cases, the bigger the party organization, the less influence individual members had in it and the more power fell to the men running the central office: ultimately the general secretary of the party committee, after 1922 a Georgian, Joseph Stalin (1879–1953).

Stalin: A Man of Steel

A lonely, harsh and self-sufficient man, Stalin was one of the few Bolshevik leaders who did not really know the West. Trained in a hard school, he had left an Orthodox seminary for the dangerous life of an underground organizer, occasionally spiced with banditry to replenish party coffers, and paid the penalties of his grim, gray devotion in prison and Siberian exile. Commissar for National Minorities after the November Revolution, he was accounted a figure of the second class, less brilliant than Trotsky or Bukharin, less articulate than Zinoviev, less learned or

Warder Collection

Joseph Stalin and party officials in the late 1920's.

intelligent than any. Experience showed him to be cruel, vindictive, un-scrupulous, cunning, intolerant, and ruthless; a great manipulator and a very great ruler in the Russian tradition.

It was in 1922 that the first of a series of strokes forced Lenin gradually to give up the reins of power and ushered in the struggle for succession which began in real earnest after Lenin's death in 1924. The chief apparent claimant for succession was Trotsky, the organizer of Red victory in the civil war and Lenin's personal lieutenant. Great orator and organizer, capable of inspiring devotion and hatred, moody, remarkably bad at intrigue and compromise, vain, headstrong, intolerant, un-cooperative, Trotsky was a devoted Socialist, an inspired theorist, a fine writer, but too aware of his superiorities to work well in harness with anyone he did not respect as he respected Lenin.

Between 1924 and 1927 the succession struggle rent the party, first between Stalin and Trotsky, then between Stalin and the men who had been his allies against Trotsky. The arguments exchanged in these debates are in a sense irrelevant, for men changed their arguments as they changed their sides and, finally, when he had won, even before Trotsky had been sent off into exile in 1929, Stalin was going to adopt most of his rival's case. There was one fundamental issue, however, in which Stalin triumphed. Dissidents, frequently associated with Trotsky, had asked for the possibility of free discussion *within* the party before decisions were made, though never disputing the necessity for discipline thereafter. Stalin had argued for the monolithic domination of all from the party's center. His point of view marked Russia and the party for a generation and, indeed, for more.

Stalin also got the better of the debate between the partisans of continued world-wide revolutionary endeavor and those who, like himself, felt that they had underestimated the resilience of the capitalist system and overestimated the revolutionary will or power of the Western workers. Unable to rely on the kind of aid Lenin had hoped for, Russia had to resign herself to build socialism in one country. This did not mean forever. The rise of fascist movements—especially after 1929—was taken as the last desperate attempt of the capitalist order to halt inevitable decline by using force. In time, capitalism was bound to break under the accumulated weight of its own contradictions and socialism would then inherit the earth. It was up to Communist parties to accelerate this coming and, world revolution once deferred, such parties became largely the instruments of Russian policy. But it was up to Russia to avoid the dangers of its own contradictions which had, by the late 1920's, created serious economic quandaries.

Under the market economy of the NEP, greater agricultural production could be had only by offering the peasants consumer goods that they could buy with their profits. Consumer goods could be provided in adequate quantities only by sacrificing the investment in heavy equipment and industry, without which Russia would remain a tributary of the West. In any case, the fragmented structure of peasant holdings was inefficient. Only large-scale cultivation could provide the surpluses that would feed the country and its expanding economy. And this, the theory went, could only be achieved by taking away from individual peasants the plots of land won in the revolution itself. The choice the Communist Party faced was whether to drift toward a modified capitalism, or take drastic action to turn a backward agricultural economy into an industrial power by ruthlessly cutting consumption and comforts in order to plow all capital back into industrial growth. Each alternative was fraught with danger: the way of facility would spell the doom of a Communist party which had denied the reasons of its being by jettisoning principle; the other was a gamble against the wishes of most Russian people, demanding gigantic exertions—the sacrifice of the present for a postulated future. Yet there was never really any choice. As Stalin said in a speech he made in 1931: "We are fifty or a hundred years behind the advanced countries. We must make good this lag in ten years. Either we do it, or they crush us." If Communism was to survive and prove itself in Russia, "socialism in one country" was the only alternative. And that country was one whose historical tradition had always disregarded the human cost of any enterprise. Now, Communist doctrine encouraged the leadership to disregard the sufferings of all but proletarians. And who the proletarians were, they alone defined. Costs counted little. Final accounts would anyway be balanced in the books of historical inevitability. What counted were not individuals but classes, not entities but collectivities, not the present but the future alone.

In 1928 NEP was discarded for a new socialist offensive designed to build up heavy industry and collectivize the land, according to objectives set out in a series of five-year plans. The military verbiage of battle was appropriate, for casualties were catastrophic on all fronts. An American engineer who helped to build the great ironworks of Magnitogorsk compared the losses of the enterprise to those in the battle of the Marne. In the countryside things were still worse. The *kulaks* and others who stood out against forcible collectivization were murdered or left to starve. Stubborn resistance by the peasants was fought with terror and mass deportation. Collectivization created chaos, shortages and famine led to bitterness and unrest, evoking further repression. Between 1928 and 1933 the number of horses and cattle in the Soviet Union decreased by more than half, that of sheep and pigs by two-thirds. By that time, however, that is in 1933, four-fifths of peasant households, two-thirds of the country's grain lands, were organized in collective farms. State farms held a further tenth of the land and a million workers. Supplies of grain and foodstuffs began to increase again, and there was no more fear that the cities would go hungry. When the first Five-Year Plan reached fulfillment, ahead of schedule in 1932, Russia had become the third industrial producer of the world. Between 1929 and 1939 its productivity increased 400 per cent. The thought that she had more ground to gain and that productivity per head remained lower than in the West could not obscure the fact that she was now, with the United States and Germany, the greatest industrial power in the world.

Many of the ideals of the original revolution had been sacrificed to the achievement of the Plan. A more intense dictatorship of the proletariat went along with the reassertion of lower middle-class morality, increasingly enforced against all the socially disturbing experiments of the past decade: free love, divorce, abortion, progressive education, abstract art, expressionist poetry. Even equal wages were banned, dismissed as petty bourgeois by the petty bourgeois who were busily replacing the dictatorship of the proletariat with their own. The slogan "From each according to his abilities, to each according to his needs" was rewritten to replace "needs" with "labor." Equality, branded a petty bourgeois notion, had to give way to true socialist competition; and this was prompted by incentives like piece rates and selective wages, social recognition for the hardest workers, medals, privileges, larger rations of food and better lodgings for heroes of labor, like the miner Stakhanov, who was able to do the work of nine men in one day.

It was certainly a kind of progress when heroism was connected with activities linked with construction rather than destruction; and when battle losses were incurred in building dams and steel works rather than waging war. But the costs were great. Along with the freedom of business and agricultural enterprise, freedom of labor was also stifled and labor unions became an arm of the state. Along with the discipline of the Communist Party, its control of private and public life and culture was immeasurably tightened. Lenin's huge tomb in Moscow began to look as if it were, in Isaac Deutscher's words, "only the pedestal for his successor"—but also the repository of doomed hopes for the freer society Lenin had envisaged.

Stalin's dictatorship grew, finding its justification in the dangers that increased as the international situation changed after 1932. The threat of hostile capitalist states, abated in the twenties, grew more acute after the rise of fascism. Just as the Nazis rose in reaction to the Communist menace, so the worst excesses of Stalinism followed their coming to power in Germany, Nazism and Communism reflecting each other like deforming mirror images. The USSR considered itself in a state of siege, threatened by enemies outside and treachery within. After 1934, the second Five-Year Plan (1933–1937), destined to provide some of the consumer goods (shoes, clothes) and lodgings that were so badly lacking, had to be revised in view of the Nazi danger. The tightening of a tension already hard to bear seems to have aggravated the internal strains and played a part in the great purges by which, between 1936 and 1938, Stalin eliminated critics and potential critics of his rule. Probably half or more of men and women holding key positions in industry, army, and every sector of society were ousted, deported, or killed. Two-thirds of the diplomatic corps and over two-thirds of the Communist Party Central Committee were liquidated; over half the membership of the Party were expelled. In the Red Army alone, during 1937 and 1938, the *Yezhovchina* (so named after the Secret Police head who was in due course killed himself) eliminated 3 out of 5 marshals, 13 out of 15 army commanders, 110 out of 195 division commanders and all the commanders of military districts. A fine bag!

In this light, the Western powers' reluctance to ally with Russia becomes more understandable. But it is well to look at Russian policy in Communist perspective too. As they saw it, revolution had to learn to live in a largely hostile capitalist world, to adjust its diplomacy to the standards obtaining outside Russia and its aims to isolation. Socialism in one country was possible at great cost; living alone was not. After 1921 the diplomacy of the Soviet Union was dedicated to lessening isolation and defending its regime. The Treaty of Rapallo in 1922 inaugurated a more forthcoming phase based on Russo-German collaboration. Nonaggression pacts were signed with whoever would subscribe to them. When Germany turned reactionary, Moscow was led to gradual adjustment toward the West, while trying to maintain good relations even with the Nazis until 1934 when Hitler concluded a German-Polish nonaggression pact, putting an end to the Rapallo policy. A few months later the Soviet Union joined the League of Nations, reopened formal relations with the United States, concluded mutual assistance pacts with France and Czechoslovakia (1935), tried to put teeth into the League, initiated the Popular Front policy of co-operation with anyone who opposed Fascism. But collective security failed before Franco-British appeasement, and their reluctance to co-operate with a Communist regime just involved in the great purges. So Stalin turned back toward Rapallo, fulfilling its promise, after repeated snubs from the democracies, in the German-Soviet pact of August, 1939, which brought its fruits in fresh partition of Poland, reannexation of the Baltic lands and Bessarabia, the gain of Finnish territories designed to protect Leningrad. Ready enough to supply Germany, afford her bases, support her abroad, and even hand over to Nazi revenge German and other Communists who had taken refuge in Russia, Stalin was not prepared to concede her domination in the Balkans and to turn eastward as Hitler wanted. Romania, Bulgaria, and Turkey he would not admit as parts of the German sphere. Friction over rival greeds convinced Hitler that war must come —the sooner the better. The 22nd of June, 1941, marked the end of an era and Russia was to emerge from war a great power at last.

A great power, but in a sorry state. Russian military casualties seem to have been around 10 million but some 18 million men and women had died in all and the demographic effects of these losses were still being felt in the 1960's. A quarter of all the nation's property had been destroyed: 17,000 towns, 70,000 villages, 31,000 factories, 84,000 schools, 40,000 miles of railroads, 45,000,000 horses and pigs and cattle. All was to do again. But Stalin also faced another problem. War had loosened the firm Communist structure, given more influence to the soldiers, introduced a disrupting contact with the West, threatened the rigid authority of the regime and the dominion of the party. Previous wars had brought reform or revolution. If either was to be avoided this time, Communist power must not be relaxed but consolidated; and Stalin knew only one way of doing this: by force. The Soviet Union would be subjected to a fresh repression, as murderous and brutal as the purges of the 1930's and which only ended with Stalin's death in 1953.*

Whereas after the revolution the country had taken nearly a decade to reattain its prewar production level, after 1945 this was done in four years. Russia rebuilt and simultaneously rearmed, exploding the first of its atomic bombs in 1949. The great difference now lay in the substructure of specialists and skilled men, administrators, technicians, engineers, and workers who had been lacking in the 1920's and whom the great training and educational efforts of the 1930's and 40's built up in numbers adequate to support and rebuild a great modern economy. By 1955 the population had grown beyond 200 million chiefly in the large cities,** while the industrial center shifted eastward to the Ural Mountains and beyond. The productivity now doubled every twelve years —a phenomenal rate of growth when kept up. Today, productivity per inhabitant is comparable to that of the West European countries behind which Russia had lagged so long. Indeed, by 1950 the Soviet Union ranked as the second industrial power in the world.

Russia After Stalin

Stalin's death was followed by an intricate power struggle in which personalities and factions engaged in shadowy battles for control of the state. After the elimination of Lavrenti Beria, head of the Secret Police † and of a passing figure, G. M. Malenkov, power was progressively assumed by the Ukrainian-born master of the party machine, Nikita S. Khrushchev (b. 1894). Khrushchev is best remembered for his great speech of 1956 before the Twentieth Congress of the Communist Party, with its bitter denunciations of the dead dictator and of the "personality cult" which had grown up around him. Equally crucial, Khrush-

---

* De Gaulle, who saw Stalin at the end of the war, noted the "shadowy charm" of the figure he recognized as a great Tsar. The shadows would be more in evidence than the charm in the last years of Stalin's bloody greatness.

** Characteristically, 6 per cent of Russia's population lives in two-thirds of the territory, 6 per cent of the country's territory accommodates half the population.

† When Beria was arrested and executed in the summer of 1953, subscribers to the *Great Soviet Encyclopedia* were ordered to cut out the article devoted to him, remit it to the authorities, and replace it with a description of the Bering Sea.

Nikita Khrushchev
in what became a
characteristic pose.

chev attempted to heal some of the wounds that Stalinist excesses had
left behind, releasing a good many of the political prisoners, unclamping
the stifling regime of censorship and terror, increasing the availability
of consumer goods, mending bridges broken with Tito and even with
the West, with whom he envisaged a relationship of "peaceful co-exis-
tence" that allowed for competition and subversion but stopped short
of open war.

In 1964, Khrushchev was forced into retirement by younger and more
businesslike politicians: notably Leonid Brezhnev, his second in command
of the Party Secretariat, and Nicolai Kosygin, chairman of the crucial
State Planning Commission. Even more than their predecessors, the
new rulers of a society where masters still endure though there are no
more slaves insisted on the collective nature of the political leadership.
They seem to represent the institutionalization of a revolution long past
for the majority of their subjects, a government of bureaucrats and
technicians interested more in internal efficiency and external power
than in the proletarian insurrections to which they still pay homage on
the first of May.

The Soviet Union was still behind the United States, which it longed
to overtake. In the 1960's, whereas 12 per cent of America's active
population worked in agriculture, some 45 per cent of Soviet citizens
did so. And, while collectivized agriculture had increased over-all production, it had not kept up with the growing population *or* with its
expanding needs.* But Soviet society is now modern, disposing of an
army of researchers, scientists, technicians, and engineers. It still lacks the
possibilities of free enterprise in its most fundamental sense of research,
interpretation, decision, and initiative; and it is not sure that the abundance which modern means permit and to which Russians, like every-

---

* In 1969, the Third *Kolkhoze* (collective farms) Congress, first in thirty-four years,
enlarged the area of land each farmer can work for his own account from about a half
acre to one and one-half acres. The measure was explained by the fact that over half
the eggs and vegetables, over a third of the meat, sold on the internal markets of the
U.S.S.R. are produced on these plots.

body else aspire, will be attained without it. Not only literature, scholarship, and the arts, but economics, too, are hamstrung by survivals of the Stalin age—perhaps, in the first place, by survivors guarding vested interests by repression. Lenin had defined socialism as "the power of the Soviets plus electrification." Russia has the latter, but the former is only a memory. Today, the ideology that inspired the years of revolution has long run down from dynamism to dogma. Yet the ruling Communist Party cannot dispense with it, for it provides the authority of its continued rule. Nor is it sure that an anachronistic faith cannot maintain itself and exercise a strong influence within societies which could do well without it. It was Marx who said that a people that oppresses another could not be a free people. But perhaps few peoples really care for freedom. Especially those who have never known it.

Meanwhile, the immensity of what has been achieved remains impressive. The great grandsons of serfs, the grandsons of illiterate peasants, are now sophisticated writers, scientists, and organizers. Literacy, industrialization, urbanization, emancipation from the hold of foreign capital, have turned a primitive, backward people into civilized men who can control and marshal their energies and resources to constructive ends. All this was done at immense human and material cost. While there is no compensation for human suffering, one may reflect that similar though less deliberate suffering elsewhere had produced far less.

Germany

The Weimar Republic

In January, 1919, as the Spartacists were put down by the army, Liebknecht and Luxemburg arrested and killed, a National Assembly gathered at Weimar under army guard to write a constitution. Germany now became a federal republic in which most states survived as separate units but the old privileges were replaced by universal suffrage and proportional representation. This last encouraged fractionalism and the survival of political factions at a time when unity should have been paramount. It removed all possibility of real majority government, ensuring that power would be exercised by coalitions and hence remain unstable and weak. As the republic which it consecrated was being inaugurated in the Weimar state theater, fly sheets fluttered down from the gallery nominating a mentally deranged poet for its first president. The Assembly elected Ebert, son of a tailor, himself a saddler by trade, to the presidency; and Ebert, as he had proved, embodied the traditional German spirit by now solidly established in the lower middle class.

514

The Weimar Republic lived out its short span under this contradictory aegis of a conventional spirit backed by the army and operating in the midst of Dadaist confusion. Its governments never quite accepted the terms of peace.* And the country never quite accepted its governments. Social Democrats, who had won one-third of the voters in prewar elections, won nearly half in the elections of 1919. But they were weakened by internal divisions and, after the formation of a Communist party, could never hope for a majority again. In 1921 Social Democrats were down to 20 per cent of a poll where Communists figured for almost 13 per cent; in 1928 the Social Democratic share was 30 per cent and the Communists' 10. Meanwhile, first the Catholic Center, then the Moderates increased in influence as the Reichstag (under the effect of proportional representation) divided into groups maneuvering for office in various coalitions. Seventeen coalition governments held office between 1920 and 1930: all of them—whether Socialists shared in them or not—of a conservative hue. In 1925 President Ebert died and the Left's weakness became more apparent: the Socialists by themselves received far less support than the Nationalist candidates. A hastily patched up coalition in which the Socialists supported a center candidate for a second turn was defeated when the right-wing parties put up the greatest military hero of the war, Marshal Paul von Hindenburg (1847–1934). The Centrist would have been elected had not almost two million Communist votes gone to a Communist leader. But in the eyes of the extreme Left there was no real difference between the Centrists and Hindenburg, and very little more between the Socialists and the Center.

That this had come about was partly due to the Socialists themselves. As usual, their moderate instincts clashed with their professions and thus prevented any consistent action on their part. The Left could see that the sympathies of men in power went toward Nationalists, not toward the workers. In March, 1920, the Free Corps which Socialists had helped create turned against the government, forcing it to flee Berlin. This was the Kapp putsch, named after the minor functionary whom the rebels hoped to make head of the state. The putsch was put down only by a general strike forcing its collapse. Then the restored coalition government used army units (which had neither supported Kapp nor moved against their Free Corps comrades) to put down workers who seemed too sanguine over their brief triumph, while military rebels went unpunished. A few months before, after the Red Republic in Bavaria had been crushed, 2,209 persons had been sentenced to long terms of prison or to death. Now the courts handed out one sentence only, and that for "honorary confinement."

Meanwhile, the determination of all German governments not to

---

* Philipp Scheidemann (1865–1939), a Social Democrat and Ebert's chief lieutenant during the war, became prime minister of the first Republican government in 1918 and resigned a year later, unwilling to accept the peace terms of Versailles.

fulfill the reparation clauses of the Versailles treaty, stiffened by a Nationalist terrorist campaign in which several hundred insufficiently patriotic politicians were murdered,* was bringing dire results. Reparation demands, though excessive, were not impossible to meet pending an agreement. Between 1933 and 1939 Hitler would spend seven times more a year on rearmament than his predecessors were asked to spend on reparations and did not. But, to finance payments, the tax structure would have to be seriously reformed and this the country's rulers would not do. Not only would it hit the rich too hard (as they were hit already in Great Britain), but it would imply their readiness to come to terms by showing that they could fulfill them. They preferred to default and take the consequences. In January, 1923, French and Belgian troops, claiming that Germany would not fulfill her obligations, occupied the Ruhr, center of German industry and major source of the Republic's revenues. The German government called for passive resistance and found support among all sections of the public. But the economic ruin that ensued set off serious troubles. "Red" governments appeared in Saxony and Thuringia, a separatist movement in the Rhineland, a monarchist movement in Bavaria followed by an attempted putsch led by General Erich Ludendorff and by Adolf Hitler, obscure leader of an even obscurer National Socialist German Workers' party. All failed, but all stressed the straits of the Republic.

Nine months of economic struggle came to an end when a new government headed by Gustav Stresemann (1878–1929) concluded that the country could not survive without the raw material, markets, and capital of the West, came to terms with the French, and secured American and British help in exchange for "fulfillment" in the future. Stresemann and Hjalmar Schacht, head of the Reichsbank, stabilized the situation and quickly secured a new agreement on the reparation proposals. Between 1924 and 1931 over 35 billion marks poured into Germany in foreign loans and investments, mostly from the United States. In the same period Germany paid the Allies 21 billion marks in reparations.

The second half of the 1920's was a time of prosperity for Germany and for Europe. But the scars of past years were hard to heal. We know that antireparation tactics had involved unlimited inflation of the currency, the mark. At the height of the Ruhr struggle, the mark became meaningless, prices were quoted in billions, debts and savings wiped out, *rentiers* and pensioners ruined, middle and professional classes largely displaced. All internal debts were wiped out by inflation and this meant that the great bankers and industrialists emerged from it more powerful than ever. Contractual obligations collapsed. So, in their wake, did social conduct and the sense of moral obligation which is no more than a habit learned by experience and just as easily unlearned by

---

* Among them in 1922 Walther Rathenau, chief organizer of Germany's economic war effort, guilty of being Jewish.

The aging leader of the Weimar Republic, Hindenburg, followed by Hitler, Goering, and other Nazi Party members.

same. The harvest of the inflation of 1923–1924, aggravated and fulfilled by the fresh crisis of 1929–1933, was reaped within the decade. In 1929, England was almost as hard hit as Germany, and the United States harder; but German stabilizers had been injured five years before by their own policy and four years of prosperity had not brought enough recovery to restore them. The Depression meant utter catastrophe for millions. Within two years salaries fell by half, production by two-thirds, the number of unemployed rose six- and sevenfold, 80 per cent of the Germans were what contemporary estimates call "proletarianized." By 1932, the middle-class backbone of society had been broken, and great masses of once law-abiding workers were set in motion, looking for some change where any change seemed better than none.

The Thousand-Year Reich

Dictatorship appeared the only solution and the providential man who offered to bring salvation was the same Adolf Hitler whose putsch had failed in Munich in 1923. Hitler had used his brief and comfortable stay in prison to write a book—*Mein Kampf*—about his life, his theories, and plans: a hodgepodge of the national, social, and racial doctrines which flourished in Germany and Austria since the nineteenth century. His National Socialist movement advanced only slowly during the years of prosperity but, as the thirties opened, despair turned the masses toward apocalyptic doctrines of which his own was the most extreme. It looked as if Germany was splitting down the middle, between the radical Right and Left; and funds from industrialists and bankers seeking defenders against the Reds poured into Nazi coffers, nourished the party's propaganda, equipped its brown- and black-shirted storm troopers. The Nazis, who had polled 800,000 votes in the national elections of 1928, won 6.5 million two years later, 14 million in July, 1932. With 230 seats compared to 12 in 1928, they were now the largest party in the Reichstag.

Hitler as absolute ruler reviews his passing troops.

In the new elections of November the Nazi poll fell by 2 million votes. But by that time all other combinations and permutations had been exhausted and two months later, in January, 1933, Hitler became Chancellor, heading a coalition government of Nationalists and Nazis. In the elections of February, 1933, over 17 million Germans voted for Nazi candidates. The Hitler coalition. could now boast what no German government had known: a clear parliamentary majority.

The new Reichstag voted a bill which practically abrogated the Weimar Constitution and which permitted the government to pass laws without parliamentary endorsement. Only Social Democrats voted against the bill, though even they were ready to endorse the government's assertive foreign policy and were repaid by dissolution in June, 1933—as were the Nazis' Nationalist allies. The Nationalist leaders, who had entertained some hope of manipulating the inexperienced Nazis, were soon shuffled out of the way and Nationalist troops absorbed in the NSDAP* by a government which did not mind drastic actions. The Communists were banned, the Social Democrats broken, the unions taken over and incorporated in a Nazi labor front, the separate state governments abolished and the states totally integrated in the Reich, united under a central administration for the first time in German history. Brown-shirted Nazi storm troops (SA) and black-uniformed SS elite corps supplemented police in a campaign of unlimited violence against all opponents. May Day was converted into a Nazi labor festival, industrial and employer interests thoroughly subordinated to the party. By July, 1933, Hitler could declare all parties dissolved and Germany a one-party state.

But if Germany was subordinated to the party, the party must be subordinate to Hitler. The SA was the organization of the more radical party militants: its members and its leadership were hard to keep in line. Their rowdiness and radicalism threatened to compromise Hitler's more gradual plans and his maneuvers. In 1934 the power of the SA

* National Socialist German Workers' Party.

518

was destroyed in a few bloody days when most of its leadership were massacred. Hitler was now absolute in Germany.

The Nazis were not hampered by many economic preconceptions. Advised by Hjalmar Schacht, they were quite ready to apply whatever means they might consider necessary to refloat the economy, controlling both labor and employers. The state became Germany's greatest banker, controlling two-thirds of banking capital, directing the most important sections of industry and press, introducing social reforms, using the structure of capitalist economy as the instrument of its policies. The profit motive remained the essential motor of production, but its direction was henceforth in public hands and managers themselves fulfilled a public function. Private enterprises, regarded as public trusts, were taken over, controlled at second hand, or left to operate freely, as expediency might dictate. Hitler had come to power just as the economic crisis was beginning to subside. His economic policies accelerated recovery, priming the economic pump and stimulating business. Rearmament, public works, loans and subsidies to private enterprises, began to absorb unemployment before the year was out and made for full employment by 1936. By that time industrial production had returned to the high-water mark of 1929. By 1939 it was 33 per cent higher, more than double what it had been when Hitler came to power. Labor was controlled to keep wages down, and prices were controlled to make wages acceptable. The deficit spending that had been rejected for economic reasons was enthusiastically accepted for military and patriotic ones. No one really had to choose between guns and butter: guns meant butter (or at least margarine) for far more people than had enjoyed any before. Foreign trade was managed by way of exchange controls, import and export licenses, bilateral agreements with other countries. German conquests after 1939 simply set the seal on what these economic policies had begun, completing the economic integration of a Europe focused on German needs.

Such marked success was bound to make the Nazis very popular. All Germans (except Jews and political opponents who were mercilessly persecuted) lived better, felt better, prouder, more at ease in the new society of the Nazis. Even intellectuals came to terms with it. With few exceptions most of them had opposed or ignored the Weimar Republic: too dull, too conformist, too decadent. On this Expressionists, Realists, and Idealists, Right and Left, Communists and Nazis, could agree: the Republic was not a cause fit for a man's commitment. The greatest German intellectuals—men like the historian Friedrich Meinecke, the economist Werner Sombart, Thomas Mann, and the sociologist Max Weber—distrusted democracy, which they thought ill suited to German character and tradition, preferring a regime in which the people would be represented by an elite . . . like them. Even the president elected by a direct vote (an Americanism advocated by Max Weber) was

Warder Collection

Victims of Belsen, one of Hitler's concentration camps for "political" prisoners.

not meant to reflect the opinions of the electorate but the call of collective will, a national spirit close to that which Rousseau had once imagined. Election was a kind of mystery and German intellectuals were its muddled prophets. No wonder that they found Weimar disappointing and the Third Reich which Hitler introduced much closer to their ideals, reinforcing the notion that social problems must be resolved from above.

Another German intellectual ideal fulfilled in the Third Reich was that heroic and virile concept which we find in certain works of Wagner or some youth movements of the time that dreamed of purity, of a new order, and of a providential leader who would show the way.* All this made for a tendency to purify the horrid democratic society by turning inward to secret male societies from which women (weak, corrupt, corrupting) were excluded; to suck up vitality from primitive sources and to recognize it (again) in that figure with which romantic tradition from Hegel to Wagner and Nietzsche had filled their dreams: the providential leader. Thus, many intellectuals welcomed Hitler and extolled his Nationalist revolution, pointing to Goethe and Schiller as the first National Socialists. Others, like Erich Kästner, author of brilliant, satirical children's stories, chose internal emigration, opting out while living on as best they could. Others again, like Thomas Mann, escaped abroad. But there was little danger that an active opposition should arise from this quarter.

In effect, after the first few months, Hitler met little opposition from any quarter, which must have strengthened his faith in his own star. It may even be that his fervent anti-Semitism was a device for creating

* There was a lot of this in the works of Stefan George (1868–1933), whose poems glowed with dreams of heroism and of the apocalypse. George would be quoted by Nazis and anti-Nazis, by SS, and by Count Stauffenberg, who placed the bomb that missed Hitler in July, 1944. Here is a typical passage from a poem he wrote after 1918:

When these Generals will have purged the shame
Cast from their necks the convict's chains
Nothing but honor craving in their bellies
Then, on the fields of death, in the endless tombs
Will burst the bloody light and on the clouds
Will pass the roaring armies, the fields
Shall bellow in the third assault, the supreme dread
When the dead return!

520

opponents where none existed, legislating a menace by decree in order to create and preserve that tension and struggle without which a dictatorship may prosper but a Fascist-type movement decays. Hitler had some notions of Darwin and of the struggle for existence. "Life," he once said, "is only preserved because other living things perish through struggle." The life of Germany, the life of the Nazi Party could only be ensured, like that of Aztec gods, by dint of war and blood and human sacrifice. The temples of the Nazis stood not in Munich or at Nürnberg, but in more desolate, blood-soaked places: at Dachau, at Belsen, and at Oranienburg. It is not so surprising that the concentration camp at Buchenwald should have been built around Goethe's favorite oak tree.

The Nazis and Their Prey

The crux of the Nazi regime was not its brutality (which never formed the basis of its power) but its delusions and its self-delusions. For Hitler proved that myths could be managed and stage-managed to convert a whole nation into a gigantic make-believe; and that this make-believe can create concrete results in morale, production, power, and wealth. He dipped into his own and his peers' unconscious, pulled out collective fantasies, and then proceeded to enact them, thus lending his enterprises an extraordinary force. For just as the greedy, murderous adventurers who went crusading into the Levant, the Indies, or America disguised themselves as Christian knights, so Hitler's troops and torturers put on the armor of Wagnerian heroes: Siegfried, Parsifal. We all reach back to find justification and disguise in the dressing rooms of national history; and Hitler's hordes found a martial storeroom from which they issued forth to take or break the world.

That was when the fantasies proved their power and their danger. To the Nazis the Jews were submen, bacillae, creatures of darkness, destructive and vile, a mirror reflection quite obviously of themselves. If Jews were not destroyed, they would destroy the best and highest parts of mankind and enslave the rest: just what the Nazis did propose to do. They must be massacred and those people whom they had most affected must be exterminated too, or, at least, decimated like the Russians of whom the intention was to kill 30 million, though only 20 million died in the end. Before the German millennium, then, the Jews had to be exterminated; and the war in which Germany engaged was above all meant to wipe them out, achieve that final solution of the Jewish problem which, by the summer of 1944, was having 12,000, 15,000, 22,000 Jews a day gassed, processed and cremated in Auschwitz camp alone. "The central issue of this war" repeated the Propaganda Ministry, "is the breaking of Jewish world domination." *

* That the world domination of half-witted fantasies remains unbroken was attested in Jerusalem in 1961 when Adolf Eichmann, a major cog in the extermination process, explained its failure by the fact that Hitler himself was but a puppet of "the Satanic international high finance of the Western World."

Jews, but not only Jews: men, women, children of every land and creed were scourged, tormented, delivered over to dread, degradation, death. But death itself is easy; dying, long and hard. The camps were not devoted to mere extermination, but to humiliation, torture, to the fulfillment of the guards and the dehumanization of their inmates. Hundreds and thousands were made to choke on dirt, to beg for sustenance or life or mercy seldom granted, to prey on each other—slaves tormenting slaves, mothers biting on their children's rations to gain a brief reprieve, man turning wolf to man and worse on an unheard-of scale.

What none would do to animals was done to human beings. They were drowned in cesspools, torn to pieces by dogs, strung on barbed wire, or by their fingers, or by their legs head down, raped, shot, whipped, hanged, starved to death, beaten to death, trampled to death, kicked to death, stoned to death, punched to death, frozen to death, run over by trucks or tractors, used as guinea pigs, maimed, injected with murderous drugs, castrated, sterilized, amputated, asphyxiated, electrocuted, poisoned, machine-gunned, gassed, thrown down quarries, or into pits or wells or ditches or hastily dug trenches or well prepared mass graves, or herded into ovens; but only when they had been stripped of everything, not just their personality, their dignity, their human respect, but all material things, the shabby, slender masks that we hold up toward the world: their chattels collected for the Reich's winter relief, earrings and wedding bands torn off, the gold in their teeth pried out for the Reich treasury, their hair swept into appropriate containers, their fat rendered down for grease or soap, their ashes for fertilizer.

Those who took part in this were ordinary men and women. Ordinary people who, willing or unwilling, did or helped to do these things, denouncing and arresting and marshaling and guarding and sentencing and employing and invoicing and shipping and storing; those who threw the switches for the long trains to pass, the stinking sealed long trains of cattle cars whose carriages built for eight horses or forty men held a hundred and two hundred prisoners, their refuse and their vermin, their thirst and hunger, their wailing and their fears; and all the people who stood and watched the trains go by loaded with dread; and those who read the letters from the eastern front or from the Polish occupied territories telling of these things; and those who wore the jewelry of the victims, sometimes their clothes, and knew or at least suspected what they wore; or stood and watched the great barbed wire enclosures bobbed with looming towers, saw the convoys arrive, saw the smoke rise, smelled its peculiar stench; all those who knew or guessed but did not wish to know; thousands and tens of thousands, hundreds of thousands who can still remember all these things: those who still remember them and those who have driven most of these memories out of their waking life. Many still survive, living ordinary lives, doing ordinary things in shops and factories and banks and offices and ministries and barracks and in courts of justice, bringing up ordinary children; bringing them up perhaps to think as they think themselves that all this is no more than history: dead, irrelevant, like the millions of shadowy ghosts they turned into statistics.

To Hitler, for whom God did not exist, conscience was a Jewish invention, suffering was irrelevant; only will mattered and the Providence which had assigned his mission, in whose pursuit he went his way "with the assurance of a sleepwalker." Nothing was impossible, neither the defeat of France nor the utter extermination of his enemies.* For the sake of racial principles he even sacrificed military and psychological advantages. This was what carried him first to victory, then to utter defeat. All the time the people he fascinated kept their belief in the miracles to which Hitler, like Bismarck, had accustomed them. Accepting the searing hardships of the home front, rejecting and reproving any stirring of opposition, they maintained the deadly conviction that Hitler's myths were real. After Stalingrad, German propaganda was constantly referring to the death of the Russian empress which had saved Frederick II from defeat and Prussia from division in 1762 (see p. 474). But no miraculous deaths and no miraculous weapons could intervene this time. The spirits Hitler raised now turned against him, as demons sometimes turn on witches who invoke them. In the midst of the Europe she had wasted from the Urals to the Pyrenees, Germany lay in ruins—the ruins of her dream.

Germany Partitioned

In 1945, what Hitler had described as the thousand-year Reich was divided into four zones of occupation. In the west, south, and southeast its borders returned to where they had been in 1937. In the northeast, the Russians annexed a portion of East Prussia, including the old Hohenzollern capital of Königsberg, and unilaterally endowed the Poles with all German regions east of the Oder and the western Neisse.** Meeting at Potsdam the Allies had agreed that Germany would be treated "as a single economic unit." But four-power management did not last; the Russians, remembering the devastation of their own country, treated the Germans as they had treated them: without mercy. The Westerners were more concerned about conditions in their occupation zones. Eighty

---

* In Treblinka alone, over a period of twelve months in 1942 and 1943, 800,000 Jews entered and forty survived the war. It was possible to kill 24,000 persons between 7 A.M. and 1:15 P.M. with a staff of forty SS and several hundred Ukrainians.

** The issue of Germany's eastern borders turns on whether Polish writ should run as far as the eastern Neisse, or to the western Neisse, some 200 miles beyond. In 1970, agreement between Bonn and Warsaw seemed to confirm the *status quo.*

German children help occupation forces clean military cooking utensils in return for leftover food, 1946.

cities had been partly or wholly destroyed, 600,000 civilian lives lost (ten times as many as were killed in Britain), 800,000 others maimed. A great many Germans had fled the cities that were being bombed to rubble or the advancing armies on both fronts; millions had been expelled from their homes in Czech or Polish territory. In the winter of 1946, 100,000 died of cold and hunger in Hamburg alone; in Cologne only one child in ten was of normal weight; everywhere men, women, and children lived on charity, black marketing, and prostitution, or else starved. The British and American occupiers who had been spared the experience of German occupation could not endure this prospect. They sought to set the wheels of the economy in motion and bring the people back to life again.

Soon, however, another factor entered the equation. As relations between East and West got worse, each side began to treat *its* Germans less as defeated fiends than as potential partners, handing them ever more authority over their own affairs while Cold War tension grew. The Soviet zone was given a German Communist administration. In the West, municipal government provided a base for the rebirth of national politics. Enjoying a good deal of local autonomy, the great German cities had always been the training ground of great administrators and, sometimes, of national politicians. The greatest of these would reveal himself in the Rhineland at this time. Konrad Adenauer (1876–1967) had been a Cologne municipal official since 1906, its mayor since 1917, deputy to the Prussian *Landtag* in Weimar days, and speaker of that Assembly from 1928 to 1933. Dismissed by the Nazis in 1933, reinstated in 1945 by the Americans only to be hustled out by an unfriendly British general a few months later, the authoritarian old gentleman turned from local to national politics, became leader of the newly founded Christian-Democratic Party (1948) and, in 1949, federal chancellor of the first autonomous German government—a post he retained until his reluctant retirement in 1963.

But while *Der Alte* (the old one), as he came to be known, was cast for a crucial part in the spectacular recovery of his country in the

1950's, German personalities were of secondary consequence in the decisions of the middle forties. It would be economic considerations that led to the progressive integration of the British, American, and French zones of occupation. By 1948, East and West Germany had separate currencies, governments, and economies: the Democratic Republic of Germany in the East, the Federal German Republic in the West—soon to be integrated into the economies of their respective camps, "good Germans" to their friends if not to one another.

What other Germans, after all, were left? The leading figures of the Nazi regime, tried by an Inter-Allied Military Tribunal at Nürnberg in 1945–1946 had been condemned to death (eleven cases) or to varying sentences of imprisonment. The denazification process decided by the Allies, never very thoroughly applied, affected mostly the pettier officials, those who could not hide, bribe, argue their way out or work their passage to forgiveness. Of the greatest criminals, many went underground or escaped abroad. Nor would it have been possible to do a thorough job of denazification without almost eliminating a generation that the war had already decimated.

It was natural that the men who sought to rebuild a devastated land should pay less attention to retribution than to reconstruction. Many of these men belonged to the pre-1914 generation when both Adenauer and Kurt Schumacher, who came out of a concentration camp to reconstitute the Socialist party, had begun their careers; and what they sought to restore were the virtues (and to some extent the system) of those good old days. Instead of awakening new forces they appealed to old ones: discipline, hard work, economy, respect for authority, the bourgeois virtues proved their worth even to the Social Democrats, who quietly abandoned all traces of Socialism. By the mid-1960's, far from remembering the doctrines of class warfare, Socialists had joined the Christian-Democrats in a governmental coalition; by 1969 they had replaced them as the ruling party, their leader Willy Brandt, a long-time opponent of Nazism, becoming federal chancellor.

The Federal Republic, restored to international sovereignty in 1954, had by that time recovered and multiplied the economic power which it once enjoyed. This "German miracle," as it has been called, turns out on examination to be less miraculous than it might appear. If Germany was in ruins, its industrial plant was not. Only 10 to 20 per cent of it had been put out of action and, as soon as the economy began to turn, the machines did too. As in 1923 and in 1930, financial collapse left the industrialists free of debts and the country practically free of reparations. As in the later twenties, billions of dollars in gifts and loans aided recovery. West Germany had no army and colonies to waste her money on, the sums paid for the upkeep of foreign occupation troops were almost all spent on her territory and, after 1955, her own defense expenses were lower even than the military budget of Belgium or Italy.

The Federal Republic was overcrowded. By 1970, some 60 million people lived where not quite 40 million had lived in 1949. But it could draw on a cheap, hard-working labor force, their numbers keeping down wages and hence production costs, while their demands stimulated the economy. The aid that society provided to veterans and poor was small and taxes low. Profits were plowed back into business. The large-scale industrial combines that the Allies broke up soon reformed, regaining their hold on the German market. By 1950, industrial production—in 1946 one-third of 1936—had returned to prewar figures. By 1961 the Germans were importing foreign workers to feed their factories. The standard of living rose steadily: cigarettes, which for years had replaced currency, returned to their proper use—burning; motorcycles and cars replaced bicycles; people ate fewer potatoes and more cakes, and Germany was the most valued European ally of the United States.

Here was some justification for the Russians' fears. For, while the division had come increasingly to be accepted, Communists knew that the dynamism of the great power refurbished between Rhine and Elbe might once again be turned toward its traditional frontiers in the east.

Temporary creation *par excellence,* governed from the non-capital of Bonn, once a sleepy little university town on the Rhine, the Republic's origins condemned it to run after its own definition. Adenauer thought he had found it in his dreams of a Carolingian Europe, united by common faith, from within which his part of Germany, rebuilt and consolidated, could exercise a magnetic attraction on the forsaken east. Yet this resulted only in the self-definition of an eastern rival which became the more resolute and the more conscious of its own originality the more the Federal Republic established its own. Unwilling to pay the price of the last war (that is, to accept its existing frontiers), or that of possible unification (that is, neutralization), Bonn's Germany took refuge in the good feeling that—with its free political parties (except for the banned Communists), its federal institutions, its democratic (and rather unusable) army, its parliament, and its respect for traditional virtues—it was quite unlike the Prussian-style Communist society of the GDR. But whatever its moral arguments, its best alibi rested in economic prosperity.

As the 1970's opened, the attempts of Socialist Chancellor Brandt to improve relations with Germany's eastern neighbors had eased some of the tensions, but, in a manner of speaking, the tension itself that German power generated had become a vested interest—for German nationalists and irreconcilable Communists, like those still ruling in East Berlin. The attractions of a friendly Germany might prove as dangerous, in their eyes at least, as the arms of an embattled one. It looked as if, at any rate for some time, the politics of Europe would continue to revolve around the fears of all Germany's neighbors and their anxious hope that Germany should learn to be herself not at somebody else's expense.

Italy

The 1914 war, which was highly unpopular and remarkably unsuccessful, had brought economic ruin to Italy along with formal victory. At Paris, Italian negotiators seeking to secure the payment promised in 1915 found President Wilson hostile to the secret treaty of London and its anti-Slav implications. The other powers deferred little to an ally which had been more a burden than a help. The grandiose hopes of London turned to dust: "only" some 1,000 square miles of territory, one for every 700 Italians who had died for them and scarcely worth the price. Meanwhile, the country lay in the grip of scarcity, soaring prices, and inflation. Prices in 1919 were 266 per cent higher than in 1913 (twice as much as England), the lira only a fraction of its prewar value. This stirred up fresh industrial agitation, demands for higher wages to meet the higher prices, strikes in the countryside as well as in the cities, while disaffected soldiers refused to march against the strikers. Employers, dreading the prospect of red revolution, resenting the cost of the subsidy with which the government kept down the price of bread and moderated misery and tempers, began to look toward the black-shirted bands of veterans and students which Mussolini was organizing into *fasci*.

In 1919, the nationalist poet D'Annunzio, now a war hero, led a free corps of legionaries to occupy the Istrian city of Fiume, disputed between Italians and Yugoslavs.* None dared dislodge him until 1920; and then the city was left to Italy. Lawless violence seemed to work well in the postwar world. In 1920 when the bread subsidy was cut, workers' demands for wages—more desperate than ever—led to industrial lockouts and these, in turn, to the occupation of many factories by the workers. Before the masterly inactivity of the government a near revolutionary situation simmered down into a settlement which settled nothing except that the revolutionary tide was on the wane. So was the star of D'Anunzio, who had been tossed out of Fiume ** without fighting. His failure, like the failure of the strikes, reinforced the Fascists who were busy harping on the danger—now past—of Bolshevik revolution. The "respectable" classes, landowners, employers, officers, state officials, were more inclined than ever to subsidize and support the patriotic hoodlums of the *fasci*. An influx of disillusioned followers of D'Annunzio strengthened Fascist ranks, and also their tendency to uncompromising violence coupled with heroic posturing.

---

* The Berlin Dadaists sent D'Annunzio a telegram hailing "capture of Fiume Dadaistic master stroke. If Allies protest telephone Club Dada Berlin."

** By his own government, at Allied insistence.

Since before the war the political situation had altered. Universal suffrage had turned the parliament into a more representative assembly, though hardly a more effective one. The Socialists had won nearly one-third of the seats in the elections of 1919. Then, Communist secession weakened the whole Left and in the elections of 1921 Communists and Socialists together garnered fewer votes than two years before. Their competition came from the Catholic Popular Party, appealing both to confessional loyalties and to the peasant masses eager for reform. After the beginning of the century most Catholics had entered political life as supporters of the right-wing parties. But a few of them formed a democratic wing whose sympathies went to small farmers and landless laborers against extortionate landlords and harsh authorities. In 1918 this tendency led to the organization of the Popular Party which, under the leadership of a Sicilian priest, Don Luigi Sturzo, supported peasant ownership, land and tax reform. Impressed by the possibility which Sturzo demonstrated of keeping peasants and workers out of Marxist clutches, the Vatican granted him its halfhearted blessing. The only way for the parties that stood for change to be effective would have been a united front. But while a coalition of Socialists and Populars made sense, it fell down under the weight of doctrine. The Socialists, aware of their unreadiness for revolution, adhered to it nevertheless, thus forfeiting the possibility of more moderate reforms. The Populars, who had been sanctioned specifically to bar the road to Marxism, could not cooperate with a violently anticlerical and revolutionary Left.

Meanwhile, the old parties, bypassed by new ones, sought to play the Nationalist game as loudly as the Right and bid for popular support against the revolutionaries. Mussolini's Fascists hesitated between radicalism and nationalism until they realized that the two could be reconciled in action. They proved their nationalism by beating up Socialists and Unionists, their radicalism by their brutal methods; they benefited from the support of the authorities and from their own determined tactics which terrorized opponents into silence or broke them down. And, as is usual in such circumstances, supporters flew to the aid of victory by joining them in droves when they had proved the stronger. As the domestic chaos grew, so did the uncertainty of the Left. It had preached violence, but hesitated to practice it or lost when it tried. Its opponents, more determined, garnered the fruits of its mistakes. In October, 1922, after the simulacrum of a march on Rome, the King offered the premiership to Mussolini rather than use the army to disperse his bands. By grace of Victor Emmanuel, Italy had a government which really meant to exercise power. But it moved slowly at first.

Il Duce

The Cabinet was a Fascist-Nationalist coalition, supported by the Populars whom pressures from the Vatican had pushed toward the Right,

Mussolini and his fascist followers march in Rome.

while eliminating Sturzo from their leadership. The most important measure passed at this stage was an electoral law according to which the party or coalition gaining the most votes—even if only a minority of the total—was allotted two-thirds of seats in Parliament. In the elections of 1924 the Fascist-Nationalist coalition got more votes than their other rivals and hence the parliamentary majority it needed. When the Socialist deputy Giacomo Matteotti denounced the intimidations and electoral frauds by which this majority was gained, he was promptly murdered by fascist bullies. A few years later the affair would have been hushed up. In 1924, vestiges of older decencies troubled public opinion and lent force to the protests of the parliamentary opposition. However, when unable to obtain retribution the opposition walked out of the chamber, thus leaving the field open to Mussolini. In 1925, after some hesitation, he declared them excluded from Parliament, suppressed all opposition parties, amnestied Matteotti's murderers, and installed a Fascist dictatorship at last.

Compared with the total grip of Communist or Nazi power, Mussolini's fascism appears a primitive affair. But it was the first to eliminate parliamentary institutions, subvert popular government, and proclaim the one-party state; and that, in the early 1920's, was impressive. Its structured organization, its disciplined, uniformed party, the way in which it swept laws and liberties away with impunity, and the histrionics with which it replaced them, made a great impression all around, not least on Adolf Hitler.

The leftist tendencies of many Fascists received a sop in the corporativism on which the Fascist state was founded. The corporative state was Mussolini's alternative to both capitalism and communism. It drew the collectivist conclusions of nationalist socialism, but also of a much older tradition. On the one hand, individual interests were subordinated to those of the nation; on the other, labor was proclaimed to be a social duty, as medieval theologians had taught: a part of the social good. Drawing on the Catholic doctrine that social classes are not opposed but interdependent, and on the anarcho-syndicalist idea that workers should control production, corporativism proposed to reconcile different economic and professional groups in corporative assemblies that faced and resolved the concrete issues concerning them, self-governing bodies of organized workers and employers, bypassing class conflict and co-operating to direct the country's economy.

All this, quite plausible in theory, became in practice a façade for authoritarian governments, dousing rather than eliminating class antagonisms and severely limiting the independence both of capital and labor. What Italy got, beyond the vast bureaucratic structure that corporativism called for, was a quarter of a century of industrial peace which soon brought consumption and production back to prewar levels. It also got labor tribunals to arbitrate individual grievances and collective disputes, a body of civil servants trained in labor relations and collective bargaining, protective legislation for industrial and agricultural laborers, social services, national insurance, and welfare organizations, holidays with pay, educational and recreational facilities, and a great many benefits which, largely symbolic in the prewar years, would be put to good use after the war.

In this, as in other respects, Mussolini set an example which other nationalist dictators followed in Austria and Portugal, Spain and Vichy France. Many of his measures were empty gestures. They nevertheless helped restore order and self-confidence where they did not exist before. There were some real advances: begging was suppressed, crime reduced, dirt, disease, and illiteracy pushed back, a measure of efficiency introduced into public life. While tourists praised the trains that ran on time and the new splendors of the Roman Forum, statisticians could note that a static society was getting underway under the impetus of educational opportunities: of children between five and fifteen, one in two had gone to elementary school in 1921; nine in ten would be going in 1941. During that period high-school attendance had doubled and university attendance tripled. But Mussolini's greatest contribution to politics was in the realm of constructive deception. Idle hands and minds, energies that could not be constructively employed in backward or stagnant economies, had long caused trouble and disorder. Now they were turned to marching and parading, solaced by public displays of power and purpose, salved with a vicarious self-importance. They were no less useless than they had been before; but they were harnessed and disciplined.

The coincidence of Fascist and Catholic thinking that we have seen in corporativism was not fortuitous. Conservative and authoritarian, Pope Pius XI (1922–1939) had served as *nuncio* in Poland in the difficult years before 1921 when the Bolshevik tide threatened Warsaw and perhaps the rest of Europe. He saw Fascism as a useful counter to godless Bolshevism and welcomed Mussolini as "the man of Providence" only a little after Matteotti's murder. In 1929, several years of negotiations resulted in the Lateran Treaties, which settled old feuds and granted the Church a privileged position in the state. The 108 acres of Vatican

City were recognized as an independent state, and a concordat reversed the policies of fourscore years. Until the late 1930's, when a struggle for control of youth organizations and educational policies brought Church and Fascist state to loggerheads, their entente overshadowed occasional squabbles, giving Mussolini the firm base he needed; and nuns marched past him escorting little boys in uniform giving the Fascist salute.

Against this happy background the Fascists sought to regenerate Italy by harnessing labor and employers, subordinating the unions to themselves and capital to the Chamber of Corporations, persuading a skeptical public that the strenuous life was best and that the glory of ancient Rome could someday be recaptured by its distant heirs. Here, as in Germany and Russia, we hear the vocabulary of struggle: Mussolini proclaimed the battle for wheat, the battle for coal, the battle for the lira, and, maddest of all in Italy, the battle for births (including a tax on bachelors and medals for the most productive mothers). In schools and universities, as in the state administration, loyalty oaths were imposed on all personnel; censorship in the press, secret police, special courts, completed the panoply of dictatorship by now so familiar but then still strange and, to some, exciting. But the regime's great battles ended in muddle and, soon, most Italians took refuge in cynicism. They had no long experience with representative government behind them and no particular sense that Mussolini's rule was worse than what they had before. But apathy would be replaced by growing disillusion. The glories of imperial Rome were pursued in war: first in Ethiopia (1935–1936), then in Spain (1936–1939), eventually in the annexation of Albania (1939). War expenses bore heavily on currency and on taxes, made for devaluation of the lira, levies on precious metals and on capital, heavier intakes of conscripts for the army. After 1938, the introduction of anti-Semitic measures on the Nazi pattern in a country which had no anti-Semitic tradition and few Jews, stressed the growing artificiality of Fascist notions.

New War and New Disasters

When the Second World War broke out Italy once more had the possibility of remaining neutral, and once more chose war, gratuitously and dangerously, largely for glory's sake. However, when we say "Italy" we must remember that most Italians had no more choice in their country's policies than Frenchmen had two centuries before. Italians did their ruler's bidding: the only difference was that Italy, perhaps wrongly, was considered a "freer" Western country and its people identified with their country's deeds—both by the myths of Fascism and those of national sovereignty.

The war was a disaster. By attacking France in June, 1940, Mussolini had hoped for spoils of victory without any effort or pain. His forces, unprepared for any serious fighting, did badly against the French in their short alpine campaign, worse against the Greeks in 1940–41, and could not even establish a firm hold on the Croat-Dalmatian kingdom which the Germans allotted them from the remains of Yugoslavia. By spring, 1943, the only Italians left in Africa were prisoners of war. By summer Sicily had been lost as well, and the Fascist regime had toppled over as easily as it had risen twenty-one years before. The King now hoped—and so did most Italians—that Italy would be allowed to leave the war. Instead, the armistice concluded with the Allies in September meant that the peninsula became a battleground subject to extraordinary devastation as Allied troops fought their way north with painful slowness. Not for another year was Rome free of the Germans. Not until 1945 was the country north of Florence liberated and Mussolini—who had briefly ruled as German puppet master of a rump Fascist republic—killed by partisans.

By the time peace came, to the monstrous ruin of Italian cities was added the misery of all the populace. The harvest was half what was needed to provide supplies, industrial production less than a quarter of that before the war, unemployment had soared beyond statistics. The country was flooded with worthless currency; supplies, fertilizers, and machinery lacking; the economic dislocation seemed total. Italy, like Germany, was a disaster area. The political dislocation was to scale. Political parties, suppressed for twenty years, fumbled their way into being during the years after 1943. By 1945, three major parties vied for the support of their countrymen: Communists, Socialists, and Christian Democrats. The latter, a new version of the Populars whom the Vatican had sacrificed to Fascism in the twenties, effectively governed the country until the 1960's. The royal house, discredited by its hypocrisies, was jettisoned soon after the war had ended.* In 1946 Italy became a republic. The kingdom of Italy, born in 1861, had lasted eighty-five years. Its disappear-

---

* The voting pattern reflected the peninsula's sharp split between north and south. All the northern provinces and Rome voted for the republic; all the south and the islands voted for the monarchy.

Mussolini and his mistress, killed by partisans.

ance and the recovery that followed showed that, in that time, Italy had joined the ranks of modern nations.

Italy Modernized

Within three years the economic destruction had been repaired, within fifteen national income, though still only half that of Germany or France, had risen to double the figure of 1938. The beginnings of land reform gave 100,000 families nearly three million acres whose production increased almost fourfold. Less than a third of the population now lives in rural areas, while backward Southerners have moved into the factories of the north. Meat consumption, always a suggestive indicator of well-being, is going up so fast that productivity cannot keep up with it. The country's economic growth (about 6 per cent a year between 1950 and 1960, compared with 4.5 per cent for Western Europe as a whole) allowed modernization, full employment, improved social security and public health. Italy had become an industrial nation.

The "miracle," as in Germany, was not entirely miraculous. Nationalism and militarism had consumed between 25 and 40 per cent of the country's wealth. These costly indulgences abandoned, the nation's energy and resources could turn to economic growth. Anticommunists, who had invested in fascism to ward off revolution, now invested in prosperity. Nationalists who had been fascinated by martial glory learned to expect more from production indexes. Ordinary people were glad to have jobs, houses, plumbing, and a modicum of comfort rather than colonies and parades. Population had doubled, but it no longer presented a threat to stability: rather a promise of further dynamism. What was more important, life expectancy doubled too—thirty-five years in 1880, sixty-five in 1950—even while the fertility rates had been cut in half. What had been a largely illiterate and provincial people was now better schooled (8 per cent illiteracy in 1962), accustomed to a national outlook and to the ways of the modern world.

Yet, as elsewhere, these advances created new difficulties. Italy's greatest problem remains the deep division between the more advanced and the underdeveloped regions. In the Mezzogiorno (the portion of the peninsula roughly south of Rome) and the islands, years of effort have improved conditions, but too slowly for populations that have at least learned impatience from modernity. A riot like that which caused two deaths at Battipaglia, near Salerno, in April, 1969, reflects the crisis of industrialization in progress. In 1951, Battipaglia had a population of 15,000; double that number in 1969. Marshes had been drained, industries brought in. But these very changes—the restructuring of land-holdings, the modernization of industrial and business enterprises—which give work and hope to some, have displaced others. Instead of 15,000 underemployed and hopeless people the population had come to number some 3,000 unemployed, and many more who were simply impatient for better conditions: no longer peasants, but not yet an industrial proletariat. The problems have changed but they are, if anything, more pressing, more explosive. The divorce between the good words of politicians, the good intentions of a public opinion fundamentally indifferent, and the realities of sagging enterprise, unemployment, emigration (northward), and economic colonization by the more advanced sections of the country, resented as intolerable, helps recruit rioters and create an explosive situation.

Democracy is being sought beyond the anachronistic structures and the authoritarian bureaucratism of state employees. But the channels of reform are clogging. Since 1962, the Socialists have joined the Catholics in governmental coalition, the Communists are resolutely reformist, the extraparliamentary opposition hampers reform in universities and administrative structures where reform is badly needed and provides a convenient alibi for reactionaries who reject all change. Few of the numerous dissatisfied join the small bands of Left or Right extremists, but all provide kindling for their fires. In 1969, some observers considered Italy to be in a prerevolutionary situation; but Italians, experienced in political acrobatics, hoped that expanding possibilities would catch up with the expectations they had sparked.

France

France had come out of the First World War victorious but badly weakened: of all Western nations, she had suffered the highest losses in proportion to her population—eight million had been mobilized, five million killed or wounded. Two out of every ten young men had died,[*] another three had been somehow disabled. Industrial production was 60 per cent less than prewar and the franc worth about one-fifth of what it had been. The tax structure was uncertain, with income taxes—introduced only in 1916—providing less than a quarter of total revenues between the wars. The public wanted high prices for its products and low living costs—high wages, shorter working hours, yet higher productivity and lower taxes. These inconsistencies passed unobserved for some years. Governments, subsisting on loans, had to reconcile lenders, not frighten them with talk of taxes or devaluation. This made for recurrent economic crises, more easily settled in the 1920's while the economy still flourished, but presenting insoluble difficulties when France's economic weakness caught up with her at last.

We have already seen that France remained an agricultural country far

---

[*] Among those of military age, the figure was near one in three.

longer than her neighbors. Urban population only equaled rural in 1928; in 1939 it stood at 53 per cent, only slightly above numbers in the countryside, much of it in sleepy burgs which were urban in name only. This meant that the Depression came late to France; but also that it stayed longer. While other countries devalued their currencies to give their goods a better chance on the international market, pressure from the saving public prevented such a measure until fall 1936, when it was too little and too late to help an antiquated and undercapitalized industry. French policy reflecting the will of the majority, struggled to maintain the old social and economic structures, to keep going hundreds of thousands of shops and factories whose high operating costs would have ruined them in a free market but which, while tolerated, enabled greater firms to make high profits by keeping their own prices unnaturally high. What triumphed in France was not efficiency but conservatism, dedicated to keeping alive enterprises which would succumb under competition or be abandoned in a planned society. Modern democracy could afford neither the ruthlessness of *laisser-faire* nor that of dictatorship. It was bound to founder.

Divisions and Defeat

The contradictions of French economics reappeared in French politics between the wars. As in other countries, the Socialists—who had long furnished recruits for ministerial posts—now became a governmental party, following in the footsteps of the Radicals. Their policy, like that of the Radicals, inclined toward an understanding with Germany which the Right rejected until the middle 30's when everything turned about, the Left arguing for resistance (though not for the necessary armaments), the Right for better relations *and* armaments but against the taxes that would make them possible. No party could gain a majority in parliament, no coalition could long maintain itself. There had been sixty-four cabinets between 1870 and 1920; there would be another forty-three by 1940: more than two a year. It is not surprising that in March, 1936, when Hitler reoccupied the Rhineland, and in March, 1938, when he marched into Austria, French policy was in the hands of weak caretaker governments, holding the fort between crises and ill-equipped for decisive action.

Such a record encouraged the appearance of right radical leagues, combining prewar nationalist ideas with the methods and inspiration of the Fascists. Their violent criticism of parliament was self-fulfilling, discrediting the discredited Republic even more. But, while creating trouble, the leagues never made a revolution, for their supporters wanted not radical change but more stability. The torch of revolution had passed to the Communists, in whom, as Robert Wohl has put it, French workers and intellectuals saw not the totalitarian tendencies of Moscow

Warder Collection

Léon Blum at a meeting of the national council of the Socialist party, 1936.

"but their own revolution, the one they had failed to make in 1919–20," the one which they would always fail to make. After the rise of Hitler, Communist policy, previously hostile to any *entente* with "Social Fascists" immediately to the right, endorsed the notion of a Popular Front that would unite Radicals, Socialists, and Communists against the conservatives and reactionaries who had long held the upper hand. In the 1936 elections the Popular Front won a victory which brought a left-wing government to power, headed by the Socialist Léon Blum.

The uneasy coalition soon foundered under the strain of internal divisions and the difficulties of foreign policy. It gave way to more moderate cabinets whose fate was to stumble uneasily to war. Before it died, however, after a year of power, Blum's Popular Front coalition had passed a series of social measures which, while they hampered the production of armaments for the coming war, did at last lead the working class into the twentieth century: the forty-hour week, higher wages, compulsory arbitration, paid holidays, and the nationalization of certain industries. By 1938, though fewer French homes had electricity, indoor sanitation, running water, or any other comforts than those in Germany or Britain, most of the poorer Frenchmen lived better, ate better, and dressed better than they had done a decade or two before. But Frenchmen were even more disunited. The failure of the Popular Front, combined with the international situation, stressed the discord between workers and employers, revived the agitation of the leagues and of the Communist Party, and further strained relations between Frenchmen.

France entered the second war divided against herself. Yet it was not her divisions but the incompetence of her generals (and allies) that ensured defeat within five weeks of the German offensive of 1940.* But it was the conservatives who feared social revolution who induced the government of Marshal Pétain to conclude an armistice which left the country at Germany's mercy.

---

* In this, the Communists, bound by the German-Soviet Pact, had done their best to help by defeatist propaganda and sabotage. After June, 1941, they would become the backbone of resistance.

Pétain was eighty-four years old in 1940 and his government, at Vichy, reflected the fact. Its slogan, "Labor, Family, Fatherland," went back to an earlier age to which it hoped to return the country, making it once again an agricultural economy endowed with gilds and corporations, educated in religious faith and bourgeois virtues. It was too late for that. France became the stake of a struggle between the Germans and the Allies in which each camp had its French supporters: on one side more or less enthusiastic collaborators with the Nazis, on the other the Resistance —Communists, patriots, democrats, all finally (if temporarily) embodied in Charles de Gaulle's Free French. "You think too much about the French," Pétain's aide-de-camp told him in 1942, "and not enough about France." The reverse was true of the lanky brigadier who had escaped from his surrendering land in June, 1940, to continue the fight from London and from France's overseas territories. Upon his figure there would eventually concentrate the hopes of Resistance fighters recruited from all prewar factions, few and isolated at first, more numerous after 1942, armed and equipped from London which they supplied with valuable information.

For most resisters, getting rid of the Germans was only a step toward a complete national renovation. Purged in the fires of suffering, the country would at least have shed the rotten old order and its discredited representatives, would be ready for new economic and political structures that could realize the democratic ideals to which prewar institutions had only paid lip service. The ideology of the resistance combined humanism and collectivism in a vague revolutionary synthesis, too uncertain to provide a common program but sufficient to provide a common hope. The hope and the credit of it were going to be captured by politicians: Communists, Gaullists, even prewar ones. Before that, however, they sufficed to recruit impressive numbers to the underground. Resistance brought repression which in turn fed the flames of resistance even more. Two hundred thousand French men and women were deported to Germany, four out of five fated to die there; twenty thousand were shot by the occupying forces, aided at times by French militiamen. Despite—or perhaps because of—this, by the time Allied forces landed in Normandy, tens of thousands of armed, organized resisters were in a position to give real help, harassing enemy troops and hampering their movements by sabotage and guerrilla activity.

Yet, whatever their heroism, in the end the country's fate was decided not by Frenchmen but by the fortunes of other people's wars in which they played only the part they were permitted. France was liberated in 1944 to the accompaniment of purges that killed between 40,000 and 80,000 persons who had collaborated with the Germans or were suspected of having done so, while twice as many were imprisoned or otherwise penalized. It was no longer a great power. The first challenge of peace was that it must learn to live with this new fact.

The Fourth Republic

Simply speaking, French politics under the Fourth Republic (1944–1958) were the parliamentary politics of the past rendered chaotic by the problems of the present. A parliament elected by proportional representation could not be made to work—the more so when a quarter of the electorate elected Communists who unbalanced it still further. It followed that France was run less by squabbling politicians and impermanent governments than by permanent civil servants whose freedom and initiative were all the greater for the impotence of the country's elected representatives. The Fourth Republic would boast twenty-five cabinets with an average life of six months. Even the most determined premiers, like the Radical Pierre Mendès-France (June, 1954–February, 1955), whose decisiveness extricated France from Indochina and began to ease her out of North Africa, left less of a mark than great administrators like Jean Monnet, architect of European union. This is what made for a situation often described as one of great stability below an anarchic surface.

The greatest positive contribution of this period was to turn another legacy of the war days into reality: the idea of European union, which German propaganda had exploited for its own ends, became the redeeming dream of the Resistance leaders. The war had demonstrated that industrial and political power were one. But Europeans could hope for neither without organization, concentration, and co-operation across national borders. France and Germany must learn to co-operate. Whatever their divisions, they had more in common than each had with other powers that had not shared what they had gone through. This was the only way in which Europe could hope to play the major world role to which its component parts no longer could aspire separately. It would be Frenchmen like Monnet and Foreign Minister Robert Schuman who launched the plans from which European integration arose; it would be France which drew the most important profits from them.

But such advances were less apparent than the problems the Fourth Republic faced. Liberation coincided with the reversal of the demographic trend of a century and more. In the ten years following the war French population increased about 10 per cent, by over four million: a tide of youth which continues to rise today (though more slowly) so that soon one Frenchman in two will be under thirty-two. Expanding economy and expanding population upset the stagnant balance of several decades, encouraged economic growth and social mobility, created great demands for housing, schooling, and mass-produced consumer goods, but also new tensions, inflation, dissatisfactions, all aggravated by psychological crisis. France, we have said, was no longer a great power. But she had fallen in the world so suddenly that many Frenchmen could not accept the thought, especially when challenged by the population of their colonies, asking for freedom in their turn. The cost of warfare in Indochina (Vietnam) and then Algeria increased inflation; and failure increased instability. A million French settlers in Algeria prevented negotiation with Nationalist Algerian rebels. France was stretched on the rack of a colonial war which threatened to turn into a civil one (1954–1962).

De Gaulle and a New France

The Republic and its political masters could neither tame their rebels nor free themselves from them. They would be replaced by a man who could do both: Charles de Gaulle (1890–1970), who cared for France more than for any party, for France's anxious glory more than for its possessions. An actor and a poet with a sense of history, de Gaulle descended from a long line of men who had served the state. Inspired by Barrès and Maurras, he had made a religion of his fatherland. Here was a seventeenth-century figure, born in the nineteenth to serve the twentieth. Too authoritarian and unbending for democratic politics, the General, who had become head of state at the liberation, had resigned in 1946. Since then he had survived as a great memory and a disrupting influence. In 1958 he returned to head a new government, to extract France from its Algerian anthill and from further colonial entanglements. The Fourth Republic collapsed under its confusions to be succeeded by a Fifth built on the economic edifice of the previous decade.

Thus the Fourth Republic proved both a dismal failure and a startling success. Years of political instability and running inflation hid from sight great advances in power production and the modernization of key industries. In 1958 the Fifth Republic inherited an economy whose dynamism, ignored by a public fascinated by political hassles, surprised everybody. Its task would be to secure the stable conditions in which an ever-growing section of the population could concentrate on the exhausting but increasingly satisfying pursuit of money.

As for de Gaulle, he concentrated on the state. A sound, or sounder economic structure; the final settlement of the suppurating Algerian conflict in 1962 and the resettlement of nearly a million refugees; a wary entente with Germany, preferred to more powerful allies; the classic ideas of balance of power applied in improved relations with Russia—all these permitted a more independent foreign policy, a firmer tone with the United States. The General shared his countrymen's resentment of overweening allies, their reluctance to go in too deep with one side and lose all touch with the other. Above all he wanted to preserve his country's freedom of maneuver, prevent her from becoming the vassal of more powerful friends, place her in a dominant position within the limited European sphere which could still be hers, and reassert her influence wherever the French language carried. Given peace, good management, and luck, the policy worked well enough, providing the prestige and the recognition which France had long been denied, securing a greater apparent independence than France's European allies enjoyed.

The year 1968 would show up the fragility of a bid for power resting on shaky foundations. In May, pressure of numbers, insufficient facilities, anachronistic structures, led to serious explosions within the great centralized nationwide structure of the University. Briefly but unforgettably, a generation which never knew what it was like to be occupied by the Germans set about showing the country what being occupied by the French was like. Parallel to this, inflation led to lasting and widespread strikes in spring, and the settlements that followed the strikes encouraged further inflation and migration of capital, threatening the stability of the franc by fall of that year. The General's insistence that France could go it alone had to be toned down as nationalistic pride gave way to anxiety and disturbance.

Visiting Romania in May, 1968, de Gaulle had hailed "the healthy wind rising from one end of the continent to the other," and reaffirmed the need of reuniting Europe from the Atlantic to the Urals, with no iron curtain in between. Now, hardening Soviet policy seemed to refurbish the iron curtain; Russian occupation of Czechoslovakia made nonsense of the thaw he hoped for, embarrassing the Franco-Russian *rapprochement* that French foreign policy had leaned on; the drain of dollars and of gold reserves after the events of May put paid to aggressive independence asserted against the United States; the rising winds blew little good to France, less to her president.

Gaullism—the policy, or lack of policy, of the General's varied but numerous followers—united authoritarian progressivism and liberal (that is, conservative) opportunism in uneasy harness. Governmental authority and stability, greater than France had known for a century, seemed to produce only piecemeal initiatives and spasmodic improvements. Little had been done to prepare the succession of a man who, like all great men, believed himself irreplaceable and therefore did not bother with what might follow his passing. Hampered in part by anti-European parochialism, economic momentum was running down. Financially, France was well off despite the run on its money. But unemployment and productivity gave cause for concern, labor and white-collar workers clamored for a greater share of national wealth, and so did students and peasants. France suffered the acute discomfort that goes with growth and change. Men with one foot in traditional society and another in the modern world showed the strain of such schizophrenic conditions. Shopkeepers rebelled against the pressure of large stores spreading at last throughout the provinces and the fiscal burdens of a costly state; peasants rioted against the competition of large-scale farms and the costs of modernization; everyone felt the difficulty of adjusting the mentalities of one age to the techniques of another.

There was little a government could do about problems of that nature. But de Gaulle always regarded politics as a personal affair. Eager to reassert his authority, he insisted on a referendum which was in effect a plebiscite: that is, a request for a confidence vote. But confidence was lacking. Some of the great barons of the regime, like ex-Premier Georges Pompidou, gave only halfhearted support. The Jewish community, mortified by the General's brutal break with Israel and support of the Arab cause, opposed him. The partisans of order feared he had lost his grip, the partisans of change doubted he could adjust to the new world around. De Gaulle's foreign policies raised fears of French isolation, his internal ones raised prices and taxes both. Above all, de Gaulle had ruled too long: longer than anyone since Napoleon III. He was getting old, clinging too hard to office. The disorder he had replaced forgotten, many judged his order the more harshly, dismissed it more easily.

In April, 1969, not quite eleven years after he had grasped political power, the General was out of it by the will of that people to which he had always turned for confirmation. But the majority that had united to turn him out was a conglomerate of many trends, ranging from extreme Right to extreme Left, and quite incapable of offering an alternative when de Gaulle resigned his office. Parliament retained a strong Gaullist majority held together by common interest in administrative efficiency, political effectiveness, and the perquisites of power. Whether under new president, Georges Pompidou, or another, Gaullism without de Gaulle seemed the fate of France for some time to come.

Britain

Victory in 1918 had proved a costly bauble. Three-quarter million dead, one and a half million wounded, the domestic and foreign debt ten times greater than in 1914, revenue from foreign investments cut by almost half, workers and veterans clamoring for social reform, taxpayers for lower taxes, these were some of the facts confronting a government torn every which way. In 1920 the French ambassador to London told Winston Churchill: "In the twenty years I have been here I have witnessed an English revolution more profound and searching than the French Revolution itself. The governing class has been almost entirely deprived of political power and to a very large extent of their property and estates; and this has been accomplished almost imperceptibly and without the loss of a single life."* By 1937 5.6 per cent of the national income had been redistributed from rich to poor. In 1939 there were 7,000 people in England with net incomes after taxes of $30,000 or more. In 1949 there would be seventy.

All this was in part the work of the Lloyd George budget of 1911, with its heavier taxes and its death duties, especially for higher income brackets. It was even more the result of war and the greater equality induced by shortages, rationing, wage rises, and the shrinking number of domestic servants. The war effort absorbed both men and women who were reluctant thereafter to reassume their servitude. The number of domestic servants in 1920 was half that of 1914; it would continue to fall, and particularly after 1940. But, though even the lowest wages were now above starvation level, A. J. P. Taylor reminds us that in 1920 1 per cent of the population still owned two-thirds of the national wealth while 0.1 per cent owned one-third of the nation's wealth **—the changes England underwent in the First World War were far from the catastrophic character of the 1940's. As England entered the 1920's democracy was still limited by institutions, custom, and deference; plural voting continued to 1945; women over thirty received the vote in 1917, those over twenty-one only in 1938; the same classes kept their hold on the levers of power. In a period when Conservatives ruled most of the time, two-fifths of the members of Parliament belonged to families with a hereditary title, and a quarter of them between 1918 and 1939 had been educated at Eton or Harrow.

Still, the Labor Party, which had never got more than half a million votes before the war, was emerging as the main opponent of the Tories. The Liberals, having exhausted their program in 1911, crumbled away as their chief vote-getter, Lloyd George, shifted toward a "national"— that is, conservative—platform. In 1918, while Lloyd George's national coalition got five and a half million votes, Labor got two and a half million and the Independent Liberals only a million and a half. In 1922, though the Conservatives stayed well ahead, Labor doubled its poll and more than doubled its seats in Parliament. In 1924, with Liberal support, Labor would form the government (though only for ten months). A cabinet in which the Home Secretary had been an ironworker, the Chancellor of the Exchequer a former clerk, and the Prime Minister, Ramsay MacDonald, the illegitimate son of a domestic servant: this had the

* W. S. Churchill, *My Early Years* (London: 1947), p. 90.
** "Even this was an improvement on pre-war when 88% owned nothing." A. J. P. Taylor, *English History 1914–45* (Oxford: 1965), p. 171.

A scene during the general strike in London. Police escort wagons attempting to make deliveries in spite of the protests of strikers.

value of a symbol. But it did not last and, under the Conservative government that succeeded, Labor agitation grew apace. An attempt at a general strike in 1926 was soon defeated; but the general elections of 1929 brought a Labor majority to Parliament and a fresh Labor government, installed that year, had to bear the brunt of the Great Depression. Labor governments have seldom been lucky. After 1929 unemployment soared, made worse by the drastic economies which were the only policy the government could think of,* and the Labor Cabinet was soon succeeded by a national coalition and then by Conservatives.

Over one man in five was unemployed and many of an age to work had no idea what steady work was like. But they received the dole—unemployment insurance payments—and need not starve, just lose their self-respect. The government would not consider the investment policy that the economist John Maynard Keynes proposed to refloat the economy, but it was willing to pay to keep the unemployed from despair. It seemed to men like the Conservative Chancellor of the Exchequer Neville Chamberlain (Prime Minister 1937–40) that it cost four times as much to put a man to work as to keep him out of it. So, many stood idle on the dole and what they might produce, or earn, or spend had they been employed, never came into existence to provide work for others. Yet this policy meant that the British masses were spared the wretchedness that drove the Germans to radical lengths. Theirs was a quieter dejection and one that was partly remedied as the economy slowly recovered. By 1937 unemployment was "only" 12 per cent; and by 1939 preparation for war created full employment. But men remembered the bad years between the wars, the general strike, the dole, the unemployment. Such memories would emerge in 1945 in a determination not to have these things happen again even at the cost of restrictive union practices which increased costs and lowered productivity.

* Only Sir Oswald Mosley, a junior member of the Labor Cabinet, fought for a bolder policy supported by the left-wing—Lansbury, Strachey, Bevin. Mosley resigned from the government, was narrowly defeated at the Labor Party Conference, resigned from the party in 1931 and set up The New Party, which soon turned into the British Fascist Party, destined for historical oblivion.

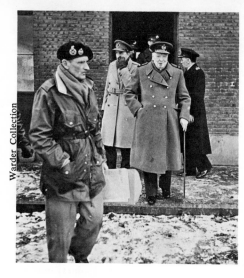

Warder Collection

Winston Churchill during a wartime visit to the Western Front. In the foreground, Marshal Montgomery.

Increasingly England turned in upon herself. Economically and spiritually she lived on capital, her old dynamic wasted. In 1936, as German troops reoccupied the Rhineland, as Popular Front governments appeared in France and Spain and civil war broke out in the latter, none of these events captured the popular imagination or the attention of politicians so much as the issue whether the new forty-one-year old king might marry a commoner who was both American and divorced. Since Victoria, Edward VII (1901–1910) and George V (1910–1936) had ruled over the kingdom. Neither mattered much politically, any more than Edward VIII or his successors were to do. But the private affairs of a monarch are just as fascinating as those of a film star and lend themselves to more acute moralistic considerations. In December, 1936, Edward VIII abdicated and his younger brother succeeded him as George VI (1936–1952). Such were the things that mattered.

With leaders whose chief concern was to keep spending down—as their electors wanted—no positive position was possible in international affairs. The Labor opposition, pacifist on principle, called for resistance to Fascism but opposed rearmament. The Conservative majority, more consistent, preferred a combination of economies and appeasement. In 1933 an event showed the way the wind was blowing among the cream of the nation's youth. A debate in the Oxford University Union ended in victory for the motion that students would *not* "fight for king and country." Why should they when Wilsonian aspirations had stumbled to apparent failure, when war had failed to end war or save the world for democracy, when peace had built no homes fit for heroes to live in, when their elders had shown their incapacity to lead and their fellows their unwillingness to die?* Even more characteristic was the Peace Ballot, an enterprise of the League of Nations Union, whose results were announced in June, 1935. Almost all who answered, and they num-

---

* Within a very few years most of the motion's supporters would be in uniform, fighting and dying as bravely as their forebears.

bered close to twelve million, voted in favor of the League of Nations, disarmament, and economic sanctions against aggression. Far smaller numbers envisaged military measures to deter aggression. Fewer still would pay for the armaments without which no forceful measures would be possible. Here was the cue for what we call appeasement: a policy which, setting aside its moral aspects, was largely a refusal to pay the costs of strength, a choice between armaments and certain social measures (Chamberlain was a great municipal reformer), and a refusal to choose between irreconcilable principles as the Left insisted stubbornly on both disarmament and anti-Fascism and the Right just as blindly on economy and security.

Only a small group of men around Winston Churchill (1874–1965) opposed the weak and vacillating policy this made for, calling for the re-armament without which there could be no firm, consistent policy. But they were excluded from the seats of power in favor of more sensible politicians. It was only when the Germans had invaded Holland and Belgium that Neville Chamberlain resigned and was succeeded by Win-ston Churchill. Churchill's old-fashioned pride in Britain and his belief in his country's destiny, the very fact that his mind was naturally closed to certain possibilities while open to every consideration and combina-tion that might bring victory, made him an ideal leader in a desperate situation. Today we cannot recreate the loneliness of England's stand, without resources, friends or—really—any reasonable hope, while one after the other European countries fell to German arms. For a year, for two, the situation got steadily worse while only unreasoning con-fidence counseled resistance. Protected by the Channel, by the R.A.F., and by the confidence that Churchill fanned, the United Kingdom was able to hold out and to emerge victorious from the conflict.

The Search for Stability

Not only victorious, but ruined. Not only ruined, but more of a social whole than it had ever been. During the war, the bloodless revolution had advanced with giant steps throughout a people mobilized for life-or-death resistance. The vast experience of wartime rationing proved that physical fitness and productive efficiency were related and that well-fed workers meant more regular timekeeping, greater output, lower absentee-ism and sickness rates. Planning and direction of industry and labor had been almost total and had contributed to victory; they were now en-listed to rebuild the country. Taxes which had soared to finance war ex-penses were turned toward a vast social and economic revolution. This was the program of the Labor government which, in July 1945, won a tremendous electoral victory, defeating Churchill's Conservatives be-cause they refused to acknowledge that things had changed and the need to change them more radically still.

But Labor faced a gigantic task. Britain had lost half her merchant tonnage and almost all remaining revenues from abroad. Industrial production, totally concentrated on armaments, had to be reconverted to a peaceful use. Fifty million people, crowded into an island a little bigger than New England, had to find the exports to pay for the raw materials and the food almost all of which came in from abroad. The Labor government tried to achieve recovery and social security side by side, and it went far in both directions, with the aid of heavier taxation, American aid, and an austerity program which extended wartime rationing and weary working hours until 1950. Banking, transport, key utilities and industries were nationalized; education and national health insurance extended to provide opportunities and security for all. When in 1951 a Conservative government succeeded Labor, it would do little, in effect, to reverse the socialization of the national economy.

But, somehow, the country seemed to have lost the sap which had coursed so briskly through it during several centuries. In a way, Britain found herself in a situation similar to that of France twenty-five years before: she had fulfilled her aspirations, she had exhausted her resources, she wanted to preserve her rank in the world, she felt her security depended less on her own power than on her allies', she hoped to preserve a *status quo* rapidly slipping into revolutionary changes, she sought to shut herself off from the irritating influences of the outside world; but, unable to face the costs of power, unwilling to pay its price, she did not know how to react coherently to her crumbling international status. The effort the country exerted during the war exhausted its last resources. Worse, perhaps, its victory in 1945 and its position through the following decade as the only excombatant who had not somehow been overrun, devastated, and humiliated, encouraged the persistent illusion of great power status now that she was no more than America's tarnished second.

Britain had come out of the war a very little power still shouldering the burdens and world responsibilities of the great power she had been, still nursing the belief that she dominated Europe and cherishing the antiquated ways *despite* which she survived. She could not face the prospect of political or economic equality with her neighbors on the continent, or of close co-operation with them, preferring her special relationship with the United States (more interested in Germany) and with the Commonwealth (more interested in the United States).

When the European Common Market was set up Britain kept out of it. As a result, though still the greatest trading nation in Europe, Britain lagged terribly behind her continental rivals in economic growth, productivity, exports, wealth, and dynamism. In 1950 she produced 10.3 per cent of the world's steel and built 37.7 per cent of its ships. By 1961 these figures had fallen to 6.1 per cent and 14.8 percent respectively. The change from Labor to Conservative government in 1951, from

Conservative to Labor in 1964, made little difference to a nation oscillating with remarkable cheerfulness between comfort and crisis. National revenue growing more slowly than that of any Western country (11 per cent against 23 percent in the Common Market), lagging industrial productivity (up 30 per cent between 1953 and 1962, as compared to 100 per cent in West Germany and 90 per cent in France), too many imports chasing too few exports with consequent balance-of-payments crises and devaluations of the pound sterling, withdrawal from outpost after outpost of Empire marked by some last imperialist hurrahs (notably at Suez in 1956), withal complacency, armaments and colonies draining funds needed at home: Britain's story in the last decade is one of dreary stagnation turning in the mid-60's to exuberant decadence.

While the economy declined, the nation furnished the deer park of Europe, a happy hunting ground for tourists, the Venice of the twentieth century. It is possible that economic stagnation and the freedom and public decency the country still enjoys go together; that the kind of government which would increase economic growth would also cut into public liberties; that the many institutions whose interests are vested in the present situation can only be set aside by something like a dictatorship; and that a dictatorship might suppress liberties without necessarily putting an end to stagnation. England, whose political and social institutions may be too advanced, too developed, to permit adjustment to the challenges of the present, poses one of the great conundrums of our day: is stability the greatest danger of modern society?

Spain

Spain's policy of neutrality throughout the First World War allowed Spanish industry to develop further and, with it, social tensions and the influence of Socialists and Anarchists. The movement for the autonomy of Catalonia, where much of this industrial growth took place, also advanced and broke into mutiny and separatist revolt in 1923 on the occasion of one more disaster in Morocco. This was met by a military coup establishing the dictatorship of a general supported by King Alfonso: Miguel Primo de Rivera, who, with French help, settled the Moroccan conflict while suppressing free press, free courts, free institutions, and the liberal opposition at home.

Primo's dictatorship, which lasted from 1923 to 1930 saw a desperate and partly successful effort to modernize the economy, increase production and improve the conditions of the working classes. Roads and dams were built, rural electrification schemes developed, industry protected,

547

railways modernized, rivers used for hydraulic power. Order helped the work and prosperity lasted until it collapsed with the world depression. But the military factions were getting restive and students and intellectuals soon stirred again. Primo, discouraged and ill, resigned in 1930. His fall was shortly followed by that of the king who had backed him and who now shared his discredit. In 1931, municipal elections resulted in overwhelming victory for the Republicans who called for Alfonso's abdication. The King left Spain and a republic was bloodlessly installed, accepted by the soldiers who would attack it within a few years.

But Spain was too divided for anything to hold it together except force. Extreme Right and Left both rejected the bourgeois republic from the beginning; army and property owners soon turned against it when military expenses were pared down and land reform plans threatened large estates. The basic break, as in the French revolution, came on the religious question. The Republicans, wanting to separate Church and State and to diminish clerical privileges, shocked the "respectable" Catholic middle classes. These could not stomach such atheistic and Jacobin measures or the government's incapacity to prevent sporadic attacks on churches, convents, and convent schools attended by their offspring. Eager to do the right thing but not to do too much, to reform but not alarm, to advance but not disturb, the Republicans discontented their critics, disappointed their supporters, and frightened the rich and respectable without weakening them. The recipe was made for trouble, and trouble came in 1936 when a coalition of center and left-wing parties—the Popular Front—won the elections. Coalition governments can seldom act with firmness. In Spain's troubled situation, the triumph of the Popular Front only accentuated internal divisions without imposing order. Soon, the debate passed from *córtes* into streets, and the resulting anarchy called forth the traditional pronunciamento.

Only this time when the military conspirators, led by General Francisco Franco (b. 1892), revolted, the government held its own in some of the major cities, particularly Barcelona and Madrid. A new political factor had arisen: the organized, class-conscious workers, unwilling to allow political decisions to be made without them. The insurgency controlled most of the army and the air force. The government, supported by the parties of the Left, organized forces of its own. What had begun as one more classic coup, which had gone wrong because neither side was strong enough to gain a quick decision, now turned into a conflict of ideologies, with foreign powers intervening on both sides and the outcome decided finally by the more effective foreign aid. The Republicans and their allies of the Left fought bravely but they were starved of help, internally divided by profound dissensions between the partners of the Popular Front, and were progressively driven back. Little help came from abroad. The United States, dreading all foreign

Left: Nationalist troops move through Madrid, November 1936. Franco and one of his generals dining during the Spanish Revolution.

entanglements, drew back its skirts from the horrid conflict. The Popular Front government in neighboring France, hamstrung by internal dissensions, was powerless to give effective help. The British, eager to appease the Axis, launched a nonintervention policy which only they and the French observed. Mexico and Soviet Russia sent some aid, but never enough to be effective. Meanwhile, Fascists and National-Socialists recognized their own. Franco's Nationalists, with strong support from Germans and Italians, pressed steadily forward.

The Legacy of Civil War

The Spanish civil war was more than an opportunity for Communists and Fascists to confront each other and for the Axis powers to try out their weapons at other men's expense. It was, for thinking people throughout the West, the traumatic experience that made their quandary clear, the quandary created by the persistent failure of the democratic powers to live up to their responsibilities, to face fascism and oppose it with a positive gesture or idea of their own. The year 1936 was in many ways a turning point. In March the Germans had finally revealed their aggressive intentions, in May the Popular Front in France had won the elections there, in July Franco's insurrection had broken out in Spain, in November the Rome-Berlin Axis had been openly proclaimed and it had recognized a protégé in Franco. Here, at a time of great popular hopes and fears, the contradictory forces and ideas of the past decade came to a head in a conflict between what looked like popular democracy and constitutional government on one side and the old order represented by its most classic symbols on the other. It was not quite like that, but that was how it looked to Hemingway, Malraux, and Brecht, and Orwell and Picasso, who saw open cities like Guernica ruthlessly bombed or shelled into ruins from the sea, and who exulted to see themselves at last fighting side by side with workers and peasants for democracy and against the Fascism that their own governments were too weak to face.

While over 10,000 Germans and seven times that number of Italians

Guernica, by Pablo Picasso. On extended loan by the artist to the Museum of Modern Art, New York.

supported Franco,* thousands of volunteers from all over Europe and America flocked to the International Brigades on the government's side. Many of them were refugees from Fascism, many were ordinary men—students, workers, intellectuals—who saw in Spain the secular plight of democracy and social justice assailed by brutal force. Some came to look on communism as the only political system that would stand up to it, but some learned a different lesson. Just because the Spanish war was the peak of a social commitment into which Western intellectuals could enter unhampered by the considerations that arose in the case of a national war, it provided not only a challenge but a touchstone of political purity, on which many intellectuals swung back from idealism to deception, from commitment to detachment and skepticism.

On the Left men like Stephen Spender or George Orwell, on the Right convinced Catholics and Royalists like Georges Bernanos, discovered that reconciling liberty and justice with modern warfare and political maneuvers was more difficult than they had ever thought: that there are not two sides but many, or one only in which all massacre, all suffer, and all are finally united in the death and the human condition that Bernanos depicted in his terrifying book *The Great Graveyards under the Moon* (1937), or Spender in the poem where

> Clean silence drops at night when a little walk
> Divides the sleeping armies, each
> Huddled in linen woven by remote hands.
> When the machines are stilled, a common suffering
> Whitens the air with breath and makes both one
> As though these enemies slept in each other's arms.

* Weapons were even more important than men. German and Italian tanks, planes, and guns, along with the specialists to man them, proved decisive in the end.

The political game on either side was not as clear or simple as had been imagined. Both sides wreaked destruction, took hostages, imprisoned suspects, raped, and murdered; both stifled the idealists in their own camp to serve what they conceived to be political or military efficiency. The Communists sacrificed all hope of social revolution on the Republican side to reassure the middle classes in Spain and abroad. The calculation failed: the workers were discouraged and the bourgeois hardly reassured. Franco eliminated and imprisoned his more radical supporters as being too disturbing for the conservatives he wooed. But the ideals of the Right—order, church, and the preservation of property—could reconcile themselves more easily to this state of affairs than those of the Left. Many liberals discovered with dismay that the faults they knew and criticized at home, the injustice or bad faith of their own governments, existed also in the "popular" and "democratic" regimes of Spain or Russia.

There was little reason, or so it seemed, to place faith in democracy's power to withstand evil; but there was not much hope in communism either. Protected by Soviet Russia—the only major power to aid the Republicans—the Communist Party, small and weak in 1936, came to dominate the Left, purging its armies and counsels of all who would not toe the party line. The purges in Spain echoed those then decimating Russia. Acquaintance with all the dirt and treachery of politics broke some of the last illusions of social and political-minded intellectuals. The year 1936 had been a time of hope in danger. The years that followed saw exasperation turning to despair. Many shared the feeling Orwell described in *Homage to Catalonia* that volunteers like him had become "pawns in an enormous political game."

"There is no use any longer," concluded Stephen Spender, "in taking sides with those politicians who seem a little nearer to the truth than the others." They might be just a little nearer, but they were almost as far away. So, many poets, thinkers, artists, who had briefly descended into the marketplace and onto the battlefield, beat a retreat. These were the years of the "God that failed." * Years of disillusion but of clarification too, when erstwhile Socialists, Liberals, and even Fascists decided that in the end, when all the words had been spoken and all the gestures made, what counted was "the decency of human beings" (Orwell), "man's dignity" (Silone), his "self-possession" (Malraux), his self-respect (Bernanos).

But such soul-searching, though important for Western thought and self-awareness, was for the few as yet. For the Spaniards there was suffering and devastation. When in the spring of 1939 Madrid at last surrendered and the United States recognized Franco's new regime a week before his adhesion to the German-Italian-Japanese Anti-Comintern Pact, some 700,000 lives had been lost in battle, some 50,000 more in air

---

* A book of that name, edited by Richard Crossman, was published in 1958.

raids, executions, and simple straightforward murders. Hundreds of thousands escaped to foreign exile. Catholicism was back in seventeenth-century garments, its control over schools and minds restored and supported by an official censorship which Raymond Carr tells us was designed to crush "pornography, Marxism, and dissolvent Liberalism." Nearly a million prisoners languished in Franco's jails. Many have died, many were released, some remain there still. The country had peace at last: a time to lick its wounds and to recover.

The convalescence has been slow. Spain became a monarchy again, but the pretender waited in exile while Franco ruled.* Despite misconceptions, Spain is not a Fascist country. Its native Fascist movement, the *Falange*, never very strong, had been domesticated by Franco, who turned it into a tame militia, never allowing it to do more than suited his policy. Franco was part of an older Spanish tradition: an authoritarian conservative, paternalistic and patriotic. He kept his country out of the Second World War * * and navigated the rapids of the peace until his steadfast anticommunism won American favor. Deprived of free institutions, almost thirty years of peace have given Spain the modest beginnings of prosperity. There have been significant efforts to reconcile a divided people, but extremes of wealth and poverty have not been eliminated and every step toward a more liberal regime tends to be followed by two steps back toward repression. There is no knowing whether Spain after Franco will break into civil war again. What she will make of herself and of her future remains to be seen.

Austria

Of seven and one-half million Austrians, over two million lived in postwar Vienna, which was given the status of a separate province in the New Republic. Most of the rest lived on the land or in small towns, provincial, backward, and strongly influenced by the Catholic Church. Between the provinces and the cosmopolitan modern capital a deep divide developed. After 1920, "red Vienna" run by Social Democrats stood in permanent opposition to the rest of the country governed by clerical governments reflecting rural opinion, reactionary and poor. In Vienna the Socialists followed in Lueger's footsteps, developing an impressive program of municipal socialism and public works. But Vienna, like the whole country, had lost its economic hinterland and was eco-

* Before dying in 1941, Alfonso XIII had designated his son, Don Juan, to succeed him. But the real pretender, since 1954, has been the latter's eldest son, Don Juan Carlos, born 1938, now officially designated as Franco's successor.

** Yet German soldiers were garrisoned on Spanish soil and British aircraft that strayed beyond the *campo neutral* separating Gibraltar from Spain were shot down by anti-aircraft guns built in bunkers facing the Rock.

nomically unbalanced. Austrian welfare now hung on foreign loans. When foreign credit was withdrawn in 1929, the economy began to crumble, sought to save itself by concluding a Customs Union with Germany (1931), which international intervention prevented, and collapsed into political as well as financial chaos.

By then the country was astir with paramilitary formations: the Socialist *Schutzbund* in the major towns, the Christian Socialist *Heimwehr* patronized by landlords in the countryside, and, everywhere, the burgeoning brown shirts of the Nazis. Heimwehr and Schutzbund had clashed for several years, with the Socialists losing ground as Catholic governments supported the Heimwehr against them. The Depression accelerated their decline. In 1932, a Christian Socialist Cabinet under Engelbert Dollfuss sought to stabilize the situation. In 1933, challenged by growing Nazi agitation which Hitler's rise to power in Germany encouraged, Dollfuss suspended parliamentary government, dissolved the Nazi Party, and established a dictatorship which the Socialists tried to challenge in 1934 only to be crushed. Within a few months Dollfuss himself had been murdered in a clumsy Nazi coup whose perpetrators were routed and executed by the Heimwehr. Authority now passed to Dollfuss's close collaborator Kurt Schuschnigg, who, for the next few years, maintained Austrian independence with the support of Italy.

Schuschnigg's corporative state, backed by all conservative elements and placed directly under the authority of God, allowed for no elections or plebiscites. It held little attraction for the young, the nationalists, and the unemployed, who, now that the Left had been eliminated, leaned increasingly toward the Nazis, still banned but increasingly influential. In 1937, the conclusion of the Rome-Berlin Axis removed Schuschnigg's Italian backing against Germany, just at the time when Hitler was making ready to forestall a possible restoration of the Habsburgs. In March, 1938, while drawing closer to Czechoslovakia and to France, Schuschnigg tried to call a plebiscite on the question of Austrian independence, was faced with a German ultimatum to resign, did so under menace of invasion, and National Socialists took the country over. The postponed plebiscite, now administered by Nazis, produced a vote of 99.75 per cent in favor of union with Germany; and Austria was incorporated into the Reich where she remained until 1945.

The country which enthusiastically welcomed Hitler and which accounted for about 8 per cent of the Third Reich's population, furnished a higher proportion of Nazis—one in every ten—than Germany. Among the murderers of the SS one in three were Austrians; among their Jewish victims almost half were killed by Austrians. Eichmann, who shipped thousands to their death, was an Austrian; so was Gestapo Chief Ernst Kaltenbrunner, and so, of course, was Hitler. Nazism was particularly lively in this lovely country and it has remained so since the war, when political power has been shared between Catholics and Socialists while Nazi survivors control the balance between the two camps.

Hungary

Hungary came out of the First World War still a semifeudal country. In October, 1918, the kingdom had broken off from Austria and signed a separate armistice. In November a republic was proclaimed under the presidency of the liberal count Michael Karolyi, who hoped to conclude peace on the basis of new national policies and thoroughgoing land reforms. As subject nations broke away, the possibility of such policies succeeding vanished. Socialist and Communist agitation spread before Karolyi could introduce his land reforms and democratic franchise. In March, 1919, Karolyi resigned rather than evacuate the areas which the Allies destined for Romanian occupation, and a dictatorship of the proletariat was set up almost by default. Its chief, Béla Kun, blundered badly when he announced that his government would not distribute land but nationalize it, thus forfeiting the support of peasants who lost interest in the conflict. Romanian troops marched into Hungary, occupied Budapest, ousted the Kun regime, and cleared the way for a reactionary takeover.

There was little Wilsonian self-determination about the peace which Hungary signed at Trianon (1920). Hungary lost three-fourths of her former territories and two-thirds of her former population. About three million Magyar-speaking persons now lived in Czech, Romanian, and Yugoslav territory. One injustice had replaced another, an even more virulent irredentism succeeded the national irredentisms of before the war.

Devastated by war, civil war, invasion, red and white terror, plundered by Romanians and amputated by the peace, the country would now be ruled by men who had led the anti-Bolshevik forces in the days of Kun. The republic, associated with revolution, was abolished; the kingdom of St. Stephen was re-established, but not for a Habsburg any longer. The kingdom without a king was to be ruled by an admiral without a fleet: its regent would be Miklos Horthy (1868–1957), erstwhile commander of the Imperial Navy in the Adriatic.

Impoverished by war, hard hit by inflation and by the loss of savings invested in the bonds of the vanished Empire, the middle class was also overcrowded by an influx of refugees from the successor states, embittered by the loss of posts, businesses, and homes. It would prove fertile ground for archconservatism rivaled only by movements of the radical Right. Revisionism became the touchstone of Hungarian politics. Even the

Socialists were Magyar irredentists. This meant that talk of agrarian or electoral reform could always be submerged by cries for the recovery of the *irredenta*. Three million landless peasants out of a population of eight million were of less importance than three million Magyars under the foreign yoke, suffering rather less than their present oppressors had suffered under that of Magyars.

When modest recovery in the later 20's stumbled into depression, the country turned from conservatism to racist protofascism, orienting itself ever more firmly toward the revisionist alliance first of Rome and later of Berlin. Anti-Semitic measures took people's minds off more material issues, while native National Socialists called for land reform and social legislation to bring relief to the industrial and agrarian proletariat. In the absence of a radical Left the extreme Right assumed the radical role which conditions in Western countries often obscured or made secondary. But Horthy was firmly in the saddle and his more conservative authoritarianism seemed to pay off when in 1939 Hungary reacquired Ruthenia from the Czechoslovakia Hitler had dismembered, in 1940 Transylvania from Romania (by Hitler's award), and in 1941 some of the territories that Yugoslavia lost.

This last act meant war with the West and in due course with Russia, collapse in 1944, and occupation by the Russian troops. It also meant that, by co-operation with the Germans, several hundred thousand Jews were deported and exterminated. The peace treaties of 1947 restored the borders set at Trianon, with the exception of some Transylvanian districts and small further losses to the Czechs. By that time the country was run by a "workers' bloc" of Communists and Social Democrats. By 1948 the Communists had taken over entirely, the economic system began to be Sovietized, and collectivization of the land was introduced. In 1956, national revolution indicated the force of the resistance. Revolt grew out of intellectual circles, their unrest spreading to the students and workers of Budapest and to the peasants who promptly began to divide the lands that had been gobbled into collective farms. The explosion that began in late spring was symptomatic of unrest that has since surfaced in other satellites (see below, pp. 968–972). The manner in which the West stood by while Soviet tanks mastered the rebels proved that it would not dispute Russian domination over the sphere of influence they had been tacitly conceded. The Hungarians, like their neighbors, continued to be treated as pawns in the political games of greater powers.

Nevertheless, revolution crushed, a milder regime appears to cause less frustration. Hungary, like most of her East European neighbors, was never quite free in the Western sense of the term. It is hard to say whether she is less free now than in the 1930's.

Eastern Europe

After 1918, out of the defeat and disintegration of the eastern empires the map of this whole region was recast. Estonia, Latvia, Lithuania were no longer Russian provinces but independent states. Poland was a republic, uniting the portions which its partitioning neighbors had carved out of it in the past 146 years. The ancient kingdom of Bohemia and Moravia now took new shape in a Czechoslovak republic. Romania doubled in size with territories acquired from Russia (Bessarabia), Hungary (Transylvania), Austria (Bukovina), and Bulgaria (Dobruja). The South Slavs were united around Serbia in a Yugoslav kingdom including not only Austro-Hungarian spoils but also part of Bulgarian Macedonia and the small principality of Montenegro.

Here was a treasury of future trouble not only between victors and vanquished, but among the successor states themselves. Whether regarded on ethical or ethnic lines the state of Eastern Europe was uneasy. The Poles held the corridor between East and West Prussia and parts of Silesia which the Germans thought were theirs. They held a large chunk of Ukraine, well beyond the ethnic line Lord Curzon had suggested in 1920 as a roughly fair border between them and Russia, which meant additional friction between the Catholic majority and the six million Ukrainians and White Russians who were either Orthodox or Uniate. They also held the city of Vilna, which they had seized from Lithuania. The Czechs held Teschen, useful for its coal and iron, coveted by the Poles. Lithuania had seized the German port of Memel for an outlet to the sea; and German Danzig, severed from Germany under a League of Nations commissioner, stood as a free city within Polish borders. There were three million Germans in Czech territory, Hungarians and Ruthenians in Slovakia, Hungarians and Germans in Transylvania, Ruthenians in Bukovina, Ukrainians and Russians in Bessarabia, Turks and Bulgarians in Dobruja.

Yugoslavia had the most serious national problems internally, her politics between the wars bedeviled by struggle between Serb Centralists and other nationalities led by the Croats, who wanted a federalist state allowing greater provincial autonomy. The clash between Croats and Serbs made parliamentary government impossible and eventually led to King Alexander's coup in 1929, abolishing the constitution and taking power into his own hands—a royal dictatorship only slightly modified when Alexander was murdered by a Croat terrorist in 1934. The Croats would secure autonomy in their own province in 1939 and then, again, after 1945. But every country had similar troubles: the Czechs plagued by their increasingly obstreperous Germans, the Bulgarians by Macedonian terrorists who demanded independence, dominated their part of the countryside, collected their own taxes, and set up their own courts.

All countries, above all, feared the rise of communism or its arrival on Soviet bayonets. Economic conditions were certainly propitious—a breeding ground for dissatisfaction, and irredentist problems were aggravated by economic backwardness. Three-quarters of the population of the area drew its meager living from the land. After the war there had been much talk of land redistribution and great domains had been dispatched or nibbled at in varying degrees. But large estates were few south of the Danube and, to the north, Hungary and Poland left most of them untouched. Only in Romania, where in 1920 sixty-three landowners still held one-third of all cultivated land, was a real effort made to gain over the peasant veterans. By 1925, about 6 million acres had been distributed to 700,000 families. Within a few years agricultural statistics showed that—with far more land under wheat than before the war—production for the market had diminished by a vast amount. This provided opponents of small peasant properties with impressive arguments against continuing the process. They forgot that the first thing the peasants did was eat a little better and bring less food to market. In any case, while they were given land, the farmers had neither capital for seed, fertilizer, and equipment, nor credit facilities. The old masters or new ones were soon back in the saddle, renting them seed, tools or money at usurious rates, which left the small owners almost as poor and backward as they had been before. In 1939, production per acre in Romania and Yugoslavia was less than a third that in Denmark, infant mortality three or four times that in western Europe.*

Ailing Nations

Industrialization, as far as it took place, was often divorced from local possibilities and needs, concerned with national prestige and armaments, regional rivalries, and an impossible desire to be self-sufficient. Industrial development was so slight that, everywhere but in Bohemia, less than one man in ten could find work in factories, mines, or transports. By 1939, Poland—rather more advanced than most of her southern neighbors—was less productive than its three separate fragments had been in 1914, with average output per worker about one-third that to be found in Italy, one-sixth that in Germany, and one-thirteenth of North American rates. In any case, industrially, these countries were colonies of foreign trusts and banks. In Romania, Poland, Yugoslavia—wherever mineral resources could not be developed without foreign capital—alien

---

* In Romania infant mortality in 1940 was 188 per 1,000: comparable to the French rate a century before and higher than that of contemporary India.

companies controlled the more important half of industry.

While foreigners and their agents dominated the economy, governments controlled their peoples. An illiterate peasantry, a miserable proletariat, provided no basis and little support for democratic government. In the Hungarian countryside and in the Yugoslav kingdom after 1931, voting was open, the secret ballot unknown. Equally open everywhere were intimidation, violence, and electoral fraud. Police and hooligan bands kept opponents from the polls, imprisoned or beat up unwanted rivals, and made quite sure that peasants voted as local bosses or the gentry wished. Sooner or later political instability in every country was "solved" by coups, which were generally directed by soldiers like Jozef Pilsudski in Poland and Joannis Metaxas in Greece, or by kings like Alexander in Yugoslavia and Carol in Romania. Everywhere except in Czechoslovakia embryo democracy gave way to government by cliques or colonels, militaristic, authoritarian, inefficient, and yet supported by large sections of the property-owning classes.

Peasant parties were either powerless or, in other cases, ineffective. The Communists were outlawed everywhere, the Socialists an insignificant minority of middle-class intellectuals. Sometimes university students provided the only opposition, going to the peasants or the workers, braving the police, often in the wake of their professors. In the absence of any organized Left, students and such other radicals as existed often took up National Socialist positions, drawing the collectivist conclusions of their patriotism and founding movements of the radical Right as violent as the tone of local politics. Such movements, always in conjunction with anti-Semitism, arose in every country; the most notorious being the Romanian Iron Guard, a militant Christian populism which attracted impressive numbers of intellectuals, workers, and poor peasants. But though the Iron Guard briefly attained power in 1940, when in the wake of grave territorial losses the king (Carol II) was forced to abdicate, it could not maintain itself any more than any of the others. In Romania, as in Hungary and elsewhere, conservative authoritarians controlling the armed services held on to power and were confirmed in it even by the Germans who preferred order to social revolution. It would be the conservatives, not the fascists, who joined Germany against Soviet Russia and who, in due course, lost.

Realignments

After the war was over, East European countries were either annexed or occupied by Russia, or else became its satellites. It made no difference whether, like Poland or Yugoslavia, they had fought against the Germans or, like the others, with them against Russia. The three Baltic states, which the Soviets took over in 1940 and lost again in 1941, were reoccupied a few years later. Poland, which had enjoyed a generation of independence between 1918 and 1939, emerged from the war a Russian vassal, amputated of her eastern provinces but enlarged toward the west at Germany's expense. The Oder-Neisse line of her new German border remained up to 1970 a bone of contention with Germany, ensuring Poland's reliance on Russian support against a possible revision. Eastern Germany, Hungary, Romania, Yugoslavia, Bulgaria, and Albania—some hundred million people—also depended on Russia's will. In 1948, the last free country of the area—Czechoslovakia—toppled into the Russian camp as a result of a coup executed by local Communists backed up by Soviet pressure.

Czechoslovakia excepted, all these lands faced gigantic problems. Almost one-third of Poland's prewar population were dead: murdered, executed, or killed in combat. More than half her buildings were in ruins, some towns almost wholly destroyed, three-quarters of the railways out of use, half the bridges blown up, vast patches of cultivable land sown with mines. On a less catastrophic scale the same conditions existed everywhere else. Inflation was rampant, dislocation rife. Of the millions of Jews who had inhabited Europe's eastern borderlands few survived except in Romania: only a few thousand out of two million Polish Jews, scarcely a few hundred of the thousands south of the Danube. National elites, never very numerous, had been decimated by warfare, exile, and the deliberate policies of the occupants—German or Russian. Cultured or not, here were peoples caught, torn between East and West, most of them speaking an Eastern language while using a Western alphabet; living an Eastern life while, in many cases, they worshiped in Western churches; belonging to an Eastern bloc but looking westward whence they had drawn their culture before they were dismembered; ambivalent, unquiet, confused, and frequently heroic to the point of anachronism.

However much resented, the territorial changes imposed by the Soviets meant that all these countries, once a national jigsaw, enjoyed greater homogeneity. Wartime devastation in some, Communist pressure in all, made for industrial development and land reform, redistributed populations internally, changed the proportion of urban to rural dwellers. In 1945, urban population still accounted for less than a quarter of the country's population in Romania and Yugoslavia, less than half in Poland and Hungary. Now, at last, it changed in favor of the cities. More schools, more electricity, more industrial power, vast capital investments painfully squeezed out of poor economies, provided the equipment first for recovery and then for growth. By 1950, in most places, industrial production was double that of 1938, and illiteracy shrinking fast. Starting from misery and chaos, the Communist countries of Eastern Europe have maintained a high rate of growth, about 6 or 7 per cent every year, higher on the whole than the average for Western Europe and North America.*

---

* Significantly, this applies to the more backward countries which had more ground to cover. Czech growth rates consistently lagged behind those of their neighbors and

The Fate of Popular Democracies

The most interesting fate was that of Yugoslavia. Self-liberated by Marshal Tito's forces, the Yugoslavs organized a federal state, redistributed land, and nationalized industry. Completely devastated by the war which had cost the life of one peasant in ten and caused losses equivalent to four years' national income, the country set out to rebuild itself, broke with the Cominform in 1948, secured Western credits one year later, traded with the West and, eventually, with her Eastern neighbors too, developed an orginal Communist order which tried to associate the masses to the socialism it sought to build, replaced collectives by co-operatives and mitigated Communist dictatorship. The Yugoslavs showed their Communist comrades that socialism was capable of development in other ways than Moscow envisaged, that even a poor country could aspire to political independence and integrity. The last few years suggest that, given time and freedom, some of their neighbors would try to follow this trail, though they might not succeed.

The year 1956 would furnish illustration of this point in the twin risings that shook Poland and Hungary: "spring in October," as Warsaw radio put it when, for one brief exultant moment, it seemed as if liberation had really been achieved—from the occupying Russians, but also from the despotic, stultifying official bureaucracies that personified not the dictatorship of the proletariat but its stupefaction.

The great changes of the later forties—land reform, expropriation of private property, forced collectivization, impetuous industrialization, mass education—had been imposed from outside but widely approved. As late as the mid-fifties a popular Polish poet still hailed the days "when Communism was the supreme poetry and effort of every day, and poetry the road to Communism, life for Communism." Yet gradually, through the excesses of senile Stalinism, as their bureaucracies hardened into corruption and brutal paranoia, the Communist regimes came to devour their subjects, and, first among them, their most devoted sons. A generation that had grown up under socialism began to feel that it was forced to live a travesty of the ideas taught in the schools, ever-repeated by party mandarins but honored rather in the breach than the observance.

Between June and October 1956 in Poland, June and December 1956 in Hungary, petitions, speeches, demonstrations, strikes, degenerating into large-scale violence affirmed Socialist hopes against the harsh reality of Communist regimes. First the rebelliousness, then the rebel-

---

Czech national output actually fell in the 1960's. Communism, apparently appropriate for backward countries determined to lift themselves by their bootstraps into the modern world, seems less useful in a developed economy. Furthermore, Italian productivity has risen faster during the 1950's and sixties than that of almost all East European countries.

Hungarian freedom fighters in Budapest, 1956.

lion of factory workers, miners, students, journalists, and intellectuals brandished the principles of Marxism itself. "This state of policemen and bureaucrats must go," proclaimed the Hungarian writer Tibor Déry, an old Communist himself, to the enthusiastic approval of the young Communists of the Petöfi Circle. Such rebels referred to the Yugoslav experience, appealed to the nationalist and anti-Russian traditions, but remembered above all the ideals professed by the very regimes that they attacked. They failed. The Russians were too near. In Hungary there was fighting, bloodshed, brutal repression. In Poland (perhaps because of the Hungarian lesson) there was compromise, ending in the gradual elimination of would-be reformists by other reformists (like Wladislas Gomulka), shrewder and readier to work with Moscow. In Warsaw as in Budapest, October's spring did not last for long.

Among the results of these events—apart from 200,000 Hungarian refugees—there would be a muddy and uncertain thaw, greater discretion on the Russians' part in the exercise of their dominion, some patchy and hesitant relaxation in the party's grip, but no weakening of the Communist hold on Eastern Europe. In his analysis of the institutionalization of what had been a revolutionary movement, *The New Class* (1957), the Montenegrin Milovan Djilas drew the conclusions of the whole experience: "International Communism . . . at one time the task of revolutionaries, . . .became the common ground of Communist bureaucracies, fighting one another on national considerations." This would be still more clearly demonstrated a dozen years later when one more spring blossomed only to wither in yet another Communist capital: Prague.

Among the popular democracies of Eastern Europe, Czechoslovakia was the most modern, boasting the longest acquaintance with democracy and industrialism. Its decline since the Communist takeover in 1948 illustrated the deadening effects dogmatic Communism could have on advanced economies, and the slight chances of even *Communist* opposition to Soviet imperialism. In 1968, the Czech economy was still the fifth in Europe for coal production per head, the fourth for steel, the sixth for cement. But would-be Czech reformers, like the economist Ota Sik, were pointing out that emphasis on productivity in purely quantitative terms

561

ignored consumer needs. The country's great industrial machine was engaged in production for production's sake, a race against ever-higher production norms that paid no heed to demand or quality, contributing nothing to the life of the Czechs themselves.

The ruling fascination with sheer output and statistics allowed machines to grow prematurely old, and turned production records into fakes. Where American metallurgy needed 272 pounds of steel to turn out 1,000 dollars' worth, the same job in Bohemia took 870 pounds of steel. In 1938, building a home had taken an average of 1,392 working hours; thirty years later it took 330 hours more. The atomic power station of Trnava, begun in 1958, still stood unfinished ten years later. In the United States a power station of the same potential would generally be finished in three years and a half. Czech productivity per head is 20 per cent higher than in France, yet Czech economists estimate French living standards to be well over twice as high as theirs: six times higher for engineers, double for factory workers. Something was surely wrong.

Just as important, Czech students and intellectuals in their turn were starting to react against the stifling regime to which they were subjected. It hardly seemed to them that the communism, socialism, and democracy they believed in need be expressed only in equality of dreariness and oppression. Under their impulse, with the support of factory workers and mere men-in-the-street, the Czech Communist Party went through an internal revolution, replacing its long-time Stalinist masters with new men, just as Communist but younger and more liberal minded. From January to August, 1968, "the spring of Prague" excited the hopes of Czechs and Slovaks, the sympathy of the world, the fear and the reproof of uneasy neighbors in Poland, Hungary, and East Germany.

While Moscow stayed its hand, it briefly seemed as if Communist regimes responding to the popular will could really become dictatorships of the proletariat, carrying out policies that found as much support in the trade unions and the Communist Party as in the countryside, the universities, and the national press. Supported by a great surge of national enthusiasm, guided by free discussion as it went along, the (communist) government proceeded with plans to modernize the economy, liberalize institutions, expand trade beyond the limited scope of the Communist bloc, permit a cooped-up people to travel abroad rather than merely flee. Such goings-on could not be tolerated long. In August, 1968, at long last, the country was invaded by a Communist force of 650,000 men, greater than the American armies at that time in Vietnam.* Passive resistance petered out before this overwhelming force and, on October 16, 1968, a treaty signed in Moscow legalized the country's occupa-

---

* On September 9, 1968, most Czech newspapers featured the words of Russian Army Marshal Gretchko, condemning the United States for "wishing to stifle by force of arms the love of a people for its liberty and independence."

Russian tanks enter Prague,
August, 1968.

tion by the Russians for an indeterminate length of time. Czechoslovakia, in its turn, ceased to be one of the rare European countries permitted to "edify its socialism" in the absence of the Red Army.

Moscow had energetically affirmed what is now known as the doctrine of limited sovereignty: the sovereignty of their satellites, its limits set by Moscow's appreciation of the superior interests of international communism. In 1968 as in 1956, these interests had been threatened by the liberal evolution of a neighboring Communist regime whose unforeseeable outcome might endanger the authority of dictatorship in Russia itself as well as the security of Russia's borders. As a Soviet spokesman explained,* "bourgeois" democratic liberties are a good thing in capitalist society, but bad in socialist society "for they are inevitably used by the remains of exploiting classes against the workers' interests." In actual practice, the men who crushed attempts at liberalization within their sphere acted in the tradition of the authoritarian rulers, feudal lords, and great bourgeois they once displaced, regarding the slightest reform as prelude to disintegration and trusting their fortune and their privileges only to the army and police.

What conclusions can one draw from such experience? It seems to follow that a Communist regime demands the lasting maintenance of censorship, of constraints, of the internal cold war that the Communist ideal once hoped to do away with. A revolution, said one Czech intellectual, makes sense only if it produces a better system than the one it overthrows. Communist revolutions, at least in Eastern Europe, seem to produce neither freedom nor well-being, their fragility turns attempts at self-expression into a menace and the criticism even of their own militants into subversion.

Nevertheless, even as Russian satellites, the Eastern Europeans continue to affirm their national personalities. Yugoslavia, of course, carries on the experiment on which it embarked in the mid-1940's. Romania carries on a subtler campaign of national emancipation, affirming her independence from the COMECON—the common market of the Soviet bloc—and doing her best to establish diplomatic and trade relations with

* *Le Monde,* Paris, September 20, 1968.

non-Communist countries, including France, West Germany, and Israel. The economic and industrial reforms that Ota Sik suggested, and that the Czechs tried in 1968, were introduced in Hungary as early as 1966 and Sik's writings are still used in courses at the University of Budapest. Since Hungary discreetly introduced her liberal reforms, industrial productivity has gone up by 30 to 50 per cent, trade balances have become more favorable, wages and prices have remained stable. One may expect other Communist satellites to imitate her methods. The collaborationist rulers of occupied Czechoslovakia themselves are sometimes anti-Stalinists, as concerned to get the Russians out of their land as they are to keep their clique in power. The 650,000 Russian and East German soldiers sent to do away with dangers symbolized above all by a free press can be taken as much for a promise as for a threat. Spring, after all, is a recurring phenomenon.

Turkey

Despite divisions and defeats, the years of the Young Turks saw many positive changes. Modernization proceeded, middle-class education got a serious start. A gendarmerie was created to keep the army out of politics, a measure of land reform begun, municipal reform brought drains and even garbagemen to cities like Constantinople. But the new men were unable to solve the basic problem of an Ottoman nation hard put to enlist the loyalties of its subject peoples. They had sought to apply nationalistic doctrines evolved in culturally homogeneous nations to an empire not only multinational and multiracial but multireligious too. Could Muslims and non-Muslims live as equals, when the Muslim faith said no? Were they, indeed, to identify themselves as Muslims or, above all, as Turks? These were almost insoluble questions until the nationalists realized that they could best imitate Western nationalism not by trying to copy Western models but by being themselves.. The turn from Ottoman hangovers to Turkish nationalism was facilitated when defeat in 1918 brought final collapse of the anachronistic Empire and loss of its non-Turkish territories.

Allied with the Central Powers, Turkish troops had fought stoutly on several fronts, beaten off an attempted allied landing at Gallipoli, and even forced a British army to surrender in Iraq. But—though they put on as good a show as their Russian enemies and kept it up longer than the Russians—the strain proved too much for the farflung realm which lacked the administrative and industrial substructure for a modern war. As Germany and Austria weakened, as French and Greek troops drove the Bulgarians back from the Aegean coast, the Turkish front crumbled

Mustapha Kemal (Ataturk) at the window of his personal train car.

before British armies driving north from Mesopotamia and Palestine. Soon, English, French, Greek, and Italian troops were occupying the country which seemed to have disintegrated completely. Then, in the highlands of Anatolia, Turkish nationalism regathered its forces under the leadership of the country's only victorious general: Mustafa Kemal (1881–1938)—the future Ataturk. The stubborn courage of the Turkish troops, the generalship of Kemal (already responsible for Turkish success at Gallipoli), supplemented dissensions among the victors who quarreled over spoils. British, French, and Italians withdrew, leaving the Greeks, who dreamed of a new Byzantium, to face the Turks alone. By 1922 the Greeks had been defeated and, in 1923, the Treaty of Lausanne set the borders of the new Turkish nation where they stand today.*

The great losses of Ottoman dominions in Asia were compensated by the national revival which, in a few years, had shaken off all traces of foreign domination. Turkey was now a republic, the Ottoman dynasty was banished, the capital was no longer in cosmopolitan Constantinople (renamed Istanbul) but in Anatolian Ankara; Kemal was president. His dictatorship would be nationalist, secular, and progressive, breaking with the past and modernizing the country as fast as it could bear—in many cases faster. The Gregorian calendar was introduced, the twenty-four hour clock, Western dress; the fez and the veil were driven to oblivion, religious law was abandoned and religious courts replaced by the Swiss civil code, polygamy was excluded, and equal rights were introduced for all religions, the Latin alphabet replaced the Arabic, women were given the right to vote, surnames and weekly holidays were introduced and titles abolished. Before his death in 1938, Ataturk, the most beneficial of dictators, had not only remade his country but dragged it grudgingly, reluctantly, into the twentieth century.

Such measures were slow to take effect. Literacy, about 10 per cent

* The Treaty of Lausanne acknowledged Turkey's hold of eastern Thrace up to the Maritsa Line, leaving better than one million Greeks in Turkish territory and half that many Turks in Greek areas. The problem was solved by a vast exchange and resettlement of populations which, after the first difficulties, allowed the Greco-Turkish rift to heal until the recent Cyprus troubles.

in the 1920's, was only 35 per cent in 1950. But, where in 1926 there were six times as many wooden plows as iron, today the wooden plow has disappeared and agricultural production rides forward into the age of tractors and combines. Still poor, backward, overpopulated for its underdeveloped resources, Turkey is nevertheless the most advanced and stable of Islamic nations, and this must be attributed to Ataturk's policies.

A crucial component of these policies was the reassertion of an independent state, establishing good relations with the neighbors who had been the Empire's subjects or its enemies. Relations with Communist Russia remained distant but not unfriendly, for Turkey, well aware of the territorial ambitions of her ancient rival, had no particular fear of Communist doctrines and no great fear of the Soviets until their power and expansionism revived. It seemed more urgent to keep southeastern Europe outside the scope of the power struggle developing in the 1930's. Toward this end Turkish diplomacy created the Balkan Entente of 1934, from which Albania and Bulgaria were kept by Italian pressure but which Romania, Greece, and Yugoslavia joined. If the Entente did not succeed in keeping war out of the Balkans, Kemal's heirs at least kept Turkey itself out of the war. Professor Bernard Lewis quotes a Turkish saying during the Second World War: "What we would really like would be for the Germans to destroy Russia and for the Allies to destroy Germany. Then we would feel safe."

Torn between sympathy for the Allies, traditional fear of Russia, and even greater fear of costly involvement, the Turks maintained a difficult neutrality until February, 1945, when, like other neutrals, they declared war on Germany in order to join the United Nations conference. The end of war meant new concerns for safety, however, for the German threat had been replaced by that of Russia, now an expansionist power once again, particularly dangerous since Communist propaganda could hope to get a hold on the half-educated masses of a partly secularized land. Reluctantly, the Turkish government abandoned its nonalignment policy, accepting American aid and, in due course, American military bases.

Partly as a result of these new orientations the ruling dictatorship relaxed its hold. In 1950 the country's first free and fair elections brought the opposition Democrats into power after twenty-seven years of rule by Kemal's Republican People's Party. Events would show that political democracy was not so easy to maintain and that the ultimate decisions still rested with the army. A two-party system and a hesitant advance toward freer political activity have marked the last few years. On the other hand, freedom of expression (however relative) has allowed reaction against the forced march into the twentieth century to assert itself. Turkey exports emigrant laborers to the West, and very little else. The country is declining once again into traditional torpor, a return that suggests that—like certain wines—Western political institutions travel badly and that, perhaps, Western views on the virtues of productivity, efficiency, or, even, simply work, find it hard to take root in unfamiliar ground.

The United States: A Special Case

If anyone doubted that the United States was one of the world's great powers, they could not continue to doubt it after the First World War. American supplies and loans had been decisive in the survival of the Allies, American intervention in the defeat of the Central Powers, American diplomacy in the drafting of the peace treaties, American internal policy in abandoning Europe to its own devices. President Wilson was a great reformer but a tactless, single-minded man. His failure in political maneuver, his zealous prickliness, ensured defeat first in Congress and then in national elections. The crusading policies he represented were voted down, business as usual voted back again in a succession of conservative presidents who believed with Calvin Coolidge that "the business of the United States is business," not costly meddling in world politics. This meant that the foreign policy of one of the world's great powers affected international affairs between the wars chiefly by abstention— or, more correctly, by continuous attempts to keep out of things.

The United States, like King Canute, made resolute moves to order back the tide of modern life. It curbed the flow of immigrants ("America must be kept American": Coolidge), smiled on the Ku Klux Klan with its "white, gentile, Protestant" membership, legislated against the teaching of evolution in schools, prohibited (by the 18th Amendment to the Constitution, 1919–1933) "the manufacture, sale or transportation of intoxicating liquors," and did its best to design legislation meant, as one historian has described it, to keep the country out of the war of 1914.

The war had bitten deeply into European investments. By 1918 the 6.5 billion of 1914 had been cut by half. The United States was now the world's greatest creditor, having lent nearly 2 billion to her allies in 1917–1919 and invested another 9 billion in Europe in 1919 alone. But the political mentality with which she approached the postwar world had been developed in the debtor era and reflected the defensiveness of mortgaged farmers, developing industries, and debt-ridden utility companies. Here lay the rationale of protection which wrecked all possibilities of sensible arrangements by which the outer world could have bought U.S. industrial products and settled accounts by exporting its crops and less sophisticated goods.

Yet, if Americans did not wish to buy, they were quite willing to invest. After the First World War (and especially after the Second), American capital supplanted European as the dominant economic power south of the Rio Grande, seeking to organize the vast region according to the needs of American industry. About one-third of the capital invested in Latin America comes from the United States, with which a great proportion of the continent's foreign trade is conducted (90 per cent of Mexican imports, 75 per cent of Mexican exports). In Cuba (1930) American sugar companies owned one-fifth of the land surface, two-thirds of the sugar refineries. while most of the remainder depended on U.S. credits. In Central America, the United Fruit Company owned more land than the whole of Belgium, operated most of the railroads, employed armies of laborers, and dominated national production. In Venezuela, where 17 per cent of the world's oil is produced, American companies controlled its exploitation.

Franklin Roosevelt's Good Neighbor Policy, restraint in intervening, tactful diplomacy, improved relations between the Northern and Southern Hemisphere until, in 1945, all American nations signed the Act of Chapultepec, which, in effect, discarded the unilateral use of the Monroe Doctrine in favor of a regional security system within the United Nations. But latent hostility persisted and the U.S. tendency to intervene when its interests were threatened persisted too. The supremacy that soon became clear in the U.S.'s back yard would take longer elsewhere, but would be as firmly asserted. Until the late 1920's, the resources that the European economy needed to rebuild itself came in good part from American banks. Then, a speculative boom based on security prices inflated beyond any reasonable expectation of earnings, stanched and reversed the flow. In 1928 American capital which had sought profits from European (especially German) investments began to find that it could make a better profit right at home. In 1929 the precarious credit structure on which the boom was based collapsed, and American investors had to scramble for any liquid funds they could get their hands on, recalling short-term loans and, of course, investing no more. The consequent economic depression made payment of Allied war debts even more difficult, at the very time when America's own problems made her even more determined to fend off products which could have paid the interest. "The debts of the outside world to us are ropes about their necks, by means of which we pull them towards us," declared the president of Chase National Bank in 1930. "Our trade restrictions are pitchforks pressed against their bodies, by means of which we hold them off."

Except for Finland, all of America's debtors defaulted on their debts; upon which Congress took steps to see that such a situation would not recur again, by prohibiting all defaulting nations from floating loans or securities in the United States (Johnson Act, 1934). But prevention was even more important than revenge. The United States must not again, at any price, become involved in the profitless conflicts of the outer world. A Gallup Poll showed that 70 per cent of Americans thought it had been a mistake to enter the Great War. In the summer of 1935, while

Mussolini made it clear he was about to break the peace, Congress adopted the first of a series of neutrality measures prohibiting credits, loans, export of arms or implements of war to belligerents, and making very clear American unwillingness ever again to become entangled in a foreign conflict—including, said an act of 1937, the kind of civil war then raging in Spain.

What had been made between 1934 and 1937 had to be unmade as best as President Roosevelt could in 1940, when German victory in Europe indicated that American security could not be cut off from world affairs. The U.S. aided Britain (Lend-Lease) and extended aid to Russia when she was attacked. But the Germans, remembering their earlier mistake, stayed their hand. It was the Japanese who forced it. The Japanese trying to conquer China, felt that only U.S. support permitted it to hold out against them. The United States refused to curb their aid to China or make concessions to Japanese needs. On December 7, 1941, the Pacific fleet at Pearl Harbor and the air force base at Manila were destroyed from the air and, within a few days, the United States, unprepared for the actions her politics precipitated, found herself at war with Japan and with Japan's German and Italian allies.

This time, victory found the United States quite willing to face her responsibilities throughout a world in which she now towered as the richest, strongest power. Unfortunately, as an opponent of German colonial policy once remarked, "World politics is for a nation what megalomania is for an individual." General de Gaulle complained about President Roosevelt's "will to power cloaking itself in idealism"; and this would be increasingly felt about Roosevelt's country after Roosevelt's death, as the will to power began to wear through the ideals. Ignorance, benevolence, self-interest, good intentions, a rough-and-ready naïveté, and the readiness to believe that arms could solve problems which wealth could not cure, characterized American politics into the 1960's.

There was nothing particularly wicked about this, only a giant's fumbling joy in his force and natural confidence in his own judgment. The United States is only the latest inheritor of an imperial role which others before her have handled with alternative presumption and dismay under the suspicious, wary, or hostile eyes of the other powers. The natural expression of power, riches, and abounding energies is never really matched by wisdom or foresight to everyone's satisfaction. It only becomes significant when its results affect not only a restricted area but the world itself, and this is truer today than it ever was.

Chapter 13

THE MATERIAL
REVOLUTION

Technology and Production

In 1776 when Adam Smith wanted to demonstrate the wonders of modern mass production he used the example of ten workers producing 48,000 needles a day. A hundred years later a machine turned out 180 needles a minute, so the ten workers would have produced 2 million needles a day. The textile worker who turned out 9,600 yards of cotton in a thirteen-hour work day in 1840 was turning out 300,000 yards in ten hours in 1880. Cyrus McCormick's Harvester allowed one American farmer to harvest seventeen acres in the time that one European scythed through one.

The marvels of eighteenth-century technology were dwarfed by the nineteenth century, as these in turn were due to be left behind by the twentieth. The high priest of this acceleration was the engineer, whom Tennyson hymned in his *Mechanophilus*.

> Now first we stand and understand,
> And sunder false and true,
> And handle boldly with the hand,
> And see and shape and do.
>
> Dash back that ocean with a pier,
> Strow yonder mountain flat,
> A railway there, a tunnel here,
> Mix me this Zone with that!

The engineer's product was the machine, turning out more machines, ever more precise, ever more interchangeable, ever more productive.

Without specialized machine tools there could be no mass production of goods on a modern scale, without the high precision of their construction there could be no mass production of machines themselves, no replaceable parts, none of the fine and complex web of industry that we associate with the modern age. Improved machines allowed their own materials to be turned out in greater quantities and at lower prices. Coal —"the modern philosopher's stone," whose gas was used for light, whose tars went into benzine and anilines, whose elements could be used, like picrates for explosives and which itself provided fuel for power, heat, and locomotion—was being mined in greater quantities: 90 million tons in 1850 (ten times the total of sixty years before), 1 billion in 1900, 1.5 billion in 1950. Iron: 5 million tons in 1850, 44 million in 1900, 130 million in 1950.* In 1875 Sidney Gilchrist Thomas discovered a process for refining phosphoric iron ores, thus making available great deposits of previously useless ores like the *minette* of Lorraine just acquired by Germany. And, just as England had been responsible for the avalanche of cheap iron that covered the nineteenth century, so it would be an English engineer, Henry Bessemer, whose converter (1856–1858) turned hitherto rare steel into a democratic commodity, not only six or seven times more resistant than iron but now accessible in price. From 1825 to 1866 the price of iron had fallen by two-thirds. In the next fifteen years steel followed suit, and in America, where technological expertise was most advanced and production highest, the price of steel rails fell 90 per cent between 1875 and 1898.

Mass production, of course, depends on mass consumption. The most striking evidence of the machines' success at the everyday level was the increased availability of consumer goods of the most ordinary kind— soap, chocolate, cheap paper, or beef extract—none of which had been so ordinary in earlier days. The lead pencil, developed in the eighteenth century, was only mass-produced after the 1850's. So was newsprint (15

* In terms of volume, nine-tenths of all the world's mining—not just coal or iron— would be carried out after 1800.

A mechanized bakery. A dog-powered treadmill outside the building operates the kneading machines illustrated here.

cents a pound in 1867, half that price fifteen years later). Pens with steel nibs, used in the first half of the century in lieu of quills, also became cheaper: 2 dollars a gross in 1830, 12 cents a gross in 1861. Fountain pens, appearing in the 1830's, became generally available in the 1880's, at the same time as inexpensive watches. Very costly portable cameras were metamorphosed by 1900 into the Brownie box camera which anyone could buy for 5 shillings or a dollar.*

In 1850 Isaac M. Singer marketed the first practical sewing machine, providing a great spur to ready-made clothing, whose value in production doubled within the decade. By 1880 boot and shoe manufacturers had applied similar machines to their needs, reducing the cost of sewing them some twenty-seven times. At first, home seamstresses could not afford to buy sewing machines and lost a lot of trade, while workshops, prisons, and convents that installed them competed with home dressmakers.** By the 1860's sewing machines began appearing in private homes, first in the United States, then throughout the world. Another humble engine which had a great impact was the velocipede: "Machine equipped with two, three or four wheels, activated by the feet and which permits one to move faster than a horse." The original high-wheeled bicycles with solid rubber tires were soon replaced by modern types with pneumatic tires and proper brakes. In the 1890's a bicycle was still a middle-class article, costing in France about 500 francs or $100—equivalent to two months of a lieutenant's pay. By 1900, at a third of this price, it had become accessible even to workers.

On its own humble level the bicycle was an invention as revolutionary as the automobile, opening distance to persons who had seldom gone far beyond their homes for lack of individual means of locomotion. Village swains could get on their bicycles on Sundays to court girls who lived in another valley, five or ten miles away. Women, long restricted in their movements, could mount their pedaled steeds and leave the chaperone behind. Physical mobility was the symbol of social and economic mobility, the prelude of more. By 1900, a million bicycles were being turned out in the United States.

This was the period when machines began to invade the home and office: carpet sweepers, washing machines, telephones, all in the 1870's, electric bells in 1880, electric fans, vacuum cleaners, and phonographs (invented by Thomas Edison in 1878) in the 1890's, refrigerators after 1900. The house, no longer a mere shelter as it had been until then, became a comfort, a machine for use and pleasure as very few of our ancestors could enjoy or imagine. White transparent window glass, a conquest of the seventeenth century which must have made an immense

* In 1884, Pope Leo XIII, who liked photography, had one of the Vatican galleries embellished with frescoes of religion blessing the arts, including Photography with her attendant cherub holding a large camera.

** Incidentally, this explains the hostility of many workers in European countries to the competition of convents and charity workshops.

A patent office illustration for an early motorized vacuum cleaner.

difference to domestic comfort, was still lacking in most peasant houses by 1800, when shutters, boards, or other means closed the scarce openings. By 1900 the poorest could enjoy it. Running water, central heating, electric light, the facilities offered by modern utilities, not to speak of air conditioning, were all conquests of the last century which may have affected our lives more than the airplane or the cyclotron.

Most of the new inventions depended not on steam but on electric power: not least electric light, made possible partly by Edison's invention of the incandescent lamp in 1879. While gas light continued to light streets and homes well into the twentieth century, the 1880's would see public and private buildings lit by electric light and electric traction motorizing first streetcars, then underground railways. The Chicago World's Fair of 1893 included the exhibition of a model electric kitchen: the shape of things to come, but not at once.

In 1886, Monsieur de Goncourt visited an American lawyer in Paris to sign a contract concerning one of his plays and reported that "the act was printed on a little piano." The typewriter had become a commercial possibility in the 1870's. It would soon be joined by calculating machines, cash registers, and tabulators—ancestors of the first modern computer, which IBM developed in 1943. Soon the question would arise of reconciling men and machines, fitting them one to the other, designing machines for the best results, training their users to use them to the best advantage. The notion would be first applied to adjust workmen as thoroughly as possible to the potentials and needs of their machine. Around 1900, an engineer, Frederick Taylor, raised the efficiency of coal shovelers by analyzing their movements and cutting out all unnecessary ones; another engineer, F. B. Gilbreth, did the same for bricklayers by reducing stooping and arranging their tools in a more practical way. Taylor initiated "time and motion studies," first at Bethlehem Steel, then elsewhere, to determine the standard time of each workman's task and to increase the productivity of workers. By 1907 Taylor's methods were applied by men like Henry Ford, who introduced a moving assembly line to turn out his Model T, cutting assembly time from 14 hours to 93 minutes per car. Europeans, who denounced Taylorism for turning the workman into a cretinized automaton, were not long in learning the lessons of "scientific management" when they found that it worked, and that in plants where it was applied the production index soared even while, as in the case of Ford, the wages could be higher for fewer hours of work.

New Links, New Trails

Alfred Marshall, the economist, remarked in 1890 that "the dominant economic fact of our age is the development not of manufacturing but of transport industries." The greatest of these in Marshall's day was still the railroads—the first great web in which nineteenth-century man organized his space and eventually, as we shall see, his time. "All railways," asserted a member of the British Parliament in 1844, "are public frauds and private robberies." But he was a lonely holdout. Forty-five thousand miles in 1860, 450,000 in 1895, 700,000 in 1910, steel rails spread their tentacles over the world. Great tunnels through the Swiss and Austrian Alps (Mont Cénis in 1871, Saint Gotthard 1882, Arlberg 1884, Simplon 1906) linked France and Italy, Germany and Italy, Switzerland and Austria, facilitating exchanges between North and South, East and West, and making Switzerland the turntable of Europe.

Charles Dickens, visiting America in the 1840's, already reports passenger cars with corridors and sleeping arrangements. G. M. Pullman's first sleepers appeared in the early 60's, his dining car in 1867. Europe was slower: sleeping cars appeared on trains in 1883 and dining cars in 1884, at the same time as great international expresses like the Orient Express, whose luxuries caught the popular imagination. But local passenger services were even more important. Cheap workmen's fares, "to

Warder Collection

A contemporary illustration of one of the first Pullman sleepers.

encourage the migration of the working classes into suburbs" and relieve housing congestion in the center, came in during the 60's and the 70's. Elevated and underground railways, appearing in the 1860's, extended the urban area and created new residential districts. Tramways, which have been called the gondolas of the people, also cut the time workers needed to get to work while helping bring new areas like public parks and sports grounds within their reach.

The trains wore down distinct regional cultures based on isolation and a large measure of self-sufficiency, fused separate regions divided as much by different rates of change as by cultural divisions, broke down local markets. The introduction of rail freight cut shipping costs by half to three-fourths in the earliest days and, shortly, far more than that. In 1817 it cost $140 to ship a ton of freight from Pittsburgh to Philadelphia; seventy years later $3 or less. In Nigeria, in 1926, a man could still choose between porters, trucks, and rail in cost proportions of 15 to 6 to 1. In remote regions where the high cost of porterage had made only the shipment of very costly goods (ivory, gold) economic, railroads—however expensive to build and operate—revolutionized the carriage of bulk freight. Where the trains went, local building materials were supplanted by cheaper bricks and slates, later by cement. The trains, which facilitated migration and hence cosmopolitanism, also facilitated the tendency to industrial concentration and specialization, accelerated the growing uniformity of the economic and cultural landscape. Rails turned the states they bound together into nations—Germany, Italy, the United States, Canada, Russia, India—with common concerns and a common center of gravity.

Timetables played their part in standardizing time itself, which had long differed from place to place. On England's Great Western Railway a timetable of July 30, 1841, indicates in a footnote that "London time is about 4 minutes earlier than Reading time, 7½ minutes before Cirencester, 14 minutes before Bridgewater." Engineers and travelers had to make their own adjustments until, in the early 1850's, the telegraph allowed time signals to be sent from London with which all stations could synchronize. From that point on, "railway time" spread from station into village, town, and hinterland, gradually bringing London time—that is Greenwich Standard Time—to every place.* No wonder that colonial powers, which wanted to assert their control over the vast spaces they possessed and harness their potential to their needs, built railroads like the Russian Trans-Siberian or the British over India, which by 1940 still had more railway mileage than all the rest of Asia. No wonder either that, with over a third of the world's railroads in North America and another third in Europe, the Western world outstripped all other areas in wealth and in cohesion.* *

* With the exception of holdouts like Christ Church Cathedral in Oxford, whose clock still clings to local time.

** By 1920, total African and Asian mileage was less than a third that of the United States.

Technology was advancing on the seas as well, forging new links between the continents. In 1620 the *Mayflower* had taken 66 days to cross the Atlantic. In 1776 news of the Declaration of Independence took 44 days to reach Europe. Mid-nineteenth-century packets were taking 21 days, the fastest clippers 14 days or so, iron steamships 9 or 10. The 1930's would cut the length of passage to 4 days. But steam took a long time supplanting sail, and the world's steam tonnage only caught up with that of sailing ships in 1893. The real advantage of steamships was that, no longer dependent on wind, they could hold a schedule which sailing ships could not be sure of doing. But for a long time fuel problems made them relatively uneconomic until, in the 1860's, new screw propellers replaced paddle wheels and new compound engines, demanding less fuel, left more space for cargo. This was when rates on bulk freight began to fall, and export of wheat, meats, and minerals to soar, turning the whole world into one great marketplace.

A great spur to overseas trade came with the invention of refrigeration. Ice cut from lakes and rivers, preserved in ice houses, exported all over the world in special storage tanks, had been for some time a minor American industry. American home consumption in 1876 had been more than 2 million tons, and the industry employed 10,000 men and 4,000 horses. Artificial ice began to be manufactured in the 1860's, mechanical refrigerators for the house in 1900, but not in mass production until the 1920's. The first refrigerated steamers sailed to Europe in 1877 carrying frozen mutton. In 1883 the first modern packing plant was set up near Buenos Aires. By that time refrigerated shipments of fruit and dairy products, as well as meat, were coming not only from America but from New Zealand and Australia.

The real breakthrough came when the Suez Canal, opened in 1869 (with Verdi's *Aida* written especially for its inauguration), cut the distance between Europe and China by 3,000 miles. In 1862 the journey from Marseilles to Bombay had taken 26 days; in 1872 Jules Verne's Phileas Fogg took 18 days from his London club (and 80 days to go around the world). Ten years after the opening of the Suez Canal, freight rates between Europe and India had fallen to a quarter of their previous cost. Other canals followed: in 1893 the Corinth Canal that Nero had dreamed of digging linked the Aegean and the Ionian Seas; in 1895 the Kiel Canal shortened the distance between the North Sea and the Baltic; in 1914 the Panama Canal joined the Atlantic and Pacific Oceans. The dreams of the Saint-Simonians had been realized. The volume of international trade grew fiftyfold between 1800 and 1900.

By then the internal combustion engine was replacing steam in ships as on the land. Worked on throughout the 1860's and the 70's by men in Germany, Austria, and Italy, the internal combustion engine and the carburetor were first patented by Gottlieb Daimler in 1885. His automobile inspired other engineers, like René Panhard and Armand Peugeot in France, Karl Bentz in Germany, R. E. Olds, J. W. Packard, and the Dodge brothers in the United States to build models of their own. Rudolf Diesel—a German born in Paris—would develop his oil injection engine in 1893. Horses and carriages—dust on hedgerows and on roadside grass in summer, mud that stuck carriages in winter, click of horses' hooves and clatter of wheels over paving, smell of horse manure—still dominated the railway age: coach and cab, berlin, barouche, daumont and Landau and phaeton and coupe, rolled and rattled over country lanes and through city streets. By 1900, however, some 4,000 autos were running over city cobbles or country ruts, exhilarating to their drivers, a dangerous nuisance to everybody else. By 1914 there were two million of them, and they could reach speeds as high as 50 m.p.h.

The auto industry stimulated other enterprises: tarred roads which made auto movement possible ended the dust problem of the early days, the rubber industry which had developed pneumatic tires for bicycles (1885) now found a growing market in automobiles (Dunlop pneumatic tires, 1900) and increased demand for its raw materials from South America, India, and Southeast Asia; manufacturers of steel, glass, plastics, electrical accessories, and machine tools all profited. So did newly motorized bandits. But the greatest beneficiary was the petroleum industry, which had appeared in the 1850's to supply paraffin and kerosene for lamps and stoves, petroleum as a lubricant, and oil for ship's boilers.

Oil, preferably derived from sperm whales, began by being used mostly for lubrication and to fuel oil lamps. When in mid-century whales began to run out, interest shifted to mineral sources meagerly tapped in France and England, the United States, and eastern Europe. Romania produced crude petroleum in 1857, but the first commercial production of it came in Pennsylvania at the end of that decade. Soon other countries were following suit, especially Russia, whose oil fields

Warder Collection

Victoria Embankment in London during the early 1900's.

The Wright Brothers'
first flight at Kitty
Hawk, North Carolina.
Opposite: a Fokker F-
32, one of the most pop-
ular early commercial
planes, which accommo-
dated 32 passengers.

National Archives

around Baku in the Caucasus produced more crude oil than Americans did by the beginning of our century. Though still mostly used for lighting and lubrication, world crude oil production rose from half a million barrels in 1860 to 400 million in 1914. By then it was being used to feed the growing appetite of cars, ships, trains, and even airplanes. By 1962 the world production of crude oil would be over a billion tons a year * and the United States (since 1902 the leading producer) accounted for almost a third of it.

The internal combustion engine increased mobility and opportunities even more than trains. Regular motor omnibuses began to run in London in 1904 and 1916 saw the last horsedrawn bus. Motor taxis were replacing hansom cabs; in 1912 a hansom was placed in a London museum. In 1911 the London Fire Brigade abandoned horses for internal combustion engines. Motor buses provided the poor with the first real opportunity for day trips to seacoasts or countryside that most had never seen before, and stressed the opportunity to escape from towns to suburban living. So did cars which supplemented commuter transport, creating the tentacular suburban spreads characteristic of the twentieth century, new settlements "composed," as A. J. P. Taylor puts it, "of little more than individual motor cars come to rest." The effects were revolutionary. Most of the children in John Steinbeck's *Cannery Row* (1944) were, as he says, "conceived in Model T Fords and not a few were born in them. The theory of the Anglo-Saxon home became so warped that it never quite recovered." The automobile could also be highly destructive. Today, 200,000 people die and 5 million are maimed yearly in road accidents: more in all, so far, than all the casualties of both world wars.

Sea and land transportation were not alone affected: the internal combustion engine also made possible the control of flight. We have seen that balloons, born before the French Revolution and put to use in its wars, had caught the popular fancy. But their use was strictly limited by steerage problems. During the siege of Paris in 1870, when balloons provided the only means of communication with the outside world, carrying 2.5 million letters, 400 pigeons, 102 passengers, and 2 dogs, of 66 balloons launched from Paris only 58 landed safely. The rest ended in

* In 1956, at the time of the Suez crisis, the non-Communist world consumed 690 million tons of oil turned out by an industry with assets of 38 billion dollars. By the Middle East War of 1967 both these figures had doubled, and they are expected to double again by 1980.

Prussian territory, out at sea, in Holland, Munich, and one even in Norway some 2,000 miles away.*

In 1900 a retired German cavalry general, Count Ferdinand von Zeppelin, conceived and built the first heavier-than-air dirigible airship, almost concurrently with the first powered, sustained, and controlled flight of an airplane made by the Wright brothers at Kitty Hawk, North Carolina (1903). Airships would carry over 20,000 persons before 1914 and render great services during the First World War; but their advantages were less than the dangerous flammability of the gases in their skin, and they were ultimately abandoned in favor of the airplane, whose development proved incredibly swift. In 1909 a Frenchman, Louis Blériot, flew the English Channel. The First World War gave aircraft a great impetus, confirming high expectations of their more murderous possibilities. The 1920's would see airplanes entering into general use, the building of airports serving the cities, the first nonstop flight from New York to Paris,** the development of air mail and of passenger transport. By 1933 the airplane had cut Phileas Fogg's record of sixty years before by nine-tenths, circling the world in less than eight days. However, the routines we take for granted today are very recent. In 1946, the Dutch National airline KLM established the first regular flights between Europe and New York; in 1947 Pan American began scheduled round-the-world flights. Where air travel had logged 8 billion passenger kilometers in 1945, it counted 275 billion in 1967, not including Russia and China.

There was yet a faster means of communication: telegraphy. In 1860, messages were still relayed by the same means as Caesar used. While stagecoaches still took three weeks from St. Joseph, Missouri, to San Francisco, the pony express proved that it could carry urgent dispatches in half that time. Within one year the transcontinental telegraph had put it out of business by taking only seconds for the job. The telegraph was not new in 1861. The new development of the mid-nineteenth century was its extension, in part by underwater cables which linked Europe to England in 1851, to the United States in 1866, to India in 1870, to Australia in

* Pigeons supplemented balloons in carrying letters for which a microfilm process was developed. Every pigeon carried six tiny films, each containing 5,000 letters. While the Prussians used hawks against the pigeons, Krupp developed a special anti-aircraft gun to check the air lift.

** By Colonel Charles Lindbergh in 1927. Two Englishmen had made the first crossing of the Atlantic from Newfoundland to Ireland in 1919.

The Material Revolution

1871. "They have killed their father Time," wrote Rudyard Kipling of *Deep Sea Cables:*

> . . . Hush! Men talk today o'er the waste of the ultimate slime,
> and a new Word runs between: whispering, "Let us be one!"

Ocean cables set up a novel and extraordinary link between different continents. An urgent message from London or Paris to New York could not be answered in less than three weeks before 1866; one to India in less than two months before 1870; one to Australia in less than four months before 1872. After those days they took minutes.* The result was a revolution in trade, diplomacy, and news-gathering of every kind. The price of commodities and grain, the evolution of a political situation, could be followed hour by hour rather than after laborious delays. Orders could be placed, commodities bought, ships redirected—and this was further facilitated by the use of radio telegraphy. G. Marconi sent the first radio message in 1894, his first trans-Atlantic signal in 1901. In 1900 Emil Rathenau, president of the great German electrical trust of AEG, set up the first radio aerial on the roof of his Berlin building, and within a few years radio contact had been established with Germany and the world. By then, ships at sea could get radio messages, the importance of which was publicized when the "unsinkable" *Titanic* sank in 1912.**

Improved communications meant that every kind of postal service grew apace: gummed stamps and the penny post had multiplied the number of letters sent in England to over half a billion a year by 1860. The Germans, who in 1840 dispatched 1.5 letters per inhabitant, were sending about 60 per inhabitant yearly in 1900. The U.S. Post Office sold 1.5 million stamps in 1850, 4 billion in 1900, six times as many in 1960. Europeans, who sent 9 million telegrams in 1898, were sending nearly 400 million before the First World War. There were 12 million telephones in 1908, 171 million in 1964 (nearly half of them in the United States). Materially the world was contracting, its separate parts being pulled closer to one another, the great trade fairs of the Middle

* Shortly the cables would also be used for telephones: a London-Paris telephone line opened in 1891.

** Radar, which uses a directional radio impulse to find the range and bearing of aircraft, ships, or other moving objects, and television were further developments of the discovery of how to transmit sound waves by electrical impulses. The first ship equipped with radar appeared in 1938, the first transmission of television signals was made in 1927, the first commercial television program was broadcast in the late 1930's after the Olympic Games held in Berlin in 1936 had been televised. Meanwhile, electronic research developed tubes capable of emitting ever shorter waves. After 1932, electronic optics developed electronic microscopes (capable of distinguishing to 1/100,000 of a millimeter), telescopes (which can work 120 times as rapidly as their predecessors), spectrographs, photoelectric cells (electric eyes) used in sound film, radar, and TV. Norbert Wiener developed cybernetics based on the analogy between electronics and the human brain.

Ages replaced by a spate of international exhibitions, the international rivalries overlaid by international agreements: to treat wounded and medical personnel decently in war (1864), standardize weights and measures (1875), establish a world postal union (1878), protect works of literature and art by copyright (1886), settle conflicts by international arbitration (1907), or, if unsettled, fight them out according to accepted rules (1907).

Industrial Progress and its Problems

The world of 1900 was more complicated than it had ever been. Men —even enemies—had to co-operate in order to function. All this resulted from technological changes taking place gradually but with increasing acceleration. On the European continent and in North America the years to 1870 or so saw only the beginnings of industrial revolution: the basic accumulation of equipment, the growth and reinvestment of capital, the rapid rise of population and its migration from country to towns, the increasing supply of consumer goods and, more slowly, of agricultural products. After 1871, the application of electricity in industry and the rise of industry in central Europe ushered in a second industrial revolution, marked by an immense development of synthetic products, dyestuffs, cosmetics, insecticides, drugs, plastics, synthetic rubber or fabrics, but, above all, by a shift in the source of industrial power from steam to internal combustion and diesel, from coal to oil and electricity. This meant that the balance of economic power shifted from the older industrial countries to new ones which adjusted more rapidly (Germany and Japan) or which enjoyed richer sources of new power (the United States and Russia), and the balance of industry shifted from railways to automobiles and tractors and trucks and airplanes.

The new industrial revolution was backed by the spread of machinery to the land, and the consequent rise in agricultural production and fall in food prices. While the population stabilized, removing the pressure of new mouths, the living and consumption standards of the popular masses, which had been little improved or adversely affected by the first industrial stages, bettered markedly despite—and sometimes because of—the brutal break of the First World War. The depression which began in 1929 masked the technological developments that would accelerate economic progress, bring new and basic changes in the ways and standards of all whom they affected—largely beginning around 1950. A second century of technological progress opened, whose crux seems to be its—painful—spread to vast areas which have remained in an earlier stage of economic development. Obviously, India or China live in conditions similar to those obtaining in the days of Frederick the Great and, while the majority of English or French people are just gaining the comforts which most Americans of the late 1930's took for granted, the economic level of Spain or Greece today is better compared with that of Bismarck's Europe.

Historically, this too is a new situation precipitated only in the last two centuries. In 1700, at least as regards essentials—that is, food—all the world's peoples faced similar circumstances. By 1800 this was no longer so even in Europe; by 1900 the differences were startling. It now looks as if the closing of the gap, which we have observed first within industrial societies, then within the area of their influence, will be the chief purpose and, it is hoped, the main effect of future technological developments. The crux of these lies in productivity; for it is interesting to note that whereas the indispensable raw material of the first industrial revolution was human, after 1913 not manpower but machine power accounted for increased production. Tractors, reapers, and other gear turned farmers into mechanics and agricultural labor into something performed largely by machines. In Russia 90 per cent of the sowing is now done by tractors, in the United States more than that. Cows are now milked and products processed by machines. The armaments industry is almost wholly automated. Where once twenty-three men produced 900 grenades per hour, now only two are needed. In the grenade factory at Rockford, Illinois, "no human hand touches the product from the time when blocks of steel enter the manufacturing process to the time when the finished weapons have been packed." In Ford's automated plant at Cleveland, forty-one men do the work that three times that number accomplished under the conveyor belt system. In the phonograph recording industry, five times as many records are turned out every day by four operators instead of 250 in the 1930's. Between 1880 and 1953 the productivity of men at work in an average European industry had doubled. It doubled again between 1953 and 1962, achieving as much progress in nine years as had been logged in the preceding seventy.

Such progress in turn creates serious problems, for modern industrial economy is eating into the resources on which it has been built. As the nineteenth century ended, the annual paper consumption of a successful Paris daily chewed up the equivalent of a 25,000-acre forest. The United States used more metals and mineral fuels since World War I than the whole world has used through all its history up to 1914. Shortages which develop as more advanced societies consume ever more of the world's raw materials cause the cost of supplies to rise, even in the case of industrial water of which it takes 20 cubic meters to refine a ton of petroleum or sugar, 150 cubic meters (some 250 tons) to make one ton of steel. The need of water per head of population has grown fifty times in as many years. Before 1914 water consumption was about 20 pints a day for every member of mankind. Today the figure stands around 800 pints.

We are outgrowing our usable resources. People can eat just so much.

But they aspire to ever higher living—that is, consumption—standards in manufactured goods and, there, supplies are being reduced to the point where rising costs may curtail their use.

Consumption of energy has soared in the past century, eating up in one year the fossil fuels accumulated over several centuries. The world's consumption of energy, 12 million kilowatt-calories per inhabitant in 1953, had risen to 20 million by 1968. Sooner or later coal, oil, and gas reserves will be exhausted. Humanity is trying to devise ways of tapping alternative sources of energy—solar or atomic. This last, if properly harnessed, holds out extraordinary possibilities. Thus in 1954 U.S. power plants generated 410 billion kilowatt-hours. If the nuclear fusion reaction now used in bombs could be manipulated as a source of controlled energy, a single cubic mile of sea water would yield five times as much. While such developments remain in the realm of fantasy, six years after Hiroshima the first EBR-1 reactor was generating electricity from nuclear power and, by 1966, twenty-one nuclear power plants had been ordered by public utility companies in the United States, the rest of the world following along behind.

But while we know that there are alternative sources of power and that man-made materials can be, and are being, fashioned to replace those that we exhaust, basic natural resources are being lost, polluted, or dangerously mutated. The earth's atmosphere is vast but not limitless. In time, it can become saturated with the toxins that we send up in it, just as the world's waters are beginning to be poisoned. And, while serious changes take place in the air and waters that surround us, the ground beneath our feet shifts under the weight of great masses of water gathered behind our dams, trembles at the nuclear blasts set off in its bowels, imbibes the noxious fallout of above-ground explosions, staggers and sometimes gives way before our assaults. Sooner or later there is retribution and, usually, though the fathers ate the grapes it is the children's teeth that are set on edge. On October 21, 1966, 144 inhabitants of the village of Aberfan in Wales, among them 116 children, died crushed by the sudden slide of a mountain of mining refuse. Accumulated in a century or more, the great mound—720 feet, one million tons—long loomed over the village before it fell on it, treated with the indifference

An atomic power plant under construction in Scotland.

of habit: a manmade volcano ready to erupt but, unlike a volcano, the creation of man's indifference to the results of his own handiwork.

Imponderable things are also being lost, whose disappearance statistics do not mention. "Cultural treasures" are destroyed by the world that worships them and destroyed the faster the richer the society: the mosaics of Ravenna, the sculptures of the Acropolis, shaken to pieces by passing planes; the paintings of Lascaux and of the Catacombs defaced by tourist scribbles; acres of frescoes ready to fall off their walls because of the tremors of passing traffic; gardens of castles in the Loire Valley decaying because neighboring factories deprive them of water; stones rotting and disintegrating under the chemicals in the air around them; the pines of Rome dying from too much hydrocarbon and Venice itself threatened by the waves of its vaporettos.

Problems of this order are far from insoluble. The social investments they suggest—not just the schools, hospitals, and highways we now take for granted, but relief of asphyxiated cities, of threatened countryside, of torn or eroded lands, protection of natural and artistic resources, the battle against pollution of water and air—could easily play the role of economic motor that defense now plays in many developed economies. Only time will show whether the immense potential we have begun to tap on every level will be applied to make life better or put an end to it.

Medicine and Hygiene

Medicine has always been a field in which art and science meet, but imagination had long prevailed over precision. As the nineteenth century opened, the practice of medicine in the West had only recently freed itself from earlier "harmonies" which related metals, humors, elements, and passions with the signs of the zodiac. Diagnostics no longer took account of the position of the stars, prescriptions no longer included pounded toad or the excrement of cats, academic considerations ignored the symbolic relation between bodily functions and the planets. Medicine could now turn from affirmation to observation, from observation to definition and experiment, from experiment to application on a quantitative and scientific plane.

There were certain drawbacks. Since its birth medicine had reflected the common culture of the educated, had been pursued as a kind of dialogue between patient and physician, both speaking a similar language and sharing much the same basic knowledge. Medicine was an aspect of philosophy, a kind of applied psychology or science in which the bodies of men, their pathology, their biology, intruded only slowly and late. In Restoration France, Balzac's Country Doctor still had to guess a patient's trouble from his account of it. Soon thereafter doctors began to use clinical thermometers to examine patients, to put their ear or their stethoscope on back and chest to hear the sound of heart and lungs, to draw their own conclusions. Thereafter, the gap between the patient and his impressions and the doctor and his diagnosis grew to a point where communication broke down almost entirely: the patient reified by the technical competence of the doctor. Men became cases, the sick man disappeared behind his sickness.

But, if the sick became increasingly *objects* of their doctors' care, sickness and pain were effectively pressed back. The first medical revolution had come with a vaccine early in the nineteenth century. Some 60 million persons had been killed by smallpox during the eighteenth century. In the nineteenth, wherever vaccine was adopted, mortality from smallpox became negligible.* The great medical breakthroughs were still to come: antiseptics and anesthetics lie at the basis of the modern world as much as steam. There were great delays between their discovery and their application. Chloroform, found in 1831, was first used as an anesthetic in Edinburgh in 1847 (American surgeons had started using ether in 1844); carbolic acid, discovered in 1834, was used as an antiseptic after 1865. Part of the delay stemmed from superstition, as when relief of pain in childbirth by unnatural means was opposed on religious grounds even after Queen Victoria accepted chloroform in 1853 for the birth of Prince Leopold. More stemmed from inertia and ignorance in the medical profession. As late as 1868, doctors still treated hepatitis complicated by serious lung infection by using leeches, cupping, and lancing to "draw off the bad blood"—a method compared to which the scapulars and holy water that Catholics recommended might prove less murderous.

Florence Nightingale's *Notes on Hospitals* (1859) opens with a revealing phrase: "It may seem a strange principle," she writes, "to enumerate as the very first requirement in a hospital that it should do the sick no harm." In practice, mortality in hospitals was higher than outside, because elementary sanitary precautions were ignored and, when the nineteenth century ended, 50 per cent of hospitalized cases still died of infections caught in the hospital. One of the few positive results of the Crimean War was Florence Nightingale's campaign to establish nursing as a profession. But, even as trained nurses trickled into wards and, eventually, into the countryside as well, better ventilation, greater cleanliness, improved food and drainage, could have saved thousands. Their virtues would not be seriously considered until the 1880's, or still later when the magic evoked in Thomas Mann's *Magic Mountain* began to be tapped, and tubercular patients were sent to sanatoria chiefly to get lots of pure fresh air.

While hospitals could remedy the woeful lack of nursing personnel and

* During the war of 1870–71, in the German army, where vaccination was compulsory, 297 died of smallpox; in the French army, where vaccination was not compulsory, 23,400 died of smallpox.

Florence Nightingale.

provide their patients with real nurses' care after the 1870's, they could not triumph over the conditions in which they operated until their basic environment was changed. The drains and sewers of the larger cities were well described by the London woman who, when asked if her house had drains, answered, "No thank God, Sir, we have none of them foul stinking things here!" In London in 1849, when over 14,000 persons died of cholera, sewers poured more than nine million cubic feet of muck and sludge into the Thames, whence came the city's water described by *The Spectator* as "a more or less concentrated solution of native guano." Legislation began to remedy the situation in the 50's but river windows of the House of Commons remained steadfastly closed and in 1858 there was serious talk of moving Parliament away from the unbearable stench of the river.

A great campaign for better drains in the 1870's gradually drove back typhoid fever, headaches, sore throats, and nausea, along with rotten pipes, damp, dankness, rats, and unsanitary drains. It was only thus that the soaring death rate of all cities could be lowered. Public drains called for private plumbing. If he could not be a prince, declared the future Edward VII who nearly died of typhoid fever in 1871, he would wish to be a plumber. And, on his humble level, the plumber appears as very much the guardian angel of late nineteenth-century hygiene. Plumbers made possible "public conveniences," which, first installed in the Crystal Palace (1851), helped diminish what the *Official Report* of the Exhibition called "the sufferings which must be endured by all, but more especially by females, on account of the want of them." Plumbers, installing running water in private dwellings, also made possible bathing, first in hip baths—which were recommended as "very beneficial in various forms of cholera, colic, liver complaints, diarrhea and disordered conditions" —then in tubs and bathrooms. In the 1880's one out of six urban residents in North America could boast a bathtub and, by that time, the possibilities of thorough washing had been supplemented by the greater availability of soap, which only became accessible to the poorer classes in the last thirty or forty years of the century.*

Against this slowly brightening backdrop the progress of medicine took place. In the 1860's and 70's Pasteur in France, Lister in Scotland, Koch in Germany established that diseases caused by microbes can be fended off by inoculation and asepsis. Where these were applied, legislated, and enforced as in England, the death rate which had hovered around 22 per 1,000 since 1840 fell to 18 in 1890 and 15 in the 1900's, and average life expectation grew by 10 years. In Russia where little was done on these lines, the death rate in 1890 was still 35 per 1,000. Meanwhile, mortality was being forced back in other quarters. In the early eighties German researchers identified the bacilli of typhoid, diphtheria, and cholera; in 1894 the French that of the plague; in 1898 the Japanese that of tetanus. Before the century ended the Caesarian operation had been developed, forceps gave gynecologist or midwife a better chance of delivering the baby, an artificial incubator which Pasteur developed preserved infants prematurely born, and baby foods improved the prospects of the infant's health. German researchers like Robert Koch and Paul Ehrlich, employing aniline dyes to identify bacteria, suggested the possibility of chemotherapy, using chemical agents to kill noxious microscopic organisms without hurting body tissues. Ehrlich dreamed of a "magic bullet," discovered Salvarsan in 1909, and laid the groundwork for later sulfa drugs and antibiotics. Medicine was now aided by biochemistry, discovering vitamins whose absence from our diet causes deficiency diseases: scurvy, rickets, pellagra; and hormones: adrenaline (isolated 1901), insulin (1922) for diabetes, cortisone (1936) for arthritis. In 1910, the discovery of different groups of blood made blood transfusions safe, while surgical possibilities increased with the development of machines for artificial respiration.

The results of all this are recorded in dry statistics. Between 1870 and 1905 England saw deaths from typhoid fever reduced by nearly seven-eighths, from tuberculosis by more than half. In Italy where in 1887, 836 per million had died of typhoid, 595 of malaria, 534 of smallpox, 115 of pellagra, twenty years later these figures had been reduced to 225, 125, 13, and 48.

During the twentieth century even greater advances would be made—greater it has been said than in all the ages since the world began. Biological and physiological discoveries, psychopathology, modern surgery

* Toilet products remained luxuries. Artificial hair dressing (as opposed to bear grease) appeared in 1793 with Rowland's Macassar Oil, to be mentioned in Byron's *Don Juan* and Lewis Carroll's *Through the Looking Glass,* and survives in the term "anti-macassar." Cutthroat razors appeared in the fifteenth century, special shaving soap in the seventeenth century. Razor strops date from the eighteenth century and the first safety models from the same time; but private shaving remained exceptional until K. C. Gillette's invention of the nineteenth century, which passed very quickly from an exorbitant five dollars to ten cents. Modern toothbrushes appeared in the nineteenth century, until which time mouth wash was used to supplement a cloth or a sponge with which the teeth were wiped.

and anesthesia, endocrinology, serums, sulfamides, hormones, antibiotics, preventive methods, equipment and research, all made giant strides. Sulfa drugs after 1935, antibiotics in the 1940's (beginning with penicillin in 1941) reduced infectious illness—typhus, typhoid, tuberculosis, cholera, syphilis. Surgery and prosthetics have surged forward, as has the use of physical agents—radioactivity, electric waves, sound waves, etc.

In 1835, a French expert had written that to find a hundred men fit for military service one needs 135 conscripts of the middle and upper classes, or else 343 of the poorer classes. At Mulhouse in Alsace, at about that time, life expectation for offspring of the rich was twenty-eight, for those of textile workers one year and three months. Among the latter, for every 100 births, 30 died in the first month, 20 in the following nine; only 27 reached the age of ten, 17 got to twenty, 6 got to forty, one sometimes lived to sixty. This level of 500 deaths per 1,000 matches the worst plague years of the eighteenth century. The difference in death rates between rich and poor persisted into the twentieth century, but much attenuated; so that the poor in France today have a life expectancy of over fifty.

Given the high mortality of—say—the year 1700, out of 1,000 living babies only 475 could be expected to reach the age of twenty, when a person begins to think and act independently. Of these, only two-thirds would see their fortieth birthday, only one-third their sixtieth. Today, 960 out of 1,000 are likely to complete their studies and can look forward to forty or fifty years during which they may contribute to society as well as enrich their own lives. The social gain that derives from this is immense, contributing, in effect, to the other sources of capital accumulation from which we benefit.

Some of the most remarkable improvements have come after 1930, when state intervention brought the masses (most of whom hardly saw dentist or doctor unless they were gravely ill) within the scope of medical and social care. Infant mortality, 142 per 1,000 in the United Kingdom in 1900 was 31 per 1,000 in 1950; in Sweden it was 21 per 1,000. Yet, even so, in 1958 about one-third of Britain's buildings were still bathless, nearly 50 per cent in some poorer quarters. In Western Germany, a few years ago, 200 homes in one town were found to have 125 TV sets and 3 baths. Even in the United States, while 42,400,000 (84 per cent) of the nation's homes had TV, a million fewer had bathtubs. When Stalin died in 1953 with the most modern medical equipment in his room, his doctors were still prescribing cupping. In France in 1950, about 12 per cent of national revenue went to consumption of alcoholic beverages, 4 or 5 per cent to the country's medical needs—which did not prevent the cost of the latter being attacked harder than that of the former.

It is true that medicine has become much more costly and that its very advances make life itself more costly: keeping people alive who without it would die of illness or of age. Old-age pensions, better hygiene and food, prolonged life, raise the porportion of aged to adults in the community, impose heavy social costs, affect activity, enterprise, attitudes, politics, and public life. Improved drugs mean that men live longer, that the sick suffer longer, that the unfit survive to procreate, to spread infections, or, simply, to be an added burden on society. The wonders of medicine are its hazards too.

Once upon a time, circumstances favored the survival and multiplication of those who were stronger, fitter, or better adapted to the world's demands. Now, society intervenes to help the weak and the ill-adapted —not necessarily to lead better lives, but—at least to survive. Genetic laws which worked in favor of the strong are being reversed as prudence, skill, and initiative are enlisted rather in preventing conception than in ensuring it. The most advanced societies may have evolved a process of natural selection in reverse.

But, if survival presents problems in the most advanced countries, it has catastrophic effects in backward ones. In India, whose population growth rate only passed that of Europe in 1921, the 300 million-odd inhabitants of the century's beginning have, by today, increased by almost two-thirds. Latin-American population has practically doubled in fifty years. These abrupt changes, not compensated by a parallel productivity of either food or goods, threaten dire consequences and create the explosive situation with which the second half of the twentieth century must learn to cope.

Science and Thought

Evolution

In 1859, Charles Darwin (1809–1882), son of the poet-doctor-member of the Lunar Society, published the results of many years of work in a book entitled *The Origin of Species,* in which it was suggested that living organisms, including men and other animals, had come into existence not as a result of special creation but by a process of evolution and natural selection. The work was but a stage in the long process of inquiry and definition which we have seen proceeding in earlier years (pp. 635–637). Its impact was the greater because the ground had been prepared for it and because, while it threatened many preconceptions of the day, it fitted many others.

By 1859 time had been recognized as a crucial factor in history as much as in astronomy: now first geology, then biology followed suit.

The notion of evolutionary growth had become commonplace in a society which believed in progress because it actually saw progress taking place. It became shocking when applied to Bible and to man, denying the literal truth of one and the special dignity of the other. Tennyson asked if really man

> Who trusted God was love indeed
> And love creation's final law—
> Tho' nature, red in tooth and claw
> With ravine, shriek'd against his Creed—

was just another animal fated to die like them. Not God but apes, not apes but sperm, not sperm but slime, here lay the ancestry of man: from dust to dust was more than a formula, and all of wisdom was but chemistry. This was hard to take.

But a dynamic world could not hold out long for static theories. Darwin's hypothesis was better suited to minds prepared by Malthus and by their own grim struggles to glory in natural selection when they could no longer boast of privileged creation. Even Fabians saw social change and reform as an accumulation of minute variations eventually and inevitably changing the face of society. And Oswald Spengler, in his *Decline of the West* (1918), would use the biological analogy for life and death of civilizations and cultures which behaved like living organisms in their passage from birth to death.

The very dismay that many felt before the crumbling of the old authorities; the sense that

> . . . We are here as on a darkling plain
> Swept with confused alarms of struggle and flight
> Where ignorant armies clash by night. . . .

reinforced a fresh will to believe and to obey new gods and new authorities. Where should these be found but in the science which had denounced the old? Even in 1848, the French philosopher Ernest Renan had seen that "Science is a religion; science alone leads man to resolve the eternal problems of which his nature imperiously calls for a solution." Twenty years later Renan's beliefs had penetrated the popular mind in the guise of scientism. Dazzled by the technical applications of scientific discoveries, public opinion was converted to a creed of science, progress, and the future of humanity, all borne out by steam, internal combustion, and electricity, by medical advances and inventions of every sort.

The Cult of Science

Science fascinated everybody. History, politics, economics became social sciences; philosophy became a moral science. It was still very hard to tell just what science was and what was scientific. Many had recourse to pseudo-sciences like phrenology: a method of telling the personality and ability of a person by examining the bumps on their skulls;* and pseudo-faiths of a mystic nature: spiritualism, table rapping, crystal ball gazing, medium experiments, and the like. Table turning and the evocation of spirits from another world fascinated high society from Victor Hugo to Empress Eugénie, a very superstitious lady. Perhaps these were the late nineteenth century's substitute for a near-exploded faith: new superstitions to replace the old. The healing work of magic and of faith was also carried on by patent medicines providing spells and love potions for their aficionados, fairy tales for commercials, and immense profits for their manufacturers without doing too much harm. Though dandruff, baldness, or halitosis persist, men and women often feel better if they think they should be feeling better and, within limits, that is worth the price.

One thing, however, seemed increasingly apparent: God, who had been banished from laboratories could now be dispensed with in an outer world which traced its origins to other sources. In 1865 a French medical student called Georges Clemenceau, obtained a doctorate with a thesis entitled *The Generation of Anatomical Elements*. which indicated the biological irrelevance of God. The issue was more clearly stated shortly after by one of Darwin's strongest advocates: Ernest Haeckel (1834–1919). "The cell," declared the German biologist, "consists of matter called protoplasm, composed chiefly of carbon, with an admixture of hydrogen, nitrogen, and sulfa. These component parts, properly united, produce the soul and the body of the animated world, and suitably nursed become man. With this single argument the mystery of the universe is explained, the deity annulled and a new era of infinite knowledge ushered in."

Many popular prophets busied themselves explaining how infinite the possibilities of knowledge and control now were. For Victor Hugo, the progress of chemistry revived the dreams of ancient alchemists. By the twentieth century chemistry would actually realize Doctor Faustus' dreams and transmute mercury into gold. For the growing number of science-fiction writers—Jules Verne (1828–1905), Arthur Conan Doyle (1859–1930), H. G. Wells—science suggested new possibilities: flying to the moon, sailing under the sea, navigating in time, rounding the world in the ridiculously short space of eighty days, making war with flying ships, rockets, or land cruisers (tanks), eventually destroying cities and perhaps the world. Nothing was beyond human ingenuity: not even man himself.

"All human facts, moral and physical, being bound up with causes and subject to laws," wrote Hippolyte Taine in 1870, "It follows that

---

* Prince Albert took phrenology very seriously, and had the royal children undergo periodical examinations.

Charles Darwin, by John Collier.
National Portrait Gallery, London.

all works of man, art, religion, philosophy, literature, moral, political or social phenomena, are but the results of general causes that must be determined by scientific methods." Scientific methods meant above all measurement for those who believed that progress would eventually connect all knowledge in one great integrated science, based on mathematics and able to account for man and cosmos and life and even God. A French chemist, Marcelin Berthelot, good friend of the philosopher Renan, affirmed: "Science is the benefactor of humanity . . . under her impulse, modern civilization marches with ever faster step." Science eased labor, created human brotherhood, " a new conception of human destiny, directed by the fundamental notions of universal solidarity between all nations." The methods of the natural sciences used in pursuit of the laws determining human behavior suggested a mechanistic view of life and man, in which all actions are determined by previous actions, in which we could calculate destiny out of the mass and motions of particles in the universe, in which (thought men like Taine) brains secreted thought much as the liver secretes bile.

Science and Society

The first great formulator of this point of view, prophet of nineteenth-century positivism, had been Auguste Comte (1798–1857), appropriately a teacher of mathematics at the Paris Polytechnic School. Comte's approach applied scientific methods not only to nature but to society as well, where history provided the laboratory of man's social experiments, a laboratory whence observation could extract the basis of a correct social morality. For Comte history passed through stages, each colored by the way in which men explained and handled phenomena about

them: the first *theological* stage was largely animistic, the second—
metaphysical—still preferred abstractions to realities, the third and last
was the *positive*, examining phenomena in relation to all other phenomena and in connection with general laws.

Auguste Comte offered a great vision of inevitable progress, humanity
moving onward and upward past successive barriers of ignorance and
superstition to the positive truths of science. Scientific methods could
and would reveal the laws of social organization and individual behavior, laws which magicians and priests still hid from sight. The task
was twofold: discover and formulate these laws by "the exact study of
facts and things" (Zola); assert them against obsolete metaphysical survivals from the past. Because of its anticlerical overtones, positivism
would become a fighting creed in those societies where liberalism came
up most forcefully against the church: in Turkey and in Catholic countries like Italy, France, Mexico, and Brazil. And Freemasonry, which had
developed to improve the world of man, took up this task like a
crusade.

Clearly, the wonders achieved by scientific methods in the realm of
nature could and should be repeated in the social sphere. A science of
society would parallel the sciences of nature. Comte had sought to do this
by his kind of historical psychology that focused on the experience and
the mind of man. An alternative notion was proposed by Social Darwinists like Herbert Spencer (1820–1903), who saw society passing from a
military and despotic to an industrial and democratic phase, condemned
state interference with the struggle for survival, and preached a robust
individualism that appealed especially to the more successful members
of the middle class. Society, said Darwinists like Spencer, cannot safely
ignore the principle of natural selection by artificially nurturing and
preserving those of its members who cannot take care of themselves.
"The poverty of the incapable, the distresses that come upon the imprudent, the starvation of the idle, and those shoulderings aside of the
weak by the strong which leave so many in shallows and miseries are
the decrees of a large, far-seeing benevolence." Millionaires were also a
product of natural selection. So were states—"the organized control of the
minority over the majority," as an Austrian sociologist described them—
resulting from a conflict between social groups in which one group,
superior in intelligence and ability, hence fittest to rule, had triumphed.

Here was an approach which allowed for variations. Karl Marx was also
an admirer of Darwin. In 1867 Marx had wanted to dedicate the first
volume of *Das Kapital* to Darwin, who declined the honor. In 1883, speaking at Marx's funeral, Engels stressed the connection: "Just as Darwin
discovered the law of development of organic nature, so Marx discovered
the law of development of human history." For both, change came
through conflict: class war being the social counterpart of the struggle for
existence and survival. But Marx despised the psychological intellec-

tualism of Comte and regarded the optimistic vitalism of Spencer as superficial. His science rested on economic development and on the classes which this forged, classes whose struggle and self-affirmation were the solid substance of history. Hegel had seen history as the fulfillment of abstract ideas embodied in the state. Marx would see it as the conflict of very concrete interests and forces embodied in social classes.

Unfortunately, his observations were founded on an early stage of British industrial development, when the working people were indeed turned into a vast undifferentiated mass. Hence Marx's classes were monolithic, not prone as they have proved to ever greater differentiation. He saw economic development increasingly depersonalizing the individual, battering him into his class like a gigantic power hammer, opposing impersonal mass and impersonal capital. And even as developments, first in Britain and then in other industrially advanced countries, were contradicting Marx's conclusions, other countries just entering the industrial race seemed to prove him right, winning him votaries in underdeveloped areas while the developed ones moved toward revisionism. The Marxist analysis which fitted the England of the 1840's, fitted the Germany of the 70's and 80's, the France of the 90's, the Russia of prewar years. Here was a materialist philosophy for materialistic times, a religion of inevitable progress for a progressive age.

From Determinism to Relativism

Marx's death in 1883 marked the beginning of a great reaction in which the clear, determined, progressive universe of positivism crumbled away under a bombardment of new discoveries and of their implications. Nineteenth-century rationalism was founded on Newtonian mechanics operating in a world of matter which was conceived as continuous and permanent. The world was made up of chemical elements, and elements of atoms; but in between, completing the continuum, lay an invisible ether which rendered motion possible by displacement of matter in space. In 1887 a series of experiments conducted in Chicago by Michelson and Morley emptied the Newtonian universe of its invisible ether stuffing, and left people wondering what was there instead. In 1895 the German W. K. Roentgen discovered X rays which could traverse apparently solid matter. Within a few years the work of the Curies in France, of Rutherford in England, revealed the instability and disintegration of radioactive atoms. Atoms which had been believed to be the firm, indivisible base of the material world, could split, releasing a quantity of energy in the process.

The idea of continuity had been fundamental to classic theories of light, energy, and matter. Now, Max Planck (1858–1947) suggested that when bodies emit light they actually radiate energy, pulsating in infinitesimal measures, or *quanta,* proportional to the frequency of the

Albert Einstein broad-
casting a warning on
the terrors of the hy-
drogen bomb. Right:
Max Planck.

radiation. All energy is ultimately quantified: emitted not in rays but in this discontinuous radiation.* One after the other, the solid notions which paved the floor of science seemed to melt away. A new physics suggested new hypotheses about the structure of the universe, of matter, of perception. The mechanical principles of Newton, the mathematical determinism of the past 300 years, were being rewritten into a new relativism.

In 1905, the theory of relativity which Albert Einstein (1879–1955) formulated suggested that neither time nor space were absolutes. Time has not the absolute character we imagine, but passes at different speeds according to whether the observer stands still or moves at great speed. This fact suggests that space also is a relative notion. Albert Einstein's studies of accelerated movements, discovering that the mass of a body varies with its speed, led to the formulation of the general relativity theory (1915) asserting the equation of energy and mass ($e = mc^2$). A body radiates energy at the expense of its mass, and matter is itself a form of energy. Matter could turn into energy; and the basic component of matter—the atom, a tiny compound of compressed energy—could turn into light, or into heat, or both. The atom was not solid, but made up of electrons revolving around a kernel; and these electrons, said the Dane Niels Bohr, could jump from one atom to another, emitting energy as they did. Indeed, the jumps—the transmutation of matter and the release of energy incidental to it—could be set off by bombarding atoms with radioactive rays. In 1932, the first cyclotron was built to accelerate this bombardment. It was also found that in the case of atoms of certain elements like uranium, their disintegration was accompanied by a chain reaction—the emission of neutrons causing the split of further atoms emitting yet more neutrons—and that such splits were accompanied by the intense emission of energy. This was the basis of the 400-pound bomb

* In 1923 Louis de Broglie provided a fresh notion of continuity by arguing that the little particles of light or matter are part of the propagation of a wave, and thus created undulatory mechanics.

which on August 6, 1945, destroyed Hiroshima.

Many years passed between the 1880's when this process started and the 1940's when it seemed to culminate. But, as its implications trickled into public consciousness, the mechanical universe began to crumble and, with it, an element of psychological security. A good expression of the traditional view of how the world was ordered can be found in Ecclesiastes I, 4–9:

> One generation passeth away and another generation cometh: but the earth abideth forever. The sun also ariseth and the sun goeth down and hasteth to his place where he arose. The world goes towards the South and turneth about unto the North; it whirleth about continually; and the world returneth again according to his circuits. All the rivers run into the sea; yet the sea is not full: unto the place whence the rivers come thither they return again. All things are full of labor; man cannot utter it: the eye is not satisfied with seeing nor the ear filled with hearing. The thing that hath been, it is that which shall be; and that which is done is that which shall be done: and there is no new thing under the sun.

There was no basic change in this world view when the seventeenth century established the laws of permanence in a moving world. Matter, space, and movement were all constant, and even the laws which Newton postulated were only constants to be discovered, not changes to be traced. Time, space, and movement were absolute quantities. If logic suggested that this might not always be so, God was there to correct accidents and make sure His grand machine worked as it should. The discoveries of the nineteenth century would throw a wrench of doubt into the works. The world was made of matter. But over great areas of space, such as the sky, this matter is invisible. Newton had postulated that the space across which forces of gravity operate was filled with ether, a compound of infinitesimal particles. We have seen that in 1887 Michelson proved that ether does not exist. Physics was at a loss. The material universe collapsed. Not immediately or in all its parts, but in the sense that "exact science" acknowledged an element of unpredictability about its calculations and that this element was enhanced by the work of Planck, Einstein, and Bohr, until exactness became an approach rather than a fact, and relativity replaced absolutism as the dominant of modern scientific thought.

After Einstein, neither time nor distance were absolute values any more. After Planck, measurements were understood to be affected by sensations. After Paul Langevin (1872–1946), matter and energy became identical. The world today is neither set nor stable. Space or distance may alter with density. Hence the world may well expand as its mass rarefies. In this variable universe, compound of solid laws, Newtonian survivals and relativism, only mathematical representation independent of the observer retains objective meaning. Experience reveals only the relative. Only concepts may permit an objective view, founded on experience maybe but transcending it.

This was more disturbing than evolution in which natural philosophers believed long before Darwin: it contradicted evolution by painting a nature proceeding not in a continuous line but in bounds, discontinuous and perhaps dialectical as well. Worse still in some respects, the realities Einstein and Planck revealed were expressible only in mathematical symbols and abstract formulae. It may well be that abstraction "is the normal and fruitful course of the scientific spirit," as a philosopher of science has recently asserted, but the evolution from more or less visual geometry toward the complete abstraction of mathematical equations removed it from the ken even of cultivated persons. Science, which had been part of educated men's equipment, became an arcane field for initiates, its mysteries and its revelations all the more disturbing for their inaccessibility.

While the debate as to the meaning of their theories divided physicists, its echoes shattered large panes of the optimistic rationalism that had grown up around them. Scientism, having battered down religion, had affirmed that it carried the keys to truth. Now it had to admit what most scientists had known all along: that "formulae are not true; they are useful," and to insist that science did not really explain the nature of things but only their relations. The philosophers of science offered little comfort. G. E. Moore's *Principia Ethica* and Bertrand Russell's *Principles of Mathematics* (both published in 1903) argued essentially that men perceived not objects as wholes, not things in themselves, but shapes, colors, images, as real in dreams or hallucinations as in waking sensation. Things *are* because we see them so, as Berkeley had once said; and the world is no more than an infinity of particular perceptions. Science thus became "a system of relations," scientific certainty became probability, and ordinary men were left panting for a faith that would reassure, a system that would reorder their disordered world.

It seemed as if Prometheus had overreached himself. Science was to have made man autonomous. The doubts its progress raised made him querulous. A French Catholic critic, Charles Brunetière, proclaimed "the failure of science"; a neo-Marxist like Georges Sorel denounced the illusions of progress; human science, affirmed Pope Leo XIII in 1902, cannot "quench the thirst for truth, for divinity, for infinity, which devours us." That was not what human science had set out to do. To the extent that its advocates had claimed too much, their dogmatic scientism was breaking down, making way for a new irrationalism less favorable to reason than to faith. The mysticism of Leo Tolstoy or Rabindranath Tagore, the philosophies of action like those of William James and Georges Sorel, and those of intuition like that of Henri Bergson, who suggested that real continuity lies only in our consciousness; the phenomenology of Edmund Husserl, arguing that reality cannot be

William James.   Henri Bergson.

shown by rational explanation or evidence but through some structural intuition; the relativism of existential philosophy which recognizes no objective truths; the theology of Karl Barth and Karl Jaspers calling for acts of faith based on no rational certainty, as an escape from the unstructured absurdity of the material world: all spring in one way or another from this collapse of the house that Galileo, Descartes, and Newton built.

Rationalism Qualified

The first great philosophy of action was what William James (1842–1910) formulated as pragmatism. James realized that men need to believe more than they actually know, or can hope to know. You cannot act only on knowledge that can be proved rationally, because then you would act very little. You must act on beliefs, justified by need or practice. "An idea is true because it is useful; it is useful because it is true." In any case, said Bergson (1859–1941), intellect distorts reality, which only intuition can grasp. The will, responding to the needs of the struggle for existence, suggests the aspects or interpretations of reality that it most needs. Bergson's early work dates back to 1889; but his most revolutionary book was published in 1907: *Creative Evolution*. In it and in his exceedingly popular lectures at the Collège de France, Bergson reacted against the reigning rationalism and demolished it with reference to the new indeterminacies that scientific discoveries suggested. Bergson appealed from materialism and rationalism to those vital forces which drive us and which alone can reveal us to ourselves, rehabilitating intuition against the excesses of reason, pointing out the force of instinct, of chance, the superiority of metaphysical over merely physical truth.

Verbiage? But expressed in a fascinating, deceptively clear style which came as a relief after the Germanic obscurities of so much nineteenth-century philosophy. Above all, verbiage which—when science was going through a revolutionary change—reflected the anti-rationalist reaction of its time: a reaction very evident in literature and politics, as in

598

the Catholic revival—not only that of the masses drawn to new devotions and pilgrimages, but that of poets like Charles Péguy and Paul Claudel, philosophers like Jacques Maritain, painters like Georges Rouault, musicians like Georges Auric, César Franck, and Vincent D'Indy, whose *Schola Cantorum* dates back to 1896. Like his contemporary, Sigmund Freud, Bergson set obscure forces in motion simply by plumbing them. The eloquent philosophy of freedom, which he drew from the collapse of scientism, became the inspiration of an anti-intellectual offensive that rejected the works of reason as distortions of living experience and obstacles to intuitive perception. Reality lay not in the mind and in its apprehensions but in a "life force" that intuition tapped and that will alone expressed in acts and gestures. Living reality could not be encompassed by logical formulae: "All that is vital is anti-rational," declared Miguel de Unamuno, one of the intellectual leaders of twentieth-century Spain.

But, in denying reason, the anti-intellectual intellectuals were denying the characteristic equipment of man himself; were admitting that, after all, man is not free to be free. They ushered in the time of disillusion for the few, who would eventually communicate their disillusion to the many; the time when man begins to think of himself as an incidental occurrence and of mankind as a passing phase of a perpetually changing world. The mood of such intellectual circles was well summed up in a statement of the Italian philosopher Benedetto Croce:

> We no longer believe . . . like the Greeks, in happiness of life on earth; we no longer believe, like the Christians, in happiness in an other-worldly life; we no longer believe, like the optimistic philosophers of the last century, in a happy future for the human race . . . we no longer believe in anything of that, and what we have alone retained is the consciousness of ourselves.

Soon this last, too, came under fire. The war of 1914–1918 emphasized and broadcast the conviction that men were playthings of "other" forces before which their consciousness, let alone their will, was powerless. And yet some of the most obvious of these "other" forces were the work of men. In this connection, the general public now discovered the work of Sigmund Freud, whose basic research into hidden emotional energies and their effect on man's conscious acts had been completed just before the war, but who spoke most clearly to the postwar mood. Freud's psychoanalytical approach formulated for the individual what Marx had formulated for society half a century earlier: a theory which sees men moved by forces of which they are unconscious, their culture, morals, institutions, beliefs shaped by interests and repressions they ignore, and the discovery of this situation as the first step toward liberation.

Philosophers, sociologists, and anthropologists took similar lines to Freud's—the social scientists proceeding to analyze the subterranean currents that make societies, men, and cultures be what they are, and change as they do. But the first and most striking of these revelations, dissolving the solid structures of the psychological universe much as the physicists had destroyed those of theirs, came from the psychoanalysts. Freud's speculations on dreams and the unconscious, Carl Jung's ideas of the collective unconscious and inferiority complexes, Alfred Adler's theories of compensation, and Erik Erikson's identification of an identity crisis, were so many revelations battering at established attitudes and constraints, from logical reasoning to sex, from women's inferiority to parental superiority and paternalism in industry or politics. That the new techniques were revolutionary soon became clear—at least to insurrectionists like Trotsky, who hoped to synthesize the work of Marx and Freud, and to Béla Kun who, during the Hungarian revolution of 1918, set up in Budapest the first institute for the training of psychoanalysts. To analysts like Wilhelm Reich, who joined the German young Communists, material and sexual misery appeared as one. And the revolutionary implications of psychoanalytical ideas were just as clear to great reactionaries like Stalin and Hitler, both of whom condemned Reich's essay of 1932, *The Sexual Struggle of Youth*.

Realism Under Fire

As established notions of reality crumbled away, the arts followed the reaction against nineteenth-century realism and rationalism, abandoning space or scale, perspective or harmony as artificial conventions, in favor of self-made rules or models in a new relative world which all could reconstruct according to their vision. Abstract artists like Jean Arp, Alexander Calder, and Piet Mondrian deliberately referred to science which shows no ultimately established nature and suggests that solid appearances conceal a mobile reality. The work of Piet Mondrian (1872–1944), for instance, reflects the impact of the world around him, insisting first on mass and absence of detail, later on the increasing abstraction that can be observed in his *Composition in White, Black and Red*. A work like his *Broadway Boogie-Woogie* reminds one that a Frenchman of the same generation, the painter-architect Le Corbusier, once described Manhattan as hot jazz in stone. Thus, nonfigurative artists set out to evoke things and create them rather than reproduce them. The new mood was expressed by writers as varied as James Joyce (*Ulysses*, 1922), Sinclair Lewis (*Babbitt*, 1922), T. S. Eliot (*The Waste Land*, 1922), all of whom denounced the futility of life, of man and of society. In 1924 the *Surrealist Manifesto* articulated this "refusal of traditional humanism" with its institutions and its ways of thought and feeling, and announced the foundation of an Office of Surrealist Re-

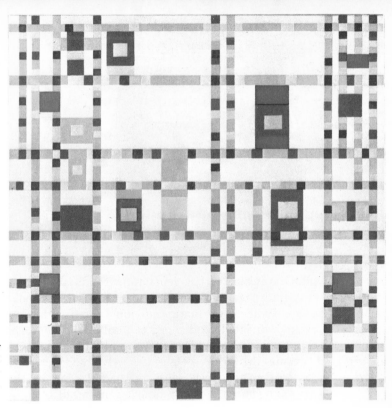

Broadway Boogie-Woogie, by Piet Mondrian. Museum of Modern Art, New York.

search concerned with the question of how sincerity could be recaptured by escape from the "deforming influence of reason."

Surrealism, after all, was not surprising, in an age that made Oedipus complexes available to all and when, in the words of an English moralist, "even typists knew that they were not fond of apples for nothing." But there was more to it. Less than five centuries after European sailors looking for Asia found America in their way and went beyond it to circumnavigate the world, their descendants would set foot on the moon. The acceleration of scientific knowledge and techniques was not only frightening or exhilarating: it soon became overwhelming. Ninety-three per cent of all the full-time scientists who ever lived are alive today. But, while the world's population doubles every thirty-five years, the mass of science and technology doubles twice as fast and its demands are beginning to nudge the limits of our resources in money and mind. The results of the cumulative scientific knowledge whose rate of increase has been doubling every decade for the past three hundred years have placed culture in what has been called a state of permanent mobilization. Unwilling to live in a continuous cultural crisis, some persons have reacted exactly as they would react when personal tensions and crises grow too great, by taking refuge in defiant stolidity or exaggerated irrationalism. But even the well-intentioned become uneasy, find it increasingly hard to tell just who or what they are supposed to be, and what they are supposed to do. Such issues

601

Jean-Paul Sartre, photographed in front of his portrait by Picasso.

seldom arose for earlier generations conditioned by habits and customs that rapid change has rattled to pieces in the modern West. But contemporary men—the static individual faced with a dynamic society, the private individual condemned to public solitude, the singular individual offered only techniques. and laws applicable to masses—are disconcerted. They are driven to define themselves as members of bodies which seem to them endowed with more solid contours than their own personality: a church, a party, a movement, an ideology.

It would be in this context that Jean-Paul Sartre formulated the challenge of his existential philosophy: man's choice between letting himself become what others see in him—the image of a false and abstract notion: Jew, Negro, waiter, bourgeois, traitor, thief—and choosing a role which he himself defines and acts out with all its implications. Condemned to freedom and to loneliness, both absurd and both absolute, Sartrean man finds that his condition can be transcended by himself alone as he endows life, events, above all himself, with a meaning that he weaves like a spider out of his own resources. Looking around at a world in which he finds neither norms nor faith, Sartre rejects despair for an affirmation arising precisely from despair, leading to choice, to action, and to the creation of one's own destiny.

Against this last assertion of free will, the "new philosophy" of structuralism, connected with the French anthropologist Claude Lévi-Strauss and anthro-analyst Michel Foucault, approaches man as one more source of data for computers. Three-quarters of a century after Nietzsche's "God is dead," Foucault declares that man is dead as a subject, as a whole being. The man of "humanism" and of the humanities is no longer a fit subject for literature or drama, or of knowledge for philosophers. He is dis-integrated into series, gestures, moments, fitted into abstractions to which living individuals are marginal if not irrelevant factors. Structuralism is an attempt to classify societies and cultural systems, decode their particular myths, languages, and structures, produce (as it were) an entomology of men: an exact, descriptive, comparative, and analytical science directed not at the way in which men live but at the structures in which their lives are cast, not at the way societies change but at the way they are ordered. If we believe the structuralists, a whole conception of man, of the world, of human being and relations, is coming to an end.

Meanwhile, the professional scientists have carried on their work and science has recaptured the belief in reason which most scientists never lost. Those who proclaimed their failure had no share in, and little understanding of, scientific life. As the world settled uneasily to relativity, the religion of science waned along with the impossible notions of perfection that its supporters and detractors had entertained. Today, critics of science attack it not because it has failed to explain the world but because it has played and plays such an essential part in the making of it. Science and technology are rejected to the extent that the modern world seems frightening: not only by its wars, which scientific discovery has made more destructive, but by the threat of dehumanization, of technological enslavement it holds out. Unfortunately, those who doubt man's capacity and future have little better to propose than a recapitulation of his past.

Religion

If the nineteenth century was not an age of faith, it was at least an age of conformity. Christian values were basic social currency, Christian morals were the foundation of ethics and of socially acceptable behavior. Even cultivated liberals in the 1890's "did not see how an *atheist* could at bottom be an honest man." Church attendance was a mark of respectability in the middle classes and above, churches and chapels were built and restored, crowded every Sunday, bookshelves filled with sermons, devotional literature, and religious tracts. In England and Wales, in 1851, out of a population slightly below 18 million, 4.5 million went to church on Sunday morning, 3 million in the afternoon, 3 million in the evening. But the same religious census that produced these figures (not less impressive if we realize that in many cases the same persons went several times a day) revealed great deserts of paganism in the cities, where fewer than one in ten attended church on Sunday. No wonder that Florence Nightingale, who knew something about the urban population from her nursing work, told Cardinal Manning that "the most thinking and conscientious of the artisans have no religion at all," the most intelligent of urban workers have "almost entirely gone over to atheism" and would only look at a book about religion if "it were *against* the Bible." No wonder either if some sermons had a defensive shrillness. Even before Darwin, authority was threatened, orthodoxy shaken, most intellectuals qualified their faith or doubted altogether.

Orthodoxy Challenged

Skepticism had long sapped the foundations of religious belief, and critical studies rejected a literal reading of the Bible. In 1835 a disciple of Hegel, D. F. Strauss, had published *A Life of Jesus,* treating Christ as a human being so impressive that messianic and miraculous myths crystallized around him. In 1863, Renan's *Life of Jesus* abandoned Hegelian mythology for a purely historical interpretation: Jesus was a very great man, but a man nevertheless. When, before publication, Renan expounded these views at the Collège de France, his lectures there had to be suspended; not because of official prejudice (the Minister of Education agreed with him) but because public and students objected in "noisy demonstrations." As always, it was less the upper than the middle classes that resented novelty. The Bible was still considered to be an authoritative historical account of ultimate truths: the age of the world, the process of creation, the fall, these could not be denied. But geology with its awkward fossils and strata, history with its distressing chronologies, physics and biology with their uniform laws of nature were sapping it. Philosophies of science (like that which Comte proposed) claimed that what could not be proved by scientific methods was not true knowledge.

Darwin's work made it impossible to ignore biological evolution. His theory that not only primates but man too evolved from lower forms of life in a great struggle for existence struck fatal blows to Genesis, to traditional doctrines of the Creation and the Fall. If there was no creation then there was no fall, and if there was no fall then there was no original sin. The origin of man was like that of other species, and his character was not revealed in the Bible but in a Hobbesian history of struggle. "The principle of natural selection is absolutely incompatible with the word of God," wrote the Bishop of Oxford. A powerful argument but one which, when the principle came to be admitted, would turn against the word of God. The debate was bitter: "Leave me my ancestors in Paradise and I will allow you yours in the zoological gardens," pleaded one defender of traditional beliefs.

The Darwinian controversy was spiced by publications like *Essays and Reviews,* in which well-known members of the Church of England, such as Benjamin Jowett, master of Balliol, and a future archbishop of Canterbury, Frederick Temple, argued for the right of free discussion within the Church and suggested that the Bible account of Genesis might be regarded as a Hebrew myth. The greatest arguments raged around the suggestion of Bishop Colenso of Natal that logistical considerations rendered the story of Noah's Ark incredible. Temple and Huxley, Colenso and Darwin, were all put in the same basket and their daring to question the literal reading of the scriptures castigated: "Revelation neither invokes human science to confirm its truths, nor does it challenge human science to disturb them. It does not stoop to notice science at all. . . ." * That was telling them. But it was not enough. By 1872 Winwood Reade's *Martyrdom of Man* concluded with a paean to the coming age when purgatory-earth would become paradise, freed from hunger, disease, hard labor, with wide-ranging men mastering nature, becoming "manufacturers of worlds. Man then will become perfect; he will then be a creator; he will therefore be what the vulgar worship as a God."

Protestantism had claimed that *its* theology rested on reason. Now reasonable doubts pecked at its foundations; moral laws were seen to rest on blind faith and social utility.** Protestantism would never recover from the blow. Rome did better. It had always limited the province of reason. Now it opted out of the modern world, thus minimizing its impact but also that of its own creed, exchanging reasonableness for obscurantism.

The Church

Shocked by his experiences of 1848, Pius IX (who held the papal throne longer than any other pope) would spend the last thirty years of his reign as a confirmed reactionary, treating all liberals as revolutionaries, all revolutionaries as devils, and liberal Catholics as simple traitors. Liberal Catholic groups in France, England, and Germany were censured in 1864 when the encyclical *Quanta Cura* was accompanied by a *Syllabus* of "the principal errors of our times," including Bible societies, communism, freedom of conscience, of discussion, of the press, religious toleration, rationalism, naturalism, socialism, Freemasonry, separation of Church and State, and condemning above all the proposition that the Pope "can and should reconcile himself to and come to terms with progress, liberalism and recent civilization." No reconciliation or agreement was possible with them.

The Pope had opted for the Middle Ages, and his opponents were delighted to see their worst predictions confirmed. The General Council of the Catholic Church which met in 1869–70 confirmed them further, by proclaiming the dogma of papal infallibility to the discomfiture of

---

* J. R. Young, *Modern Scepticism* (1865), quoted in James Laver, *The Age of Optimism* (London: 1966), p. 129.

** Even the arguments of the religious suggested as much. Reviews of Darwin's *Descent of Man* in 1871 criticized an author who revealed "his zoological conclusions to the general public at a moment when the sky of Paris was red with the incendiary flames of the Commune." Darwin endangered faith, faith bolstered patience, obedience, and duty, its crumbling could only mean dire danger for society: radicalism, free-thinking, social revolution.

Pope Leo XIII.

liberal Catholics. The day after this decree had been voted in the midst of a thunderstorm, war broke out between France and Prussia. Within a few weeks French troops, which had protected papal power since 1849, were withdrawn from Rome and, by September, 1870, Italian troops occupied the city. The temporal power of the papacy was ended, the kingdom of Italy—at last united—had recovered its ancient capital. But the impression Pio Nono left on Catholicism was only emphasized. Despite reforming popes and active social movements, the image of Catholicism allied to reaction persisted into the twentieth century.

It seemed that there could be no conciliation between a totalitarian Church and a state not only indifferent to its claims but nursing totalitarian ambitions of its own. Nor, apparently, could there be conciliation between the anachronistic cultural concepts formulated in the *Syllabus* and the technical civilization of the modern world. This was the point of the *Kulturkampf*, a point significantly formulated by a famous pathologist, Doctor Rudolf Virchow, in the Prussian Chamber. In 1878, Leo XIII's encyclical *Quod Apostolici Muneris,* which condemned socialism, communism, and nihilism as deadly plagues "tainting society to its very core and bringing it to a state of extreme peril," reinforced the censures of the *Syllabus*. This would have wide effects.* Christian Socialists had to abandon their label and any identification with socialism; the radical Christianity of Lamennais was discredited again; socialist movements were confirmed in their hostility to religion in general and Catholicism in particular. On the other hand, the condemnation of tendencies and ideas reproved in all respectable quarters was not a barrier but a bridge between the Vatican and large parts of conservative society. An encyclical of 1888, *Libertas,* denied that the Church "looks unfavorably on *most* modern political systems and rejects *all* the discoveries of

---

* When in 1880 an eminent Dominican preaching in a fashionable Paris Church urged the reconciliation of Church and modern society, he was denounced by his congregation and banished to Corsica. Both sides in France agreed: you had to be either a Christian or a Republican.

contemporary genius." Leo XIII (1878–1903) supported the reconciliation of French Catholicism to the Third Republic and, eventually, the participation of Catholics in Italian politics, permitted after his death but in his spirit. He tried to come to terms with moderate political movements and with modern learning, opened the Vatican Archives to scholars, encouraged the revival of Thomistic studies which tried to reconcile science and theology, faith and reason. Most interesting to many, in 1891, his encyclical *Rerum Novarum* set out a social doctrine in which the ideologies of revolution and class war were challenged by reassertion of original Christian principles on which a practical social policy could be based.

Rerum Novarum condemned capitalist exploitation of human beings as if they were just another commodity, and declared that the state had a right and a duty to legislate against economic oppression and find remedies to social needs. Catholics now need no longer opt out of their age. They could form Christian unions, fight for social justice, appeal to workers, work with and for them; and though in its beginnings, before 1914, the echoes of *Rerum Novarum* touched only narrow circles, its principles prepared more widespread and effective action after the First—and especially after the Second—World War.

But even Leo reacted violently when the climate that he helped create encouraged Catholics to apply critical methods to the Bible or go too far in their advocacy of social reform. The modernist movement, which tried to reconcile modern scholarship and traditional tenets, was reaching dangerous conclusions in the work of men like Alfred Loisy (1857–1940) and George Tyrell (1861–1909). Dogma, they suggested, is not an unvarying truth but something that grows and changes with the times. Revelation is not an unchanging formula, but a living experience. Leo XIII's successor, Pius X (1903–1914), would not accept such notions. In 1907, the modernist movement was suppressed by papal pronouncement (*Pascendi*), modern velleities broken, and tight conformism reimposed. A kind of fatality hovered over the great institution which, based on dogma and authority, could only liberalize itself at the expense of the cement that bound it. Allied so often with those who were rich and mighty like itself, the Church over and over had to suppress movements for social justice among its own faithful.*

The quandary affected all churches in some degree, during an age which no longer took their authority for granted. Atheism, by its very denial of God, seemed to take Him seriously. Agnosticism—the term itself

---

* This did not prevent confessional parties and trade unions, both Catholic and Protestant, from mobilizing quite a bit of working-class support in Holland, Belgium, France, Italy, and Germany, thus splitting workers without bringing them any compensating influence. Such confessional parties and unions were controlled by conservative personalities or interest groups connected with the Church hierarchy, who would have the last word in policies which, in the last resort, tended to conservatism. This was shown in the case of the worker priests in France, a hopeful experiment of the 1940's disowned in the 1950's after numerous complaints from employers' organizations.

coined only in 1869—affirmed only doubt. This could make God irrelevant. Their supernatural authority increasingly questioned, the churches had to justify their existence on the same ground as any social institution. They found this ever more hard to do. "We'll not refute you: we'll explain you," had said John Morley. Christian apologists spluttered but failed to explain themselves, to adjust theology to new knowledge and currents of ideas, or to meet their challenge. Religion, already identified with political reaction, became identified with intellectual reaction and sterility as well, with opposition to modern science and education, with pietistic revivalism akin to superstition. When Gambetta proclaimed "Clericalism, there is the enemy!" he spoke for more than French republicans, in so far as the clergy, which refused to allow religious concerns to rest in private spheres, too often hampered social activities and progress. Politics competed with religion by suggesting another form of hope.

Dechristianization

By 1939, when the *Times Literary Supplement* reviewed T. S. Eliot's *Idea of a Christian Society,* written between Munich and the invasion of Poland, it had to remark that intelligent men seldom admit even the possibility that Christianity "is a system of truth from which flow inexhaustible principles in metaphysics, ethics and politics." Hardly anyone would have doubted the thought half a century earlier—at least not in public. But the half century had seen great changes. The dechristianization of Western Europe advanced with rationalism and even with irrationalism, as the latter grew more eclectic. Devotion and piety were relinquished to the simple mind. The number of religious ordinations fell as the rewards of a clerical vocation shrank in proportion to other opportunities—in the liberal professions for the middle class, in teaching, government service, and trade unions for the poorer—and the social authority of priests and ministers was diluted by the competition of other professional classes. The number of parishes without a priest increased nearly fourfold in France in the half century before 1900, and further still in the twentieth century. In Portugal, by 1930, the Archdiocese of Lisbon had only 320 priests for one and one-half million people. Priests were less educated, their sermons less inspiring, so were church art and music; people went less to church as other amusements became available. Country weekends among the upper classes, religious doubts among the middle classes, the rise of the labor movement, refusal or inability to find a penny for the collection plate among the urban and especially the rural poor, diminished church attendance. Greater material possibilities on earth meant less need for solace in the hereafter. On the other hand, Christian charity was called into question.

The political and national commitments of churches—priests taking sides with a particular party or blessing their nation's arms—discredited religion. Above all, alternatives now offered for the many services—social and psychological—which the Church alone had offered in the past.

Every civilization, Victor Hugo said, begins in theology and ends in democracy. While the evolution did not seem very clear, current experience convinced a great many that theology and democracy were mutually exclusive. The process of dechristianization was as other-directed as religious conformity had been in the past. People had gone to Church with and like their neighbors; when enough of them stopped going, whole neighborhoods fell away. People had enjoyed the comforts of belief. Now they enjoyed the comforts of indifference. A great deal is written—even today—about the pangs of loneliness without a God, nothing about the relief and release of getting rid of the jealous, frowning Lord, terrible in his wrath and holding out more hell than heaven, the problems of continual self-examination and emotional fear, the growing problems too of intellectual doubt, of reconciling religion and science. Agnosticism or atheism could be pragmatically justified. To a great many they brought release, relief, and new hope: "the daring which goes forth into the sunshine and under the stars, to study and enjoy, without leave asked or fear of penalty." So noted Harriet Martineau in her *Autobiography* (II, p. 56), while Tennyson in his "Despair" reflected

And we broke away from the Christ, our human brother and friend,
For He spoke, or it seemed that He spoke, of a Hell without help, without end.

Everywhere religious practice declined and conformity became increasingly occasional. In London, by 1902, only about two out of eleven residents went to Church on Sunday. In central France, the proportion of children left unbaptized rose from 2 per cent in 1899 to 40 per cent in 1914; that of civil marriages increased from 14 to 60 per cent. Men went to church far less than women, workers far less than the middle classes, young people less than the old. In Spain, in 1933, most cities were pagan and only 5 per cent of parishioners went to Easter Mass. In Italy, the number of communicants fell by half between 1938 and 1948. Today, in Belgium about a quarter of Catholics go to Mass, in West Germany about 50 per cent, but only half that in cities; in France between 20 per cent in middle-class and 5 per cent in working-class parishes. In Austria, where 86 per cent of the population is Catholic, only 20 per cent of the population goes to church. The same is true of Protestants. About 5 per cent of England's population, 20 per cent of Scotland's, belongs to any church at all. In the United States less than half the grownups surveyed declared that they belonged to a church of any kind.

Pope John XXIII.

Theology for Today

Yet through the centuries the message of the Scriptures has provided ground for radical criticisms of the way life in society is lived. Of recent years, in Europe as in Latin America, clergy and laymen jostled by the world around them have insisted once again that religious beliefs are related to contemporary problems. The "revolution" revealed in the papacy of John XXIII (1958–1963), and in the Vatican Council that met in 1962 at his behest, had been going on unnoticed for a long time, individual Christians questioning the established order in its injustices and their churches in their conservative orientation: a slow, unspectacular process, but leading in our day to the presence of more progressive personalities in positions of authority within the hierarchies of their churches and to the progress of an ecumenical movement devoted to the collaboration and union of divided Christians.* This evolution is particularly noticeable in the ranks of the Roman Church, whose members—Young Catholics, Syndicalist Catholics, Worker Priests, prelates, and laymen—are often found in the van of social rebellion (as in France, Italy, Spain, and Latin America), making a point which had been long forgotten: that, as the title of a recent book affirms, *God Is Not Conservative.***

The word *religion* comes from a Latin term meaning "to bind" and, if the mystic bond is that between man and God, the social bond is that

---

* Under the rule of Paul VI, the Church applied the brakes on its progress into the twentieth century, while its membership urged it forward. The Pope resisted pressure to allow the marriage of priests; less reasonably, the Vatican opposed attempts to legalize divorce and the sale of contraceptives in Italy, thus reviving the image of a Roman Catholicism determined to beat back even the most moderate reforms.

** A tract circulating in Lisbon in May, 1969, and reproduced in the Paris *Monde* of May 13, 1969, p. 11, states: "Reward to those furnishing information leading to the capture of a certain Jesus Christ, accused of sedition and conspiracy against the established order. Frequents workers, homeless persons and vagrants, dangerous professional agitator."

between men who share a common faith and, hence, a common set of values. With the religion of the West decaying, disgruntled men and women inevitably sought reassurance in substitute bonds and systems of identification: on the religious plane the mass of sects and churchlets which would begin to swarm late in the nineteenth century,* on the political plane a common worship of certain great abstractions—people or nation, proletariat or race—whose destiny could lend an eschatological meaning to their times and lives. "When people cease to believe in God," remarked G. K. Chesterton, "they don't believe in nothing, but—what's far worse—in anything." Fascisms and communisms are also great religious movements of our time to which individuals could give the loyalty and veneration they once accorded an established church, in which they could find the total revelation, dogma, and reassurance that another kind of worship provided their ancestors. Creed, since the Reformation polycentric, became polymorphous too, and the cultural divisions of Western society were reflected in the diversity of its beliefs.

While institutional Christianity decayed, the spiritual quest of many was offered answers tempered by new experiences. Lonely individuals, faced with the responsibility of choice without authorities to guide them, could not be satisfied either by traditional forms or by the liberal theology in which "a God without wrath brought men without sin into a kingdom without judgment through the ministrations of a Christ without a cross." ** Domesticated, institutionalized, its hair combed, its teeth filed, its claws trimmed, its brightness tarnished, Christianity had been tamed into a social custom, the resplendence of its original madness dulled down to bearable proportions, the logic of its peculiar folly—the folly of the cross—abandoned for that of everyday reason and compromise, the paradox and scandal on which Paul of Tarsus throve rendered irrelevant. This was the sense of the message that the new theologians refurbished.

The answer to man's religious problems did not lie in a theology where sin and salvation, good and evil, were happily reconciled in a harmonious transition from darkness to self-knowledge. This feeling had led Søren Kierkegaard (1813–1855) to turn violently against the theological counterpart of the optimistic rationalism of his day. Majority rule was a snare ("Truth is always in the minority") and "sciencemongery" a delusion. The human personality could not be explained or manipulated in mechanistic terms. Kierkegaard's vision stressed not

---

* This is not to mention the growing mass of private enterprise catering to popular superstition. "There will come a time," wrote Voltaire, "when all people will have discovered the roguery of all astrologers." Today there are a thousand professional astrologers in Paris alone, some 50,000 in all of France, counting seers, card, coffee, and crystal ball gazers; There is a union of 120,000 occultists in Italy; 60 per cent of French people read astrology forecasts regularly; German businessmen consult astrologers (as did Hitler), and one English astrologer counts among her regular clients fifty British and forty-nine foreign firms.

** Richard Niebuhr, *The Kingdom of God in America.*

gradual transition but moral struggle. Only hard, abrupt decisions could deliver men from sin. The way to salvation could not be taught or reasoned. There was, there is, no intellectual proof of Christianity or of any other ultimate truth. Faith is an act of will, not of understanding. A conventional, respectable, established Church is a hollow fake, for the truth it promises cannot be found in its pews but only in the night of man's own soul, "through fear and trembling."

Ignored in his own time, Kierkegaard was rediscovered when confidence in reason, convention, conciliation, hit rock bottom and much of Europe lived in fear and trembling. After the First World War, Kierkegaard became a patron saint of existential philosophy and of the theology of crisis, both of which stressed the view that ultimate truth cannot be accepted from outside, but only apprehended by living it out in a total existence. Under the pen of men like Karl Barth and Karl Jaspers, the gospels turned into "special delivery letters to the 20th century." Men were challenged to jettison easy routine and acceptance in favor of free choice. Faith, they were told, cannot be reached by any human road: "It is a leap in the void. And it is possible for all only because it is equally impossible for all."

An absurd world had found a theology in its own image.

The Way They Lived

The Countryside

Most people's lives reflect their work: its circumstances and its wages. In this respect, one of the greatest changes of this period lies in the shrinking of the portion of the population making its living on the land. In 1900, only the nations of North and Western Europe could show less than half the active population employed in agriculture. By 1950, less than four in ten of all active Europeans (two in ten in the north and west) worked on the land. The peasant of the old regime "dressed all in canvas like a windmill," as the saying went, was disappearing. Peasants were still, as ever, dissatisfied, embittered, rapacious, hopeful, clinging to every bit of earth and greedy for more, humble and assertive, submissive and tough. But they were learning to fill in official forms, to use new foods and buy their trousers in the markets, to ignore older authorities and to respect new ones. Rural conditions were still much worse than urban ones, agricultural laborers still the worst paid of all salaried workers, untaught, unwashed, and unenterprising.

As in many countries of Southern Europe today, the rustic cottages, the pretty countryside romantic to outsiders, hid abject poverty and chronic want for most peasants at least as late as 1914. An English union ballad described the laborer tramping

> . . . Off to his work while townfolk were abed,
> With nothing in his belly but a slice or two of bread;
> He dined upon potatoes and he never dreamed of meat
> Except a lump of bacon fat sometime by way of treat . . .

The peasant's staple diet into the 1870's consisted of broth, potatoes, and bread, and remained almost wholly meatless except for diseased meat, or game snared despite the severe laws against poaching. Fresh air and, where it existed, sunshine did not make up for insanitary lodgings and shortage of water. Nostalgic references to horse-and-buggy days forget that manure in the home, yard, or village street is no less nauseous and insanitary for being natural.

Rural living was distinguished less by health and good cheer than by rudimentary education, limited horizons, and a high incidence of illegitimate births. "Fornication and adultery, incest and murder, abortion and poisoning—all the tangled annals of the poor—this is "Our Village" at work, this is Christian and happy England," remarked the *Saturday Review* of March 3, 1857. No wonder that those who could went to the towns much as rivers run into the sea. Not into the small provincial towns, though, which held out little opportunity and little enough change, where there was no excitement except the feuds and gossip of a narrow world, where there was no variety except for seasons, and ageing. They went into the cities, where there was employment and life and growth. By 1930 about one-fifth of people in the world dwelt there, while most of the rest lived in conditions much closer to those of ancient Romans or Egyptians than to those of Kentish or Midwestern farmers. And, since it was mostly the young who left, over the years small towns and villages became places where the retired and the old predominated, leftovers of a slower-changing world whose ways increasingly contrasted with those of the modern city.

The Cities

In 1801, Europe boasted twenty-one cities with populations over 100,-000; in 1900, 147. Where less than 2 per cent of Europeans had lived in cities over 100,000, now the proportion was 15 per cent and higher than that in the Atlantic West. The population of Paris doubled, that of Berlin quadrupled in the last half of the century. In 1837, the year of Queen Victoria's accession, only six British cities had more than 100,000 inhabitants. By the century's end there were twenty-four. By then, 15 per cent of Englishmen and Welshmen lived in London, one Scotsman in five lived in Glasgow. Human groups seemed to exercise a magnetic force proportionate to their mass.

The cities grew like coral reefs, ramparts giving way to broad new boulevards, roads, rails, and aqueducts reaching out for food—and even more for water, which had to come over great distances to satisfy a level of consumption that seemed almost to double decade by decade. The urban reefs spread outward in irregular accretions, with bits of blighted country in between, swallowing up what had been isolated villages (Montmartre, Passy, Kensington, Islington), allowing new slums to rise in formerly elegant quarters, turning undeveloped land on the outskirts into suburbs, some—similar to medieval *faubourgs*—sheltering the shanties of those who could not find room within the city, others accommodating the flight from smoke and noise, the quest for new amenities like fresh air. "I am alien to what is coming, to what is here already," grumbled Goncourt in his *Journal* (November, 1860), "like these new boulevards with no turnings, with no adventure of perspective, implacable in their straightness, which retain nothing of the world of Balzac, which make one think of some American Babylon of the future."

The high pressure of city life, its nervous rhythm and hurry, evoked particular comment. Oscar Wilde, lecturing in New York in 1882, found its inhabitants all "in a hurry to catch a train;" and an American doctor coined the term "neurasthenia" to describe a malady arising typically out of the noisy, crowded city streets. Cities frightened the beholder and they thrilled him. Jefferson had called them "ulcers on the body politic." Rousseau believed that they corrupted. "Men," he insisted, "are not made to be crowded together in anthills." A popular mid-nineteenth-century novelist thought that they were "the results of the Fall." Cities were rough, dirty, dangerous, dissolute. They were overcrowded. Some parts of Liverpool had a density of 1,200 persons to the acre; some suburbs of London, six and ten persons to a room. Planning and rebuilding, inspired by the work of Haussmann in Paris, fascinated civic

Mansell Collection

Glasgow tenements during the mid-19th century.

reformers as far apart as British Birmingham and Chicago, Brussels and Barcelona. But rebuilding created difficulties of its own:

> Who builds? Who builds? Alas, ye poor!
> If London day by day "improves,"
> Where shall ye find a friendly door,
> When every day a home removes?

The masses added new dimensions to old fears of frightening mobs. "The population is hourly increasing in breadth and strength," noted a Victorian. "It is an aggregate of masses, our conceptions of which clothe themselves in terms which express something portentous and fearful." They intrigued and titillated romantic imaginations spurred by ignorance of depths, dark and unrevealed as the unknown wastes of Africa and Asia to which they were often compared. In 1890, General Booth of the Salvation Army published *In Darkest England,* comparing the slums of London with the regions which Stanley had just penetrated. Another author had just remarked that the same sun which never set on the Empire never rose on the dark alleys of London's East End. T. H. Huxley, Darwin's champion, compared Polynesian savages and London slum dwellers. It is hard to say how far all this reflected ignorance of how the other half lived, even more than any real parallels. The new masses seemed to pose a special threat to the politics of personal influence which had developed on quite a different scale, and many expected (as many hoped) that they would soon use their strength of numbers to secure radical—or even socialist—ends.

The Working Classes

How did these people live? What did they do? Their clothes, their food, their living quarters and outward surroundings improved in mid-nineteenth century and after. But the intensity of their working effort, the strain during working hours, the stress of urban living itself, the time spent getting to and from work also increased. Women were generally paid half a man's wages even for doing the same job. And a woman usually had to work to supplement her husband's pay. Insecurity was the watchword of the worker's life, at the mercy of accident, illness, depression, unemployment. True, savings banks flourished, but so did grog-shops. The workman felt the need for protection and sought it in unions and associations, harking back to old traditions but also to present habits of a collective life not only in the workshop but in the pub, or bar, or coffee shop that offered refuge from cold, uncomfortable, ill-lit lodgings; warmth, company, the opportunity to read a paper or to discuss current events and common concerns. Unions were born in pubs but grew in didactic enterprises like the French Ligue de l'Enseignement or the English Workers' Institute. Education was the workers' major weapon of self-help; organization was another.

Among the more frugal and industrious of the skilled workers in mines, shops, and factories, who could pay cash for what they bought and even save a little, the Cooperative Movement prospered. In England, where it had begun in the 1840's, 1914 saw it reach a membership near 4 million and an annual turnover of over 500 million dollars. The same skilled workmen, afraid of being swamped by the unqualified masses, launched the first trade unions in the 1850's and 60's. There seems to have been a certain consensus in liberal societies that unions were justified. "Our only chance," declared a workman in a mid-nineteenth century English novel, "is binding men together in one common interest; and if some are cowards and some are fools, they must come along and join the great march whose strength is numbers." Thomas Hughes, who was not only the creator of that model of Anglo-Saxon enterprise—Tom Brown—but also a member of Parliament, agreed: "Under a system which professes the right or rather the duty of all men peacefully to pursue their own interests for themselves, unionism appears to us the exact correlative of competition."

Unions achieved legal recognition in France between 1864 and 1884, in Belgium in 1866, in Austria and Britain after 1870, in Spain after 1881, in Germany in 1890, in Russia after 1906. First in Germany, then in Britain and in a number of other countries, the unions became vast enterprises running a variety of insurance systems, administering large treasuries, and augmenting property in buildings, hospitals, recreation centers, eventually even investments in industrial or trading companies. Their members, and especially their managers, were thoroughly identified with the existing system; their officials, accountants, and bureaucrats were little different from those of the companies with which they bargained within the framework of the existing—capitalist—order.

As we may imagine, the basic attitude of such bodies was apolitical. Most of their members were neither socialist nor Marxist, and they kept out of politics whenever they could. Two factors forced them into political action. The first was the struggle to gain recognition for themselves and for characteristic activities like picketing and strikes. This could only be achieved by legislation which came in response to political pressure at the polls or in the streets. The second factor was that the makeup of labor and of industry were both changing. During the prosperous years of the mid-nineteenth century, workers who shared the general feeling that technical progress, material improvements, and better living standards all went hand in hand, accepted the ruling faith in progress even for themselves. Experience apparently confirmed this. Visibly, workers could become managers, shopkeepers, manufacturers, and even millionaires. In 1872, 80 per cent of masters had begun as workmen, 15 per cent were the sons of workingmen. But this was the last generation to stem from the working class. Economic conditions which permitted such social and economic promotion began to alter, economic expansion lagged, relations between patrons and workers grew rarer, education and capital needed for success rose to a higher order, the worker felt he would not get the chance his predecessors enjoyed. Industrial expansion was mobilizing a different kind of workman in ever greater numbers—less skilled, less secure, more aware of the gap between his earnings and those of his employers. The concentration and growth of industry were separating worker and master, the latter increasingly distant from his employees, the masters becoming an invisible presence in the Board room, with whom relations could only be in class terms, far from the old personal ties however hostile these may occasionally have been.

In this changing context, the mass unions were well adapted to mediate between the increasingly distant and hostile parties. They did their work well: their first aim, and that of the Second International founded in 1889, was to cut working hours. These, which were patterned after those of agricultural labor, beginning at dawn and ending at dusk, amounted to 3,500 or 4,000 hours a year—12 hours or more a day for 6 days a week. The agitation to reduce the work week to 60 hours had brought its first results in the United States, where the 60-hour week was introduced in the 1860's. The new International made its demonstrations so impressive (the May Day was launched in 1890 as the first of them) that Kaiser Wilhelm II called an international conference that year to consider possible labor legislation * and by 1900 the 60-hour week was almost general. It fell to 48 or 50 hours after World War I, and lower still between the 1930's and the 1950's. As a result, most twentieth-century workers enjoyed far greater leisure than their ancestors. The average sixty-five-year-old man retiring in 1900 had worked about 220,000 hours of his life; the average Western workman of our day at retirement will have worked 100,000 hours or less.

Real wages were improving (70–90 per cent between 1866 and 1936). Conditions of life and labor were getting better. There were many poor, but even the poorest were consumers now. They bought pins and buttons, tea or candles. The remainder simply bought more. In other words, vast numbers of people appeared, most of whom had never existed (numerically) in previous centuries, most of the remainder of whom had never existed as consumers of anything but basic foodstuffs—millions and millions of consumers of manufactured products whose very existence created the demand which gave them the jobs, hence the wages, hence the means to carry out their consumer's function.

Higher wages did not only keep up with higher prices but also with increased expectations. Bread consumption remained steady while that of meat, wine, and beer went up. In the 1850's and 60's, 61 per cent of

* *Rerum Novarum* was another response to the agitation for social reform.

Pit boys at the Derbyshire coal
mines in the early 1900's.

the French working-class budget still went for food. But the poor were
beginning to actually buy clothing—though still generally secondhand
—instead of relying only on charity. Soon living standards improved:
fewer children, fewer married women, went out to work; working hours
were reduced; real wages edged up as prices of consumer goods went
down; so did the size of the average family, falling from five or six
to four in the last decades of the ninteenth century. The very poor
were still very poor, but there were fewer of them. Meanwhile, more and
more were being reconciled to a society in which conditions of life and
work were notably improving, life expectation going up, elementary
education provided for every working child. In the 1880's English
workers began to take holiday trips like their social superiors. Manners,
behavior, public safety improved; streets were cleaner, better lit and
paved, safer at night; there were more parks, better drains and sewers,
more stringent inspections of working conditions, food purity, weights
and measures: all of which made life better for a lot of people, quite
apart from wages.

More, the income gap between rich and poor was narrowing. A textile
worker of the Second Empire had to work 15 days for a good pair of
boots, which his descendant earns today in as many hours. A Berlin
dressmaker around 1900 put in 7 hours' work to buy a pound of beef,
seven times more than her granddaughter today. A suit which would take
a well-paid miner 12 days' work to buy before 1900 could be acquired
with one day's wages today. The bicycle which cost a Frenchman the
equivalent of 100 work days in 1900, cost only 10 in 1938. In 1900 the
inner tube of a bicycle cost 40 hours' work: today only 2 hours.*

* It is interesting to glance at the relative cost of various products, not in time but
space, in the 1950's, and to note, incidentally, that costs in what economists call tertiary
or service categories differ little: one pair of shoes costs 7 hours' work in Chicago, 15 in
Paris, 54 in Moscow; one pound of bread costs 7 minutes' work in Chicago, 15 minutes
in Paris, 25 minutes in Moscow; however, a seat at the opera costs 8 hours' work in
Chicago and Paris and 7 hours' in Moscow, while a medical consultation costs the
equivalent of 5 hours' work in each of these cities.

618

This closing of the income gap between rich and poor has been one of the greatest changes of the past century. Economists like Jean Fourastié have calculated that in 1800 the income of a senior judge was fifty times that of his janitor; in 1950 it was only four or five times greater, while the proportion of the hours they worked respectively (2,000 a year for the one, 3,000 or 3,500 for the other) has changed considerably. Comparing the salaries of a higher public servant and those of an industrial worker, the ratio alters from 55:1 in 1800, to 13:1 in 1900, and 7:1 in 1960. Of course, what matters is buying power; and everybody knows that if the workman's mean hourly wage has increased a thousandfold since the day of Louis XIV, so have prices. But not all prices have gone up in the same proportion: the price of mirrors, for instance, proportionate to hourly wages has been immensely reduced, while that of personal services has not. In 1700 a mirror six feet square cost relatively as much as a Cadillac does today. At that time, and until the beginning of the nineteenth century, half or more of a working-class family budget might go for bread alone. By 1831, only a quarter of such budgets went for bread. By mid-twentieth century bread figured for only 3 per cent in a French worker's budget and for 1 per cent in a New Yorker's, while in both cases nine-tenths of food expenses now go for things which made rare or no appearances on working-class tables a hundred years ago: meat, fruit, milk, and fresh vegetables.

The large proportion of expenses which food took up is now devoted to new comforts, like refrigerator or washing machine, auto or television. The very *standard* of living has utterly changed from times when comfort meant sufficient heat, when clothes and lodging accounted for a tiny proportion of the budget and meager household equipment for even less. The level of what we regard as a minimum has soared to include far more things, and men's capacity of paying for these things has improved too—though proportionally more so among the former underprivileged. Thus, while between 1830 and 1960 the nominal income of a French factory hand increased from 60 to 64,000 (index points), that of a colonel or an office manager went up just half that much: from 60 to 32,000. And, while such a salary in 1950 stood for 2,250 working hours a year, its counterpart in 1831 had to be earned in 3,600 hours.

But class differentials, if smaller, clearly subsist. Thus, in pre-1914 years, while a French miner came to earn 20 per cent more, his employer's profits doubled. On the eve of that war in Britain, 5 per cent of the population owned 85 per cent of the national wealth. To the extent that wealth and well-being increase, that of the wealthy increases faster. In 1954, in Paris, infant mortality for children of unskilled workers was more than double that of the children of the managerial staff; and four times as high for children of laborers as for the children of doctors or lawyers.

Food (and Drink)

Nothing can illustrate the improvements that have taken place so well as changes in food habits.

In 1842, many poor townspeople lived entirely on potatoes and porridge, eking these out with rotten vegetables and vegetable refuse. Consumption of tea increased so much partly because many people could not get milk and looked to the tea for warmth. After 1860, things improved, but bread remained the mainstay until the end of the century. Toast is probably an English invention, made to disguise the taste of stale bread. In 1864, the typical Lancashire worker's diet consisted mainly of bread, oatmeal, bacon, perhaps a little butter, treacle, tea, and coffee. Skilled workmen did better, getting butter and Sunday meat. When fuel was dear and weariness overwhelming, most people could afford only two or three hot meals a week; and these were cooked on an open fire or baked in a brick oven. Closed ranges began to show up in middle-class kitchens in the 1860's, and domestic gas ovens, which appeared about the same time, only came into general use at the end of the century. They were for a long time out of reach of poor people, who could not afford their price and that of cooking utensils. What with inadequate water supplies, limited means, and little time, no wonder cookshops flourished.

So did drink shops. In 1860 there was one for every seventy French men, women, and children. Even in the London of 1900, one house in seventy-seven was a public house. A third to a quarter of a working-class family's income seems to have gone for drink—a welcome argument for those who attributed the poverty of the poor to their own improvidence. But drink, like gambling, is typical of a search for satisfaction or relief not otherwise available to people with no reason to believe that gratification may be deferred. Also, more simply, poor working people could seldom find snacks or meals elsewhere than in taverns. It would be the awareness of this fact among temperance workers, shocked first of all by the large number of drunken children, that produced concrete results (first in England after the 1850's) in chains of cafés, refreshment houses, and temperance restaurants, where one could order food or nonalcoholic beverages at very moderate prices.*

The temperance movement was only one reflection of a growing, sometimes muddled but ultimately effective, awareness of social problems—prison abuses, juvenile delinquency, prostitution, and alcoholism. The awareness was emphasized by the crusading propaganda carried out

* The temperance movement also sparked the foundation, in 1880, of the first temperance music hall, which—situated in a popular quarter of London—would become the Old Vic Theatre.

A British institution and the gathering place of the whole neighborhood: the pub.

in books and pamphlets. There were those meant for children, some selling by the million, all fully equipped with dramatic conversations and death scenes, but well informed about the condition of the destitute, especially the young, which were graphically described. There were books for grownups: the accounts and surveys appreciated by the age, and novels like those of Charles Dickens. Today we find much of their tone pathetic and rather overdone. But as a later critic, the novelist George Gissing, pointed out: "such pathos is called 'cheap' . . . In Dickens's day the lives, the happiness of children were very cheap indeed and . . . he had his purpose in insisting on their claims to attention." The same might be said about the sordidness that seems to overflow from the naturalistic novels of the 1870's and after. They, too, like the pathos of their predecessors, had a social purpose and achieved it.

By the 1880's a social conscience had become fashionable. The American Society for Prevention of Cruelty to Animals had obtained conviction of a parent who starved and beat his child, by claiming that the child was an animal in distress. In 1884, the London Society for Prevention of Cruelty to Children was founded. In the same year the *Oxford English Dictionary*, which had defined the word "slumming" as "frequenting slums for discreditable purposes," added a new variant: "to visit slums for charitable or philanthropic purposes, or out of curiosity, especially as a fashionable pursuit." Middle-class intellectuals and idealists were going to the people, beginning to work and teach in the slums of Paris and London, as the Narodniks were trying to do in the Russian countryside.*

After the 1880's a new recession prompted a new look at conditions of working-class life. The facts produced by contemporary surveys suggested that poverty was not due to improvidence or sin as had been com-

* Yet neither rich nor poor questioned the assumption that they were different races, each fated to a different place in the world. Equality was an idea entertained only by those above the poverty line, not below it.

fortably supposed, and placed in relief the sufferings of the very old and the very young—the latter could hardly be charged with improvidence, except in being born. The Young Men's Christian Association, which had been founded in 1844, was now followed by the YWCA, set up in 1877 as a prayer union for young girls. Then, in 1883, came the Boys' Brigade, designed to teach poor boys "drill, physical exercises, punctuality, cleanliness and obedience to command." * More important perhaps, the social conscience found a wide open field in the realm of food and drink, where fraud, adulteration, and exploitation abounded. When the controls, inspections, and regulations of the bad old days before Adam Smith had been removed, competition became a vicious spiral in which little men survived only by undercutting their fellows, overworking their employees, deteriorating their wares, and defrauding their customers. One Liverpool firm even took out a patent in 1851 for a machine which could compress chicory into the shape of coffee beans, to cheat the buyer. Manufacturers, brewers, vintners, wholesalers, retailers, all set out to press back the limits of private enterprise. The public—especially the ignorant and poor—paid. Chronic gastritis, characteristic of the nineteenth-century urban populations, was only one result of a diet containing alum, plaster of Paris, lead, mineral dyes, and any number of poisons introduced in search of profit and under the cover of a vast conspiracy of silence.

First Englishmen, then Americans, then others, began to be informed that their breakfast sausage was a mess of spiced and flavored putrid meat, their coffee grains were mixed with dried blobs of horses' blood from the knacker's yard, the cream on which they smacked their lips was thickened with calves' brains, their sweets bore poisonous decorations, their infusions were for a good part sweepings, their tea gum and dust, their bread loaves only partly wheat, and all their food a major carrier of disease and dirt. The campaign against this and the legislation it set off achieved many improvements in the quality of food. Commercialism now intervened to show that it was profitable to sell pure foods—if at a higher price—and, by the 1880's, increasingly effective laws made adulteration dangerous and unprofitable. Packaged foods (tea, sugar, flour) appeared as a first result of some manufacturers' determination to see their products reach the consumer in a pure state. Breakfast foods, probably first developed in the United States to provide pure food for Seventh Day Adventists waiting for a second coming, began to appear in Europe. Infantile mortality fell, partly as a result of movements to supply unadulterated milk free to poor mothers. France, then England and

* This soon had a membership in the tens of thousands and helped to inspire boy scouting, which appeared around 1907, making its appeal to the middle classes. The poor could not afford to join, since scouts had to read, write, and own a small sum in savings, while the uniform cost too much for children whose only clothes were hand-me-downs.

Holland, established milk dispensaries, followed by health visitors and infant welfare centers. Milk *was* getting purer and its consumption rising. But it was still relatively expensive, and figures for 1902 show that while middle-class English families consumed six pints per head per week, the lower middle-class consumed four, artisans less than two, and laborers less than one pint.

The best will in the world could not furnish food where there was none, or no means to get it. Prosperity and technology worked hand in hand to provide these. Substitutes like margarine, invented by a Frenchman, developed by the Americans and the Dutch, became an important part of working-class diet. A vast increase in processed foods made ready-made eating possible. The difficulty of transporting meat was tackled first by salting and drying, then by canning, always with highly unappetizing results. Canning processes had been invented and used during the Napoleonic wars. The California gold rush, the Crimean War, and the Civil War in America had provided them with a further impetus. Prejudices against canning still persisted; and British sailors, referring to a woman who had been cut into small pieces in a famous murder case of 1867, called their canned meat "Sweet Fanny Adams," an expression that survived until the First World War. Then, in the 1880's, the problems of refrigeration were solved, introducing really cheap imported meat and, also, adding fresh fish to the salted or pickled herring to which the working classes had been restricted until then. One has to remember how narrow the margin is between the slaughter of an animal and its putrefaction, the picking of a fruit and its rotting, the milking of a cow and the milk's turning, the freshness of butter and its rancidness, to get a sense of what the world gained from refrigeration.

We have already seen that, as incomes generally rose, a smaller proportion of them was spent on food. In England of 1885, while the working classes spent three-fourths of their earnings on food and drink, the middle classes spent 44 per cent. At the same time, as they became better able to choose—that is, afford—more people shifted from dark bread to white, from bread, potatoes, and other fillers to meat, from carbohydrates to proteins, from make-dos to luxuries: tea, coffee, cocoa, chocolate, sugar, eggs, jams. In all, to more variety and better nutrition. The consumption of food increased with the buying power of the masses: between 1890 and 1914 the consumption of wheat doubled in Belgium, trebled in Germany. The average Englishman who had eaten 6 pounds of sugar a year in 1800 was eating 80 pounds in 1900, the Frenchman had been promoted from 4 to 46. Sugar consumption seems, incidentally, to provide a very accurate reflection of industrial prosperity. Its spread among the poorer classes and the comparative figures of average consumption in the early 1880's per head of population range themselves in a hierarchical table of industrial and social advances at that time:

623

Spain	5.1 lbs. per head per year
Italy	7.6 lbs. per head per year
Russia	7.7 lbs. per head per year
Austria	13.2 lbs. per head per year
Germany	15.0 lbs. per head per year
France	22.6 lbs. per head per year
Denmark	38.0 lbs. per head per year
Great Britain	68.8 lbs. per head per year

Nevertheless, although conditions had been steadily improving throughout the century, for millions of men and women the wartime rations of the First World War were far better than anything that they had known before. During the Boer War, army recruiters lowered the minimum height to five feet, and still had to reject two men in every five for physical deficiencies. In Leeds (1902) half the children in the poorer quarters had rickets; in Britain as a whole (1904) one-third of all children "were undernourished in the sense that they actually went hungry," and the average height of boys at private schools was 5 inches greater than that of boys at council (or public) schools. 1906 and 1907 brought school meals, medical and dental treatment, infant welfare clinics, followed by old-age pensions (1908), health and unemployment insurance (1911). Poverty and disease could only be tackled on the public level: a fact which Communists and National Socialists recognized, but which the free economies accepted only after 1940 when shortages were turned to dietary improvements and rationing was deliberately used to change the health and habits of the popular masses.

Today, almost all of Europe has sufficient food. Dietitians tell us that the average daily ration of a normal population ranges between 2,700 and 2,800 calories. This range has by now been attained even in poor countries like Italy or Greece—although statistical averages do not show how much overconsumption in certain quarters balances the hunger of other men. Even so, counting all of Europe, all of Soviet Russia, the United States, and the white dominions of the British Empire, this accounts at most for half the population of the world. The other half still lives, hungry or undernourished, in the conditions Europe left behind with Louis XIV. There are perhaps a few hundred thousand people among the scores of millions of the West who eat as little and as badly as the average man of Asia's 700 or 800 million. Until this disparity has been effaced, their hunger must influence not only the conscience but the stability of the world.

The Bourgeoisie

If the outstanding characteristic of the past century has been the rise and assertion of the masses, the most articulate and constructive roles would still be played by the *bourgeoisie,* however general or misleading the term: people living in cities as a rule but who, particularly, do not derive their living from manual labor, whether they be landowners, *rentiers,* clerks, bankers, manufacturers, shopkeepers and employees, lawyers, or veterinarians. The *bourgeoisie* allows for subdivisions—high, medium, petty—among those who have a fortune, those who are building one, and those who have no hope (and perhaps no ambition either) of ever attaining it. But it does set itself apart from those who work with their hands in industry or on the land, and also from those who derive their status specifically from birth: the landed aristocracy.

The latter's social significance diminished to the point of irrelevance halfway through this period. Over most of Europe their wealth, the revenues of their estates and of the property they held in and around the fast developing cities, enabled the aristocracy to retain social and economic predominance until 1900 or 1918. The horse and carriage, the notion of gentleman derived from landed values, remained symbols of social standing into the twentieth century. But the majority among the nobility—pompous, shallow, narrow-minded and ignorant—looked increasingly like an anachronistic polyp on the body politic. Hunting and gambling seem to have been their greatest passions and while the latter ruined only the players, the former caused vast hecatombs whose results can still be viewed by wondering tourists in the eerie stuffed-corpse-lined chambers of some hunting lodges and castles.* But the trend of the age toward investment and management rather than pomp and circumstance emphasized wealth as the base of status rather than birth. Aristocracy was being pressed back by plutocracy, and rich aristocrats simply melted in it. It was also being sapped by bureaucracy and specialization.

Society was becoming increasingly complicated, requiring and recruiting immense numbers of men to make it run. Between 1880 and 1910, in Germany alone, the number of postal and railway employees increased from 245,000 to 700,000. New professions, new pursuits appeared: policemen, sanitary inspectors, medical officers, permanent professional officials, colonial and other civil servants. There and in teaching, science, and technology, amateurs were steadily replaced by specialists; and the new structure called for educated men to run it. Men of background and breeding were preferred, of course, but there were not enough of them. A wider elite was taking shape, appealing to capacity —as when the British Civil Service began to be recruited by competitive examinations—and sometimes forming it by scholarships and grants. The hierarchies of money and of social function would gradually eliminate the hierarchy of birth.** On the other hand, the industrial condition

---

* Between 1867 and 1900 a keen but not exceptional hunter of his day, Lord Ripon, slaughtered 142,343 pheasant, 97,759 partridge, 56,460 grouse, 29,858 rabbit, 27,686 hare, 97 wild pig, 19 sambur, 12 buffalo, 11 tiger, and 2 rhinoceros: nearly 30 lives a day for 33 years.

** However, as this happened, the importance of decorations and titles also grew: in England, elevation to or promotion within the peerage; in France appointment to some order, especially the Legion of Honor; in Germany and Austria not only ennoblement

A piano of the 1860's which converts to a bed, a bureau, and two closets.

out of which they grew also reduced the distance between classes, offering all the same increasingly showy, shoddy goods, creating a common taste for the fashionable and the superficial, which most men could increasingly indulge. Mass production laid the groundwork for a new mass age: refining the people, vulgarizing their masters, imparting to both a certain identity of tastes and manners even while it differentiated their material situations.

This can be seen quite plainly in their homes and dress. Perhaps the most widely recognized form of self-expression the last century knew was spending money.* The bourgeoisie, General de Gaulle once remarked "is wealth: the consciousness of having it, or the desire to acquire it." Conspicuous consumption became a badge of rank, as it had been a responsibility of rank in earlier days. Objects poured forth to fill once empty rooms and cupboards, parlors became teeming hoards of loot both from the past and from the farthest corners of the earth, as mixed and crowded as purse and ingenuity could achieve. Men and things responded exuberantly to the possibilities held out by the new machines: in furniture, spring upholstery made possible by cheap metal springs was an immense advance in comfort but a failure in looks. In decoration, design gave way to mass-produced adornments to satisfy an ever-growing number of uneducated customers. The ingenuity of ornament turned into a kind of game where every object concealed its function in an alien shape: embroidered spittoons, antler hatstands, stuffed bears to hold umbrellas, doilies concealing tables, flowers opening to embrace toothpicks, gothic bookcases, baroque tubs: the more machines could multiply ornaments, the uglier ornaments seemed to be. This was the essence of the "home, sweet home"—the song of which name became almost the anthem of English-speaking countries in the nineteenth century.

but, even more, honorary and other ranks in the civil service; these rewarded political utility as much as they did service to the state. Differentiating labels would be as rife in the modern world as in the old.

* The decree appointing Giuseppe Verdi a senator in 1875 spoke first of the amount of tax which the composer paid and only second of his services to music. The order, which shocked some music lovers, was highly indicative of the contemporary and especially Italian atmosphere.

But homes are relatively private; and people outside their homes were most easily set apart by dress. Until the 1880's, men of the "respectable" classes—although less and less differentiated among themselves by their dark, drab clothes—were easily identified by the frock coats and top hats which they wore, it seems, on all occasions.* Thereafter, with the spread of ready-made wear, workmen abandoned their smocks and corduroys and men began to shift toward the modern practice of dressing differently for different activities—sports, labor, lounging, or formal wear occasions.

They could afford to do so, for they retained a formidable agent of conspicuous consumption in their womenfolk. The clothes that wives and daughters wore would testify to the wealth of their more drably garbed husbands and fathers. The well-upholstered shapes of womankind answered the well-upholstered furniture in the parlors, in the same spirit: showing off. But here the problems involved led to sartorial escalation.

Women's fashion magazines, appearing early in the nineteenth century, had brought information to circles which would never otherwise have had it, so that even tradesmen's daughters could wear the same costume as their betters. Cheap textiles contributed to this, and one contemporary complained that "while expensive silks were worn they could not be attained by persons of small means, but when a few shillings could purchase a muslin gown quite in the fashion every woman could command one. . . ." As ready-mades and patterns encroached on society, *ladies* preserved their prerogatives by extravagance. Fashionable glamour became increasingly expensive, out of the reach of smaller purses. The dimension of clothes came to indicate social importance, the latter increasing with the diameter of the crinoline or the bulge of the bustle.

Fashions were the more exclusive the more useless they rendered their wearer. It was a long cry from the ladies' dresses of the beginning of the century when a young girl at a London ball could ask her partner: "Pray, Sir, do not tread on my dress and tear it, for as you can see I have nothing on underneath." Now women's bodies were swaddled like Chinese ladies' feet, and with the same debilitating results. As late as the 1870's, a girl asking her mother what "abdomen" meant was told that no lady needs to know about something only found among the lower orders. No wonder that women who did not know about abdomens—let alone other parts—suffered gastric troubles, acidosis, various results of poor diet, tight lacing, and general bad hygiene.

Wasp waists, corsets, bustles, crinolines were said "to restrain the impulses of one sex while arousing those of the other." "The crinoline," wrote a guide to etiquette in the 1870's, "is an ever present monitor indirectly bidding its wearer to exercise self-restraint; it is evidence of a well-disciplined mind and well-regulated feeling." But, if tight

---

* Millais' portrait of Ruskin shows him on a mountain walk in black frock coat and top hat (1854); much later Lord Salisbury went rabbit shooting in the same garb.

A group of women tram conductors in Edinburgh. Right: a woman chimney-sweep in London.

lacing meant that no woman so bound could stoop to conquer, no more could she stoop to dust. Burdened by 20 yards of heavy material, cut and deformed by steel-hard stays,* trammeled and hamstrung by a wealth of lace, fancies, and trimmings, the late-nineteenth-century woman of fashion was a triumph of artifice, the walking Christmas tree of her menfolk's thrift. Now it was time for her emancipation.

Women

The story of the emancipation of women is seldom mentioned in the same breath as that of other submerged groups, like workers or colonial peoples. Yet it should be. For, sometime at the turn of the nineteenth into the twentieth century, a process started which, by today, is well on the way to liberating half the human race. There was a great deal more than clothes from which women had to be liberated. Existing legislation tended to treat them as objects or, at least, as subjects of their masters' will. They were chattels of their fathers, transferred eventually to a husband's rule. In a novel of 1897, a father who breaks off his daughter's engagement is asked what she thinks. "She's got nowt to think," he answers, "I'm her father, I think for her." Marx denounced bourgeois marriage as prostitution, in which a woman sold her body for her keep. Tennyson slashed at "the woman markets of the West/where our Caucasians let themselves be sold." It certainly looks as if the love match that we more or less take for granted was almost a nineteenth-century invention; and that the widespread tendency of young people

* A letter from a schoolgirl, published in *The Englishwoman's Domestic Magazine* in the mid-sixties, mentions that at her boarding school stays are compulsory, sealed up by a mistress on Monday morning, removed on Saturday for one hour "for the purposes of ablution." The result: a 23-inch waist at fifteen was reduced to 13 inches by seventeen. Sleeping in tight-laced stays, remarks one mother, "carries no hardship beyond an occasional fainting fit."

to marry without dowry, contract, or marriage settlement only came in much later, with full employment and social security. As for spinsters, "devoured by little black relations just like fleas," many of them were simply murdered slowly by families that turned them into maids of all work.

All this applies in practice to the middle classes rather than the poor, to whom material considerations and contracts remained irrelevant. But, while among the poor the woman remained a workhorse, among the better off she was condemned to triviality. The bourgeois helpmate was rendered futile by domestic help, the active woman stultified by respectability. The ideal of nineteenth-century womanhood was sensitive, delicate, and useless: for what greater luxury could a man afford? She sighed, fainted, suffered from the vapors, dissolved into tears at the slightest provocation. Although some, like Florence Nightingale, ate like horses and lived to be ninety, many, like Flaubert's Madame Bovary, lived mostly in a dream world, unfit for anything but fantasies.

Emancipation came partly with the opportunities that the economy offered to the poor, partly with the self-assertion of the better off. The economic and educational issue here was crucial. In most European countries high-school education for girls became available only in the 1880's and 90's. Opportunities for independent work were slight. Respectable women took work at home in secret (sewing, embroidery, copying), taught music or languages at minimal fees. No woman could expect to live on her own earnings: prostitution or marriage were her only hope. One other opportunity lay in domestic service, which constituted the second largest occupation in England in 1851 and still employed one and a half million before the First World War, when the *Ladies' Home Journal* rightly but unbelievably predicted "we are gradually coming to the abolishment of a permanent serving class in our homes."

In the 1880's, telephonists, secretaries, and woman office clerks appeared. Between 1890 and 1900 the proportion of female clerks rose from 8 to 18 per cent; by 1911 one-third of all clerks were women. In England, women—even fashionable women—could now run shops (milliners, dressmakers), become professional photographers, doctors (212 in 1901), dentists (140 in 1901), or accountants. Erstwhile maids and cooks found that factories offered more freedom and sometimes better pay. The post office, the schools, opened their doors to cheap female labor.

Women were becoming more independent, using the trams and the omnibuses launched in 1870, setting up committees, turning toward higher education, asking for the vote. The first women's colleges in the United States date back to the 1830's, in England to the 1870's; the first teachers' training colleges in France to the 1880's. Women's dress was also becoming simpler, more practical, if only relatively and slowly. Until the appearance of the reticule in the 1890's, women had only a hidden pocket *under* the skirt. The reticule, forerunner of the handbag, permitted money, keys, card case, and purse—eventually cigarettes and cosmetics—to be carried in comfort and used without embarrassment. About the same time, knickers began to replace petticoats, lightening the load of material that women had to carry, eventually permitting shorter skirts and greater freedom of movement. The tailor-made dress with its efficient look reflected the new mood with its assertion of equality and emancipation. So did the safety bicycle, which freed women from their chaperones and encouraged the emancipating trend. One sometimes thinks of Ibsen's Nora slamming her way out of the *Doll's House* (1879) and riding off into a broader life mounted, quite likely, on a bicycle.

Women were going in for sports, playing golf, tennis, hockey, and, in England, cricket. They dueled or went in for Greco-Roman wrestling. They jettisoned social constraints to take on a new, slender, fluid shape, that of the hermaphrodite dear to the aestheticism of the 1880's and nineties. One of the literary heroes of the day * is smitten by a Miss Urania, a circus acrobat: "And as he admired her suppleness and strength, he could see an artificial change of sex taking place in her." This kind of allusiveness (with its picture of women becoming more masculine) was somewhat premature. Nevertheless, by 1900, women, still tightly bound by their garments and hobbled by their skirts, were striking out in ever new directions. Tearooms were offering them a respectable public meeting place unescorted by husband or brother; hotel dining rooms saw the first cigarettes being lit, perhaps in London's *Savoy* in 1896; ** powder compacts began to come out in public places; suffragettes (whom *Punch* wanted to call *Insuffrabelles*) were fighting for the vote which they would get in England in 1917.

The feminists set out to secure not advantages but equality: the recognition that a woman's sex was no reason for subjection, no mark of inferiority. They had achieved successes, attained greater legal independence, seen divorce laws enacted, but all by the "generosity" of the males. They would be satisfied only by equal rights, and these they would obtain by fair means and by foul. By 1914, women had voting rights in New Zealand (1893), Australia (1902), Finland (1907), Norway (1913), and in eleven Western states of North America. After the war they were enfranchised—though sometimes with reservations—in Soviet Russia, Germany, and all West European countries except for France (1945), Italy (1946), Belgium (1948), Spain (where they got the vote under the Republican Constitution of 1931 and lost it with Franco), Portugal, and Switzerland. By 1924 the first woman was holding office as cabinet minister (in Denmark). In 1950, except for Switzerland, Portugal, and Spain, women had the vote in all European countries. Their influence made the electorate more conservative but also more interested

---

* Des Esseintes in J. K. Huysmans' novel *Against the Grain* (1884).
** In 1864, three young ladies had been arrested for smoking in the Tuileries Gardens.

in social security, family allowances, pensions, health schemes, and public education: trends which connect with modern politics.

The greatest single factor in the emancipation of women, however, was not the vote but birth control. The most common form of birth control in all ages has been abortion, always widespread, nearly always illegal. But in the eighteenth century, when mortality rates were falling, the better off—finding that the greater number of surviving children created problems—began to have recourse to contraceptive methods. Once the fatality of death was placed in question, the fatality of birth could be questioned too. Now that survival was no longer subject *only* to chance, the notion of family planning became possible. At the same time, greater interest in individual children, greater concern for their welfare and character, encouraged parents to limit families.

A diversity of factors spread these practices beyond the upper classes. In the French countryside, the provisions of the Napoleonic Code which stipulated that land must be divided among all heirs, discouraged large families if a workable holding was to be held together. In industrial societies Thomas Malthus argued that excessive numbers make for misery and, in his wake, there came the first deliberate propaganda for birth control.* But theoretical arguments were less convincing than experience. In the second half of the nineteenth century, the spread of child labor laws and compulsory education were turning the children of the poor from a potential source of profit into a burden, those of the rich into a luxury. Surveys of working-class families found that their circumstances were more strained in proportion to their size. Middle-class families, struggling to keep up appearances, found that the cost of educating children accounted for about one-fourth of their budget. Cheap servants were getting harder to find, large apartments were expensive.** Tutors, dancing, drawing, language and music lessons could be a sound investment but proved a heavy charge. Greater expectations of comfort provided an added inducement for family planning, while the decline of religious authority, the spreading capacity to plan ahead, the availability of contraceptive devices and information about them, all contributed to a declining birth rate in the more advanced nations of the West.

Middle- and upper-class families now shrank from twelve or seven to two or three children, and their staff, houses, and stables shrank with them. Between 1851 and 1950 birth rates per 1,000 fell from 34 to 16 in England and Germany, from 32 to 16 in Sweden, from 48 to 26 in Russia. The greatest drop came in the twentieth century when really effective contraceptive devices became available, and when the more

* James Mill wrote an article about it in the *Encyclopaedia Britannica* of 1818, recommending chastity and abstinence. The labor leader Francis Place, more realistic, recommended contraception.

** The Victorian precept that children should be seen and not heard reflects the defensive needs of adults at a time when the average family had five or six children and *kept them in the house.*

backward countries joined the others. Between 1905 and 1950 the Italian birth rate fell from 32 to 19, Spanish and Greek from 34 to 20, Hungarian from 36 to 21. Given the choice, more and more people were limiting their families or avoiding children altogether, to the benefit of their living standards and of their independence. They were still, mostly, members of the social groups best able or most inclined to take advantage of such opportunities. It turned out that the more skilled and prosperous had fewer children, the poorer and less educated had relatively more. Contraception furthered the survival of the unfittest. It also, very likely, in its imperfect stage between the 1880's and the 1940's, caused frustrations which might have been reflected in the nerves and temper of widening sections of the population of the West. But it did a great deal to better the lot of women, to turn them into free or *freer* agents, to introduce a great element of choice into their lives.

So did the possibility of divorce which, like family planning, introduced an element of deliberation in what has been called the successive polygamy of earlier days, when high mortality rates made for frequent remarriages of widowers and widows.*

Of course, greater choice was paralleled like everything else by less security. The family, kept together by the economic dependency of almost all its members, broke asunder: "The young men and women of our day are parting fast from their parents and each other," declared an English novelist as early as 1851. Neither men nor women have found it easy to adjust to a situation in which true equality of the sexes, at least in advanced societies, becomes really feasible. But it is possible to imagine that, just as the emancipation of the working class has mobilized vast new energies for social use, so the probability of women finding other purposes in life than childbearing and rearing, another fulfillment than the strictly biological, will enrich the world rather than impoverish it.

The Victorians

As the twentieth century grows ever more complex and insecure, the nineteenth appears ever more attractive, a haven of security and straightforward situations. In the last decades of the twentieth century many have begun to look somewhat wistfully toward a period which their parents and grandparents emphatically rejected. This epoch, best de-

---

* Such mortality may have been spurred by the fact that, until the liberalization of divorce procedures, chiefly after 1920, divorce was so hard to come by that poisoning of spouse was probably the shortest way out of unhappy marriages. Poisoning was one of the most frequent marital crimes, and mid-nineteenth-century legislation like the English Arsenic Act, took cognizance of the temptation.

scribed by the term "Victorian," runs roughly from the middle to the end of the nineteenth century and does not concern only England, from whose sovereign it derives its name, but most of the middle and upper classes of Europe, which seem to have borrowed its values and mentality. It is in this sense that we use it here.

Today, the term "Victorian" begins to acquire all the rather hazy aura that we associate with the good old days, *la belle époque,* which ended in the First World War. It had not been so to many of its more thoughtful contemporaries. H. G. Wells thought it a slovenly and wasteful age. For Leslie Stephen (1832–1904), who fathered the *Dictionary of National Biography* and also Virginia Woolf, nobody would ever want to revive what its biographer, Lytton Strachey, later called its "slow funereal barbarism." In fact, as always, it was all things to all men, and curiously like our own time. It was not a contemporary commentator but a country doctor who, in a book of 1860, denounced the unbearable social pressures under which his patients labored: "The craving lust for gold, the restless goading of ambition, and the insatiable yearnings for display, these march hand in hand with an unscrupulous and reckless luxury and with new, artificial and intolerable anxieties, in the wear and tear of which the human machine prematurely breaks down."

"We live sadly too fast," complained social commentators of the 1860's in articles with titles like "The Sad Intensity of Modern Life." A scheme was mooted to erect a statue to Worry in the city of London. Worry can never have been absent from the city of London or anywhere else; but anxiety, insecurity, fear of failure and of the morrow (as well as hope), must have taken very concrete forms in an age when limited liability was mostly lacking until mid-century, and bankruptcy meant not only ruin and the likelihood of jail, but loss of social status: coming down in the world and sinking to the dread condition of the poor. Hence the pace of life and business constantly on the run, the rising incidence of heart disease after 1850, the discovery of "neurasthenia," the new interest in nervous disorders—not only in Victorian London, where Beatrice Webb found people with "no roots in neighborhood, in vocation, in creed, or for that matter in race," but in every other city where the same situation prevailed. Hence the self-analysis and introspection which, complained an observer in 1868, were being "pushed to the verge of monomania." Hence the "ennui and depression" which Matthew Arnold in his inaugural lecture at Oxford in 1856 found to characterize contemporary literature and, obviously, people too. Frustration, discontent, hopelessness recurred under the pens of undergraduates and men of letters in the 1850's as they had done in the 1820's, as they would do in the 1920's and 1960's.

> For what wears the life of mortal men?
> 'Tis that from change to change their being rolls;

'Tis that repeated shocks, again, again
Exhaust the energy of strongest souls . . .

Like children bathing on the shore,
Buried a wave beneath,
The second wave succeeds, before
We have had time to breathe.*

They reeled under "a thousand facts and notions, which they know not how to classify, pouring in on them like a flood."** "They hear so much said," noted J. S. Mill in his diary on January 13, 1854, "or find that so much can be said about everything, that they feel no assurance of the truth of anything." Perhaps this is why home was so sweet: a symbol of stability, a world enclosed, secured, that one could hope to encompass and to dominate. Perhaps this is why the activity of men was so feverish: work could keep doubts at bay. While they worked, they need not think or worry; after they had worked, they were too tired for it. A modern student of the Victorian frame of mind, Walter Houghton, attributes the immense productivity of many "Victorian" writers to "their frantic need to bury their doubts and anxieties" beneath an equally frantic activity.

The hold of traditional values and beliefs declined. The classes which traditionally forged these values or endorsed them—clergy and aristocracy—also declined. Bereaved of authority, men were thrown back on themselves to make the best of their own judgment. Those who could not, must refer to others: to political prophets, to literary and intellectual figures like Carlyle or Tolstoy, or simply to one of the periodicals which now began to "teach the multitude of men what to think and what to say" (1850).

Here were the antitoxins. Convention, conformity, the pressure of public opinion, acquired a new importance as other cohesive or stabilizing forces wore away. Mrs. Grundy, born in a play of 1798, had become a power half a century later. People who had cast off the tyranny of kings bent 'neath that of their neighbors. Men were free, but not of public opinion: "It exacts obedience to itself," wrote Walter Bagehot, "It requires us to think other men's thoughts, to speak other men's words, to follow other men's habits." Ambitious men and women, climbing or trying to climb into new spheres, unsure of what obtained and seeking to conform, would naturally look around and do as others do. As for the others, most of them, they were unsure too. In 1845, to quote him once again, Matthew Arnold deplored their "want of independence of mind, the shutting their eyes and professing to believe what they do not, the running blindly in herds, for fear of some obscure danger and horror if they go alone. . . ."

* Matthew Arnold, *The Scholar-Gipsy* (1853).
** Charles Kingsley, *Yeast* (1851).

And so society became a lot of people, uncertainly looking to one another for reassurance or a lead, and duty became "complying with whate'er is expected here." All this conformity, pretension, and evasion only increased the tension between head and heart, between emancipation and dependence. Repressed sensuality turned to greed, either for food or objects; faith, doubt, tension, dissolved into sentiment and were superficially resolved in it; sentiment turned to sentimentality, to tears, to supersensitivity, and vapors; duty turned sour in hypocrisy. Much of the smugness, dogmatism, and self-assurance that we detect in the Victorian temper masked self-doubt, bewilderment, and even skepticism. In reading men like Carlyle or Ruskin, Nietzsche or Tolstoy, one gets a feeling that the more they doubted the more passionately they insisted that they *knew,* the more insecure they felt the more positive they acted (with respect to God, Society, Truth, or Beauty), the more shaken they might be the more inflexible their views on religion, morals, or reform became. All stood at Armageddon and battled for the Lord. The issues seemed to warrant such a stand: God, Society, the Nature of the World and Reality were at stake. No wonder that arguments tended to be dogmatic and the debaters rigid.

The great barrage of criticism, of critical analysis, of doubt, of private judgment, to which the social and the private conscience were subjected stirred up inevitable reaction. High-flown idealism, anti-intellectualism, irrationalism, bear harsh witness to the relentless intellectual and rationalist offensive which upset and endangered most people's peace of mind. Threatened by arguments like those of John Stuart Mill asserting liberty against conformity, like those of Darwin and the Darwinists against orthodoxy, a great many people reacted like Ulysses among the deadly Sirens. Like him they bound themselves to a dogmatic mast to withstand the temptations of unbelief or, like his crew, stopped up their ears with wax.

The differences among educated people encouraged the uneducated to think that they might be as right as any, even if they thought not at all. If every authority was being contradicted by some other authority, then what authority was left, how could one discriminate between them, why should one try? The open mind became an empty mind or, rather, one in which contending notions and ideas clashed, rattled, and jangled with only the vaguest attempt at reconciliation or at synthesis. This became known as reaching one's own conclusions. Self-educated, half-educated people ignored the lengths and depths to which real study and thought could go, the true value of evidence. Shallow judgments were good enough for them. The possible contribution of books began to be underrated. Everyone ignored what had been done or said. Limited and indiscriminate learning, encouraged by the limitations of the publicists, critics, journalists on whose work it fed, produced a bumptious, insensitive (or possibly oversensitive) mentality: that of our own day.

The Modern Age

By the time Queen Victoria died, society had been democratized willy-nilly by the continuous change that turned traditional privilege, estate, or even heritage into fluid and transitory things. Men were no longer defined by birth or status but free to become what they could, and what passing opportunity offered. They were individuals and had to assert that individuality by rational means, because routine and tradition could no longer be trusted to cope with situations as they arose. Democratic, individualistic, and rationalistic, this society was also the counterpart of all these things: increasingly specialized, class-conscious, and elitist, ever more conformist, conventional, and other-directed, less and less likely to follow rational arguments under the pressure of mass emotions and mass appeals.

Almost all the changes that are connected with the postwar years had germinated in the decade preceding 1914: the reluctant but final acceptance of parvenus in high society, the emancipation of workers and of women, the stirrings of irrationalism in philosophy and politics and art, the expanding scale of politics and the contracting scale of family life. Even the local color of the 1920's—jazz, cocktails, looser clothes —made its appearance in the prewar years, along with the mad "abandoned" dances of the modern age: first the Boston, then the Turkey Trot and the Bunny Hug, finally "the terrible Tango."

Drugs also became fashionable at this time. They had been common enough, not only for poets seeking new sensations, but for invalids and housewives seeking relief. It almost appears, if the term be allowed, that in a nineteenth century where no (or few) laws regulated the activities of pharmacists, drugs were a drug on the market. Cordials containing morphia, physics laced with laudanum, sedatives prepared with opium, alleviated the pains of the incurable, quieted squealing children, or soothed the nerves of their harassed mothers and nurses. Then their significance began to be realized, and from commonplace they became wicked—hence titillating. Paul Poiret in *My First Fifty Years* claims that in Paris "opium dens were in full blast everywhere"; and London's *Punch* (July 12, 1911) showed two ladies talking at a garden party: "If it were only chloral; or even morphia. But Laudanum, my dear— Laudanum is so frightfully middle class."

Too little liberty in the nineteenth century brewed up too much license in the twentieth. Or maybe just enough. For most people most of the time prefer to seem better than they are, not worse; and conformity, less strenuous than cynicism, provides a better conscience. Hence the frantic wildness and self-assertion of the postwar years were on the whole the franchise of the few, more people lived like Babbitt than like Gatsby. So the revolt and glumness of the 1920's, which have left their mark on the collective memory, were only representative in a minor key. The bitterness of the articulate partly reflected resentments among the upper and middle classes whose comforts were shrinking; the fact that, as A. J. P. Taylor reminds us, more lawyers and doctors and professors now had to do their own dishwashing, the fact that—while class consciousness persisted—economic, sartorial, and educational differences between the classes were becoming smaller.

Zip fasteners, first manufactured in the United States in 1917, made their contribution to simpler dresses and to their emancipation from hooks and maids. Artificial silks and other fabrics made both stockings and dresses cheaper and inspired the poet to sing

> Whenas in silk my Julia goes
> That nothing to the silkworm owes,
> But is compact of cellulose;

> Then, when I note the moderate fee
> Charged for the same by Jules and Cie,
> O, how that cheapness taketh me!

Clothes becoming simpler could be easily copied at home or in ready-made models. Upper- and middle-class people worked in shops and offices, like everybody else; workers went hiking and eventually traveling abroad wearing clothes very similar to their "betters"; elegance was no longer ornate but simple and casual like a Chanel suit; understatement became fashionable. Cruises, which had begun before 1914 for people who could not quite afford their own steam yachts, became popular for inexpensive middle-class holidays, before being enlisted for the workers by Nazis and Communists. Standards of comfort also differed less, as fewer families kept servants or sent their children to private schools, as more families ate and lived better, and hoped that their offspring might obtain not only secondary but higher education.

The middle class was expanding but, even as it did, its status was shrinking with its income, bitten into by death duties and higher direct taxes, which before 1914 had accounted for a negligible proportion of budgets but which would thereafter constitute between 10 and 20 per cent of total expenses. There were other factors too: before 1914 the difference between comfort and straitened circumstances often lay in a source of private revenue: income from dowries, inheritances, land, rents, or interest which could provide all or most of a middle-class family budget, and generally provided a portion of it. The role and proportion of such unearned income shrinks as the twentieth century advances, that of salaries or other returns on work done rises fast. An engineer or lawyer, half of whose income might, before 1914, have come from his wife's dowry or his own inherited wealth, would get only a quarter or a third of his income from such sources by the 1930's, less in postwar years. In other words, earned income takes over from unearned: another equalizing factor when one considers that most great fortunes are inherited.

Inflation also played a most important part in the disappearance of savings. It was becoming increasingly apparent that, while enterprise could still make money, prudence and thrift no longer could. When money kept its worth a lifetime through, not only members of the middle class but even workers could save their way to retirement. After the 1920's this was no longer true. No wage earner could henceforth feel secure by his thrift alone. This meant that unemployment, sickness, and age became community problems whose cost further cut down the income of the rich, whose benefits supplemented the income of the poor, and whose effects narrowed the economic gap between the classes further.

All this was relative but still significant. The average consumer is a myth. But even the destitute and the poor in the hard years of the 1930's were less destitute, less poor than they would have been even a generation before. They drank two pints of milk a week when the rich drank five, they ate one or two eggs a week when the rich ate four, but these themselves were things regarded as luxuries by their forebears. Overcrowding and malnutrition continued to exist even in industrialized countries, but they were being pressed back. Above all, the standards by which they were defined were rising. The miseries of the nineteenth century had disappeared outside the undeveloped countries of the South and East. In 1939, A. J. P. Taylor reminds us, half the population of England never left home even for a single night. But holiday travel— a middle-class habit in the nineteenth century—caught on in countries where the 1930's brought holidays with pay—day trips for some, holiday camps for others, and cruises. By mid-century, the novelty of one generation was treated by another as a natural right.

Buying on the installment plan, introduced in the 1930's, generalized in the 1950's, gave poorer people a chance to obtain things whose price they could never scrape up at once—household goods, automobiles, and even homes—and the increased demand thus tapped when things really got going in the 1950's stimulated production in its turn. Even the modern cult of slimness, the increasingly obsessive concern with weight, reflected a new well-being in which all could eat their fill and then some. By 1939, the working classes were better fed, housed, and clothed than their parents. A generation later this could be said of all. And workers of one kind or another accounted now for most of society.

The Public and its Servants

Sports and Entertainment

The equalization of the classes becomes particularly visible in the great public sectors of sport, entertainment, and education. Sport for a long time had been a preserve of the rich, who could afford it and who had time for it.* Tourneys and hunting had provided substitutes for the fighting and warfare of earlier days. Physical satisfaction, the sense of danger and adventure, had been channeled into less destructive directions. Team sports played similar roles in debrutalizing the masses, filling their leisure time, and offering opportunities for distinction with less regard to class (or race) than might reign otherwise.

The first of these sports was football (soccer); which English schoolmasters of the nineteenth century came to encourage as an antidote to immorality and a lesson in discipline. Eager to keep their charges from drinking, poaching, gambling, teachers saw a valuable substitute in limited mayhem on the playing field, and then began to think that games could inculcate positive virtues too: team spirit, a sense of loyalty, co-operation, and self-sacrifice—all the things exalted in Kipling's novels, like *Stalky and Co.,* the moral virtues that Sir John Squire sings in his poem *The Rugger Match*:

> A selfless flinging of the self in the fray,
> Strength, compassion, control, the obeying of laws,
> Victory and a struggle against defeat.

But all this was still for the rich, until the Factory Act of 1847 prohibited the employment of women and children on Saturday afternoons. Soon the men were freed too. Here was a new weekly holiday to be filled, and one of the major contenders for filling it was football. In the 1860's the rules of Association and of Rugby football were stabilized, in 1871 the Football Cup competition was established, by 1905 England could boast 10,000 member clubs, one in almost every English village. More and more working-class clubs appeared which, by the 1880's had come to dominate the game. Along with the clubs, the number of watchers rapidly increased. Socially select clubs could draw only on a small public. Popular clubs attracted a much larger audience. By the mid-80's attendance figures at important matches ran in tens of thousands (the Cup Final of 1901 drew over 110,000). Generations of football watchers

---

* Under the Tudors, the lower classes were supposed to stick to useful sports like archery, while gentry could indulge in bowls or tennis.

grew up who lacked room to play the game themselves, but had little else to do in their free time. Men began to be paid to play, and 1885 saw professionalism recognized as a fact and regulated. Games, no longer played only by amateurs for their own sake, became mass entertainments, masterfully handled for profit by skillful athletes and their managers.*

Thus, while the unprofitable pursuits like hunting and tennis remained mere games, football was the first to serve the needs of the industrial society in which it grew, itself becoming an industry and a business. By 1950, 86 million in Britain alone watched football matches through the year.* * Every week more than 6 million paid for their tickets, while 7 million played the football pools which have become one of the largest industries in Europe—employing over 100,000 people in England alone. The only greater entertainment and source of revenues was cinema, which (to take the same British statistics for 1950) had sixteen times more viewers and twelve times more revenues than football, serving nearly one and a half billion patrons and making gross receipts of some 300 million dollars.

The cinema was born of two inventions: that of photography and that of celluloid, which permitted the making of film strips whose rapid projection gave the beholder the illusion of a moving image. The first public projection seems to have taken place in Paris in 1895. Very soon the process was being imitated all over the world, and some of the films' great classics were made before 1914. After 1927, the appearance of sound and the need for large capital investment this created ensured the industry's domination by banks and by a few large concerns which turned it, as Erich von Stroheim put it, into a giant sausage machine. Nevertheless, films offered better entertainment than either church or tavern. They also offered pleasures that men and women could enjoy together —unlike the sports or the carousing that had separated them. A century ago, the greatest entertainment centers of the world—London, Paris— catered to no more than two or three thousand persons nightly. Today, tens of thousands sit in cinemas and millions watch television everywhere, any night of the week.

Technology, a German philosopher once suggested, is simply a trick designed to arrange the world so that we do not have to experience it, but only reproduce various experiences. The cinema is one of our liveliest art forms. It also became our greatest step toward the industrialization of dreams. In its darkened temples men and women grasp at real life substitutes, find an escape valve from dreary existence, experience vicarious enjoyment of power, beauty, and riches beyond their grasp.

* English experience was repeated on the continent only after 1920 or so, partly because working hours were longer and were effectively limited only much later, but partly too because sports were regarded as a prerogative of the ruling classes, training their scions to meet the rising challenges of democracy.

** That same year 50 million attended greyhound races, 12 million speedway races, 5 million cricket matches.

640

They also learn how unknown classes and distant peoples live. Which means that the cinema suggested new desirabilities and standards, first in the West, then all over the world, spreading its stereotypes across class or national barriers.

Education and Popular Culture

More stereotypes would grow from education. For the romantic humanist, education had been the great liberating and creative force by which man discovers his true nature and thereby gains his freedom. "The powerful travail of self on self," as Michelet had called it, made "every man his own Prometheus." This lyrical vision would be paralleled by a more utilitarian one. Man, said the sociologists of the modern age, is not the work of nature but of society. His shape changes according to society's intentions, particularly the pressure of deliberate education designed to turn out citizens in its own image.

The image that the nineteenth century conceived was that of disciplined, useful, patriotic citizens. The educational structures set up on the continent in Napoleon's wake treated adolescents much like soldiers, put them in uniforms, trained them to perform a socially useful function as rationally and obediently as they could. This tendency went furthest in the German schools and, after 1871, the French—claiming that the Prussian victory was due above all to Prussian schoolmasters—set out to imitate them. But Prussian schoolmasters had not been active only in *gymnasia*: they had taught the common people, among whom illiteracy had been pressed far back. Here, too, there was work to be done; here, too, the basic arguments were utilitarian. It was not only that a man who could read, write, count, would make a better workman or soldier. He would also be a better citizen: indeed, become the citizen he wasn't. Adam Smith already had pointed out that, while the division of labor is the source of "universal opulence," it makes the laborer "as stupid and ignorant as it is possible for a human creature to become." Laborers were being turned into productive animals at the expense of their human and civic qualities, just when their growing numbers and concentration made such developments dangerous. Education could prevent this. State investment in it would protect the masses from "the delusions of enthusiasm and superstition which, among ignorant nations, frequently occasion the most dreadful disorders," make them more apt to think, less open to seditions and factious arguments, "less apt to be misled into any wanton or unnecessary opposition to the measures of government."

Malthus, too, had felt that education would make the common people "bear with patience the evils which they suffer," and realize "the folly and inefficacy of turbulence." By 1848, the Chartists were complaining that men moved by these motives "would educate us not, as you sometimes pretend, to fit us for the exercise of political rights, but to make us indifferent to these rights." There must have been less consciousness and more good intentions about educational ventures than the suspicious thought. There was the simple hope of improving man and life by mechanical means. There was the dream of a richer life achieved by the mobilization of social potential which had long lain dormant. There was the simple yearning to increase the dignity and capacities of human beings. There was belief in progress, of which knowledge was seen as an intrinsic part. And there was, ultimately, a real and wide-felt need to adapt the newly significant masses to life in newly created national states: not only in the nineteenth-century creations like Belgium and Italy, the German Empire, or the French Republic, but in older societies turning into nations: Norway, Denmark, Holland, and even Spain.

This was the task of free, compulsory elementary education, which had become general in most Western countries by 1900, and of its carriers, the schoolteachers. Secular public schools which taught not only reading, writing, and counting, but morals and civic sense, were a major instrument in developing patriotism, spreading common notions and a common language, ousting religion from its near monopoly of popular education, and opening new avenues for rising in the world.

The first to benefit were the teachers themselves. In the 1870's and 80's teaching became a promising occupation for the bright, ambitious sons and daughters of workmen or peasants whose horizons had been limited heretofore by domestic service or a clerical career. Teachers were ill-paid, but they enjoyed prestige and social status. They were particularly influential in small villages and towns, where the intellectual credit and strategic position of the teacher challenged older authorities like landlord or priest. Their sons, with an even better education, became professional men, entered the civil service and the universities. A vast proportion of twentieth-century professors and intellectuals are sons of elementary teachers; and teachers traditionally play a role in democratic politics quite disproportionate to their numbers. Thus, under the Third and Fourth Republics in France, while only one Frenchman in 3,000 or more was a teacher, one deputy in every twenty or so had at some time taught.

Education made a crucial contribution to the social mobility which we have seen increasing in our time. Educational opportunities meant social and economic opportunities. Professional and technical schools proliferated. More high schools were created and scholarships opened them to poorer students too. Thousands whose parents never learned to read could now at least *aspire* to higher education. Evening and correspondence courses reached out to many who had had to miss, or drop out

Boys in the Cloisters of the Blue-
coat School in England.

of, school. Free public libraries encouraged study and reading. By 1914 among French conscripts, one-fourth of whom could not read or write in 1863, the illiteracy rate was only 2 per cent. In 1880 one in six Frenchmen, one in three Frenchwomen, could not sign their marriage license. By 1939 the figures would be about one out of 120. By 1950 the estimated adult literacy rate in North and Western Europe was 99 per cent, in the Soviet Union 90 per cent, in the European South 80 per cent.

The only Western country that lagged for a long time in this process was the United Kingdom, which lacked an elementary or secondary network comparable to those in France or Germany, let alone adequate systems of industrial or technical education. In 1903, while Germany led Europe in the number and quality of its 22 universities, Britain had only 13, receiving two-thirds less public aid than German ones.* This was in part the reflection of a public in which plain men took pride in successes achieved by uninstructed common sense and lack of study. They knew their opinion to be as good as anybody else's, despised teachers and theorists because they were not men of action, insisted that "those who can, do!" Reading, thinking, talking were not necessities but ornaments, more suitable for women and for idle men. Education made sense as long as it had a practical application, but studies which were not clearly or immediately useful only distracted men from the main object of life which was to earn money, amass property, get on in life. The British upper classes were accommodated in private schools, where they were taught the classics, sports, and leadership. Little was done for others until the twentieth century. The price of such neglect was paid by British industry, which fell behind its competitors in equipment, inventiveness, and the trained skills of its available work force.

But even in England, as education improved with the new century

* At that time, Italy counted 21 universities, France 15, and the United States 134.

and the population of secondary and grammar schools went up, its effects were being felt. By 1913, more than twice as many books were being published than a decade before, more than twice as many were being borrowed from public libraries. Then, as now, the favorite reading of workers and the lower middle class tended toward crime stories, sentimental romances, popular novels quite forgotten today, moralistic or political pamphlets. Only exceptional men went further; and it has been claimed, perhaps with justice, that the educational process which, it was hoped, would widen their horizons, merely equipped them for conformity.

The twentieth century, which saw the triumph of formal education, would also witness reading and writing becoming increasingly irrelevant and twenty-year olds who forgot the unused skills with which they had left school at fourteen. Recent French surveys show a frightening number of conscripts who have *forgotten* how to read or write. Nevertheless, by 1960 the least schooled of European countries, Portugal, had a higher proportion of schoool-age children sitting in its schools than any African, Asian, or Latin American country.* At the same time, however, means of communication had become increasingly verbal and visual. Telephone, radio, motion pictures, and, in due course, television, escaped the limits and disciplines of writing while abandoning its lasting power. As Gide noted in his *Journal*: "How many fine letters lost in talks over the telephone. . . ."

Ideally, modern education sought to inculcate awareness of our limits, permit men to discover the liberating quality of intellectual activity, the capacity to be most fully themselves, taking pride in human talents which alone permit the affirmation and organization that are specifically human. What it produced, only too often, were simplification and vulgarization: charlatans masquerading as experts, and experts learning to talk as charlatans. Already in the 1880's Nietzsche was complaining that, far from enabling man to become richer and greater, education was "essentially the means of ruining the exceptions for the good of the rule. Higher education: essentially the means of directing taste against the exceptions for the good of the mediocre."

Learning itself, people complained, was being killed by *degrees,* used to turn out cogs for the wheels of the social machine, standardized products with standardized minds for an increasingly standardized way of life. How true this is we simply do not know. But there is no need for quantity to stamp out either quality or independence. If a majority of the products of modern education are more conformist and mediocre than it had been hoped, a majority of mankind has always been this way. A larger proportion of the world being educated must mean that a large proportion of the educated will show signs of conformism and mediocrity. It also means, however, that many more—though not necessarily a ma-

---

* Forty to 60 per cent of Portuguese and Mexican children of school age go to school; 25 to 30 per cent in Latin America; less than 20 per cent in Africa and Asia.

William Randolph Hearst

jority—discover possibilities which had remained unsuspected both in themselves and in the outside world. And that, as long as Western man continues to be curious, must be counted as clear gain.

The Popular Press

The most impressive and sometimes depressing monument to mass education was the popular press. Newspapers that wished to sell more than a few thousand copies had to catch the eyes of those whom George Gissing in his *New Grub Street* (1891) called the quarter-educated: "The young men and women who can just read but are incapable of sustained attention." Throughout the 1880's men sought a formula that catered to a public which knew how to read, but little else. The American "yellow press" had found it: scandal, rumor, trivialities, "revelations," issues picked to the extent that they helped circulation, stirring sensation or public interest. Here was the stuff of life or, at least, the stuffing. The name of William Randolph Hearst (1863–1951) had come to represent low but profitable journalistic standards. Lurid illustrations, glaring headlines, sensationalism, and jingoism built up unprecedented sales—over a million and a half a day for his *New York Journal* in 1896.

That year, Alfred Harmsworth's *Daily Mail* introduced the formula to England. It worked. By 1901 the sales of the *Daily Mail* had risen to a million copies a day. The paper, which an English politician described as written by office boys for office boys, was rather by and for the semi-educated. Women, servants, tradesmen, all those who—outside their particular concern—retained the minds and tastes of twelve-year olds, bought it, read it, liked it. Bright, bitsy, predigested, the *Daily Mail* and the numerous progeny it spawned throughout the rest of Europe assumed that serious news or interpretation would bore a public whose attention span was very short indeed.

By 1900, rotary presses, type-setting machines, the linotype turned out the printed pabulum of the masses. The expense of such equipment for mass production was very great. This meant that more than ever a

645

newspaper cost more than it could earn. A sheet which sold for a penny in the street would bring its publisher only two-thirds of that and probably cost a penny and a quarter to turn out. The gap between the moderate price without which there could not be large sales and the high costs of production was filled by advertising. Publicity had also grown with the buying public and, as the nature of customers changed and simplified, it had created a fresh art style expressed in posters and eventually in print.* The publicists, like the newspapers, had to catch attention in a flash, make an impression which would help their product. To this purpose they created a visual universe which has taught the twentieth-century world to experience most things—from washing machines to sex—less through the rational mind than through the eye.

Essentially, most publications depend on subsidies and cater to subsidizers. Since newspapers wanted all the advertising they could get, they too found that they had to cater to the widest public. Most of the advertisers were (at least relatively) politically neutral, and they objected to any orientation that might alienate possible buyers. Distinct political views became increasingly rare. The press became an industry like any other and, like all other industries, increasingly concentrated under the ownership of powerful financiers or groups.

With brand-name goods being sold from one end of the country to another, national advertising increased in scope and scale. The national press that carried it gained ground at the expense of local papers and of the smaller, uncompetitive sheets. As more and more publications were swallowed or scuttled, variety of opinion notably decreased. In Britain between 1920 and 1945 half the morning papers, a quarter of the evening papers disappeared. In France, which had 238 dailies in 1939, 1953 saw only 164. In the United States in 1955 fourteen men controlled 25 per cent of daily sales. The need to cut costs, to please the many and displease only few, made for standardized agency fare, widely syndicated and reproduced, the reign of comic strips and of innocuous, vapid stuffing for heads that asked no better, supplementing the vast periodical industry that turns out women's weeklies and cheap sentiments, vicarious sensation or conformist thrills.

Literature and the Arts

Artists and writers are less "the unacknowledged legislators of the world," as Shelley had it, than its mirrors (perhaps deforming mirrors), reveal-

---

* Just over a century old, the publicity poster is, like the film, an integral part of the modern world, which would be very bare and very different without it. Designed to make a brief, sharp appeal, posters were first to accustom the general public to a shorthand and synthesis of image and of message, familiarizing it with elliptic modern art styles it would never have accepted otherwise.

ing aspects of a time, suggesting possibilities and perspectives which, without them, might well remain unnoticed. When there is a direct relation between artists and their public—that is, when the number and choice of both are still restricted—the work of art reflects the taste and the ideas of its time; or, rather, of that small elite in which cultural life is concentrated. The moment this limited balance breaks, when the elite is paralleled or supplanted by a wider public, this changes. Potential opportunities encourage some men to strike out on their own. This means that some among them—those who, like Rembrandt, Blake, Van Gogh, or Cézanne, persistently ignored the demands of society around them for the sake of a personal quest or vision—become heretics and rebels, departing from convention and risking misery. This situation, exceptional before the eighteenth century, became the norm in the nineteenth when a restricted market for works of literature, music, or art became an open marketplace where everyone could vie for public favor. In a hundred years, the once limited aristocratic public grew in number and proportion as the middle classes grew, until by the twentieth century all of society became potential patrons. This immeasurably increased the opportunities of all artists. But it also meant (as we have already seen in the romantic era) a definite break between the art tradesmen catering to current tastes and the independents who pursued a vision of their own.

The new art patrons of the nineteenth century were rich but hard-working—enjoying little of the leisure their clerical and aristocratic predecessors had enjoyed. For men of little time and little taste, art had to speak loud and fast, offering striking effects and reassurance of a good money's worth: plenty of paint, of effect, of anecdote, or ornament. Weary men did not want to think. They wanted to escape their hard, ugly world and find a substitute paradise in a painting or book, or to relax listening to undemanding music. All these would be appreciated for the soft glow they could bring, rather like a good meal, the entertainment or the reassurance that they might provide.*

It follows that the great painters, novelists, often musicians also, whom we today remember, found very little favor in their time. Their appeal was always restricted, while the popular artists and best sellers are nearly all forgotten today or looked at only for their period flavor. In all the arts, the contemporary period stands out by the "divorce between what is officially and socially successful and what is aesthetically good." This was the age when many concert societies were founded to react against bad public taste, when anti-exhibitions rebelled against academic conformity, when public protests kept the impressionists out of French museums and forced Edvard Munch to withdraw his paintings from a Berlin exhibi-

---

* They would also, at least in theory, have to preach the moral lessons respectable people respected in public and sometimes in private too: "The art that doesn't serve to ennoble and purify and help us in our lifelong struggle with sin and evil," wrote *Christian Remembrances* of April, 1854, "however beautiful, however serene and majestic, is false and poor and contemptible."

tion, when both Flaubert and Baudelaire would be condemned in court. Hence, the present section deals in large part with *unrepresentative* works and figures.

Realism and Naturalism

A great deal of nineteenth-century art, for instance, reflected the contemporary interest in accuracy, the yearning for scientific objectivity, the progressive tendency to edify and reform. With Honoré de Balzac (1799–1850) the romantic searchlight moved from the rural landscape to the urban, and from high society to middle and lower classes. Part of the romantic thrill had always been the exploration of unknown regions, which the novelist revealed to a curious public. This was now complemented by a documentary approach, as novels rivaled contemporary reports and blue books, producing studies of society in the making and of its reefs and shoals, documents reflecting change in time or political pamphlets about conditions that must be .changed. Balzac had led the way in shifting the novel from private life onto a social stage, insisting on the growing role of *things,* of money, and of a society in which man himself (and woman even more) became a negotiable object. Friedrich Engels would remark that he had learned more from Balzac "than from all the works of the historians, economists and professional statisticians put together."

Society novels became social novels. Dickens' introduction to *Oliver Twist* (1841) proposed a "service to society" by offering not descriptions of picturesque scenes but of the "cold, wet, shelterless streets of London." This was the particular effect of mid-century positivism. The people who are generally labeled realists (Flaubert, Courbet) or naturalists (Zola) followed the same course, trying to abandon the last bits of lyricism and color and to describe actions and things as objectively and precisely as they could. Like scientific researchers, they set out to observe and note their observations. Human beings, they and their interpreters reasoned, are feeling, thinking bodies, provided with organs, moved by passions, feelings, ideas, and needs. Their fate and their behavior are determined by natural laws—heredity, environment, causality. It is up to the novelist or playwright to study these elements as a psychologist or a pathologist would; and try to represent them in reality.

This is what Gustave Flaubert (1821–1880) did in his novel *Madame Bovary* (1857): a kind of documentary of small-town life and ways in mid-nineteenth-century France, which shows pretentious, petty people, living on some small income, gorging themselves on commonplaces and on platitudes. Although Flaubert is often labeled a realist, *precisionist* might be a better term for this meticulous stylist who reacted against romantic passion and expressiveness by tying a cannonball to his quill. Perhaps the most realistic thing about Flaubert's novel is the romanti-

648

Honoré de Balzac, by Auguste Rodin. Right: Gustave Flaubert.

cism of his characters. On the one hand ideas *about* life, on the other hand life itself. On one hand books, education, prejudices, and on the other reality. There is no reconciling the two, either for Madame Bovary or for the idealistic hero of *A Sentimental Education* (1869): both disintegrate rather than take shape under the battering of experience and of time. Where the romantics had painted a lost generation of fallen angels and fiery rebels, that of the realists had a flaccid cast, less strong, less cultivated, and more hopeless.

Some painters also turned to characters and scenes from everyday life, which they depicted in all reality or, as contemporaries claimed, in all vulgarity. In the late 1840's the painters of the "school of Barbizon" (a village not far from Paris) escaped from the artificial light and scenery of the studio to paint simple, familiar landscapes in the open air. Camille Corot (1796–1875), insisting that "nature must be interpreted artlessly," produced fresh, spontaneous pictures still filled with the light of limpid afternoons. J. F. Millet (1814–1875) glorified farmers and laborers to such an extent that he was accused of being a socialist. Less sentimental, more brutally realist, Gustave Courbet (1819–1877) rejected all idealization. He painted priests with red noses, prostitutes, vigorous ugly workers, the face of people plain. His letterhead proclaimed "Gustave Courbet, Master Painter, without ideals and without religion." No wonder that Napoleon III's Minister of Fine Arts saw realism as "democratic painting"; and he was right, for Courbet would become the Fine Arts Commissar of the Paris Commune.

Men like Courbet and like the naturalists who came after him reacted, of course, against the monumental fantasies of the established order. But their purpose was fundamentally ethical. The object of their rebellion may be seen by a quotation from an English novel of 1851,* in which a painter who has just painted a gamekeeper in the fashionable heroic style of the day is asked by an artless girl: "Why have you been so un-

* Kingsley's *Yeast,* Chapter 3.

Giraudon

The Gleaners, by Millet. Louvre, Paris.

faithful to your original? Why have you, like all artists, been trying to soften and refine on your model?"—"Because my dear lady, we are bound to see everything in its ideal—not as it is, but as it ought to be, and will be, when the vices of this pitiful world are exploded." This dialogue illuminates the character of Podsnap in Dickens' *Our Mutual Friend* (1864), who does not want to know, discuss, or admit anything that spoils his comfort: poverty, injustice, faults in the system or society.

Here the subversive character of naturalism becomes clear; not only in aesthetics but in politics too. The plays of the Norwegian Henrik Ibsen (1828–1906) showed the social possibilities of modern theater, exploring all the themes that preoccupied society in this time: the limitations and potentialities of man (*Peer Gynt,* 1867); feminine emancipation (*A Doll's House,* 1879); heredity and syphilis (*Ghosts,* 1881); social hypocrisy (*An Enemy of the People,* 1882); artistic integrity (*The Master Builder,* 1892). In France, the great exponent of the naturalist creed was Émile Zola (1840–1902). His novels and especially the twenty-volume cycle of *The Rougon-Macquart* published between 1871 and 1893, followed the fortunes of a family right through the Second Empire. Zola's works, in which heredity and environment, the taints and corruption of society and human beings, helped to reveal each other, shocked the public with their insistence on sex and violence, their subversive pounding at ignorance, prudery, and evasions.

Even more deliberately revolutionary would be the Germans, to whom naturalism came late. Gerhart Hauptmann's play *The Weavers* (1892), which has no human hero, dwells rather on the inarticulate tragedy of

The Port of La Rochelle, by Corot. Louvre, Paris.

a wretched Silesian village where all—workers, rebels, and exploiters
—are playthings of mechanisms they can neither master nor comprehend.
Here was a prediction of the new mass age, passing from the particular
to the general, and of a literature of impotence that our century knows
well. This last found its first expression in Russia, where contact between
the cultivated classes and reality was slight and ineffectual, and where
control over one's fate seemed far more faltering than in the West. The
plays and stories of Anton Chekhov (1860–1904) mirror the futility, the
isolation, and the boredom of Russian living (*The Three Sisters,* 1900);
the impossibility of communication (*The Sea Gull,* 1898, *Uncle Vanya,*
1898); the decline of the landowning family whose cherry orchard is
sold to be cut down (*Cherry Orchard,* 1904). They all expressed an
attitude which the turn of the century saw spreading: creeping despair
about man's ability to manage his affairs, expressed more stridently in the
works of men like August Strindberg (1849–1912) and in a conciliatory
vein by Leo Tolstoy (1828–1910), perhaps the greatest novelist of modern days (*War and Peace,* 1869; *Anna Karenina,* 1877). Tolstoy's answer
to the human predicament was to reject the constricting scale and absurdity of society and history, seeking salvation in homely happiness—
the goodness and naturalness of simple lives.

Whatever the variety of solutions they proposed, many such works carried an aesthetic radicalism just as shocking to a public used to the
lies and evasions of academic art as the socialism which some artists es-
poused. The artist's political opinions did not really matter. Daumier,
Courbet, Pissarro, Morris were for revolution; Degas, a reactionary; Flau-

Chekhov, Gorki, and Tolstoy.

bert and Monet solid bourgeois; and many others indifferent to politics. What mattered was that, in opposing truth to falsity, artists attacked the basis of convention. Anna Karenina, Madame Bovary, Courbet's lascivious women, Manet's Olympia in her disturbing nakedness, were all unorthodox, all challenged visual, social, or literary patterns, and thus threatened stability. A selfish, acquisitive society wanted reassurance not reminders, its conscience salved not stirred. Ends should be happy, and horrors swathed in sentiment as bees neutralize disconcerting foreign bodies by covering them with wax. Flaubert, Zola, and even Tolstoy were too sad, too harsh, for a sad, harsh world. No wonder they were greeted with hostility. No wonder that they were slow to find success.* No wonder a Russian minister of education once remarked that he would only be able to sleep soundly when there was no longer any literature at all.

The strange detachment that we sense in Chekhov and in Tolstoy mirrored the intellectual situation of societies in which theology and science clashed and deadlocked. Deprived of a clear, authoritative reality or truth, many artists, like other people, denied any responsibility to a superior truth, turned toward "beauty" or their perception of it. If life was meaningless, a moment's beauty could be fixed by art. In 1842, the young Karl Marx, writing in the Rhenish *Gazette* on freedom of the press, had already affirmed that "the writer doesn't look on his works as a *means*. They are ends in themselves. . . ." Paul Cézanne (1839–1906)

* Millet had to sell his drawings to buy shoes, Auguste Renoir's family went without food, Claude Monet had to stop painting for lack of money to buy paints. All of them sold their pictures at ridiculous prices. Millet's *Angelus* sold by him in 1859 for $360 was bought by a millionaire in 1881 for $320,000. In the late 1870's Monet's paintings were selling for less than 200 francs: about 40 dollars. In 1884 the contents of Monet's studio were sold by his executor. Among them *Olympia* fetched $2,000, *Le Bar aux Folies Bergères* $1,170, *La Servante de Bocks* $500, *Le Balcon* $500. By 1924 they were going to sell at prices a thousand times greater.

agreed: "Painting," he said, "is its own end." It was not supposed to represent an anecdote, a moral lesson, a conversation piece, a historical or religious memory. The subject, treated for its own sake (whether a patch of light, a flower, or a hunk of beef) became autonomous. This was the point of view of those who practiced "art for art's sake."

Impressionism

First, and today most familiar, among these are the impressionists who, like naturalist writers, refused to paint "noble" subjects, preferred the commonplace. The academic art of the day combined photographic exactness and arbitrary subjects. After the 1870's, persuaded that photographs provided a more exact reproduction of reality and that the world held as much beauty as the imagination, painters turned away from a pursuit in which they were outmatched by cameras: from form to color, to light, and to suggestion. They let their eyes roam freely and sought to catch the moment on the wing. The canvases that Pissarro, Monet, Renoir, turned out shimmered with light and color but were considered vulgar because they failed to provide the idealized pictures which the public had been used to. The things impressionists painted were neither clear nor detailed. They did not look finished or conform to the "law of appearances," complained the critic Ruskin comparing them with the grotesque pictures of the Chinese that lacked all linear or aerial perspective. Their subjects, too, were vulgar: streets, suburban scenes, railroad stations—an urban landscape now incorporated in the domain of art. To the impressionists, industry had a magic of its own: cotton and iron garbed and encoiled the world. Their distant adventures and mysterious destinations suggested romance to color-hungry producers in the livid North. Why not, then, the same treatment for cityscapes which held the excitement and mystery of frenzied movement, belching smoke, hazy steam, thickets of chimneys, cliffs of houses, the color and bustle of endlessly drifting crowds?

But patrons would not buy them because, as one explained, "When you have daughters, you have to have a solid-looking house." And when, in 1877, Renoir asked his friend Gambetta for a helpful article about the Impressionist Exhibition of that year: "It would be impossible," the editor told him, "It would be scandalous! Don't you realize that you are revolutionaries?"

Abstract Art

Yet it would shortly seem that naturalists and impressionists were the last accessible—understandable—artists of an age whose search for novelty and expression turned ever to new sources and new idioms, abandoning the material for the abstract, the objective for the subjective, the descrip-

Émile Zola, portrait by Manet which includes a miniature reproduction of the artist's painting, *Olympia.* Louvre, Paris.

tive for the evocative, leaving behind narrative, form, melody, representation, for symbol and allusion. Impressionists and naturalists had made the world their own and glorified it. Even their criticisms implied acceptance, suggested the potential of goodness and beauty in the world. Henceforth the tendency would be to retreat into the self and into art which can make life livable, but on the most personal plane alone. "The artist should not even glance at nature," declared the visionary painter Rodolphe Bresdin (1825–1885), a favorite of Odilon Redon, Gustave Moreau, and J. K. Huysmans: "He has everything within himself." He can plumb reality with the help of drugs and of the visions they entail, of alcohol, of strange evocative cults, like Satanism, of the exploration of dreams, mental maladies and alienation.

This was the mood of Aestheticism, Decadence, Symbolism, Art for Art's Sake—different labels for a common flight from and rejection of the world, which found its patron saint in Charles Baudelaire (1821–1867). Once experience had been valued for its fruits. Now it would be valued for itself, like Art. What counted, counseled the Oxford Aestheticist Walter Pater (1839–1894), was "to catch at any exquisite passion . . . stirring of the senses, strange dyes, strange colors and curious odors, or work of the artist's hands, or the face of a friend," anything that might set the spirit roaming for a moment. The world was full of mysterious analogies, harmonies, connections: colors, shapes, sounds related to each other and to states of mind. Man was a wanderer through "a forest

A Young Woman in the Sun, by Renoir. Jeu de Paume, Paris.

of symbols," each one an intimation of a great many things if he could but perceive them.

Science seemed to be turning from objects to sensations, from the stable to the relative, from the whole to the parts. The world was an illusion: senses provided the only reality. Where there was no coherence, the part must be greater than the whole, and immediate sensation counted more than any possible significance. It was up to the poet and painter to transmute the beautiful into its possibilities, increasingly musical, increasingly abstract; to create Harmonies, Symphonies, Nocturnes, as James Whistler (1834–1903) called his paintings; to explore the possibilities of optics and sensation (Georges Seurat 1859–1891; Paul Signac 1863–1935), discover the emotions that shapes and colors can evoke (Paul Gauguin 1848–1903), search for the geometrical symbolism underlying nature (Paul Cézanne); reveal the magic possibilities of words, when statements lost their meaning (Stéphane Mallarmé 1842–1898, Arthur Rimbaud (1854–1891); or do in tone what painters did on canvas: use pure colors to produce delicate, luminous sounds (Claude Debussy 1862–1918).*

* Debussy, a friend of Mallarmé and of the symbolists, tried not only to conciliate literature and music but to express contemporary scientific tendencies in a new musical technique. Works like *Pelléas et Mélisande* (1902) or *La Mer* (1905) introduced the use of whole scales, new harmonies and dissonances, helped suggest the rhythm and tonality of Igor Stravinsky (b. 1882: *The Firebird* 1910, *The Rites of Spring* 1913), and prepared us for the musical expression that we know today.

The Material Revolution

The classic or traditional style, image, or melody corresponded to a stable, orderly universe in which thought and expression were tamed and disciplined. The chaotic universe we discern around us calls for an equivalent reflection that we can recognize in Joyce and Schönberg, Cézanne or Mathieu, dismantling erstwhile structures into an intuitive chaos analogous to that around us. In modern science, statistics take the place of laws and working probabilities take the place of absolute certainties. Art can no longer imitate a nature that physics reveals in movement, biology in evolution, psychology in depth, philosophy in process of becoming. What art does now is to follow the new ways of nature, the elasticity of space, the deformability of forms, the possibilities which the new probability theories open up. Paul Klee (1879–1940) looks through a microscope and draws his strange subjects from histological slides. Vasili Kandinsky (1866–1944) paints the geometry of diatomic algae. Franz Marc (1880–1916) declares "Instead of contemplating the world, we x-ray it." Arnold Schönberg rejects traditional tonality and the chromatic scale, the composer's hand, in favor of new forms suggested by mathematics. Melody is jettisoned in favor of logical constructions: the twelve-tone scale, serial music, obey external laws. Like Cézanne, Henry James (*The Turn of the Screw*, 1898) is fascinated by the "multiplicity of the aspects of vision."

Color bites into forms; things pulse and vibrate; shapes disarticulate like syntax. And, just as the rational Renaissance setting out to encompass the world had produced both double-entry bookkeeping and perspective, so the increasingly hurried and abstract modern world of speed and symbols would see the generalization of shorthand in business and in art along with the increasing abstraction of both. "Do not copy too much from nature," advised Gauguin. "Art is an abstraction. Draw it from nature while dreaming before it." It was the dream that counted, not the nature: nature that was bent and twisted to the haunting dream whose intensity could sometimes end in madness, as with Vincent Van Gogh (1853–1890). Like the symbolists, Van Gogh appreciated the symbolism of movement and of color. The flame that burned him licks over his canvas, whirls in the branches of his trees, convulses his skies, glows in the harsh tones of his oils.

The Arts of Anarchy

Unnoticed behind the politics of pre-1914 Europe, the movements of the future were taking shape in deliberate attacks on established structures and categories. The influence of Cézanne was prompting Georges Braque and Pablo Picasso to the distortions and simplifications of modern cubism. Categories began to mix and mingle. In 1910 the Russian composer Alexander Scriabin included projections of colored lights in the performance of his symphony *Prometheus;* in 1911 (probably)

Picasso (or Braque) first introduced newsprint and wallpaper into an oil painting; in 1917 Erik Satie would introduce a typewriter into the orchestra; in 1918 Guillaume Apollinaire's typographic venture, *Calligrammes,* began the association of the poetic and the graphic image. Why not? Metal and string, sand and wood, could henceforth be incorporated in a painting just as a shotgun or a vacuum cleaner could play its part in a musical composition, or a waterfall in the design of a millionaire's living room. Incongruity in art articulated the incongruous and complex world whose categories and hierarchies commingled in collapse.

The art of the impressionists had been contemplative. The language of twentieth-century art would be critical, exasperated and tormented by the great cities that the poet R. M. Rilke damned, where "unsatisfied men labor to live and die not knowing why they've suffered." The "infernal chaos of rhythms and images" about us echoed in art and music which grimaced back at a grimacing world: *The Cry* of Edvard Munch (1893), the "Howling Wave" of Alban Berg's opera *Wozzeck* (1921), *The Cabinet of Doctor Caligari* (1919) with its dissonance, its shadows, its equivocal madness, reflecting its time and rejecting it, prophesying the rise of fascisms, violence, and irrationality. The years before the war had seen a last attempt to reconcile art and the modern world. The futurists were affected by the revival of aggressive and nationalistic sentiments in a young generation excited by the political friction of its time and tired of the rationalism of its teachers. They saw modernity breaking through old forms, everything in motion, turning on wheels and axles, beating with pistons and hammers, whirling with propellers, running with tramcars and railway engines, flashing with lights, roaring with crowds and with cannon. They tried to substitute this sense of masses and of movement, of action and of power to the static techniques of the day, by exploiting the audio-visual possibilities of the phonograph and the film. Their painting (like the contemporary world) subordinated form to motion, attempting to capture the simultaneous quality of films and affecting future surrealists like Marcel Duchamp (*Nude Descending a Staircase,* 1911).*

The war of 1914 put an end to thoughts of conciliation. The futurist influence endured in its most violent aspects, in its advocacy of action for action's sake, dissonance, and motion. All these were now intensified by the war. German Expressionism, for instance, formulated well before the war, rose to frenetic rebellion and rejection when it ended. So did Dada, likewise born out of prewar experiments but even more out of the fire and blood of war. To the murderous absurdity perpetrated or

* Much twentieth-century music seems to derive from futuristic *bruitism* (noises) devised as artistic provocation by Futurists in pre-1914 years. Luigi Russolo had built a noise organ (1911) which could produce distracting sounds. Edgard Varèse incorporated these sounds into his music, while Bunuel and Dali used them in the sound track of their film *L'Age d'Or* (1930).

Nude Descending a Staircase, by Marcel Duchamp. Philadelphia Museum of Art: Louise and Walter Arensberg Collection.

abetted by the respectable public, Dadaists answered with harmless but shocking absurdities of their own. Society was led by criminals and lunatic muddlers. The Bible in one hand, a cleaver in the other, generals and politicians were driving mankind to perdition with their claptrap of reason, patriotism, and logical purpose. If the most sensible and responsible men devoted themselves to destruction and mayhem, the only answer lay in salvation through nonsense. Developed in wartime Switzerland by a Romanian, Tristan Tzara, an Alsatian, Hans Arp, and a German, Hugo Ball, Dada was nihilistic, opposing art, coherent creativity, and, above all things, reason.* It simply held all existing values up to ridicule, and Dada groups appeared in Germany and France even before New York discovered it in Marcel Duchamp's contribution to the Independent Show of 1917: a plain marble urinal entitled *Foun-*

* The *Cabaret Voltaire* where Dada was born in 1916 stood at number 1 of the Spiegelgasse in Zurich; Lenin lived across the street at number 12. The police were more suspicious of the Dadaists then of the "quiet, studious Russians": Lenin, Radek, and Zinoviev.

Vincent Van Gogh, a self-portrait. Jeu de Paume, Paris.

tain. But, since it was destructive and nonsensical, Dada could neither last nor create. It would give way to an offspring whose members wanted to build as well as to destroy: surrealism.

Like Dada, surrealism was founded by angry, unknown young men: André Breton (1896–1966), Jean Cocteau (1889–1963), Louis Aragon (b. 1897), Paul Éluard (1895–1952), most of whom had been involved with Dadaist demonstrations. Like Dadaists, surrealists rejected cultural norms, conventions, commonplaces of society for spontaneity, immediate experience, subjective impulses and fantasies. Like Dada, they subjected the world around them to a semantic bombardment under which order, meaning, and perspective disintegrated, revealing the inherent absurdity of life. But, unlike Dada, surrealism was hopeful as well as destructive. Surrealists believed in "truth" and the possibility of attaining it with a key furnished by André Breton, himself an analyst: they set out to apply the lessons of Freudian psychoanalysis in art, by the use of automatic writing, of free association, of methods designed to break through the crust of convention and illusion to the reality of the unconscious mind. The method, which certainly had a reinvigorating effect on art, did not as the surrealists hoped affect society and the public mind in any particular way, since it was—like most original concepts—good only for elites.

The free association surrealists proposed depended on the wealth and the variety of the practitioner's imagination and was then extended

Jean Cocteau with one of his ceramic pieces, "Three Eyes."

to depend on, or to appeal to, the same capacities in beholder or listener. The drawback of the method was that, since most people are quite limited, free association was little freer than habitual or conditioned association; and little wider either. In most cases, after the first shock wore off, it was seen that one narrow, conventional mode merely succeeded another. While those who *could* appealed to interior riches and broke into original patterns and connections (like Breton or Max Ernst), most would-be surrealists expressed themselves even better as their forms became more organized (e.g. the American poet Ezra Pound or the Spaniard Salvador Dali).

Nevertheless, surrealism did see itself as a revolutionary movement, out "to change life" (culled from Rimbaud) and "to transform the world" (culled from Marx), which meant that a number of its adherents eager to smash the old bourgeois values entered revolutionary politics. Some (Aragon, Éluard) joined the Communist Party, some Trotskyist groups, some tended to anarchism (Dali, Cocteau), some went through all these stages before being adopted by the Establishment and the art dealers (Dali, Cocteau, Joan Miró), emphasizing the paradox of the last twenty to thirty years in which the avant-garde is swallowed by public taste before it has had time to get far ahead. Nowadays publicity lights up "arts" like fashions, in a situation where everything goes and in which the survival of avant-garde artists is based on the support of businessmen who sell them and the appreciation of rich connoisseurs who buy them.

The Meaning of Modernity

Art and literature, which had once described man in his greatness, began to seek him in his privacy, perhaps because great deeds are so often bloody and blood has become once more, along with violence on every kind of scale, a commonplace of everyday experience. Display gave place to introspection, confession to analysis, concrete things melted into abstractions, wholes dissolved into parts, experience turned to fragmented sensations, like a vast puzzle disintegrates into its components in some surrealist cartoon that leaves us with an impression of shapes, colors, moods, but with no stable, tangible image. Painters abandoned the imitation of nature for what E. H. Gombrich * calls "a man-made construction, a colored canvas." From illusion to painting deliberately man-made constructs on canvas, from content to configuration: planes, textures, lights, and shades, assembled first according to the creator's will and later according to chance, would take the place of narrative or message. No more illusion. No more perspective. No more the artifice of the image that brings together the disparate multiplicity of what we witness. Instead, the artist's act and the beholder's reactions exist in separate worlds.

Victorian society believed in order and so did the philosophers, the writers, and the artists who sprang from it. Today, neither society nor the men and works that reflect it conceive of order as more than something arbitrary, imposed from outside. The art of the future, Strindberg had prophesied, "will, like nature, leave a lot more to chance." Chance meant the end of choice and of discrimination. The reign of randomness was translated from the laboratory to the studio and, hence, to the eye and mind of the beholder. How indiscriminate taste has become can be seen from the recent fortunes of nonfigurative art, moving from one simplification to another, toward ever greater abstraction: from the first compositions of Kandinsky in 1910, divorcing color and form from the world of nature, through the reconstructed Cubism of Mondrian in the 1920's, to the calligraphic abstractions of Tobey, Hartung, or Soulages in the 1950's. Object and subject have been so manipulated in the past eighty years that they have finally vanished altogether in works which seem the very essence of art for art's sake. And in the last stages of rebellion, nonfigurative art returns to the realism it had abandoned. Sculptors take over all the offal and waste of industry, enlist the flotsam and wreckage of an object-bound world. Painters now imitate real materials or use them in their compositions. Finally, neo-realists like Bazaine insist on the intrinsic abstraction of *all* painting, since it merely uses objects as starting points of "the plastic invention." There is no point, they say, in nonfigurative art, since even the figurative is abstract.

Certainly, labels become irrelevant when faced with action painting, minimal painting, primary structures, pop, op, mec, or cynetic art, and happenings, all of which seek less to express anything than plunge men into a "situation" where they can play at being free and take a passing

* In his great work *Art and Illusion* (New York, 1960).

cure of nonconformism. Derivative, repetitious, romantic, vulgar, this is an art for amusement parks and fair grounds, occasionally amusing for that very reason. The question arises whether crushed cars are sculpture, whether programmed silence or noise are music, and so on. The only answer possible is the one given by Stravinsky,* that "it is still generally thought of as art if it is shown in a gallery, and as music if it takes place in premises traditionally associated with concerts; which is hardly an answer, but in the absence of identifying rules and conventions, and at a time when an aesthetic object may be anything at all, the limits of art are not only not air-tight but indefinable."

One wonders whether the highly individualistic tradition of Western art is not giving way beneath the pressures of modernity: the burden of research, of learning, of discovery, of creation, has become too much for individuals, has been passed to teams—of scientific researchers, of artists, or of scholars. Even musical composition becomes corporate, even the work of art—once the expression of a single genius—turns toward mixed media put together by several cooks. All this stresses and enhances the gulf which opened in the nineteenth century between intellectuals and society, between intellectual and artistic life and the remainder of an increasingly fractured existence. Music, literature, or painting appeal to initiates, and their obscure idioms widen the gulf between their adepts and the rest, even though within two generations they have permeated western cultural fabrics, become the commonplaces of a consciousness divided between beliefs it has retained in science and in progress and the contemporary philosophy of relativism and doubt.

Contrasting with the plastic arts, the great *writing* of the twentieth century would be social and, hence, political and ideological. We have seen that the novel turned from individual psychology and restricted games played within the limits of a social group to description of social

* *New York Review of Books,* June 1, 1967.

Warder Collection

W. H. Auden

problems, culminating in the great crusading works of naturalism. But even most of these presupposed a change of heart, of mind, of luck, of opportunity, rather than of the social order. After the First World War this changed radically. Thomas Mann's hero, Hans Castorp, descends from his Magic Mountain into the battered plains of war and politics, Dada turns to surrealism and surrealism to revolution, the detached observers of an earlier day—delineators of men and society in decay and isolation—decide that only political action can change society, and that they must take sides in the political battle.

Surrealist fantasies were enlisted to articulate *The Waste Land,* in which more men than T. S. Eliot found themselves:

> A heap of broken images, where the sun beats,
> And the dead tree gives no shelter, the cricket no relief,
> And the dry stone no sound of water . . .
> Hooded hordes swarming . . .
> Falling towers
> Jerusalem Athens Alexandria
> Vienna London
> Unreal.

The nightmares of 1925 became the realities of the 30's, when the works of W. H. Auden (b. 1907) crept and seethed with secret conspiracies, hidden guerrillas, dangerous frontiers, industrial ruins, in which events to come were outlined with prophetic lunacy: "A preliminary bombardment of obscene telephone messages for not more than two hours, destroys the morale already weakened by predictions of defeat made by wireless controlled crows and pack cards. Shock troops equipped with wire cutters, spanners and stink bombs penetrating the houses by infiltration silence all alarm clocks, screw down the bathroom taps, and remove plugs and paper from the lavatories. . . ."

Depression, fascism, Nazism, purges, concentration camps, defeat, betrayal, the collapse of one world, the need to build another, echoed through the 30's and the 40's: Malraux, Silone, Brecht, Koestler, Steinbeck, Hemingway, Orwell, culminating in Sartre and Camus. Statements of failure all—failure of synthesis or communication (Eliot, Pound), failure of decency or faith (Malraux, Orwell), failure of man and society (Camus, Auden), failure of logic and coherence (Sartre, Breton), failure of trust or will (Silone, Koestler)—and yet, illogically, statements of a new commitment, hopes renewed, the necessity of decision when all alternatives fail, the ultimate assertion with Albert Camus that—isolated in an alien world, meaningless, unless he introduces meaning into it— man can and must assert himself. Sisyphus, condemned everlastingly to roll his rock to the mountain's top only to see it roll down again, finds that "the struggle itself towards the heights is enough to fill a man's heart. One must imagine Sisyphus happy."

Chapter 14

THE LATEST AGE:
1945 TO THE PRESENT

The Ebb of Empire

The year 1945 was the end of a period and also of a way of life. The war had shaken the earth like a great earthquake and nothing after it would be the same again. The age of European dominance was over. The supremacy of European countries, based as much on prestige as it had been on power, could not survive the blow it had received. Great colonial empires, sapped in earlier years by declining confidence among the masters and ever more strident appeals to the liberal doctrines which the masters taught, would quickly fall to pieces when the economic and military power that had won and held them disappeared. The confidence that made Europeans shoulder the white man's burden uninvited, long before the concept itself was formulated, broke down. The war had shown that the seats of power now lay outside strictly European limits, above all within her two great offspring—the Soviet Union and the United States—and that the new power conflict would be reflected in their rivalries.

A New China

Indeed, the effect of these rivalries would be to raise up a third and further rival and one whose titles as a non-European power could not be gainsaid. No greater proof could be demanded that European empire was on the ebb than the revival of the great Far Eastern power which, having long withstood Western cajolements and pressures, had crashed down at the turn of the century. A more powerful dissolvent than Western guns, the nationalist ideas the West brought to China or that China borrowed from the West, had put an end to the last imperial dynasty, and to Chinese unity for half a century.

The imperial unity of China went back to the days of the Roman Empire and beyond. But since 1644 a foreign dynasty of conquerors from Manchuria ruled in Peking. The nationalist movement, led by foreign-educated students, attacked the corrupt and reactionary Manchus as instruments of the foreigners and of national decadence. In 1908 both the Emperor and his mother (who had kept him imprisoned over the past decade) died suddenly, leaving the throne to an infant. The central administration now disintegrated completely, local warlords setting themselves up as independent rulers in various provinces. In 1911 a republican revolution broke out, led by Sun Yat-sen (1866–1925), a peasant's son, converted to Christianity and trained as a surgeon by missionaries, who would devote his life to revolutionary activity. In 1911 Sun became president of a newly proclaimed republic and the revolutionary society he had founded in the 1890's became the Nationalist Party, or *Kuomintang*. The Kuomintang stood for opposition to the foreigners and the Manchus, and for three positive principles: nationality, democracy, and a livelihood for all. The program was easier to formulate than to apply. For several years, the Republicans were but one more faction struggling against various warlords to control the central government in Peking to which the foreigners remitted revenues from the international customs they controlled.

Then came the First World War and, though Sun joined the Allies, Japan pulled greater weight in their councils. While Western powers were otherwise engaged, the war years saw Japan enforce her supremacy

Sun Yat-sen, leader of the Kuomintang, surrounded by his military staff.

Warder Collection

over China's ports. As a result, the Chinese nationalists turned to Moscow. The Communists had a simple view of colonialism which Lenin formulated in 1916. According to this, imperialism was simply the highest stage of capitalism. Industrially developed countries were plundering backward ones, growing fat on their exploitation, avoiding the collapse which contradictions inherent to the capitalist system would otherwise bring about, keeping up living standards at home by securing cheap raw materials and easy markets in colonies. The Western workers who benefited from this were themselves accomplices of capitalist imperialism. Hence Communists supported national or independence movements in all colonial territories, and attempted to emancipate weak or backward countries from great power domination, as they did in China.

With Russian help, the Kuomintang was reorganized on Soviet lines. In 1926, its Bolshevik-trained army, led by Sun's political heir, Chiang Kai-shek, imposed itself at last. Central authority over the provincial warlords was reasserted, Western tutelage cast off and, shortly after, the Communists themselves were murdered or expelled. But China was not to know peace or independence quite so easily. In 1931 she had to face Japanese aggression, designed to bring a new order to Asia in which a Japanese-dominated "co-prosperity sphere" would give Japan an even greater empire than that which the West had dominated not long before. Long years of warfare, during which the Japanese occupied large parts of North and Eastern China, ended only with Japanese defeat in 1945, but their elimination did not put an end to war.

Not all Communists had been destroyed in Chiang's great purge. Some who survived, having barely escaped annihilation by flight into the far north of China, reorganized their forces by enlisting the peasants to their cause. Led by Chiang's classmate Mao Tse-tung, another product of Soviet tutelage, and with little or no support from Moscow, which (rightly) suspected the orthodoxy of their Marxism, they devised a new revolutionary strategy based not on the urban proletariat but on the rural disinherited. Wherever they went, the Communists made war on landlords and usurers, gave land to the smaller peasants, allowed them a say in local government, defended them against exactions and pillage. Unlike other soldiery China had ever known, the Red Army behaved correctly toward civilians. Such tactics, along with superior discipline and training, enabled the Communists to attract recruits and gain the sympathy of most intellectuals and nationalist democrats disgusted with the corruption, nepotism, and inefficiency of the Kuomintang dictatorship and its subordination to foreigners (chiefly Americans) who furnished its arms and money.

The Kuomintang had never established its authority over the whole of China. While attempting a number of reforms (undertaken partly in order to please his foreign friends), Chiang never managed to extirpate

EAST ASIA TODAY

Communist

Non–communist

0   1000 miles

the wide-ranging corruption of the administration he controlled, let alone the brutal anachronisms surviving in the quasi-independent fiefs of warlords who paid him only the vaguest homage. Great armies marched under Kuomintang banners; but they were ill-trained, often ill-armed, and their loyalty was as uncertain as their pay. Unable to hold the countryside against the Red guerrillas, the Kuomintang gradually lost the cities too. In 1949 Chiang's two remaining strongholds fell—

the capital. Peking, in the north and the great port of Canton in the south—and the dictator was forced to take refuge on Taiwan (Formosa), an island colony whose attempt to achieve independence he had crushed only shortly before. The mainland remained in the hands of the Communist "People's Republic of China." Since then, the Communist attempt to reorganize and industrialize the country, using its human resources as basic capital, has subjected China to the agonies which Russia had to face thirty years before, revealed the possible pattern of an original kind of national revolution, and alarmed the world at the prospect of the resurgence of a major power in Asia, a power now vying with Russia for leadership of the Communist camp.

India

The great Japanese imperial venture, while it crashed down in 1945, had weakened the Western hold on Asian lands beyond repair. One of the first casualties had been Britain's Indian Empire. The British certainty that they were in India to stay, their willingness to give the upper classes education but refuse them responsibility, allow them liberty but not effectiveness, made the worst of a bad situation. If ruthlessness could have kept the Indians down, indifference could have left them alone when they ceased to be profitable. Imperial inertia radicalized the moderates and opened the way to more extreme groups, especially to the leadership of Mohandas Gandhi (1869–1948). This seditious saint, as Churchill called him, who opposed every form of alien "progress"—machines, speed, urban growth and the increasing drift away from land, tradition, and religion—advocated the development of village industries (particularly handloom weaving), the vitalizing virtues of goat's milk, the political uses of nonviolence and civil disobedience.* After

---

* Between the wars, an American newspaper would write of him as "the only figure of world importance operating practically naked."

Opposite: Chiang Kai-shek, leader of the Nationalist Chinese and Mao Tse-tung at a desk in his cave headquarters during the Communist takeover of 1948. Right: Mohandas Gandhi and his political heir, Jawaharlal Nehru.

1907, Gandhi's *Satyagraha* campaign of passive resistance furnished a base for the increasingly revolutionary agitation of the National Congress. The struggle between India and Britain was further complicated by a rift between the Hindu and Muslim communities, each after 1906 endowed with separate electorates, each growing increasingly aware of cultural differences, until only partition or civil war could settle their divisions.

There would be Indian soldiers in Flanders in 1914, twenty-four centuries after Indian archers opposed Greeks at Plataea in 479 B.C.—their first appearance on a European battlefield. But the end of the First Great War only saw national agitation grow worse, and the communal rift grow wider. The Second World War made it clear that Britain would be unable to hold on to India much longer. Not that most Englishmen wanted to do so.

Partition and civil war followed in 1947, when predominantly Hindu India, Muslim Pakistan, and the island of Ceylon severally received their independence. The British had taken over a war-torn, miserable, and divided land. They left it torn by war and by communal strife, marked by inequities and disillusion. In 1948, Gandhi was murdered by a Hindu nationalist and the subcontinent's chances of peaceful evolution diminished still further.

In the new India most people are still underfed and hungry, misery is still a way of life, 2 per cent of the population drain half the national revenues. An educated middle class finds no opportunities to employ its limited talents. A superstitious populace finds no relief in the administrative structure inherited from the British. One thing the foreigner could not achieve was to reform the religious and caste system which

Ho Chi Minh.

contributes to the country's inability to cope with its own problems—especially soaring birth rates and lack of initiative. Nearly two centuries after the battle of Plassey, India is equipped with the administrative structure the British have left, with modern laws and railroads, ports and industries, but with less than 1 per cent of its 300 million working in industry and 80 per cent or more of its population dependent on the backward agrarian economy Britain had maintained.

Southeast Asia

Far beyond India and far more than there, Southeast Asian nationalists had welcomed the Japanese co-prosperity sphere. Despite its racialist militarism, Japanese occupation seemed preferable to Western imperialism. To opponents of European and American colonial power in Manchukuo, India, Indochina, Malaya, Burma, Indonesia, or the Philippines, Japan appeared (however briefly) as a friend because she opposed the whites who had too long dominated Asian affairs. After Japan had been defeated, any national government seemed (and still seems) better than the most enlightened colonial administration. Nor were the old colonial powers in a position to hold out against such feelings. The immense Dutch empire in Indonesia, harking back 300 years and incorporating myriad islands—some 735,000 square miles of land stretching out for nearly 3,000 miles—acquired independence in 1949. The Philippines had reached independence in 1946; Burma, conquered piecemeal between 1824 and 1886, gained independence at the same time as India in 1947. Malaya, which took longer to achieve independence, became a British dominion ten years later.

The greatest problems arose in Indochina. In 1885 China had recognized French supremacy there and the provinces of Tonkin, Annam, Laos, and Cambodia had become part of the French colonial empire soon thereafter. There as elsewhere colonization ruined village economies and communal institutions, favored usurers who alone could provide money to pay taxes at 10 per cent a month, turned farmers into tenant laborers and sharecroppers. Japanese occupation followed by collapse of French authority encouraged the proclamation of independence in 1945 by Emperor Bao Dai and the king of Cambodia, while nationalists, chief among them the Communist Vietminh led by Ho Chi Minh, fought both the French and the Japanese. The Japanese defeat allowed the setting up of an independent government which resisted French attempts to re-establish their rule in the colony. Guerrilla war led the French to try to restore the former collaborationist Bao Dai, but this failed. The Vietminh were everywhere, the French and their collaborators restricted to the towns. The battle of Dien Bien Phu in 1954 determined the end of a war unpopular in France; and the Geneva Agreements of that year, while paying lip service to eventual unification, patched up a compromise peace that left the north to the Vietminh and the south to a "representative" regime surviving only with American aid. Since then, both parts have been the prey of civil war which threatens to leave both devastated, a war moreover which has come to involve half a million U.S. troops and the diplomatic or military intervention of a score of other nations.

It is unclear whether China, preoccupied with her own revolution, has any serious designs on Southeast Asia, an area which the automobile revolution, emphasizing oil, tin, and rubber, has made the richest in the world in relation to its size. It would seem rather that most of the countries of this region cherish traditional particularisms of their own. But it would not be surprising if China, like Japan, expressed the self-confidence of economic upsurge and national revival in imperialist aspirations. If it did, it would only be doing what we have seen the Western powers do in their time of energy and expansion. But one may pause to think how little this phase has lasted,* how soon the conquering countries lost their energy and their political hold, how quickly they learned that the most effective means of domination lay not in fleets and armies but in subtler relations.

The Middle East

One region that illustrates both these points is that between the Tigris and the Nile, stage of kaleidoscopic changes for a quarter of a century.

The discovery of oil fields in Persia, Iraq, and Arabia had turned the backward Middle East into a focus of power politics, the prize of struggles to control an area that became crucial after 1913 when the

---

* Germany's colonial period ran from 1884 to 1917, Italy's from 1885 to 1941, that of the United States from 1898 to 1947. Of the old colonial powers, Portugal and Spain still hold certain African territories, Holland retains only the island of Curaçao in the Caribbean, France and Britain retain small parcels of the vast empires they accumulated during centuries. In the past twenty-five years over fifty new states have sprung from these colonies.

British Admiralty decided to convert its ships from coal to oil. In one generation the Middle East passed from the Biblical age of asses and camels into the age of trucks, buses, and refineries. By developing communications and stirring up the population, technology replaced the community of Islam with national aspirations learned from the West. Egyptian and Turkish nationalisms had appeared before 1914, proportionate to Western influences. After the Great War, during which the Allies had competed for Arab support against their Ottoman rulers, Arab states were set up in which nationalist politics directed against French and British domination were always sure of a following: the more extreme the better. The combination of unlimited aspirations and limited capacity to fulfill them provided a constantly explosive fuel for the region's politics.

In 1944, the Arab League joined together the Arab states of the Middle East in uneasy pursuit of common objectives. The first of these was to get rid of foreigners. The old colonial powers, whose determined pupils they had been, had lost their force and, what was worse, their self-confidence. The French sourly withdrew from Syria and Lebanon in 1945, the British reluctantly and gradually were pressed out of the region by 1956.* As they went, chaos and disunion too often took their place.

There could be little community between a rich paternalism like the sheik of Kuwait's and the fly-ridden savagery of Iraq, the prosperous cosmopolitanism of Lebanon and the isolated puritanism of Saudi Arabia, the national-socialism of Damascus ideologues who leaned on Moscow and the medieval court at Riadh, relying on tribal loyalties and oil revenues. Cairo and Baghdad have traditionally been rival poles of attraction in Islam, not allies. Syria fears the possible domination of Egypt, Lebanon apprehends Syrian greed, Jordan—torn between native Bedouin and rebellious Palestine refugees—subsists by an effort of her sovereign's will. Egypt itself—the leading power of the region, by dint of numbers and by the personality of its former president, Gamal Abdel Nasser (1918–1970) —is hardly an "Arab" power. Though Muslim in their majority, Egyptians never considered themselves to be Arabs before the 1930's.

Confusion was compounded by conflict in Palestine, between Jews and Arabs: long, bitter, and apparently inextricable. It had begun when, in the course of the First World War, the British government sought Jewish support by holding out the hope of a national home in Palestine—then a Turkish province. Influenced as much by Old Testament memories as by the needs of war, the Balfour Declaration of 1917 thus promised the Jews a homeland that Britain did not own, and which it only came to control by right of conquest.

This fulfilled a long-standing aspiration of the Jews, one which the

* With the exception of Aden, which was only evacuated in December, 1967, when the area was incorporated into a newly independent South Yemen Republic.

Nehru with Egyptian leader Gamal Abdel Nasser.

Zionist movement had articulated late in the nineteenth century and had begun to carry out in the colonization of Palestine even under Turkish rule, so that the Jewish population of that province, 24,000 in 1882, stood at 85,000 in 1914. But it clashed with promises other British emissaries had made to the Arabs, whose risings contributed to Turkish defeats.

Serious trouble might still have been avoided if immigration to Zion had not been spurred by flight from a Europe darkened by Nazi persecution in Germany and rising anti-Semitism elsewhere. 150,000 in 1927, the Jewish population of Palestine had trebled by the thirties' end. The competition between modern methods which the Jews employed and the traditional methods of the Arab population, the friction of rival nationalisms, each of which came to regard the other as the beachhead of alien culture, made trouble inevitable or, at least, predictable. Threatened in their homeland, the Arabs reacted with wild, sometimes blind, violence: riots, arson, murder. The British authorities were caught between Arabs who blamed them for letting in Jews and Jews who blamed them for not admitting more. The Arabs spoke of their rights in what was still their country. The Jews of life and death, only alternatives seemingly open in Hitler's Europe. Between 1944 and 1948, terror and counter-terror competed in a now-familiar crescendo, nationalist terrorism turning increasingly against the British occupants against whose prohibitions of illegal immigration was being pursued. *Mutatis mutandis,* the activities of terrorist groups like the Stern Gang or the Irgun Zvai Leumi did not differ greatly from the crimes their Palestinian Arab foes were to perpetrate twenty years later. Against the British in Ireland, against the Germans in France, soon against the French in Algeria, patriots demonstrated that—however much conditions might differ—the terrorism of small, scattered bands could dent the inertia of the majority and harry an occupying power into recruiting enemies by repression.

Jewish nationalists found widespread support in a world horrified by Nazi crimes and eager to help Jewish survivors in search of shelter find that shelter in Palestine, rather than elsewhere. The debt that Europe

673

owed the Jews, much aggravated by common responsibilities in Hitlerite horrors, would be paid at someone else's cost, creating an unending source of resentment and conflict. One could count the establishment of Israel as an independent republic in 1948 as a clear gain, were it not for the rancors that fester on, for the hatreds that still rage unabated.

Three wars, in 1948, 1956, and 1967, have opposed Israel and its Arab neighbors, each an Arab defeat, none an Israeli victory beyond the battlefield, all falling far short of a solution to the region's problems. Israel is too strong for her enemies; the Arabs are too numerous for their foes. A detailed account of their struggles would be irrelevant, for facts have little hold on this head-on encounter of the rival rights (and wrongs). Only some things are certain: that the new state of Israel will not be eliminated short of annihilation; that the economic and the human drains of war threaten the stability of every Arab state; and that the needs of warfare increase the contestants' dependence on alien powers which alone can subsidize and arm them.

In 1956, a last attempt to reassert the traditional imperial influence ended less with a bang than a whimper, when a joint Franco-British invasion force had to leave Egypt under the threat of United Nations sanctions. Yet more illuminating than the humiliation were the conditions of their failure. For the Franco-British expedition against Suez harked back to glorious days when denunciation of a contract or failure to pay a debt by some small state would bring French or British gunboats to Greece, Egypt, or Mexico, to enforce the interests of their subjects. In this case, President Nasser, angered by refusal of Anglo-American aid for the building of Egypt's high dam at Aswan, had prematurely abolished the Suez Canal Company's ninety-nine-year lease. The interests involved were slight. The costs of the canal had long been paid off; revenues were now sheer profit, but they would end in 1968 in any case. Nationalization was only twelve years ahead of the contract's expiration. What was at stake was not profit, but a state of mind. And clearly, in Paris and in London this state of mind was muddled. For what appeared as a Franco-British initiative was a by-product of the struggle between Washington and Moscow for influence in Egypt, of Egypt's efforts to arm itself against Israel, of Israel's attempts to seize the initiative against Egypt. The combined operation that was launched from Cyprus against Nasser's troops reflected less what France or Britain wanted than what others had done or wished to do.* It ended ingloriously when Washington and Moscow forced them to halt and remove their troops from Egypt. And the only ones to benefit were the Israelis, whose forces had

* The Americans sought to recruit Egypt for a regional defense pact directed against Russia, the Russians to keep it from any such alignment; the Egyptians wanted arms against Israel, Israel wanted an end to Egypt's blockade of her crucial Red Sea port at Eilat. When the United States refused Egypt the arms it wanted, Egypt got them from Communist sources, thus raising Washington's ire and making it withdraw its promise of support for Aswan, a project which Moscow quickly undertook.

THE MIDDLE EAST

Territory occupied
by Israel, 1967

Israeli troops move to the Egyptian border during the 1948 war.

performed with their usual brio, and who had succeeded in opening the way to their vital port at Eilat.

But the withdrawal of the Europeans, which the Suez fiasco symbolized, left the area free for the confrontation of the Soviet Union and the United States. Riven by internal dissensions, torn by external temptations, the Middle East could not stand by itself, could certainly not learn to act as an independent entity. New imperial interests moved in to replace the old. Nature abhors a vacuum of power.

Dependent Independence

It is clearly possible to control other countries by economic influence rather than by conquests, by use of loans or investments which would affect their policies, by the penetration of industrial methods and products which shatter native economies frequently already in decay and keep them as the lenders' vassals until they rebuild their own power or break away by revolution or war. Actual practice is more complex.

As communications were shrinking the world, and trade tying its disparate parts together, the need of industrial nations to interfere with those less developed increased—if only because without their products and their markets (but especially the former) the industry was liable to run down. On the other hand, more backward countries—Turkey or China, Egypt or Peru—could only hope to match their exploiters in wealth and power by developing capital and skills which they could only secure by enlisting Western aid: that is, by facilitating even greater foreign meddling in, and control of, their affairs. The West could not be kept out without Western techniques, and these could not be acquired without bringing in the West. This was a quandary. But while, as we have seen, such changes meant social and cultural revolution for the adjusting economy, they need not always mean political subjection. Even a poor country like Algeria today can limit the influence of foreign investors if it wills; even a capital-poor country like the United States of the nineteenth century can develop its equipment and resources almost wholly on a flood of foreign loans, and yet maintain its political and diplomatic independence. A country sufficiently determined could adapt its borrowings to its peculiar needs as did Japan, could expropriate foreign capital as did Mexican revolutionaries or Russian Bolsheviks,

676

could assimilate it by bankruptcies as did the United States, could try to do without it almost altogether as does Communist China, or rely on it utterly and yet control it as Israel does today.

What has been called economic colonialism is seldom the result of economic conquest and much more often that of a native default: the failure to develop possibilities which may be realized and yet ignored, not for lack of means but because those who have the means have no wish to use them in the public good. Foreign capital is thus attracted to do things that national capital does not care to do.

In this connection we should do well to remember the words of John Stuart Mill, like his father before him an official of the East India Company: "One people," wrote Mill, "may keep another for its own use, a place to make money in, a human cattle farm to be worked for the profit of its own inhabitants," but not for that of the subjects. Whatever motives moved the empire builders, Mill's words proved terribly true in Asia as elsewhere. But everywhere, as in India, Europe trained the leaders and inspired the ideologies that would first challenge and then displace its power.

The Protean Conflict

On the night when the Japanese had attacked Pearl Harbor, General de Gaulle, then head of the Free French Committee in beleaguered London, had rejoiced. "The war is now definitely won." As for the future, he went on to predict two phases: Germany restored by the Allies and a great war between Russia and America. The first proved true within half a dozen years. The second was only avoided by dint of mutual fear.

Only a few men could be so clear-sighted. The exuberance and the needs of combat fought in common toned down the differences between reluctant partners whom Hitler turned to allies. Most of the American people, like the British, impressed by Russian sufferings and valiance, could not conceive that they and the Soviets need ever again be foes. In 1942, to General Douglas MacArthur as to his countrymen, "the hopes of civilization" appeared to "rest on the worthy banners of the courageous Russian army." Men like President Franklin Delano Roosevelt and his chief advisor, Harry Hopkins, seem to have felt that the United States and Russia had more in common in some ways than either had with more old-fashioned countries maintaining social hierarchies at home and colonies abroad. Men like Churchill, Roosevelt felt, desperately clutching at the past, would attempt to reimpose the anachronistic values of another world, reinstall royalist or conservative regimes, restore imperial structures. Against such aims Russia and the

677

United States could co-operate, all the better if Russia's legitimate concerns for her security and welfare were satisfied. Even Americans who did not think this way seem to have held that the successful conduct of the war came before any consideration of postwar policies. Until the end, American leaders like the commander of the Allied armies in Europe, General Dwight D. Eisenhower, regarded military victory as prior to and distinct from political decisions, which meant that American policy was to win the war and hope for the best thereafter.

This is not to say that the British, the Americans, and their allies gave no thought to the world which they hoped to build once peace had come. The Allied leaders—Churchill, Roosevelt, Stalin, joined sometimes by leading figures and representatives of friendly countries—met frequently for talks and conferences which would define war aims and postwar actions. One of the concrete results of such talks was the foundation of the United Nations, set up on American initiative to replace the defunct League of Nations in which Roosevelt had lost all faith.

The League of Nations had not lived up to its supporters' expectations. It had provided a platform for the lesser nations and a meeting ground for members, accustoming statesmen to continuous negotiations and playing a useful part in its nonpolitical organizations for health, labor, or drug limitation on the international plane. But it had shown that peace could only be maintained with the co-operation of the greatest powers, whose support it lacked. Only co-operation could defeat Fascism; only continued co-operation could maintain peace. Roosevelt proposed to abandon his country's policy of isolation and, with the support of his greatest allies, provide the basic structure of a world where democracy would prevail and aggression be suppressed once for all. The United Nations, whose declaration was signed shortly after Pearl Harbor (1942) and which came into being three years later, was endowed with a Security Council of six nonpermanent members and five permanent ones (the Soviet Union, the United States, Britain, France, and China), who could only act in unanimity against aggression (hence the veto);* and a General Assembly in which, despite Stalin's objections to giving little countries (like Albania) which he despised the same rights as those of the greater powers, every member nation had an equal vote. The United Nations would, in due course, become less the peace-keeping agency of Roosevelt's dream than a forum of international affairs. But it was hardly, then or in retrospect, more than a hopeful gesture toward a better peace, a sop ceded to Roosevelt by the Russians who were preoccupied by far more concrete things.

In any case the wartime and postwar conferences, conducted in haste and under pressure, aimed rather at agreement on common formulas than at definitions which would clarify and settle the differences be-

---

* In 1966 the Security Council of the U.N. was enlarged to fifteen, and the Big Power veto abandoned.

A meeting of the United Nations Security Council.

tween the parties present. While all agreed that the new world should be democratic and that the peoples of liberated Europe were entitled to self-determination, no one quite knew or perhaps wished to know what such terms implied. Peoples, democracy, self-determination, had different meanings for each party. For Communists, in any case, words and gestures had no intrinsic meaning, only a dialectic value arising out of the aims and realities of a given moment and passing away with it. This was something Roosevelt would learn too late. But if the Russians were the most ruthless both in fact and doctrine, the Americans and British also bent ideals to particular ends: in Greece, where in 1944 a Communist rising was suppressed by the British army; in Yugoslavia, where Churchill backed the Communist Tito against both Germans and pro-British royalists, only to find him assert his independence of British plans as he would later of the Russians too; in Poland, where "compromise" allowed the Russians a government which would be at their beck and call; and everywhere that great power decisions settled the fate of peoples without real reference to their wish.

While the Americans were chiefly interested in somewhat abstract notions of international security and justice, the Russians understood only the politics of power. Like their allies, the Russians were determined that Germany, once vanquished, should never rise again. But they also nourished the thought for themselves of a protective rampart against any revived threat to their security. In other words, they wanted to control Eastern Europe, partly because its states affected the security of their borders (Finland, Poland, Romania), partly because they were traditional protégés (Bulgaria, Yugoslavia), partly because they lay athwart strategic routes toward Germany (Hungary, Czechoslovakia). Moreover, by 1945, all these states between the Greek and Finnish borders were occupied by Russian troops and the temptation of "what we have we hold" was very great. "This war is not like those of the past," Stalin told Tito in 1945, "Whoever occupies a territory imposes his own social system upon it. Everybody imposes his system as far as his army can advance."

Yet unilateral decisions could not hold without some consent of the other powers; and these were bound by principles and treaties to quite a different set of views. The independence of Poland in particular, for whose sake the war had started, could not be easily abandoned. Churchill himself in 1944 had agreed with Stalin on their respective East European zones of influence, a deal in which most of the countries along Russia's borders became in effect Russian satellites, while Greece became a protégé of Britain. But even Churchill fought hard to let the Poles choose their own government as they wished. This was a point which the Russians—having killed, arrested, or otherwise eliminated most of that country's non-Communist leadership—never would concede. The first years following the war were marked by desperate and unsuccessful attempts by the Western powers to prevent Eastern Europe and especially Poland from falling entirely into Russian hands. By 1948 their failure and Russia's establishment of its effective hold upon this region determined the complete breakdown of the wartime alliance and its division into hostile camps.

The roots of this division went back to the great conferences of Teheran (1943) and Yalta (1945) in which the leaders of the Allied powers bargained for the world. Yalta is a good case of the dangers of leaving such large decisions to the debate of a few powerful but fallible individuals.* Here, Roosevelt's rather naïve expectation that he could hold the balance between British imperialism and Soviet Communism, reconciling the Russians to the "one world" he had in view,** in which lions would work with lambs in the United Nations, came up against the grim realism of Stalin. The future of Germany was settled and its division into Allied zones of occupation confirmed; it was agreed that Russian intervention against the Japanese would take place shortly after the end of hostilities in Europe; but no agreement could be reached on Poland, which Stalin regarded as an avenue through which the Germans might again attack Russia. There was little opposition to his proposal that Poland's eastern border should be approximately on the Curzon Line, while she received compensation in the west at Germany's expense, but no settlement as to his determination that the Polish government must be in hands on which he could rely. Indeed, the most striking thing about the outcome of the talks at Yalta, as at every other summit conference, is not what was decided but what was left undecided.

Perhaps this is easier to understand if one bears in mind the brutal changes and the multitude of problems that faced the victorious peacemakers. As Winston Churchill told the House of Commons on his return from Yalta: "We are now entering a world of imponderables, and

---

* Of the major participants at Yalta, Churchill was, according to the American Secretary of State, Stettinius, going through his menopause; Roosevelt, very ill, maintained only a brittle contact with life; his chief adviser, Harry Hopkins, was dying of cancer; only Stalin was in fine fettle.

** A term coined by his unsuccessful Republican rival in the presidential election of 1940: Wendell Willkie.

Big Three representatives—Stalin, Roosevelt, and Churchill—dine at Livadia Palace during the Yalta Conference. In the left foreground is Secretary of State Edward Stettinius, and to the right of Churchill is Soviet Foreign Minister Molotov.

at every stage occasions for self-questioning arise. It is a mistake to look too far ahead. Only one link in the chain of destiny can be handled at a time."

But such self-questioning seems to have been limited to the West. For, as soon as the conference had ended, the Russians took steps to collect on the half-concessions which they had managed to secure. Within a few weeks, their hold on Bulgaria, Romania, and Poland was affirmed, despite the protests of their Western allies. It would be solidly established in the next two years, as not only national leaders but also Communists whose complete devotion Stalin doubted were eliminated one by one. As Marx had prophesied in the New York *Tribune* of April 12, 1853, the western borders of the Soviet Empire now stretched "from Stettin to Trieste." Along them, declared Winston Churchill in a great speech at Fulton, Missouri, in March 1946, an iron curtain cut off the peoples of the East from freedom.

Yet, as it had been during the war itself, the crux and focus of international tensions and great power rivalries was Germany. There, the occupation zones hardened into a division of the country between the western part under British, French, and American occupation, and the eastern, where the Russians established the rule of local Communists everywhere but in the provinces beyond the Oder and Neisse rivers, which were handed over to Polish administration. By 1948, friction between the occupants on economic and political questions (reparations, monetary reform, the fate of Berlin) led to a confrontation focused on the old capital which was under their joint administration. The Allied position in Berlin, a hundred miles within Communist territory, marked the city out as a permanent sore, and one which the Russians could scratch whenever they wished. Angered by unilateral Allied currency reform in the West, the Russians sought to close their access to Berlin. Cut off by land, the Westerners survived by means of a giant airlift: 300,000 flights and over 2,000,000 tons of supplies between July, 1948, and May, 1949.

But Berlin, like Poland, Greece, or Turkey, was only one point where friction turned to crisis, where constant Communist probing had to be

681

withstood. Here was an unheard-of situation: neither peace nor war but a world-wide struggle in which every possible weapon was used short of a frontal attack that would lead to major conflict. Local wars, insurrections, political and ideological infiltration and subversion, propaganda by every available means, political and economic pressures, added up to what the American Bernard Baruch described in a speech of 1947 as the "Cold War."

The Lagging Unification of Europe

The Cold War was a conflict which the impoverished survivors of Western European power were in no position to maintain. Only the United States could face Russia in defense of areas as yet free from Communist rule. In 1947, President Harry S Truman announced American military aid to Greece and Turkey then under heavy pressure from the Communists. Then, in February, 1948, a Communist coup took over Czechoslovakia, the last country in Eastern Europe to preserve its recovered independence. The democratic government in Prague was sympathetic to the Soviet Union which had opposed the betrayal of Munich, and had done its best to function as a kind of bridge between East and West. The native Communist Party was numerous and Soviet prestige high, but public sentiment favored social democracy rather than proletarian dictatorship. Nor did the Communists have the excuse of oppressive government or social injustice, since the country's institutions and her industrial structure were among the most progressive in Europe. But in the struggle between East and West there was no room for neutrality. Moscow had no use for an uncommitted neighbor or for a government that did not reflect the wishes of the local party. Backed by the presence of Soviet troops at the border, armed Communist militia took over the country. Czechoslovakia was part of Russia's defensive pattern; she became, for twenty years at least, the most docile of Stalin's satellites.

Her rape, followed in short order by the blockade of Berlin, made 1948 a very nervous year. Soviet armies could have overrun Western Europe with little opposition from existing European or American forces, and the Soviet Union was seen as a serious threat to independence and free institutions everywhere. Nor could the Europeans be sure that the distant United States would use her atom bombs to defend them. It was as a first step in their own defense that Britain, France, and the Benelux countries signed a fifty-year defensive treaty in March, 1948. Within a year, with North American encouragement, this grew into a wider alliance including the original five, the United States, Canada, Denmark, Iceland, Italy, Norway, and Portugal all of which signed the North Atlantic Treaty in April, 1949. Greece and Turkey would join in 1952. The expenses of the North Atlantic Treaty Organization (NATO) were largely borne by the United States, but its structure took some time to crystallize. Then, in 1950, the conflict feared in Europe broke out at the other end of the world with the invasion of South Korea by the Russian-trained troops of her sister state in the North.

Annexed by Japan in 1910, the Koreans had never given up their struggle for national independence. In 1945, they had proclaimed a People's Republic that surprised all the allies, who had envisaged a long-term trusteeship that would prepare the peninsula for self-government. Russian occupation of the country north of the 38th parallel and American occupation south of it had resulted in rival regimes: Communist in the north and National-Conservative in the south. Attempts to unify the peninsula under a single government naturally failed and the equally oppressive and unrepresentative rulers of the two sections faced the familiar alternative of turning temporary division into permanence or modifying it by force. When the North Koreans took the initiative in the latter, the United States was able to enlist United Nations opinion in favor of defending the *status quo*. The common "police action" decided upon lasted three years and cost some three million casualties among the military and civilian populations involved, including 140,000 Americans, the U.S. having contributed the largest contingent of the U.N. Expeditionary Force.

Peace negotiations begun in 1951 ended in 1953 in an armistice that has been uneasily maintained ever since. But the fears excited by the conflict, the passions aroused by Chinese intervention on the North Korean side, the difficulty of fighting the kind of limited war of containment that General Douglas MacArthur (for a time commander of the U. N. forces) denounced as "a war without victory," seemed to bring world conflict very near. At the same time, the outbreak of the war in 1950, with the demands it made on American resources and the additional strain it imposed on Europeans contributing their share to the Korean enterprise, had spurred the NATO powers into fresh initiatives. Most particularly, the pressing danger argued for greater manpower that could only be contributed by a (West) Germany rearmed and integrated into the military alliance of her victors. Prolonged negotiations for an all-European army having collapsed in 1954 before the objections first of the British, then of the French, Germany entered NATO and the Western alliance system as a full-fledged member in 1955.

In 1969, members of the Atlantic Alliance celebrating its twentieth anniversary could pride themselves that the fear of Russian aggressiveness which presided over NATO's foundation had given way to a more relaxed attitude; and certainly compared to 1949 both Eastern and Western camps seek to avoid tension and to encourage appeasement in

Europe. Yet, if it has kept the peace, the Alliance has hardly preserved the freedom of the nations it was also designed to protect: neither that of member states like Portugal or Greece, nor that of the Czechs whose loss of liberty in 1948 precipitated the Alliance in the first place.

But, even to achieve very limited successes, military aid was not the only way. The Communists did best where economic and social dislocation on a major scale wore down the middle class and discontented labor, creating social grievances that they could utilize. The anti-Communists had to make war on poverty, unemployment, and hunger. In June, 1947, the U.S. Secretary of State, General George C. Marshall, announced a new policy: "directed not against any country or doctrine but against hunger, poverty, desperation and chaos. Its purpose should be revival of a working economy. . . ."

The Marshall Plan worked. The actual financial aid which it provided was somewhat less than the American aid that Europe had received up to the time it started.* But previous aid had been distributed haphazardly; the new aid would be coordinated by the Europeans themselves. Indeed, the greatest function of the Marshall Plan was to promote European co-operation in the establishment of a common recovery program (1948), which, by 1951, brought industrial output back to prewar levels.

Within a series of international agreements ** Western Europe tried to leave behind the conflicts of national claims and ambitions which had shaped and scarred it over the past century and a half, and moved toward political and economic integration managed by supranational institutions. It is unlikely that this would have developed without the original American initiative; or, one would think, without the stubborn policy of Stalin, who was determined to keep his part of Europe out of it. The advance of West European integration and of Communist policy developed in a kind of counterpoint. Marshall aid itself a counter to Communist progression; a tightening of Stalinist reins on Eastern satellites in answer to it culminating in the abolition of Czech independence in 1948; the struggle over Berlin in that same year encouraging the creation of a North Atlantic security pact; the outbreak of the Korean War in 1950 speeding the emancipation of West Germany, whose manpower and resources could not be spared and leading to the recognition of a sovereign Federal Republic in West Germany in 1952 and of the rival Democratic Republic (GDR) in the East. This German resurgence, in turn, suggested the pooling of coal and steel resources of Belgium, Holland, Luxembourg, France, and Germany in the Euro-

* U.S. aid to Europe before the Marshall Plan amounted to about 17 billion dollars; Marshall aid provided approximately 11 billion dollars: a quarter to Britain, a fifth to France, 11 per cent to West Germany, 10 per cent to Italy.
** Organization for European Economic Cooperation (OEEC) 1948; European Coal and Steel Community (ECSC) 1951, European Economic Community (EEC) 1957, European Free Trade Area (EFTA) 1959, and many others.

pean Coal and Steel Community, which restrains German economic activity in a freely negotiated settlement. Finally, there would develop out of this a European Economic Community (1957), establishing a common market with common tariffs, ensuring the free movement of capital, labor, and goods, and working out common social and economic policies.

If the challenges of recovery and the aid of the United States played important parts in this process, a significant and unexpected force working for European integration was to be found in the Vatican. Remembering the days before the sixteenth century when national divisions counted less than the bonds of widely shared religion and culture, the Catholic Church looked with sympathy upon ideas of European union mooted with particular urgency since the First World War. It so happened that the late 1940's saw Christian-Democratic (that is, Catholic) parties and leaders in dominant positions, notably in Germany, where Konrad Adenauer remained in power from 1949 to 1963; Italy, where Alcide de Gasperi held the premiership from 1945 until his death in 1953; and France, where Robert Schuman was a constant member and sometimes head of successive cabinets from 1946 into the early 1950's.* These men and their supporters realized that if Europe did not somehow unite, its energies, unable to express themselves effectively, would curdle into the same old parochialism and lead to the resurgence of national rivalries which had already cost it dear. Paradoxically enough, the promoters of this initiative—the most progressive that Europe had known in centuries—were old men: Adenauer, born in 1876, de Gasperi, born in 1881, Schuman, born in 1886; they had all grown up at a time when nationalisms had not yet hardened into myth, had been formed in a Catholic bourgeois tradition where common interests and beliefs counted for more than passports.

The first move in this direction would take place in 1948, year of the Communist coup in Prague and of the Berlin blockade, when arguments for European unity carried particular conviction. A thousand delegates, twelve ex-premiers, forty ex-cabinet ministers, belonging to nineteen European countries, presided over by Winston Churchill, who had made himself the unexpected champion of a United States of Europe, gathered in the Hague and called for new unitary institutions. Governments responded promptly, the French and Belgians taking the initiative, the British hanging back. In a series of official committees, the hopes of 1948 were pared down to purely consultative institutions: there would be no federal union, no European government. But on May 5, 1949, the Council of Europe was set up "to ensure a closer union of its members," originally Belgium, Denmark, France, Ireland, Italy, Luxembourg, Holland, Norway, Sweden and the United Kingdom. Twenty years later,

---

* All came from border zones: Schuman and Adenauer from opposite sides of a Rhine which has traditionally served more as a highway than a border, de Gasperi from the Trentino; all were especially aware that frontiers of the modern kind were a new invention, artificial sunderers of normal relationships.

Jean Monnet.

the original ten had become eighteen, including all non-Communist European nations except for Finland, Portugal, and Spain. The Council's structure could be used to advance political integration when Europeans were ready for it, while committing them to nothing for the present.

Meanwhile, European ideas were to be carried into action by a less public figure: the Frenchman, Jean Monnet (b. 1888). Monnet had made his career as a supranational technocrat and administrator, first in the League of Nations, then in the commissions that negotiated economic agreement with Britain and the United States. It was he who, in 1940, as his country was being overrun by German armies, invented the proposal fruitlessly advanced by Winston Churchill that France and Britain should be fused in one, with a common citizenship for their peoples. Now he felt that the reconstruction of Europe offered an opportunity to restructure national into international institutions, beginning with economic integration but leading to political union. He proposed that this should begin where interdependence was already most evident, in a supranational authority controlling the continent's great coal-producing areas in the Saar and Ruhr and regulating the coal, iron, and steel industries of the West. Adenauer and Schuman agreed; Italy, Belgium, Holland, and Luxembourg followed suit; only the British held out.

There were many reasons for London's attitude: among them, suspicion of an initiative launched by politicians who were not only Catholic (hence tarred by historical memories with the brush of reaction) but overt supporters of capitalism and free enterprise. As a member of the British Cabinet later explained, the Labor Government "were determined not to allow interference by a European Committee with our full employment policy, our social services, our nationalized industries, or our national planning." No Socialist Party, stated a Labor pamphlet, "could accept a system by which important fields of national policy were surrendered to a supra-national European representative authority, since such an authority would have a permanent anti-Socialist majority and would arouse the hostility of the European workers." British Conservatives agreed for reasons of their own. For Churchill, speaking in the House of Commons, Britain "could not be an ordinary member of a federal union limited to Europe" and excluding the Commonwealth and the United States. And future Conservative Prime Minister, Harold Macmillan, asserted: "One thing is certain and we may as well face it. Our people will not hand over to any supra-national Authority the right to close down our pits or our steel-works."

Insularity, pride, selfishness, understandable concern for specific orientations that were ideological and sentimental as much as economic kept Britain out; and their expressions deserve attention because they are human, natural, representative, and typical of how one day's certainties may become another's rue. At any rate, in the 1950's Britain produced half the coal and a third of the steel of Europe so that its refusal to join the proposed Authority was a serious blow. The European Coal and Steel Community (ECSC) proceeded nevertheless, its High Authority (virtually autonomous in its particular realm) fixing prices, determining production, controlling investments and imports, closing down uneconomic mines, removing internal tariffs and setting external ones as it saw fit among the six members of the Community.

It is a classic rule that unification provides a vaster market and opportunities, not only for trade but for supranational planning on a more economic scale. Monnet hoped to extend the economic harmonization worked out within ECSC to the rest of the economy of the six original partners and to work out supranational institutions on a political level that would integrate them and Europe as a whole. The European Economic Community (EEC), generally identified as the Common Market, should have been the vehicle of this new advance and did, to some extent, play this role. But Britain, concerned for her Commonwealth ties and her privileged position in relation to the United States, still unwilling to subject her policy to authorities other than national ones, remained outside the EEC until too late, organizing a rival organization: the European Free Trade Association. Then, after 1958, as the Common Market forged steadily ahead, General de Gaulle turned French policy away from further integration. Europe, he insisted, existed only as a coalition of nations united at the governmental level, but jealously retaining their separate political identities. The Council of Europe had first been watered down by the British; now it was opposed by the French, who saw to it that the meetings of the Council of Ministers and of the annual Assembly of member nations at Strasbourg should remain purely verbal affairs, lacking power or effects upon national governments.

L'Europe des patries which de Gaulle imposed upon his partners set back the prospects of thorough economic—let alone political—union transcending national boundaries by a decade. At the same time, when—in 1963—Britain, chastened by her economic difficulties, sought to join the Common Market, France's negative vote prevented her admis-

Representatives of the European Common Market countries after one of their first meetings.

sion. The Council of the EEC must vote unanimously on questions such as admission of new or associate members. There were concrete reasons that made British entry into the European Economic Community difficult to negotiate: Britain's past record and her extra-European orientation raised suspicions as to her real intentions, above all the island kingdom's reluctance to give up the domestic subsidies and the cheap food imports from the Commonwealth which permitted low food prices and, hence, relatively lower wages, thus indirectly subsidizing industrial exports. But General de Gaulle's veto prevented the question from being decided on its merits. His fall from power in 1969 reopened the possibility of negotiations, without removing the obstacles in the way of Britain's admission. The major problems now were no longer in the agricultural field, but in that of currency and balance of payments. Members of the Common Market had reason to fear the weakness of the pound sterling, a currency with interests and vagaries of little profit to the Six. Yet the changing factors—from agriculture to currency—suggest that when objections of principle are removed, the problems to be solved fall in the realm of those everyday issues that all economies constantly face; experience indicates that, in or out of the EEC Club, the fates of sterling, franc, dollar, and mark are inextricably entwined; and one imagines the admission of Britain and her European Free Trade Association partners to a growing European Community to be henceforth a matter of time and perseverance.

Meanwhile, EEC and EFTA have continued to co-operate within the Organization for European Economic Cooperation, established in 1948. By 1960 their consumption, their productivity, the level of their living standards, had doubled compared to prewar days. Western Europe, with only 3 per cent of the land and 10 per cent of the population of the world, had 20 per cent of its food, 25 per cent of its total output, 40 per cent of its trade. One can see that the eighteen members of the OEEC, if they were really united, would be the most powerful economic unit in the world today. But also the most vulnerable: dependent on foreign trade, on raw materials, on continued peace, above all on adjustment and response to the challenges that face it.

From Cold War to Coexistence

The Cold War redefined and restricted the meaning of the West as that part of the world where Soviet writ did not run—thus including Turkey but not Czechoslovakia, Spain and Portugal but not Finland, Australia but not India, eventually Japan and Formosa but not Cuba. The social and political structures of these "Western" nations varied widely; but in all the capitalist system had been and was being steadily modified. In most of them, either between the wars or after 1945, a certain degree of nationalization had taken place. Railroads, industries like steel or armaments or aviation, mines, public transport, utilities, banks, insurance companies, tobacco companies, match manufactures, automobiles—all or some of these were taken under state control, either as public corporations or in some other way. War, Marx once said, is the forcing house of democracy. The Cold War was that too. And, while the Western world moved ever further from the capitalist model Marx and Lenin described, the Soviet world has moved closer to the kind of old regime it professes to replace, complete with intellectual slavery, terror, and power hunger.

By the 1950's, each side had come to regard the other as an incarnation of evil and itself as the champion of justice and truth. In the nineteenth century Tocqueville had seen the future world divided between Americans and Russians, one party standing for liberty and the other for servitude. But now the almost pathological hostility between the rival camps rose to fantastic heights. It was sharpened by common terror of the weapons which a new war might bring into use. War, which had been temporarily excluded from the everyday experience of nineteenth-century men, now became a way of life as in the Middle Ages and, more: a total threat. The United States in 1952, the Soviet Union in 1953, possessed hydrogen bombs. By 1957, the Soviet ICBM which could lift an earth satellite into orbit could also carry atomic missiles to the United States.

Historical events seem to reproduce the relationship of thunder and lightning. The happening itself is a flash soon lost in darkness. But the thunder reverberates, carries on the news of it amplified to monstrous proportions. If lightning burns and scorches, it is thunder that brings fear. People knew that the power of the two bombs dropped on Hiroshima and Nagasaki was equal to two-thirds of all bombs dropped on Germany in the course of the whole war. The first hydrogen bomb tested in 1952, equaled two hundred of the earliest atom bombs; and its three megatons would be dwarfed ten years later by the Russians'

60-megaton bomb, which enlarged the destructive area of atomic power from a single city to a whole region or country. Men also knew that atomic radiation, spreading far beyond a given target, could prove more deadly than any given bomb. They knew, in fact, that a major war could easily mean the end of the human race. And such prospects of Armageddon were matter-of-factly envisaged both by U.S. Defense Secretary Robert S. McNamara describing U.S. forces in 1963 as "large enough to insure the destruction, singly or in combination, of the Soviet Union, Communist China, and the Communist satellites as national societies . . ." and by the deputy commander of Soviet missile forces answering that his rockets could "raze all industrial and administrative targets and political centers of the United States," and "completely destroy the countries on whose territories American bases are situated." Others took the likelihood of destruction with less calm. Europeans in particular tended increasingly to place their hope in a possible "third force," detached from either side, and, at least in private, to call a plague on both their houses. Still, there was little that they could do but wish: the third force that might have modified the balance of terror or escaped from it could arise only out of a united Europe, and Europe was far from that.

It seemed as if the unrelenting conflict had become an established fact of life and that Europe must learn to live ever divided in two parts Neither side, however, was as monolithic as appearance might suggest. After Stalin's death in 1953, a series of succession struggles in Russia ended, as we have seen, in the temporary victory of Nikita Khrushchev, who expressed a widespread revulsion against the rigidities of Stalinism. He would pursue a policy of coexistence, theoretically based on the certainty of eventual Communist victory but practically inspired by the balance of atomic terror.

The relative easing of international tensions was reflected in 1955 by two events: Russia's signature of a peace treaty with Austria and the withdrawal of Soviet troops from that country; and the concurrent establishment of the Warsaw Pact, which linked Moscow and her vassals in an alliance ostensibly directed against NATO but in effect permitting the continued presence of Russian troops on the territories of neighboring countries. Russian occupation of eastern Austria had justified the maintenance of garrisons in Hungary and Romania, "to guard lines of communication." Once the Warsaw Pact provided an alternative excuse for this, peace with Austria could be concluded, neutralizing the country and reassuring Marshal Tito, to whose heresies the new Russian leaders reconciled themselves, admitting that there could be different roads to socialism.

It would soon appear that liberty in this respect varied in proportion to a country's proximity to Soviet borders and to the Kremlin's estimate of its own interests. In 1956, Khrushchev's denunciation of Stalin's capricious tyranny and paranoiac murderousness before the 20th Congress of the Communist Party weakened the infallible authority of Moscow and opened the way to a new polycentrism, expressed that very year in national revolts in Poland and Hungary but, more importantly, by greater practical independence from Moscow throughout the Communist world. Crushed in Hungary, settled by intimidation and compromise in Poland, both rebellions would bear fruit: an easing of pressure on peasants, intellectuals, and the Catholic Church; increased production of consumer goods; a relaxation of the tension and oppression that had gripped these countries for a decade.

Tito's stand against Stalin was followed within a few years by the victory of communism in China. After 1956, the Communist governments of Poland, Hungary, and then Romania, while maintaining close relations with the Soviet Union, set themselves to gain the popular acceptance that would provide support in case of conflict with Moscow, relaxing some constraints and placing great emphasis on national sentiment and independence. By the later 1960's, while Communist governments ruled over a billion people in fourteen states, there would be almost as many brands of communism as there were national parties, and rival centers for differing tendencies: Moscow, Peking, Belgrade, Havana.

This meant that, in effect, the Soviet Union's pressure on Western Europe relaxed after a last flare-up of trouble over Germany. There, the Federal Republic proved too attractive to citizens of the Eastern zone who were passing in frightening numbers to the West, particularly by using the facilities offered by the joint occupation of Berlin. Formally ruled by the four Allied commanders, incorporated in neither zone, the old capital functioned as two separate entities—East and West—joined by a multitude of practical bonds and, crucially, by freedom of movement; which meant that many Berliners lived in one sector of the city and worked or walked in another. Taking advantage of this, some 4,000 East Germans a week, almost a quarter of a million yearly, had been choosing the greater freedom and comfort of the West. In the late fifties, a future British cabinet minister remarked to East German economists that if he were in their position, watching their human and financial resources seeping to the West, he would build a wall. His sally would shortly come true. By July, 1961, the emigration, which had risen to over 10,000 a week, threatened to drain the GDR of its youngest, most skilled, and enterprising inhabitants. Hence the sealing off of their last escape route by building the famous Berlin wall, separating the Soviet sector from the remainder of the city in contravention of the agreements that had maintained Berlin under the joint control of the four occupying powers.

Quickly prolonged by impassable obstacles sealing off the whole border between East and West Germany, this measure cut the manpower drain and turned the German Democratic Republic into an economically

The Berlin Wall. Right: Walter Ulbricht.

viable state. Since 1961, West Berlin has been languishing. The East Germans, on the other hand, now look upon their existence as a permanent fact rather than a temporary arrangement pending reunification. Under the leadership of a dour old Stalinist, Walter Ulbricht, they are pressing forward with long-range economic plans they had not been able to undertake in the earlier period. Thus, with the wall, the German problem was for the time being settled; not, as Russia had wanted, by Germany's subjection but by its division into rival states, each one a key component of its alliance system, each one viewed by its allies with mingled respect and fear.

Eastern Germany had once been the Reich's granary. But the regions richest in grain as in minerals lie in the territories forfeited to Poland; and the chief wealth of Ulbricht's realm (as, for that matter, of the Federal Republic) is its high standard of technical training and administrative skill. Technical and higher education is more modern and accessible than in the West, less restricted by considerations of .means and class (though far more so. of course, by ideological considerations). Living standards are still well below those of the West, but opportunities for personal distinction and reward are fast increasing and the defection rate is much lower even when opportunity occurs. The GDR has become a leading producer and exporter of machine tools, optical goods, office and railroad equipment, its industrial output second only to Russia's among Socialist countries. By 1963, beneath the dictatorship of its Stalinist rulers the ripples of intellectual and moral discussion were spreading as they did both east and west of an increasingly porous Iron Curtain. The new academic, technological, and managerial elite sought for a road not back to capitalism but to "a humanized and more democratic form of Socialism." Pending a mutation that may be long in coming, the country and its ruling party, no longer simple instruments of Soviet policy, becomes an ever more assertive member of its bloc. In 1968, Ulbricht appeared as the chief advocate of a tough line against the liberalizing Czechs, and his troops furnished the Soviet Army's chief support in Czechoslovakia's occupation.

The Federal Republic, meanwhile, has grown into the world's third greatest economic power, its army the most numerous contingent in NATO, its currency dominating those of its European allies. Bonn's foreign policy, long oriented toward the reunification of German territories, was expressed in what became known as the Hallstein Doctrine, from the foreign minister who enunciated it in 1955: refusing to recognize the existence of the GDR and to maintain relations with any government that did recognize it (with the exception of the Soviet Union). Recently, however, the Doctrine has begun to be quietly discarded. In 1967, diplomatic relations were established with Romania, which naturally recognizes the fellow regime of the GDR. With the accession of the Social Democrats to power in 1969, and the opening of direct talks between the two Germanies in 1970, it is probable that other exceptions will whittle down the rule.

Adenauer's Germany had been one of the most enthusiastic supporters of European Union and the Common Market, looking to them for opportunities of self-realization and vicarious greatness denied to a defeated and still-suspected land. By the 1960's, discouraged by French opposition to political integration on a European scale, the Federal Republic has shown a tendency to go it alone or seek its support in Washington. Its industrial enterprises prefer American to European alliances, its politicians often do so too. Denied the armaments in which she once sought her power, West Germany finds herself once again the dominant force in Western Europe and proud of her success. In the process, she is slowly abandoning hopes of a reunificaton rendered ever less likely as the temporary structures of the two Germanies harden into a semblance of permanence. The signature in 1968 of the Nuclear Non-Proliferation Treaty (designed to maintain Russo-American predominance by denying nuclear weapons to other powers) also consolidated the European *status quo* and the division of Germany by maintaining the country under a measure of international control and keeping it out of the nuclear club. One of the great international issues of the postwar age, the German question needs to be settled afresh every few years. For the moment, with the land divided and (relatively) unarmed, its neighbors can take advantage of the undoubted contributions Germans can make to the prosperity of the continent.

The fact that this also applies to members of the Soviet bloc, where —in Poland and Hungary, Czechoslovakia and Romania—German capital is invested and jointly operated factories are built, indicates that after the wall, paradoxically enough, the division of Europe became not more but less clear and tangible, tourism and trade between East and West increased, traditional links eliminated in 1945 were re-established,

693

so that in 1965 there were ten times as many tourists, twice as many trade exchanges, between its two parts as there had been four years before. Relations are often easier where limits are clearly drawn; but these limits themselves are slowly giving way to the reassertion of national interests and local tendencies within each bloc and across its borders.

In a world where one year's records are tomorrow's anachronisms, one year's crises are next year's good old days, exchanges between the two camps were growing. The level of industrial development seems more important than ideological coloring and, as the economies of Eastern Europe advanced, their integration with those of their Western neighbors became more difficult to avoid. Joint enterprises—Italo-Russian, Franco-Romanian, German-Polish—linked the interests of capitalist and noncapitalist countries. In the Soviet Union a new (or newly articulate) economic school, associated with the name of Professor E. Liberman of Kharkov, argued successfully for the introduction of the profit system into state enterprises, greater managerial initiative, attention to consumer demand rather than norms set by the State Planning Commission and other planning enterprises that still employ some ten million persons. In the German Democratic Republic managers were paid by results and workers' wages geared to the profits of their enterprise. Romanians and Russians were invited to lend their savings to the state at 4 per cent interest. In 1968, the Secretary of the Central Committee of the Hungarian Workers' Party declared: "Profit is the only true indication of what an enterprise is worth." "We know that bourgeois liberties are partial, often false or truncated," declared a Russian student to the correspondent of a foreign newspaper: "But give them us all the same!"

The admission that the Communist world could counter the superior attractions of the West only by force was followed in 1962 by the further admission that such force as the Communists had would not (at least for the moment) be used in a nuclear conflict. In October, 1962, the great race for strategic superiority between Americans and Russians culminated in Khrushchev's attempt to place missiles in Cuba and his surrender to an American ultimatum.

The origins of the crisis went back to 1956 when a young Havana lawyer, Fidel Castro, began a guerrilla campaign against the Cuban dictator Fulgencio Batista. By 1959 Batista had been expelled from Havana and Castro embarked on the more difficult campaign to modernize Cuba, give it a viable economy, and free it from dependence on foreign business interests. Under the pressure of native anti-Americanism and of American suspicions of his own national-socialist inclinations, Castro's revolution—originally idealistic and middle-class—quickly turned toward the extreme Left. Concrete disputes over agrarian reforms that affected powerful U.S. corporations merged with ideological differences, and Castro was driven to seek support from native Communists and lean ever

Fidel Castro.

more heavily on ideological revolutionaries like his old guerrilla companion, the Argentinian Ernesto (Che) Guevara.

Before long, Cuba became a base for armed revolutionary attacks on other Latin American dictatorships (notably Nicaragua and the Dominican Republic), and for virulent propaganda against other conservative-reactionary regimes, its activities a serious source of concern to the United States. In 1960, the nationalization of American-owned properties * and trade agreements with the Soviet bloc intended to free Cuba (and especially its mammoth sugar industry) from dependence on the U.S. market, added fuel to the fire. Unhelpful but conciliatory to begin with, the Americans became ever more intransigent. Communism in Latin America, declared the State Department, was not negotiable. The Cuban example could endanger more important American interests in other parts of the Southern hemisphere. Arms and training facilities were made available to Cuban refugees planning to dislodge Castro. Then, in 1961, economic warfare turned to open fighting when an American-supported expedition attempted to land in the Bay of Pigs on the island's coast only to be repulsed with heavy losses.

It was in the wake of this that Cuba had taken the final steps to enter the Communist camp, acquiring Soviet arms and persuading the Russians to place nuclear missiles on the island as a credible deterrent to the aggressive intentions evidenced by their mainland neighbors. The United States could not tolerate the presence of these missiles only miles from its territory. Challenged by President John F. Kennedy, Khrushchev backed down and removed them (possibly in exchange for a secret understanding that Cuba would not be invaded). Nuclear war had been very close but, the crisis settled, the air was clearer for the mutual (if tacit) admission that one great power would tread very lightly or not at all in areas vital to the other. Before long, American

* With the compensation values to be assessed on the basis of the figures the companies themselves had provided in the past for their tax returns!

695

missile bases near the Soviet border (rendered out of date by the development of longer-range weapons) were also being abandoned. Other steps followed in the same direction. By 1963, Americans, British, and Russians could sign an agreement banning nuclear tests in the open, symbol of their appeased relations and of the fact that the participants considered survival more important than competition. Equally significant, that same year a special "hot line" provided a direct link between the Kremlin and the White House, both equally eager to avoid fatal errors of judgment by keeping in contact.

Since that time, the polycentrism that we noted in Communist politics has spread to both camps and—as we saw—to fields other than doctrine. The French, also a nuclear power, and the Chinese, who exploded an atom bomb in 1964 and a hydrogen bomb in 1967, refused to sign the nuclear test ban. The treaty, which was less an effective gesture than the indication of a change in mood, calmed some fears while verifying others. The Nuclear Non-Proliferation Treaty of 1968, again refused by China and by France (along with other not-yet-atomic nations) seemed to confirm the common interests of Moscow and Washington in restricting the membership of their exclusive "club." The Cold War, once clear and definite, was becoming vaguer if not less dangerous; and it appears that, once again, the Soviet Union and the United States have more in common than each has with its fresh potential enemy in Asia.

Polycentrist tendencies themselves were to receive a brutal rebuff in 1968, when Czech attempts to liberalize one of the longest-lived Stalinist regimes in Europe and broaden the scope of their economic activities at home and abroad were crushed by invasion and occupation. Six hundred thousand Russian, Polish, Bulgarian, Hungarian, and East German soldiers reasserted Moscow's tenuous hold on its uncertain vassals; their impunity proved the unwillingness of the Western allies to intervene in the "internal" affairs of the rival bloc. It was within the latter that reactions to the aggression proved the divisions among Communists themselves. Romanians and Yugoslavs held off, while showing all the sympathy they dared for the oppressed Czechs; Hungarians and Poles continued their relatively independent economic activities, while lending a loyal hand to their Russian allies. The members of the Warsaw Pact were far from the "mere purveyors of raw materials" that Peking Radio accusingly described. Within the limits of discretion, each followed its own interests, getting the most for itself out of its neighbor's discomfiture.

The Czech invasion confirmed the non-Communist Left and wide sections of the Communist world in their suspicion of the Russian oligarchy and of its good faith. To Milovan Djilas, sometime vice-president of Communist Yugoslavia, it proved the abandonment of ideological dynamism for imperialist interests. To the Communists of Peking it demonstrated the re-establishment of a "bourgeois dictatorship" appealing to Socialist dogma for private ends. In Peking the Soviet government is officially regarded as counter-revolutionary: "a new Tsar" oppressing the peoples of Europe and its own subjects too, "social-imperialist, social-fascist, colonialist and aggressive." The conclusions that the Chinese and their supporters draw from this are far-reaching. Premier Chou En-lai has described (September 30, 1968) how "American imperialism and Soviet revisionism struggle and collaborate in a vain attempt to delimit their zones of influence and redivide the world."

The new situation suggests the possibility of tactics in which the policy of "peaceful coexistence" for which Peking long reproached Moscow may now be wielded by the Chinese to divide their two chief enemies. To China, Russia is not only a foreign enemy and a rival for colonial possessions that run the whole length of the two powers' Asian frontiers. She is also and above all the symbol of a great revisionist menace—a revisionism that slumbers apparently even in the best of Communists and against which China's cultural revolution was launched in 1966–68 to prevent the bureaucratization and embourgeoization of its own revolution. Russia is therefore an internal as well as external danger, more threatening than the American representatives of an alien system. No longer able to carry the banner of ideological cold war, long overtaken by radicals more revolutionary than its own leaders, Russia is condemned to seek some kind of *entente* with its recent rivals in order to face more pressing challenges elsewhere.

All this has accelerated another phenomenon: the tendency for Communist parties in Western countries, such as Italy and France, to become less revolutionary and to take up the stance of a responsible opposition following the parliamentary road to socialism. Socialist parties, of course, had participated in governments since the First World War. By the late 1960's, in Belgium, Germany, and Italy, coalition governments of Christian-Democrats and Socialists reflected the increasing similarity of majority parties that differed about the degree and tempo of reform, not about the principle of reform itself. One result of this has been the appearance of an extraparliamentary opposition, representing the active minority disillusioned with existing parties and particularly embarrassing to the Communists who see themselves overbidden by "adventurist and anarchic leftists." The latter have done their best to contest the established order and its reformist machinery, precipitating the long series of disturbances which have marked 1968 and 1969 and which the Italians describe as *maggio strisciante,* or "creeping May," from the French riots of May, 1968.

Too weak for effective revolution, the pressure of the leftist forces has nevertheless encouraged an acceleration of reform (which leftists reject), for instance in many universities, and—more important—a rethinking of the programs and responsibilities of left-wing parties, including Communists no longer regarded as the revolutionary, liberating force they once appeared to be.

697

All in all, the internal and external power blocs first precipitated in the late 1940's by the conflict between the U.S. and the U.S.S.R. have both hardened and weakened. Their appearance reflected the exhaustion of a Europe which had been unable to free itself from Nazism by its own forces, and the weakness of governments unable to maintain themselves without the aid or protection of powers one of which was only half-European, while the other was not European at all. The division of Europe naturally ran along the demarcation line between their rival occupation troops and reflected not only the balance of power but the aspirations of Moscow and Washington to dominate the world. Today it rests on a common incapacity to provide for its own security in the nuclear era by setting up a confederation sufficiently strong to be a nuclear power in its own right.

The Atlantic Treaty of 1949 had sought "a just and lasting peace founded on appropriate guarantees" for the security of its members. The signers of the Warsaw Pact of 1955 had claimed as much, adding that they would be glad to abolish their treaty as soon as a system of European security could be set up. Thus, the negotiations envisaged by both sides in 1969 to achieve a real *détente* in Europe have a common aim. There is no reason why a working settlement should not be achieved. The soaring recovery of the 1950's could not have been foreseen in 1948, nor the progressive emancipation of Eastern European countries in 1956. In this perspective, the union of Western—and perhaps of Eastern Europe too—seems far from impossible.

This is perhaps the best indication of the hazards of history written too soon after events. For, while the sense and proportion of things that happened long ago seem clear in adequate perspective, those of the events of yesterday remain obscure. Things which loom large seen from nearby appear in quite another light when time has placed them in a vaster complex. This is, really, why the present chapter has been more narrative than interpretative or, at least, why the former can be provided more easily than the latter. For interpretation, like Athena's owl, only takes its flight when the dust of the past has settled.

The Third World

One of the great novelties of the postwar era has been the appearance and progressive self-assertion of a "third world" born of the dissolution of erstwhile colonial empires. At least fifty new republics have joined the ranks of the United Nations since 1945. By 1970, the only colonial empires left to Europe were those of Russia and of Portugal. The physical holdings of France or Britain are scarcely worth mention, let alone comparison with those of countries like China, Brazil, South Africa, Indonesia or, even, the Sudan. Europe's age of territorial imperialism seems to be over and that, itself, is a remarkable change. But—leaving aside new variants of colonialism and domination—the colonial enterprises of the past have left their mark behind them. Today, as in the nineteenth century, the impact of harder, better-armed cultures remains as evident as it appears unavoidable. Whether they came, as they still come, to heal, teach, order, or exploit, the Europeans were bound to revolutionize (when they did not destroy) the societies, peoples, cultures that they touched.

Benevolent, indifferent, or selfish, some actions can have dire effects if based on an inappropriate estimate of what is good. Condensed milk for babies, solid meals for starving men, cold water for the overheated, can hurt or kill. Similarly, so can constitutions and other alien imports, like a determined desire to introduce efficiency. European technology always brings with it European ideas of much broader scope. You cannot introduce machines and factories without implicit concepts of what man can or should do; or social services without attendant ideas about what man needs and what man is. One materialism ushers in another, one ideology elbows out another and imposes itself, even when its importers are basically defensive or hostile.

To take only one example, European ideas concerning property proved as much a dissolvent as European arms and techniques. When land, like any other object, was treated as private, separate pieces of property subject to sale or transfer or mortgage by one particular owner, then different forms of land tenure were torn to shreds and, with them, the societies, crafts, and tribes which had evolved quite different structures. Like land, labor too had to be brought in line with European concepts and European needs. Money wages, open markets, regular hours, above all the notion of work as a value rather than as a demeaning necessity, replaced older forms of labor organization—sometimes forcibly. Barter or subsistence were replaced by money, self-sufficiency by exchange, tens of millions who had seldom or never used currency were initiated into its delights or pressured by taxes and other obligations into cash-producing activities. Efficiency replaced haphazardness, secularization replaced traditional magic observances, laws and administration replaced custom, incorruptibility replaced compromise and convention, impersonality replaced face-to-face relationships.

Some of this was an improvement; all was upsetting. In Asia, Africa, America, one society after another was affected by alien concepts generally applied with little understanding of the historical conditions behind existing institutions and the stability provided by existing practices. Men who knew what they wanted and who subordinated their activities to their ends, triumphed over societies whose members subordinated their actions to their habits. Weapons counted in this, but states of mind

699

counted even more. Men who had operated time out of mind as parts of the customary cultures were introduced to the possibilities and insecurities of change. They became subjects and, faced with their new masters' formidable power, sought refuge in migration, in idleness, in religions that provided an excuse for evasion, before finally turning from religion to politics as a substitute for hope. But the colonial process is not as simple as it is often painted, and it does not operate in one direction alone. The occupier does not simply rule the occupied, he haunts him, fascinates him, infiltrates his consciousness and his life, takes hold of him inside and out. Yet the process works both ways and, in this kind of coupling, it is hard to tell after a time which of the parties has sucked the other's blood, which has contaminated the other, which (in the precise sense of the terms) is oppressor and which oppressed.

All this indicates the possibility that technological society did not destroy values but rather suggested new ones. Contract replaced tradition, the free-moving, free-wheeling individual replaced the static family or tribe, democracy with all its drawbacks and opportunities replaced the stable hierarchies of status and of birth. Changing legal structures transformed society and social attitudes, technological innovations turned congeries of provinces into countries, spread modern skills, suggested the revival of native industry and enterprise in a new guise and on a new scale. The implications of these changes—equality before law and politics, for instance—are making themselves felt even in nontechnological societies; and so are those arising from the technologically induced shrinkage of a world more truly and more uncomfortably *one* than ever in its history.

Nothing illustrates this better than the principal quandary of our world, which is the disparity between the advanced European and Europoid countries and all others, the imbalance between the industrialized "West" and the agrarian remainder of the world. It must have become clear in chapter after chapter that the greatest distinction between our society and previous ones lies in the quantitative factor. In the first place there are simply more men. More human beings were being born between 1870 and 1914 than between Adam and Newton. But material commodities have increased too: not only their use, but the volume of their production. During the last four centuries the volume of coal production increased 3,000 times, that of iron production 4,000 times, that of glass 5,000 times. And yet we know that this applies in practice only to limited sections of the human race. We know that time has not unreeled at the same rate for men in every country—as it seemed to do, generally speaking, until 100 or 200 years ago, when most men everywhere still lived approximately in similar circumstances. Today, a glance across the world reveals extraordinary differences which neither Herodotus nor Marco Polo would have encountered: differences more on a scale of time than space. Thus, one can say that life in Britain or France today is similar to that which the United States knew in the 1930's; that life in Spain or Turkey has striking analogies to that of France in the 1860's; that life in India or Sumatra continues in conditions not very different from those of Peter the Great or Louis XIV. The number of doctors per inhabitant is very revealing in this connection. The progression runs from one for 700 in the United States, to one for 1,400 in France and Germany, one for 3,000 in Poland, one for 4,500 in Egypt, one for 10,000 in Iraq, one for 50,000 in Indonesia; and it varies within the countries themselves according to local wealth. The practical reflection of this can be seen in the fact that where life expectancy in the mid-twentieth century was 67 years in Canada, 70 in Holland, 58 in Japan (where it had been 48 in 1930), it was 44 in Egypt and 32 in India. Where three out of four Dutch babies can expect to live to 60, only one out of two Indian babies can. In other words, a uniformity of techniques and values leaves room in some respects for a much wider diversity of evolutionary stages.

Behind this lies the fact that, while all the world advances, its most advanced areas advance the fastest. Asia, Africa, Latin America, are increasing their production, but not nearly as much as Europe and North America, which have less than 30 per cent of the world's population and produce 80 per cent of its income. In 1962, Asia, with more than half the world's population, had 3 per cent of its motor vehicles; Africa and Latin America, with more than one-third of the world's land, had 7 per cent of its surfaced roads. The amount of world trade has increased tremendously, about sevenfold in the last fifty years—most of it since the last war. But in 1960 Europe and North America still accounted for two-thirds of it and Western Europe for two-fifths. Indeed, the post-war recovery of Europe (including Russia) becomes clear when one considers that its share of world trade—46 per cent in 1937, 33 per cent in 1947— was 53 per cent by 1960. Despite the appearance of non-European trading powers like Japan, Canada, and the United States, Europe continues to consume the greatest share of the surplus foods and raw materials of the world and to provide the leading exporters of manufactured goods, just as she had done in 1900.

The great change which has taken place since then is that, whereas in the earlier period manufactures were mostly exchanged against primary products from more backward countries, today the mass of exchanges takes place between the industrial nations themselves. Europe, which took three-fourths of the world's raw materials in 1913, only took half of them in 1953. This suggests that primary producers in Asia, Africa, and South America, with their rubber and oil and tin, do less trade and do it on worse terms than before because demand for their products is shrinking, or is only maintained by artificial means. A country like Ghana produced more cocoa in 1964 than in 1954 but earned less than half what she had earned a decade before. In effect, nonindustrial economies, no

GREENLAND
(Denmark)

ARCTIC OCEAN

ICELAND

NORTH
SEA

NORWAY

SWEDEN

FINLAND

DENMARK

UNION OF SOVIE

IRELAND

GREAT
BRITAIN

NETHERLANDS
BELGIUM

WEST
GERMANY

EAST

POLAND

LUXEMBOURG

CZECHOSLOVAKIA

AUSTRIA

HUNGARY

FRANCE

SWITZ.

ROMANIA

ITALY

YUGOSLAVIA

SPAIN

BULGARIA

ALBANIA

GREECE

TURKEY

BLACK SEA

CASPIAN SEA

GIBRALTAR
(Br.)

TUNISIA
1956

MALTA
1964

CYPRUS
1960

MEDITERRANEAN
SEA

SYRIA

LEBANON

IRAQ

IRAN

A T L A N T I C

MOROCCO
1956

IFNI
(To Morocco, 1969)

ALGERIA
1962

LIBYA
1952

U.A.R.
(EGYPT)
1953

ISRAEL 1948

JORDAN
1946

KUWAIT
1961

SPANISH SAHARA

MAURITANIA
1960

MALI
1960

NIGER
1960

SAUDI ARABIA

RED SEA

SENEGAL 1960

GAMBIA 1965

PORTUGUESE GUINEA

GUINEA
1958

SIERRA LEONE
1961

UPPER VOLTA
1960

CHAD
1960

SUDAN
1956

YEMEN

SOUTHERN YEMEN
1967

MUSCAT AND OMAN

O C E A N

LIBERIA

IVORY
COAST
1960

GHANA
1957

DAHOMEY 1960

NIGERIA
1960

CENTRAL AFRICAN
REPUBLIC
1960

ERITREA

AFARS AND ISSAS
(Fr.)

ETHIOPIA

TOGO
1960

CAMEROON
1960

EQUATORIAL
GUINEA
1968

GABON
1960

CONGO REPUBLIC 1960

DEMOCRATIC REPUBLIC
OF THE CONGO
1960

UGANDA
1962

KENYA
1963

SOMALIA
1960

CABINDA
(Port.)

RWANDA
1962

BURUNDI
1962

TANZANIA
1964

ANGOLA
(Port.)

ZAMBIA
1964

MALAWI
1966

MOZAMBIQUE
(Port.)

MALAGASY
REPUBLIC
1960

MAURITIUS
1968

SOUTHWEST
AFRICA
(S. Africa)

BOTSWANA
1966

RHODESIA
1969

THE DECLINE OF COLONIALISM
AFTER WORLD WAR II

SWAZILAND
1968

LESOTHO
1966

SOUTH AFRICA
1961

Independent since 1945

Remaining dependent

WESTERN HEMISPHERE

GULF OF MEXICO

BAHAMAS
(Br.)

ATLANTIC OCEAN

CUBA

PUERTO RICO
(U.S.)

BR. VIRGIN IS.
ST. MARTIN (Neth. and Fr.)

HAITI
DOMINICAN
REP.

U.S. VIRGIN IS.
ST. KITTS (Br.)

BRITISH
HONDURAS

JAMAICA
1962

GUADELOUPE (Fr.)

CARIBBEAN SEA

MARTINIQUE (Fr.)

HONDURAS

NETHERLANDS
ANTILLES

BRITISH
WINDWARDS

BARBADOS
1966

NICARAGUA

CANAL ZONE
(U.S.)

TRINIDAD AND TOBAGO
1962

COSTA RICA

PACIFIC OCEAN

PANAMA

VENEZUELA

GUYANA
1966

COLOMBIA

SURINAM
(Neth.)

FR.
GUIANA

OCIALIST REPUBLICS

U.S.S.R.

MONGOLIA
1947

N. KOREA
1948

S. KOREA
1948

JAPAN

AFGHANISTAN

CHINA

PACIFIC OCEAN

WEST PAKISTAN
1947

NEPAL

E. PAK.
1946

INDIA
1947

BURMA
1948

TAIWAN

HONG KONG
(Br.)

N. VIETNAM
1954

LAOS
1954

BIAN SEA

BAY OF BENGAL

THAILAND

S. VIETNAM
1954

CAMBODIA
1953

PHILIPPINES
1946

CEYLON 1948

REPUBLIC OF
MALDIVES
1965

BRUNEI
(Br.)

INDIAN OCEAN

MALAYSIA
1963

SINGAPORE
1965

NEW GUINEA
(Aust.)

INDONESIA
1948

PAPUA
(Aust.)

TIMOR
(Port.)

AUSTRALIA

longer limited or self-sufficient, have become even more unstable than the industrial economies on which they depend; especially so when they have focused on a single product, as in the case of Mauritius, 99 per cent of whose exports is sugar; Bolivia, 97 per cent of whose exports is tin; Liberia, 95 per cent of whose exports is rubber; Egypt, 87 per cent of whose exports is cotton; Colombia, 86 per cent of whose exports is coffee; Ghana, 85 per cent of whose exports is cocoa; Ceylon, 85 per cent of whose exports is tea. All in all, over a score of countries still depend on a single product for over half of their export trade and lead a precarious existence, teetering on the brink of catastrophe with every oscillation of world commodity prices.

Meanwhile, the inflationary effects of incipient industrialization and urbanization affect backward states much more than more developed ones. The cost of living index is a highly artificial but nevertheless suggestive indicator of this. It shows that, while between 1958 and 1968 the cost of living went up from 100 to 110 in the United States, 119 in Germany, 122 in Britain, 131 in Italy, and 133 in France, it rose to 149 in India, 202 in Ghana, 250 in Yugoslavia, 879 in Argentina, and 2,260 in Brazil, all countries where anachronism and modernization are at odds.

Inflation is only one aspect of economies caught between soaring demand and insufficient supply, a demand created not only by higher expectations but by the human avalanche which modern sanitation has released upon these countries—that is, by overpopulation. The traditional world of limited resources, such as that which Western Europe left behind after 1848, balanced demand and supply by dint of high mortality rates. These have now been pressed back with the result that in most parts of the world far more people stay alive than can be adequately fed.

History, said Voltaire, is only a pack of tricks that we play on the dead. How far, one may ask, is it a pack of tricks the dead play on us and of which we become aware as one hidden mine or firecracker after another goes off unexpectedly? At any rate, in the realm of overpopulation, many have tried to warn that we are advancing through a mine field. In 1933, a noted Australian scientist reporting to the Rockefeller Foundation on the results of campaigns against malaria, pellagra, and hookworm, remarked that "in 10 years the Foundation would be spending more money in dealing with the results of its successes than in dealing with disease itself." It took less than a decade for his prediction to prove correct.

Lower death rates in countries with high fertility rates, the introduction of industrial sanitation techniques in countries with an agricultural mentality and a lagging technology, meant that demographic changes which took centuries in the West were carried through in less than a decade in certain Asian or South American countries, far faster than the population could adjust to the conditions thus created. The continents least able to bear it find their population rising fastest. Asia, with 50 per cent of the world's population, has 11 per cent of its revenues; North America, with 7 per cent of the world's population, has 45 per cent of its revenues. In Ceylon, for instance, when DDT wiped out malaria after the Second World War, the death rate was almost halved in seven years (1945–52). This compounded a population explosion already set off by the control of other diseases so that the population of Ceylon, which had been growing about five per 1,000 at the end of the nineteenth century, was increasing at the rate of nearly 3 per cent by 1950. The population of many countries grows at an even faster rate: North Vietnam's at 3.6 per cent, the Philippines' at 3.7 per cent, Mexico's at 3.8 per cent, Venezuela's at 4 per cent. At 2 per cent a population doubles every 35 years, at 3.5 per cent every 20 years, at 4 per cent every 15 years. India, with a population nudging 550 million, is expected to double her numbers to over a billion within 25 years.

Men have multiplied for 200,000 years to reach the present three billion mark, but short of catastrophe they will double that in forty years. It was pointed out in 1967 that one human being in two once lived under Western rule, one in three lives in a Communist regime, one in four is Chinese, and two in three are short of food. Yet these hostile or demanding masses, which are no longer powerless or silent, which grow because of our medical advances, which ferment because of our transistors, cannot afford our comforts, our cars, our nourishment. Discontent can spread more rapidly than prosperity. As Nehru once remarked, "What is new in India is not misery, but the consciousness the Indian people has of it today and its impatience to be free of it." Yet, while an American farmer can feed forty-four persons, a Frenchman twelve, a Russian five, the average producer in an undeveloped country can generally feed only himself, at best one other person. It takes fifteen Indian cows to give as much milk as one American cow, seven acres of Vietnamese ricepaddy to harvest the same quantities as those produced by one acre in Australia.

Two-thirds of mankind are hungry all the time: which is why, when traveling in underdeveloped countries, one has the impression that people are always eating something. Undernourishment makes for the "apathetic" character of so many peoples, which needs to be stimulated with drugs, alcohol, or spices, the weak constitutions that leave them at the mercy of epidemics or contagious diseases, and the difficulty of extracting hard and sustained work from them. There is little reason to think that the hungry countries whose population by 2000 A.D. will be over 5 billion (four-fifths of the total foreseen for the whole earth) can be modernized fast enough to keep them from becoming a miserable, suffering, and explosive sore. The greater the population, the less likely their living standard is to improve. The less the living standard improves, the less chance there is of lowering the birth rate. The greater the population pressure on available resources, the fewer resources can be spared to increase productivity, to better living conditions, and to create possibilities and attitudes conducive to limiting the population.

All this has lent itself to much debate. One side argues that population is not outstripping resources, that the latter are simply being mismanaged by those who control them. The 27 million people in northeast Brazil would not suffer from hunger if the region's agronomical possibilities were rationally developed. Millions of Indians would not be left to starve or vegetate if dams controlled water, if one grain out of four was not left to be eaten by rats, monkeys, or sacred cows, if a fertilizer industry existed. Another side answers that the fault rests with lack of international solidarity, with failure to accept that everyman's death diminishes *me*. It does not explain, however, how such solidarity can be reconciled with national sovereignty and with its vagaries: preferring to invest resources in armaments, prestige schemes, heavy industry, or let them scatter in popular but unproductive directions, or again to serve vested interests, avoid needed reforms, let the rich become richer and the poor vegetate.

Overpopulation, of course, is a relative affair which comes down to the capacity to organize the population productively. Every West European country today supports a population which would have been unthinkable in the age of Malthus—let alone before him. It is possible to increase food production—as Israel has shown by raising its own by nearly 9 per cent a year for the past fifteen years. The area of the world's cultivated lands can be tripled, productivity greatly intensified, new aliments tapped in the seas and in laboratories. A fuller, more balanced diet might even cut down the demographic flood. Recent experiments suggest that hungry societies whose diet is deficient in proteins may be particularly prolific, while protein-rich diets reduce the fertility rate. It is possible also to bring the birth rate down to compensate the lower death rate, as Japan has shown since the war. It is possible to enlist science in solving the problems of subsistence, production, and population. But capital and technology depend on human attitudes and decisions. The goods and services men want, the price they are prepared to pay for them, the sacrifices to which they will consent, reflect their abstract and social values. Production and consumption answer not only hunger, but needs and formulas that change with every culture, so that the hungry and backward countries of the world challenge the industrialized West to aid them while accusing it of ignoring or destroying their peculiar culture and their values.

Between 1950 and 1963 the fifteen industrialized countries of the Organization for Economic Cooperation and Development contributed some 50 billion dollars in gifts and loans to less-developed countries. But a Danish report (*Le Monde,* October 6-7, 1968) indicates that in 1959 countries of the third world spent a total of 19 billion dollars on armaments (which are all imported, since none produces its own) while, during the same period they received from abroad only 4 billion in loans and subsidies to increase living standards. Though more recent figures are lacking, everything suggests that this disproportion has grown greater in the last decade. Once again, political decisions command material possibilities; cultural and ideological orientation affects and directs the uses of the means at a society's command; and, from this point of view, the most dramatic angles are oft, alas, obtuse.

It is quite possible that such dire prospects will melt away before developments that we no more suspect than Malthus could foresee the solution of the problems of his time. It is equally possible that populations will be limited by traditional means—famine, war, plagues, and self-destruction—and that the same great factors which set off the demographic avalanche may actually intervene to break it up. Historians are only the prophets of the past. The future, perhaps fortunately, remains obscure. "The wind bloweth where it listeth and Thou hearest the sound thereof, but canst not tell whence it cometh and whither it goeth" (John 3:8).

The Revolt of Youth

Another revolutionary development of the postwar era would be the changed social role of young people, a group whose significance we have seen growing over the past 150 years, but who had never done more than walk on the stage in obedience to the injunction that they were more properly seen than heard. The demographic explosion of the postwar years turned under-25's into near-majorities of their national populations, while prosperity afforded them unusual opportunities for self-definition and independence. Most important perhaps, where in earlier times the immense majority of young people, forced to work from an early age, merged into the surrounding adult world, today an ever-greater proportion of them was condemned or privileged to the relatively irresponsible isolation of higher education. Between 30 and 45 per cent of their age group in the United States, 15 or 20 per cent in the U.S.S.R., students accounted for 10 to 15 per cent of their coevals in other parts of the West, where they had seldom reached 1 per cent at the turn of the century and little more than that in 1940.

The growth of student numbers created a special "class," consuming high proportions of the national budget, responsible for a good part of the national market, a class which sociologists had not envisaged and whose particular originality lay in its constant renewal. By the late 1960's it was impossible to ignore the rise of a generation which had not known the war nor, often, the hard times that followed; for whom Hitler and Stalin were names and the past increasingly irrelevant in the light of a kaleidoscopic present.

Youth is the personification of permanent revolution, hardly significant when it lacks autonomy and self-consciousness, highly significant when it has both. Traditionally, the rebellion of youth had expressed itself in sporadic gestures of violence and nonconformity. In the postwar society, these were found increasingly impossible or unsatisfactory. Heresy is meaningful only against dogma, nonconformity against conformism; and these have lost their hold on a West that has abandoned the rigid standards and conventions of the past. Only in the bosom of Communist parties and extremist sects, last bastions of conservative conventions, can real heretics indulge their vocation and pay some kind of price. Elsewhere, tolerance eases their lot, indifference makes them irrelevant, generalization conventional. Their would-be unconventionality frustrated, their natural turbulence repressed in an increasingly orderly society, some young people began to break out in unexpectedly violent forms of nonconformism—provos in Holland, hippies in the United States, drug-taking—whose common basis was a rejection of the surrounding society.

The year 1968 would see this tension explode into rebellion all over Europe and all over the world. In Warsaw and Madrid, in Belgrade and Paris, in Prague and in Berlin (as in Rio, Tunis, and Tokyo), serious troubles threatened and sometimes shook men and regimes in power. Their origin was novel, for they broke out in times not of penury but of prosperity, and they reflected less economic grievances than ideological ones. In every case, their dynamo lay in the universities, in every case their original militants were students and intellectuals, most often very young.

The University: An Incubator

This youthful insurrection marked the gradual emancipation of another portion of society claiming its rights after workers and women had established theirs. The universities, tremendously expanded in the years since 1950, their population greater than ever before, played the role that factories had played in nineteenth-century working-class history. They concentrated young people, gave them a sense of difference from surrounding society, the confidence of numbers, and a base of operations.

708

Parisian policemen armed with helmets and shields against the rebelling students, May, 1968.

H. Roger-Viollet

Schools, but above all universities, taught the values the community claimed to respect and the techniques which society needed in order to operate and to expand. They also analyzed the communities in whose midst they rose, revealed how these failed to live up to their own principles, suggested values higher than those by whose application or whose breach they thrived. In itself, this was nothing new. Long before Socrates, thinking men must have threatened the routines and acceptances of their time. Thomas Hobbes, himself no mean iconoclast, found that "the core of rebellion [against his Stuart patrons] are the universities." Men, he suggested, are only too inclined to think well of their wits.* Once educated, they imagine they can run the country. Drawing the practical conclusions that many statesmen followed in centuries to come, one of Charles II's advisers suggested halving university admissions and cutting school intakes too.

Despite such views—sometimes put into practice—most twentieth-century universities continued to furnish a sanctuary for critics and heretics, a repository for every sort of idea, a kind of privileged haven and debating ground. This was particularly true in Western Europe and North America in the years after 1945 and, though far from affecting all students or all teachers, it had its effect both within and without university walls—though never as sharply evident as in 1968.

The revolt of youth against authority is, of course, a revolt against paternalism at every level, against the very notion of adult civilization and of adulthood itself. The demands voiced for abolition of examinations, for instance, reject not only an established test of social selection, but—as a writer in the Paris *Monde* put it in May, 1968—"the capital initiation rite of modern society," the rite of passage into "the adult's adulterated universe." What this manner of rebel seems to want is a kind of permanent adolescence not very different from the permanent revolution that Trotsky preached.

Revolt of youth against age, rejection of the old for new, has flourished particularly since the romantic tide of the nineteenth century. It has

* One hundred years later, Diderot's views on the university were no different: "That's where they teach the art of speaking before the art of thinking," he said, "that of expressing oneself well before having any ideas to express."

709

been alimented by disillusionment in the wake of revolutions (after 1815 or 1848) or of wars (1918, 1945) expected to usher in better days, and by the "modern" feeling that the old dates very quickly and that change is somehow good for its own sake. At the same time, prosperity and full employment diminished the dependency of young people on their elders, released ever more of them for longer periods of study or leisure, turned adolescence from a purgatory into an enjoyable condition, and one whose prolongation appears both feasible and desirable.

Sustained revolutionary action has ever been the province of the uncommitted: those who have not yet been integrated in society, who do not have to earn a living or cannot, who have not taken up or have been refused entry to a career. The reservoir of such people, once full of vagrants, unemployed, or social rejects, came to be found among the growing numbers of the young whose irresponsibility and uncommitment society or parents prolonged by their subsidies, and whose idealism was little diverted by concern for necessities of life.

Idealistic youth found plenty to criticize. "The international of the twenty-year olds," declared an Italian weekly in 1968, "shares the same ideological masters, brandishes the same flags, holds to the same ideas. They are disillusioned by a democracy often only formal, and they reject a socialism suspicious of intelligence." Democratic ideals, praised in both capitalist and communist countries, appear little in evidence as they look around them. Postwar European economies are planned and directed. Whether in Germany or France or Britain, half or more than half of capital investments are financed by the state. Created by revolution or imposed by conquest in the case of Communists, established or attempted by fiat in the Fascist dictatorships between the wars, collectivism now springs from the needs of large industrial units and corporations, from the calculations of modern industrial states, establishing everywhere its managers, its bureaucrats, and its planners. Like the modern industrial state, the organized parties of the Left have developed bureaucratic structures that both paralyze and conserve them. The power of the people gives way to the power of an elusive oligarchy.

The new industrial state, writes the American economist J. K. Galbraith in a book of that title, turns us into the servants of the machine we created. Economic objectives replace all other aspirations, and the ultimate question becomes what a man does to increase the gross national product. "If you own something," proclaims the advertising of a German bank, "you are something." It is such attitudes and such effects that the rebels spurn—forgetting that they had been quite typical of other societies too—and that they rise against. Petrels of a longed-for storm, they condemn the continued exploitation of the working classes, of underdeveloped countries, of outcast races, imperialist wars abroad or social injustice at home, but, above all, what they regard as an impersonal and inhuman power, a welfare state in which quantitative satisfactions stifle qualitative needs.

710

Many who felt this way found their justification in the works of a German philosopher who had taken refuge in the United States from Nazi persecution: Herbert Marcuse. Born in 1898, Marcuse's chief references are drawn, very appropriately, from the two main authorities of our time: Marx and Freud. For Freud, the history of man had always been the history of man's repressions, the tale of aimless animal drives transmuted into societal instincts, of the pleasure principle blindly seeking satisfaction transmuted into the reality principle. The drive for immediate personal gratification, Freud had taught, is culturally destructive. Sublimated, it creates civilization, art, a working and productive society.

For Marcuse, the impressive results of this process in the West have created an increasingly unsatisfactory situation. Man is in a position to achieve what Marcuse calls "the rational organization of the realm of necessity." But he lets himself be taken over by his means. Technology itself has taken on the appearance of a new necessity. "The instruments of productivity and progress, organized into a totalitarian system, determine not only the actual but also the possible utilizations." In his most explicit attack on this state of affairs, *One Dimensional Man*, Marcuse avers that "advanced industrial society is approaching the stage when continued progress would demand the radical subversion of the prevailing direction and organization of progress." Once agents of hopeful change, science, technology, democratic institutions, political emancipation, have turned into stabilizers. "The status quo defies all transcendence," digests all digressions, assimilates alternatives, contains all change but that which suits its limited ends, discourages those internal oppositions and criticisms which made for a healthy dialectic, in favor of a one-dimensional society with room only for one-dimensional men. Capital and labor, *bourgeoisie* and proletariat, Establishment and opposition, even the United States and Soviet Russia, no longer clash as agents of historical transformation; unhealthy fat has stifled the dialectic. As opposites are unified and qualitative change counteracted by common interest in preserving and improving what already exists, even affluence, freedom, tolerance, become the vehicles of a totalitarian universe where opposition, criticism, life itself are killed by kindness but killed nevertheless.[*]

Only sheer and total negation of the administered good life—the good in it as well as the bad—can counter the deadening forces, break through the illusions of advanced industrial society, reject the rules of a game rigged from the start, reopen the possibilities of real change, for better or for worse.

Fortunately, our technological successes, while stifling in their effects, have created the preconditions for abandoning or rejecting the restraints that made them possible, the repressions without which our conquest of nature (including our own) could not have been carried out. "The continued rule of the performance principle as the reality principle . . . has

---

[*] The quotations are from *One Dimensional Man* (1954), pp. 235, 255, 16, 17.

perhaps created the preconditions for a qualitatively different, non-repressive reality principle."* The struggle for existence no longer calls for a repressive organization of the instincts. Contemplation, enjoyment, acceptance of what the world has to offer, could now replace struggle and constraint. Repression and renunciation are presently being justified no longer by objective needs but for their own sake. They could be abandoned, and freedom, fantasy, transcendence, allowed to reign instead.

Not surprisingly, such views appealed to young intellectuals, to students, to all those who in every generation cannot but find fault with their world and time, and who will strive to replace it with something that is not just better but ultimately good.** Affluent heirs of an opulent culture, glutted with the wealth of their collective past, they proposed to reject it now for more sober fare, which, on examination, bears within it many ingredients of the past—not least romanticism—but unacknowledged.

The University: A Target

But if the universities appeared as breeding grounds of criticism and revolt, they soon became its targets.

> I turn my eyes to the Schools and Universities of Europe,
> Works of many Wheels I view, wheel without wheel, with cogs tyrannic
> Moving by compulsion each other: not as those in Eden, which
> Wheel within Wheel in freedom revolve in harmony and peace.

What William Blake had viewed better than a century and a half ago still seemed as real to his visionary successors, and to many who were not visionary at all. Numbers overwhelming facilities, classes overflowing lecture halls, professors invested with enormous authority, wielding autocratic powers over students they ignore, absentee teachers indifferent to their charges, courses irrelevant to subjects—let alone to life or work. Slow to change their ways, highly elitist and hierarchized, European universities suffered from institutional rigidity and from a kind of self-imposed isolation from the world around. In 1966, an academic conference held in France called them the last refuge of feudalism in Western Europe. Yet, as they sought to modernize themselves and follow in the footsteps of American universities, it was found that the "adjusted" university turned into a "knowledge factory," chiefly devoted to producing the "useful" knowledge required by society, industry, the military, to training its managers and indoctrinating its members.

The old schools of humanistic learning and culture have become mul-

---

* Herbert Marcuse, *Eros and Civilization* (1955), p. 129.

** Neither they nor Marcuse, however, could explain how the gifts of high productivity could be enjoyed while ignoring the discipline and restraints which maintain that productivity.

tiversities, dedicated to teaching not minorities but majorities, geared to mass production and mass consumption, increasingly structured, bureaucratized, and impersonal, like the rest of the world. Their academic staffs, in turn, have become the clerks of the modern world, furnishing its basic wisdom, the authority for its actions, the advice for its leaders. And, critics complain, just as the clergy had become the tamed, institutionalized servants of religious and secular institutions, so today university faculties have turned into just another kind of civil service: a bureaucracy of the intellect has succeeded a bureaucracy of the spirit.

In fact, things are more complicated. Universities are caught between growing demand for university education and growing reluctance of taxpayers to foot the costs this entailed; between the number of their students and the number of openings available to them on graduation; between growing expectations of students from faculty and growing preoccupations of a faculty increasingly involved in the surrounding world.

In Europe and elsewhere, universities displease the many they cannot accommodate and some of those who, having been accepted, are sent out with degrees but with no place to use them. And those who do not resent being ill-adapted to society's needs fear that they will become too well adapted to the one-dimensional standards of bureaucracy and technology. In other words, some want the university to adapt itself to modern life, while others blame it for being too well adjusted, reject the life it trains for as repressed, repressive, sordid, and mean, seek not integration into adult society but escape from its corrupting embrace, denounce in the same breath rotten liberals and "Stalinist blackguards." "The path of excess leads to wisdom," asserts a French student sticker. It would certainly lead to agitation throughout 1967, and particularly in 1968, when Europe's universities suddenly boiled over.

The trouble had started in 1967 at the Free University of Berlin, where students and a few of the younger faculty attacked inadequate and anachronistic structures particularly out of place in the most modern of German academic institutions. It spread to Italy in the winter, where students took a leaf out of the syndicalist notebook to occupy the faculties in great sit-in strikes; and to Spain, where the University of Madrid was officially closed for part of the academic year. It would culminate in France in the spring of 1968, where student revolt precipitated the strike of nearly ten million workers, clerks, and civil servants, and seemed about to topple the Fifth Republic. A generation which had known no war devised mini-conflicts to its measure by building barricades as symbolic as they were anachronistic. But, as Alexis de Tocqueville, the most perceptive observer of the revolution of 1848 once remarked, "in a rebellion as in a novel, the most difficult part to invent is the end."

Very soon, students realized that the changes they sought within the university structure had to be related to broader changes within the state itself. The teaching methods and the academic obstacle course which they critized, reflected the authoritarianism and the class barriers of surrounding society; the institutions of representative democracy outside the university gates were reproduced by student representative bodies, just as irrelevant to student realities, just as far removed from the needs of their electorate, just as absorbed in sterile political-party games.

Thus, from parochial claims, student movements progressed to a criticism of the university's function in society and then to criticism of society itself. In Berkeley, Paris, or Berlin they rejected the consumer society. In Madrid, Prague, and Belgrade they refused the yoke of police and censorship. In Warsaw and Moscow they criticized regimes which seem to organize production for penury. The points they raised were different; the dissatisfaction, the refusal, the same. Alienated by economic mechanisms that lead them to consume what they do not want, or by political mechanisms that force them to think and do what they do not want, they condemned both. They condemned the structures which, they fear, will swallow and use them, along with the institution that provides both a temporary refuge from the world outside and a conditioning agent for it. "We believe that the university is an essential element supporting society. We are convinced that the sole way of solving the problems at all levels is to take part in the destruction of the system" (*Le Monde,* May 29, 1968). Turning in the easiest direction first, they sawed off the branch on which they sat, smashed the bed of Procrustes, as the first gesture of rebellion against a fate they would not accept.

The fate which they rejected was not theirs alone, but that of the oppressed everywhere. "We think that the struggle of French workers and students is one with that of the peoples of Latin America," declared an Argentine admirer of the revolutionary guerrilla leader Che Guevara. Wherever possible, students connected their aspirations with those of black men, of the North Vietnamese, of the agricultural and industrial proletariat. The latter, long cast in the role of a progressive force, would be crucial to their ambitions . . . and their miscalculations. In Italy and Spain, in Germany and in France—where the greatest and most publicized outburst of spring, 1968, snowballed into near civil war—student rebels supported labor claims or, more often, spurred them on, striving to unite student and labor action.

The "revolution of 1968" was directed less against the consumer society (to which workers seek admittance and from which students profit) than against organized society, highly structured and bureaucratized both in East and West, in capitalist and socialist countries. Yet structures and administrations which flatten men also fatten them. Industrial societies cannot operate or expand without them. Their rejection by a utopian or anarchist Left is almost the counterpart of their rejection by a reactionary Right dreaming of a return to nature, of bygone nonexistent ages of happy peasants and artisans.

714

Che Guevara shortly before his death.

Furthermore, if student claims were largely ideological, those of labor remained steadfastly utilitarian. The students opposed both university and society, the workers sought material gains within the existing system. If the former were revolutionary, the latter were not.* The seeds of the "revolution's" failure lay in its irreconcilable aims, in the inner contradictions of a movement that sought to change men and had to use them as they were, which rejected industrial society but not the advantages it offered, which scorned the Communists and the unions as too conservative but could supply no alternative organization, and no slogans beyond those of romantic self-indulgence: "It is forbidden to forbid"; "The duty of every revolutionary is to make the revolution"; "Imagination has seized power"; or "Be realistic, demand the impossible."

The failure of such efforts in the West appeared to show that the conjunction between labor and youth was spurious. It indicated also that these—like other—fighters for a better world were more impressed by action than by thought. Paradoxical in intellectuals (or would-be intellectuals), this was reminiscent of other modern movements that preach and sometimes practice action for action's sake. And, indeed, those who affirm the primacy of action over thought make an important point. Reflection slows you down, often paralyzes. A search for motives, an examination of alternatives, a balancing of factors and of possible effects, prevents the decisive act. Action, on the other hand, carries its meaning (and reassurance) with it. Hence, Goethe's Doctor Faustus replaces *word* with *deed* in the old wisdom: "In the beginning was the act." Explanations and a search for meanings only too often hamper. Our activists have learned Faust's lesson, and that of the world around.

There was another lesson in the spring of revolution, if one looked hard enough. For the first time since 1848,** the actions of a few students had precipitated major changes in the political scene. The United States, France, Czechoslovakia, bore witness to the possibility that a few determined wills could sensibly affect the course of history. This would, in

* Moreover, from a worker's perspective, the students rioting in universities were like mice rioting in a cheese. And left extremism achieved the paradoxical result of enacting in reverse the class war that it preached, when lower-class police and gendarmes (and factory workers) turned on the privileged revolutionaries of the "upper" or educated classes.

** With the exception of 1956, when the Hungarian revolution also grew out of student and intellectual circles.

due course, color existing interpretations of political action and its possibilities. To understand just how, we must retrace our steps and recapitulate the fortunes of the revolutionary idea in the modern world.

The model of revolution that Karl Marx designed suggested that the most advanced nations would develop a technology and means of production so collectivized that workers would be able to take them over, eliminate private ownership, and, turning private property to public ends, turn productive processes to social ends. Lenin's success in Russia and the failure of communism in Germany and Italy suggested a variant model, according to which revolution could only succeed in technologically backward societies, where the government's means of defense could not operate and the causes of general dissatisfaction could be harnessed to social-revolutionary ends.

The experience of France in 1968, though limited, went far to revalidate Marx's original version. Where managers have taken over, where production depends on technocrats and society on bureaucrats, where private property has been depersonalized and the small property owner turned into a wage earner, corporate and state collectivization may be turned into a political fact by spontaneous revolution. The revolutionary struggle of a conscious minority may yet spread awareness of real democracy and turn formal democracy into real democracy, formal socialism into real socialism. This could apply as easily to Russia as to France. The depersonalized rule of privileged bureaucrats and managers who monopolize public force and public power, enjoying economic and social privileges at the people's expense, could be shown up for the fake it is and wrested from them in a great explosion of popular will.

Thus the theory. But now the theory referred to an experience. And if the experience seemed disillusioning, it would not discourage the revolutionaries bred in the ever-replenished reservoir of youth. As J. M. Keynes once noted of his own early years, youth is "an age when our beliefs influenced our behavior, a characteristic of the young which it is easy for the middle-aged to forget."

An Interim Report

If every man is not yet, or not quite, his own historian (as Carl Becker suggested), every age is: rewriting, reinterpreting history to fit its needs. That simply means that men, as always, turn to the past—as they do to the world around them—for answers to the questions that concern them here and now. The peculiar needs and formulas that change with every culture provide the sieve that retains experience, or lets it run through and down the drain. As the culture alters, so does the sense it seeks and finds in cultures and experiences of the past.

The twentieth century has proved an age of speed, an age in which the rate of physical movement which we have come to take for granted is paralleled by the acceleration of history and of change itself, the rapidly growing distance between us and the past, the realization that the experience of our grandparents may have been closer to that of Cardinal Mazarin than to our own. The universe has grown smaller but also larger. Larger because it was realized that the world is part of a galactic universe about 100,000 light years in diameter, itself but one of 100 million or so galaxies of about the same size, the nearest of them about 500 million light years away. The order of magnitude involved in this appears from the term "light year" itself, invented to cope with these astronomical distances and denoting the space which light, traveling at 186,000 miles per second, covers in one year.

In the last hundred years cultural changes such as these have come thick and fast, faster than man has ever known before. Under their bombardment the questions men have asked of history have altered too until, in certain cases, the history of a generation or of a decade has come to seem irrelevant to the next—let alone to peoples somewhere else. In this respect, all that the historian may hope to do is to record a passing point of view as honestly and as thoughtfully as he knows how: not to provide a chronicle of facts or cut a slice out of the pie of Truth, but to suggest plausible interpretations to his time and indicate to others who come later how his own age mirrored itself in its past.

This has now been done. For better or for worse the story of the last 600 years, beginning in the days when Europe became conscious of its forces and of itself, ending when its power to control the world collapsed, has been told. From where we stand it seems to be a whole, comprising (as we see it) a beginning, a middle, and—in 1945—an end. What follows after is not so much past as process: things still becoming, impossible to envision in perspective, to record in more than the most passing shape. A history of Europe written in the 1950's could only conclude with its decline and fall. A similar history written ten years later can dwell not only on fall but on recovery. And it is hard to tell what yet one more decade will add, but easy to insist that these things too will justify no more than mere conjecture.

The politics of Europe now, its trade, its industry, are part of the pattern of the world. This too is changing rapidly. Ten years ago it could be seen and told in terms of the great rivalry of the United States and the Soviet Union. Now this polar pattern shifts, as the forces of other continents come into play, as the dilemmas and hostilities that we have known in our small corner of the world are reproduced with world significance elsewhere. All we can say with any certainty is that .where, once, the struggles and rivalries of European powers echoed through the world, today they have been relegated to provincial states. France, Britain, Germany, may still go to war. But general war can only rise from decisions arrived at somewhere else.

Yet, paradoxically, the end of Western Europe's dominion of the world comes at a moment when the whole world has come to bear its mark. Attitudes, values, techniques, even ways of life, evolved in a few cities at the Western end of the Eurasian land mass prevail everywhere, even among their foes. And the superpowers, whether in Asia, in America, or in Eastern Europe, run on ideas and on a dynamism which Western men taught or imposed not so long ago.

The great peculiarity of European culture is that it developed the belief that fate "rests not in our stars but in our selves," that men, not superhuman powers, are a crucial part of their own destiny and that of others. The story of the last six centuries is the evolution and the assertion (sometimes in brutal, overweening, murderous ways) of humanism: respect for man and for his capacity to make himself great, forge his own destiny, free himself, and assert his personality on the world around. The price of such ambition is, sometimes, success. This, as Prometheus discovered, carries its discomforts. Most notable among them has been the need to adjust our lives and minds to the conditions that technological progress has created, the problems of abundance rather than scarcity and, possibly, of leisure rather than toil.

As long as human productivity remained constant—that is, as far back as recorded history goes—wealth that went beyond the most modest limits could arise only from the exploitation and deprivation of others. The great novelty of our times is that it is possible to enrich *all* members of a given society by successive improvements in the techniques, the instruments, and the organization of labor, that the wealth thus produced can furnish the means of yet further developments, and that this process can be both rapid and indefinite. Of course, this does not happen everywhere or affect everybody, but the phenomenon is sufficiently widespread to have a serious impact on modern mentalities and practices. What St. Paul and Karl Marx once cited as a law of nature—the obligation or the right to work—is being mitigated, affected by the social virtues of consumption, disrupting the value systems of societies and men conditioned by the experience of ages. Free time becomes a problem: in literature, in the films of Fellini and Antonioni, in the discourse of politicians and social critics. Education, once designed to teach skills, is being redesigned in part to train men and women for leisure.

But, while the material reality in industrially developed societies changes, old-established attitudes persist—not least the belief in the virtue of toil ("He who works prays"). Like anesthetics or contraceptives, material plenty seems to go counter to the higher will of nature. Taking man out from the rule of necessity appears a kind of blasphemy, not only against God who ordered us to make our living by the sweat of our brow, but against the wisdom of centuries that connected virtue with effort, with suffering, and repression of the instincts. As misery decreased, as famines and plagues disappeared, as material well-being spread, moralists and social critics thought they discerned the ebbing of faith and higher values too. Material abundance brought spiritual decadence. Bread and bathrooms for all wore down the tragic sense of life. Comfort made placid. In 1966, Michael Harrington's *Accidental Century* analyzed the reactions to this aspect of modernity, all the way from Dostoevski and Nietzsche to Ortega y Gasset and T. S. Eliot. Harrington quotes Robinson Jeffers' attack on "the new abundance:"

> Blind war compared to this kind of life
> Has nobility, famine has dignity.

Here was a kind of fat boy's revolt: an elitism of the sated. With plague and famine no longer endemic in the West, those who were spared them could afford to think them a spiritual advantage, regret the loss of moral fiber that went with great trials, consider the ages when they still endured to have been more vital and fine than ours. And even though over most of the world hunger persisted, and even when men proved that terror and tragedy had hardly relaxed their grip, poets and thinkers continued to feel that the society they lived in was barren and the lives they lived in it absurd. That was in part, at least, because they had the energy and leisure to spend on critical thought. In part because they knew that many lacked their advantages, hence felt embarrassed and guilt-ridden about the false peace and comfort permitting some to write or appreciate art while others suffered and died. In part, however, also because—as more men came to die in bed rather than through some irrational catastrophe—a certain tension had gone out of life. Man has gone far toward mastering the irrationality of nature. He is still prey to irrationalities of his own.

Even without this, the problems he must face suffice to make him uneasy. The speed of jets and rockets is reproduced in the speed of social and technological change: the gap between the evolution and the application of scientific theories narrows, the time span shortens between laboratory, factory, and general use, the results of technological progress are in all hands within years where once they could have taken centuries, are enjoyed quickly and widely, cast off just as quickly, replaced by fresh triumphs of skill and imagination fated like them to early obsolescence. Our mental equipment, like that of our daily lives, grows out of date before we have time to die. Education for living is not the once-for-all training that it used to be, but an awkward, never-ending readjustment to social and material activities on a stage where the scenery, the rules, even the language of the play, are in constant motion.

Our cities, the core of our civilization, alter. The modern metropolis is a place whose scale makes it different in kind from those the past world knew. Ancient Rome had a million inhabitants, but they could still walk from one part of the city to another, or out into the countryside. Today, even a car may take hours to achieve such a feat. By the end of the century, most people of the world may live in still vaster metropolitan complexes, ranging from 10 to 20 million and covering areas wider than those that appall us now.

The modern industrial system changes too. Industry has come a long way from the free enterprise to which it pays lip service, dominated by tremendous corporations dedicated to planning their activities and organizing relations between one another, between themselves and government, themselves and organized labor, rather like states in international affairs. Union contracts eliminate the uncertainties of the free labor market. Government intervention eliminates fears of collapsing demand. Publicity and market research eliminate uncertainty and condition the consumers. Planning restricts the free play of the economy to safe limits, that is, narrow ones. Problems like those of transport, communications, or urban land development cannot be left to individual initiative: road traffic or air traffic, for example, *have* to be planned on a very large scale. The development of backward areas or social groups will not occur by itself: industry, for instance, tends to locate where markets and facilities are most developed, and incentives have to be artificially provided to encourage it to settle somewhere else.

In such a situation, where scale introduces a difference of kind rather than degree, the whole tends to overshadow the part in ways that a world where everything was man-size could hardly have imagined. The tendency toward abstraction that we can see in economics and arts, in the nature of our currency, the shape of furniture, or the issues of political debate, appears in every other aspect of a life in which nations or classes take precedence over their individual members, entities or concepts tend to be more real and certainly more important than people, statistics take the place of a reality that outruns our capacity to grasp it. In other words, means become ends at every level, taking on a life of their own until even wars and revolutions count more than any purpose which they may be held to serve. The impersonality of abstractions helps to explain the facility of modern mass murder, itself a simpler and less obtrusive operation than leaving people workless or letting them starve to death.

Within this world, once-solid institutions are giving way. Society, which briefly visualized itself as a community of people similar in attitudes and values and objectives, has had to accept itself as a much looser conjunction of people with common habits and rules but whose relations are close rather because they live together than because of a deliberate and sustained choice: conscripts in the same company rather than partners in a marriage. The atoms of social reality, on which society's superstructure rose, disintegrate in the reactors of social and economic change. Family, age, experience, knowledge itself, crumble into apparent irrelevance. Thus, we have seen that the old, through most of history, had an important function. They had survived, hence were a rarity; also a source of wisdom (knowledge, memory) not otherwise available, and possibly of power—controlling property or authority for which others had to wait their turn. Today their survival is hardly an achievement, more a burden; their knowledge is available to all and, anyway, out-dated: property and authority spread far more widely. The old are more distinguished by their needs than by their contributions.

Similarly, the family household in which most people lived was also the basic social unit of production. People had to work together in order to survive. No wonder they stayed together. The young were the insurance of the old, the old at times the reassurance of the young. In modern urban society this is no longer so. The family consumes but it does not produce: it has lost a sense of necessity, it has lost its focus and it is fast disappearing except as a way station to emancipation. Even the ancient rites of breaking bread together, perpetuated in the family meal, decay and wane. Families that had eaten from a common dish first learned to dine round a common table, before even this commensality declined to snacks, to meals taken on the run, and the communal ceremony turned to the bare gesture of feeding.

Along with unifying facts or rituals there also wanes the old sense of individual responsibility, affected by the eruption of chance into a world of will, of self into a world of social duty. Politics, which was the luxury of an elite, has become the condition of men's lives, the arena where fundamental decisions are taken in societies where everything has to be decided afresh all the time. Even so, most groups and individuals are indifferent to politics until dissatisfaction brings them into it; political activity is chiefly the expression of sectional or fractional dissatisfactions. This can mean that politics serves as a safety valve and echo chamber of social tensions, a valve that some regimes know how to turn on and off, while diverting outward the tension it alleviates or easing it by the judicious use of bread and circuses.

Responsibility to God, then to the city or the state, are gone as comprehensible and accepted choices (at least for most men). There are more duties but fewer responsibilities. First adults, then adolescents, have drawn the conclusions of a situation in which they find themselves, affluent but ineffective, able to assert themselves largely in games, illusions, fantasies, while real decisions are made beyond their ken. The modern world is, by contemporary definition, a place where not production but services are economically predominant. Of all these the most important are those that furnish packaged irresponsibility: entertainment, drugs, alcohol, the vehicles of vicarious experience and of escape from reality—that is, from morality, which is about how to come to terms with reality, not abandon it.

The tensions of this kind of living have lent themselves to a great deal of talk, either in sorrow or in anger, while its advantages have attracted far less comment. It is a fact that what has been called the open society in which we live is an unstable, impermanent succession of situations and arrangements that make many men terribly uneasy. Perhaps because they know that the competition on which it is based means elimination, that the competence which is its norm means selection, that

721

the specialization which is its core means eventual obsolescence. More likely, though, because they do not know their place in a world where the very notion of a "place" is either transitory or anachronistic. Once upon a time the effective unit of production and of action was, by our standards, very small: the family or clan. It could not easily be larger, since large groups could not be fed or moved or controlled with any ease, so that cities or armies were small, and self-assertion or defense did not require great numbers. This changed, as means of communication improved and possibilities of organized production and control improved with them. The scale of states grew, nation states appeared, regional structures lost their independence, and men forfeited the power to operate within the accessible confines of small-scale hierarchies. They found some reassurance in transferring their ideological allegiance to the nation which now superseded kinship as a means of identification. Irrelevant in the mass, men discovered vicarious relevance for themselves as members of the nation which was the effective working unit of a larger world and, within it, of various groups linked by more or less abstract ideologies, like political parties. The more impotent people felt as individuals, the more they stressed their importance as members of a group. Now that the nation is being superseded by supranational entities, while the scale of politico-economic effectiveness increases, men have to adjust again, adopt some other notion that will alleviate their impotence and give them meaning.

Technology has outrun the world's ability to cope with its advances. Much of mankind reacts with a nostalgia often amounting to aggressive longing for what is past and lost. This easily leads to falsification; to pretending that what is, is not, because we wish it different; to the substitution of delusive meanings for a straightforward look at what lies around.* The crackpot creeds that flourish in our day are evidence of the helplessness that many feel about the possibility of acting sensibly in a world where, like little children, they find effectiveness far beyond their grasp. They may well represent attempts to adjust to new situations, nets to catch men and organize them in some way, at a level they find comprehensible and at which they can feel effective. There is a tension here between the demands of growing scale which call for commensurate ideologies and those of individuals dwarfed and dismayed by the process. On one hand a tendency to the particularism in which reality remains accessible if, sometimes, unreal; on the other the need to transcend the sense of helplessness and borrow power from identification with a yet wider solidarity.

---

* It also leads to a running fight between two rival cultures, rather than an attempt to reconcile them and come to terms with their implications. Or to the kind of bitter detachment that a contemporary of Jonathan Swift expressed nearly 250 years ago: "For my part," wrote Lady Mary Wortley Montagu, "as it is my establish'd Opinion that this Globe of ours is no better than a Holland Cheese and the Walkers about in it Mites, I possess my Mind in patience, let what will happen, and should feel tolerably easy though a great Rat came and eat halfe of it up."

The problem modern people face is not lack of freedom, for they are freer of their biological trammels than ever in the history of mankind. The problem is how to apply their power and their knowledge without abandoning or denying the very capacities that increased them so. This brings us back, however reluctantly, to politics, which are, as Napoleon once said to Goethe, the fatality and also the tragedy of our time, because they reveal in the most public and dramatic fashion the fatal gap between what one wishes, what one says, what one does, and what eventually happens.

There is—there has always been—something strange about the way we look at history. We live on the conquests of our mind, yet gaze fascinated upon the glamorous catastrophes produced by our passions. Out of the past, we cherish less the constructive than the destructive: wars, murder, mayhem, the battered abysses on whose rim we still teeter today. Lord Macaulay remarked that times which are exciting to write about are not good to live in. We are in a position to confirm this. Surgeons have learned to replace vital organs; biologists synthesize life artificially in test tubes and prepare to affect the genes which control our physique and, perhaps, our personality; bioculture can affect not only environment, but life: manipulate it and preserve it. It cannot govern it. Nothing fails like success.

Yet, as Einstein once said: "The most extraordinary thing is that the world certainly has a meaning." Perhaps that meaning is the one with which we endow it: like the Indian sage who had the gods whose images watched over the sacrificial tables of the temples replaced by mirrors. Thus, man's suggestions are more important than his certainties and his questions mean far more than the answers he may hazard. But even the value of questions—like that of sincerity—lies not in themselves (as some seem to believe), but in what they may reveal.

It is reassuring and convenient to pretend that, in the end, nothing really changes very much except appearances. Human nature remains much the same. Soviet Russia carries on the work and methods of Tsarist Russia, as the Fifth French Republic continues the evolution of the Fourth. And yet, in fact, after evolution or revolution, reconstruction or stabilization, nothing is quite the same, nothing is quite finished, nothing is quite set. The social changes that we mark with suspicion or with satisfaction bear in themselves further awarenesses, dissatisfactions, claims, and emancipations. The dialectic of history does not consent to halt, nor lend itself to more than limited foresight—let alone prophecy. The only thing that one can say for sure is that however fair the moment, no Doctor Faustus can stay its passing. That men will go on being born, suffering, and dying. And that this—men, the things they do, they think, they feel and say—will be the stuff of history as long as there are men and as long as they continue to invent themselves.

E quindi uscimmo a riveder le stelle.

GENEALOGICAL
TABLES

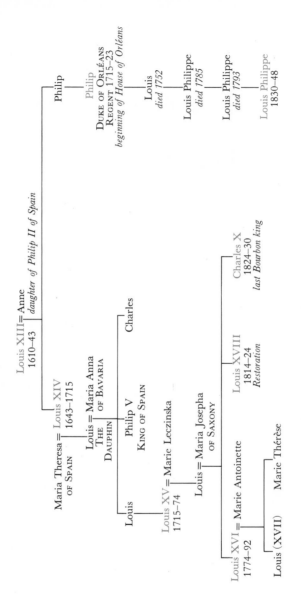

THE FRENCH SUCCESSION • 1610–1848

(House of **Bourbon**)

Louis XIII = Anne
1610–43 *daughter of Philip II of Spain*

Maria Theresa = Louis XIV   Philip
OF SPAIN   1643–1715

Louis = Maria Anna   Philip
THE   OF BAVARIA   DUKE OF ORLÉANS
DAUPHIN   REGENT 1715–23
                          beginning of House of Orléans

Philip V   Charles   Louis
KING OF SPAIN   *died 1752*

Louis   Louis Philippe
                                   died 1785

Louis XV = Marie Leczinska   Louis Philippe
1715–74   *died 1793*

Louis = Maria Josepha   Louis Philippe
        OF SAXONY   1830–48

Louis XVI = Marie Antoinette   Louis XVIII   Charles X
1774–92   1814–24   1824–30
                               Restoration   *last Bourbon king*

Marie Thérèse

Louis (XVII)

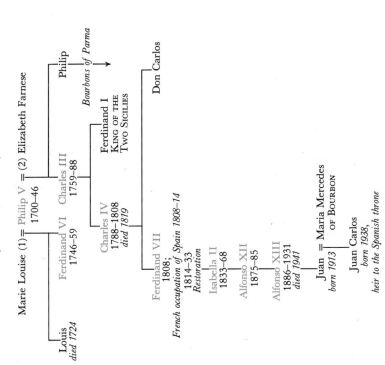

THE SPANISH SUCCESSION • 1700–1972
(House of **Bourbon**)

Marie Louise (1) = Philip V = (2) Elizabeth Farnese
                      1700–46

Louis
died 1724

Ferdinand VI
1746–59

Charles III
1759–88

Philip

Bourbons of Parma

Charles IV
1788–1808
died 1819

Ferdinand I
KING OF THE
TWO SICILIES

Don Carlos

Ferdinand VII
1808;
French occupation of Spain 1808–14
1814–33
Restoration

Isabella II
1833–68

Alfonso XII
1875–85

Alfonso XIII
1886–1931
died 1941

Juan = Maria Mercedes
born 1913   OF BOURBON

Juan Carlos
born 1938,
heir to the Spanish throne

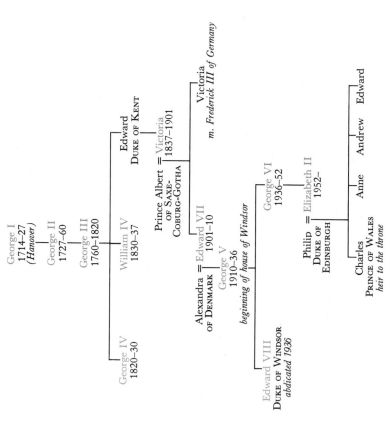

THE ENGLISH SUCCESSION • 1714–1972

George I
1714–27
(*Hanover*)

George II
1727–60

George III
1760–1820

George IV
1820–30

William IV
1830–37

Edward
DUKE OF KENT

Prince Albert = Victoria
OF SAXE-   1837–1901
COBURG-GOTHA

Victoria
m. Frederick III of Germany

Alexandra = Edward VII
OF DENMARK   1901–10

George V
1910–36
beginning of house of Windsor

Edward VIII
DUKE OF WINDSOR
abdicated 1936

George VI
1936–52

Philip = Elizabeth II
DUKE OF   1952–
EDINBURGH

Charles
PRINCE OF WALES
heir to the throne

Anne   Andrew   Edward

THE HOUSE OF HABSBURG • 1619–1918
(Holy Roman Emperors in blue)

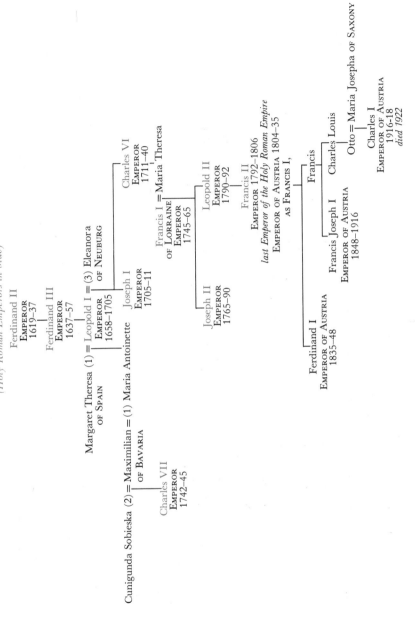

Ferdinand II
EMPEROR
1619–37

Ferdinand III
EMPEROR
1637–57

Margaret Theresa (1) = Leopold I = (3) Eleanora
OF SPAIN   **EMPEROR**   OF NEUBURG
        1658–1705

Cunigunda Sobieska (2) = Maximilian = (1) Maria Antoinette
           OF BAVARIA

Charles VII
EMPEROR
1742–45

Joseph I
EMPEROR
1705–11

Charles VI
EMPEROR
1711–40

Francis I = Maria Theresa
of LORRAINE
EMPEROR
1745–65

Joseph II
EMPEROR
1765–90

Leopold II
EMPEROR
1790–92

Francis II
EMPEROR 1792–1806
last Emperor of the Holy Roman Empire
EMPEROR OF AUSTRIA 1804–35
AS FRANCIS I,

Ferdinand I
EMPEROR OF AUSTRIA
1835–48

Francis

Francis Joseph I
EMPEROR OF AUSTRIA
1848–1916

Charles Louis

Otto = Maria Josepha OF SAXONY

Charles I
EMPEROR OF AUSTRIA
1916–18
died 1922

THE HOUSE OF BONAPARTE

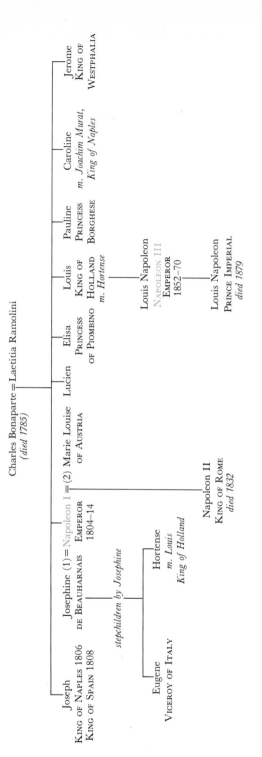

THE HOUSE OF HOHENZOLLERN • 1619-1918

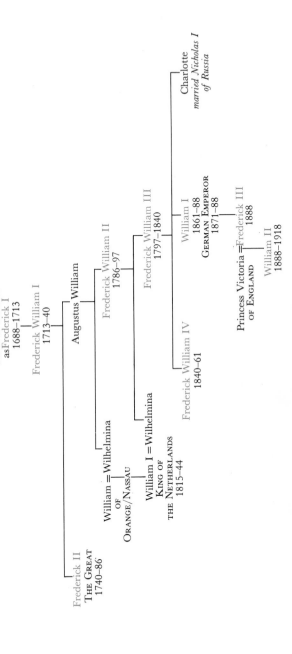

George William
ELECTOR OF BRANDENBURG
1619–40
descendant of Frederick I Hohenzollern, Elector 1415–40

Frederick William
THE GREAT ELECTOR
1640–88

Frederick II
KING OF PRUSSIA
asFrederick I
1688–1713

Frederick William I
1713–40

Frederick II
THE GREAT
1740–86

Augustus William

William = Wilhelmina
OF
ORANGE/NASSAU

Frederick William II
1786–97

William I = Wilhelmina
KING OF
THE NETHERLANDS
1815–44

Frederick William III
1797–1840

Frederick William IV
1840–61

William I
1861–88
GERMAN EMPEROR
1871–88

Charlotte
*married Nicholas I
of Russia*

Princess Victoria =Frederick III
OF ENGLAND   1888

William II
1888–1918

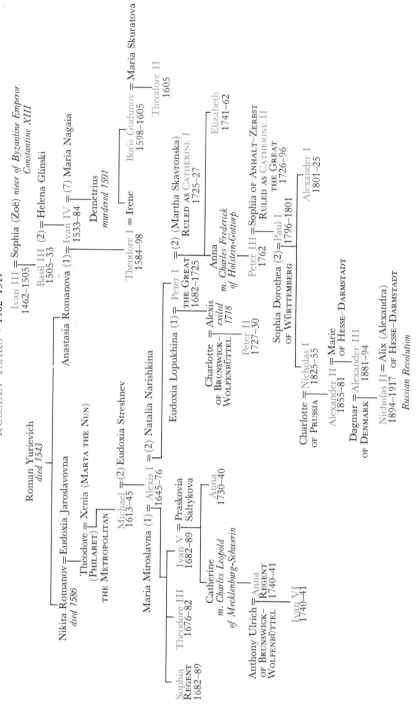

RUSSIAN TSARS • 1462–1917

Ivan III = Sophia (Zoë) *niece of Byzantine Emperor*
1462–1505 *Constantine XIII*

Basil III (2) = Helena Glinski
1505–33

Roman Yurievich
died 1543

Anastasia Romanova (1) = Ivan IV = (7) Maria Nagaia
1533–84

Demetrius
murdered 1591

Theodore I = Irene
1584–98

Boris Gudunov = Maria Skuratova
1598–1605

Theodore II
1605

Nikita Romanov = Eudoxia Jaroslavovna
died 1586

Theodore = Xenia (MARTA THE NUN)
(PHILARET)
THE METROPOLITAN

Michael = (2) Eudoxia Streshnev
1613–45

Maria Miroslavna (1) = Alexis I = (2) Natalia Narishkina
1645–76

Eudoxia Lopukhina (1) = Peter I = (2) (Martha Skavronska)
THE GREAT   RULED AS CATHERINE I
1682–1725   1725–27

Ivan V = Praskovia
1682–89 Saltykova

Anna
1730–40

Charlotte = Alexis
OF BRUNSWICK– *exiled*
WOLFENBÜTTEL *1718*

Peter II
1727–30

Anna
m. Charles Frederick
of Holstein-Gottorp

Peter III = Sophia of ANHALT–ZERBST
1762   RULED AS CATHERINE II
          THE GREAT
          1726–96

Elizabeth
1741–62

Sophia Dorothea (2) = Paul I
OF WÜRTTEMBERG 1796–1801

Alexander I
1801–25

Theodore III
1676–82

Catherine
m. Charles Leopold
of Mecklenburg-Schwerin

Sophia
REGENT
1682–89

Anthony Ulrich = Anna
OF BRUNSWICK– REGENT
WOLFENBÜTTEL 1740–41

Ivan VI
1740–41

Charlotte = Nicholas I
OF PRUSSIA 1825–55

Alexander II = Marie
1855–81   OF HESSE–DARMSTADT

Dagmar = Alexander III
OF DENMARK 1881–94

Nicholas II = Alix (Alexandra)
1894–1917 OF HESSE–DARMSTADT

Russian Revolution

BIBLIOGRAPHY

General works

It would be useless to list all the good books concerned with the general problems of European history. The few that follow provide sound points of relevance and suggestions for further study. An asterisk (*) indicates that the book is available in paperback.

*Carlo Cipolla, *Economic History of World Population* (1962) (Penguin) and B. H. Slicher van Bath, *Agrarian History of Western Europe, A.D. 500–1850* (1963) are excellent accounts of economic history. See also Shepard B. Clough and C. W. Cole, *Economic History of Europe*, 3rd ed. (1952). *John U. Nef has given us a good general survey in *Western Civilization Since the Renaissance: Peace, War, Industry and the Arts* (1963) (Harper Torchbook) and a fresh point of view in his essay *War and Human Progress* (1950) (Norton). Since the present book is much concerned with intellectual history, the following works may prove useful: Bertrand Russell, *History of Western Philosophy and Its Connection with Political and Social Circumstances from the Earliest Times to the Present Day* (1945); Franklin L. Baumer, ed., *Main Currents of Western Thought*, rev. ed. (1964); *Jacob Bronowski and Bruce Mazlish, *The Western Intellectual Tradition: From Leonardo to Hegel* (1960) (Harper Torchbook); Crane Brinton, *Ideas and Men: The Story of Western Thought* (1963); and Hugo Leichtentritt, *Music, History, and Ideas* (1950). Political ideas may be explored further through George Sabine's classic, *History of Political Theory* (1937) and John Bowle, *Western Political Thought: An Historical Introduction from the Origins to Rousseau* (1948). In the realm of the plastic arts, *Arnold Hauser's *Social History of Art*, 4 vols. (1951) (Vintage) is a suggestive reflection of the dialectical materialist approach, best read in conjunction with the critique of E. H. Gombrich, in his *Meditations on a Hobby Horse and Other Essays* (1963). The latter's *Story of Art* (1956) (Praeger) is probably the best existing treatment of art history in a social and intellectual context. On a simpler level there is a good revised edition of William Fleming, *Arts and Ideas* (1966).

Certain series maintain a high standard of excellence. One may turn to them with confidence for basic facts or thought-provoking interpretation. Thus *The New Cambridge Modern History*, most of whose fourteen volumes are already in print, while hardly a bedside book, is convenient, informative, and readily accessible. So is the Cambridge Economic History of Europe, whose sixth volume, in two parts, edited by H. J. Habakkuk with M. M. Postan (1965), is entitled *The Industrial Revolutions and After*. Although a trifle dated and still incomplete, the volumes of the Rise of Modern Europe series, edited by William L. Langer, are learned, readable, and provide handy bibliographies. *The Norton History of Modern Europe series, Felix Gilbert, General Editor, 6 vols. (1970) also maintains a high standard of excellence. The best sources of bibliographical information are the two Clio series published by the Presses Universitaires de France: the older in the 1930's (revised after the Second World War); the new—Nouvelle Clio—in the 1960's, comprising more volumes and much up-to-date data and discussion of work in progress.

The French publishing house of Albin Michel publishes two series inspired by the school of Annales, which has done more than any other to enrich the study of history in the past half-century: L'Evolution de l'Humanité, founded by Henri Berr, and Destin du Monde, directed first by Lucien Febvre and after his death by Fernand Braudel. The volumes of the latter are sumptuously illustrated, as are those in the Histoire Générale de la Civilisation, directed by Maurice Crouzet, and the less expensive volumes of the History of European Civilization, edited by Geoffrey Barraclough. Lastly, an impressive series—Arts, Idées, Histoire—published by the Swiss publisher Skira, sets out to link art and architecture to the tendencies and atmosphere of particular epochs.

When all is said and done, historical narrative or interpretation cannot by itself come as close to reality as the documentations of the time, which may be found in many good collections of readings but, above all, in contemporary works like *Chaucer's *Canterbury Tales,* *Cervantes' *Don Quixote,* *Grimmelshausen's *Simplicissimus,* *Goethe's *Werther,* *Stendhal's *The Red and the Black,* *Flaubert's *Sentimental Education,* *R. M. du Gard's *Jean Barois,* or *Simone de Beauvoir's *The Mandarins.* Each in its own way recaptures and reflects attitudes, problems, and atmosphere peculiar to its own place and time. There are many similar works: too many to list but generally revealing, the most accessible dating from the last two hundred years, when novelists began to hold up more or less distorting mirrors to society.

Novelists have also contributed imaginative reconstructions of historical situations, and some of these reveal far more than any textbook. *Helen Waddell's *Peter Abelard* (1933) (Compass) or *H. F. M. Prescott's *Man on a Donkey* (1952) (Ballantine; Collier) are splendid reconstructions of the living past by important scholars. More straightforwardly combining use and enjoyment are the works of men like Alfred Duggan, Maurice Denon, and C. S. Forester. Unfortunately, some of the great practitioners of the art have concentrated on portions of history preceding the period we are studying, but Mary Renault, Robert Graves, Marguerite Yourcenar, and Frans G. Bengtsson can be read with pleasure and profit, whatever their immediate relevance.

PART I

An Age of Revolution

For general information regarding European history during the eighteenth century the following works are recommended: Albert Sorel, *Europe under the Old Regime* (1947); *Walter L. Dorn, *Competition for Empire, 1740–1763* (1940) (Harper); *Leo Gershoy, *From Despotism to Revolution, 1763–1789* (1944) (Harper); *Matthew S. Anderson, *Eighteenth-Century Europe, 1713–1789* (1966) (Oxford); *Leonard Krieger, *Kings and Philosophers, 1689–1789* (1970) (Norton); and *Charles Breunig, *The Age of Revolution and Reaction, 1789–1850* (1970) (Norton). The diplomatic problems of this period are discussed briefly in Arthur H. Buffinton, *The Second Hundred Years War, 1689–1815* (1929) and at greater length in Robert B. Mowat, *A History of European Diplomacy 1451–1789* (1928) and Arthur Hassall, *The Balance of Power, 1715–89,* 5th ed. (1960).

The world-wide revolutionary tendencies and implications of the age have been traced by *R. R. Palmer in his *Age of the Democratic Revolution, 1760–1800,* 2 vols. (1959–1964) (Princeton). *J. Christopher Herold, ed., *The Horizon Book of the Age of Napoleon* (1963) (Dell) teases both eye and mind. The Congress of Vienna and its aftermath may be followed in *Harold G. Nicolson, *Congress of Vienna: A Study in Allied Unity, 1812–1822* (1946) (Compass); *Guglielmo Ferrero, *The Reconstruction of Europe: Talleyrand and the Congress of Vienna, 1814–1815* (1941) (Norton); G. de Bertier de Sauvigny, ed., *France and the European Alliance, 1816–1821* (1958); Hans G. Schenk, *The Aftermath of the Napoleonic Wars* (1947); and *L. C. B. Seaman, *From Vienna to Versailles* (1956) (Harper). For the period after 1789 see *E. J. Hobsbawm,

The Age of Revolution: Europe from 1789 to 1848 (1969) (Mentor); Irene Collins, *The Age of Progress: A Survey of European History from 1789 to 1870* (1964); *Jacques Droz, *Europe Between Revolutions, 1815–1848* (1968) (Harper Torchbook); and *J. L. Talmon, *Romanticism and Revolt* (1967) (Harcourt, Brace & World)—this last highly speculative. George T. Romani's study, *The Neapolitan Revolution of 1820–1821* (1950) shows the reasons for its failure which can be applied to other contemporary rebellions. *Benedetto Croce's *History of Europe in the Nineteenth Century* (Harcourt, Brace & World) (1933) remains an interesting interpretation of the period, although the information is a bit dated. *Frederick B. Artz, *Reaction and Revolution, 1815–1832* (1935) (Harper); *Arthur J. May, *The Age of Metternich, 1814–1848*, rev. ed. (1964) (Holt, Rinehart & Winston); and John W. Dodds, *The Age of Paradox: A Biography of England 1841–1851* (1952) deal with various aspects of European history during the first half of the nineteenth century. As far as diplomacy is concerned, René Albrecht-Carrié's *A Diplomatic History of Europe since the Congress of Vienna* (1958) is still the best work.

For the revolutions of 1848 see François Fejto, ed., *The Opening of an Era: 1848* (1950); Priscilla Robertson, *The Revolutions of 1848, A Social History* (1952) (Princeton); *Lewis B. Namier, *1848: The Revolution of the Intellectuals* (1946) (Anchor); Reuben J. Rath, *The Viennese Revolution of 1848* (1957); Joseph Redlich, *Emperor Francis Joseph of Austria* (1929); Jerome Blum, *Noble Landowners and Agriculture in Austria, 1815–1848* (1948); *Cecil B. Woodham-Smith, *The Great Hunger: Ireland, 1845–1849* (1963) (Signet); and E. E. Y. Hales, *Pio Nono* (1954).

The World and Its Horizons

Industrial Revolution   A general survey has been given by *T. S. Ashton, *The Industrial Revolution, 1760–1830* (1948) (Oxford) and *Paul Mantoux, *The Industrial Revolution in the Eighteenth Century* (1937) (Harper Torchbook). For particular aspects see William O. Henderson, *Britain and Industrial Europe, 1750–1870* (1954) and *Philip A. M. Taylor, ed., *The Industrial Revolution in Britain: Triumph or Disaster?* (1958) (Heath). E. E. Lampard, *Industrial Revolution: Interpretations and Perspectives* (1957) is brief but illuminating; *W. W. Rostow, *The Stages of Economic Growth* (1960) (Cambridge) is controversial but suggestive. See also *John H. Clapham, *The Economic Development of France and Germany, 1815–1914*, 4th ed. (1937) (Cambridge); Abbott P. Usher, *A History of Mechanical Inventions*, rev. ed. (1954); and Arthur L. Dunham, *The Industrial Revolution in France* (1955).

Agricultural Revolution   For agrarian changes, see N. S. B. Gras, *A History of Agriculture in Europe and America*, 2nd ed. (1940) and M. Augé-Laribé, *La Révolution Agricole* (1955). There are many works on the general economic history of this period. Among the more useful are Witt Bowden, Michael Karpovich, and Abbott P. Usher, *An Economic History of Europe since 1750* (1937); A. Philip, *Histoire des faits économiques et sociaux de 1800 à nos jours* (1964); Rondo E. Cameron, *France and the Economic Development of Europe, 1800–1914* (1961); *Carlo Cipolla, *The Economic History of World Population, 1750–1918* (1962) (Penguin); *Karl Polanyi, *The Great Transformation, 1750–1918* (1957) (Beacon); and Daniel T. Jack, *Studies in Economic Warfare, 1789–1815* (1941).

Society and Societies   The history of social classes could be approached through M. C. Buer's *Health, Wealth and Population in the Early Days of the Industrial Revolution* (1968). For the nobility see especially *Albert Goodwin, *The Euro-*

pean Nobility in the Eighteenth Century (1953) (Harper Torchbook); Esmé C. Wingfield-Stratford, *The Squire and His Relations* (1956); *Franklin L. Ford, *Robe and Sword: The Regrouping of the French Aristocracy after Louis XIV* (1953) (Harper Torchbook); Robert Forster, *The Nobility of Toulouse in the Eighteenth Century* (1960); and M. Reinhard, "Elite et noblesse dans le seconde moitié du 18ᵉ siècle," in *Revue d'histoire moderne et contemporaine,* Vol. III, January, 1957. *Elinor G. Barber, *The Bourgeoisie in 18th Century France* (1955) (Princeton) is excellent. *Gwyn A. Williams, *Artisans and Sans-Culottes* (1969) (Norton) compares the working classes in eighteenth-century Britain and France, while Duncan Bythell, *The Handloom Weavers: A Study of the English Cotton Industry During the Industrial Revolution* (1969) is the most recent study of those whom the new technology displaced. Among the accounts of working-class life, *Edward P. Thompson, *The Making of the English Working Class* (1964) (Vintage) and L. Chevalier, *Classes laborieuses et classes dangereuses à Paris pendant la première moitié du 19ᵉ siècle* (1958) are the best, but they should be complemented by contemporary pictures of life in the industrial revolution: *Friedrich Engels' classic *Condition of the Working Class in England in 1844* (1845) (Stanford); *Mrs. Gaskell's *Mary Barton* (1848) (Norton); or *Victor Hugo's *Les Misérables* (1862) (several editions).

Slavery has been extensively studied by Gaston Martin, *Histoire de l'esclavage dans les colonies françaises* (1948) and Hugh A. Wyndham, *The Atlantic and Slavery* (1935), while Eric E. Williams, *Capitalism and Slavery* (1944) presents the case for the prosecution. For some of the other problems treated in this chapter, see R. Priouret, *La Franc-maçonnerie sous les Lys* (1953); George N. Clark, *Science and Social Welfare in the Age of Newton,* 2nd ed. (1949); and R. H. Shryock, *The Development of Modern Medicine* (1947).

Enlightened Despotism   See *Geoffrey Bruun, *The Enlightened Despots,* 2nd ed. (1967) (Holt, Rinehart & Winston); *Roger Wines, ed., *Enlightened Despotism* (1967) (Heath); John G. Galiardo, *Enlightened Despotism* (1967); and Fritz Hartung's fine pamphlet, *Enlightened Despotism* (1964). For more detailed studies: Franco Valsecchi, *L'Assolutismo illuminato in Austria e in Lombardia* (1931) and Helen P. Liebel, *Enlightened Bureaucracy Versus Enlightened Despotism in Baden, 1750–1792* (1965).

Internal and Constitutional Changes

England   English political history could be approached through the readable works of J. H. Plumb, one of the greatest interpreters of eighteenth-century England: *England in the Eighteenth Century* (1950) (Penguin), *Chatham* (1953), *The First Four Georges* (1956) (Wiley), *Sir Robert Walpole* (1956); and Erich Eyck, *Pitt versus Fox: Father and Son, 1735–1806* (1950). *Ian R. Christie, *Crisis of Empire* (1966) (Norton) is an illuminating summary of events between the 1750's and the 1780's, with excellent bibliographical notes. Social history is well served by Dorothy Marshall, *English People in the Eighteenth Century* (1956) and *M. Dorothy George, *London Life in the XVIIIth Century* (1925) (Capricorn). Sound information and interesting points of view may be found also in Derek Jarrett, *Britain, 1688–1815* (1965); Denis G. Richards, *Britain 1714–1851* (1961); *Asa Briggs, *The Age of Improvement* (1959) (Harper Torchbook); and Stanley E. Ayling, *The Georgian Century: 1714–1837* (1966).

The nineteenth century is covered more extensively in Ernest L. Woodward, *The Age of Reform, 1815–1870* (1938); David Thomson, *England in the Nineteenth Century (1815–1914)* (1964); and John W. Derry, *Reaction and Reform, 1793–1868* (1963). Social and political changes of the nineteenth century may be followed in the writings of John L. and Barbara Hammond: *The Village Labourer, 1760–1832* (1920), *The Town Labourer, 1760–1832* (1917) (Anchor), *The Skilled Labourer, 1760–1832* (1919), *The Bleak Age* (1934); in M. C. Buer's

Health, Wealth and Population in the Early Days of the Industrial Revolution
(1968); and in *Edward P. Thompson's vigorous and fascinating *The Making of
the English Working Class* (1964) (Vintage). See also *Peter Laslett, *The World
We Have Lost* (1966) (Scribner) and Reginald J. White, *Waterloo to Peterloo*
(1957). Among the best biographies: John Osborne, *William Cobbett* (1966);
Michael S. Packe, *The Life of John Stuart Mill* (1954); G. D. H. Cole, *Life of
Robert Owen* (1930); and John L. and Barbara Hammond, *Lord Shaftesbury,*
4th ed. (1936).

Imperial ventures are treated in *Charles E. Carrington, *The British Overseas*
(1950) (Cambridge); Leland H. Jenks, *The Migration of British Capital to 1875*
(1927); and Alfred L. Burt, *The Evolution of the British Empire and Commonwealth from the American Revolution* (1956).

The United States   It is not the purpose of this book to analyze the history of
the United States—only its connections with Europe. In this context, one may
consult *Michael Kraus, *The Atlantic Civilization* (1949) (Cornell); *John R.
Alden, *The American Revolution, 1775–1783* (1954) (Harper Torchbook); *Clin-
ton L. Rossiter, *Seedtime of the Republic: The Origin of the American Tradition of Political Liberty* (1953) (Harcourt, Brace & World); *Edmund S. Morgan,
Birth of the Republic 1763–89 (1956) (University of Chicago); *Carl L. Becker,
The Declaration of Independence: A Study in the History of Political Ideas
(1922) (Vintage)—all readable and authoritative. The relation of American
events to the mind and politics of Europe appears in *Lewis B. Namier, *England
in the Age of the American Revolution* (1930) (St. Martin's); Herbert Butterfield,
George III, Lord North, and the People, 1779–80 (1949); Charles R. Ritcheson,
British Politics and the American Revolution (1954); Werner Start, *America:
Ideal and Reality: The United States of 1776 in Contemporary European Philosophy* (1947); *Durand Echeverria, *Mirage in the West: A History of the French
Image of American Society to 1815* (1957) (Princeton); Lewis R. Gottschalk, *The
Place of the American Revolution in the Causal Pattern of the French Revolu-
tion* (1948). See also *Charles M. Wiltse, *The New Nation, 1800–1845* (1961)
(Hill & Wang); John Dos Passos, *The Shackles of Power: 3 Jeffersonian Decades*
(1966); and *Russell B. Nye, *The Cultural Life of the New Nation, 1776–1830*
(1960) (Harper Torchbook).

France   Paul A. Gagnon, *France since 1789* (1964); Gordon Wright, *France in
Modern Times* (1960); and John Lough, *An Introduction to Eighteenth Century
France* (1960) are clear, knowledgeable surveys providing handy bibliographies.
C. E. Labrousse, *La Crise de l'économie française à la fin de l'ancien régime et
au début de la révolution* (1944) remains the fountainhead of most recent works
on that subject. Diverse aspects of the old regime are treated in Henri E. Sée,
Economic and Social Conditions in France during the Eighteenth Century
(1927); *Elinor G. Barber, *The Bourgeoisie in 18th Century France* (1955)
(Princeton); John McManners, *French Ecclesiastical Society under the Ancient
Regime* (1961); Douglas Dakin, *Turgot and the Ancien Régime in France* (1939);
E. Faure, *La Disgrace de Turgot* (1961); E. G. Leonard, *Mon village sous Louis
XV, d'après les mémoires d'un paysan* (1941) and *Le Protestant français* (1953);
and Herbert Luthy, *La Banque protestante en France,* 2 vols. (1959–1961).

Three of the most revealing works, however, are the contemporary account of
*Arthur Young, *Travels in France during the Years 1787, 1788, 1789* (many edi-
tions) (Anchor); *Alexis de Tocqueville's classic *The Old Regime and the French
Revolution* (Anchor), written over a century ago; and *Georges Lefebvre's won-
derfully compact and perceptive *Coming of the French Revolution, 1789* (1947)
(Princeton).

On the revolution itself, the best account remains that of Georges Lefebvre,
The French Revolution, 2 vols. (1961–64). *R. R. Palmer, *Twelve Who Ruled*

(1941) (Atheneum) provides illuminating biographical studies. See also *Crane Brinton's comparative *The Anatomy of Revolution* (1938) (Vintage); George F. E. Rudé, *The Crowd in the French Revolution* (1959); A. Soboul, *The Parisian Sans-Culottes and the French Revolution, 1793–4* (1964); J. M. Thompson, *Robespierre* (1936) or, briefer, *Robespierre and the French Revolution* (1953) (Collier); *J. L. Talmon's controversial but suggestive *Origins of Totalitarian Democracy* (1952) (Norton); and Jacques L. Godechot, *France and the Atlantic Revolution of the Eighteenth Century, 1770–1799* (1965). In *The Vendée* (1964) (Wiley) *Charles H. Tilly has undertaken a sociological study of the counter-revolution of 1793. See also *Alfred Cobban, *The Social Interpretation of the French Revolution* (1964) (Cambridge) and *Aspects of the French Revolution* (1968) (Norton).

For Napoleon and the Napoleonic era, see F. M. H. Markham, *Napoleon* (1964); a good survey, *Geoffrey Brunn, *Europe and the French Imperium, 1799–1814* (1938) (Harper Torchbook); and J. Christopher Herold, *Bonaparte in Egypt* (1962). The changing aspects of the Napoleonic myth are analyzed in *Pieter Geyl, *Napoleon: For and Against* (1949) (Yale). The changing aspects of life in *Crane Brinton's *The Lives of Talleyrand* (1936) (Norton).

The years after 1815 should be tackled first in G. de Bertier de Sauvigny, *The Restoration* (1967). Other evaluations may be found in Douglas W. J. Johnson, *Guizot* (1963). Stanley Mellon, *The Political Uses of History* (1958); Frank E. Manuel, *The New World of Henri Saint-Simon* (1956) (Notre Dame); John P. Plamenatz, *The Revolutionary Movement in France, 1815–71* (1952); T. E. B. Howard, *Citizen-King: The Life of Louis-Philippe, King of the French* (1961); and (fascinating for the revolutions of 1848) *The Recollections of Alexis de Tocqueville* (1948), edited by Jacob P. Mayer.

Spain *Harold V. Livermore, *A History of Spain* (1968) (Minerva); Rafael Altamira, *A History of Spain, from the Beginnings to the Present Day* (1949); and Salvador de Madariaga, *Spain* (1958) are convenient general surveys. For the eighteenth century, the basic works are J. Sarrailh, *L'Espagne éclairée de la seconde moitié du 18ᵉ siècle* (1954) and (in English) *Richard Herr, *The Eighteenth-Century Revolution in Spain* (1958) (Princeton). See also A. Ramos Oliveira, *Politics, Economics and Men of Modern Spain, 1808–1946* (1948) and Gabriel H. Lovett, *Napoleon and the Birth of Modern Spain* (1965).

Italy *René Albrecht-Carrié, *Italy from Napoleon to Mussolini* (1950) (Columbia) and *Arthur J. Whyte, *The Evolution of Modern Italy, 1715–1920* (1944) (Norton) are useful general works. The eighteenth century could be approached through O. Barrié, *L'Italia nell'Ottocento* (1964) and the very good collection of lectures given at the Italian Institute in London in 1957–1958, published under the title *Art and Ideas in 18th Century Italy* (1960). For the nineteenth century and especially for the Risorgimento, see C. Giardini, *Il Risorgimento Italiano, 1796–1861* (1958) and Kent R. Greenfield, *Economics and Liberalism in the Risorgimento,* rev. ed. (1965). The history and the role of the church are discussed by E. E. Y. Hales, *Revolution and Papacy, 1769–1846* (1960) and *Pio Nono* (1954). For the intellectual history of Italy see G. Maugain, *L'Evolution intellectuelle de l'Italie de 1657 à 1750* (1909). More detailed aspects are to be found in H. M. M. Acton, *The Last Medici,* rev. ed. (1959), *The Bourbons of Naples (1734–1825)* (1957) and *The Last Bourbons of Naples (1825–1861)* (1962); George T. Romani, *The Neapolitan Revolution of 1820–1821* (1950); A. J. P. Taylor, *The Italian Problem in European Diplomacy, 1847–1849* (1934); and the first volume of Bolton King, *A History of Italian Unity* (1923).

The Germanies For Prussia, see *Walter H. Bruford, *Germany in the Eighteenth Century* (1935) (Cambridge); *Gordon A. Craig, *The Politics of the*

Prussian Army (1955) (Oxford); *Sidney B. Fay, *The Rise of Brandenburg-Prussia to 1786* (1937) (Holt, Rinehart & Winston); and William F. Reddaway, *Frederick the Great and the Rise of Prussia* (1904). Pierre Gaxotte's biography *Frederick the Great* (1942) is highly readable, if biased. Essential for eighteenth-century Prussia is H. Brunschwig, *La Crise de l'état prussien à la fin du 18ᵉ siècle et la génèse de la mentalité romantique* (1947), which links the history of institutions with that of political and social thought; and *Hans W. Rosenberg, *Bureaucracy, Aristocracy and Autocracy* (1958) (Beacon). See also Robert R. Ergang, *The Potsdam Führer, Frederick William I, Father of Prussian Militarism* (1941) and Peter Paret, *Yorck and the Era of Prussian Reform* (1966).

The Austrian empire has been chronicled in Paul Frischauer, *The Imperial Crown* (1939) and *A. J. P. Taylor, *The Habsburg Monarchy, 1809–1918* (1949) (Harper Torchbook). For the eighteenth century one may consult Heinrich Kretschmayr, *Maria Theresa* (1925); George P. Gooch, *Maria Theresa, and Other Studies* (1951); Saul K. Padover, *The Revolutionary Emperor: Joseph the Second, 1741–1790* (1934); and François Fejtö; *Un Habsbourg Révolutionnaire, Joseph II: Portrait d'un despote éclairé,* (1953)—all excellent. For the history of the peoples which were part of the empire, see William E. Wright, *Serf, Seigneur, and Sovereign* (1966) on the agrarian problems and reforms of Bohemia; Henrick Marczali, *Hungary in the Eighteenth Century* (1910), an old work but still unreplaced; Carlile A. Macartney, *Hungary: A Short History* (1962); Robert J. Kerner, *Bohemia in the Eighteenth Century* (1932); and R. W. Seton-Watson, *A History of the Czechs and Slovaks* (1943).

The ideas and politics of the early nineteenth century are well treated in *Theodore S. Hamerow, *Restoration, Revolution, Reaction: Economics and Politics in Germany, 1815–1871* (1958) (Princeton); J. G. Legge, *Rhyme and Revolution in Germany 1813–1850* (1918); *Arthur J. May, *The Age of Metternich, 1814–1848* (1933) (Holt, Rinehart & Winston); and Richard H. Thomas, *Liberalism, Nationalism and the German Intellectuals, 1822–1847* (1952).

The Eastern Borderlands Stanislaw Arnold and Marian Zychowski, *Outline History of Poland* (1962) and William F. Reddaway, ed., *The Cambridge History of Poland*, 2 vols. (1941, 1951) are sound general works. For the eighteenth century and certain less-known aspects of the Enlightenment, see J. Fabre, *Stranislas-Auguste Poniatowski et l'Europe des lumières* (1952). For the partitions of Poland, see Robert H. Lord, *The Second Partition of Poland* (1915) and Herbert H. Kaplan, *The First Partition of Poland* (1962). The later period is covered in William J. Rose, *The Rise of Polish Democracy* (1944) and R. F. Leslie, *Polish Politics and the Revolution of November 1830* (1956). Later developments are treated in R. W. Seton-Watson, *The Historian as a Political Force in Central Europe* (1922). For Hungary, see the references for the Austrian empire in the preceding section on the Germanies.

Russia For general narratives see the works of Bernard Pares and N. Riasanovsky. The reign of Peter the Great should be approached through B. H. Sumner's *Peter the Great and the Emergence of Russia* (1951) (Collier) and *Peter the Great and the Ottoman Empire* (1950). *Marc Raeff's *Peter the Great: Reformer or Revolutionary?* (1963) (Heath) reviews the controversial aspects of the reign of the creator of modern Russia. For his successors, see George P. Gooch, *Catherine the Great and Other Studies* (1954); Gladys S. Thompson, *Catherine the Great and the Expansion of Russia* (1950); Ian Grey, *Catherine the Great* (1962); and Constantin de Grunwald, *Tsar Nicholas I* (1955). Already cited, James H. Billington, *The Icon and the Axe* (1966) and *Jerome Blum, *Lord and Peasant in Russia* (1961) (Atheneum) are basic for cultural and agrarian history respectively. Hans Rogger, *National Consciousness in Eighteenth-Century Russia* (1960) traces the relationship of westernization and national feelings. Leonid I. Strakhovsky sketches an uncertain personality in *Alexander I of Russia* (1947). Mikhail O. Zetlin's *The Decembrists* (1958) goes beyond the unsuccessful rising to the general unrest affecting Russian society at the beginning of the nineteenth century. See also R. Portal, *L'Oural au 18ᵉ siècle* (1950), useful for the origins of Russian industrial development; Robert J. Kerner, *The Urge to the Sea* (1942); and Frank A. Golder, *Russian Expansion on the Pacific, 1641–1850* (1914).

The Ottoman Empire A general bibliography for the empire and the countries controlled by the Turks has already been given. One should add some works regarding the beginning of the process of modernization and the impact of the West upon the southeast part of Europe. Useful remarks and bibliography may be found in the book edited by Charles and Barbara Jelavich, *The Balkans in Transition* (1963). One may also consult Wesley M. Gewehr, *The Rise of Nationalism in the Balkans, 1800–1930* (1931) and R. W. Seton-Watson, *The Rise of Nationality in the Balkans* (1917). *Bernard Lewis, *The Emergence of Modern Turkey* (1961) (Oxford) and H. A. R. Gibb and Harold Bowen, *Islamic Society and the West*, 2 vols. (1950–1957) are basic. J. A. R. Marriott, *The Eastern Question*, 4th ed. (1940) surveys Ottoman decline and its effects on the international plane. The Turkish point of view has been presented by Halide Edib Adivar, *Conflict of East and West in Turkey* (1935). For one of the most important events of the early nineteenth century, affecting not only the Balkans but all Europe, see C. M. Woodhouse, *The Greek War of Independence* (1952).

Sense and Sensibility

Science and Technology For general surveys regarding the role of science and technology in modern civilization, see *Alfred R. Hall, *The Scientific Revolution, 1500–1800* (1954) (Beacon); Abraham Wolf, *A History of Science, Technology and Philosophy in the Eighteenth Century*, 2 vols. (1961); Charles J. Singer, Alfred R. Hall, and Trevor I. Williams, eds., *A History of Technology*, Vol. IV (1958); *Lewis Mumford, *Technics and Civilization* (1963) (Harcourt, Brace & World); Archibald and Nan Clow, *The Chemical Revolution* (1952); L. T. C. Rolt, *The Aeronauts: A History of Ballooning, 1783–1903* (1966). Stimulating: *Charles C. Gillispie, *The Edge of Objectivity* (1960) (Princeton) and G. Bachelard, *La Formation de l'esprit scientifique* (1960). *Charles C. Gillispie's *Genesis and Geology* (1951) (Harper Torchbook) is excellent for the impact of scientific discoveries upon religious belief in the decades before Darwin. For the impact of Darwinism itself see *Loren C. Eiseley, *Darwin's Century* (1958) (Anchor) and *Gertrude Himmelfarb, *Darwin and the Darwinian Revolution* (1968) (Norton).

The Enlightenment and the *Philosophes* Good introductions to the general history of ideas and thought during the period are found in *Paul Hazard, *European Thought in the Eighteenth Century* (1954) (Meridian); Gerald R. Cragg, *Reason and Authority in the Eighteenth Century* (1964); and Lester G. Crocker, *An Age of Crisis: Man and World in 18th Century Thought* (1959). For the Enlightenment, see *Peter Gay, *The Enlightenment: An Interpretation* —Vol. I, *The Rise of Modern Paganism* (1966) (Vintage) and Vol. II, *The Science of Freedom* (1969), and *The Party of Humanity: Essays in the French Enlightenment* (1963) and *E. Cassirer, *The Philosophy of the Enlightenment* (1955) (Beacon, Princeton), all basic. René Mauzi, *L'Idée du bonheur au XVIIIᵉ siècle* (1960) is heavy going but worthwhile for the serious student. *Carl L. Becker, *The Heavenly City of the Eighteenth-Century Philosophers* (1932) (Yale) should not be missed—delightful reading, best followed by a look at Raymond O. Rockwood, ed., *Carl Becker's Heavenly City Revisited* (1958). Other general works: *Frank E. Manual, *The Age of Reason* (1951) (Cornell); A. Bruno, *Car-

tesio e l'illuminismo (1949); Geoffrey Clive, *The Romantic Enlightenment* (1960); and Louis I. Bredvold, *The Brave New World of the Enlightenment* (1961). For the old discussion concerning the impact of enlightened thought upon the French Revolution, see Alfred Cobban, *In Search of Humanity: The Role of the Enlightenment in Modern History* (1960) and *William F. Church, ed., *The Influence of the Enlightenment on the French Revolution: Creative, Disastrous or Non-existent* (1964) (Heath). Other suggested works: Eric W. Cochrane, *Tradition and Enlightenment in the Tuscan Academies, 1690–1800* (1961); M. Fubini, ed., *La Cultura iluministica in Italia* (1957); George M. Addy, *The Enlightenment in the University of Salamanca* (1966); and Henry Higgs, *The Physiocrats* (1952).

Among the best biographies: Robert Shackleton, *Montesquieu* (1961); *Henry N. Brailsford, *Voltaire* (1935) (Oxford); and *Peter Gay, *Voltaire's Politics* (1959) (Vintage); Lester G. Crocker, *The Embattled Philosopher: A Biography of Denis Diderot* (1954); *Frank E. Manuel, *The Prophets of Paris* (1962) (Harper Torchbook) for Turgot, Condorcet, Saint-Simon, Fourier, and Comte; Jacob S. Schapiro, *Condorcet and the Rise of Liberalism* (1934); J. Christopher Herold, *Mistress to an Age* (1958), a splendidly readable biography of Madame de Staël; Richard Friedenthal, *Goethe: His Life and Times* (1965); Henry N. Brailsford, *Shelley, Godwin, and Their Circle* (1969); and Michael S. Packe, *The Life of John Stuart Mill* (1954). More revealing than any biography are the autobiographies of *Edward Gibbon (1961) (Meridian) and *John Stuart Mill (several editions).

Other Philosophies For ideas and systems of thought other than those of the Enlightenment, see *Robert L. Heilbroner, *The Worldly Philosophers,* rev. ed. (1967) (Clarion); Godfrey E. Elton, *The Revolutionary Idea in France, 1789–1871* (1969); Simon Maccoby, *English Radicalism:1786–1832* (1956); *Guido de Ruggiero, *The History of European Liberalism* (1927) (Beacon); Harold J. Laski, *The Rise of Liberalism* (1936); *Harry K. Girvetz, *The Evolution of Liberalism* (1963) (Collier); Donald G. Rohr, *The Origins of Social Liberalism in Germany* (1963); and Leonard Krieger, *The German Idea of Freedom* (1957).

Utilitarianism, at least in its British aspects, is well treated in Leslie Stephen, *The English Utilitarians,* 3 vols. (1900); John P. Plamenatz, *Mill's Utilitarianism: Reprinted with a Study of the English Utilitarians* (1949); and *Elie Halévy, *The Growth of Philosophical Radicalism* (1955) (Beacon). The best Owen biography is Margaret I. Cole, *Robert Owen of New Lanark* (1953). A good short introduction, *Hegel* (1883) is by Edward Caird. For the evolution of historical ideas, see Sherman B. Barnes and Alfred A. Skerpan, *Historiography Under the Impact of Rationalism and Revolution* (1952).

Good analyses of European conservatism and of traditionalist thought are to be found in *Peter Viereck, *Conservatism Revisited: The Revolt Against Revolt, 1815–1949* (1949) (Free Press); John Morley, *Edmund Burke* (1924); Alfred Cobban, *Edmund Burke and the Revolt Against the Eighteenth Century* (1929); and Ernest L. Woodward, *Three Studies in European Conservatism: Metternich, Guizot, the Catholic Church in the 19th Century* (1963). See also *Michel Foucault, *Madness and Civilization: A History of Insanity in the Age of Reason* (1965) (Mentor); J. L. Talmon, *Political Messianism: The Romantic Phase* (1960); *Alexander R. Vidler, *The Church in an Age of Revolution* (1961) (Penguin); and Kathleen Heasman, *Evangelicals in Action* (1962).

The Romantic Reaction

Rococo The Rococo could be approached through the following works: A. Schönberger and H. Soehmer, *The Rococo Age: Art and Civilization of the 18th Century* (1960); A. Anger, *Literarisches Rokoko* (1962); and *Michael Levey,

Rococo to Revolution: Major Trends in 18th Century Painting (1966) (Praeger). The vogue of Asia, and particularly of China, is discussed by H. Cordier, *La Chine en France au 18e siècle* (1910) and William W. Appleton, *A Cycle of Cathay: The Chinese Vogue in England During the Seventeenth and Eighteenth Centuries* (1951).

Rousseau For Rousseau, the best English work is Frederick C. Green, *Jean-Jacques Rousseau* (1955). See also Alfred Cobban, *Rousseau and the Modern State* (1934); and *Ernst Cassirer, *The Question of Jean-Jacques Rousseau* (1954) (Indiana) and *Rousseau, Kant, Goethe* (1945).

Romanticism For Romanticism see *Jacques Barzun's *Classic, Romantic and Modern* (1961) (Anchor), a new edition of his earlier *Romanticism and the Modern Ego* (1943); *Kenneth Clark, *The Gothic Revival* (1950) (Penguin); P. Moreau, *Le Romantisme* (1957); *M. H. Abrams, *The Mirror and the Lamp: Romantic Theory and the Critical Tradition* (1953) (Norton). David O. Evans, *Social Romanticism in France, 1830–1848* (1969) and *Hans Kohn, *The Mind of Germany* (1960) (Harper Torchbook) help one to understand the relationship between Romantic ideas and political commitments. For different aspects of Romantic theory see E. Newton, *Romantic Rebellion* (1962); Allen F. Casebier, *The Historical Conception of Romanticism* (1964); Theodore H. von Laue, *Leopold Ranke, The Formative Years* (1950); J. Fabre, *Lumière et romantisme: énergie et nostalgie de Rousseau à Mickiewicz* (1963); J. Bousquet, *Les thèmes du rêve dans la littérature romantique* (1964); and *Kathleen M. Tillotson, *Novels of the Eighteen-Forties* (1954) (Oxford). The Romantic background can be found in *Eugen Weber, ed., *Paths to the Present* (1960) (Dodd, Mead).

Nationalism *Hans Kohn, *The Idea of Nationalism: A Study of its Origins and Background* (1961) (Collier) is the best beginning, along with *Boyd C. Shafer, *Nationalism: Myth and Reality* (1955) (Harcourt, Brace)—clear and succint. See also E. H. Carr, *Nationalism and After* (1945) and the older work by C. J. Hayes, *The Historical Evolution of Modern Nationalism* (1931). For an extensive bibliography see Karl W. Deutsch, *Interdisciplinary Bibliography on Nationalism* (1955).

New Public and New Culture

*George Rudé, *The Crowd in History* (1964) (Wiley); A. Brulé, *Les Gens de lettres au 18e siècle* (1929); and M. Glotz and M. Maire, *Les salons du 18e siècle* (1949) all help one to understand the problems discussed in this chapter.

Education Robert F. Butts, *A Cultural History of Western Education,* 2nd ed. (1955); William Boyd, *The History of Western Education,* 8th ed. (1966); and Brian Simon, *Studies in the History of Education, 1780–1870* (1960) are all dependable works. So is John W. Adamson's older *Short History of Education* (1920). For the history of pedagogical ideas see G. Snyders, *La Pédagogie en France au 17e et 18e siècles* (1965); Frederick Mayer, *A History of Educational Thought* (1960); and W. A. C. Stewart and W. P. McCann, *The Educational Innovators, 1750–1880,* 2 vols. (1967). A. Babeau, *L'Ecole de village pendant la Révolution* (1885) and E. Philip Trapp, *The School Teacher* (1957) are recommended for the problems regarding education in rural areas. Hugh M. Pollard, *Pioneers of Popular Education, 1760–1850* (1956) is also useful.

The Writing Trade Convenient for reference are Alfred Hessel, *A History of Libraries* (1950); Elmer D. Johnson, *A History of Libraries in the Western World* (1965); Herman J. Vleeschauer, *History of the Library Since the French Revolu-*

tion (1965); Irene Collins, *The Government and the Newspaper Press in France, 1814–1881* (1959); and G. Weill, *Le Journal: origines, évolution et rôle de la presse périodique* (1934). For writers themselves see the works of Arthur S. Collins, *The Profession of Letters* (1929) and *Authorship in the Days of Johnson* (1929); James Hepburn, *The Author's Empty Purse and the Rise of the Literary Agent* (1968); Robert J. Cruikshank, *Charles Dickens and Early Victorian England* (1950); and Monica Stirling, *The Wild Swan: A Life of Hans Christian Andersen* (1965).

The Public Arts Francis D. Klingender, *Art and the Industrial Revolution* (1947) discusses the impact of social realities on art and artists. Of the innumerable books on various aspects of European art during the eighteenth and nineteenth centuries, the following are among the most useful: *Michael Levey, *Rococo to Revolution* (1966) (Praeger); Marcel Brion, *Romantic Art* (1960); *Eric Newton, *The Romantic Rebellion* (1963) (Schocken); E. de Kayser, *L'Occident romantique, 1789–1850* (1965); and J. Starobinski, *L'Invention de la liberté, 1700–1789* (1964).

David Ewen, ed., *From Bach to Stravinsky* (1933) is an excellent general work. See also Alfred Einstein, *Music in the Romantic Era* (1947) and J. Chantavoine and J. Godefroy-Demombynes, *Le Romantisme dans la musique européenne* (1955); or for an introduction to musical ideas, Donald N. Ferguson, *A History of Musical Thought*, 2nd ed. (1948). *Alfred Einstein, *Mozart, His Character, His Work* (1945) (Oxford) is an excellent biography of the great composer; Francis Toye, *Rossini* (1963) is a splendidly readable introduction to the world of Italian opera; while *Jacques Barzun, *Berlioz and the Romantic Century*, 3rd ed. (1969) (Meridian) illuminates the whole Romantic period through the life of its most representative composer.

Fiction The best and pleasantest way of entering into the life and problems of a given time is through its literature. The eighteenth and early nineteenth centuries offer us a new vehicle for this purpose: the novel. The shady life of Louis XV's France is reflected in *Abbé Prévost, *Manon Lescaut* (1731) (several editions); the questing, moralizing skepticism of the Enlightenment in *Denis Diderot's *Rameau's Nephew,* written in the 1760's and best tackled in Jacques Barzun's edition of 1956 (Bobbs-Merrill); the amoralism of late eighteenth-century society in *Pierre Choderlos de Laclos's *Liaisons dangereuses* (1782) (Signet); the sentimentalism blowing out of Germany in *Johann Wolfgang von Goethe's *The Sorrows of Young Werther* (1774) (several editions), and the Romantic world-view even better in his *Wilhelm Meister* (1796) (Collier).

However, a new society was taking shape and sparking a new kind of social novel, less fantastic and closer to life. After the turn of the century, contemporary reality is mirrored in the works of *Jane Austen—*Pride and Prejudice* (1813) (several editions), *Emma* (1816) (several editions)—and especially in those of two great Frenchmen, Stendhal and Balzac. Stendhal (the pen-name of Marie Henri Beyle), writing mostly in the 1830's, has left us three masterful accounts: *The Red and the Black* (1831) (several editions), of the frustrated yearnings and rebellious stirrings of the post-1815 generation; *The Charterhouse of Parma* (1839) (Signet, Penguin), of antediluvian institutions and youthful idealism in anachronistic Italy; and (unfinished) *Lucien Leuwen* (New Directions), about the 1830's themselves. His contemporary, Honoré de Balzac, survived him; but some of Balzac's most revealing novels (*Lost Illusions, *Eugénie Grandet, *Père Goriot*) were also written in the thirties. They give us the richest and truest picture of life and values of those days.

743

PART II

The Age of Masses

For a general approach see N. Ponente, *Les Structures du monde moderne, 1850–1900* (1965). Quincy Howe, *A World History of Our Own Times,* 3 vols. (1953); and Frank P. Chambers, *This Age of Conflict,* 3rd ed. (1962). Concerning population and population movements, see M. Reinhardt, *Histoire de la population mondiale de 1700 à 1948* (1949); Alexander M. Carr-Saunders, *World Population* (1936); Julius Isaac, *Economics of Migration* (1947); Donald R. Taft and Richard Robbins, *International Migrations* (1955). Specifically concerning the role of the masses, see Henry P. Fairchild, *People: The Quantity and Quality of Population* (1939); Robert E. Dickinson, *The West European City* (1951); Gustave le Bon, *The Crowd,* new ed. (1925); *José Ortega y Gasset, *The Revolt of the Masses* (1932) (Norton); and William L. O'Neill, ed., *Echoes of Revolt: The Masses, 1911–1917* (1966). *Peter N. Stearns, *European Society in Upheaval: Social History since 1800* (1967) (Macmillan) is the first attempt to provide students with a synthesis of the subject. Another crucial connection is treated in *Carlo M. Cipolla, *Literacy and Development in the West* (1969) (Pelican).

The International Scene Most of the problems included in this chapter will be discussed in detail in later sections. Nevertheless, for a very general survey, one can turn either to the relevant volumes of the New Cambridge Modern History (X, XI, XII, and especially the last, edited by David Thomson, *The Era of Violence, 1898–1945* (1960); to A. J. P. Taylor, *The Struggle for Mastery in Europe, 1848–1918* (1955); or to *Felix Gilbert, *The End of the European Era, 1890 to the Present* (1970) (Norton).

For the economic aspects of the international scene, there are several excellent works: among them William Ashworth, *A Short History of the International Economy Since 1850,* 2nd ed. (1962); Michael Tracy, *Agriculture in Western Europe* (1964); M. Lévy-Leboyer, *Les Banques européennes et l'industrialisation internationale dans la première moitié du 19e siècle* (1964); *Herbert Feis, *Europe, the World's Banker, 1870–1914* (1930) (Norton); *C. P. Kindleberger, *Economic Growth in France and Britain, 1851–1950* (1964) (Clarion); and Eugene Staley, *War and the Private Investor* (1935). *Lewis Mumford, *Technics and Civilization* (1934) (Harcourt, Brace & World); Ludwig F. Haber, *The Chemical Industry During the Nineteenth Century* (1958); Walter Henry Green Armytage, *A Social History of Engineering* (revised 1961); and N. G. B. Pounds and W. N. Parker, *Coal and Steel in Western Europe* (1957) are also suggested, along with *John H. Clapham, *The Economic Development of France and Germany, 1815–1914,* 4th ed. (1935) (Cambridge) and Gustav Stolper, *German Economy, 1870–1940* (1940).

Politics for Masses

Liberalism Harold Laski's works, especially *The Rise of Liberalism* (1936), are basic. Also good, *Guido de Ruggiero, *The History of European Liberalism* (1959) (Beacon); John H. Hollowell, *The Decline of Liberalism as an Ideology* (1943); and Harry K. Girvetz, *The Evolution of Liberalism,* rev. ed. (1963). For liberal perspectives see the optimistic book of Joseph Grimond, *The Liberal Challenge* (1964).

Bibliography

Anarchism This should be first approached through the general work of G. D. H. Cole, *Socialist Thought: Marxism and Anarchism, 1850–1890* (1954). Among specific works devoted to the subject see *James Joll, *The Anarchists* (1965) (Grosset & Dunlap); *George Woodcock, *Anarchism* (1962) (Meridian); R. Gaucher, *Les terroristes* (1965); *E. J. Hobsbawm, *Primitive Rebels* (1959) (Norton); and Jean Maitron's vast *Histoire du mouvement anarchiste en France* (1955). Good biographies of the founders of the movement are D. W. Brogan, *Proudhon* (1936); George Woodcock, *William Godwin* (1946) and *Pierre-Joseph Proudhon* (1956); E. H. Carr, *Michael Bakunin* (1937); G. P. Maksimov, ed., *The Political Philosophy of Bakunin* (1953); and *Peter Kropotkin, *Memoirs of a Revolutionist* (1899) (Dover).

Socialism The basic work on socialism is G. D. H. Cole, *A History of Socialist Thought*, 4 vols. (1953–1956). Among others: *Norman I. Mackenzie, *Socialism: A Short History* (1950) (Harper & Row); Carl Landauer, *European Socialism*, 2 vols. 1959); and *Alexander Gray, *The Socialist Tradition: Moses to Lenin* (1946) (Harper Torchbook). *Edmund Wilson, *To the Finland Station* (1946) (Anchor) is the clearest and most readable discussion in English of "the revolutionary tradition in Europe and the rise of Socialism," but *George Lichtheim, *The Origins of Socialism* (1969) (Praeger)—less discursive and more scholarly—is almost as readable and more tightly argued. For national aspects see Henry M. Pelling, *A History of British Trade Unionism* (1963); Val R. Lorwin, *The French Labor Movement* (1955); Harvey Goldberg, *The Life of J. Jaurès* (1962); *George Lichtheim, *Marxism: An Historical and Critical Study* (1961) (Praeger); and *Peter Gay's account of revisionism in *The Dilemma of Democratic Socialism* (1952) (Collier).

The Catastrophic Heroes The theoretical backgrounds of Nazism and fascism are discussed in *Peter Viereck, *Metapolitics, from the Romantics to Hitler* (1941) (Capricorn), *Ernst Nolte, *Three Faces of Fascism* (1966) (Mentor); Franz Neumann, *Behemoth: The Structure and Practice of National Socialism, 1933–1944* (1944) (Harper Torchbook); * George L. Mosse, *The Crisis of German Ideology: Intellectual Origins of the Third Reich* (1964) (Grosset & Dunlap). See also Louis L. Snyder, *German Nationalism: The Tragedy of a People* (1952); Michael Curtis, *Three Against the Third Republic: Sorel, Barrès and Maurras* (1959); and Eugen Weber, *The Nationalist Revival in France, 1905–1914* (1959). For the intellectual history of the past fourscore years, a stimulating introduction may be sought in two works by H. Stuart Hughes, *Consciousness and Society: The Reorientation of European Social Thought 1890–1930* (1958) (Vintage) and *The Obstructed Path: French Social Thought in the Years of Desperation, 1930–1960* (1969) (Harper Torchbook), and in *Gerhard Masur, *Prophets of Yesterday* (1961) (Harper & Row).

Anti-Semitism For a general outline: Leon Poliakov's *The History of Anti-Semitism*, 4 vols. (1965); *Norman R. C. Cohn, *Warrant for Genocide* (1967) (Harper Torchbook); James W. Parkes, *The Emergence of the Jewish Problem, 1878–1939* (1946); and Koppel S. Pinson, ed., *Essays on Antisemitism* (1946). Works concerning individual countries include Paul W. Massing, *Rehearsal for Destruction: A Study of Political Anti-Semitism in Imperial Germany* (1949); Robert F. Byrnes, *Antisemitism in Modern France*, 3 vols. (1950); and *Peter Pulzer, *The Rise of Political Anti-Semitism in Germany and Austria* (1964) (Wiley). On some of the causes of anti-Semitism, see Nathan W. Ackerman and Marie Jahoda, *Anti-Semitism and Emotional Disorder* (1950); Rudolph M. Loewenstein, *Christians and Jews* (1951); Peretz F. Bernstein, *Jew-Hate as a*

745

Bibliography

Social Problem (1951); Jules Isaac, *The Teaching of Contempt: Christian Roots* of Anti-Semitism (1940).

Europe and the World Overseas

Europe Explodes Herbert Feis, *Europe, the World's Banker, 1870–1914* (1930) (Norton) is still very good on Europe's role in the development of the world. The colonial problem should be approached through the following works: René Maunier, *The Sociology of Colonies: An Introduction to the Study of Race Contact,* 2 vols. (1949); Mary E. Townsend, *European Colonial Expansion Since 1871* (1941); Heinrich A. Wieschoff, *Colonial Policies in Africa* (1944); John T. Pratt, *The Expansion of Europe into the Far East* (1947); Christopher Hollis, *Italy in Africa* (1941); *Archibald P. Thornton, *The Imperial Idea and Its Enemies: A Study in British Power* (1959) (Anchor); John F. Cady, *The Roots of French Imperialism in Eastern Asia* (1954); and *David S. Landes' brilliant *Bankers and Pashas: International Finance and Economic Imperialism in Egypt* (1958) (Harper Torchbook). See also the special issue "Colonialism and Colonization in World History" of the *Journal of Economic History,* XXI, No. 4, December, 1961, and the works of A. Grenfell Price: *The Western Invasions of the Pacific and Its Continents: A Study of Moving Frontiers and Changing Landscapes, 1513–1958* (1963) and *The Importance of Disease in History* (1964).

Imperialism William L. Strauss, *Joseph Chamberlain and the Theory of Imperialism* (1942) is still a good theoretical introduction, while William L. Langer, *The Diplomacy of Imperialism, 1890–1902,* 2 vols. (1935) provides practical exemplification of what imperialism was. For the same period see C. J. Lowe, *The Reluctant Imperialists,* Vol. I (1969); John Atkinson Hobson, *Imperialism: A Study* (1902), pioneer of the economic interpretation, *V. I. Lenin, *Imperialism, the Highest Stage of Capitalism* (1939) (China Books); *Joseph A. Schumpeter, *Imperialism and Social Classes* (1919) (Meridian); Earle M. Winslow, *The Pattern of Imperialism* (1948); Archibald P. Thornton, *The Imperial Idea and Its Enemies: A Study in British Power* (1959); and Richard Koebner and Helmut D. Schmidt, *Imperialism* (1964). For the reaction of the colonized, see *Frantz Fanon, *The Wretched of the Earth* (1965) (Grove).

India Percival Griffiths, *The British Impact on India* (1952) is good on the problem of contacts between different types of civilizations. *Stanley A. Wolpert, *India* (1965) (Spectrum) provides the best brief introduction. Thomas W. Wallbank, *India: A Survey of the Heritage and Growth of Indian Nationalism* (1948); Charles F. Andrews and Girija Mukerji, *The Rise and Growth of the Congress in India* (1938); and *Percival Spear, *India, Pakistan and the West,* 4th ed. (1967) (Oxford) are also recommended.

The Far East Good introductions may be found in Cora A. Du Bois, *Social Forces in Southeast Asia* (1959); Maurice Zinkin, *Asia and the West,* new rev. ed. (1953); Jan Romein, *The Asian Century: A History of Modern Nationalism in Asia* (1962); and Paul H. Clyde, *The Far East: A History of the Impact of the West on Eastern Asia,* 2nd ed. (1952). The role of the West is discussed also by G. B. Sansom, *The Western World and Japan,* and Edwin O. Reischauer, *The United States and Japan,* rev. ed. (1957). Brian Harrison, *South-east Asia: A Short History* (1954) should be used for that area of the continent. China is best approached through *Kenneth S. Latourette, *A History of Modern China* (1954) (Penguin); S. H. Tang, *Communist China Today: Domestic and Foreign*

746

Policies, 2nd ed. (1961); and *John K. Fairbank, *The United States and China,* rev. and enl. (1958) (Compass). For two illuminating biographies, see Emily Hahn, *Chiang Kai-shek: An Unauthorized Biography* (1955) and *Benjamin I. Schwartz, *Chinese Communism and the Rise of Mao* (1951) (Harper Torchbook).

Europe 1848–1914 For the second half of the nineteenth century there are good general accounts in Robert C. Binkley, *Realism and Nationalism, 1852–1871* (1935); *Norman Rich, *The Age of Nationalism and Reform* (1970) (Norton); and *C. J. H. Hayes, *A Generation of Materialism, 1871–1900* (1941) (Harper & Row). The Crimean War provides the background for *Cecil Wood-ham Smith, *The Reason Why: An Exposé of the Charge of the Light Brigade* (1953) (Dutton), an exposé also of the incompetence of those responsible for the conflict. *Michael Howard has written a good account of *The Franco-Prussian War* (1961) (Collier). See also Edgar Holt, *The Boer War* (1958); Heinrich A. Wieschoff, *Colonial Policies in Africa* (1944); *Erich Eyck, *Bismarck and the German Empire* (1950) (Norton); and William L. Langer's massive studies of diplomatic history, *European Alliances and Alignments, 1871–1890* (1931) (Vintage) and *The Diplomacy of Imperialism, 1890–1902,* 2 vols. (1935). Finally, ample and useful, Oron J. Hale, *The Great Illusion, 1900–1914* (1971).

War, 1914–1918 *Barbara Tuchman, *The Proud Tower: A Portrait of the World Before the War, 1890–1914* (1966) (Bantam) and *The Guns of August* (1962) (Dell) are readable accounts of the years when war clouds gathered, and of 1914, when they burst. Among the myriad studies of the war's origins, the most accessible is Nicholas Mansergh, *The Coming of the First World War* (1949). For the German and French views, well stated, see Erich Branden-burg, *From Bismarck to the World War* (1927) and Pierre Renouvin, *The Immediate Origins of the War* (1928). On the fighting itself, *Cyril B. Falls, *The Great War* (1959) (Capricorn) and Hanson W. Baldwin, *World War I: An Outline History* (1962) (Grove) are both sound general surveys. For the position and role of the United States, see *Ernest R. May, *The World War and American Isolation, 1914–1917* (1959). (Quadrangle). Other aspects of those years are treated in Frank P. Chambers, *The War Behind the War* (1939); *Arthur Marwick, *The Deluge* (1966) (Norton)—both on civilian society— *Alistair Horne, *The Price of Glory: Verdun, 1916* (1963) Harper & Row); and Bernard Bergonzi, *Heroes' Twilight* (1966), a study of the literature of the war.

Peace H. W. V. Temperley's *History of the Peace Conference of Paris,* 6 vols. (1920–1924) is a mine of information but without a general theoretical view; Thomas A. Bailey, *Wilson and the Peacemakers* (1947) focuses on the U.S. role in the peace conference; *Harold G. Nicolson, *Peacemaking, 1919* (1939) (Grosset & Dunlap) is a handy brief account by a British participant. Thomas Jones's biography *Lloyd George* (1951) provides information on another dominant figure of the conference. The economic debate on the wisdom of the peace terms is best followed in John Maynard Keynes, *The Economic Consequences of the Peace* (1920), a brilliant criticism, and *Etienne Mantoux, *The Carthaginian Peace: or The Economic Consequences of Mr. Keynes* (1946) (University of Pittsburgh), an attack upon it. The role and the destiny of the smaller nations at the conference table should be approached through Stephen Bonsal, *Suitors and Suppliants: The Little Nations at Ver-sailles* (1946). Paul Birdsall, *Versailles—Twenty Years After* (1941) is a stimulat-ing appraisal of the far-reaching effects of the peace settlements.

The Twenty Years' Armistice *A. J. P. Taylor's *From Sarajevo to Potsdam* (1966) (Harcourt, Brace & World) is brief and readable. See also the general works of M. Baumont, *La faillite de la paix 1918–1939* (1945); *E. H. Carr, *The Twenty Years' Crisis*, 2nd ed. (1946) (Harper Torchbook); and Ephraim Lipson, *Europe, 1914–1939*, 7th ed. (1957); and the satirical social history by *Robert Graves and Alan Hodge, *The Long Week-end* (1941) (Norton). The hopes and the failure of the League of Nations are well described by F. P. Walters, *History of the League of Nations*, 2 vols. (1960). *John Kenneth Galbraith, *The Great Crash, 1929* (1955) (Sentry) helps one to understand the troubled events which led to the rise of Nazism and the Second World War. The period preceding this last is analyzed by *John Wheeler-Bennet, *Munich: Prologue to Tragedy* (1948) (Compass) and in two collections of essays by Lewis B. Namier: *Diplomatic Prelude, 1938–1939* (1948) and *Europe in Decay: A Study in Disintegration, 1936–1940* (1950).

The End of Liberalism *Elizabeth Wiskemann, *Europe of the Dictators, 1914–1945* (1966) (Harper Torchbook) is factual and useful. See also Alfred Cobban, *Dictatorship: Its History and Theory* (1939); G. W. F. Hallgarten, *Why Dictators?* (1954); and Carl J. Friedrich and Zbigniew K. Brzezinski, *Totalitarian Dictatorship and Autocracy* 2nd rev. ed. (1956). *Erich Fromm, *Escape from Freedom* (1941) (Aron) argues that modern man, unable to bear the burden of freedom and self-definition, desires to escape into irresponsible mass movements. *Barrington Moore, Jr., *The Social Origins of Dictatorship and Democracy* (1966) (Beacon) attempts a comparative study of the process of modernization in different countries, suggesting why this led to fascism, communism, or democracy.

Communism The practical aspects of communism, especially in Russia, will be discussed in another chapter. For a theoretical interpretation see *G. D. H. Cole, *The Meaning of Marxism* (1964) (University of Michigan); *Alfred Meyer, *Marxism: The Unity of the Theory and Practice* (1954) (University of Michigan) and *Marxism Since the Communist Manifesto* (1961) (Service Center for Teachers of History). There is a good life of Marx by *Isaiah Berlin, *Karl Marx* (1939) (Oxford), while *Franz Mehring's sympathetic *Karl Marx: The Story of His Life* (1957) (University of Michigan) is very thought-provoking.

See also *Massimo Salvadori, *The Rise of Modern Communism*, rev. ed. (1963) (Holt, Rinehart & Winston); Kermit E. McKenzie, *Comintern and World Revolution* (1964); and R. N. C. Hunt, *Theory and Practice of Communism* (1950). *Hugh Seton-Watson, *From Lenin to Khrushchev: The History of World Communism*, 2nd ed. (1960) (Praeger) is a sound, readable survery.

Fascism Some of the relevant works are listed under national rubrics. But studies of the fascist phenomenon as such have increased in number during the 1960's. Works like *Franz Neumann, *Behemoth: The Structure and Practice of National Socialism* (1942) (Harper and Torchbook) and *Hannah Arendt, *The Origins of Totalitarianism*, 2nd enl. ed. (1958) (Meridian) are basic. *Ernst Nolte, *The Three Faces of Fascism* (1966) (Mentor) is a philosophical discussion of the Fascist syndrome. *Eugen Weber, *Varieties of Fascism* (1964) (Van Nostrand, Reinhold), and *Hans Rogger and Eugen Weber, eds., *The European Right* (1965) (University of California) describe the variety of a many-faceted phenomenon and its relations with traditional Left and Right.

World War II *A. J. P. Taylor's controversial *Origins of the Second World War* (1962) (Premier) is strongly recommended but should be read critically. Further, on the causes of war see Cyril B. Falls, *The Second World War*, 3rd ed. rev. (1950); and especially *Lionel Kochan, *The Struggle for Germany,

1914–1945 (1963) (Harper Torchbook). Herbert C. O'Neill, *A Short History of the Second World War* (1950) and J. F. C. Fuller, *The Second World War, 1939–45* (1949) are comprehensive general works. The most readable and effective account of the whole war, however one-sided, remains *Winston Churchill, *The Second World War,* 6 vols. (1949–1952) (Bantam). Jon Kimche, *The Unfought Battle* (1968) deals with the phony war of 1939–1940; *M. L. B. Bloch, *Strange Defeat* (1949) (Norton) is a moving analysis of France's surrender in 1940. *Alexander Werth, *France, 1940–1955* (1956) (Beacon) and *Robert Aron, *The Vichy Regime 1940–45* (1958) (Beacon) provide good accounts of subsequent events there. The broader scene is well covered in *Chester Wilmot, *The Struggle for Europe* (1952) (Harper); *Herbert Feis, *Churchill, Roosevelt, Stalin* (1957) (Princeton); *Gordon Wright, *The Ordeal of Total War, 1939–1945* (1968) (Harper Torchbook); and *R. J. C. Butow, *Japan's Decision to Surrender* (1967) (Stanford).

Internal and Constitutional Affairs

Russia An excellent survey is *Lionel Kochan, *The Making of Modern Russia* (1962) (Penguin). For the pre-Soviet period see the survey of Mikhail M. Kapovich, *Imperial Russia, 1801–1917* (1932); *Bernard Pares, *The Fall of the Russian Monarchy* (1939); *Hugh Seton-Watson, *The Decline of Imperial Russia, 1855–1914* (1952) (Praeger); and Thomas C. Masaryk's old but valid *The Spirit of Russia,* 2 vols. (1919). Further, Launcelot A. Owen, *The Russian Peasant Movement, 1906–1917* (1937); *Franco Venturi, *Roots of Revolution* (1960) (Grosset & Dunlap); Werner E. Mosse, *Alexander II and the Modernization of Russia,* (1966) (Collier). For the Revolution and the Communist Regime, see *John Reed, *Ten Days that Shook the World* (1919) (several editions); *Bertram D. Wolfe, *Three Who Made a Revolution* [*Lenin, Trotsky, Stalin*], 4th rev. ed. (1964) (Delta); E. H. Carr, *A History of Soviet Russia, 1917–1926* (1950–1952); Leon Trotsky's own account, *History of the Russian Revolution* (1932) and his autobiography, *My Life* (1930); and the vivid biographies of Stalin (Oxford) and Trotsky (Vintage) by *Isaac Deutscher. Estimates of achievements and further outlook are to be found in Walter Laqueur, *The Fate of the Revolution: Interpretations of Soviet History* (1967); *Isaac Deutscher, *The Unfinished Revolution: Russia 1917–1967* (1967) (Oxford); and the essays *The Impact of the Russian Revolution, 1917–1967: The Influence of Bolshevism on the World Outside Russia,* issued under the auspices of the Royal Institute of International Affairs (1967) (Oxford). For institutional history see John Hazard, *The Soviet System of Government,* rev. ed. (1960). * George F. Kennan, *Russia and the West under Lenin and Stalin* (1961) (Mentor). Franz Borkenau, *The Communist International* (1938) and *European Communism* (1953); and Robert D. Warth, *Soviet Russia in World Politics* (1963) will be useful for international issues.

Germany Ernst Kohn-Bramstedt, *Aristocracy and the Middle Classes in Germany, 1830–1900* (1937) provides a fine introduction to social history. For the making of imperial Germany see *Michael Howard, *The Franco-Prussian War* (1961) (Collier) and the following biographies of Bismarck: *Erich Eyck, *Bismarck and the German Empire* (1950) (Norton) and Otto Pflanze, *Bismarck and the Development of Germany: The Period of Unification, 1815–1871* (1963). William H. Dawson, *The German Empire, 1867–1914* (1919) is still a readable survey, to be conplemented by *J. Alden Nichols, *Germany after Bismarck* (1958) (Norton) and Alexander Gerschenkron, *Bread and Democracy in Germany* (1943). For the period immediately preceding the First World War, Michael Balfour, *The Kaiser and His Times* (1964) is the best English biography of William II. *Carl E. Schorske, *German Social*

Democracy, 1905–1917 (1955) (Wiley); Peter Gay, *The Dilemma of Democratic Socialism: Edouard Bernstein's Challenge to Marx* (1952) (Collier); and Mary E. Townsend, *The Rise and Fall of Germany's Colonial Empire, 1844–1918* (1930) discuss various aspects of the prewar years, while *Fritz Fischer, *Germany's Aims in the First World War* (1967) (Norton) illuminates the coming of the war itself and its ends.

*Richard Grunberger, *Germany, 1918–1945* (1964) (Harper & Row) and *Erich Eyck, *A History of the Weimar Republic*, 2 vols. (1963) (Atheneum), one brief, the other detailed, and *S. William Halperin, *Germany Tried Democracy* (1946) (Norton) are recommended for the times following the collapse of 1918.

For the collapse of the Republic and the rise of National Socialism, see *George L. Mosse, *The Crisis of German Ideology* (1964) (Grosset & Dunlap); *Fritz R. Stern, *The Politics of Cultural Despair* (1961) (Anchor); *Robert G. L. Waite, *Vanguard of Nazism: The Free Corps Movement in Postwar Germany, 1918–1923* (1952) (Norton); John W. Wheeler-Bennett, *Wooden Titan: Hindenburg in Twenty Years of German History, 1914–1934* (1936); Klaus W. Epstein, *Matthias Erzberger and the Dilemma of German Democracy* (1959); and *Gordon A. Craig, *The Politics of the Prussian Army, 1640–1945* (1955) (Oxford), already cited. Also good are Walter Z. Laqueur, *Young Germany: A History of the Germany Youth Movement* (1962); *Klemens von Klemperer, *Germany's New Conservatism* (1957); (Princeton); A. Mendelssohn, *The War and German Society* (1937); *Siegfried C. Kracauer, *From Caligari to Hitler: A Psychological History of the German Film* (1947) (Princeton).

William Sheridan Allen has described the gradual aspect of *The Nazi Seizure of Power* (1955) as it affected a small German town. The years of the Third Reich may be approached through *William L. Shirer's popular *Rise and Fall of the Third Reich* (1960) (Crest; Simon & Schuster); Konrad Heiden's *History of National Socialism* (1935); *Franz Neumann's *Behemoth* (1942) (Harper Torchbook), already cited; or the collective study cited by M. Baumont, J. H. E. Fried and Edmond Vermeil, *The Third Reich* (1955). The destructive aspects of Nazism are revealed in E. Crankshaw, *Gestapo* (1956) and *Eugen Kogon, *The Theory and Practice of Hell* (1950) (Medallion); its more positive side in *David Schoenbaum, *Hitler's Social Revolution* (1966) (Anchor). The best biography of Hitler is *A. L. C. Bullock, *Hitler, a Study in Tyranny*, rev. ed. (1964) (Harper Torchbook), while his end and that of the regime are vividly sketched in *H. R. Trevor-Roper, *The Last Days of Hitler* (1947) (Collier).

The postwar period is examined in Henry C. Wallich, *Mainsprings of the German Revival* (1955); Edgar Alexander, *Adenauer and the New Germany* (1957); and Grant S. McLellan, ed., *The Two Germanies* (1959).

Italy Good general surveys are to be found in Denis Mack Smith, *Italy: A Modern History* (1959), and (from the economic aspect) Shepard B. Clough, *The Economic History of Modern Italy* (1964) and Maurice F. Neufeld, *Italy: School for Awakening Countries* (1961). G. M. Trevelyan, *Garibaldi and the Thousand* (1909); Denis Mack Smith, *Garibaldi* (1956); Raymond Grew, *A Sterner Plan for Italian Unity* (1963); John A. Thayer, *Italy and the Great War: Politics and Culture, 1870–1915* (1964) carry the story through to the rise of fascism. Renzo di Felice's great history of Mussolini's Italy, *Mussolini il Fascisto* (1968), has, in its second volume, reached the end of the 1920's. The best English biography of Mussolini is by Ivone A. Kirkpatrick: *Mussolini: A Study of a Demagogue* (1964). His regime should be approached through the works of Federico Chabod, *A History of Italian Fascism* (1963); and Richard A. Webster, *The Cross and the Fasces: Christian Democracy and Fascism in Italy* (1960); Roman Dombrowski, *Mussolini: Twilight and Fall* (1956); and Dante L. Germino, *The Italian Fascist Party in Power* (1959). For the foreign policy of

Fascist Italy see Elizabeth Wiskemann, *The Rome-Berlin Axis* (1949). Muriel Grindrod, *The Rebuilding of Italy: Politics and Economics, 1945–1955* (1956) and *A. J. White, *The Evolution of Modern Italy* (1965) (Norton) deal with the postwar period. A stimulating overview of recent historical orientations can be found in Leo Valiani, *L'Historiographie de l'Italie contemporaine* (1968).

France Edward M. Earle, ed., *Modern France* (1951) is still one of the best introductions to most aspects of French life, thought, and politics. Also excellent are J. E. C. Bodley's old *France* (1898); Gordon Wright, *France in Modern Times: 1760 to the Present* (1960); *John C. Cairns, *France* (1966) (Spectrum), a brief, wise, readable essay; and *Stanley Hoffmann, ed., *In Search of France* (1963) (Harper Torchbook). Good works on Napoleon III and his times: George P. Gooch, *The Second Empire* (1960); *James M. Thompson, *Louis Napoleon and the Second Empire* (1955) (Norton); Theodore Zeldin, *The Political System of Napoleon III* (1958); Albert J. Guérard, *Napoléon III* (1943). For a recent assessment, see Theodore Zeldin, *Emile Ollivier and the Liberal Empire of Napoleon III* (1963); while the watershed of 1870 is described in *Roger L. Williams, *The French Revolution of 1870–1871* (1969) (Norton).

Two important works are René Rémond, *The Right Wing in France* (1966) and Paul M. de La Gorce, *The French Army* (1963). Guy P. Chapman, *The Third Republic of France: The First Phase, 1871–1894* (1963) is excellent, as is the brief illuminating essay of *David Thomson, *Democracy in France Since 1870*, 4th ed. (1964) (Oxford). The best account of the Dreyfus crisis is by Douglas Johnson, *France and the Dreyfus Affair* (1966). The years between the wars are somberly depicted in Alexander Werth, *The Twilight of France, 1933–1940* (1942); their economic aspect in A. Sauvy, *Historie économique de la France entre les deux guerres*, 2 vols. (1965/67). The politics of the first half of this century are reflected in *Eugen Weber, *Action Française* (1962) (Stanford) and in several good biographical studies: Harvey Goldberg, *The Life of Jean Jaurès* (1962); Joel Colton, *Léon Blum* (1966); P. Miguel, *Poincaré* (1961); Rudolph Binion, *Defeated Leaders* (1960). War and its aftermath are reflected in *Robert Aron, *The Vichy Regime* (1958) (Beacon); *Alexander Werth, *France, 1940–1955* (1956) (Beacon); Herbert Lüthy, *France Against Herself* (1955); Philip M. Williams, *Politics in Post-war France* (1954); Nathan C. Leites, *On the Game of Politics in France* (1959); *Dorothy M. Pickles, *The Fifth Republic* (1960) (Praeger); and *Jean Lacouture, *De Gaulle* (1966) (Discus). On the latter, the brightest light is shed by his own memoirs.

Britain General works: R. C. K. Ensor, *England, 1870–1914* (1949); Charles L. Mowat, *Britain Between the Wars, 1918–1940* (1955); Keith Hutchinson, *Decline and Fall of British Capitalism* (1950); A. J. P. Taylor, *English History, 1914–1945* (1965). Henry R. Winkler, *Great Britain in the 20th Century* is an excellent pamphlet. The Victorian age should be approached through *George M. Young, *Victorian England: Portrait of an Age* (1954) (Oxford); Asa Briggs, *Victorian People* (1955); F. M. L. Thompson, *English Landed Society in the Nineteenth Century* (1963); and Cecil B. Woodham-Smith's rich biography, *Florence Nightingale* (1950). Simon H. Nowell-Smith, ed., *Edwardian England, 1901–1914* (1964) is basic for the beginning of the twentieth century. Also recommended: Mary E. Edes and D. P. Frasier, eds., *The Age of Extravagance: An Edwardian Reader* (1955); *George Dangerfield, *The Strange Death of Liberal England, 1910–1914* (1935) (Capricorn); and *Anne Fremantle, *This Little Band of Prophets: The Story of the Gentle Fabians* (1960) (Mentor).

The interwar years are covered by *David Thomson, *England in the Twentieth Century, 1914–1963* (1964) (Penguin); *Arthur Marwick, *The Deluge: British Society and the First World War* (1965) (Norton); *Robert Graves and

Alan Hodge, *The Long Week-end: A Social History of Great Britain, 1918–1939* (1941) (Norton); and the biographies of James Ramsay MacDonald by Godfrey E. Elton (1939); of Stanley Baldwin by George M. Young (1953); of Neville Chamberlain by Keith G. Feiling (1946); of John Maynard Keynes by *Roy F. Harrod (1951) (St. Martin's); and of Ernest Bevin by Alan Bullock (1960). The postwar years are treated by David Thomson (above); Francis Williams, *Socialist Britain* (1949); and Ernest S. Watkins, *The Cautious Revolution* (1950).

For the history of the empire, its rise and fall, see Charles F. Mullett, *The British Empire-Commonwealth, Its Themes and Character* (1961) or the works of Nicholas Mansergh, *The Multi-racial Commonwealth* (1955) and *Commonwealth Perspectives* (1958).

Spain   Raymond Carr, *Spain, 1808–1939* (1966) is the basic source of information. John B. Trend, *The Origins of Modern Spain* (1934) may still be usefully referred to. See also A. Ramos Oliveira, *Politics, Economics and Men of Modern Spain, 1808–1946* (1948). The important period of the Republic and the Civil War is treated in the following works: *Gabriel Jackson, *The Spanish Republic and the Civil War, 1931–1939* (1965) (Princeton); José M. Sanchez, *Reform and Reaction: The Politico-Religious Background of the Spanish Civil War* (1964); *Gerald Brenan, *Spanish Labyrinth: An Account of the Social and Political Background of the Civil War* (1960) (Cambridge); and *Hugh Thomas, *The Spanish Civil War* (1961) (Harper & Row). See also *George Orwell, *Homage to Catalonia* (1938) (Harcourt, Brace & World); *Stanley G. Payne, *Falange: A History of Spanish Fascism* (1961) (Stanford) and Payne's *The Spanish Revolution* (1970) (Norton); and, for later events, *Herbert L. Matthews, *The Yoke and the Arrows: A Report on Spain* (1957) (Braziller).

The Habsburg Empire   *A. J. P. Taylor's *The Habsburg Monarchy, 1809–1918* (1948) (Harper Torchbook) provides an excellent short account, while *Arthur J. May gives a detailed one in *The Hapsburg Monarchy, 1867–1914* (1951) (Norton). For the major problem of the monarchy, see Robert A. Kann, *The Multinational Empire: Nationalism and National Reform in the Habsburg Monarchy, 1848–1918,* 2 vols. (1951). The fall of the empire is well described by *Oszkar Jaszi, *The Dissolution of the Habsburg Monarchy* (1929) (Phoenix) and, more recently, by *Edward Crankshaw, *The Fall of the House of Habsburg* (1963) (Popular Library).

Austria: The economic consequences of the Empire's disruption are reflected in Leo Pasvolsky, *Economic Nationalism of the Danubian States* (1928); the history of the Austrian Republic itself, in Mary MacDonald, *The Republic of Austria, 1918–1934* (1947); Charles A. Gulick, *Austria from Habsburg to Hitler,* 2 vols. (1948); Julius Braunthal, *The Tragedy of Austria* (1948); and Gordon Brook-Shepherd, *Anschluss: The Rape of Austria* (1963).

The Hungarian Lands   C. A. Macartney, *A History of Hungary, 1929–1945,* 2 vols. (1957) is fundamental. See also the good book badly written by Rudolf L. Tokes, *Bela Kun and the Hungarian Soviet Republic* (1967); Owen Rutter, *Regent of Hungary: The Life of Admiral Nicholas Horthy* (1939); and, for very recent history, Leslie B. Bain, *The Reluctant Satellites: An Eyewitness Report on East Europe and the Hungarian Revolution* (1960); or François Fejtö, *Behind the Rape of Hungary* (1957).

Eastern Europe   *Hugh Seton-Watson, *Eastern Europe Between the Wars, 1918–1941,* 2nd ed. (1946) (Harper Torchbook) is an excellent introduction, along with his *The East European Revolution* (1956) (Praeger). For more recent developments see *C. A. Macartney and A. W. Palmer, *Independent Eastern Europe* (1962) (St. Martin's) and *Stephen A. Fischer-Galati, ed., *Eastern Europe in the Sixties* (1963) (Praeger). Samuel H. Thomson, *Czechoslovakia in European History*, 2nd ed. enl. (1953) and Elizabeth Wiskemann, *Czechs and Germans* (1938) are useful for the troubled history of Czechoslovakia. Polish history should be approached through the good brief survey of Hans Otto Meissner, *A History of Modern Poland* (1966), and Titus Komarnicki, *Rebirth of the Polish Republic* (1957). For the dark years of the war see Tadeusz Cyprian and Jerzy Sawicki, *Nazi Rule in Poland, 1939–1945* (1961).

For more recent events: Paul Zinner, ed., *National Communism and Popular Revolt in Eastern Europe* (1956), whose documents help one to understand Flora Lewis, *A Case History of Hope: The Story of Poland's Peaceful Revolutions* (1958). *Leften S. Stavrianos, *The Balkans, 1815–1914* (1963) (Holt, Rinehart & Winston) is a handy synthesis of complex problems. So is *Robert Lee Wolff, *The Balkans in Our Time* (1967) (Norton). R. W. Seton-Watson, *A History of the Roumanians* (1934); Thad W. Riker, *The Making of Roumania* (1931); and Henry L. Roberts, *Rumania: Political Problems of an Agrarian State* (1951) are recommended for Rumania, whose Communist period is reflected in Ghita Ionescu, *Communism in Rumania, 1944–1962* (1964). For Yugoslavia, see Jacob B. Hoptner, *Yugoslavia in Crisis, 1934–1941* (1962); George W. Hoffman and Fred W. Neal, *Yugoslavia and the New Communism* (1962); and Fred W. Neal, *Titoism in Action* (1958). More general, but highly readable: *Rebecca West, *Black Lamb and Grey Falcon: A Journey Through Yugoslavia* (1941) (Compass).

Turkey George E. Kirk, *A Short History of the Middle East*, 4th ed. rev. (1957) should be useful, along with *Bernard E. Lewis, *The Emergence of Modern Turkey* (1961) (Oxford). The meeting of Turkey and the West, and subsequent developments, may be traced through William Miller, *The Ottoman Empire and Its Successors, 1801–1936* (1966); Roderic H. Davison, *Reform in the Ottoman Empire, 1856–1876* (1963); Joan Haslip, *The Sultan: Life of Abdul Hamid* (1958); Serif Mardin, *Genesis of Young Ottoman Thought* (1962); Arnold J. Toynbee, *The Western Question in Greece and Turkey* (1922); and Donald E. Webster, *The Turkey of Ataturk* (1939).

The United States James G. Randall, *Civil War and Reconstruction* (1937) is still dependable. Also interesting are Donaldson Jordan and Edwin J. Pratt, *Europe and the American Civil War* (1931) and Julius Pratt, *America's Colonial Experiment* (1950). On American expansionism, see *Albert K. Weinberg, *Manifest Destiny* (1935) (Quadrangle) and Walter Millis, *The Martial Spirit* (1931). For Latin America, see Daniel Dawson, *The Mexican Adventure* (1935), concerning the French fiasco of the 1860's; James F. Rippy, *Latin America and the Industrial Age* (1944); and *Herbert L. Matthews, ed., *The United States and Latin America*, 2nd ed. (1963) (Spectrum).

The Great Crash, 1929 (1955) (Sentry) by John Kenneth Galbraith, discusses the traumatic breakdown of 1920's prosperity. Two good works on the New Deal are *The Era of Franklin D. Roosevelt*, by D. W. Brogan (1950), and *William E. Leuchtenburg, *Franklin D. Roosevelt and the New Deal* (1963) (Harper Torchbook). See also *Allen Guttman, ed., *American Neutrality and the Spanish Civil War* (1963) (Heath) and *Richard Fenno, Jr., ed., *The Yalta Conference* (1955) (Heath).

The postwar posture of the United States is treated in *Eric F. Goldman, *The Crucial Decade and After: America 1945–1960* (1960) (Vintage) and John Kenneth Galbraith, *The Affluent Society* (1958) (Mentor). For a more general evaluation, see *George F. Kennan's brief and lucid *American Diplomacy, 1900–1950* (1951) (Mentor).

Bibliography

The Material Revolution

Technology and Production William L. Thomas, ed., *Man's Role in Changing the Face of the Earth* (1956) is a massive volume, packed with information about every aspect of this problem. An optimistic view of the impact of technology upon social life is J. Fourastié, *Machinisme et bien-être* (1951). Other aspects and other views are to be found in Kingston Derry and Trevor I. Williams, *A Short History of Technology* (1961); *Sigfried Giedion, *Mechanization Takes Command* (1948) (Norton); Ludwig F. Haber, *The Chemical Industry in the Nineteenth Century* (1958); and *Lewis Mumford, *Technics and Civilization* (1934) (Harcourt, Brace & World). See also Frederick Pollock, *The Economic and Social Consequences of Automation* (1957); Thomas C. Cochran, *The American Business System: A Historical Perspective 1900–1955* (1957); *Frederick Lewis Allen, *The Big Change* (1952) (Harper & Row); and Michael Tracy, *Agriculture in Western Europe* (1964).

Medicine and Hygiene Among works on modern medicine and its role in modern society, the following are the most useful: Richard H. Shryock, *The Development of Modern Medicine,* rev. and enl. (1947); Howard W. Haggard, *The Doctor in History* (1934); *Paul de Kruif, *The Microbe Hunters* (1939) (Harcourt, Brace & World); R. Sand, *Vers la médicine sociale* (1948); Nathaniel W. Faxon, ed., *The Hospital in Contemporary Life* (1949); and *Charles Wilcocks, *Medical Advance, Public Health and Social Evolution* (1966) (Pergamon).

Science and Thought For a basic reference work, consult *John T. Merz's monumental *History of European Thought in the Nineteenth Century,* new ed., 4 vols. (1924) (Dover). See also Carl T. Chase, *The Evolution of Modern Physics* (1947); *Leopold Infeld, *Albert Einstein: His Work and Its Influence on Our World* (1950) (Scribner); *Bernard Barber, *Science and the Social Order,* rev. ed. (1962) (Collier); *Jacob Bronowski, *Science and Human Values,* rev. ed. (1965) (Harper Torchbook); *Arthur S. Eddington, *The Expanding Universe* (1958) (University of Michigan); W. P. D. Wightman, *The Growth of Scientific Ideas* (1951); William Esslinger, *Politics and Science* (1955); and J. A. Y. Butler, *Science and Human Life* (1957). For more specific problems see John C. Greene, *The Death of Adam: Evolution and Its Impact on Western Thought* (1959); Walter Hollitscher, *Sigmund Freud: An Introduction* (1947); *Benjamin N. Nelson, ed., *Freud and the 20th Century* (1958) (Meridian); *Ernest Jones, *The Life and Work of Sigmund Freud* (1961) (Anchor); *Philip Rieff, *Freud: The Mind of the Moralist* (1959) (Anchor); *Paul A. Robinson, *The Freudian Left* [Reich, Roheim, Marcuse] (1969) (Colophon).

Religion Revealing and still important is *Andrew D. White, *A History of the Warfare of Science with Theology in Christendom,* 2 vols. (1896) (Dover Free Press). James H. Nichols, *History of Christianity 1650–1950* (1956) is a factual and reliable general work. See also John N. Figgis, *Churches in the Modern State* (1913); Waldemar Gurian and Matthew A. Fitzsimons, eds., *The Catholic Church in World Affairs* (1954); *Karl Jaspers, *Man in the Modern Age* (1957) (Anchor); *Walter Rauschenbush, *Christianity and the Social Crisis* (1963) (Harper Torchbook); Adrien Dansette, *Religious History of Modern France,* 2 vols. (1961); Michael P. Fogarty, *Christian Democracy in Western Europe, 1820–1953* (1957); Kenneth S. Inglis, *Churches and the Working Class in Victorian England* (1963); Reinhold Niebuhr, *Faith and History* (1949); and the essays in *Sidney A. Burrell, ed., *The Role of Religion in Modern European History* (1964) (Macmillan).

The Way They Lived

The Countryside *Robert Redfield, *Peasant Society and Culture: An Anthropological Approach to Civilization* (1956) (Phoenix) is a theoretical study. More factual are Hubert H. Tiltman, *Peasant Europe* (1934) and H. Pourrat, *L'Homme à la bêche: l'histoire du paysan* (1949), as well as M. Augé-Laribé, *La Révolution agricole* (1955), already cited. For more specific studies, see R. Thabault's wonderful *Mon Village* (1944); *Gordon Wright, *Rural Revolution in France: The Peasantry in the Twentieth Century* (1964) (Stanford); *Lawrence W. Wylie, *Village in the Vancluse* (1957) (Harper & Row): and Edgar Morin, *Commune en France* (1967).

The Cities Govind S. Ghurye, *Cities and Civilization* (1962) is an excellent introduction, along with *Constantinos A. Doxiadis and Truman B. Douglass, *The New World of Urban Man* (1965) (United Church); William E. Cole, *Urban Society* (1958); Paul K. Hatt and Albert J. Reiss, eds., *Cities and Society,* 2nd ed. (1957); and *H. Wentworth Eldredge, ed., *Taming Megalopolis,* 2 vols. (1967) (Anchor). Two classic works deserve attention: *Max Weber, *The City* (1958) (Free Press) and Lewis Mumford, *The Culture of Cities* (1940). H. Lavedan, *Histoire de l'urbanisme,* Vol. II, *Epoque contemporaine* (1952) is also useful. Colorful details in Lawrence Wright, *Clean and Decent: The Fascinating History of the Bathroom and the Water Closet* (1960) (University of Toronto), and Alison Adburgham, *A Punch History of Manners and Modes, 1841–1940* (1961) and *Shops and Shopping* (1964). See also Hans Selye, *The Stress of Life* (1956).

The Working Classes Gilbert Stone's *A History of Labour* (1922, rather old) is still useful. More up to date is Walter Galenson's *Labour in Developing Economics* (1962). Very interesting and more theoretical are H. Dubreuil, *Le Travail et la civilisation; esquisse de l'histoire et de la philosophie du travail* (1953) and A. Touraine, *La Conscience ouvrière* (1966). Also suggested: Robert Theobald, *The Rich and the Poor* (1960); *Andrew Shonfield, *The Attack on World Poverty* (1960) (Vintage); and *Lee Rainwater and Karol K. Weinstein, *And the Poor Get Children* (1960) (Quadrangle).

For concrete social conditions, see G. Duveau, *La Vie ouvrière en France sous le second Empire* (1946); M. Collinet, *Essai sur la condition ouvrière, 1900–1950* (1951); Ferdynand Zweig, *Men in the Pits* (1948); *Val R. Lorwin, *Labor and Working Conditions in Modern Europe* (1967) (Macmillan); and John Hilton, *Rich Man, Poor Man* (1944).

Food John Burnett, *Plenty and Want: A Social History of Diet in England from 1815 to the Present Day* (1966) and Richard O. Cummings, *The American and His Food; a History of Food Habits in the United States,* rev. ed. (1941) are factual and interesting. Norman W. Desrosier, *Attack on Starvation* (1961) and the older book by Frank Carpenter, *How the World Is Fed* (1928) have a more general scope. See also Noel Curtis-Bennett, *The Food of the People* (1949) and the pioneering study of R. N. Salaman, *The History and Social Influence of the Potato* (1949)—not limited to this period.

The Bourgeoisie *Charles Morazé, *The Triumph of the Middle Classes* (1967) (Anchor) traces the rise and growth of the bourgeoisie. Lewis Corey, *The Crisis of the Middle Classes* (1935) marks the beginning of its decline. P. Bleton, *Les Hommes des temps qui viennent; essai sur les classes moyennes* (1956) and especially Nikolai Berdiaev, *The Bourgeois Mind* (1934) are strongly recommended. Also useful, Joseph A. Banks, *Prosperity and Parenthood: A Study of Family Planning Among the Victorian Middle Classes* (1954).

Bibliography

Women See Joseph A. and Olive Banks, *Feminism and Family Planning in Victorian England* (1964) and the works of Cecil W. Cunnington: *English Women's Clothing in the Present Century* (1952), *Feminine Attitudes in the Nineteenth Century* (1936), *The Perfect Lady* (1948). Specifically on the theme of emancipation, see *Eleanor Flexner, *Century of Struggle: The Woman's Rights Movement in the U.S.* (1968) (Atheneum); Aileen S. Kraditor, *Ideas of the Woman Suffrage Movement, 1890–1920* (1965); William L. O'Neill, *Woman Movement: Feminism in the United States and England* (1969) and *Everyone Was Brave: The Rise and Fall of Feminism in America* (1969); Page Smith, *Daughters of the Promised Land: Women in American History* (1970); Kate Millett, *Sexual Politics* (1970). Basic sourcebooks are *Mary Wollstonecraft, *A Vindication of the Rights of Woman,* edited by Charles W. Hagelman, Jr., first published in 1792 (1970) (Norton); *John Stuart Mill, *Subjection of Women,* first published in 1869, included in several collections; *Simone de Beauvoir, *The Second Sex* (1953) (Bantam); *Betty Friedan, *The Feminine Mystique* (1963) (Dell). Irene Clephane, *Towards Sex Freedom* (1935) is relevant but thin. The following may also be of use: *Mary Ellmann, *Thinking about Women* (1968) (Harcourt Brace Jovanovich); Virginia Woolf, *A Room of One's Own* (1929) and *Three Guineas* (1938); Arthur H. Hirsch, *The Love Elite: The Story of Woman's Emancipation and Her Drive for Sexual Fulfillment* (1963); *Helen Gurley Brown, *Sex and the Office* (1964) (Pocket Books); Adele B. Lewis, *From Kitchen to Career* (1965).

The Victorians See *G. Kitson Clark, *The Making of Victorian England* (1962) (Atheneum); *Steven Marcus, *The Other Victorians* (1966) (Bantam); Peter C. Quennell, *Victorian Panorama: A Survey of Life and Fashions from Contemporary Photographs* (1937); *Walter E. Houghton, *The Victorian Frame of Mind, 1830–1870* (1957) (Yale); *William L. Burn, *The Age of Equipoise: A Study of the Mid-Victorian Generation* (1964) (Norton); and Asa Briggs, *Victorian People* (1955) and *Victorian Cities* (1965) (Harper & Row).

The Modern Age

See Hajo Holborn, *The Political Collapse of Europe* (1951); *George Lichtheim, *The New Europe: Today—and Tomorrow* (1963) (Praeger); *Richard Mayne, *The Community of Europe* (1963) (Norton); and Michael Shanks and John Lambert, *The Common Market Today—and Tomorrow* (1962). For a more speculative approach, see Eric Fischer, *The Passing of the European Age: A Study in the Transfer of Western Civilization and its Renewal in Other Continents,* rev. ed. (1948). R. L. Delevoy, *Dimensions du XXᵉ siècle, 1900–1945* (1965); Henry S. Hughes, *An Essay for Our Times* (1950); Kenneth W. Thompson, *Political Realism and the Crisis of World Politics* (1960).

Education and Popular Culture For the complex problems of modern education, see the works of Frank P. Graves, *History of Education in Modern Times* (1915); Adolph E. Meyer, *The Development of Education in the Twentieth Century* (1939); and G. A. N. Lowndes, *The Silent Social Revolution* (1937). Widely differing examples of excellent educational history are David Newsome, *Godliness and Good Learning* (1961), about the way in which the ideal of muscular Christianity evolved in British schools; and A. Prost, *L'Enseignement en France, 1800–1967* (1968). See also Howard C. Barnard, *Short History of English Education* (1947); Stanley J. Curtis, *Education in Britain since 1900* (1952); F. Ponteil, *Histoire de l'enseignement, 1789–1965* (1966). The phenomena of popular culture should be approached through the studies of *Raymond Williams, *Culture and Society, 1780–1950* (1958) (Harper Torchbook) and *The Long Revolution* (1961); *Bernard Rosenberg and D. M. White, eds., *Mass Culture*

(1957) (Free Press); and *Lee Loewenthal, *Literature, Popular Culture and Society* (1961) (Pacific Books). More specific, but very interesting, *Henry N. Smith, *Popular Culture and Industrialism, 1865–1890* (1967) (Anchor). *Sui generis* speculations on contemporary trends are in *Marshall McLuhan, *Understanding Media* (1964) (McGraw-Hill) and *The Medium is the Massage* (1967) (Bantam). Fascinating and also more comprehensible: *Richard D. Altick, *The English Common Reader: A Social History of the Mass Reading Public, 1800–1900* (1957) (Phoenix) and Richard Hoggart, *The Uses of Literacy* (1957), on changing tastes in reading and entertainment among the working classes. There are no good works on entertainments as social phenomena, but one can refer to Ronald H. Coase, *British Broadcasting: A Study in Monopoly* (1950); or consult the encyclopedic *Histoire des Spectacles* (1965), edited by Guy Dumur.

Concerning sports, the works of Peter C. McIntosh are the most useful: *Sport in Society* (1963); *Physical Education in England since 1800,* rev. ed. (1969), whose scope is broader than the title suggests; and *Landmarks in the History of Physical Education* (1957). There are two compendious works in French: B. Gillet, *Histoire du Sport* (1965), brief and handy; R. Caillois, ed., *Jeux et Sports* (1967). See also Eugen Weber, "Pierre de Coubertin and the Introduction of Sport in France," *Journal of Contemporary History,* Vol. 5, No. 2 (1970) and "Gymnastics and Sports in fin-de-siècle France," *American Historical Review,* February, 1971.

Literature and the Arts The best introductions here are the works themselves. More generally, however, reference can be made to *Eugen Weber, ed., *Paths to the Present: Aspects of European Thought from Romanticism to Existentialism* (1960) (Dodd, Mead); *E. H. Gombrich, *The Story of Art* (1956) (Praeger); and *Sigfried Giedion, *Mechanization Takes Command* (1948) (Norton), cited previously. Beyond these see Stephen T. Madsen, *Sources of Art Nouveau* (1957); Nikolaus Pevsner, *Pioneers of the Modern Movement* (1937); *Alfred H. Barr, Jr., *What Is Modern Painting?,* 10th ed. (1968) (Mus. Mod. Art); Theodore M. Finney, *A History of Music,* rev. ed. (1947); Hugo Leichtentritt, *Music, History, and Ideas* (1950); Mary G. Colum, *From These Roots: the Ideas That Have Made Modern Literature* (1944); *J. M. Richards, *An Introduction to Modern Architecture* (1956) (Penguin); *Helmut and Alison Gernsheim, *A Concise History of Photography* (1965) (Grosset & Dunlap).

There are convenient volumes on various artistic movements in the World of Art Library: François Mathey, *The World of the Impressionists* (1961); Hans Richter, *Dada* (1965); *Patrick Waldberg, *Surrealism* (1965) (McGraw-Hill); and *Lucy R. Lippard, *Pop Art* (1967) (Praeger). John Rewald has written two beautiful and detailed studies: *The History of Impressionism* (1946) (Mus. Mod. Art) and *Post-Impressionism from Van Gogh to Gauguin* (1956). *Herbert E. Read's *Concise History of Modern Painting* (1959) (Praeger) provides a handy survey.

More details are furnished by good biographies of leading composers: Lawrence and Elisabet Mary Hanson, *Tchaikowsky* (1965); Siegfried Kracauer, *Orpheus in Paris* (1938), on Offenbach; *Winton Dean, *Bizet* (1948) (Collier); *Ernest Newman, *Wagner as Man and Artist* (1924) (Vintage); George Martin's excellent *Verdi* (1963); or *Igor Stravinsky's own *Autobiography* (1936) (Norton) and his other vivid writings—or see the biographies of leading literary figures.

Fiction Until their slow death in the 1950's and 60's, novels of the past century have piled up in such numbers that we can give here only a highly selective list of those most revealing for the social historian.

For provincial life under the Second Empire, *Gustave Flaubert's *Madame Bovary* (1857) (many editions) provides a classic picture. Less read but perhaps more revealing is his *Sentimental Education* (1869) (Penguin), whose hero's moral disintegration under the impact of reality culminates in 1848 and soon after. Flaubert's nephew, *Guy de Maupassant, would carry on the family tradition of social criticism—especially in *Bel Ami* (1885) (Popular Library). Contemporary English life and values are reflected in the works of William Makepeace Thackeray and Charles Dickens; a somewhat later German period in a novel like *Theodor Fontane's *Effi Briest* (1894) (Penguin; Unger). The greatest literary achievements of the style would come from Russia, where *Leo Tolstoy portrayed the society and life of his own time in *Anna Karenina* (1875) (many editions).

Conditions of working-class life in the late nineteenth century are grimly described by Emile Zola in *The Dram-Shop* (1877); *Germinal* (1885) (Penguin; Scribner). The rather grosser life of the German bourgeoisie in the novels of Heinrich Mann are more useful to the social historian than those of his more famous brother. Both men wrote their best works before 1914. In the case of *Thomas Mann, *Buddenbrooks* (1901) (Vintage) is the tale of a bourgeois family's decline; *The Magic Mountain* (1924) (Vintage) that of the confusion of a whole civilization. One may compare this with *Jean Barois*, by R. M. du Gard (1913, 1969) (Bobbs-Merrill), the story of a Frenchman's life through the half-century preceding the First World War (and through the Dreyfus affair), facing all the problems of the *fin de siècle*.

The depression is better understood from novels than from economic analyses. See Hans Fallada, *Little Man, What Now?* (1932) for Germany and Walter Greenwood, *Love on the Dole* (1933) for England.

The intellectual quest for commitment can be traced through *André Malraux, *Man's Fate* (1933) (Vintage); *Ignazio Silone, *Bread and Wine* (1937) (Signet); *Ernest Hemingway, *For Whom the Bell Tolls* (1940) (Scribner); *Arthur Koestler, *Darkness at Noon* (1941) (Bantam); to the utter despair of *George Orwell's *1984* (1949) (Signet). The pattern of hope and disillusion behind that evolution is spelled out most clearly in *R. H. S. Crossman, ed., *The God That Failed* (1950) (Bantam; Harper & Row).

The Latest Age

For the aftermath of the war, see Wilfrid F. Knapp, *A History of War and Peace, 1939–1965* (1967); *Richard F. Fenno, Jr., ed., *The Yalta Conference* (1955) (Heath); *Herbert Feis, *Between War and Peace: The Potsdam Conference* (1960) (Princeton); *Arnold J. Toynbee, *The World and the West* (1953) (Meridian); *George Lichtheim, *The New Europe: Today—and Tomorrow* (1963) (Praeger); Jacques Freymond, *Western Europe since the War* (1964); Hugh Seton-Watson, *Neither War nor Peace: The Struggle for Power in the Postwar World* (1960); and Robert C. Mowat, *Ruin and Resurgence, 1939–1965* (1966), providing general surveys of the situation, of which Lichtheim's is the most suggestive. *David Rees, *The Age of Containment: The Cold War* (1967) (St. Martin's), and John A. Lukacs, *A New History of the Cold War*, 3rd ed. (1966) focus on that particular struggle. On the problem of European unity: L. Armand, *Le Pari européen* (1968) is excellent.

Some of the major issues facing us are tackled in *Herbert Marcuse's *One Dimensional Man* (1964) (Beacon) and *Reason and Revolution*, 2nd ed. (1963) (Beacon), strongly recommended for understanding the philosophy of a scholar whose influence upon the present generation has been great. Beyond Marcuse and more optimistic is *Michael Harrington, *The Accidental Century* (1965) (Penguin), a brilliant and incisive discussion of our times, their dangers and their promises. Some of the tendencies they criticize have been described in works like *David Riesman et al., *The Lonely Crowd*, rev. ed. (1950) (Yale); William H.

Bibliography

Whyte, *The Organization Man* (1957) (Anchor); and *Vance O. Packard, *The Status Seekers* (1959) (Pocket Books), studies of American society leading the way, where Europe and the rest of the world are likely to follow. Other aspects of our time are discussed in Eric Fischer, *The Passing of the European Age,* rev. ed. (1948); *Robert L. Heilbroner, *The Great Ascent: The Struggle for Economic Development in Our Time* (1953) (Harper Torchbook); *Raymond Aron, *The Century of Total War* (1954) (Beacon); Andrew Shonfield, *Modern Capitalism* (1966); *M. M. Postan, *An Economic History of Western Europe: 1945–1964* (1967) (Barnes & Noble). For the politics of developing nations, see the book of that title edited in 1968 by Gabriel A. Almond and James S. Coleman. Also R. Dumont and B. Rosier, *Nous allons à la famine* (1965), John Russell, *World Population and World Food Supplies* (1954), and the various writings of Jacques Berque.

On the revolt of youth, the best running comment may be found in the pages of periodicals of the 1960's—especially *Encounter* through 1968–70. For the New Left of the late 1960's, see *Paul Jacobs and Saul Landau, eds., *The New Radicals* (1966) (Vintage), and *New Revolutionaries. Left Opposition* (1969) (Apollo), edited by Tariq Ali. For a swift general report, see *Stephen Spender, *The Year of the Young Rebels* (1969) (Vintage). The American situation has been described in a plethora of books and articles—among them *Kenneth Keniston, *The Young Radicals* (1968) (Harcourt, Brace & World). For what happened in France see *H. Bourges, ed., *The Student Revolt* (1968) (Hill & Wang), which also reproduces a rather famous interview between D. Cohn-Bendit and Jean-Paul Sartre. For criticism of radical views: R. Aron, *La Révolution introuvable* (1968); for the comments of a friendly but critical witness: Epistémon, *Ces Idées qui ont ébranlé la France: Nanterre 1967–68* (1968).

The Third World The literature on this score becomes out of date as fast as it is printed. But here are a few suggestions: on the evolution of East and Southeast Asia, see George M. Kahin, ed., *Governments and Politics in Southeast Asia* (1959); Frank M. Trager, ed., *Marxism in Southeast Asia* (1959); *Amry Vandenbosch and Richard A. Butwell, *The Changing Face of Southeast Asia* (1966) (University of Kentucky); Charles A. Fisher, *Southeast Asia: A Social, Economic and Political Geography* (1964); Harold C. Hinton, *Communist China in World Politics* (1966); and Hugh Borton et al., *Japan Between East and West* (1957).

On Africa, some of the most stimulating works are in French: for example, R. Dumont, *L'Afrique Noire est mal partie* (1966), and G. Balandier, *Sociologie actuelle de l'Afrique Noire* (1955). But see also *D. O. Mannoni, *Prospero and Caliban* (1964) (Praeger), an analytical view of relations between colonist and colonized; P. Gordon Walker, *The Commonwealth* (1962); and J. Dufey, *Portugal in Africa* (1962). Richard Bourne, *Political Leaders of Latin America* (1970) and the works of L. Mercier Vega, *Roads to Power in Latin America* (1968) and *Guerrillas in Latin American* (1969) are skeptical and thought-provoking. An original work whose suggestions go beyond the area it covers is *John J. Johnson, *Political Change in Latin America: The Emergence of Middle Sectors* (1958) (Stanford). Boris Goldenberg, *The Cuban Revolution and Latin America* (1965) is reasonably dispassionate on a passionate subject. Equally involved are those writing on the Middle East, a subject on which most people take sides or are pushed into doing so. See Don Peretz, *The Middle East Today* (1963); Bernard Lewis' expert *The Middle East and the West* (1964); John Marlowe, *Arab Nationalism and British Imperialism* (1961); and, dealing specifically with Israel, Christopher Sykes, *Crossroads to Israel* (1965) and Walter Z. Laqueur, *The Road to War 1967* (1968). One might also consult the interesting geopolitical essay of *John P. Cole, *Geography of World Affairs,* 2nd ed. (1963) (Penguin).

759

INDEX

Index

Black, Joseph, 226
Black Dwarf (Cobbett), 282
Black Hundreds (organization), 430
Black Sea
  Crimean War, 344–45
  World War I, 367
Blake, William, 647, 712
Blanc, Louis, 155
Blanqui, Louis Auguste, 24, 155, 317, 391
Bleichröder, Gerson, 325
Blériot, Louis, 579
Blum, Léon, 387, 536
Boccherini, Luigi, 159
Boer War, 335–36, 410
  British recruits, 624
Bohemia, 176, 177, 445, 455, 490, 556, 562
  Austro-Prussian War (1866), 347
  industry, 439
  serfdom, 56
  technological institutes, 229
Bohr, Niels, 595, 596
Boileau, Nicolas, 226
Bolingbroke, Lord Henry, 53
Bolívar, Simón, 165
Bolivia, 704
Bologna
  risings of *1830*, 172–73
Bombay, India, 339
Bonald, Louis de, 149, 257
Bonaparte, Jerome Napoleon, 384
Bonaparte, Joseph, 162, 166
Bonaparte, Louis, 382
Bonaparte, Louis-Napoleon, *see* Napoleon III
Bonaparte, Napoleon, *see* Napoleon I
Bonaparte, Pauline, 134
Bonaparte family, 129, 134
Bonapartism, 149, 172
Bonington, 272
Bonnet, Georges, 489
Booth, General William, 615
Borghese, Prince Camillo, 129
Borneo, 328
Borodino, Battle of (1812), 136
Bosnia, 350, 440
  Austrian annexation of, 356, 449
Boston (dance), 636
Boston, Massachusetts, 79–80
Boston Tea Party, 79
Boswell, James, 37, 74
Botot, 224
Boucher, François, 33, 102, 263, 288
Boulanger, General Georges, 397–98
Boulton, Matthew, 7, 221
Bourbon family, 63
  ouster of (1830), 93
  restoration, 142, 143, 145, 146–52
    end of, 152; settlement of property rights, 150–51; ultra-royalism, 149–50
Bourgeois Gentilhomme, Le (Molière), 294
Bourgeoisie
  de Gaulle on, 626
  Marx on, 219, 628
  19th and 20th centuries, 624–28
  Sorel on, 320
Boutmy, Emile, 384
Boxer Rebellion, 340, 341
Boyle, Robert, 226
Bradlaugh, Charles, 377
Brandenburg
  Thirty Years' War, 66
Brandt, Willy, 525, 526
Braque, Georges, 656–57
Brazil, 165, 328, 593, 699
  agricultural plantations, 44
  British exports to, 9
  cost of living index (1958–68), 704
  Euro-African society, 44
  guerrilla warfare, 413
  mining industry, 44
  Polish emigration to, 446
  population, 166
  Portuguese monarchy, 166
  slavery, 44, 48
  sugar trade, 44
Brazza, Pierre Savorgnan de, 332
Breakfast foods, development of, 622
Brecht, Bertolt, 549, 663
Bresdin, Rodolphe, 654
Brest-Litovsk, Treaty of (1918), 369, 370, 436–37
Breton, André, 323, 659, 660, 663
Brezhnev, Leonid, 513
Bridgewater, Duke of, 6, 268–69
Bridgewater Canal, 6

Bright, John, 96
Bristol, England, 45
British and Foreign Bible Society, 90
British North America Act of *1867*, 336
Broglie, Louis de, 595
Brooke, Rupert, 363, 367
Brown, Ford Madox, 329
Brown, Tom, 98, 616
Brown Shirts (Nazi organization), 517, 518–19, 553
Brunetière, Charles, 597
Brunswick, province of, 117
Brussels, 615
  carrier-pigeon service, 287
Bucharest, Treaty of (1918), 369
Buchenwald (concentration camp), 521
Buckingham, Duchess of, 89
Budapest, 443, 600
  communist uprising (1918), 452
  Jewish population (1900), 443–44
  Revolution of *1848*, 212; of *1956*, 555, 560–61, 691, 715
Buddhist Sanskrit literature, 338
Bülow, Bernhard von, 407
Buenos Aires, 576
Buffon, comte de, 220, 227
Bugeaud, General Thomas, 28
Bukharin, Nikolai, 507
Bukovina, province of, 556
Bulgaria, 351, 556, 566
  autonomy, 446
  Balkan Wars (1912–13), 356–57, 447
  communism, 681
  dictatorship (1934), 482
  independence, 350, 449
  internal affairs (1848–1918), 445; (since 1918), 556, 557
  minorities, 455
  trade with Germany (1934–38), 467
  Turkish suzerainty, 350
  Versailles Treaty, 452
  World War I, 367, 564–65
    peace treaty, 453
  World War II, 495, 511
Bunny Hug (dance), 636
Bunuel, Luis, 657
Buonarotti, Filippo, 218
Burckhardt, Jacob C., 191
Bureaucracy
  Colbert on, 105
Burgoyne, General John, 80
Burke, Edmund, 38, 73, 85, 87, 140, 141, 196
  American colonies and, 79, 258–59
  conservatism, 259
  on equal rights, 74
  on French Revolution, 123
Burma
  colonialism, 670
  imperialism, 338
  independence, 670
Burnett, John, 36
Burney, Charles, 226
Burnham, James, 462
Bute, Earl of (1713–92), 73
Byron, George Gordon, Lord, 197, 272, 587
  death of, 210

Cabinet of Doctor Caligari, The (1919), 657
Cadets (political party), 430
Cádiz
  Cortés of *1812*, 269
  republican societies, 145
Caesar, Julius, 579
Caesarian operation, development of, 587
Calabria, feudalism (19th century), 414
Calas, Jean, 236
Calculating machines, development of, 573
Calder, Alexander, 600
Calendars
  French Revolution, 122
  Gregorian, 436, 565
California, 84
  atrocities against Indians, 328
  concentration camps (World War II), 498
  gold discoveries, 303–4, 623
  proposed Mexican sale of, 408
Calonne, Charles de, 106
Calvinism, 197
Cambodia, 670–71
Cambridge University, 278, 279
  exclusion of Jews, 279
Camden, Lord Charles, 79
Camus, Albert, 663

Index

Index

Index

Index

Index

Index

Index

Index

storm troopers, 517, 518
Third Reich, 517–23
youth movement, 520
Necker, Jacques, 106, 240
dismissal of, 110
recalled, 111
Nehru, Jawaharlal, 337, 669, 705
Nelson, Lord Horatio, 128
Nero, Emperor, 576
Neruda, Jan, 439
Nerval, Gérard, 272
Netherlands, 182, 351
Agricultural Revolution, 16, 18
Austrian rule, 65, 68, 182
civil wars (1783, 1787), 68
colonialism, 43, 307
Asia, 49; Indonesia, 670
Common Market, 684–88
confessional parties, 607
Congress of Vienna, 143
Constitution, 156
dairy industry, 16
education, 642
as French satellite (1795), 118
life expectancy, 701
monetary stability, 52
NATO, 682–84
Philip II and, 182
population shifts, 19
revolt of *1789*, 182
slave trade, 45, 48
abolition of, 48
Social Democracy, 318
Spanish rule of, 182
suffrage, 460
World War II, 402, 493, 545
Neuilly, Treaty of (1919), 452
Neutrality, 82, 547
New Guinea, 496
New Harmony, Indiana, 248
New Mexico, 84
New Orleans, Battle of, 82, 83
New Science (Vico), 231
New Zealand, 576, 630
immigration, 96
Maoris, 328, 329
self-government, 336
settlement of, 328
Newcastle, Duke of, 73
Newcomen, Thomas, 7, 8, 224
Newfoundland
Barbary pirate raids, 39
Newgate Prison, 269
News agencies, 287
Newspapers, 645–46
and advertising, 287, 646
beginning of, 284, 285–86
carrier-pigeon service, 287
mass production, 645–46
news agencies, 287
price of newsprint, 571–72
sensationalism, 645
See also name of newspapers
Newton, Sir Isaac, 229, 243, 256, 596, 598, 700
influence on *philosophes*, 230–31
mathematical theories, 225
Ney, Marshal Michel, 126
Nibelungen (saga), 188
Nicaragua, 695
U.S. intervention (1912–33), 343
Nicholas I, Tsar of Russia, 197, 204, 206, 210, 423
Nicholas II, Tsar of Russia, 375, 423
abdication of, 369, 433
accession of, 427
murdered, 437
St. Petersburg riots, 429–30
World War I, 432
Nicolson, Harold, 492
Niebuhr, Richard, 611
Niepce, Joseph, 293
Nietzsche, Friedrich, 321–23, 421, 520, 635, 719
on education, 644
on God is Dead theology, 323, 602
Superman theory, 322–23
Nigeria, 575
Nightingale, Florence, 94, 345, 585, 586, 603
Nihilism, papal condemnation of, 606
Nile, Battle of the (1798), 129, 130
Nine Sisters (Masonic lodge), 241–42
Nineteenth century, *see* Eighteenth and nineteenth centuries
Nobel, Alfred, 315, 461

Non Expedit (papal decree), 415
Non-Intercourse Act (1809), 82
Nono, Pio, 606
Normandy
World War II, 499, 537
North, Lord Frederick, 80
North Atlantic Treaty Organization (NATO), 682–84, 690, 698
members of, 682–83
North German Confederation, 318, 401
North Korea, 683
North Vietnam, 705
Northern Ireland, 380
Norway, 642
Constitution, 156
NATO, 682–84
Social Democracy, 318
suffrage, 460, 630
World War II, 492, 494
Notre Dame Cathedral, 122
Novalis, 272
Nuclear Non-Proliferation Treaty (1968), 693, 696
Nuclear test ban, 696
Nürnberg
Inter-Allied Military Tribunal (1945–46), 525
public baths, 33
Third Reich, 521

Oath of the Horatii (David), 269, 270
Oberkampf, Christophe, 14, 104
Obrenovitch, Kara George, 208
Obrenovitch, Milos, 208
Odessa, 202, 209
naval mutiny, 430
wheat exports, 19
Oerstedt, Hans Christian, 227
Oil industry
development of, 577–78
first commercial production, 577
Middle East, 671–72
production (1914), 578
Romania, 444, 577
U.S., 577
U.S.S.R., 577–78
Olds, R. E., 577
Oliver Twist (Dickens), 648
Olmütz, Agreement of (1850), 399
Olympia (Manet), 652, 654
Olympic Games, 580
Omnibuses, invention of, 32
On Germany (Staël), 260
On Libery (Mill), 309, 310, 374
Op Art, 661
Opera
Romantic, 267, 287, 289, 290
Opium War, 49, 50, 340
Orders-in-Council (England), 82, 133
Oregon, 84
Orfeo ed Euridice (Gluck), 267, 289
Organization for Economic Cooperation and Development, 707
Organization for European Economic Cooperation (OEEC), 684
Orient Express, 574
Origin of Species, The (Darwin), 406, 589
Orléans family, 99–101, 149, 152–55, 245, 246, 386, 392
Ortega y Gasset, José, 160, 421, 422, 478, 719
Orwell, George, 549, 550, 551, 663
Ossian, 271
Otis, James, 79
Otto I, King of Greece, 210
Ottoman Empire, 56, 66–68, 197, 207–11, 344
agriculture, 566
balance of power (18th and 19th centuries), 207–11
Balkan Wars (1912–13), 356–57, 447
censorship, 448
Chios massacre (1822), 209, 210
Committee of Union and Progress, 449
conquest of Egypt, 129
education, 208, 448
exports, 207
first newspaper, 208, 448
first printed books, 207
foreign investments in, 330
Greek independence and, 208–10
internal affairs (1848–1918), 447–49
Islam, 447, 448, 449
janissaries, 208
Jews, 207
railroads, 448

Index

Index

Index